The Regiment

The Definitive Story of the SAS

MICHAEL ASHER

PENGUIN BOOKS

PENGUIN BOOKS

UK | USA | Canada | Ireland | Australia
India | New Zealand | South Africa

Penguin Books is part of the Penguin Random House group of companies
whose addresses can be found at global.penguinrandomhouse.com.

First published by Viking 2007
Published in Penguin Books 2008
Reissued in this edition 2018

003

Printed and bound in Great Britain by Clays Ltd, Elcograf S.p.A.

A CIP catalogue record for this book is available from the British Library

ISBN: 978–0–241–98593–9

www.greenpenguin.co.uk

MIX
Paper from
responsible sources
FSC® C018179

Penguin Random House is committed to a
sustainable future for our business, our readers
and our planet. This book is made from Forest
Stewardship Council® certified paper.

THE REGIMENT

Michael Asher has served in the Parachute Regiment and the SAS Regiment, and studied English at the University of Leeds. In 1979, he went to work as a volunteer teacher in the Sudan, where he learned Arabic and made dozens of expeditions by camel. He later gave up teaching to live for three years with the Kababish, a traditional nomadic people of the desert. In 1986–7, he and his wife, photographer and Arabist Mariantonietta Peru, made the first recorded west–east crossing of the Sahara desert by camel and on foot, a distance of four thousand five hundred miles in nine months. The author of twenty-four books and presenter of six TV documentaries, he was made a Fellow of the Royal Society of Literature in 1996. For his writing and travels, he has been awarded the Lawrence of Arabia Memorial Medal of the Royal Society for Asian Affairs, the Mungo Park Medal of the Royal Scottish Geographical Society, and the Ness Award of the Royal Geographical Society. He lives in Nairobi, Kenya.

To the men of all ranks and nationalities
who have served in our Regiment

The term SAS was never used in Hereford, and to turn it into one sound – 'sass' – was sacrilege. It was referred to as 'The Regiment' by anyone who had actually been part of it.

Robin Horsfall, *Fighting Scared*, 2002

Contents

List of Illustrations

Section Three

Maps

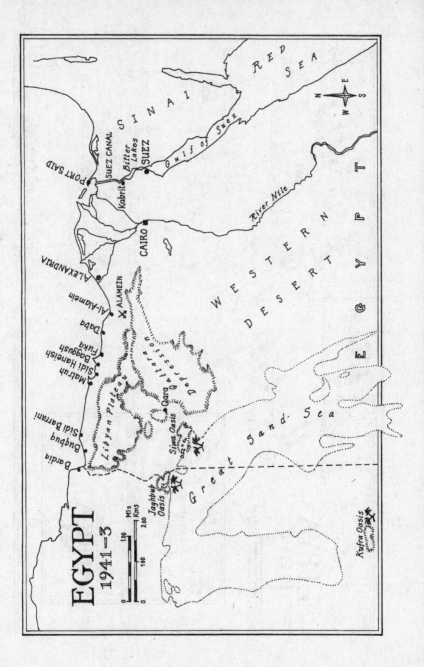

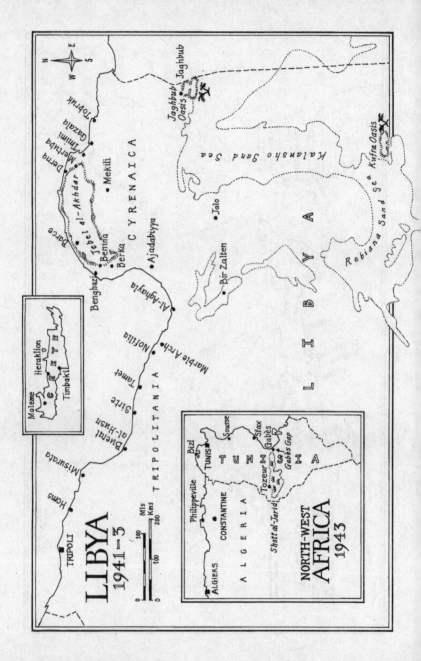

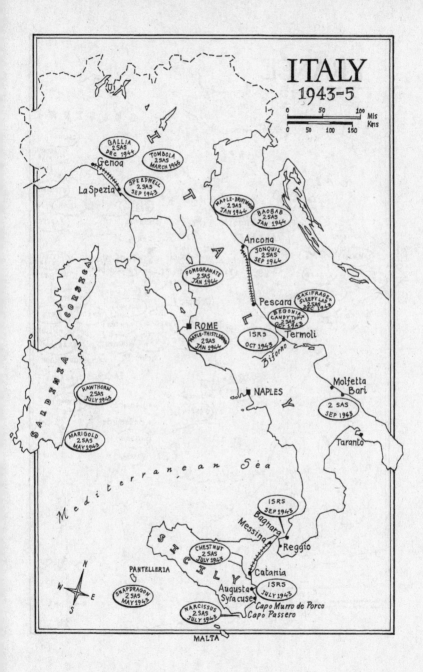

ITALY
1943–5

GALLIA
2 SAS
DEC 1944

TOMBOLA
2 SAS
MARCH 1945

Genoa

SPEEDWELL
2 SAS
SEP 1943

La Spezia

MAPLE-DRIFTWOOD
2 SAS
JAN 1944

BAOBAB
2 SAS
JAN 1944

Ancona

JONQUIL
2 SAS
SEP 1944

POMEGRANATE
2 SAS
JAN 1944

CORSICA

I T A L Y

Pescara

SAXIFRAGE
SLEEPY LAD
2 SAS
DEC 1943

BEGONIA
CANDY TUFT
2 SAS
OCT 1943

ROME

MAPLE-THISTLEDOWN
2 SAS
JAN 1944

1 SRS
OCT 1943

Termoli

Biforno

SARDINIA

HAWTHORN
2 SAS
JULY 1943

MARIGOLD
2 SAS
MAY 1943

NAPLES

Molfetta
Bari

2 SAS
SEP 1943

Taranto

M e d i t e r r a n e a n   S e a

1 SRS
SEP 1943

Baghara

Messina

S I C I L Y

CHESTNUT
2 SAS
JULY 1943

Reggio

PANTELLERIA

N
W   E
S

SNAPDRAGON
2 SAS
MAY 1943

Catania

Augusta
Syracuse

1 SRS
JULY 1943

NARCISSUS
2 SAS
JULY 1943

Capo Murro de Porco
Capo Passero

MALTA

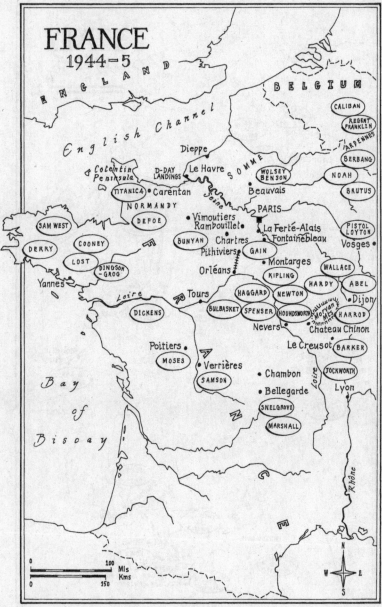

FRANCE
1944–5

ENGLAND

English Channel

BELGIUM

Dieppe

Cotentin
Peninsula

D-DAY
LANDINGS

Le Havre

SOMME

CALIBAN

REGENT
FRANKLIN

ARDENNES

BERBANG

TITANIC4

Carentan

WOLSEY
BENSON

Beauvais

NOAH

NORMANDY

Seine

PARIS

BRUTUS

SAM WEST

DEFOE

Vimoutiers
Rambouillet

La Ferté-Alais
Fontainebleau

PISTOL
LOYTON

DERRY

COONEY

LOST

BUNYAN

Chartres

Pithiviers

GAIN

Montarges

Vosges

DINGSON
– GROG

Orléans

KIPLING

WALLACE

HARDY

ABEL

Yannes

Loire

Tours

HAGGARD

NEWTON

Dijon

DICKENS

BULBASKET

SPENSER

HOUNDSWORTH

Nevers

Morvan
Mts

HARROD

Château Chinon

Poitiers

Le Creusot

BARKER

MOSES

Verrières

Chambon

JOCKWORTH

Bay

SAMSON

Bellegarde

Lyon

of

SNELGROVE

MARSHALL

Loire

Rhône

Biscay

0   100   Mls
                   Kms
0   150

N
W   E
S

NORTHERN
EUROPE
1945

Kiel

Wilhelmshaven
LARKSWOOD

HAMBURG

AMHERST

HOWARD

H O L L A N D

LARKSPUR

Ems

Bergen-
Belsen

Nienburg

Celle

KEYSTONE

• Apeldoorn

Neustadt
■ HANNOVER

Emmerich

Nijmegen •

ARCHWAY Munster • Rhade

• Wesel • Schermbeck

B E L G I U M

G E R M A N Y

Rhine

Weser

LUXEMBOURG

0   20   40   60   80   100 Mls
0   40   80   120   160 Kms

N
W   E
S

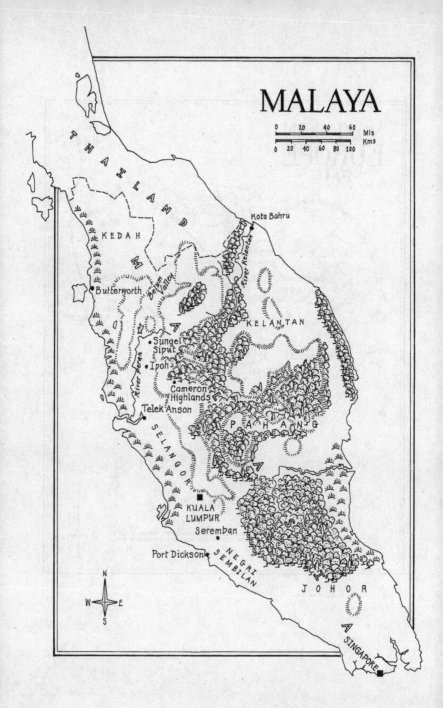

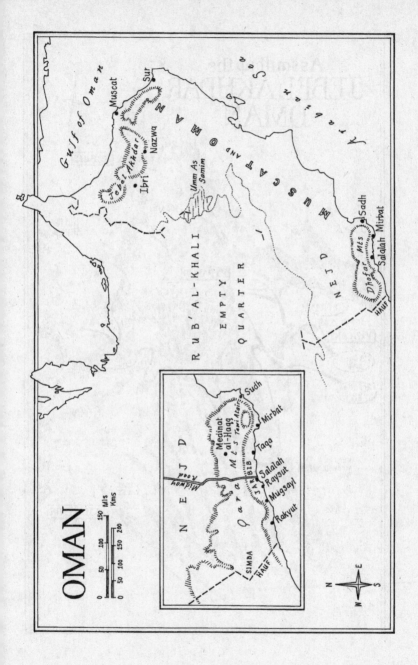

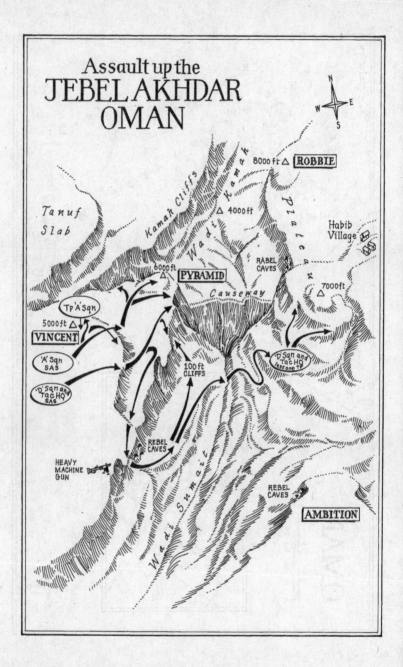

Assault up the
JEBEL AKHDAR
OMAN

N

ROBBIE
8000 ft △

Tanuf Slab

Kamah Cliffs

Wadi Kamah

△ 4000ft

Plateau

Habib Village

6000ft △   PYRAMID

RABEL CAVES

Causeway

Tp 'A' Sqn

△ 7000ft

5000ft △

VINCENT

'A' Sqn SAS

100 ft CLIFFS

'D' Sqn and Tac HQ zero one

'D' Sqn and Tac HQ SAS

REBEL CAVES

HEAVY MACHINE GUN

Wadi Sumail

REBEL CAVES

AMBITION

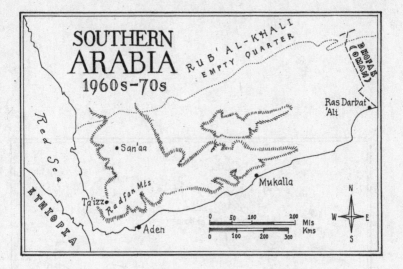

SOUTHERN ARABIA
1960s-70s

Rub' Al-Khali
Empty Quarter

DHOFAR (OMAN)

Red Sea

Ras Darbat 'Ali

San'aa

ETHIOPIA

Radfan Mts

Mukalla

Ta'izz

Aden

0 50 100 200 Mls
0 100 200 300 Kms

N W E S

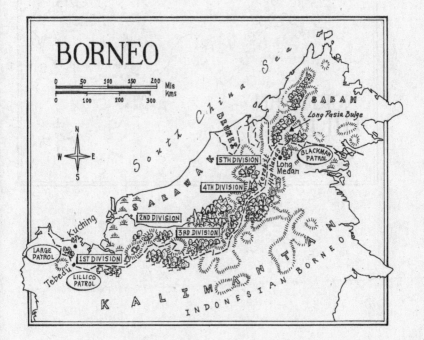

BORNEO

0 50 100 150 200 Mls
0 100 200 300 Kms

South China Sea

SABAH

Long Pasia Bulge

BRUNEI

BLACKMAN PATROL

5TH DIVISION

Keratin Highlands

Long Medan

N W E S

SARAWAK

4TH DIVISION

2ND DIVISION

Kuching

3RD DIVISION

LARGE PATROL

1ST DIVISION

Tebedu

LILLICO PATROL

K A L I M A N T A N

INDONESIAN BORNEO

NORTHERN
IRELAND

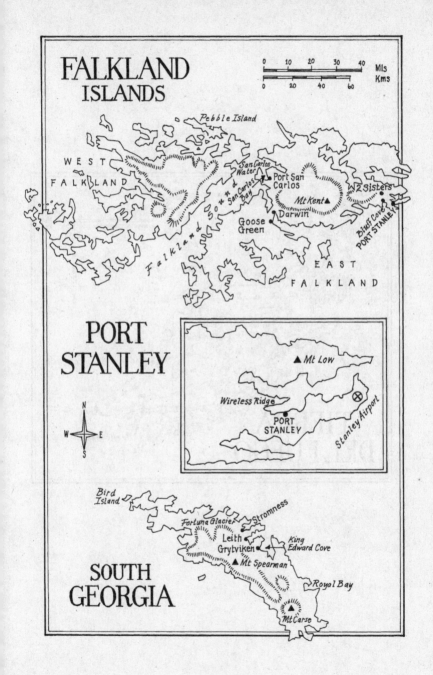

TIERRA
DEL FUEGO

Acknowledgements

My sincere thanks to David List, formerly of 21 SAS Regiment (Artists'), currently the leading authority on the SAS and one of very few SAS historians to appreciate the distinction between history and hagiography. Much of the new material presented here on the early years of the Regiment is due to his refusal to accept myths at face value, and his painstaking research over many years.

I am also grateful to Nigel Morris, for his interviews, especially with Major Clive Fairweather, former second-in-command, 22 SAS Regiment. I would like to thank Major General Tony Jeapes, CB OBE MC, former commanding officer, 22 SAS Regiment, for his assistance. I am grateful for the help of Lorna Almonds Windmill, both in correspondence and for the diary of her father, Major Jim Almonds MC and bar, of L Detachment and 1 SAS Regiment. I would like to thank Major Peter Ratcliffe DCM, former Regimental Sergeant Major, 22 SAS Regiment, both for *Eye of the Storm* – possibly the best book of memoirs ever written on 22 SAS – and for personal contributions. My thanks also go to John Kerbotson, formerly of B Squadron, 23 SAS Regiment, for his support.

My deepest thanks to my long-standing editor at Penguin, supreme professional Eleo Gordon, and to my ever-patient agent, Anthony Goff of David Higham Associates, and his assistant Georgia Glover. I would also like to thank my wife, Mariantonietta, and my children, Burton and Jade, for their understanding.

Michael Asher
Frazione Agnata, Sardinia
and Langata, Nairobi

Prologue:
'I always knew you would do a good job, but I never knew it would be this good'

On the morning of 30 April 1980, Major Clive Fairweather, second-in-command, 22 SAS Regiment, received a phone call from an old mate named Dusty Gray. Fairweather knew Gray from the secret SAS campaign in Dhofar – an experience that had forged a special bond among the so-called 'Storm Veterans' who had shared it. An ex-D Squadron corporal, noted for his Groucho Marx moustache and his sense of humour, Gray was now out of the army, working as a dog-handler with the Metropolitan Police. He told Fairweather that a terrorist situation was building up in central London.

This was the second call Fairweather had received about conditions in the capital that morning. Minutes earlier, his fiancée had reported that there were 'lots of police about in Princes Gate, Kensington'. She was having a hard time getting round the roadblocks. Fairweather knew that the Princes Gate area was favoured by foreign embassies. He had a feeling that something serious was going down.

Fairweather was holed up in the 'Kremlin' – the ops room at Bradbury Lines, the Regiment's base in Hereford. His main job that day was to move the SAS Special Projects counter-terrorist team, codenamed Pagoda, to Catterick in Yorkshire. It was scheduled to spend the rest of the week on a hostage-negotiation exercise. The four sabre squadrons of 22 SAS, A, B, D and G, rotated through the counter-terrorist role in six-month tours. It was currently the turn of B Squadron, which had taken over from G at the start of the month. The SP (Special Projects) unit was divided into Red and Blue Teams. One generally remained on stand-by at Hereford, while the other was out rehearsing terrorist scenarios in different parts of the country. At that moment, the

Pagoda boys were drinking tea in the Blue Team stand-by area with their Range Rovers and Ford Transit vans lined up outside.

Fairweather, ex-King's Own Scottish Borderers, a thirty-six-year-old Scotsman from Edinburgh with a long record of service in the Regiment, was faced with a dilemma. Though he now had two bites of information about a possible terrorist scenario in Princes Gate, neither was official. If he sent the team to Catterick, and a job did develop in London, the extra two hours' driving time might prove of life-and-death importance. After pondering it for a minute, he phoned B Squadron's OC, Major Hector Gullan, and told him that the exercise was postponed. Then he went home for a bowl of soup.

He never finished it. While he was eating, he heard a report on the radio about an incident that had occurred at about 1120 hours. Half a dozen Arabs had stormed the entrance of the Iranian Embassy in Princes Gate. Momentarily repulsed by the sole guard, forty-one-year-old Police Constable Trevor Lock of the Diplomatic Protection Group, one of them had fired three rounds from a Browning 9mm pistol. The shots had shattered the glass doors and temporarily blinded the policeman. Lock hadn't managed to draw the six-shot .45 calibre Smith & Wesson revolver he wore under his overcoat. Instead, he set off an alarm concealed in his lapel. Unheard by the terrorists, the alarm alerted the Diplomatic Protection Group HQ in New Scotland Yard.

The Arabs took Lock hostage. His face streaming blood, he was bundled into an upstairs room together with BBC producer Chris Cramer and sound-man Simeon Harris, who happened to be at the embassy chasing up visas. There were twenty-two other hostages, including chauffeur Ron Morris, other embassy staff, and visiting journalists.

The terrorists claimed to belong to an organization called the Democratic Revolutionary Front for the Liberation of Arabistan, an ethnically Arab province of western Iran, known officially as Khuzestan. Their spokesman, twenty-seven-year-old Baghdad-born trader Awn 'Ali Mohammad, made three demands. The first was the restoration of human rights to the people of Arabistan.

The second was freedom, recognition and autonomy for the region. The third was the release of ninety-one Arabistan political prisoners in Khomeini's jails. If these demands weren't met by noon on Thursday 1 May, he said, the embassy and all the hostages would be blown up.

Rushing back to his office, Fairweather called off the Catterick exercise. He phoned his commanding officer, Lt. Col. Hugh Michael Rose, who had been out of camp that morning. A forty-year-old ex-Coldstream Guardsman, Rose had been CO of 22 SAS for less than a year. The Indian-born stepson of author John Masters, of *Night Runners of Bengal* fame, he had studied at both Oxford and the Sorbonne, and had done stints in the Territorial Army and the RAF Volunteer Reserve before joining the Guards.

Rose did two things. First, he put a helicopter on stand-by to fly him to London for an immediate recce. Then he contacted the Director of the SAS Group, Major-General Peter de la Billière, at Group HQ in King's Road, Chelsea. He asked the Director for official confirmation from the Ministry of Defence that a major terrorist incident was brewing. De la Billière was as keen to get Pagoda in the picture as Rose was. A forty-six-year-old SAS veteran, he had served as squadron commander, second-in-command and CO of the Regiment, and had been instrumental in setting up an SAS counter-terrorist role almost a decade earlier.

At noon, the SP team was given a preliminary briefing in the tea-room by B Squadron OC Hector Gullan, a gruff ex-Parachute Regiment officer who had helped set up the first SAS counter-terrorist squad seven years earlier.

The men were raring to go. '[We were] secretly hoping beyond hope that this would really be it,' said a member of Blue Team, Trooper Robin Horsfall, a twenty-three-year-old former boy-soldier and ex-Para. '. . . Such an incident had never happened before in the UK.'[1]

By early afternoon Mike Rose was on the ground liaising with the police. No answer had come back from the Ministry, but Rose ordered Fairweather to move Red Team nearer the capital anyway. An official from the Cabinet Office phoned Bradbury Lines six

hours later, requesting SAS assistance at Princes Gate, and Fairweather took great satisfaction in telling him, 'We're already there.'
Hearing the 2IC's Scots brogue, the official inquired disbelievingly
if he could talk to 'a proper officer'.

The team had split up into small groups and left Hereford by
different routes. They met up at the Army School of Languages at
Beaconsfield, on the outskirts of the capital. 'Surprise was the key
to success,' Fairweather recalled, '. . . and I didn't want to alert the
media that the SAS were en route to London . . . I worried that
the Range Rovers would be spotted . . . but we succeeded in
getting the whole team in without any fuss.'² By midnight they
were setting up a tactical HQ at Regent's Park Barracks, in Albany
Street. Peter de la Billière had spent most of that afternoon
attending an emergency session at COBR – the Cabinet Office
Briefing Room – with Home Secretary Willie Whitelaw. He
was certain that the siege would end in carnage. Prime Minister
Margaret Thatcher had made it clear that, though she expected
the police to negotiate for as long as it took to achieve a peaceful
solution, the terrorists were subject to British law, and there was
no way they would leave the country. De la Billière believed that
the Arabs would never surrender because of the loss of face it
would entail.

Mike Rose was carrying out an unobtrusive recce around
Princes Gate, looking for a forward holding area nearer the target
– now referred to as 'the Stronghold'. The embassy itself was one
of a terrace of solid early Victorian town-houses on the one-sided
road running parallel with the main thoroughfare, Kensington
Road. The main road fell gently past the rotunda of the Albert
Hall on the left, Kensington Palace on the right, and the church
of St Mary Abbots, where it merged with busy High Street Kensington. On the opposite side of the road lay the lawns, lakes and
maples of Hyde Park. The trees weren't yet in full leaf, but since
the front windows of the embassy faced squarely across Kensington
Road, Rose thought they would make perfect hides for snipers.
The Stronghold was bigger than it looked from outside. Built in
the 1850s, it contained fifty-four rooms on four floors, its façade

embellished with a pillared portico, huge sash windows and ornate balconies.

Rose finally chose the Royal College of General Practitioners, at Nos. 14–15 next door, as the team's holding area. The college could be approached by a concealed route through some flats, across a garden, and down a basement passage. He knew it would be crucial to keep the movement of the SAS under cover, not only for their protection, but also to prevent the media spotting them. There were at least three television sets in the embassy, and the last thing Rose needed was for the terrorists to learn what the SAS was doing on TV.

In the early hours of 1 May, the two dozen men of Red Team brought up their equipment in Avis rentatrucks. They smuggled it into the college by the concealed route. Two hours later they had installed themselves in their new forward holding area, and were kitting up for a possible assault.

At this stage the SAS had two plans, a hasty one and a deliberate one. 'The hasty plan required speed and stealth,' Fairweather said. '[It] would have been carried out if hostages were imminently at risk in the first few hours. This plan would [probably have] involved a frontal assault.'[3] Nobody wanted to use the hasty plan if it could be avoided. It would mean going in blind without reliable intelligence or a detailed knowledge of the target's layout. The casualty projection for the hasty plan was ninety per cent.

The deliberate plan required the gathering of detailed information. 'We needed to know how many rooms there were,' Fairweather commented, 'how many storeys, what were the buildings either side, could we get along the balconies, could we get on the roof, what the light was like inside, which ways the doors opened . . . And we needed to know how many people were inside, how many terrorists, who they were, what weapons they had, what they wanted – the list went on and on . . .'[4] Both plans would be in a continuous state of revision as new intelligence came in.

The team's intelligence section, run by Sgt. Joe 'S', had already started constructing a model of the Stronghold. Shortly, Sgt. 'S' was able to give the team an initial intelligence brief, with an outline of the building plan, and mug-shots of the six terrorists. 'We spent a lot of time studying them in order to be able to separate the bad from the good if we went in,' Horsfall recalled. '. . . One mistake and I could find myself shooting a hostage, or get shot myself as a result of hesitating.'[5]

'Shooting a hostage' was the SP team's *bête noire*. They had practised hostage-rescue drill day-in day-out in the close-quarter battle range at Hereford, known as the 'Killing House'. With their preferred weapon, the MP-5 Heckler & Koch 9mm sub-machine gun, SAS shooters could put a three-round burst through a 10cm circle at five metres without using the sights. The Special Projects team had drilled with it until the weapon became an extension of themselves. Over and over again they had practised in rooms where dummy 'terrorists' had to be instantly distinguished from dummy 'hostages', and taken out with a four-inch group to the head. They had also rehearsed different scenarios with live 'hostages', each of the team playing 'hostage' in turn.

The Pagoda crew wore 'black kit' weighing about 15 kilos, specially designed for the anti-terrorist role. It included a standard NATO carbon-lined nuclear-biological-and-chemical (NBC) warfare suit with a hood and an SR-6 respirator. They had requested Nomex fireproof overalls, but had been told that they were too expensive. Instead, they wore ordinary black overalls, with body armour that included 'trauma-plates' capable of stopping high-velocity rounds. On exercises, few of the Special Projects boys liked to wear the heavy trauma-plate, but now everyone was scrabbling for one. They became, commented Horsfall, 'as rare as rocking-horse shit'.

Over the 'flak-jacket' came a suede utility vest with pouches for a pair of 'flashbang' stun-grenades and a shell-dressing, a leather belt carrying a pouch that held three thirty-round magazines for the MP-5, and a quick-release holster holding a 9mm Browning automatic pistol with a special twenty-round magazine. They also wore personal radios with earpieces and throat-microphones that were tuned to a communal net, so that everyone could hear everyone else talking.

In this 'black kit' the SAS looked more like aliens from a *Star Wars* epic than down-to-earth regular soldiers. This was no coincidence. The 'Darth Vader' style kit was tailored as a psychological weapon – a return to pre-camouflage days, when the idea of military dress was to intimidate the enemy.

Next morning, Home Secretary Whitelaw belatedly authorized the SAS to move nearer the target. In a hangar at Regent's Park barracks the Assault Pioneer Company of the Irish Guards had started constructing a flimsy full-sized mock-up of the Stronghold out of plywood and hessian, aided by blueprints and the embassy's caretaker. Later that day they were supplied with up-to-date information from one of the hostages, BBC producer Chris Cramer, who had been unexpectedly released. Cramer and the other three British captives had decided that one of them had to get out. Finding himself 'rather conveniently ill', Cramer – a future managing editor of CNN International – 'ramped it up a little' by collapsing into screaming convulsions. Alarmed, the gunmen agreed to let him go.

The police had cut the embassy's communications with the outside world. That morning they handed in a field telephone and opened negotiations with the terrorists' spokesman, Awn 'Ali Mohammad. The noon deadline passed without incident, but Awn – codenamed 'Salim' by the police – continued to make demands. Red Team were up and down like yo-yos. It was not until 0330 hours the following morning that they were relieved by Blue Team. By then, they had been on stand-by for twenty-three hours. From now on, Red and Blue would alternate on eight-hour shifts.

The following day officers of Scotland Yard's C7 technical support division attempted to drill into the Stronghold's thick granite walls to insert microphones and fibre-optic cameras. They requested COBR to find ways of increasing ambient noise to cover the operation. They were obliged by a gas company team, who got a pneumatic drill thumping in Princes Gate. When this only succeeded in irritating the terrorists, COBR had civil aircraft change their flight-path into Heathrow and zoom low over Hyde

Park instead. Neither of these measures prevented the terrorists from detecting noises in the walls. When one of them asked Sim Harris what he thought the noises were, he put his ear to the wall and told them gravely, '*Mice!*'

The observation devices weren't entirely successful. They did reveal, though, that the gang were occupying all three upper floors of the building. The hostages had been divided into male and female groups in two separate rooms on the first floor. If the SAS went in, they would have to enter these rooms at precisely the same moment to stop the gunmen murdering the hostages. It became clear that the enemy were well armed, with sub-machine guns, Browning 9mm pistols, a .38 revolver and some Russian-made grenades. Whether they had the means of blowing up the building remained unknown.

The 'deliberate plan' had been formulated by last light on Saturday, when both teams assembled for a briefing by squadron commander Hector Gullan. If an assault was ordered, Gullan told them, the large number of rooms to be cleared meant that the entire team would have to be deployed. Standard operating procedure required a 'fire group' covering the attack. This would have to be supplied by trained SAS snipers who were not part of Pagoda. They would be sited in adjacent buildings, and in nearby Hyde Park.

The task of raising the additional men wasn't easy, as the other three regular SAS squadrons were occupied elsewhere. Fairweather, whose job it was to provide them, was also concurrently managing a delicate SAS anti-terrorist operation in Northern Ireland. 'One of my biggest headaches was finding all the extra manpower,' he said, 'as we had guys scattered throughout the world.'[6] In the end, he managed to pull in a dozen permanent staff instructors from 21 and 23 SAS, the Regiment's territorial units.

The plan was for a standard building-assault on a vertical plain. The main difficulty would be to breach every entrance point, on each of the floors, at the same time. A major complication had come from the information that the first- and ground-floor windows were bomb-proofed. The SAS had themselves done an inspection of the building in the days when it belonged to the Shah. They had recommended that such windows be installed, but no one knew if their advice had been taken. It was a small but vital point. If the windows were bomb-proof they would need to be blown in by specially designed 'frame-charges'. If not, a sledgehammer would suffice. The SAS decided to play it safe and make up the frame-charges anyway.

The assault group would be backed by a support group tasked with pumping CS gas shells through the windows. The assault group itself was divided into five teams of four men each. Team No. 1 would cross the roof and lower two special stun-charges down into the stairwell that occupied the centre of the building. They would detonate with ear-splitting thumps that would distract the terrorists from the other entrances. The SAS team would move down a staircase from the roof and clear the top floor.

Team No. 2 would abseil down the rear of the building from the roof, alight on the second-floor balcony, blow in the windows and clear the floor. Team No. 3 would jump across from next door's balcony at the front, and clear the first-floor area. Team No. 4 would blow in the rear doors on the ground floor and secure the stairs, while Team No. 5 would enter via the same doors and clear the basement. A reception party of two men would remain outside to receive the hostages. 'Success depended on every SAS man knowing his task precisely,' de la Billière said, 'the soldiers had to be able to pick out the terrorists, recognize every hostage . . . and keep within pre-set boundaries so that there was no chance of shooting each other.'[7]

The aim of the assault, if sanctioned, was to rescue hostages, not take out the gunmen. Army legal experts were brought in to remind the SAS troops that the law only permitted them to kill the 'bad guys' if their lives or those of others were threatened. 'In our hearts we wanted to kill the terrorists and then save the hostages,' Horsfall admitted. 'What was important was that we knew what to say if something went wrong.'[8]

Police dialogue with the Arabs followed a well-rehearsed pattern. Never losing their cool, the police negotiators, 'Ray' and

'Dave', played cat and mouse, making offers, stalling, then offering again. The object was to chip away at morale. The police believed they were slowly winning the psychological battle. On Sunday 4 May, though, the mood changed abruptly. A hostage – embassy chief press officer Abbas Lavasani – became incensed over graffiti insulting the Ayatollah Khomeini that the gunmen had sprayed on the walls. He hurled himself at one of them. His fellow hostages overpowered him, but Lavasani became a marked man after the attempted assault.

The following day was a Bank Holiday. At about noon, Peter de la Billière visited the control room in the college, where he met Mike Rose. The Director had a feeling that events were about to accelerate. 'All morning the terrorists had been giving out new deadlines for action,' he said. 'They had grown extremely edgy. Salim, the leader, came on [the phone] to say that they proposed to kill one of the hostages.'[9] Twenty-five minutes later, de la Billière and Rose heard two shots from the direction of the embassy. The shots were separated by a twenty-second interval, and from their timing, Rose was certain that someone had been killed. De la Billière hot-footed it back to COBR to meet Whitelaw, who had just been driven at breakneck speed from his official residence at Dorneywood, near Slough. The Home Secretary had already laid down that the SAS would not be deployed unless at least two hostages had been executed. This seemed like squinted logic, but the rationale was that one death 'might be an accident'.

No one knew at this stage if a hostage actually had been killed. Rose was sure of it, and if he was right it increased the likelihood of Pagoda's intervention. De la Billière explained to the Home Secretary that despite the care they had taken with the plan, they could still expect 40 per cent casualties. Whitelaw told him graciously that once the SAS were in play he would not interfere, and that he would take responsibility if anything went wrong. Although Rose had managed to hide the SAS presence from the media, there had been speculation in the press for days that the Regiment would be called in. Reporters had even stationed themselves outside Bradbury Lines in Hereford, waiting for the teams to emerge. On the ground, police had confined TV cameras to a small area called 'Pressville', about a hundred metres west of the Stronghold. They had considered screening off the entire area, but decided against it. The official reason for this was tactical – it might alert the terrorists to the fact that an assault was building up. Others later claimed that the exposure was deliberate policy. The government, they said, wanted the world at large to see how it dealt with terrorists.

The lack of screening meant that, if the SAS went in, it would be operating for the first time in its history in the full glare of the world's media. The story was being covered by all the networks. It was a Bank Holiday, when millions of Britons would be at home with their TV sets on. De la Billière said later that he accepted the necessity of 'a degree of public presentation'. Neither he nor Rose could possibly have predicted the massive impact these TV cameras, and this day, would have on their lives, their Regiment, and the world.

At 1820 hours that evening, while Awn was in the middle of an argument about Islam with the Imam of the Regent's Park mosque, three more gunshots were heard from inside the building. Awn announced that a hostage had been executed. Another, or others, would be killed within half an hour: 'all the hostages together,' he added. Ten minutes later the embassy door opened and the body of Abbas Lavasani was flung into the street.

The cadaver was spirited away by police, and an autopsy later showed that Lavasani had been dead for hours. He was not the victim of the most recent gunshots, which turned out to be a bluff. The police, though, had heard two sets of shots and had one body. It seemed enough to fulfil Whitelaw's 'two deaths' rule.

At COBR, Whitelaw phoned Prime Minister Margaret Thatcher, who was in her car being driven from Chequers to London. Thatcher didn't respond immediately, but answered on the second attempt. She gave her consent. Whitelaw put the phone down. 'Right,' he told de la Billière, 'you can send them in.'[10] At precisely seven minutes past seven, the senior policeman on the spot, Chief Superintendent John Dellow, handed Rose written permission to unleash Pagoda.

Police negotiators went all out to engage the attention of the terrorists, promising them a bus to Heathrow. The SAS encroached on the Stronghold. They lowered the stun-charges into the stairwell. They fixed their abseiling ropes. They sneaked along the basement alley. They prepared to cross to the front balcony with their specially designed frame-charges. In Hyde Park, and on the roofs of nearby buildings, the snipers took up their posts.

Robin Horsfall was with Team No. 4, at the rear of the embassy. He thumbed the safety-catch on his MP-5 to make sure it was off. The only sounds he was aware of were the mush in his radio earpiece, the thump of his heart, and the howling of police dogs in the college. He wished to hell they would shut up. 'My greatest fear now was of making a mistake that might endanger a life,' he wrote, 'especially mine.'[11] As his team moved out towards the back door, time wound to a halt. Sounds were magnified. There was a sudden tinkle of glass above him, and he looked up to see four men of Team No. 2 rappelling down from the roof. The Red Team leader, Staff-sergeant 'M', had stuck on his rope five metres down. He had put a rubber-soled boot through a window.

Awn, in the middle of a dialogue with police negotiators, also heard the smashing glass. 'There is suspicion!' he snapped. He broke off the conversation and stalked off to investigate with his .38 revolver and a grenade. Trevor Lock and Sim Harris tagged along behind him. Realizing the assault was a hair's breadth from compromise, Hector Gullan, in the control room next door, grabbed the microphone from his operator and yelled. 'Go! Go! Go!'

That instant a deafening wallop ripped through the stairwell. One of the two stun-charges went off, so loud that it was heard miles away. On the front first-floor balcony, Team No. 3 – Lance-Corporals Mac'A' and Mac'D', and two troopers – were setting their frame-charge in the full view of whirring TV cameras. The ghostly face of Sim Harris materialized suddenly on the other side of the window. They screamed at him to get back and down. At that moment, a window on the second floor above them creaked open and a terrorist leaned out and dropped a grenade. It was his last move. A split-second later a deadly accurate single round from a sniper in Hyde Park smacked into his skull. The grenade bounced off the balcony but failed to explode – he had forgotten to pull the pin. A policeman in the street below saw it clatter across the pavement. At the same time he noticed a kitbag being lowered from a tree in Hyde Park, followed by a figure in a camouflaged suit. The camouflaged shooter collected his gear and walked briskly away.

Mac'A' detonated the frame-charge. It exploded with a whoomph and a mushroom of smoke, taking out not only the window but, unseen by the TV cameras, part of the balcony floor. The team had to jump across the gap to get into the building.

At the back, Blue Team couldn't blow in the ground-floor doors for fear of injuring the staff-sergeant dangling above them. 'M' roared to the men still on the roof to cut him down. The rest of his team landed on the second-floor balcony. They demolished the windows with sledgehammers and lobbed flashbangs into the room. A second later they were inside. Their grenades had set the curtains ablaze, and as the fire licked upwards, it enveloped the hanging team-leader's legs. M kicked frantically outwards to avoid being roasted alive.

Horsfall looked up to see that two men on the roof were trying to saw through M's nylon rope. The pendulum motion made it difficult. If they severed the rope at the wrong moment, he would miss the balcony and plummet twenty feet to the concrete steps beneath. Horsfall heard his screams, but realized there was nothing he could do. He and his oppo, 'Ginge', focused on the stairs, waiting to see what would come down. Awn and Lock were in the room at the front, next to the one where Team No. 4 were making their entry across the balcony. Awn, at the window, drew a bead on Mac'A' and his men. Suddenly Lock leapt on him, deflecting his aim and pinning him down. To Awn's astonishment, Lock produced a pistol from under his overcoat. He held the muzzle to Awn's head. Just as Lock was wondering whether or not to pull the trigger, the door burst open. Lance-Corporal Mac'D' and his mate stepped in coolly and yanked Lock out of the way, yelling, 'Trevor, leave off!' As Awn tried to get up, they pumped fifteen rounds into his head and chest.

Across the landing, at the door of the ambassador's office, Mac'A' and his comrade found themselves facing twenty-one-year-old Thamir Mohammad Hussain, armed with a Browning 9mm pistol. Mac'A' threw a flashbang, and his comrade fired his MP-5 twice. Thamir retreated, probably wounded, and disappeared into the smoke.

Moving into the room, Mac'A' suddenly got a whiff of CS gas through his respirator and backed out, coughing. A sergeant from Team No. 4, who had just come up the stairs, joined his mate, and they entered the room together. Thamir crouched on a sofa by the window, pointing his pistol at them. They opened fire with their MP-5s, drilling his body with twenty-one rounds.

Team No. 2 had broken into an empty office with locked doors. The flames were spreading and the room was already filled with smoke. A moment later M's rope was cut. He crashed on to the balcony behind them, and staggered in through the broken windows. The team shot out the door locks with their MP-5s, but the doors were barricaded from outside, and refused to give.

One of the team, Trooper Robert Palmer, backtracked to the balcony and leaned over to peer in through the window of the next-door room. He clocked one of the terrorists, twenty-three-year-old mechanic Shakir Sultan Said, attempting to set fire to a pile of paper with matches. Palmer smashed the glass and tossed in a flashbang. Shakir leapt up and grabbed his pistol. Palmer squeezed the trigger of his MP-5, but there was a dry click as the weapon jammed. Growling with frustration, Palmer drew his Browning 9mm. He burst through the window and pursued Shakir out of the room.

In the first moments of the siege, twenty-one-year-old 'Faisal' Shakir 'Abdallah Radhil, No. 2 in the terrorist team, and his comrade, Fawzi Badavi Najad, had opened fire on the male hostages in the telex room. They killed one of them, 'Ali Samad Zade, and badly wounded two others, including embassy medical officer Ahmad Dadgar. A third was miraculously saved when a round was deflected by a fifty-pence piece in his pocket. Shakir ramped through the telex room door with Palmer in hot pursuit, and found that Faisal and Fawzi had gone. They had left another man, Makki Hanun 'Ali, to guard the surviving hostages. Exactly what happened there in the next few minutes is uncertain. It must have been a scene of utter confusion – shrieks of pain and terror, bodies writhing, blood pooling on the floor, smoke and CS gas swirling about. All that is known for sure is that neither of the terrorists left the room alive. Shakir's body was found to have a single entry wound under the left ear, with an exit wound in the temple. Both wounds were caused by a round from Palmer's 9mm pistol. Makki was shot in the back, his body riddled with bullets from Red Team leader's MP-5.

On the stairs the other SAS teams formed a human chain. They began to shove the hostages roughly down, bundling them from man to man. They were aware there was still a chance of the terrorists detonating explosive devices that would blow everyone sky-high. They wanted to clear the building as soon as possible.

In COBR, de la Billière was tuned into the net. He was trying to make sense from the confusion of voices and to give a running commentary for Whitelaw's benefit: 'At least one hostage is dead . . . but the majority are alive . . . The terrorists don't seem to be doing too well . . .'[12] On the ground floor, Horsfall and his mate, 'Ginge', were at the base of the chain. They were feeding the hostages out into the garden, where the reception party was waiting. The five women hostages had been liberated from the cipher room on the second floor by M, the injured staff-sergeant. M shortly fainted from his burns. He refused to let anyone help him, but got up and made his way down to the door with glazed eyes.

As the women were stumbling downstairs, Horsfall heard someone shout, 'Watch out, he's a terrorist!' He glanced up to see one of the team, 'Soldier I', smash the butt of his MP-5 into the neck of a tall, frizzy-haired terrorist. It was Faisal, who had sprayed the hostages with rounds from his SMG. 'Soldier I' had spotted a grenade in his hand but couldn't shoot because the team in the foyer was in his line of fire. 'I raised the MP-5 above my head,' he said, '. . . and brought the stock of the weapon down on the back of his neck. I hit him as hard as I could . . . He collapsed forward and rolled down the remaining few stairs . . .'[13]

Horsfall saw the grenade and fired a short burst of four 9mm rounds into Faisal's chest. There was a staccato bipping of fire as his mates also opened up. Faisal jerked and lay still. He didn't spurt blood or spasm. One of the SAS team grabbed his hand and inserted it under the body so that if the grenade went off they would be shielded from the blast. They waited nine seconds and nothing happened. They relaxed. Faisal lay dead with at least twenty-seven 9mm slugs in his body.

The shooting petered out. The fire raged. Nineteen hostages lay spread-eagled on the lawn with their hands bound behind them, encircled by police dog-handlers. The second floor was wreathed in flames and smoke. Among the prostrate hostages was the sole survivor of the terrorist gang, Fawzi Badavi Najad, who had been hidden by one of the women. He was fingered by Sim Harris. According to Horsfall, he was pulled to his feet by one of the SAS reception team, 'Big Tony', and marched back towards the door of the embassy. Horsfall and another mate, 'Ivan', stopped him. 'We never knew for sure what Big Tony had in mind,' Horsfall said. 'But I had my suspicions.'[14] The last of the teams was pulling out. At COBR, de la Billière put down his headphones. He told Whitelaw the operation had been largely successful. There were ecstatic cheers, and a round of whisky. Then the Director SAS and the Home Secretary hurried to Princes Gate, where Mike Rose had already handed control back to the police. Operation Nimrod, the most celebrated action in special forces history, had lasted just eleven minutes.

The teams were back in the holding area, stripping off respirators and body-armour, and giving each other high-five hand-slaps. When Whitelaw arrived to address them minutes later, he was dewy-eyed. 'I always knew you would do a good job,' he said, 'but I never knew it would be this good.'[15] He wanted them to go outside and take a bow before the world's cameras. OC Hector Gullan demurred. Five minutes later, the Pagoda boys were moving in their Avis rentatrucks to Regent's Park Barracks, where Prime Minister Thatcher called in to see them with her husband, Denis. She shook hands with each man and was filmed cheering along as they watched themselves in action on TV.

This image, of the heroes applauding their own existence on television, is a curiously apt one. It was a tacit acknowledgement of the truth in the saying that, in our age, 'nothing is real unless it's on TV'. Although it was later claimed that the TV coverage had been unplanned, and Mike Rose had deliberately concentrated most of the action away from the mass of cameras, there was clearly a degree of collusion. An astute politician, de la Billière recognized that the government needed full media exposure to convince the taxpayers that the incident warranted the use of military force. He also admitted that for months he had been looking for a way of showing that the SAS were not 'shady behind-the-scenes opera-tors, but first class soldiers'. The opportunity had fallen like a ripe peach into his hand: 'All at once,' he said, 'the real value of the SAS to this country . . . was manifest.'[16]

Those eleven minutes in front of the TV cameras transformed the SAS. It had never been a secret organization, but until then most people had been unaware of its existence. That had changed. It was not only, as de la Billière said, the 'surgical precision' of the operation that impressed the watching millions, but the visual effect, the frisson of menace, of terrible purpose, that exuded from these men in their black suits, hoods and masks. It was something that touched deep into the collective unconscious. Nothing quite like it had ever been seen before.

Operation Nimrod was the single most important event in SAS history. The TV cameras robbed the Regiment of its anonymity and converted it from 'a shady presence' to a national icon. They launched what was to become no less than the great warrior-myth of the late twentieth century.

In an era when warfare was the domain of 'smart bombs',

multi-billion-dollar defence systems and hierarchies of faceless technocrats, the SAS soldier was a reversion to the idea of individual chivalry. Invulnerable and unstoppable, swinging on ropes, leaping balconies, rescuing the innocent, doling out death to the villains, SAS-men became instant folk-heroes. Here was a heady mix of true grit, cyber-tech and derring-do that came straight out of a James Bond movie. As Margaret Thatcher proclaimed, it 'made you proud to be British'. In the public consciousness, the SAS was where Robin Hood and the Knights of the Round Table met Spiderman, the Ninja assassin and the Last of the Jedi: 'heroes with halos, monkish militiamen', as one *Guardian* journalist said.

While de la Billière revelled in the new high profile, many of the rank-and-file saw the writing on the wall. '[The Iranian Embassy] was the best – and worst – thing that ever happened to the Regiment,' said SAS veteran of twenty-three years' service Ken Connor. '. . . Everyone and his dog knew about the SAS. From then on every fact, every rumour about the Regiment, would be seized on by the media . . .'[17] 'Before the siege very few people had heard of the SAS,' Robin Horsfall commented. 'Now the whole world wanted to know us . . . we were turned into a performing circus, demonstrating our techniques to any interested member of the Royal family and their corgis. Our standards dropped appallingly.'[18]

From the sublime pinnacle of the super-hero, there was still the mundane question of the inquest to be dealt with. SAS-men had never appeared in a public court before. In February 1981, the Westminster coroner concluded that they had used reasonable force. All five dead terrorists were victims of justifiable homicide.

Outside the court, though, questions were raised. The first semi-official accounts of what happened in the telex room, for example, suggested that Shakir had been shot while hurling a grenade. Makki had been taken out making a sudden threatening movement while being searched. Later accounts held that the SAS had demanded, 'Who are the terrorists?' and executed the two men pointed out to them. 'Both were sitting there and put their hands on their heads,' said embassy doctor Ahmad Dadgar. 'Then several SAS-men came in . . . they took the two terrorists and pushed them [against the wall] and shot them.'[19]

This was never proved. In answer to allegations that Margaret Thatcher had tacitly ordered the team to kill the gunmen, regardless of the hostages, Clive Fairweather said that all the team's orders had been videotaped, and the tapes sealed by lawyers immediately afterwards. Such an order would therefore have been impossible. 'People thought the message from Thatcher was to waste them,' he commented, 'but that wasn't true. The message was to rescue the hostages, not kill the terrorists. The strategy was to avoid bloodshed.'

That there were those among the anti-terrorist team who weren't happy with this strategy was clear from Robin Horsfall's account of the booze-up that followed the operation back in Hereford. 'What . . . caused me to leave early,' Horsfall said, 'were the recriminations that were already beginning to circulate . . . "Ivan" was criticized for preventing "Big Tony" from topping the last terrorist . . . I realized that because I was involved in saving [him] I too would be a subject of criticism behind my back. It depressed me that such an occasion should be demeaned by such petty minded behaviour . . .'[20]

Ironically, despite the presence of multiple eye-witnesses and TV cameras, what actually happened inside the embassy will never be known for sure. No one, not even those who took part in the assault, experienced more than a small part of the operation. It happened so quickly that a precise ordering of events is impossible. Perhaps the most mysterious factor is that while de la Billière stated that 'a single shot by a sniper in Hyde Park accounted for one of the terrorists as he leant out of the window, and four were killed by precision marksmanship inside the building',[21] the sums do not add up. Two terrorists were killed on the first floor by the assault teams, two in the telex room, one at the bottom of the stairs: one survived. The existence of the ghostly 'seventh terrorist' shot by the sniper at the telex room window has never been explained.[22]

For the Regiment such quibbles were now academic. The SAS

cult had taken on a life of its own. In the decade before the Iranian Embassy siege, the SAS had been on the verge of disbandment for lack of a role. Now, its future was assured. The same month had witnessed the abysmal failure of the Regiment's American twin, Delta Force, to rescue hostages from the US embassy in Tehran. Operation Nimrod was a vindication of something the British had always believed about themselves: that they were 'exceptionally good at this sort of thing'. From now on, everyone else agreed. 'Shown live around the world on primetime TV,' a BBC report ran, 'the storming of the Iranian embassy made the SAS a brand name for military excellence.'[23]

In the years following Nimrod, other states began to covet that 'brand name'. Britain might no longer rule the waves, but now she was number one on the counter-terrorist market-place. SAS training became the beau idéal of every foreign special forces outfit, and turned into a major British export. Training teams started to claw back vast sums for the exchequer. Black-clad, hooded figures popped up on streets all over the world. On the home front, the Iranian Embassy success provided a stark deterrent to terrorists, but above all, it restored national pride. Britain still had something the rest of the world envied: daring, dash and ingenuity – qualities that big bucks alone couldn't buy. 'For behind all the specialist weapons, assault equipment, technical devices and so on,' said de la Billière, 'are the SAS . . . a living embodiment of the individualism of the British.'[24] The SAS had proved that the right man was mightier than technology, and that small was beautiful in the special forces world.

It was an axiom that one man, who had watched the assault quietly on TV in the bar of White's Club that evening, had been extolling all his life. A retired lieutenant-colonel with the Distinguished Service Order, six foot four and remarkably strong for a quasi-pensioner, he was a legend among the cognoscenti. Once known as the 'Phantom Major', he had also been called 'the most under-decorated officer of the Second World War'. A former officer of the Scots Guards, he had first become a member of White's during his cadet days at the Guards Depot at Pirbright in

1940. By coincidence, Home Secretary Willie Whitelaw had been one of his intake. Whitelaw remembered him as a cadet who would 'simply ignore duties and go off to a party in London . . . quite incorrigible'.[25]

As the TV coverage came to a close that evening, the 'incorrigible' ex-Guardsman may have reflected that it was here, in White's bar, that a meeting with a man called Bob Laycock had sent him on the journey that had changed his life. The storming of the Iranian Embassy he had just witnessed was, in a sense, the outcome of that journey – the culmination of events that he had set rolling in Cairo, Egypt, thirty-nine years before.

PART ONE

North Africa 1941–3

1. 'The sort of plan we are looking for'

In July 1941, the British in Cairo felt they had been granted a reprieve. The summer season was as gay as ever. Officers in starched khaki drill rubbed shoulders over cocktails in the Continental and at the Long Bar at Shepheard's, tucked into dinners of roast pigeon at the Roof Garden, and packed the belly-dancing cabarets in Ezbekiyya Square. Enlisted men queued to watch talkies at the Metro, quaffed beer and tea in Groppi's, the Tipperary, or Forest Hills Tennis Club, argued with vendors in the Muski, or played football and cricket on vacant lots near the waterfront, where urchins yelled 'Sieg heil' at them and ran away. In the bars there was talk of the attempted suicide of Major Orde Wingate, victor of the Gideon Mission in Ethiopia, who had shut himself in his room at the Continental, and slit his own throat with a bowie knife.

Middle East Headquarters was sited at 10 Tonbalat Street in the leafy district of Garden City, amid palaces and villas – a five-storey art nouveau block known in dispatches as 'Grey Pillars', and to senior officers simply as 'No.10'. The mood there was sombre but optimistic. Back in April, General Erwin Rommel's Afrika Korps had been expected at the pyramids any day, but the immediate threat had evaporated. Rommel was obsessed with Tobruk, the only port on the coast of Cyrenaica still in British hands. Though Battleaxe, Commander-in-Chief General Sir Archibald Wavell's attempt to relieve Tobruk, had failed in June, with the loss of ninety-one tanks and a thousand men, Rommel had baulked at invading Egypt.

The real reprieve, though, had come on 21 June, when Hitler launched Barbarossa – his invasion of the Soviet Union. The eye of the storm had shifted abruptly away from the Mediterranean, and in London, Winston Churchill was rubbing his hands and urging Wavell's replacement, General Sir Claude 'the Auk' Auchinleck, to hit Rommel while his divisions had no chance of reinforcement.

Auchinleck, a square-jawed, dignified man with a deep confidence in his own judgement, refused to budge until he was fully prepared. On 15 July he sent a long cable to Churchill, explaining that there could be no offensive until his tank crews had been fully trained – that would not be until the end of October, maybe later. While he was dictating the signal that morning,[1] there was a scuffle outside GHQ ME. A tall young subaltern in battledress, wearing the Scots Guards badge on his field-service cap, approached the security barrier on crutches. When the military warden demanded his pass, the officer failed to produce it. Sent packing, he dumped his crutches outside the barbed wire, jumped over the fence, and sprinted to the door with a bawling warden in hot pursuit.

Outrunning the guard, the officer made his way up to the third floor and barged his way into the office of Major General Neil Ritchie, Auchinleck's Deputy Chief of General Staff. As Ritchie glanced up in surprise, the subaltern fumbled a salute, stammered apologies for bursting in, and held out a paper for the DCGS to read. Ritchie had a reputation for being 'an awfully nice chap', if a little slow. 'He was very courteous,' the young officer remembered years later, 'and he settled down to read it. About halfway through, he got very engrossed, and had forgotten the rather irregular way it had been presented.'[2]

When the DCGS had finished reading, he glanced at the lieutenant and said, 'I think this may be the sort of plan we are looking for. I will discuss it with General Auchinleck and let you know our decision in the next day or so.'[3]

The subaltern could hardly contain his excitement. He had entered the office of the third most senior man in the British army in Egypt, without an appointment or even a pass, and had induced him to read a proposal for a new concept in warfare, badly scrawled in pencil. The 'incorrigible' young officer had not been prepared for such a swift and positive reaction. His name was David Stirling and he was twenty-six years old. He had just taken the first step in the creation of the SAS.

2. Bands of brothers, packs of hounds

Although his uncle, Simon Joseph Fraser, had founded the famous Lovat Scouts in the Boer War, few of his comrades would have put money on David Stirling as creator of a unit that would change the face of modern warfare. Among the most enthusiastic revellers at the Continental and the cabarets, his main pastimes were drinking and gambling. On graduation from the Guards Depot at Pirbright, he had been classed as an 'irresponsible and unremarkable soldier', who flouted authority, neglected his duties, and spent every free moment partying.

Stirling had once, it was said, knocked out the horse of a Cairo cabby in protest against the excessive fare. After a night on the tiles he would sleep off his hangovers at the 15 Scottish Military Hospital, reviving himself next morning on shots of pure oxygen begged from a nurse. He would return to duty late, with a doctor's note citing 'pyrexia of unknown origin' as an excuse. Since arriving in Egypt in March that year he had spent so much of his time on sick-leave that he was under investigation for malingering – in wartime tantamount to cowardice.

Stirling had left Britain the previous January, as an officer in Layforce – the fifteen-hundred-strong commando brigade earmarked for the invasion of Rhodes, off mainland Turkey. The commandos had been forged in Britain's blackest hour – the summer of 1940 – when Hitler's armies were massing across the Channel, facing Britons with the prospect of invasion for the first time in a thousand years. Determined that the nation should not sink into the slough of despond that he thought had scuttled the French, Winston Churchill demanded that 'enterprises must be prepared, with specially trained troops of the hunter class . . . who can develop a reign of terror on these coasts'.[1]

A week earlier, a third of a million Allied troops had been scooped off the beaches of Dunkirk by an armada of little ships. British forces had sustained a shock to their morale, and were poorly equipped and unready. Churchill was convinced that the only way to slow down the German machine was with guerrilla attacks by 'lightly equipped, nimble forces accustomed to work like packs of hounds instead of being moved about in the ponderous manner [of] the regular formations'. 'We must have at least ten thousand of these "bands of brothers",' he wrote, 'who will be capable of lightning action.'[2]

Three days after Churchill's 'hunter class' declaration, the War Office issued orders instructing each British regional command to supply the names of forty officers and a thousand other ranks ready to volunteer for 'striking companies' to be deployed on unspecified mobile operations. It was an ambitious gambit – no one quite knew how these 'packs of hounds' were to be trained or used. General Sir John Dill, Chief of the Imperial General Staff, delegated the task to his military assistant, Lt. Col. Dudley Clarke, a Royal Artillery officer of uncommon subtlety.

Clarke not only came up with the name 'commandos', but also penned the first specifications for special forces troops. They would all be volunteers, he said, as fit as professional athletes, trained to perfection in the use of infantry weapons. They would be capable of killing quickly and silently, would operate by night rather than by day, and would be familiar with ships and the sea. They would be able to fight alone or in small groups, to use independent initiative, and would think of warfare only in terms of attack.

The commandos were a new kind of army. Regular soldiers trained to fight like guerrilla bands, they would operate without heavy weapons, artillery or air-support. They would be trained to endure fatigue, face overwhelming odds and persevere to the end. The commando course emphasized comradeship between officers and men, self-reliance and individualism among all ranks. Commando units were flexible and mobile, unencumbered with barracks, cookhouses, HQ offices or rear-echelon staff. Being volunteers, there was no need for traditional military discipline –

the ultimate sanction for misbehaviour was RTU, 'Return to Unit' – a humiliating expulsion from the elite force that the commandos came to consider a fate worse than death.

It took three months to train the commandos, and by the time they were ready for action, the situation had changed radically. The Royal Air Force had won the Battle of Britain, and the immediate threat of invasion had receded. The 'bands of brothers' were raring to go, but suddenly there was nothing to shoot at. The focus of the war had already relocated from Europe to the Mediterranean theatre. In North Africa, Wavell's field commander, Lt. Gen. Dick O'Connor, had thrashed Mussolini's Tenth Army in Libya, and captured a hundred and thirty thousand Italian troops. Seaborne special forces might be useful in securing key Mediterranean islands to support O'Connor's advance.

In October it was proposed that the commandos should launch an assault on the island of Rhodes, to maintain British control in the eastern Mediterranean. On the last day of January, the Special Service Brigade, codenamed 'Force Z', comprising numbers 7, 8 and 11 (Scottish) Commandos with elements of 3 Commando, was dispatched from the Isle of Arran in Scotland to Egypt, in two landing ships, *Glengyle* and *Glenroy*. By the time the ships had reached their destination the brigade had been re-christened Layforce, after its commander, Col. Bob Laycock, of the Royal Horse Guards. David Stirling, an officer in 8 Commando, had left Arran on board *Glenroy*.

When Layforce arrived in Egypt that March, a British victory in the Mediterranean theatre looked almost certain. Rommel had changed all that. By the end of April, all the gains O'Connor had made in six months had been reversed. The Rhodes operation had become untenable. Instead, 7 Commando had been squandered fighting a defensive action on Crete, 11 (Scottish) Commando had suffered more than twenty-five per cent casualties during a botched landing at the Litani River in Syria, and 7 and 8 Commandos had failed in three raids on the coast of Libya. By mid-June, Layforce had lost half its fighting strength, and was no longer a viable unit.

3. 'The landing of small parties by night will clearly be most effective'

A month before his meeting with Ritchie, Stirling and four other commandos had made history by executing the first recorded parachute descent on the African continent. They had jumped from a Vickers Valentia a thousand feet above Fuka – a railhead on the Mediterranean coast. The others had landed well, but Stirling's canopy had snagged on the aircraft's tailplane, ripping out the panels. Later, all he remembered was the ground rushing up to meet him before he piled into it like a wrecking ball.

The drop was the idea of John Steel 'Jock' Lewes, a twenty-eight-year-old lieutenant in the Welsh Guards, who was the first to jump that evening. Stirling and his companion, Sgt. Barney Stone, had muscled in on the party by claiming that they were planning an operation in Syria. Lewes resented their interference. An intense Oxford graduate with a puritanical streak, he had a tendency to make savage moral judgements on those who failed to live up to his ideals. Stirling certainly fell into this category. Lewes knew him as an idle, cynical, sybaritic 'Cheekie Laddie' from a privileged background, who had never managed to settle down to anything, and who was so notorious for over-sleeping that on *Glenroy* he had acquired the nickname 'The Great Sloth'.[1]

Lewes, who had left a sweetheart at home, and wrote romantic poetry, looked like a man constantly grappling with an internal chess problem. He was in many ways Stirling's opposite: serious, single-minded, systematic and analytic – not the kind to be caught propping up bars in Cairo, or having a flutter at the racecourse. Lewes had volunteered to carry out tests with a consignment of fifty parachutes diverted to North Africa from India, and had plans to execute an airborne operation with a troop of fifty selected commandos.

The experiment had been sanctioned by A Force, a secret psy-ops division with an office at 6 Shari' Qasr an-Nil, Cairo. The brainchild of Lt. Col. Dudley Clarke, the same heterodox thinker who had named the commandos, A Force was engaged in dropping squadrons of dummy parachutists over Helwan, south of Cairo, for the benefit of enemy informers. This fictitious unit was designated '1 Special Air Service Brigade': Clarke was keen on having some real parachutists to back up the charade.

Lewes's initial jump was successful – Stirling was the only casualty. He hit the ground hard and lay in the crater his body had gouged in the gravel, his legs paralysed, his eyes blinking sightlessly up at the darkening skies. An hour later he was slotted into a military ambulance and carted off to 15 Scottish General Hospital in Cairo. By the time he arrived there his eyesight had cleared, but the blindness had been replaced by a crippling headache. He still couldn't move his legs. He was suffering low blood pressure, and was diagnosed as having sustained severe spinal shock.

Stirling was in bed for about a week before the sensation started returning. Among his first visitors was Lt. Evelyn Waugh, ex-Royal Marines and 8 Commando. Already a famous author in civilian life, and one of the stars of the Cairo cocktail circuit, Waugh had seen hard fighting on Crete in May, as Layforce Intelligence Officer. He brought news that, while Stirling had been messing about with parachutes, Wavell had decided to disband the Middle East commando force.

Stirling had already heard rumours about the breakup of Layforce, but the fact that it was now certain came as a shock. It could mean returning to his parent unit, the Scots Guards, and either shipping back to Blighty or settling down to a conventional war of platoons and companies. Though he came from a military family, Stirling had never envisaged a career as a soldier: he lacked the authoritarian pose. So quietly spoken that others were often unsure if he was actually talking to them or not, he also radiated warmth and bonhomie. 'He had the knack of conning you into anything,' said Ernie Bond, an early SAS recruit, who had known Stirling in the Scots Guards. 'He was such a charming gentleman . . . He never gave you an order – it was sort of a suggestion . . .'[2]

Born in 1915, educated at Ampleforth, Stirling was one of four sons and two daughters of Archibald Stirling, retired general,

Member of Parliament, and Deputy Lieutenant of Perthshire, with an impeccable Scots-Catholic pedigree. His mother, Margaret Fraser, was the daughter of the 16th Baron Lovat.

Stirling's early ambition had been to become an artist, and after being sent down from Cambridge for gambling, he joined the Bohemian community of Paris with a view to making himself one. Advised by his tutor that he lacked the requisite drawing skill, he quit the artistic life in high dudgeon, and decided instead to become the first man to climb Everest. As part of his training regime, he spent seven months in the Canadian and American Rockies, and six months in the Swiss Alps. The Everest expedition was cut short by the outbreak of war.

It was Stirling's social position that gained him entry into the commandos. He had passed no more stringent a selection test than downing gin-and-tonics alongside 8 Commando's socialite commanding officer, Lt. Col. Bob Laycock, at the bar of White's. Stirling's case was not unique – Laycock believed in going to war among friends, and many commando officers, including Waugh, had been recruited in the same way. The 'Bar of White's' became a legend among the well-heeled young subalterns of the commando, projecting exactly the right brand of gentlemanly amateurism. Some of these officers were of real quality, but many were unable to pay more than lip-service to the ideals of the new unit.

Lt. David Stirling had been one of them. It was only when faced with the prospect of RTU that June that his mind began racing over new possibilities for the deployment of raiding units behind enemy lines. Within a few days of Waugh's visit he had come up with the blueprint for the SAS.

What this memo actually contained has been the subject of some confusion, mainly because most SAS historians have been under the impression that the original paper was lost. This is not the case. In fact, a typewritten copy, dated 16 July 1941, bearing Stirling's name, and the stamp of the Chief of the General Staff, has always been extant. Filed not with the SAS records, but in the A Force dossier, it was recently rediscovered by SAS scholar David List, when the A Force records were released into National Archives.

David Stirling's proposal was for a small parachute unit that would drop behind enemy lines, sabotage aircraft, vehicle parks, water, ammunition and supply dumps, and withdraw on foot. Entitled *Case for the retention of a limited number of special service troops, for employment as parachutists*,[3] his paper suggested that while seaborne commando operations were restricted by weather conditions, this factor would not apply to parachute drops. The range of airborne troops would be much greater than that of seaborne commandos, because they would not be confined to areas within reach of the sea, and they could be tasked at much shorter notice.[4] As the first paragraph makes clear, the memo was stimulated directly by the demise of Layforce:

Now that Layforce has finally been disbanded, there remains no ad hoc organisation for raiding enemy lines of communication . . . This unit is being dispersed at a moment when the enemy is being forced . . . to fulfil his total commitment to Russia – a time which seems totally propitious for these raids . . . The landing of small parties by night on a wide range of objectives will clearly be most effective, in Lybia [sic] and elsewhere, so long as the enemy is finding difficulties in replacing material and in reinforcing troops.[5]

Stirling knew that another drag on seaborne operations was the reluctance of the Royal Navy to commit ships without adequate air-support. His idea was to deploy parachute commandos in tiny groups. They would not seek to confront the enemy, but would operate like ghosts, coming silently out of the desert by night, laying demolitions charges on any available targets. By making full use of stealth and the element of surprise, Stirling thought, a small section of highly trained men could swing a hammer out of all proportion to its size.

As the numbness in his legs thawed, he began to pen out his proposal on a memo pad. The more he scribbled and pondered, the more certain he became that his idea would work. After Waugh, he had a string of visitors, among them Jock Lewes, who was now bound for beleaguered Tobruk to carry out raids on Axis troops.

Stirling had a certain awe of Lewes, and desperately needed his approval. Though an 8 Commando officer, Jock was anything but a 'Bar of White's' recruit. Born in India in 1913, he was the son of Arthur Lewes, a chartered accountant of Calcutta. A lean, classically handsome six-footer with dazzling blue eyes and a long-ranging stride, he had spent his childhood in Sydney, Australia, but had moved to Britain to study Modern Greats – Philosophy, Politics and Economics – at Christ Church, Oxford. Unlike Stirling at Cambridge, Lewes had not only stayed the course, but had distinguished himself as President of the University Rowing Club. Under his leadership, in 1937, the Oxford team had broken a long string of Cambridge victories in the boat race, winning by three lengths. Lewes had earned himself a Blue and undying fame in rowing circles.

Commissioned in the Welsh Guards, Lewes had been accepted by Bob Laycock as a subaltern in 8 Commando, and had joined the unit for training at Burnham-on-Crouch, where he found himself a fish out of water. 'Jock Lewis [sic], the wiry Australian,' wrote a comrade, Carol Mather, 'surveying his companions knocking back their pink gins, muttered into his beer that after the war "all this would change" – meaning that society would change and us with it, that our . . . privileged lives might be cruelly shattered.'[6]

Now Lewes considered Stirling's proposal with critical acuity, and saw that he had not thought the problems through. Stirling was interested in patterns and concepts rather than nuts and bolts. When discussion came down to times, distances and details, his eyes would glaze over. 'Stirling wanted the action without the preparation and training,' Ernie Bond commented. '. . . Jock was the thinker, he used to think the "whys and wherefores".'[7] They were the perfect complement. 'The chat with Jock was the key to success,' Stirling admitted. 'I knew I had to have all the answers to the questions he had raised if I was to get anywhere.'[8]

Stirling's initial plan was that his air-commando would attack a range of enemy targets within weeks of its formation. He later realized that this was aiming too high, and evolved a specific scheme to coincide with Auchinleck's big push – Operation Cru-

sader, due at the beginning of November. The raid would kick off
two days before the offensive, when sections of his parachutists
would drop on Axis airfields at Gazala and Tmimi, on the coastal
plain of Cyrenaica, near Tobruk. The raiders would lie up for a
day observing their targets, and go in silently at night, sabotaging
every enemy aircraft they could find. They would then leg it back
to their own lines, or get picked up by submarine. Stirling later
modified the submarine idea – probably at Lewes's suggestion. He
proposed instead that his squads could be extracted by the Long
Range Desert Group, a mobile force equipped with Ford trucks,
already operating deep behind Axis lines.

Stirling later said that Lewes was the 'brains' behind the SAS
scheme: '. . . the proposal was largely based on Jock's ideas,' he
wrote, 'and was merely an application of them on a unit basis.'[9]
An analysis of the original document suggests that while its frame-
work was Stirling's, the solid detail came from Lewes. Lewes later
acknowledged that Stirling's great quality was his ability to see the
big picture, and to 'appreciate the long-term value of my experiment more accurately than I'.[10] It was out of the tension between
these two very different personalities – the analytic perfectionist
and the romantic visionary – that the SAS was born.

4. Friends in high places

The date of Stirling's discharge from 15 Scottish Military Hospital
in Cairo is unknown. Stirling exaggerated the time he was there,
claiming that it was two months, though it is unlikely to have been
more than three weeks. On 16 July he wrote to his mother that
he had recovered from the back injury 'quicker than expected',
and had been 'on leave' in Cairo for a month.

By the second week in July, he was staying with his brother,
Peter, Third Secretary at the British Embassy, who had a flat at
Qasr ad-Dubbara, a short taxi ride from Grey Pillars. The flat
was shared with a third Stirling brother, Bill, currently assistant to

General Arthur Smith, Chief of the General Staff. It was here, amid the Victorian chaos of books, maps, papers, weapons, shell-cases and overflowing cocktail cabinets, that David, puffing pensively on a pipe stuffed with Dark Empire Shag, considered the best means of introducing his proposal to the high command.

To present the plan through the usual channels would be fatal. It would get swamped in the slough of bureaucracy – what Stirling would later call 'layer upon layer of fossilized shit'. He needed to hand it to a senior officer face to face. Top brass didn't usually talk to lowly subalterns, but if he could get near enough to establish his social credentials, he would be in with a chance. There is no independent corroboration, though, that he actually did vault over the wire at GHQ and elude the wardens. As a romantic, Stirling undoubtedly saw the mythic possibilities in presenting the creation of the SAS as the result of a daring 'raid'. It is at least possible that he was not challenged at all.

Whatever the case, there is certainly a vital element missing from his original account. His arrival in Ritchie's office was no accident. Stirling admitted later that the Deputy Chief of the General Staff had always been his target. Ritchie was a man noted for 'friends in high places', and what he saw when he glanced up from his desk that morning was not just a lanky young officer, but a familiar face. He had shot grouse with Stirling's father before the war, and certainly recognized the scion of a noble family when he saw one.

The day after the first meeting, Stirling talked to his force commander, Bob Laycock, at the Long Bar of Shepheard's. Laycock was about to leave for Britain by air to make a case to Winston Churchill for retaining commandos in the Middle East. Stirling's parachute idea dovetailed neatly with his own objectives. They discussed which officers would be suitable for the new unit. Stirling asked for Lewes, and Laycock suggested Lt. Robert Blair Mayne, an officer of 11 (Scottish) Commando who had distinguished himself in action at the Litani River in Syria a few weeks earlier.

Claude Auchinleck had inherited from his predecessor, Wavell, a scheme to establish a parachute training-school in the Middle East. The plan had been booted around for a year, but had gone into abeyance. The C-in-C leapt on Stirling's proposal as a way of reviving it. For Auchinleck, it was a no-lose deal. The Parachute Unit project would be attached to Dudley Clarke's deception programme. If it succeeded, it might deliver a genuine strategic advantage. If not, it would still show the enemy that the Allies really did have an airborne capacity. Auchinleck told Ritchie he would see Stirling right away. They met at Grey Pillars, probably on the morning of 18 July, and Stirling saw at once that he'd hit paydirt. Not only were Auchinleck and Ritchie there, but also Ritchie's immediate superior, CGS Arthur Smith. Auchinleck authorized the recruitment of sixty-eight men and seven support staff; Ritchie told Stirling he could recruit from the whole of the defunct Layforce. The unusual number was dictated by the capacity of the RAF Bristol Bombay transports assigned to parachute operations. One of the officers Stirling had consulted about his plan, Group Captain Ronnie Guest, RAF, who worked with A Force, had assured him that Bombays would be available for training and operations, and may also have pointed out that they carried only eleven men. The Parachute Unit would, therefore, be divided into six sections of ten men, each with one officer.

Stirling said later that one major proviso was that the force must come directly under the Commander-in-Chief. The Parachute Unit should have a strategic role, and should not be 'acquired' by any other department, such as Combined Operations, which directed commando ops, and others. It seems likely that Auchinleck accepted this in principle, but for practical purposes, Stirling's early missions would come under the General Officer Commanding the Eighth Army, Lt. Gen. Sir Alan Cunningham.

That evening, a signal left GHQ bound for the War Office in London, asking for authorization to create the new unit. Stirling quit No. 10 promoted captain, elated but troubled by the tall order he had just imposed on himself. He had only three months to create from scratch an entirely new unit. He had bluffed his way into the highest circles with his rhetoric and social connections, but without the training skills of Jock Lewes, the unit was unlikely to get off the ground.

5. 'Jock wanted to be sure I was going to stay with it'

The night before Stirling met Auchinleck, Lewes had been in action near Tobruk, when a sixty-strong detachment of 8 Commando raided the 'Twin Pimples' salient. Lewes, a section commander, led his men to within thirty yards of the Italian rear under the cover of an artillery barrage. A sentry popped a shot. The commandos strafed him with .45 calibre Tommy-guns and .303 rifles, exploding into a ferocious charge with bayonets fixed. The twenty Italians on the knoll bolted to their sangars. The commandos lobbed in grenades, and gouged the enemy with bayonets as they stumbled out. In four minutes the hill was bloody with Italian dead. The commandos pulled back – only just in time. Before they'd made a hundred yards, enemy artillery and machine-gun fire blitzed the salient from adjacent positions. Five of the commandos were hit before they slipped away into the night.

The Twin Pimples raid achieved nothing of strategic importance, but it was a sorely needed morale-booster for the besieged garrison. Tobruk was manned by twenty-three thousand troops, Australian, British and Indian. Conditions there were oppressive. The town stood on white cliffs over a blue bay whose pellucid waters concealed the dozens of ships that had been sunk by Axis dive-bombers. The British perimeter was a thirty-five-mile crescent under daily attack from tanks and artillery – and from aircraft based so near that the troops could hear them taking off. Most of the men lived in dugouts and stone sangars, assailed by hordes of flies and fleas, riddled with dysentery and desert sores.

It was in this warren of defences that Stirling visited Lewes. He tried to persuade him to become the first recruit in what was to be known formally as 'L Detachment, 1 Special Air Service Brigade'. Dudley Clarke, Director, A Force, had offered to give Stirling as much help as he needed on the understanding that his parachute unit came under his non-existent SAS. Since there were already fictitious 'J' and 'K' Detachments, 'L' Detachment seemed appropriate. Stirling said later that he accepted Clarke's suggestion 'just to humour him'.

Lewes listened to Stirling's proposal. His answer, Stirling said, was 'No way.' He knew the principle was sound – the plan had, after all, been based on his ideas – but he didn't trust Stirling's commitment. He also resented the fact that while GHQ had scrapped his own operation, they had accepted a similar idea proffered by a known wastrel, with no experience of combat, whose only advantage was 'the old school tie'. In a few short weeks Lewes had gained a reputation as the boldest patrol-leader in Tobruk. He was loath to hand himself over to a cynical upper-class layabout, who had as yet scarcely heard a shot fired in action.

Stirling saw Lewes's refusal as a challenge to his credibility. He was so desperate for his comrade's approval that he returned to Tobruk twice. 'Jock wanted to be sure that if we got the thing working, I was going to stay with it,' he said, 'and also tackle the enormous problems at GHQ, which he possibly foresaw more clearly than me – he just didn't want to get involved if it was going to be a short-term flight of fancy.'[1]

Lewes held Stirling at arm's length. While his reputation was mounting in Tobruk, Stirling went ahead and recruited his first fifty men. On 27 July he attended a conference at GHQ's Training Branch, with eleven other officers, including Deputy Director of Military Training Col. J. A. Baillon, Adjutant General Lt. Col. Frederick H. Butterfield, Lt. Col. Dudley Clarke, and Major Vivian Street, Special Duties.

Adjutant General Butterfield told Stirling that he had a list of some hundred and twenty ex-Layforce men from whom he could make his selection. Stirling replied cheekily that Ritchie had authorized him to choose from the whole of Layforce. In any case, he had already acquired twenty-one ex-commandos from the Scots

Guards, and another eighteen from the Infantry Base Depot at Geneifa. He added that he could probably obtain the final eleven men he needed from the same sources, but preferred to wait until the 'specially trained Layforce personnel' were released from their patrol duties at Tobruk.

Red-faced at this impertinence, Col. Joe Baillon snapped that he should acquire his recruits 'through the proper channels' and ordered him to discuss the matter further with Butterworth. It was probably from this moment on that Stirling and the Adjutant General's office became bitter enemies.

The conference debated scales of weapons, ammunition and equipment, and Stirling was allocated a training-camp on a site at Kabrit in the Suez Canal Zone, which had previously housed a commando training school. When he argued that his new unit must have a distinctive cap-badge, though, the Adjutant General snorted.

Stirling complained that he had very few officers to choose from, as the best of Layforce had already been offered other posts. According to Lt. Carol Mather, Welsh Guards, though, the truth was that he had already canvassed most 8 Commando officers, and been bluntly turned down. 'We really could not give [his scheme] credence,' Mather wrote, 'and we thought we knew David too well for it to work. Another fiasco was the last thing that anyone could take.'[2]

Almost totally bereft of officers, Stirling thought once more of the brilliant Jock Lewes in Tobruk. In late August, Lewes was posted back to Alexandria and spent a few days in hospital recovering from acute desert sores – an ubiquitous problem among the troops, resulting from the British staple diet of bully beef. Suddenly, Stirling had Lewes cornered, and was able to focus on him the full power of his rhetoric. He urged Lewes to join the Parachute Unit as training officer, with carte blanche to run the show from within. After he'd gone, Lewes thought it over. The Stirling he had encountered in his hospital room was a different kettle of fish from the 'pudding' he'd known previously. This was a Stirling whose determination and enthusiasm were irresistible –

a man inspired.³ Stirling had already proved that he had the right connections to get the project moving, and, if Lewes had to play second-fiddle in the eyes of the world, at least it would be a vindication of his ideas.

A man of very little ego, Lewes realized that, together, he and Stirling could make the perfect partnership. Stirling might be commander in name, but the character of the new unit would be Lewes's. He decided that it would be more pragmatic to accept a bird-in-hand than to hold out for his own command. When he met Stirling at Shepheard's Hotel a few days later, he capitulated. 'I have been and gone and done the very thing which I promised myself in [Tobruk] that I would never let myself in for again,' he wrote home wryly. 'The only difference . . . is that now it appears that success does depend in a very large measure on what I do.'⁴

6. 'An extremely truculent Irishman'

On 21 June, five days after Stirling had 'piled in' at Fuka, Lt. Col. Geoffrey Keyes returned to his HQ at Salamis on Cyprus, to find an 'appalling scandal' in progress. The previous evening had been Guest Night at the 11 (Scottish) Commando's officers' mess, and one of his subalterns, twenty-six-year-old Lt. Robert Blair 'Paddy' Mayne, Royal Ulster Rifles, had drunk himself into a frenzy. Called to order by the commando's acting 2IC, Major Charles Napier, Gordon Highlanders, the scion of a well-known military family, Mayne had growled threats and become 'very bolshie'.¹ Later, as Napier returned to his tent, he was set upon by a 'huge unknown assailant', and severely thrashed. Napier was certain it was Mayne but was unable to identify him in the darkness.²

Geoffrey Keyes, Royal Scots Greys, son of the Director of Combined Operations, First World War hero Admiral Sir Roger Keyes, was a bespectacled Old Etonian, who, at twenty-six, was reportedly the youngest battalion commander in the British army. He investigated the assault on Napier, and by next morning was satisfied that Mayne was responsible. On 23 June he hauled Mayne in front of the Divisional Commander, Brigadier Rodwell, who promptly RTU'd him. The orders session is recorded in Keyes's diary:

June 23: 'Produce Paddy before Div Commander, and he is rocketed and removed. Very sorry to lose him as he did awfully well in the battle and is a great fighter. He is, however, an extremely truculent Irishman when he is "drink taken" and is as strong as a bull.'[3]

11 Commando had arrived back in Cyprus only a week earlier, after its spectacular but costly landing at the mouth of the Litani River in Syria – the first opposed landing ever carried out by commando troops. Of the three hundred and eighty-five men who had struggled ashore, a hundred and four were killed and thirty badly wounded.

The Litani action was Mayne's baptism of fire, and he had acquitted himself well. His 7 Troop had engaged the enemy minutes after hitting the beach, and had ended the day with ninety prisoners, eight machine guns and three mortars. Back on Cyprus, he was recommended for a Mention in Dispatches – the first in the series of awards that would eventually put him among the most decorated men of the war.

Mayne was eleven months older than David Stirling. Born in Newtownards, Northern Ireland, where his family were Protestant businessmen and lawyers, he was the second youngest of four brothers and three sisters. Articled to a firm of solicitors, he had read law at Queen's University, Belfast, but had not completed his studies when war broke out.

He was a big man – six foot two or three, fifteen and a half stone of muscle, yet as light on his feet as a tap-dancer. He was respected by his troops, but not known for his small-talk – softly spoken, shy and withdrawn, he filled his spare moments with his head in a book and a cigarette in his mouth. He was a formidable boxer. While at Queens he had won the Irish Universities heavyweight championship and reached the final in the British Universities championship. It was rugby, though, that was his real forte. Capped six times for Ireland, and once for the British Lions, he had made his name as lock-forward against the Springboks in the Lions' 1938 South African tour.

Mayne had been commissioned in the Royal Ulster Rifles, but was 'on loan' to a Scottish battalion, the Royal Cameronians, when 11 (Scottish) Commando was formed at Galashiels. He volunteered together with a close friend from the RUR, a nineteen-year-old fellow-solicitor from a well-known Catholic family in Ulster, Lt. Eoin McGonigal. In normal circumstances, Mayne shared his culture's disdain for Catholics, but he and McGonigal were close. David Stirling was later to make the not entirely flattering observation that McGonigal was 'the one person who liked Paddy before he became a hero'.[4]

Mayne was much more than the stereotype bruiser. He was a man of sensitivity – modest, gentle, considerate, literate and intelligent. He had a profound ability to empathize. Like many shy people, though, he had a shadow side – one that, in his case, emerged during bouts of heavy drinking. This alter ego was an 'Edward Hyde' character, capable of beating others to a pulp for no good reason. When Mayne was drinking heavily he could be frightening, even to hardened soldiers. In years to come, there would be a mad scramble for cover when it was announced that 'Paddy was looking for a drinking partner'.

Mayne was interested in women, but lacked the ability to form long-term relationships. This may have been the result of his close ties with his dominant mother, around whom, according to his brother, Douglas, he 'behaved like a child . . . responding to her every whim', and who 'demanded his constant attention'.[5] Despite his athletic prowess and huge dimensions, he regarded himself as a 'big, ugly man', to whom no woman would be attracted. Stirling later ascribed the shadow aspect of his character to a frustrated creative urge, which, he wrote, 'got bottled up to an intolerable level and this led to some of his heavy drinking bouts . . . and . . . explained at least some of his violent acts and black moods'.[6]

After being RTU'd, Mayne returned to the Infantry Base Depot at Geneifa, in Egypt, where, a week later, he went down with malaria. He spent most of July recovering at No. 19 General Hospital, Canal Zone, and at a convalescent home nearby. Laycock had been on Cyprus the day Keyes had brought Mayne in front of the Divisional Commander, and knew all about the assault on Napier. He had suggested Mayne's name for the new unit, but Stirling had lost track of him. He said later that he'd discovered where Mayne was through a 'great friend' of his, and went to interview him.[7] This 'great friend' can only have been Eoin McGonigal, whom Stirling recruited for the SAS in mid-August.

Stirling's encounter with Paddy Mayne, probably at Geneifa, that August has become one of the great SAS foundation myths. Stirling himself maintained that Mayne was in military prison when they met, awaiting court martial. In fact, he was neither under close arrest, in prison, nor facing court martial. Keyes, who would have recorded any such sentence in his diary, simply wrote that he was 'removed' – RTU was the usual punishment for commando offenders.[8]

Mayne greeted Stirling with suspicion. He had a problem with authority figures, and particularly disliked 'snooty public-school types', of whom Stirling was a prime example. When Stirling addressed him as 'Paddy' he replied curtly that his name was 'Blair'. He gave out contradictory signals. On one hand, he spoke in a self-effacing way, blinking ceaselessly. On the other, there was a sheer physical presence to him that was intimidating. Stirling felt challenged from the beginning by his physical superiority, and later, unexpectedly, by his natural qualities of leadership. In months to come this would develop into a fierce sense of competition that would lead both to reckless acts. Mayne was a very different character from either Stirling or Lewes. While Stirling was a dreamer, and Lewes a thinker, Mayne was a warrior – an instinctive fighting man.

'What are the chances of fighting?' was Mayne's inevitable question.

'None,' Stirling is supposed to have answered. 'Except against the enemy.'

Mayne chortled, and agreed to join Stirling. Before shaking hands on the deal, though, Stirling demanded his word that the Napier incident would not be repeated. Mayne promised, and as Stirling later commented, 'kept the promise at least in respect of myself, though not with others'. The triumvirate of remarkable men who made the Special Air Service Regiment – the dreamer, the thinker and the fighter – was complete.

7. Wondering why he should be scared if Lewes wasn't

At about 2220 hours on 16 November 1941, five Bristol Bombays of 216 Squadron RAF banked south over the coast of Cyrenaica into a wall of Italian flares, searchlights and ack-ack fire. The aircraft were spaced out at irregular intervals, their pilots searching for separate drop-zones on the littoral plain, about ten minutes away. It was a moonless night, with rain and cloud, and below them a sandstorm was brewing. Although they could see snatches of the coast through the swirling dust, the pilots could make out neither the landmarks they had anticipated, nor the flares they had dropped to assess their positions.

The aircraft had taken off at twenty-minute intervals from Baggush, an airbase west of Alexandria, not long after sunset. At the same time Auchinleck's Eighth Army, under his field commander, Cunningham, had started rolling towards Libya, on the long-awaited Crusader offensive. Cunningham's column – six hundred tanks, five thousand lorries and armoured cars, and a hundred thousand troops – stretched through the desert for more than a hundred miles.

In the lead Bombay – No. 1 Flight – David Stirling felt the aircraft lurch as the pilot tried to put cloud-cover between the plane and the Italian anti-aircraft gunners. The RAF dispatcher had already ordered the stick of eleven men to stand up and hook up. The jump was just six minutes away.

Though Stirling didn't know it until much later, one of his five aircraft hadn't made it through the ground-defences. Minutes earlier, No. 4 Flight's pilot, Flight Sergeant Charlie West, had taken the Bombay down to two hundred feet to get a visual fix on the coast. No sooner had she shucked cloud-cover than she was hit by a burst of flak that shattered West's instrument panel and holed the port engine.

West heaved the thirteen-ton bird back into cloud, but she had lost power, and fuel was bucketing out of the wing tanks. He told the SAS section commander, Lt. Charles Bonington, that he was aborting the drop and turning back.

Paddy Mayne was on the trailing aircraft, No. 5 Flight, the last to take off from Baggush. As his Bombay dipped over the coast, he braced the open door, shivering with cold, wondering how his section would hold up in combat. His section sergeant, Edward McDonald, Cameron Highlanders, had fought with 11 Commando at the Litani River in Syria, where he had commanded a sub-section during a daylight advance on the Kafr Badr bridge. Corporal Dougie Arnold, Cameron Highlanders, known as the 'Great Escaper', had been in combat with 7 Commando on Crete. Separated from his troop, he had survived in the mountains for a fortnight before stealing a boat and navigating it back to Egypt.

Parachutist Reg Seekings, poised near Mayne at the front of the stick, had already acquired his 'red badge of courage' – he had been wounded in the thigh during the raid on Bardia. He was another 7 Commando man. A dour ex-farmhand from the desolate East Anglian Fens, Seekings had served in the Cambridgeshire Regiment before volunteering for the commandos. A fitness fanatic, keen on running and cycling, he had also been heavyweight boxing champion of his division. Seekings was living an ambition. He had been turned down for parachute training with 2 (Airborne) Commando in 1940, because he exceeded the weight limit. Now he was about to take part in the first ever SAS operational jump.

Next to Seekings was Corporal Bob Bennett, a Grenadier with the mercurial charm of a Cockney barrow-boy. Born and bred in London's East End, he had joined the Guards at the start of war but, disillusioned with 'bullshit' and what he thought were antique ideas of warfare, he and his mate, J.H.M. 'Lofty' Baker, had volunteered for 8 Commando. The disbandment of Layforce had left them high and dry at the Infantry Base Depot at Geneifa, with no parent unit serving in the theatre. Both had joined the SAS.

Behind Bennett were Parachutist Harold White, Royal Army Service Corps, Corporal Geordie White, Royal Scots (an ex-11 Commando man) and three 8 Commando veterans – Lance-Corporal Bill Kendall, and Parachutists Anthony Hawkins and Thomas Chesworth, Coldstream Guards. Chesworth, a world-class complainer, had already incurred Mayne's wrath once on the final exercise, when Mayne had shut him up by holding him one-handed over the edge of a cliff.

The last man in the stick was thirty-one-year-old Cpl. 'Honest Dave' Kershaw, another Grenadier, who had been with the 8 Commando raiding detachment at Tobruk. Kershaw, a sailor in his youth, had fought with the International Brigade against the Fascists in the Spanish Civil War. He had enlisted in the Guards, but had ditched the gloomy prospect of training recruits at Pirbright for 8 Commando and Layforce. Now he was in the SAS, waiting to leap out into darkness and a forty-mile-an-hour wind. When the green light came on, at 2230 hours precisely, there was no drama. Mayne went out first, and the section cleared the aircraft in thirty seconds.

For Jock Lewes's section, on No. 3 Flight, the situation for the past few minutes had looked sticky. His aircraft had only made it through the AA screen by the skin of her teeth. Seconds after banking, she had been illuminated by 'flaming onion' tracers, pinpointed by half a dozen searchlights and hit by streams of orange, green and yellow 20mm tracer, punching through the hull with the sound of ripping paper.

No sooner had the plane cleared the first line of defences than she was picked up by two more beams, and the clatter of ack-ack fire started up again. Now Lewes was plying through the cabin with a deliberate expression of nonchalance on his face, while his ten-strong stick battled to hook up their static lines, to stay balanced as the plane bucked, plunged and yawed, and to dodge the enemy flak coming up through the floor. Poised near the rear starboard door, Cpl. Jeff Du Vivier saw a 20mm shell burst through the aircraft's skin and plop out again, narrowly missing the auxiliary fuel tank that took up most of the cabin's space. 'The flak was terrible,' recalled Du Vivier, London Scottish, an ex-hotel clerk who had fought with 11 Commando at the Litani River. 'We were all leaning back against the side and the flak was coming up through the centre. How the hell no one got wounded I don't know.'[1]

Opposite him, twenty-two-year-old Parachutist Jimmy Storie, Seaforth Highlanders, ex-11 Commando and a former tile-fitter from Ayr in Scotland, was trying to convince himself that the men nearest him, both six-foot giants, were more likely to be hit than he was. They were Lewes's sergeants, twenty-five-year-old John 'Jock' Cheyne, Gordon Highlanders, and his friend Charles 'Pat' Riley, Coldstream Guards. Both had been uncomfortable with the fit of their parachute-harnesses, and had swapped them on the two-hour flight from Baggush. Cheyne, a good-natured Scot known for his humour, had distinguished himself with 11 Commando at the Litani, by taking command when his troop officer, Lt. Bill Fraser, had been hit and knocked out. Fraser, another Gordon, was also serving with L Detachment but had been left behind on this operation because of a broken arm sustained in training. Charles 'Pat' Riley, an ex-policeman in East Anglia and Palestine, was technically an American. Born in Wisconsin, he had been brought up in England and had enlisted in the Coldstreams at eighteen, giving false information about his nationality. He had rejoined the Guards at the start of the war but, faced with the prospect of drilling recruits for the duration, had volunteered for 8 Commando and sailed for the Middle East on *Glenroy*. Riley had seen action at the Twin Pimples, and was one of the famous 'Tobruk Four' who had patrolled with Jock Lewes behind Axis lines that summer.

Nineteen-year-old Parachutist Johnny Cooper, near the front of the stick, was convinced that the Bombay, slow and unstable at the best of times, was going to crash. A youth from Leicester with a grammar-school education, Cooper had been an apprentice wool-grader in Bradford when war broke out. Under age at the time, he had persuaded the recruiting sergeant to enlist him in the Scots Guards on the strength of five shillings and his Scottish descent. He had served in Stirling's troop in 8 Commando, and was one of thirteen guardsmen recruited from Buqbuq. For Cooper, who would end his military career a lieutenant-colonel, this was his second taste of enemy fire – his first had been with the 8 Commando raiding detachment at Tobruk. Now, he was watching Jock Lewes's placid face and wondering why he should be scared if Lewes wasn't.

Behind Cooper were Parachutist Bob Lilley, Coldstream Guards, a big, physically tough barrack-room philosopher, and another of Lewes's 'Tobruk Four'. With him were three more 8 Commando men, Corporals Johnny Rose and Jimmy Brough, both of 2 Scots Guards, and Parachutist Frank Rhodes, of the Grenadiers. The tenth man was Lance Corporal Charlie Cattell, East Surrey Regiment, who had served with 7 Commando.

The Bombay had taken a hit on the starboard wing, but was still climbing steadily up to five hundred feet. Lewes told the stick that the pilot was lost. They would be jumping blind, into a force nine wind.

Eight minutes from the drop-zone, the RAF dispatcher ordered, '*Prepare to jump.*' They were the longest eight minutes any of them remembered. It was freezing in the cabin because the door had been removed. The men were nauseated by the stink of aviation fuel and the craft's constant pitching. Jumping blind or not, they couldn't wait to get out. Then, two minutes to exit-time, the red light flashed on. Hands turned white on the static-lines. Everything went out of focus but the door of the aircraft. The green light winked. They were almost on top of each other as they dropped out into the night.

8. 'The man is the Regiment'

Almost the only thing the men of L Detachment had in common was a yearning for action. They came from different parts of Britain and from different backgrounds – from rural hamlets, suburban estates, inner-city slums. Some were teenagers not long out of school, others were men in their forties with wives and children. In civvy-street, they had been labourers, farm-hands, factory-workers, seamen, fishermen, policemen, clerks. What they shared was a contempt for the humdrum, and a need for dynamic quality in their lives. Forty-odd years on, David Stirling would comment that the 'type of chap' who joined the post-war SAS, though more politically aware, technically sophisticated, and ready to argue his corner, was 'really no different in spirit from those who came together in Africa'.[1]

Critics who dismiss special forces troops as 'adrenalin addicts' or immature characters needing to 'prove themselves' are probably acceding subconsciously to Dr Johnson's adage that 'Every man thinks meanly of himself for not having been a soldier.' Peter Ratcliffe, DCM, who started his military career as a private in the Paras, served in the post-war SAS for a quarter of a century and retired a major, spoke for almost every special forces soldier, on one level or another, when he wrote that he had joined the army to 'get away from a miserable dead-end existence', and owed to both the Paras and the SAS the fact that he was not 'still in a dead-end job'.[2] Captain Malcolm Pleydell, L Detachment's medical officer, said that his motive for joining the SAS was simply 'boredom': 'This sort of warfare possessed a definite flavour or romance,' he wrote. 'It conjured up visions of dashing deeds which might become famous overnight.'[3]

Some people are content with static lives, others endure them. Some need dynamic quality to feel alive at all. Change comes about through individuals who are not able to accept things as they are. The commando idea was itself an attempt to rid the British army of its outdated feudal ethos. It was partly to supersede the tactics of the 'thundering herd' with its mass 'suicide-charges' of the First World War that Stirling and Lewes had come up with the SAS concept in the first place. In every age there have been men who have sought the dynamic edge of reality in the warrior's path – a path on which 'the only perceived good is freedom, and the only perceived evil is static quality itself'.[4]

The original L Detachment was an elite of an elite. All its personnel were ex-Layforce, and therefore volunteers. They had made a further commitment to join the new unit. Stirling personally interviewed all potential recruits who hadn't seen combat. Those with favourable combat records were taken on automatically. There was no selection in the modern sense of a pro-active pass/fail course, but standards were high. Tough desert battle-marches organized by Jock Lewes, and dangerous parachute-training, served as satisfactory rites of passage. The idea was that the training would sort out the 'passengers' – but the men would 'fail themselves'.

Stirling understood that the quality of the SAS was the quality of its recruits. Technology and technique couldn't transform men into supermen, while for the right men almost anything was possible. 'The man is the Regiment,' he said later, 'and the Regiment is the man.'

In a speech made years later, he told his audience that the cornerstone of the SAS was and had always been the 'calibre of each individual man recruited'. His initial menu of SAS values was basically a restatement of the purity of the commando idea – a purity that had been corrupted in actual performance.

In his inaugural address to the Detachment on 4 September, he told the men that they would be expected to display self-discipline, independence, personal initiative, modesty, and the highest standards of turnout and behaviour. RTU would be the penalty for those who weren't committed, or weren't up to the training. 'We can't afford,' he said, 'to piss about disciplining anyone who is not a hundred per cent devoted to having a crack at the Hun.'[5]

There was a paradox inherent in his requirements, though. He wanted men 'who argued', who were 'not controllable, only

harnessable', who were 'individuals', yet men who would be as
rigidly disciplined as the Brigade of Guards. One of these principles
had to go, and inevitably it was the old 'bullshit' style of discipline.
'There was no bawling,' Jeff Du Vivier said, describing conditions
at the SAS base in the early years. 'None of what is commonly
known as bullshit. Drilling, saluting officers every time you passed
them, it was all forgotten . . . You had to learn to think for yourself.
If the sergeant said do this and you didn't think it was right, then
you didn't do it.'[6]

This laid-back attitude to normal discipline continued in the
post-war SAS. Charlie Beckwith, the US Special Forces officer
who served with 22 SAS, wrote that '[The SAS] shared with the
Brigade of Guards a deep respect for quality and battle-discipline,
but unlike the Guards it had little respect for drill and uniform, in
part because it approached warfare in an entirely unorthodox
manner.'[7] 'The discipline was there,' wrote wartime SAS-man
Roy Close, 'but it was unobtrusive and understood; and that is
really the hallmark of the SAS. We knew who was who.'[8]

The 'Cheekie Laddie' Stirling was himself no paragon of
Guardsman-like ways, and was certainly ill-qualified to impose this
ideal on men like Paddy Mayne, who was never cured of his
addiction to binge-drinking and bar-room brawls. Nor was it only
the officers. Reg Seekings, the quintessential SAS enlisted man,
who served in almost every major SAS action of the war and
became one of the Regiment's most highly decorated soldiers, for
example, was remembered by his comrades as a pugnacious and
prickly bruiser, who, like Mayne, was apt to settle arguments with
a knuckle sandwich.

9. 'A yellow streak a yard wide'

Stirling's first op was designated 'Squatter', and training for it lasted
ten weeks. The Detachment's base at Kabrit on the Great Bitter
Lake, Canal Zone, was little more than a patch of desert next to a

naval camp, an airstrip and a signal station. There was no view but the canal and the stony wastes of Sinai on the other side. The odours of salt-breeze and sulphur hung on the air. The canal, with its heavy shipping, was a frequent target of Axis bombing and mine-dumping runs.

The base grew by the men's own efforts from five tents and a signboard to what Stirling called 'a spectacularly effective camp'. With his encouragement, they looted most of the tents and furniture from the nearby Allied Stores Depot, and the camp of 2 New Zealand Division, currently in Tobruk. Some of the boys had qualms about this, because the Kiwis were well-liked, but it was pointed out that they also had more than they needed: 'everything but the kitchen sink'.

Although Stirling later claimed that the men never complained about conditions in Kabrit, this was not the way some of the others remembered it. Reg Seekings recalled that Stirling had promised there would be no fatigues or sentry duty, but for the first fortnight all they seemed to do was dig holes and fill them in. Eventually they started to wonder if they'd been conned. Many decided to go back to their own units.[1]

Stirling probably failed to recall this incident because he spent most of his time in Cairo, wrangling with GHQ, and was away when it occurred. Day-to-day running of the camp was left to Jock Lewes, who suddenly found himself faced with a near-mutiny. He held a meeting in the lecture-tent, and after listening to the chuntering for a few moments, leapt on a table and barked, 'The trouble with you people is you've all got a bloody yellow streak a yard wide down your backs. You just can't take it, that's your problem.'[2]

There was an incredulous silence as the men wondered if they had heard right. To soldiers who had just laid their lives on the line for special service, many of whom had already seen hard fighting in Crete, in Syria and at Tobruk, it was an almost unforgivable insult. Lewes stared back at them stony-faced, and said, 'Right, prove me wrong. From now on you'll do anything I do, and I'll do anything you do.'[3] Later, Seekings couldn't believe that he hadn't flattened Lewes on the spot. Yet it worked – the real training started from then on.

The Detachment was divided into A and B Troops, commanded by Lewes and Mayne. The troops were subdivided into sections. Stirling envisaged his eleven-man sticks being subdividable into two units of five, plus one officer, but the essence of the SAS was its flexibility. It would not fight in set formations like infantry, but its personnel could be picked and mixed according to the task. All ranks were trained in demolitions, Axis small-arms, including Beretta pistols and Schmeisser sub-machine guns, first aid and parachuting.

Lewes doubled as Training Officer, and, besides Mayne, there were three other officers on the orbat: Lt. Bill Fraser, Gordon Highlanders, Lt. Charles Bonington, General List, and Lt. Eoin McGonigal, Royal Ulster Rifles. The Company Sergeant-Major, George 'Bill' Yates, and a Company Quarter Master Sergeant, Gerry 'Daddy' Ward, had been among the first men selected. In practice, the Detachment had an operational orbat of sixty-eight men, with another twenty-six assigned for back-up and administration duties – a total of ninety-four. Captain Peter Warr, East Surrey Regiment, a trained parachute instructor, turned up at the beginning of November in time to add the finishing touches, but too late to affect the basic parachute course.

Lewes's course was commando training geared to desert conditions. The men developed the confidence to navigate across hostile terrain, with little food and water and the sketchiest of maps. Night confidence and night shooting were essential, as movement and offensive operations would take place only in darkness. They practised night movement blindfolded during the day, crawling, feeling and sensing objects, so that their instructors could watch them and point out mistakes.

They practised the recognition of sounds at night until it was second nature, and it soon became clear that operating during the moonless phase conferred considerable advantages. On moonless nights, visibility was down to a maximum of twenty yards, and the range of automatic weapons down to only ten or twenty yards, rendering enemy machine-gun posts virtually useless. For the observation phase, they were trained in recognition and memory techniques, including 'Kim's Game', and coached in writing observation reports. The dyslexic Reg Seekings found this the most taxing job of all. While the others were sound asleep, he would be poring over his notes, convinced that he would never make it.

Basic infantry skills were honed until they were perfect. Jock Lewes taught fieldcraft, Bill Fraser, map-reading, and Eoin McGonigal, weapon-training. Mayne took gruelling PT sessions and doubled as Provost Marshal – punishments usually consisted of going a few rounds in the ring with him, a daunting challenge to all but the other boxing champs like Reg Seekings and Pat Riley.

The commandos had aimed to produce men capable of marching two and a half miles an hour with full equipment, over distances of up to thirty-five miles. The endurance march was to become the key aspect of SAS training and, later, its selection course. The marches took place mainly at night, over distances of between twelve and thirty miles, carrying packs filled with sand. The men soon got wise to this, tipped the sand out, and replaced it before the end of the march. Lewes took to issuing bricks instead. The conservation of water was crucial to these marches. The men carried a water-bottle, but would be expected to have water left when they returned. They didn't drink unless instructed, and even practised washing their mouths with water and spitting it back, in the belief that swallowing it would only make one more thirsty.

In parachute-training, Lewes had to improvise from lack of experience. Requests for guidance to No. 1 Parachute Training School at Ringway, Manchester, evoked responses that were slow in arriving, and some of Lewes's do-it-yourself techniques proved counter-productive.

The training-gear was created from designs Stirling acquired. It was constructed by a self-styled 'bogus engineer' – twenty-seven-year-old Sergeant John 'Gentleman Jim' Almonds, Coldstream Guards, ex-8 Commando, and one of Lewes's celebrated 'Tobruk Four'. Almonds was to be left out of Op Squatter because his newly-born son – incidentally a future 22 SAS squadron-commander – was in hospital in Britain, gravely ill. The son of a Lincolnshire smallholder, Almonds was a brilliant improviser who had built a boat and an aeroplane in his youth. He took advice from a Royal Engineers officer, Captain Fred Cumper, and constructed training-towers, gantries to simulate parachute-canopies, and a miniature railway with a trolley that could be used for practising parachute-rolls.

When the trolley proved cumbersome, Lewes decided to have the men hurl themselves from the back of a fifteen-hundredweight truck instead. Seekings recalled jumping off at about thirty-five miles an hour and trying to land on his feet rather than rolling. 'I ploughed up the bloody desert with my face,' he remembered, 'I was in a hell of a state. That was the last time I tried to be clever. [Then] Paddy Mayne jumped out and you could hear his head hit the deck half a mile away.'[4]

The truck-jumping technique, rightly considered dangerous by professional parachute-instructors, caused injuries to more than half the Detachment, and resulted in at least half a dozen broken limbs: Jeff Du Vivier, Jimmy Brough and Lt. Bill Fraser were among the hospitalized cases.

10. 'We tried not to think about it. But we did'

The situation grew darker when the time came for aircraft jumps. Dudley Clarke had pointed out at the July conference that experience had shown the necessity of training on the same aircraft parachutists would use on operations. Stirling had managed to get the use of an RAF Bristol Bombay for parachute-training.

The Bombays were veterans, with a maximum airspeed of about ninety miles an hour in all but the most favourable conditions. They were as unstable as kites. When a parachutist wanted to go to the heads (toilet) in the rear gun-turret he had to inform the pilot, because the movement displaced the centre of gravity by eleven feet. Still, they were an improvement on the Valentia Lewes and Stirling had used on their first drop at Fuka. They had been modified with a head-level anchor-line to which the parachutes' static-lines were clipped. When the parachutist jumped, the force of the slipstream yanked him sideways and down, pulling the static-line taut and jerking open the parachute canopy. The static-line was fixed to the canopy with a tie that broke under pressure, leaving the line attached to the anchor in the aircraft, and allowing the canopy to fall free.

By the third week in October there had already been two drops. Stirling himself had jumped both times, though not all of the Detachment had yet made their first descent. One of the uninitiated was Jeff Du Vivier, who was just about to collapse in his tent one evening when someone poked his head in and told him, 'You're down for jumping tomorrow.' Du Vivier dashed over to the noticeboard and examined the manifest. His name was third on the list. That was the end of his sleep for the night. He tossed and turned till first light, and at breakfast found that he had lost his appetite. When he scanned the faces of the other condemned, he saw in them a reflection of his own.

The 16 October jump was to include multiple lifts, carrying sticks of mixed one-jump veterans and first-timers. The drop-zone was on the opposite side of the canal, on the shores of the great rocky shelf of Sinai. Du Vivier was with Johnny Cooper, Jimmy Storie and seven others in the first stick. Nineteen-year-old Cooper recalled that he was desperately afraid, but that as soon as he was out of the door and hurtling through the slipstream, the fear dissolved. As he drifted down slowly under his canopy, he took in the stunning view – the yellow-amber landmass right down the Canal to the Gulf of Suez and, on the other side, the paper-model town of Ismailiyya and the blueness of the Bitter Lakes. The first stick landed without mishap, then the Bombay picked up its second stick, and took off for another run.

As it happened, the first three men in the next stick were all ex-11 Commando and veterans of the Litani action. The first two were both ex-Seaforth Highlanders, twenty-one-year-old

Ken Warburton from Manchester and his mate, Scotsman Joseph Duffy. The third man was Parachutist Billy Morris of the Black Watch. The Bombay came in for her final run, and the green light sparked. The dun-coloured desert was only nine hundred feet below, but to Warburton, at the door, it looked a thousand miles away. The RAF dispatcher, Flight Sergeant Ted Pacey, clapped him on the shoulder and yelled 'Go!' in his ear. Warburton leapt out into the sky. Behind him, Joe Duffy hesitated. 'What are you waiting for, man?' Pacey yelled. Duffy jumped. Neither he nor Warburton were seen alive again.

On the airstrip waiting for the next lift, Bob Bennett, Dave Kershaw and Reg Seekings watched the aircraft bank around the drop-zone and head back towards them. They looked at each other, wondering what had happened. 'I'm sure I saw something come out of the plane,' Bennett told Kershaw.

'Well, if it had done there would've been a parachute,' Kershaw replied. Moments later, the Bombay landed and the stick trooped out grim-faced. Warburton and Duffy had jumped to their deaths: their parachutes had failed to open. The snap-links on their static-lines had bent and burst under pressure – there had been nothing to pull the canopies out. Dispatcher Ted Pacey, who blamed himself for the accident, had only noticed after Duffy had gone. He'd pulled the third man, Morris, back from the brink. Morris considered himself the luckiest man alive.

The attachments had actually been changed a week earlier, after a previous jump. The original system had been to fit the D-ring on the static-line strop through a shackle on the anchor-line, and screw it closed. A new snap-hook with a spring release-clip, like a dog-leash, had been introduced for convenience and speed, but the steel wasn't robust enough to take the torsion forces. Ironically, there had been a similar fatality at Ringway previously, but news hadn't yet reached the SAS. Stirling was incensed when he found out.

Jimmy Storie was one of the party detailed to bring back the bodies of Warburton and Duffy. They found them lying on their backs, side by side, as if awaiting burial. There were signs that

Duffy, at least, had attempted to pull his own canopy open as he fell. Mayne, on the drop-zone at the time, said later that he had heard the men screaming as they dropped. Their bodies were brought back to Kabrit by boat – the first two names on the SAS roll of honour.

According to some eye-witnesses, Stirling had also been on the DZ and had seen the men pile in. Seekings and Bennett, though, recalled that he was away in Cairo at the time, and on hearing what had happened, signalled back immediately that everyone would jump next day. Bennett said that it was Jock Lewes, not Stirling, who took the parade at Kabrit that evening. 'Lewes had us on parade and told us that [the accident] was due to the fact that the RAF had put the fitting in the hands of the Egyptians,' he recalled. '[Lewes] said that this would be put right. The RAF would do it.'[1] Lewes relayed Stirling's order, but told the boys that anyone who wanted to leave was free to do so.

Nobody left, but that night proved to be the severest test of the whole training course. Parachuting was unnatural enough – most SAS-men loathed it – but a chute that failed to open at only nine hundred feet was the parachutist's worst nightmare. Few of them got any sleep that night. They were issued with a tin of fifty Players' Navy Cut cigarettes each, and spent most of the night chain-smoking. It was the worst twenty-four hours of their lives. 'We tried not to think about it,' Bennett said, 'but we did.'[2]

Next morning, Stirling, back from Cairo, hooked up number one on the first lift, for what was probably the most crucial drop in SAS history. Bob Bennett, jumping for the first time, said that, when 'Action stations' was called, everyone began tugging on their static-lines frantically. Stirling went out first, and the whole detachment jumped in five successive lifts, at a thousand feet, without a hitch. Bob Bennett was so euphoric that on the way down he started playing his mouth-organ.

The deaths of Warburton and Duffy weren't entirely in vain. The episode that might have been disastrous for the SAS proved an important morale-booster. The next day's jump was, said Bennett, 'when I found out I was with a unit that meant something, because not one man backed out'.[3] Stirling's evident courage in going out first increased his standing. He had joined in virtually none of the training, and the men didn't know him as well as they knew Lewes, Mayne, Fraser and the others. Most of the time he'd been away in Cairo, and Lewes had been the real boss. 'David has been . . . absent more than not,' Lewes wrote to his mother, 'and I have been in command the while . . . We have fashioned this unit; he has established it without and I think I may say I have established it within.'[4]

Stirling admitted later that the enlisted men had been ill-at-ease with him. Some remembered him from 8 Commando days as a member of the jet-set 'Silver Circle Club' in Cairo, centred on author Evelyn Waugh and the Prime Minister's son, Randolph Churchill, whose natural habitat was the bar and the racetrack. Stirling, who had been more shaken than he showed by the accident, admitted later that he hated parachuting. The jump on 17 October, though, was the worst he ever had to make.

11. 'A nice little black pudding'

Stirling always denied that the SAS was a band of airborne saboteurs, yet at first it was in their demolitions training that they differed most from other special units. Lewes set up lectures by visiting experts, including civil engineers, railwaymen and aircraft engineers, who advised them where to lay charges for the most devastating possible results.

Lewes was aware, though, that the available five-pound charges weren't suitable for saboteurs operating on foot. They were too heavy and cumbersome. He worked out that the men would be able to carry only two charges apiece, which meant that the operation would inflict minimal damage. This was worse than useless, because the enemy would be able to get the undamaged planes airborne and pursue the raiders. Lewes had been determined from the start not to get involved in a suicide raid.

He had made it a personal challenge to develop a bomb that was light, easy to set up, and would write off an aircraft in one go. He needed a charge that would be both explosive and incendiary at the same time. A Sapper demolitions expert from GHQ told him that he was hunting the snark: bombs could explode or burn, but not both. Lewes ignored him and erected a small hut on camp as a laboratory, where he began to conduct chemical experiments. He laboured night after night, and nocturnal bangs and crashes became commonplace.

Stirling returned from Cairo one night to find the camp in uproar. Earlier, Lewes had burst into the bar shouting, 'I've got it! I've got it!' All the men had left their beer and jogged over to goggle at the new charge in operation. '[Lewes] was going nuts,' Seekings recalled. 'It was the only time I ever saw him excited.'[1]

He had invented the 'Lewes bomb' – a mixture of plastic explosive with thermite and aluminium turnings, rolled in engine-oil. It was, said 'bogus engineer' Jim Almonds, 'a nice little black pudding' that was ignited by a gun-cotton primer and a No. 27 detonator, set off by a thirty-second fuse. The thermite caused a flash that would detonate the petrol in the aircraft's fuel tank, blow the wing off, and destroy the entire plane. The bomb could also be detonated by a 'time-pencil' when longer or shorter delays were needed. A pen-sized glass tube, the 'pencil' contained a phial of acid and a spring-loaded striker held back by a strip of copper wire. When the phial was smashed, the acid would eat through the wire and release the striker – the time depending on the thickness of the wire. The time-pencils were colour-coded according to delay-times.

While conventional charges had to be tied in place, the Lewes bomb was 'sticky' – it could be moulded into position in a few seconds. It also weighed only a little more than a pound, which meant that every man could carry in his pack the means of wrecking at least eight aircraft. The Lewes bomb was literally custom-built for SAS operations, and was a brilliant feat of ingenuity. Later, the legend grew up that Lewes was an Oxford science graduate – in fact his only relevant experience was with a childhood chemistry set.

12. Rite of passage

By the end of October, Lewes felt that L Detachment was ready for its first mission. A few recruits had fallen out or been RTU'd, leaving a core of desert-hardened men who were all marching fit, demolitions-trained, and qualified parachutists.

Stirling had an idea for a gruelling final exercise. It came to him over a £10 bet with a deprecating RAF Group Captain, that his men could get into the RAF base at Heliopolis, near Cairo, and slap labels representing bombs on the aircraft parked there. The Group Captain, whose name remains unknown, was almost certainly the officer responsible for airfield security, an activity on which the RAF were currently conducting an in-depth study.

The whole operational orbat of the Detachment would trek across the desert from Kabrit, a distance of ninety miles, in three days. Hefting packs simulating the weight of Lewes bombs, they would travel in four groups, moving only by night, and lying up in daytime under a piece of hessian they each carried with them. They would be allowed only four pints of water each. The idea was to complete thirty miles a night for the first three nights, then hit the airfield on the fourth night. The RAF knew they were coming, but Stirling didn't tell them that the SAS would be arriving out of the desert.

On briefing, the men thought there would be a high drop-out rate: in the event, it went off superbly, and only one man fell out. Having covered the distance unspotted, the SAS arrived at Heliopolis at midnight on the fourth day, so feverish from water-loss that some of them were half convinced that it actually was an Axis airfield. They clipped their way through the fence and stuck their labels on more than forty aircraft. They then did a few circuits of the drome to reassure themselves that they could get away with it without being nabbed.

Stirling duly collected his £10 wager and a gratifying letter of congratulation from the Group Captain. The SAS had proved that they were capable of moving long distances on foot across the desert by night, lying up by day, and infiltrating a guarded airstrip unseen. They had undergone their ordeal, their rite of passage. They had survived hellish marches on little water, had come through parachute training that had injured many and killed two of their comrades. They had earned a special identity forged through shared hardship. They were ready for anything.

The first operation – Squatter – was to go in on 16 November against Axis airfields at Gazala and Tmimi. These were the bases for both Italian and German aircraft, including the Messerschmitt 109-Fs, state-of-the-art airpower that could fly faster and higher than RAF Hurricanes and outdated Gloster Gladiator biplanes. The 109-Fs had first been reported in Libya by British intelligence only weeks earlier, and one had been shot down more or less intact. These fighters were fitted with 20mm cannons that could outgun anything the RAF could throw at them. It was estimated that about 50 per cent of Axis single-engined aircraft would be 109-Fs by the end of October. On 10 November Stirling received his brief, instructing him that Messerschmitt 109-Fs would be his priority targets.

The operation was secret, but the existence of the SAS was not. It had come into being primarily as part of Dudley Clarke's propaganda force, and its airborne potential was to be proclaimed to the world. When Auchinleck arrived in Kabrit for his final inspection on 13 November, he was accompanied by a small army of newsmen, including two American correspondents, and a newsreel cinematographer. The cameraman shot footage of Stirling greeting the C-in-C, of Jock Lewes and his stick inside a Bombay, of the parachutists descending from two thousand feet. The footage became a four-minute film that was shown at cinemas around the world on Pathé News. This exposure was of even greater significance than the operation itself. Almost forty years before the Pagoda team appeared on the world's TV screens at the storming of the Iranian Embassy, the SAS potential as a psychological weapon had already been unveiled.

13. 'We'll go because we've got to go'

On Sunday 16 November, Stirling was at HQ RAF Western Desert near Baggush when the first weather reports came in. They were not encouraging. The weather at Baggush was fine, but the met boys were tracking a storm that would break over the target area with rain, and winds of thirty knots. Stirling was staggered. A fifteen-knot wind was enough to cancel the drop. The Brigadier General Staff coordinator, Sandy Galloway, advised him to call it off. There would be no moon, and with winds gusting that fast, the parachutists would be scattered. They would certainly sustain high casualties. 'There will be plenty of other opportunities,' Galloway told him. 'However, the decision will rest with you.'[1]

Stirling cursed his bad luck. He told Galloway glumly that he would talk it over with the boys and get back to him within the hour. The Detachment was at Baggush airfield, where they had arrived that morning, raring to go. They had been briefed about the operation only twenty-four hours earlier. The atmosphere in the lecture-tent at Kabrit had been electric when they discovered that they had been training to knock out the whole fleet of Messerschmitt 109-Fs.

In October, Stirling had conducted a night-recce over the targets, riding passenger on a Royal Navy Albacore aircraft. His final orders had come from Eighth Army Battle HQ the previous day. The SAS was to raid the airfields at Tmimi, Gazala No. 1 and Gazala No. 2, on the night of 17/18 November. The airfields would also be bombed by RAF Wellingtons and Albacores during the dates his unit was in the field. After completing its tasks, the SAS was to rendezvous with a patrol of the Long Range Desert Group early on 21 November, at a place agreed on between them. The LRDG would carry them to a fallback rendezvous, where they would find two of their own trucks in the charge of Lt. Bill Fraser. They would travel by their own transport to Jaghbub oasis on the Egyptian border, from where they would return to Kabrit by air.

The target airfields lay on the coastal strip west of Tobruk, and extended a total distance of seventy miles. The area wasn't the desert proper, but a flat, rocky plain with well-frequented tracks running east-west, grooved by shallow wadis, and covered with sedge, esparto grass and thorny acacia scrub. It was sparsely inhabited by Bedouin of the Awlad 'Ali, coastal semi-nomads who kept camels and sheep and hitched their camels to ploughs in the rainy season. It was hot and humid and subject to sea-mists. In winter, daytime temperatures got up to about 29° Celsius, and went down to 11° Celsius at night.

The Bombays would hug the coast at eight thousand feet, then wheel south over the Gulf of Bomba. They would pass over the target area, and drop the parachutists in the desert about twenty miles west-south-west of their objectives. The SAS would lie up five miles south of the airfields during the next day, and hit the targets simultaneously at exactly one minute past midnight, as the Eighth Army's tanks lumbered into battle.

Stirling felt depressed as he drove back to the airstrip. The one thing he had dreaded was a cancellation. After the final ex, the Detachment's spirits had hit the roof, but everyone had bad memories of the continuous aborted operations they had suffered in Layforce. Galloway had told him there would be other chances, but he didn't think postponement was an option. The operation had to be pulled off in coordination with the Crusader advance. Whatever the brigadier said, Stirling was convinced that if this job was called off, they would never be allowed another go.

He knew he had enemies among the 'layers of fossilized shit' at GHQ, many of whom had predicted that Squatter would fail. He was also embarrassingly aware that one of his main selling-points for the new unit had been that 'weather would not restrict their operations to the same extent that it had done in the case of seaborne special service troops'.[2] On the other hand, the allocation of five Bombays for a single special-operations mission was unprecedented. Was it right to risk five priceless aircraft and fifty-four highly trained men, when the weather conditions offered only a minimal chance of success? Sandy Galloway had left the decision with him. He knew that he was facing the gravest choice of his life.

At the airfield, Stirling called Lewes, Mayne, Bonington, McGonigal and Major F. C. Thompson – an Indian Army officer who was accompanying the drop as an observer. He put his cards on the table. He said he thought they ought to take the risk, but didn't try to argue the case. Lewes and Mayne agreed immediately, and the others concurred after a moment's hesitation. Stirling then had Sergeant-Major Yates bring in the enlisted men. Lewes explained the situation and told them that though the op could be postponed, it would not be a tactically sound option. Any man who wanted to could pull out now. The way Johnny Cooper remembered it, after Lewes had finished, Stirling stood up and said, 'We'll go because we've got to go. The job is important . . . the whole army depends on us to get in there and knock off as many of those Messerschmitt 109-Fs as possible.'[3] No one opted out. 'Rightly, people might . . . say we should never have dropped under those conditions,' commented Reg Seekings. 'But if we hadn't there would never have been an SAS.'[4]

14. Raining so hard it hurt

Of the fifty-four men who set off that night, only twenty-one came back. Those who jumped landed in forty-mile-an-hour winds that dragged them for long distances across the desert, and were flayed alive by sharp gravel and the spiky acacia bushes that covered the drop-zones. One man of Stirling's stick was blown away and never seen again. Jock Lewes had to leave his giant troop-sergeant, Jock Cheyne, on the DZ, with a broken back. Mayne had to abandon Dougie Arnold and Bill Kendall, neither of whom could walk. Dave Kershaw's arm was fractured. Stirling's stick suffered two sprained ankles, a broken wrist and a broken arm. Though he never reported it, Mayne hurt his back so badly that he was never again able to play first class rugby. There wasn't a single man in the three sections who walked away without concussion, bruises, cuts or sprained limbs. It was pitch dark on the DZs and sound was obscured by the roaring wind. They had been instructed to do everything in silence. Instead there was pandemonium as they bawled to each other and flashed torches. Though they had brought entrenching tools to bury their parachutes, many of the canopies inflated and flew off before they could catch them. It took up to four hours to clear the drop-zones, and by that time there was little chance of making their lying-up places by first light. Both Stirling's and Lewes's sticks had been dropped in the wrong place.

The fate of Eoin McGonigal's stick, on No. 2 Flight, remained a mystery for several years. It was only when one of the parachutists, Jim Blakeney, escaped from his prison camp, that the truth was revealed. Blakeney, a former Grimsby trawlerman and ex-Grenadier who, along with Riley, Almonds and Lilley, had been one of Lewes's celebrated 'Tobruk Four', reported that the stick had jumped, but that McGonigal had been killed on landing. The rest of the section had made for the meet-up place, but had been captured by the Italians on the way.

Bonington's stick didn't jump at all. After being hit by flak, No. 4 Flight headed back east for fifty minutes until the fuel gave out. Pilot Charlie West set the Bombay down on what he was certain was Allied territory, only to discover that a shard of shrapnel had lodged behind the compass-faring, and that they had flown round in a circle. Using the last of the fuel, West managed to get the Bombay airborne again, but she ran straight into a Messerschmitt 109-F, which shot her down. She crash-landed in the desert and broke up. West suffered a fractured skull, ribs and shoulder and a ruptured diaphragm. His wireless operator was badly hurt and his co-pilot killed. Charles Bonington, his troop-sergeant Ernie Bond, and the other eight SAS-men were injured, one mortally. All of them, including observer Major F. C. Thompson, were bagged by German troops.

One major tactical mistake was the system of dropping the gear separately. The men jumped with only their pistols and webbing, wearing khaki overalls over shorts and shirts, with woollen 'stocking-caps' instead of helmets. Thompson sub-machine guns, Lewes bombs, detonators and fuses, personal packs containing rations, spare ammunition, spare food, blankets and water, were packed separately in canisters, attached to parachutes. Most of them vanished into the night. Some canopies failed to open. Some detonators exploded on impact, setting the containers on fire. Plunging down under his canopy, Paddy Mayne saw the flashes and thought his section was under fire.

Mayne recovered only one of his five canisters. Lewes's men found two. Stirling's section found two, containing personal packs, six blankets, and twelve Lewes bombs with no fuses. Incredibly, though, both Lewes and Mayne decided they had enough bombs to do at least a partial job, and pressed on to their targets. Even Stirling, who lacked any explosives, and sent his stick back to RV with the Long Range Desert Group, took Sergeant Bob Tait and trekked to the coast to do a recce of Axis movements.

Stirling's later assertion that 'no party was dropped within ten miles of the selected DZs', though, was untrue. In fact, Mayne's section was dropped more or less on target. Despite depleted equipment, they actually lay up six miles from Tmimi aerodrome, and discovered by close observation that there were seventeen 109-Fs on the strip. With the sixteen Lewes bombs Mayne had retrieved, they stood a good chance of bagging almost all of them. Mayne divided his section into two four-man groups. He had already issued final instructions when the rain hit them.

The terrible rainstorm that swept the coast of Cyrenaica on the afternoon and evening of 17 November, bedevilling Cunningham's advance, has become part of Second World War legend. It came in a shock-wave – a wall of water that crashed out of the sky on the tail of cracking forked lightning and booming thunder. It sizzled across the sand, spreading like electricity into the vast network of clefts and channels, plunging downward with increasing momentum, until wadis had become swirling deep rivers hundreds of feet wide. The transformation it wrought was breathtaking. The land, till that moment still and bone dry, suddenly became a heaving monster of glistening wetness and frantic movement.

The storm was characterized by war correspondents as 'the worst storm in living memory', or 'the worst storm in forty years'. This may have been the case, but the stitchwork of deep wadis gouged across the desert was adequate indication of the part water had played in its geological history. It rained frequently in this area at this time of year – Cyrenaica averaged twenty-four inches annually, and it was by no means rare for nomads to be drowned in flash floods. No one in GHQ had anticipated it, mainly because of the enduring Western belief that the desert is a hot, dry place that can be cold at night, when in fact it is a landscape of extremes in a constant state of dynamic flux. Not even Lewes, for all his brilliance, had considered the possibility of rain – the fuses and time-pencils weren't waterproofed.

At first, Mayne's section tried to sit out the cloudburst. When it dawned on them that they were sitting in what had just turned into a fast-moving river, though, they scrambled out of the wadi to higher ground and tried to dive under their blankets. It was raining so hard that it hurt. The rain sieved out the wadi, bringing twigs and branches and animal droppings. It carried off bits of gear, it penetrated everything. At last light, Mayne found that the instantaneous fuses were soaked. He was so furious at having been thwarted at the last minute that he declared he would go ahead on his own with a couple of grenades. The others tried to talk him out of it. It was only when he realized he would have to swim a seventy-five-foot-wide wadi in spate that he gave up. Mayne was never a good swimmer. The following night the section moved out to the rendezvous.

For Lewes's section, the rain kicked in just after noon as they lay up in a wadi. They clambered to higher ground, but their fuses and time-pencils were wrecked in minutes. Until that point, Lewes had still been determined to carry out the mission. Now, he knew they had no choice but to withdraw.

Stirling and Tait managed to reach high ground from where they could see both the coast-road, the Via Balbia, and the sea beyond. There was a great deal of Axis activity on the road, and Stirling told Tait he wanted to climb down to have a closer look. They didn't make it. At about 2000 hours, just as they were starting their descent, the skies opened and the deluge began. They found themselves slithering about in a waterfall. Stirling, an experienced mountaineer, saw that they were going to end up plummeting down the escarpment. They decided to retrace their steps and make for the rendezvous.

Their destination was Rotunda Segnale, a crossroads on the Trig al'Abd (the Slave Route), a desert track in places forty miles south of the coast. Stirling had chosen it in consultation with the Long Range Desert Group, mainly because it was exactly thirty-four miles from both targets.

The squadron had rehearsed long marches on minimum water, but had never dreamed they would be marching back thirty miles *through* water that was often up to their knees. It was horrendous going, only alleviated by the thought that the rain had saved their lives. None of the sections had the full complement of water-bottles, most of which had been lost on landing. Stirling and Tait had only one full water-bottle to cover the whole distance. Thirst was further suppressed by the unbelievable night cold. The men were used to British winters, but none of them had ever experienced such cold before. 'I couldn't explain how cold it actually was,' Jeff Du Vivier said. 'To believe it one would have to experience it . . . I couldn't speak, every time I opened my mouth my teeth just cracked against one another.'[1]

15. 'Well crikey, if these people can penetrate this far . . .'

On 20 November, Captain David Lloyd Owen, MC Queens Regiment, and Trooper Titch Cave, Wiltshire Yeomanry, were lying in a desert hide, watching the crossroads at Rotunda Segnale. They belonged to Y Patrol of the Long Range Desert Group, whose thirty-hundredweight Fords were camouflaged nearby. Lloyd Owen had been with the LRDG only since September, but Cave was a veteran who had already won the MM for action behind enemy lines. Not long after first light, they clocked two men limping towards them out of the desert. They were David Stirling and Bob Tait, on their way to the rendezvous three miles further on.

Lloyd Owen accosted the two SAS-men and steered them back to his hide, where he plied them with tea laced with whisky. Stirling was worried about Bill Yates and the rest of his stick. Lloyd Owen hadn't seen them, but said that Mayne and eight men had passed by a few hours earlier. Gulping tea, Stirling told Lloyd Owen that Squatter had been a fiasco. He was especially irate about the loss of the equipment-canisters. On the other hand, he and Tait had managed to get right up to the coast-road and back again unobserved, proving that it was possible to operate in the Axis rear.

Lloyd Owen smirked at this. The Long Range Desert Group had been penetrating Axis territory with impunity for almost a year and a half. They had been set up by Wavell before Layforce had even landed in Africa, as a way of persuading the Italians that the British had large forces operating in their rear. Unlike the rest of the army, the LRDG didn't operate only on the coastal plain. They ranged thousands of miles into the deep Sahara, where in the early days of the war they had carried out some spectacular raids on Italian outposts.

Founded by Major Ralph Bagnold, Royal Signals, the LRDG was the military manifestation of the pre-war 'Zerzura Club' – a group of peacetime army and navy officers, colonial administrators and pilots dedicated to exploring the eastern Sahara. In the course of their travels, they had invented or improved the sun-compass, the expansion tank for condensing radiator water, dead-reckoning techniques, the sand-channel, the sand-mat and the supply-dump. They had worked out detailed tables of food and water consumption that Lewes would have given his right arm for. Not only had they done the seemingly impossible by driving cars and lorries across vast dune-fields like the Great Sand Sea, they had also made new maps of the Sahara and presented papers to the Royal Geographical Society. Bagnold, more a boffin than an army officer, had written a book on the physics of blown sand.

Lloyd Owen claimed later that, as he mulled over Stirling's problem, an idea struck him. 'Why shouldn't we in the LRDG take [Stirling's] men to their targets, let them do their dirty work and then transport them home again?'[1] When he suggested this, he said, Stirling muttered that trucks were too slow: his objective was surprise. Lloyd Owen countered that it was better to be certain of getting to the targets than 'to risk the whole thing going off half-cock like this last show of yours'.[2]

Stirling looked sceptical. 'Perhaps he didn't want to abandon his idea of parachuting,' Lloyd Owen commented. '. . . Perhaps also he wasn't convinced that we could do all I said we could . . . Anyway this conversation was the birth of an idea which grew to fruition in David Stirling's mind, and he never again attempted to reach his objective by parachute.'[3]

Stirling never denied Lloyd Owen's oblique claim to have been the unofficial 'godfather' of the SAS, in its role as a vehicle-borne unit. He later called the LRDG the 'supreme professionals of the desert' and 'honorary members of the SAS family'. He commented that Lloyd Owen was 'a very high-grade chap', but mentioned another LRDG officer, Jake Easonsmith, as the man who had first suggested being carried by truck instead of parachuting.

Years afterwards, he told journalist Gordon Stevens that he had known all about the LRDG before the operation, and had originally planned to make the SAS an LRDG-style force. He had been dissuaded from the idea by a fellow Scots Guards officer, Michael Crichton-Stuart, a former LRDG patrol commander, who advised him that GHQ would never accept a proposal for what would essentially be a second version of the LRDG. Instead, Stirling had written Jock Lewes's parachuting idea into his paper, not because he thought it was a more efficient means of delivery, but because it was a novel 'selling-point'; 'they could grasp the newness of the idea,' he said, '[because] it was identified by a new method of arrival. Psychologically the parachute was the ideal propaganda means of putting over the proposition of the role of the unit.'[4]

Evidence unearthed by SAS scholar David List shows that Stirling did plan more parachute drops after Op Squatter, and was dissuaded from them, not by Lloyd Owen, but by GHQ. At the same time, he was open to suggestions – a point he'd made clear at the conference in July, when he stated that while the principal aim of the SAS was parachute missions, it could also be deployed on 'any combined operation'.

The devastating result of his attempted raid can only have sunk in fully, though, when Stirling arrived at the rendezvous with Captain Jake Easonsmith's patrol later that day. Lewes was there with nine survivors – Pat Riley, Johnny Rose, Johnny Cooper, Jeff Du Vivier, Jimmy Brough, Jimmy Storie, Frank Rhodes, Charlie Cattell and Bob Lilley. Jake Easonsmith was rated as the LRDG's best patrol commander. He had kept a couple of hurricane lamps burning all night on twin ridges above his vehicle-laager, to guide the SAS parties in. At first light he brought the lamps back and replaced them with a smoky fire of desert sedge as a beacon. His orders were to ditch the camp at 0700 hours, but in view of the fact that less than half of the SAS raiders had appeared, he pulled his six Fords into cover and stayed there another eight hours. Soon after dawn, Mayne's section came in. They had spotted the lamps, but had laid up for the rest of the night in case it was an Axis trick. Mayne had eight men with him – Edward McDonald, Dave Kershaw, Harold White, Bob Bennett, Reg Seekings, Tom Chesworth, Tony Hawkins and Geordie White.

Stirling could have trekked back to the fallback rendezvous in the Wadi al-Mra, where Bill Fraser was waiting with the two SAS Bedford trucks. He and all the men preferred to stay with Easonsmith and see if anyone else arrived. No one did. Dave Kershaw, nursing his smashed arm, reported that on the march back he had spotted another group in the distance and had identified them through his binos as Sgt. Major George Yates and others belonging to Stirling's stick. He had shouted and fired his pistol, but they hadn't responded. They had been going in the wrong direction.

The men were shocked and dejected, not only by the loss of so many good mates, but by their failure to 'get a good crack at the Hun'. Mayne thought his section had held up remarkably well. He was especially impressed with his section sergeant, Ed McDonald, who would end his career as an officer. Mayne felt that given even tolerably good weather the plan could have worked. But he was also shattered by the loss of his best friend, Eoin McGonigal. Bob Bennett was convinced this was the end of the SAS. Jeff Du Vivier agreed. He thought the next move would be a general RTU. Cooper and Riley both wanted to continue, but didn't know if it was tenable.

To the enlisted men, most of whom had known nothing of the LRDG until now, the answer seemed obvious. 'Everybody said: "Well crikey, if these people can penetrate this far . . . why not get them to carry us in?"' Seekings recalled. 'We had no idea that we had patrols penetrating two, three or four hundred miles behind the enemy position, and it made the idea of parachuting in stupid . . .'[5]

16. A landscape so vast it raked the senses

It was probably while Stirling was riding back to base with Easonsmith that the full conceit of his original idea hit him. This was the first time he had been in the 'real' desert, and it was not the same place he had seen in the Canal Zone or Tobruk. This was the LRDG's desert, a landscape so vast, endless and empty it raked the senses. It was a dimension beyond time and space, whose hugeness reduced even the great columns of the Eighth Army and the Panzergruppe Afrika to the status of ants, shaming the war into insignificant pettiness.

That he had believed they could operate in this land of extremes, never having experienced it, must have begun to seem increasingly ludicrous. On the other hand, men could adapt to this wilderness. Jake Easonsmith, Royal Tank Regiment, had worked for a Bristol wine merchant before the war, and yet he led his patrol across the endless shimmering plains with the sureness of one born to it.

Stirling watched Easonsmith and his patrol, mainly New Zealanders, with interest. He observed at first hand the accuracy of their navigation, the way they could exchange information quickly using wireless, their ability to improvise solutions to mechanical problems, the facility with which they read the desert surface, and most of all, the way they seemed to blend into the Sahara rather than standing out from it.

The return was not without hazard. Next day, as the Fords were raking across the plain in a tailback of dust, there was a cry of 'Aircraft!' An Italian Savoia 70 fighter dipped over the convoy with its machine guns rattling like snare-drums, stitching a lethal pattern across the stones. The driver of the truck carrying Lewes and Riley took evasive action, and a second later the vehicle flipped over on its back, trapping the two SAS-men underneath.

They were saved from being crushed only by the Lewis gun mounted on the back. By the time they crawled out, soaked in petrol, the Savoia had melted into the blue horizon, but Easonsmith guessed it would soon be back with help. Within minutes, his team had righted the truck and got the whole patrol into camouflaged positions. When the Savoia returned forty minutes later, riding shotgun for a Heinkel III bomber, the LRDG had cammed-up so expertly they were invisible. Instead, the Heinkel dropped its payload on some derelict trucks three miles away. All the following day, though, they had to remain in cover. The skies were teeming with enemy planes.

17. 'You'll like him, and he's well placed to help'

It was not until Stirling was ushered into the presence of GOC Eighth Army Alan Cunningham at Fort Maddalena on 26 November that he fully realized how insignificant the Squatter flop was in the greater scheme of things. Cunningham was wrestling with the prospect of losing the entire battle. His plan, so uninspired it had confirmed Rommel's analysis of British tactical methods as 'stereotyped and over-systematic', had backfired badly.

He had hoped to lure Rommel into a stand-up duel at Gabr Salih, where superior British tank numbers – almost two to one – would outgun him. Instead the Desert Fox had lived up to his name as a 'general gone raving mad' and executed his notorious Dash for the Wire. Cunningham had been taken in, and had dispersed his armour. 'What difference does it make if you have two tanks to my one,' Rommel asked a captured British staff officer, 'when you spread them out and let me smash them in detail?'[1]

Stirling saw at once that Cunningham was under stress. He had expected some sort of reprimand, but the general spoke to him for no more than five minutes, and had little time to spare for the flea-bite loss of thirty-four parachutists and a Bombay aircraft, which had, in any case, been mainly a psy-ops gambit. He was only interested in whether Stirling had seen panzers on the Via Balbia, which he had not.

The SAS had arrived at Jaghbub oasis in their own lorries at 1530 hours the previous day. Once the headquarters of the Senussiyya brotherhood, the most powerful Islamic fraternity in the Sahara, Jaghbub contained the ruins of a famous Quranic school and library. Now it was significant mainly as one of the Eighth Army's forward landing grounds, and the site of a medical aid-post. After dispatching the wounded for medical treatment, Stirling received instructions to report to Eighth Army Advance HQ at Maddalena the following day. The rest of his party were to fly back to Baggush and await further orders. Stirling told Lewes to take them back to Kabrit.

He left the GOC's tent with some relief, not anticipating the swift succession of events that was to follow. That afternoon a plane landed on the airstrip at Maddalena, disgorging Chief of the General Staff Arthur Smith and his Deputy, Neil Ritchie. Smith marched smartly over to the tent and presented Cunningham with a letter from Auchinleck relieving him of command. The Eighth Army was to be handed over to Ritchie. Stirling was not altogether delighted by this development. He had no wish to face Ritchie and admit that his plan had failed. He was about to escape back to Jaghbub, when the new GOC issued a summons. He need not have worried. Ritchie, too, was mainly concerned with what he had observed on the coast-road. His only comments on the operation were ritual commiserations.

Auchinleck hadn't been taken in by Rommel's madcap Dash to the Wire. He knew that, as on other offensives, this advance would soon be throttled by over-extended supply lines. Ritchie's orders were to dispatch two flying columns across the desert to hit the Axis from the south, in support of a renewed offensive along the coast. One of these columns, E Force, under Brigadier Denys Reid, had captured the remote oasis of Jalo two days before Ritchie arrived. The second, Marriott Force, was to link up with E Force in December.

Stirling's next parachute operation was scheduled to support the joint assault with a strike at Ajadabiyya aerodrome, on the coast of Cyrenaica. Stirling hadn't lost interest in parachuting, but as he had only a handful of men left, he didn't want to risk them on a jump that might wipe them out. He had already admitted to himself that his original proposal had been too ambitious.

The formal suggestion that the SAS should accompany LRDG patrols came neither from Lloyd Owen nor Easonsmith, but from the LRDG commander, Lt. Col. Guy Prendergast, a reserved ex-Royal Tank Regiment officer who had been part of Bagnold's pre-war club. He was now the Eighth Army's desert expert and, in practical terms, the real 'godfather' of the SAS. On 28 November a signal arrived from the LRDG base at Siwa oasis: 'As LRDG not trained for demolitions,' Prendergast's message ran, 'suggest pct [parachutists] used for blowing dromes.'[2] This was followed the same day by a signal from Maddalena to GHQ in Cairo, inquiring if the Detachment had reached Kabrit. If so, they were to collect demolition equipment and report as soon as possible for a 'special mission with the LRDG'.[3]

While at Maddalena, Stirling bumped into Marriott Force chief Brigadier Sir John Marriott, whom he knew as a fellow Scots Guards officer and Commander, 22 Guards Brigade. One of the Randolph Churchill–Evelyn Waugh 'Silver Circle Club', of which Stirling himself was an honoured member, Marriott was sympathetic. According to Stirling's account, Marriott advised him to 'lie low' for a while, away from GHQ, and away from Ritchie. Reid's new base at Jalo was exactly what the doctor ordered: in the middle of nowhere, out of sight of Eighth Army HQ, out of Rommel's line of retreat, yet superbly placed as a launch-pad for mobile raids. 'If you're looking for a supply base to leech on to,' he told Stirling, 'Denys is your man. You'll like him, and he's well placed to help.'[4]

Whether this conversation actually took place is uncertain, but if so, Stirling didn't take Marriott's advice. Signals traffic compiled by David List reveals conclusively that four days after meeting Ritchie, Stirling was at GHQ in Cairo, probably to run the new idea past the operations staff. He did take on board Marriott's suggestion about moving to Jalo, though, and arrived there with two dozen SAS-men on 6 December.

18. 'Advance and attack any suitable objectives'

Jalo was not a story-book oasis. Lying two hundred miles west of the border, it consisted of a thousand palm trees, brackish springs, a Turkish fort and two mud-brick villages half buried in sand. The wind hardly ever ceased here. It whipped across the open plains, layering the air endlessly with a miasma of brimstone-scented dust. When the wind did drop, the flies moved in. The nearest sweet water was twenty miles away. Protected by a jagged hammada of angular boulders on the western side, Jalo's southern approaches lay across the Kalansho Serir – a sand-sheet of chilling monotony where a vehicle could speed on for mile after mile without encountering a tree, a ridge or a single stone. To the east lay the cut-glass facets of the Kalansho sand-sea, where the wind honed knife-blade crests on sand-plinths hundreds of feet high.

The entire operational orbat of L Detachment had been landed by three Bombays of 216 Squadron. A few familiar faces were absent, including Pat Riley, and 'Honest Dave' Kershaw, currently in hospital in Cairo. There was a handful of replacements from Kabrit, including Bill Fraser, Jack Byrne, Arthur Phillips, Ted Badger, Frank Austin and Sgt. Jim Almonds, all of whom had missed the first op. Almonds had been stunned to discover that one of his 'Tobruk Four' mates, Jim Blakeney, had been lost.

Stirling set up his headquarters in a disused warehouse. He met Denys Reid, a giant of a man with a florid drinker's face, and found him as accommodating as Marriott had claimed. Reid at once saw the value of the SAS in 'making a show' at Axis aerodromes in the Aghayla–Ajadabiyya area, to cover his December offensive. Stirling also introduced himself to Major Don Steele, commanding A Squadron, LRDG, which had arrived at Jalo a few days earlier. Steele, ex-2 New Zealand Expeditionary Force, was a veteran operator of the 'desert troops'. He had with him thirty men in three patrols – New Zealanders, Rhodesians and Guardsmen – with sixteen 30cwt Fords and a light recce vehicle. Steele's squadron had been placed under Reid's command, with orders from Eighth Army HQ to 'advance and attack any suitable objectives on enemy communications'.[1] This matched Stirling's plans perfectly.

The day after their arrival, Stirling assembled his men in the shade of a palm grove and told them the SAS was not finished. They were still a parachute force, but for now they would be operating overland with LRDG patrols. They would be going into action almost immediately.

19. Swallowed up by the huge dimensions

Stirling and Mayne quit Jalo next day with eleven SAS-men and eighteen troopers of the LRDG's Rhodesian patrol under Captain Gus Holliman, Royal Tank Regiment. Their targets were the airfields at Tamet and Sirte, almost three hundred and fifty miles to the north-west. Jock Lewes would follow with his section two days later, to bump Aghayla aerodrome, about a hundred and fifty miles away. These three raids would be synchronized for the night of 14/15 December. The raid against Ajadabiyya – four men under Lt. Bill Fraser – would not go in until a week later, to prepare the way for Reid's link-up with Marriott the next day.

Mayne's and Stirling's sections were carried in five stripped-down Fords. As the trucks fanned out into the plain north of the oasis, the SAS-men felt swallowed up by the huge dimensions of the Sahara. Minutes faded into hours. The sun rose higher, leaching the rainbow colours from the desert. The trucks were a flotilla of tiny boats cast out into a vast ocean of stippled sand, black gravel beaches, tussock grass and desert sedge, thickets of acacia as fragile and desiccated as skeletons. To the west, they could make out the splintered scabs of rubble-stone escarpments, and to the east the iridescent sand-cliffs of the Kalansho dune-field, almost translucent in the heat-haze. To the north the horizon vanished into the trembling fata morgana of spectral lakes and cloud.

Holliman, a stocky, blond Englishman, was leading the convoy with his navigator, Corporal Mike Sadler. An elvish-looking, tow-haired twenty-two-year-old, Sadler was an Englishman who had emigrated to Rhodesia in his youth to learn farming. He had been a sergeant in an anti-tank unit and was good with figures, but hadn't studied navigation before joining the LRDG. He had taken to it like a fish to water, and was already Holliman's most promising navigator.

Sadler sat next to the driver, log in hand, his eyes flicking continually from the sun-compass, a steel needle casting a shadow on the vehicle's dashboard, to the speedometer, to his watch, and back again to the compass. He plotted the course by dead-reckoning, noting every change in bearing, and logging the time and speed. At every opportunity he would mark the patrol's progress on the map.

At the evening halt, Sadler would lug out a theodolite to check the dead-reckoning position by astral fix. He took the 'shot' against the sixth pip of the Greenwich time-signal, picked up by the patrol's W/T operator on the wireless truck, noted by a time-keeper with a Zenith Chronometre stop-watch. Sadler would then match the 'shot' against RAF astronomical charts, and compare the result with his dead-reckoning fix. Despite all the trouble, the log wasn't that accurate, but if it brought the patrol to within a mile of its objective, Holliman was satisfied.

On the patches of easy going the trucks sped along at forty miles an hour in fantails of dust, drifting back and forth in open and asymmetrical formation, to present a difficult target for enemy aircraft. On straight-line runs they would make deliberate one-and-a-half-mile detours every six miles to throw off air-spotters dogging their tracks. On rocky ground or in soft sand they slowed to no more than ten miles an hour.

These Fords had reinforced springs – they were heavily laden with petrol, water, weapons and equipment, and carried .303 calibre Lewis machine guns on the back. Getting bogged down in *mish-mish* – soft sand – was a continual hazard. The LRDG crews would jump out with shovels and unload their steel sand-channels and canvas sand-mats – both devices invented by Bagnold, and by now standard issue in the desert. The crew would shovel sand from under the Ford's rear wheels and slide the steel channel underneath. The mat would go under the front wheels. Once the vehicle's back wheels got some purchase, the crew would lay successive channels until the Ford was out of the soft patch.

Mish-mish – literally 'apricots' – lay in places where the silicon particles hadn't jelled, and there were relatively big air-pockets between grains. Pressure caused the grains to compress. The

LRDG drivers could sometimes spot *mish-mish* by surface pattern – they had become expert at reading the desert 'going'. The vehicles were hard to spot from the air, but there were dust plumes and tyre-tracks that aircraft could home in on. After a contact, the patrols would go to ground in the shade of a dune or a wadi, or in acacia scrub, with camouflage-nets flung right over the vehicles. As SAS medical officer Malcolm Pleydell said later, 'There is no lesson that improves camouflage as well as a low-level machine-gun attack.'[1]

Stirling reassigned himself the role of apprentice: there was a great deal to be learned. Over the first three days the SAS started to get into the rhythm of the desert drive. The patrol travelled from sunrise to sunset, and as the heat got up mid-morning, off would come the LRDG's calf-length sheepskin coats, pullovers and shirts. They would strip right down to their drill shorts and sandals. Crossing open desert, the LRDG favoured Arab shamaghs as headgear. The SAS would later adopt the shamagh themselves, though they, like the LRDG, were careful to remove it once they were near the enemy. The LRDG had learned that by mirroring the khaki-drill uniforms of Axis troops they could often pass them quite unnoticed.

They would halt for a short break for lunch at noon, erecting a tarpaulin for shade. The LRDG had acquired and developed the 'composite ration pack', a daily ration including canned bacon, sausages, stew and canned oatmeal biscuits.

After twelve hours in the heat and the desert wind, the night halt came as a blessing. The napalm glare of the sun slowly drained away, the landscape turning by degrees to blood-red and gold. The heat dissipated quickly after dark, and greatcoats and sheepskins came back on again. The LRDG crews would cook bully beef stew in a cooker of British army devising – a petrol tin cut open and filled with sand soaked with petrol. While the meal was on the go, the W/T operator would report to LRDG base at Siwa, and the navigator take his star shot. After eating the men would squat round the fire swigging tots of army-issue rum – another special privilege of the LRDG. In the deep desert the patrols posted no sentries at night. They were confident enough of their security even to play dance music on the BBC.

By noon on 11 December they were forty miles south of Sirte when an Italian Ghibli spotter poled up suddenly out of the haze. Holliman didn't order evasive action immediately, because he knew that, nine times out of ten, enemy spotters could be persuaded the convoy was friendly if it failed to react. He saw quickly, though, that this pilot had decided already – it dropped straight into a strafing run at five hundred feet. Holliman ordered his bearded gunner, J. A. Kroeger, a South African from Pietermaritzburg, to open fire. Kroeger's Lewis rattled drumfire, quickly followed by the other Lewis guns. The gunners ripped off ear-splitting bursts, blagging out round after round until the barrels were red hot. LRDG operating procedure was to engage fighters head-on at up to two thousand feet. The Ghibli was sluggish and lightly armed, and didn't worry the LRDG squads. The Heinkel IIIs and Caproni Ca309s bombers presented a more serious threat, because they could release their payloads from five thousand feet, way out of range. In this case, the Ghibli pilot saw he was outgunned and dumped his two bombs. They went wide, detonating with a crump and kicking up wedges of pebbles and dust.

Holliman ordered the patrol back to a tangle of thorn-scrub and camouflaged up, while some of the crew brushed out their tracks. His caution proved justified. Minutes later, the Ghibli was replaced by two more. They cruised over threateningly, but the pilots failed to pick out the vehicles in the tapestry of light and shade, and in frustration beat up a vacant stretch of desert nearby with bombs and machine-gun fire.

Holliman had made a gamble earlier by breaking radio silence, and thought the Regia Aeronautica might have been alerted by the message. The Italians were exceptionally skilled at dee-effing – wireless direction-finding. In any case, the enemy now knew the patrol was there.

Stirling was piqued. His crucial op had been compromised, but he had no choice but to go on. Instead of being dropped twenty miles from Sirte aerodrome as planned, the patrol motored him in to within three miles of the target. He decided not to risk his whole section, but to slip into the airfield with only one companion, Sgt. Jimmy Brough, an old comrade from 8 Commando and the Scots Guards. Both were carrying heavy Italian packs, but it was Brough who ended up lugging the seventy-pound bag of Lewes bombs they had with them. In his customary style, Stirling didn't order Brough to carry it, but merely suggested it might be a good idea, as he would be doing the navigating. There had been a change of plan for Mayne too. Rather than hit the original target, the main airfield at Tamet, Mayne's section, including McDonald, Seekings, Hawkins, White and Chesworth, would attack a new airfield not marked on the map. This was only five miles west of Sirte, at the end of the wadi. A recce had revealed aircraft landing and taking off from there.

Stirling knew the Italians were on the lookout for raiders, and he and Brough spent some dicey moments dodging sentries. The aerodrome was wide open, without even a fence. There were thirty Caproni Ca309s bombers parked on the strip. Stirling was so excited to have got within striking distance of the enemy at last that he was tempted to lay his Lewes bombs straight away. He held back only because he knew it would jeopardize Mayne's attack the following night.

They were making their way round the edge of the airfield when they stumbled over two Italians sleeping in a hollow. One of the enemy let out a shriek, and fired blindly. The two SAS-men hared off into the desert. The airfield erupted into chaos behind them – strings of imprecations and prayers, cracks and muzzle flashes, and the rainbow tracer of a 20mm anti-aircraft gun, pumping rounds towards the sea. Stirling and Brough guessed that the Italians thought they were under attack from two sides. They grinned at each other, teeth glinting white in the darkness.

They lay up in some scrub on a ridge two miles away, and at first light scanned the area with binoculars. The day was as clear as crystal, the aquamarine sea lying heavy against the pastel shore. They could see sand-wrinkles spreading along the coast to the west, and Sirte airstrip to the east, with the cream-cake buildings of Sirte town beyond. In the limpid air, the Ca309s, with their hornbill snouts, looked huge – far bigger than they really were. The SAS-men could make no move until sunset, so they lay dozing until noon, when they were awoken suddenly by girlish voices. Stirling peered out of the bushes and saw a gaggle of Arab women working with mattocks on a postage-stamp patch of cultivation nearby. He cautioned Brough to stay quiet and they waited for the women to go. They stayed and stayed. It was 1500 hours and the sun was already dipping by the time they packed up.

An hour later they heard aircraft engines gunning. Sweeping the airstrip with his binoculars, Stirling saw with dismay that the Capronis were taking off in pairs. By last light all thirty precious targets had vanished west along the coast towards Tamet. Stirling surmised that they had been moved for security reasons, following the alert the previous night. His recce had been a cock-up.

After dark, they trudged back to the road where they had arranged to rendezvous with Holliman's patrol at 0045 hours that night. Neither of them spoke. The prize had been within their grasp, but it had slipped away through their own carelessness. Stirling was despondent. He knew that if this operation didn't come off, there probably wouldn't be another chance for the SAS. Everything now depended on Mayne and Lewes. If Mayne succeeded, they would see the flash and hear the blast of his bombs from where they were. Midnight came and nothing happened. Stirling concluded with a sinking feeling that Mayne's part of the op had also fallen through.

20. 'I saw him rip the instrument panel out with his bare hands'

Mayne's section had been dropped at last light, two miles from the target. The team moved in and lay on the dunes for over an hour, observing the airfield. The aircraft on the strip were mostly Italian Fiat C42 biplanes, but it was too dark to tell how many there were, or the dispositions of the sentries. Mayne reckoned that it would not be heavily guarded. Just before midnight the section moved out of hiding and started boxing around the landing ground in single file.

They recced the perimeter as far as the seashore, where they found a huddle of empty buildings. Mayne spotted a chink of light penetrating the blackout curtains from a Nissen-style hut nearby. He eased towards it, with the others following, and crept right up to the door. He listened. He could hear laughter and the raised voices of cheerful drinkers from within. It was the pilots' mess, he concluded, and they were having a party. He had a party-surprise for them.

Mayne stood back and opened the door, snapping it forward with a size twelve boot. For an instant, thirty faces froze in shock. Then he squeezed the trigger of his .45 calibre Tommy-gun, drumming rounds into the densest group. He heard yells and the crashing of tables, as bodies pitched in every direction. He put the last double tap through the light, and beat a hasty retreat.

The rest of the SAS team were crouching outside. 'As soon as Paddy cut loose,' said Reg Seekings, '. . . the whole place went mad – [they fired] everything they had including tracer . . . They had fixed lines of fire about a couple of feet from the ground. We had either to jump over or crawl under them . . . Chesworth came slithering over to us on all fours. I can still see him getting to his feet, pulling in his arse as the tracer ripped past his pack, missing him by inches. On a signal from Paddy we got the hell out of it.'[1]

They hurried back to the airfield, setting charges on a petrol dump, a bomb dump and some telegraph poles on the way. They trotted down the line of aircraft, sticking Lewes bombs on as many machines as they could. After an hour, Mayne sent Ed McDonald and three others back to the LRDG patrol to tell them to wait. He and Seekings stuck bombs on a last row of planes, but when they came to the final aircraft there were no bombs left. Mayne clambered into the cockpit. 'At first I thought he'd gone mad,' Seekings said. 'Then I saw him rip the instrument panel out with his bare hands. How he did it I shall never know.'[2]

The two men melted back into the night, just in time. 'We hadn't gone fifty yards,' said Seekings, 'when the first plane went up. We stopped to look, but a second one went up near us and we began to run. After a while we ... stopped to take another glance. What a sight! Planes exploding all over, and the terrific roar of petrol and bombs going up!'[3]

Five miles east, Stirling and Brough saw the starbursts of fire over the horizon. They heard the rumble of charges igniting, and locked each other's eyes: Mayne had done it. 'We didn't grab each other and dance for joy,' Stirling commented. 'But damned nearly.'[4]

Mayne and Seekings were racing for the rendezvous, with the enemy in hot pursuit. The LRDG drivers winked the Fords' headlights to guide them in, but stopped quickly when they saw enemy torches. Mayne blew his whistle and received a shrill answering call from the patrol. The LRDG men hauled them into the trucks, and in a few seconds they were roaring off into the desert.

When Gus Holliman's patrol rocketed up to collect Stirling and Brough at Sirte, Stirling told them he wanted to set mines in the road, and see if they would have any takers. Holliman agreed to wait. Stirling and Brough set the mines, and together they took cover nearby. Ten minutes later an Italian truck came rattling out of the darkness and hit a mine. Its cab was torn apart instantly, and the vehicle veered off the road in an incandescent fireball. 'That's our fun over for the evening, boys,' Holliman commented. 'Now we have to get cracking.'

The RV lay eighty miles to the south. Holliman brought Stirling's section in two hours after sunrise, after a non-stop drive. They waited an hour, two hours, but Mayne's group failed to show. When it finally arrived three hours later, Stirling's team blasted a volley into the air in relief and celebration. Mayne's news was just what Stirling had hoped for. He had destroyed or damaged twenty-four Axis aircraft, shot up a pilot's mess, and sabotaged dumps and a truck. Stirling was ecstatic. The 'truculent Irishman' had saved the SAS.

Three days after they arrived back at Jalo, Lewes came in. His team had been unlucky at Aghayla: they had found no aircraft there. They had blown up a transport park and destroyed telegraph poles instead. The SAS-men and the LRDG patrol, under New Zealander 2.Lt. Charlie Morris, had got into a contact with Axis troops and had only just avoided being encircled. In the ensuing firefight, they had killed or wounded fifteen enemy. Lewes also brought in three prisoners.

21. 'Rommel must have had a headache'

While Stirling, Mayne and Lewes were heading back to Jalo, Lt. Bill Fraser's section was making for Ajadabiyya. Though this was Fraser's first action with the SAS, he had fought with 11 Commando at the Litani, where a richochet had struck his helmet and knocked him out. An ex-Gordon Highlander, he had survived Rommel's capture of 51 Highland Division in France, and had escaped at Dunkirk. Even though he had seen more action than just about anyone in L Detachment, he was unfairly regarded as having 'yet to prove himself'.

Fraser was a dark-haired, smart-looking Scot from Aberdeen, five foot eight, with a puckish face and what one comrade would later describe as 'an irresistibly jolly expression'.[1] He came from a long line of Gordon Highlander sergeants. He was proud of being the first of his family to get a commission, but his background didn't sit well with some of the men, who suffered from the peculiarly British snobbery of despising officers not born to the 'officer class'. Apart from that, some of them thought Fraser 'strange' rather than 'jolly'. They reckoned he might be 'the other way'.

Mayne was especially guilty of this. 'Paddy used to give [Fraser] a hell of a time,' Jimmy Storie recalled, 'because he thought he was "that way inclined". Paddy could be cruel, especially after a few.'[2] Fraser wisely avoided the mess when Mayne was 'drink taken'. He preferred the company of his dachshund, Withers. Not everyone shared Mayne's view of Fraser. Jack Byrne, an Englishman who had served in the Gordons, had known him as far back as Dunkirk. Byrne thought him 'one of the best'. Fraser was shortly to prove it.

He had a good team. Sgt. Bob Tait, ex-London Scottish, a former merchant seaman, had won an MM at the Litani River with 11 Commando. Sgt. Jeff Du Vivier, London Scottish, and Cpl. Jack Byrne, Gordon Highlanders, were both ex-11 Commando men. Only Parachutist Arthur Phillips, Royal Warwickshire Regiment, a hard-drinking ex-7 Commando-man reputed to be a 'Communist', was a dark horse.

On 20 December 2.Lt. John Olivey, Southern Rhodesia Force, dropped them north of Ajadabiyya airfield and gave them their position and bearings. Fraser knew there was a lot riding on this raid – the 'show' Reid had asked Stirling for was down to the five of them.

The Chevy's engine faded, and the SAS-men stood stock-still, listening to the night, allowing their bodies to adjust to the new environment. They remained motionless for ten minutes, drinking in the smell of the sea, the desert odours of flint and dust, picking out distant voices and far-off twinkles of light. Then Fraser gave the signal to move out.

They moved in file, spaced five yards apart, with Bob Tait in the lead, navigating by compass. They covered only two miles, and lay up two hours before dawn. At first light Fraser realized their position was too exposed, and they shifted to a nearby hollow. A few hundred yards away there was a wooden building in a patch of green cultivation, which Fraser thought housed a deep-bore well. As it got light they saw a truck pull up, carrying a bunch of Arab labourers who started work in the cultivated area under the supervision of a European. They remained in cover the whole day. It rained intermittently. They couldn't see the airfield from this distance, but were able to get a compass fix for night marching from flights of aircraft they saw coming in to land beyond the skyline.

Some time that morning they heard the tinkle of sheep-bells, and saw an Arab boy grazing his flock about a hundred yards away. According to Du Vivier, the boy spotted Phillips as he was burying a Lewes bomb with a broken time-pencil. The boy climbed right up to their position to see what they were doing.

It was the classic stand-off, shepherd-boy v. SAS patrol. Almost exactly fifty years later, the failure of one of the most famous SAS desert missions of all time would be blamed on just such a scenario, and astonishingly perhaps, the name of the SAS-man who was supposedly clocked by the Arab boy then would also be Phillips. As in that future incident, though, it is uncertain whether, in this case, Fraser's patrol was actually compromised. Du Vivier said that the shepherd made eye-contact, but Fraser's official report states that the boy simply hovered within a few hundred yards of them for most of the day. If he saw them, he evidently didn't report it to the enemy.

They pulled out just after last light, carrying eight Lewes bombs each. Byrne had a Thompson, and the other four carried .45 calibre pistols. They advanced with almost excruciating slowness – they had practised night stalking with Jock Lewes until it was second nature, and knew that to rush was to produce noise and movement that might be spotted. They marched in Indian file, Tait leading, Fraser second man, with Byrne, the Tommy-gunner, as tail-end-charlie. They covered a mile an hour, pacing carefully, boxing round any obstacle. They communicated by hand-signals. Once an hour they halted and got down in all-round defence, taking turns to relieve themselves. There was one close call on the way, when the headlights of a German vehicle hit them full on. To react would have alerted the enemy, so they kept their cool, and carried on slowly until the headlights melted.

Close to the target, Fraser, now in the lead, came to a two-strand wire fence. He gave the signal to halt. The patrol crouched down, and Fraser glanced at his watch. It was 2115 hours, and the raid was due to go in at midnight. He signalled Tommy-gunner Byrne forward. Byrne moved up with his Thompson at the ready, and stepped over the fence. The others followed. At first they couldn't see any aircraft, and Fraser began to worry that they had all taken off. It took almost three hours to locate the planes. They found them just after midnight – mostly Italian Fiat C42s, but also a few Messerschmitt 109-Fs. Later, Byrne didn't remember seeing enemy personnel, but Tait recalled passing aircrew asleep under some of the Fiat bombers. 'We didn't wake them,' he said.

The aircraft were parked in clusters, about two hundred yards apart. They dealt with each batch before moving to the next, pressing the Lewes bombs into position on the wings of the bombers, or the noses of the fighters. Tait and Du Vivier came across a big transport plane with its door open and went inside, hunting souvenirs. It was too dark to search properly, so they left a bomb instead.

They crimped time-pencils. They pulled safety-pins. They worked systematically, 'leapfrogging' each other. Fraser used one charge on a dump of Breda anti-aircraft ammunition in a sand-bagged building nearby. According to Byrne, they also stuck bombs on a truck and a tractor parked in the middle of the runway.

It took forty minutes to set up the charges. When it was done, they faded quickly into the night, but had only gone a few hundred yards when there was an ear-shattering crump, and a plane erupted in a blinding cascade of flame, smoke and steel shards. Another blew apart, then another. 'The centre of the airfield was one great forest of fires,' Byrne recalled; '. . . enemy machine-guns began firing tracer-bullets on fixed lines down two sides of the airfield and partly across our escape-route.'[3] Searchlights lasered the sky, and the ack-ack guns started grinding out a bass bump-bump-bump, spritzing waves of tracer into the darkness. 'There was the most tremendous din,' Byrne said, 'with ammunition crackling in the exploding and burning aircraft . . . the enemy . . . remained in their bunkers . . . not one aimed shot came our way.'[4]

In the blaze of light, Fraser clocked eight Me 109-Fs about fifty yards away to the right. They were parked snout to tail, and they were covered in blanket-like cowlings as if they were straight off the assembly-line. Fraser shouted to Byrne to collect all the remaining Lewes bombs and follow him. There were seven bombs left. While they were sprinting to the Messerschmitts, Byrne pressed the time-pencils. Fraser stood guard as Byrne placed the bombs. Before they had made it back to the others, all seven charges had gone up.

Then the ammo dump exploded with what Du Vivier remembered as 'a blood-curdling deafening roar'.[5] It was so powerful that they could feel the concussion press on their lungs. 'By this time the whole area was in turmoil and alive with shouting and excited men,' Du Vivier said, '. . . they hadn't the foggiest idea what was going on.'[6]

The SAS team couldn't resist crowing in atavistic glee at the firework show. 'All five of us added to the bedlam by shouting to each other,' Byrne said, 'pointing out the destruction all around. The whole area was as light as day, and we must have been clearly visible.'[7]

They spread out into a line and marched unhurriedly off the aerodrome, heading for the desert track they intended to follow on the withdrawal. As they vanished into the darkness, a flight of RAF Blenheim bombers glommed overhead on its way to hit the main road, and loosed a stick of bombs on the brilliantly illuminated airfield, for good measure. By the time the SAS team made the RV with Olivey's patrol it was almost daylight. They were well overdue. When they thanked Olivey for waiting, one of the LRDG men said, 'It was such a fantastic show, we just had to stay till the end.'[8]

They drove towards the Wadi Faregh, where an hour later they encountered an armoured patrol of the Kings Dragoon Guards, outriding Denys Reid's E Force column. They exchanged recognition flares, and as they got closer the entire column came into view, hundreds of vehicles spread out over miles of desert. Soon the force engulfed them. Brigadier Reid had his driver move forward, and ran straight up to Fraser's truck. He stopped and asked him how the raid had gone. 'Very sorry, sir,' Fraser answered laconically in his Scots brogue, 'I had to leave two aircraft on the ground as I ran out of explosive. But we destroyed thirty-seven.'[9]

The massive Reid beamed and thumped Fraser on the back.

'There's nothing to stop us now!' he exclaimed. 'This was indeed a wonderful achievement by an officer and three men [sic],' Reid wrote in his diary. 'Incidentally, we heard later that Rommel had been in [Ajadabiyya] that night. He must have had a bit of a headache.'[10]

By the time Fraser's section arrived back in Jalo two days later, their exhilaration had been dampened by a blue-on-blue incident that occurred on the way back. Just after meeting Reid, the patrol halted for breakfast of tea and oatmeal porridge, and a few hours' rest. Jeff Du Vivier was shaken out of a doze by the rat-tat-tat of machine guns. He opened his eyes wide to see the blue bulk of an RAF Blenheim bomber droning in on them like a Valkyrie, while another one soared five thousand feet above. Rounds were whipping up sand in puffs all around the vehicles. Du Vivier rolled out of his blanket, almost at the same instant as the man next to him, Corporal Laurence Ashby, rolled into his place. Ashby took a couple of bullets in the chest. Another Rhodesian, Bob Riggs, leapt up and shook his fists at the aircraft, yelling and pointing at the air recognition panel the patrol had laid out. A second later he was blasted to pieces.

The Rhodesians were incensed, and irrationally seemed to blame the SAS for the deaths. When the two LRDG men were buried in the desert later, Olivey asked Fraser and the others to stay away.

Fraser's section got back to Jalo just in time for the advance Christmas party Stirling had laid on for the whole detachment. He was over the moon with Fraser's performance, not least because it was a 'textbook' SAS operation. In a few days, his handful of men – twenty-five in all – had destroyed or damaged sixty-one Axis aircraft with little cost and no casualties. At last, he felt, the epiphany he had had back in Cairo in June had been vindicated.

No one has recorded what Mayne thought of Fraser's success. Predictably, perhaps, it was his feat of shooting up the hut at Tamet that later grabbed the publicity, and his Herculean 'ripping the control panel out with his hands' that would go down in legend. While SAS historians generally mention Fraser's raid on Ajadabiyya only in passing, in terms of stealth and efficiency alone it would be equalled but never surpassed. It was as perfect a raid as any the SAS ever carried out.

22. 'When they went up, they went'

Stirling and Mayne were heading off again next morning. Stirling suggested to Fraser in his usual understated manner that it would be 'a good crack' to have a go at another airfield. Fraser had no objections. Rommel was still at Ajadabiyya, but his forces were believed to be wilting under Ritchie's new onslaught. Stirling wanted to bump airfields while the Afrika Korps was on the hop, but he was also driven by his lack of personal success. Fraser and Mayne had both made good 'bags', but his own best shot had been one enemy truck. This couldn't be put down entirely to bad luck. Stirling had felt envious of Mayne ever since he had joined the unit at Kabrit. Combat-wise, Stirling was a greenhorn compared with Mayne, Lewes, Fraser, and a lot of the men. The men knew it, he knew it, and it mattered. He was determined to have another bash.

He wanted at least one man with him who'd had experience laying Lewes bombs in actual combat. Mayne told him Seekings had done well at Tamet, so Stirling poached him. Seekings wasn't pleased. He revered Mayne, and hated Johnny Cooper, who was in Stirling's section. He had already had a run-in at Jalo with the mercurial, plummy ex-grammar-school kid over some blankets Seekings thought he had helped himself to. He had called Cooper 'a bastard' and a 'big mouth' and threatened to 'knock his bloody block off'. When he found himself paired up with the kid in Stirling's section he was appalled. They looked daggers at each other all the way to the next foray.

Stirling and Mayne's groups set off together on Christmas Eve with Holliman's patrol, to go in for the 'double whammy' at Sirte and Tamet. Stirling reasoned that the Axis would not be expecting follow-up raids so soon. On Christmas Day Lewes's and Fraser's sections would head out with Morris's patrol. Lewes would attack Nofilia. Fraser would go for an airfield sixty miles away, near Mussolini's triumphal monument, Arae Philenorum, which the British had nicknamed 'Marble Arch'.

Mayne's second Tamet raid went off as smoothly as the first. His section – Sgt. Ed McDonald, Parachutists Harold White, Hawkins, Chesworth and Bennett – hit the aerodrome on Christmas night. They blew up twenty-seven planes. Once again, the time-pencils were set to delays that were too short, and the Lewes bombs began to rip before the raiders were off the airfield. 'When they went up, they went,' Bennett recalled, 'and you had great big volumes of flame, and so we started running . . . [the Italians] started shooting. So we just ran through, throwing grenades and firing, and managed to get through and back to the rendezvous.'[1]

Stirling, with Brough, Cooper, Seekings, Rose and Cattell, was unable to penetrate Sirte airfield. A barbed-wire fence had been erected since his last sortie – probably because of it. As they boxed round it, they were seen by a sentry. They bugged out to the vehicles, where Stirling only just avoided being shot by the LRDG sentry. They piled in and bumped down the road, halting to stick Lewes bombs on two trucks whose crews were asleep. For the next twenty-five minutes they cruised along the Via Balbia in Holliman's Fords, the LRDG belting away with their Lewis guns and a Bofors, and the SAS cracking fire with their Tommy guns, zapping grenades at anything they saw. They left behind them a trail of flaming lorries and camps, and scores of Italian troops whaling about in confusion.

Heading back to the RV as magenta streaks thickened over the desert to the east, Stirling knew the damage they had done was a poor substitute for his failure to hit the airfield. Seekings and Cooper, though, were flying high. They had run the gauntlet of enemy fire together, and discovered suddenly that the bad blood between them had evaporated. Thereafter, they became inseparable. 'There was an almost intuitive rapport between them,' Stirling said. 'A marvellous team.'[2]

On the way back, Paddy Mayne ribbed Stirling unmercifully on his second failure at Sirte.

23. 'The only one to be killed and it had to be him'

Jalo felt desolate without the Indian and South African soldiers of Denys Reid's E Force. The war passed into its third year without celebration, as Stirling waited anxiously for news of Lewes and Fraser. After dark on New Year's Day, a single damaged Chevrolet limped into Jalo, carrying four LRDG troopers and three SAS-men. They were all that was left of the patrol of six vehicles and twenty-five men who had set out on Christmas Day to hit Nofilia and Marble Arch. The SAS-men were Jim Almonds, Jimmy Storie and Bob Lilley. The fourth enlisted man of their group, Cpl. Geordie White, had vanished. Bill Fraser's entire section was missing. Jock Lewes was dead.

Next morning, Stirling sent for Almonds, who marched into the CO's tent still sporting his week-old beard. Stirling was stunned by the news of Lewes's death. He wanted to know how he had died, but Almonds couldn't provide an entirely coherent answer. He told Stirling that they had lucked out on the Nofilia raid. They had found only two aircraft on the strip, with their fuel-tanks empty – the planes hadn't burst into flames when the charges detonated. They had been picked up by Morris's patrol on 30 December, and the next day set off early to scoop up Fraser and his section near Marble Arch.

It was 1000 hours. Almonds and Lilley were riding behind Lewes in a Ford with three LRDG men when the shadow of a Messerschmitt 110 passed over them like a giant bat. They watched frozen for a few seconds as she banked steeply and came in out of the sun at only sixty feet, with four wing-mounted machine guns blistering the ground. Two cannon in the rear gun-turret wheezed out incendiary shells. The drone of the engines and the tattoo of the guns was terrifying. Lilley pivoted the Lewis gun and had almost emptied the magazine before the driver braked. Everyone piled out and scattered. As he jumped, Almonds had a fleeting impression of Lewes in the front seat, 'fiddling about with some papers'.[1]

For the next few minutes Almonds and Lilley were too busy rattling Bren-gun rounds at the aircraft, and playing a hazardous game of hide and seek round a rocky knoll, to notice what had happened to Lewes. When the plane broke off her attack and vanished, Almonds was pretty sure he had snagged her rear-gunner. He sprinted back to find LRDG men milling round the truck, which was no longer where it had been when they ran for it. There was no sign of Lewes, but Almonds didn't have time to think about it, because the driver was already revving the truck's engine. He leapt in and they shot off into the desert. They covered another seven miles before a pair of Stukas rolled up, wailing like demons. The driver slammed brakes. Almonds hared off in double-quick time and sprawled in the thorn-scrub, assuming the most non-human-like posture he could, and layering himself with sand.

It was getting on for sunset before the Stukas' banshee shrieks finally went silent. By that time nine of Morris's LRDG men had simply melted into the desert, taking with them SAS-man Cpl. Geordie White. All the Fords but one were smoking wrecks. It wasn't until he met up with the truck crews again that Almonds discovered Lewes hadn't made it. He had been hit on the Messerschmitt's first run, but no one knew exactly what had happened.

Jimmy Storie[2] had helped bury Lewes's body in the interval before Almonds had returned from his fight at the knoll. Storie said that Jock had been taken out by a 20mm slug in the thigh. The exit-wound had ripped half his leg away and slashed an artery, and he'd bled to death in about four minutes. He thought Lewes had been wounded while jumping from the truck. His body had been buried in the place the truck had originally been hit.

Stirling listened solemnly, chewing at his pipe, then asked about Bill Fraser's team. Almonds had no news. After Morris and his men had managed to get the one serviceable truck running that night, they'd made the rendezvous near Marble Arch, but Fraser hadn't showed. Morris had decided they couldn't wait till first light. With one battered truck to nine men, it was touch and go as to whether they would make it back to Jalo at all.

Stirling wanted to know why Almonds hadn't brought Lewes's body back. Almonds was surprised. SAS operating procedure was to leave the dead, and even the wounded when they couldn't be carried. Lewes himself had left Jock Cheyne on the DZ on Squatter. Almonds saw how profoundly Stirling had been affected by the loss of his friend. He empathized. His own first thought on hearing the news had been, 'the only one to be killed and it had to be him. If the enemy only knew the loss to the SAS.'[3]

Reg Seekings said later that Lewes's death was such a blow to morale that some of the men wondered if it was worth going on. 'Although I never met Lewes,' wrote Malcolm Pleydell, 'I hadn't been in the SAS for long before I realized that he was the man who was responsible for its construction and organisation . . . by all accounts he was a remarkable man, possessing . . . a terrific drive of character together with a natural sense of leadership.'[4] Pleydell recalled a later recruit to the SAS, Captain Jim Chambers, telling him, '[Lewes] never had any official sort of recognition but just you listen to some of the men talking about him. Anyone would think he was some sort of a god . . . If it hadn't been for him none of us would be here now.'[5] Pleydell added that the enlisted men always spoke of Lewes with admiration and 'as much reverence as could be expressed in their rather gruff and unemotional voices'.[6] 'There is no doubt,' Stirling himself wrote Lewes's father a year later, 'that any success the unit had achieved up to the time of Jock's death, and after it, was, and is, almost wholly due to Jock's work.'[7]

24. 'The day the SAS was truly born'

During the first few days of the new year, when the seventeen-strong detachment was back from Jalo and settling into its base at Kabrit, David Stirling turned up with an unpleasant task to perform. He had just come from Cairo, and had every reason to be pleased with himself. Claude Auchinleck had been impressed with the unit's performance. Crusader was over. Tobruk had been relieved, Benghazi taken and Rommel pushed back to Aghayla, from where he had started his offensive a year earlier. The Axis had lost three hundred aircraft, and almost a third of those had been taken out by the SAS.

The Commander-in-Chief approved the new partnership with the LRDG, authorized the recruitment of thirty-three more volunteers, and agreed to Stirling's new project – a raid on shipping in the harbour of Bouerat al-Hsun, a port on the coast of Tripolitania west of Sirte and Tamet. Stirling had been promoted major and Mayne captain. Both had been recommended for the DSO.

Stirling had other promising developments in his pocket. He had come across fifty Free French parachutists of 1 Infantérie de l'Air languishing in Alexandria, under an irascible but keen-as-mustard young Gascon, Commandant Georges Bergé. With some difficulty, Stirling had persuaded the Free French commander in Cairo, General Catroux, to let them join the SAS. They would be in Kabrit shortly. He had also secured the services of Captain Bill Cumper, Royal Engineers, an explosives genius, who would fill Lewes's role as demolitions instructor.

The only cloud on Stirling's horizon as he debussed at Kabrit that day was the necessity of telling Paddy Mayne that he had been struck off the orbat for the Bouerat op. This seemed a poor way of repaying the man who had done most to reverse the fortunes of the SAS, but Stirling had decided to appoint him officer-in-charge, recruitment and training. Kabrit would soon be swelling with almost a hundred recruits, and he had convinced himself that he needed a man like Mayne to inspire them. It was a job tailor-made for Jock Lewes, but Lewes was dead.

In his tent, Stirling explained the situation to Mayne as diplomatically as he could, adding that it was 'nothing personal', and in the best interests of the SAS. The explosion he had half-expected didn't come. Instead, Mayne's eyes narrowed hazardously. He hinted obliquely that Stirling was jealous of his success. He was eliminating him from the field so as to overtake his 'bag'.

This was not as ludicrous as it sounded: Mayne and Stirling were still in their twenties. Stirling, a major at twenty-seven, had yet to make his mark in combat. Mayne had distinguished himself in action with 11 Commando, and had taken out more than fifty aircraft on recent ops. Stirling envied Mayne's intuitive battle-sense, and the way the men venerated him. While they responded to Stirling's laid-back style of leadership, Mayne had the knack, as Stirling himself admitted, of touching just the right chord in each of them. He was a natural gang-leader, a born bandit-chief. While Stirling always seemed to have his head in the clouds, looking for lessons and patterns, Mayne concentrated on the job in hand. '[Mayne] was a very good fellow to operate with,' said Mike Sadler, 'because he gave a great sense of confidence and was focused on the operation, and knew exactly what was happening in it. David obviously did too, but he didn't give you the same feeling.'[1]

Mayne may have reminded Stirling that he had joined the SAS to 'get a crack at the Hun', not to become a 'desk wallah'. Stirling stuck to his guns, and Mayne accepted the situation with bad grace, on the understanding it was temporary. He gave his CO the entirely unconvincing assurance that he would 'do his best'. Stirling admitted later that the decision to chain his best fighter to a desk was 'bloody stupid'. Despite his rhetoric about 'what was best for the SAS', though, he was at least partly motivated by his need to run an operation on which he would not, for once, be over-shadowed by Mayne.

Auchinleck had told Stirling that he would have to put the Bouerat raid in before the third week in January, when the port was scheduled for bombing by the RAF. There was no time to be lost. The op was important, in Stirling's mind, to demonstrate that the SAS had more strings to its bow than aircraft-demolition. Some elements at GHQ ME, particularly Chief of the General Staff Arthur Smith – and presumably Dudley Clarke – still saw L Detachment as a parachute unit, and wanted Stirling to re-start parachute training in April. Stirling had already been down that road. In December, Rommel had been supplied with twenty-two panzers by sea at Benghazi. This demonstrated the vital importance of shipping and harbours. Stirling had already brewed up a scheme to raid Benghazi, but it had been rendered obsolete by the Axis retreat. Bouerat still lay behind Rommel's lines, and to destroy vital fuel-tankers and fuel-storage facilities there would be a major coup.

Stirling's was the kind of mind that grasped the importance of symbolism. He had stated at the very first staff meeting that the elite unit needed a special, mystic insignia to set it apart. In Cairo, he had taken the astute step of wearing SAS wings and cap-badge during a meeting with the C-in-C. His implacable foes in the Adjutant-General's office had reminded him bluntly that the SAS was a temporary unit and couldn't have its own badge. Stirling ignored them, and the gamble paid off. Auchinleck liked it. That day, he commented, was 'the day the SAS was truly born'. He owed it to Jock Lewes's memory to crown success with 'an accepted identity of which we could all be proud'.[2] Lewes had designed the wings the previous year. They had a straight edge on top to make them distinct from the wings of other airborne units. The design was said to have been borrowed from a fresco in the lobby of Shepheard's Hotel, based on an ancient Egyptian motif of a sacred ibis. In fact, as Seekings pointed out, it was actually a winged scarab-beetle motif, with a parachute in place of the scarab. The dark and light blue backgrounds were said to be the colours of Stirling's and Lewes's respective alma maters, Oxford and Cambridge universities. So it was that emblems of two of Britain's oldest and finest institutions found their way into the insignia of a quite different but equally distinguished one. Those who qualified as parachutists could wear the wings on their shoulders, but veterans of three SAS operations had the right to wear them above the left breast-pocket.[3]

The cap-badge was the work of Bob Tait, now missing in action with Fraser, who had designed it back in October. Tait's sketch was the winner of at least a dozen entries in a competition set up by Stirling. Though it would later be familiar as the 'Winged Dagger', the badge actually symbolized the flaming sword Excalibur. Tait's suggestion for the SAS motto, 'Strike & Destroy', was vetoed by Stirling as being too value-neutral. Instead, he came up with the inspired 'Who Dares Wins' – a more robust statement of an axiom favoured by Combined Operations chief, Admiral of the Fleet, Sir Roger Keyes: 'He Most Prevails Who Nobly Dares'.

Not all Stirling's friends were impressed with it. Randolph Churchill dismissed it as 'totally rotten'. Stirling solved the carping in characteristic fashion by betting Churchill £10 he couldn't improve on it. He never did, but as Stirling pointed out in amusement later, Churchill soon became quite desperate to wear the 'totally rotten' badge himself.

While officers would wear the flaming sword on their peaked field service caps for some time to come, Stirling had got hold of some surplus snow-white berets for enlisted men. On their first leave in Cairo that January, the men got into so many fights with wolf-whistling Aussies and Kiwis that some of them refused to wear it. Eventually it was replaced with the sand-coloured beret that, with several hiccups, was eventually to become the lasting emblem of the SAS Regiment.

25. 'Surrounded by bottles, reading James Joyce'

Stirling launched the Bouerat mission from Jalo on 17 January, going in with Captain Anthony Hunter's Guards patrol of the LRDG. He had with him the now inseparable Cooper and Seekings, and two Squatter veterans who had been *hors de combat* until recently, Pat Riley and Dave Kershaw. He also had with him Bob Bennett and his mate Lofty Baker, Jimmy Brough, Charlie Cattell, Frank Rhodes, Ted Badger and Frank Austin. He had a two-man RAF intelligence team, and two canoeists from the Special Boat Section, Captain G. I. Duncan, Black Watch, and Corporal Edward Barr, Highland Light Infantry.

The Special Boat Section had been founded two years earlier by canoe-expert Lt. Roger 'Jumbo' Courtney, Kings Royal Rifle Corps. Originally part of 8 Commando, its main role was beach-head reconnaissance, but it also had a limited capability as a raiding force. The SBS operated in two-man teams, using collapsible kayak-style canoes known as *folbots*. Stirling decided to take a *folbot* with him on the Bouerat raid, and have the SBS team set limpet mines on shipping in the harbour.

Once again, he was unlucky. On the drive in, Hunter's patrol was buzzed by Stukas in the Wadi Tamrit and his wireless truck and an operator and two other men were lost. Stirling had been relying on them to relay data on the position of storage tanks and fuel-bowsers in the port from the Army Air Photographic Interpretation Unit. His chances of obtaining this data were abruptly scotched. Worse was to come. Stirling had instructed the SBS team to assemble the *folbot* before going in. The fragile canoe was smashed when the 15 cwt Ford truck the SAS were using for the final approach went over a pothole. It would not have been much use in any case, because the SAS team found no enemy shipping in the harbour. Stirling divided his raiding party into four groups under himself, Duncan, Riley and Kershaw. Sauntering past Italian sentries, who never even bothered to challenge them, they set Lewes bombs on the wireless station, cables, dumps, and eighteen petrol bowsers. The impressive firework display that lit up the night for hours afterwards didn't deceive Stirling that he had achieved his aim.

On the exfiltration, Stirling's crew were meandering along the road, having just planted bombs on Axis lorries, when they were banjoed by Italians in two guard-sangars they had passed on the way in. Then, they had appeared deserted. Now the sentries had woken up, and were pulling iron on 20mm Bredas. Rounds were skeetering at them. The situation looked critical.

The LRDG driver, Cpl. 'Flash' Gibson, Scots Guards, switched his headlights to full beam and floored the accelerator. Cooper, on the back, chunked the enemy with a Vickers K aircraft machine gun that had been fitted specially for this operation. '[I] let fly with a devastating mixture of tracer and incendiary,' he recalled, '. . . at the same time Reg [Seekings] opened up with his Thompson, and we ploughed through the ambush completely outgunning and demoralizing the Italians.'[1] Cooper and Seekings scragged at least five Italians dead. A moment later they heard the unmistakable crunch of mortar shells hitting the earth.

Stirling believed that they had done the near impossible in running the ambush unscathed, and put their survival down to Gibson's presence of mind, and Cooper's cool shooting. Gibson was awarded the MM, and Cooper the DCM.

Back at Jalo, Stirling found out why there had been no ships in Bouerat. The op was based on stale intelligence. Rommel's Afrika Korps had moved on 21 January and pushed the Eighth Army all the way to Gazala, near Tobruk. Benghazi had again fallen to the Axis. Ruminating over the recent reverses on the way back to Jalo, Stirling saw that the news wasn't all bad for the SAS. Raids on Axis ports and shipping would now be a priority. While Stirling hadn't achieved his major objective on the Bouerat raid, it had at least proved that the SAS could bring off harbour attacks.

Stirling arrived back at Kabrit with a plan for a raid on Benghazi already formed in his head. He was desperate to get Mayne's input, but there was silence when he inquired after him. He eventually tracked him down to his tent. 'I went in,' Stirling recalled. 'Paddy was surrounded by bottles, reading James Joyce.'[2] Mayne had been holed up for three days, drinking. He didn't ask how the Bouerat raid had gone, answered in grunts, and refused to look at Stirling. He had fallen into a slough of despond, brooding not only on his exclusion from the raid, but also on the loss in November of his only close friend, Eoin McGonigal.

He hadn't bothered monitoring the training, but had withdrawn into his shell. He had become bored with administration and frustrated by the bureaucracy at GHQ. Stirling could only be thankful that he hadn't ended by punching out some senior staff officer. Bergé's French contingent was only halfway through its course, and would not be ready for the next operation. There was a host of other recruits. Mayne had even let GHQ take back the priceless Bill Cumper, who was now wasting his talents 'fitting toilet-seats in Alexandria'.

Stirling quickly saw the folly of trying to tie Mayne down to an admin job, and promised him it would not happen again. According to Jim Almonds, though, the tension between them continued even after Mayne returned to an operational role. There may have been other reasons for this. With the death of Lewes, Mayne was now 'No.2' in L Detachment, yet Stirling never made him second-in-command. In fact, Stirling had recruited Lt. George, Earl Jellicoe, a member of the 'Silver Circle Club' and a fellow ex-8 Commando officer, in early 1942, as Detachment 2IC. Jellicoe said that he took up the post after being released from his battalion, 3 Coldstream Guards, on 30 April.

However, Stirling told his biographer, Alan Hoe, that he didn't appoint a 2IC in the spring of '42, because he 'had no-one at the time'.[3] It seems likely that he did promise Jellicoe the post, but never made it official. At the same time, he had his eye on LRDG patrol leader Captain the Hon. Robin Gurdon of the Scots Guards, whom he had offered the same job. Stirling rated Gurdon 'a very, very fine man' and said that by early June he had almost talked him into transferring from his current assignment. As Jim Almond's biographer, Lorna Almonds Windmill, put it, Stirling's success lay partly in his ability to 'kiss all the girls' – to back more than one horse, and to tell people what they most wanted to hear.

According to Jim Almonds it was common knowledge that Stirling didn't think of Mayne as second-in-command for the detachment. In view of Mayne's reaction to being desk-bound in Kabrit, there were obvious reasons for this, but there may also have been other, less obvious ones. Stirling admired Mayne as a fighter, but wasn't at ease with him socially. He would later declare that the SAS was a unit 'without class', where every man could aspire to become an 'aristocrat' in his own lifetime, but in practice he preferred the company of his social peers. 'He had a slight weakness for the well-heeled with the right old school tie,' said Almonds, 'and even took on one or two [officers] whose suitability some thought questionable.'[4]

Jellicoe and Gurdon didn't fall into this category, but both were the kind of upper-class officers Mayne disliked. Gurdon was killed in July 1942, before he got the chance to take up Stirling's offer, but assuming Mayne knew that Stirling had promised the post to one or both, he may well have taken it as an affront – more of the same 'old boy network' that he had experienced in the commandos, but of which he had imagined the SAS would be free.

Stirling argued later that Mayne had amply demonstrated his unsuitability for administrative duties, and that his temperament and moods made him a difficult subordinate. 'He had, I suppose, something in common with Hotspur, the young Harry Percy,' he said, 'quick-tempered, audacious, vigorous in action, but not one who took kindly to being thwarted, frustrated or crossed in any way.'[5] Stirling probably believed that only one of the 'old school' could press the right buttons in GHQ ME. Certainly, Mayne had a great many aversions, among them the English, Catholics (excluding McGonigal) and the landed gentry. He despised 'big mouths' and those he thought were 'shooting a line', but in his violent moods he picked indiscriminately on friend and foe.

Despite recent efforts to whitewash Mayne's character, the evidence is that he could be awkward even when sober, and extremely belligerent when drunk. 'When he drank you felt your life wasn't safe,' said Lt. Johnny Wiseman, a later SAS recruit, describing how Mayne once hurled him to the floor for some unknown reason, and forcibly shaved off half his beard.[6] Wiseman added that while he was superb in action, Mayne could be terrifying off duty. It wasn't a matter of blind fury: Wiseman was convinced that Mayne had a deeply ingrained destructive urge.[7] '[Mayne] was a nice, kind fellow,' Mike Sadler commented, '. . . very considerate for other people . . . but once he had gone beyond a certain point, drinking, he became somebody quite different.'[8]

Big Pat Riley, the Wisconsin-born ex-Coldstreamer, was perhaps the only SAS man who ever knocked Mayne down. He once found him drunk, beating someone so savagely it looked as if he might do him real harm. Without even thinking about it, Riley – who had been a champion boxer in the Guards, and had fought Reg Seekings in the ring before either had joined the commandos – walloped Mayne with a massive fist and flattened him. 'I thought I was in for a rough time,' Riley said, 'but not a bit of it. He stood up, looked at me for a while and then quietly went off.'[9]

It was Pat Riley, now promoted sergeant-major, and the Detachment's senior non-com, whom Stirling chose to replace Mayne as training officer. He managed to extricate Bill Cumper from his 'toilet-fitting' duties and have him permanently attached to the SAS. He had also discovered on his arrival at Kabrit that he was one good officer and four good men better off. Bill Fraser and his party – Tait, Du Vivier, Byrne and Phillips – had returned. They had been picked up south of Ajadabiyya by a patrol of the King's Dragoon Guards on 10 January, having made an astonishing eight-day trek across the desert from Marble Arch. The LRDG men who had disappeared at the time of Lewes's death had also come in, but the SAS-man with them, Geordie White, was still missing.

26. 'You can get away with it by sheer blatant cheek'

In the Naval Intelligence Office at Alexandria, a little whitewashed room stocked with maps and aerial photos, Stirling examined a scale-model of Benghazi with a recently trained officer-recruit, Second-Lieutenant Fitzroy Maclean, Cameron Highlanders. Maclean, an ex-Foreign Office diplomat, spoke German and Italian, and had travelled extensively in Russia, China and Central Asia before the war. Barred from military service by his profession, he had managed to circumvent it by getting elected a Conservative MP. A half-admiring Winston Churchill would later quip that he was a man who had 'used the Mother of Parliaments as a public convenience'.

Maclean was one of the new SAS intake authorized in January, and his first experience at Kabrit was getting turfed out of his tent by a bearded and filthy Bill Fraser, just back from his two-hundred-mile tramp across Cyrenaica. Now he was keen to accompany Stirling on a mission to Benghazi, due to take place on 21 May.

Lying about two hundred and fifty miles behind the Afrika Korps divisions pressing on Ritchie's defences at the Gazala Line, Benghazi was Rommel's main conduit of supplies. Stirling was obsessed with it. So was RAF Middle East, but the thousands of tons of high explosive they had dumped there hadn't put it out of business. Air bombardments were hit or miss affairs, and Stirling had already proved the SAS could outdo the RAF on airfield raids at a fraction of the cost. Now he was anxious to prove that he could get the same result with Benghazi's docks and shipping.

This would be Stirling's second venture into the Benghazi area. On 15 March, he and Mayne had conducted a series of strikes in and around the port. Stirling's crew had managed to get near the docks with a *folbot*, intending to limpet-mine fuel-tankers in the harbour. The plan fell through when the SBS officer in charge found the canoe parts incompatible.

Of the three attacks Stirling had planned on nearby airfields at the same time – at Barce, Slonta and Berka – only Mayne's raid on Berka achieved anything significant. Mayne, who lost Jack Byrne on the thirty-mile march-out, reported that his team had knocked off fifteen aircraft and fifteen torpedoes. The huge grin Mayne wore as he presented his report cannot have been endearing to Stirling, who had once again failed in his task. During the withdrawal another team blew up five aircraft in hangars at the Luftwaffe repair depot at Benina, a few miles east of Benghazi, but thirty planes they had spotted there earlier turned out to be dummies.

In the Naval Intelligence office, Stirling and Maclean studied the model of Benghazi. A tiny dab of yellow paint marked a narrow strip of shingle that would make the ideal launch-pad for their boats. Stirling had never liked *folbots*, and for this op Maclean had got hold of a pair of inflatable recce craft from the Royal Engineers. Stirling thought these would prove more robust. Together with Seekings and Cooper, they had practised with them, laying dummy limpets on Royal Navy destroyers riding at anchor on the Great Bitter Lake, quite unaware that the crews regularly dropped five-pound depth charges over the side as a security measure.

Stirling had chosen 21 May for the mission because it fell in the moonless period, when SAS troops could creep within feet of enemy sentries unseen. Mayne was to be excluded once again, in favour of Maclean – perhaps it was the sight of his grinning face on the last op that had clinched it. The team included Seekings, Cooper, Rose, Bennett and Lt. Gordon Alston, Royal Artillery, ex-Middle East Commando, another recent SAS acquisition, who had been with Stirling on the March raid.

Also with the team was the Prime Minister's son, Captain Randolph Churchill, 4 Hussars, who had completed a few weeks of training with the SAS. He had lost more than ten kilos, but according to Stirling was still 'damn fat'.[1] Churchill had made only one of his five qualifying jumps, but persuaded Stirling to take him on the Benghazi op. Stirling knew Randolph wrote his father daily, and could hardly refuse a chance of gaining the Prime Minister's ear. He agreed to let him come 'as an observer'. He didn't doubt that Churchill had courage, but felt he wasn't so much interested in fighting behind enemy lines as in wearing the SAS insignia – the same badge he had dismissed weeks earlier as 'totally rotten'.

Escorted by Robin Gurdon's LRDG patrol, they set off from Siwa in their own vehicle – the 'Blitz Buggy' – a stripped-down Ford V8 utility vehicle done up with Afrika Korps TAC signs. Stirling had 'found' it in Cairo and had it modified. Churchill irritated him early on by swigging rum from his water-bottle. 'We do not drink on operations, Captain Churchill,' Stirling told him, not entirely truthfully, as he snatched the offending bottle and emptied it into the desert. His plan had been to deposit Churchill at the LRDG rendezvous overlooking Benghazi, before the raid. This scheme went awry when Reg Seekings was injured by an exploding time-pencil while sorting out the Lewes bombs, and Churchill claimed the right to go in his place.

As it turned out, Churchill was the least of Stirling's worries. One of the Blitz Buggy's track-rods had been damaged in a wadi, giving the car an exasperating two-tone whine that could be heard miles away. After Maclean had used flawless Italian to bluff his way through a checkpoint, they were chased by another vehicle. They entered the town at eighty miles an hour. Having lost their pursuer in the labyrinth of streets, they heard air-raid sirens, and knowing no RAF raid was planned for that night, assumed the sirens were for them. They ditched the 'Blitz Buggy' and set a charge on her with a half-hour time-pencil. They had to remove it hastily when Maclean ascertained from an Italian *carabiniere* that the alarm really was for an air attack.

The RAF raid never materialized. Leaving the car with Churchill and Johnny Rose, Stirling found a gap in the wire around the harbour. They manoeuvred one of the packed inflatables surreptitiously down to the waterfront, weaving through cranes and railway sidings. There was no moon. The night was cold, clear and brilliant with stars. The sea was dead calm and stretched away from them like a sheet of lead. In the starlight Maclean made out some tempting-looking Axis vessels lying at anchor.

Cooper and Maclean began to inflate the boat, while Stirling and Alston went for a look-see round the docks. The foot-pump made a racket, and an Italian on watch on one of the ships shouted to inquire what they were doing. Maclean told him to mind his own business. They continued pumping away but nothing happened – the 'robust' inflatable had been punctured.

Cursing to themselves, Cooper and Maclean had to sneak back through the wire, trek a mile through the streets to the car, and get the second boat, which once again had to be ferried silently all the way to the harbour. After half an hour's pumping they realized that this one, too, wasn't inflating. 'It was heart-rending,' Maclean said.[2]

They found Stirling and Alston outside the hole in the wire, and decided against placing charges on the railway trucks, as it would prejudice their chances of carrying out a future raid. They would have to abort the mission. Stirling said they should return to the waterfront and collect all their gear, so as not to betray the fact that a raid had been attempted.

It was starting to get light. On his way back through the wire, Maclean was prodded with a bayonet by a Somali guard. He quickly cowed the colonial soldier with an indignant diatribe in Italian. He, Stirling and Cooper packed the mines and inflatables into their bags, but as they moved off they noticed two more sentries hovering behind them. This was awkward. It meant they couldn't return through the gap without alerting suspicion. Instead, they headed for the main gate, where Maclean marched up to the guard-commander and accused him of sloppiness and 'a gross dereliction of duty' for allowing the three of them to wander about without being challenged. For all the Italian knew, he said, they could be British saboteurs. The guard-commander looked suitably intimidated, and as the SAS team went out, the sentry presented arms.

They lay up for the next twelve hours in a bomb-damaged house directly opposite a building that turned out to be a German Area HQ. Stirling couldn't help chuckling to himself at the thought of the British Prime Minister's son lurking within a stone's throw of a German nerve-centre. They were disturbed only once – by an Italian sailor they thought might be a spy, but turned out to be a looter. After sunrise, Stirling went out and sauntered around the harbour mole nonchalantly with sunglasses on, and a towel around his neck, as if he were going for a swim.

Stirling said that his walk revealed two boats that were ripe for demolition, but the way Maclean remembered it, several of them went for a stroll around Benghazi after dark the following night to identify potential targets. They strolled past the Italian basilica, down the middle of the street, arm in arm, whistling, as though they owned the place. 'Nobody paid the slightest attention to us,' Maclean recalled. 'On such occasions, it's one's manner that counts. If only you can behave naturally and avoid the appearance of furtiveness, it is worth any number of disguises and faked documents.'[3]

Maclean said that they noticed the two motor-torpedo boats tied to a jetty and realized they would make good targets. They hurried back to the ruined house, where Johnny Rose had been working on the Blitz Buggy's damaged track-rod. They piled into the car and returned to the jetty with their bombs, only to find that a guard had been put on the boats. 'To bomb [them] would have been tantamount to suicide,' Cooper commented.[4] Instead, they left the town on the Benina road, passing easily through the checkpoint by tacking themselves on to an Italian convoy. On their way back to the meet-up, they set a couple of charges on some machinery at Benina landing-ground.

The bombs went off as they were motoring up the escarpment. Looking back they could just make out the spiral of smoke. It was no more than a pin-prick, Cooper admitted, 'but at least we had something to show for our persistence'.[5] Stirling's second raid on Benghazi had turned into a farce, but a useful farce. A team of SAS troops, in uniform, had entered a vital enemy port and remained there for thirty-six hours without detection. They had even completed a foot reconnaissance.

The lesson was that the chink in the enemy's armour was always the human factor: 'If you think of something the enemy would consider an impossible stupidity,' Cooper said, 'and carry it out with determination, you can get away with it by sheer blatant cheek.'[6] They laughed about it all the way back to their own lines, where the joke finally backfired on them. Overtaking a British convoy on the road between Alexandria and Cairo, Stirling clipped a lorry and rolled the 'Blitz Buggy'. Maclean suffered a fractured skull and was out of action for three months, Churchill's spine was so badly injured he had to be evacuated to Britain, Rose broke his arm and Stirling escaped with a cracked bone in the wrist. The

Daily Telegraph correspondent Arthur Merton, who had hitched a ride with them, was killed.

27. The most ambitious SAS project yet

For twenty minutes, Paddy Mayne and his three-man team had been proned out on the Berka Satellite airfield near Benghazi. A terrific fire-fight was in progress. RAF bombs were wheezing in, hammering the deck with seismic quakes, rupturing into hot shrapnel that seared around them. The night was split by the flashes of flares like lightning streaks, and the probing arms of searchlights, punctuated by the percussion of 20mm ack-ack guns thumping out streams of tracer. Mayne heard the groan of an aircraft dopplering out of control, and a moment later there was a head-pounding shock as it hit the ground and blew apart not six hundred feet away. Mayne and his men felt the heat braise their faces.

It was 2340 hours on 12 June 1942, almost a month after Stirling's aborted raid on Benghazi shipping. Mayne's attack was supposed to go in at midnight, synchronized with eight other SAS raids in Cyrenaica, and across the water on Crete. It was the most ambitious SAS project yet, and Mayne was furious that the RAF had messed up his part in it by bad timing.

This was the second time Mayne had raided Berka. The first had been back in March, when he had bagged the fifteen aircraft. Since then, the enemy had got wise to the fact that SAS raiders came at midnight during the moonless phase. They had also learned to space their aircraft out on the airfields to make them less vulnerable to air attack, and to assign individual sentries to each machine.

The bombers passed and the thump of the AA guns stopped. The downed plane was still burning. Jimmy Storie and Arthur Warburton had already set a Lewes bomb on one aircraft, and Bob Lilley crawled forward towards another. Lilley was ten yards from the plane when he was challenged by a sentry. A rifle cracked. A round soughed over his head. Almost at the same instant, a No.36

Mills grenade hurled by Mayne erupted, whacking the sentry's body apart in mid-air.

Rifles cracked. Sub-machine gun fire sizzled out of the darkness. 'The stuff was whistling over our heads this way and that,' Lilley recalled '. . . They had our range more than once as we ducked and ran for it, so Mayne shouted out to us to split into two groups and find some place to hide.'[1] Somehow the pairs got mixed up. Mayne ended up with Jimmy Storie, while Lilley stuck with Warburton.

The one aircraft they had snagged detonated and blazed up. The plain around Benghazi was lit with pinpricks of fire from the RAF bombing and the other SAS raids. Mayne could hear a furious barrage of gunshots from Berka Main aerodrome only two miles away, targeted by a Free French SAS party under Aspirant André Zirnheld. There was a smug pink frisson in the sky over Benina aerodrome, slightly inland from Benghazi town. This had been Stirling's assignment. Mayne wondered if he had scored at last.

Up on the jebel, at Barce, fifty miles away, another French SAS team under Aspirant Jaquier was heading for the aerodrome. Beyond that, far to the east, fifteen more French SAS-men had infiltrated the airfields of Derna and Mertuba, concealed in Afrika Korps vehicles. Another French group under Commandant Georges Bergé was scheduled to hit an airfield at Heraklion on Crete.

For two hours Mayne and Storie lay motionless in a ditch as the Germans tromped up and down beside them. At first light they set off towards the escarpment. They had covered only two miles when a command vehicle pulled up sharply across their line of march. They fell flat, eating dust and gravel. A troop of soldiers jumped out of the command vehicle, dressed into a neat line, and advanced straight towards them.

28. 'Give them something to remember us by'

At that moment, Johnny Cooper was raking through bush on the jebel towards the meet-up point with Robin Gurdon's patrol, in a wadi four miles away. Benina aerodrome was on fire below him, and Benghazi town, to the west, lay under a pall of smoke.

A few hours earlier, Cooper, Seekings and Stirling had raided Benina. They had knocked out at least five enemy aircraft, torched three hangars and a fuel dump, and fragged a guardhouse full of enemy troops. On the way up the hillside, Stirling's elation had been marred by a migraine so intense that for a while Seekings and Cooper had to pull him along. Cooper had left the two of them, and had gone on ahead to recce the RV.

All the previous day they had hidden in scrub a thousand feet above the airfield. This was Stirling's third attempt to hit Benina, and he knew its value as a repair-depot. Their lying-up place was close enough to hear the growl of machinery being tested in a cluster of hangars and workshops. Through their binoculars, they watched Luftwaffe engineers swarming over stripped-down airframes, fitting new engines and parts. Several planes took off, wheeled lazily round the cloudless sky like kites, and landed again.

The plain below them wasn't as arid as the coast further east. From here, it looked like a shaggy Persian kilim woven in greys and greens and duns and ochres. Benghazi port, now familiar to Stirling from the thirty-six hours he had spent there last month, lay basting in the heat, its buildings dazzling white against a wedge of jade-coloured sea. There was a lot of activity on the hillside. Arab women in rainbow skirts laboured on plots. Boys in tattered trousers sauntered behind donkey-trains. Bearded herders hustled mobs of sheep. No one spotted them. All was quiet when they moved out after dark.

It was a hard climb down through steep wadis, but they slipped into the aerodrome easily. They lay on the field and waited for the RAF sortie that was due to hit Benghazi town before midnight.

The Blenheims soared in right on cue, just before moonset, and by the time their engines had faded the night was pitch black. At midnight the SAS-men primed their sixty Lewes bombs. It was standard operating procedure to press the time-pencils after the bombs were laid, but tonight they were going in with live bombs, set to hour and half-hour delays. Once the bombs were in place, they would pull the safety-pins and hope they wouldn't blow up in their faces. The change in procedure marked the importance of the mission. 'This is a big moment in our history,' Stirling told them, 'all the way along the coast, right into the Med, now everybody's [pressing] their time pencils.'[1]

The eight SAS raids synchronized for midnight on 12 June 1942 were the mature expression of Stirling's original concept, without the parachuting element. Six of the eight SAS groups were drawn from the Free French detachment, and the other two from L Detachment veterans. The missions were strategic in nature – the outcome of the entire North African campaign might hinge on their success.

Malta, the key British supply-base in the Mediterranean, was blockaded by the Italian navy and under daily attack by the Luftwaffe. At the end of April, the island's governor, General Dobbie, wired Churchill that Malta was starving and couldn't hold out after mid-June. Churchill announced that the loss of Malta would be 'a disaster of the first magnitude to the British Empire, and probably fatal in the long run to the defence of the Nile Valley'.

The Prime Minister decreed that the supply convoys due to be sent from Alexandria and Gibraltar in the June dark-phase must get through. Some Axis aircraft that would be deployed against the convoys were based on airfields in Cyrenaica and on Crete. Stirling was tasked to hit these airfields on the night when Naval Intelligence thought a concerted air assault was most likely.

Stirling, Seekings and Cooper lurched towards the hangars hefting forty-pound packs of explosive. On the way they nearly fell into a six-foot deep silo of aviation fuel they hadn't clocked from their observation point. They stuck two bombs on it and pulled pins. They moved on again with Seekings lead-scout, their senses fine-tuned for movement. Seekings heard the tramp of a sentry's hobnail boots, magnified in the stillness. He grabbed Stirling's arm and they all froze. They squatted down till the sentry passed, then made a beeline for the first hangar.

It loomed over them, its big sliding doors closed. Stirling found the catch, but when Cooper and Seekings pushed the door open, the rollers creaked. They stood stock-still and listened. No shouts, no sudden movements. Seekings hunkered down outside. Cooper and Stirling dollied-in bombs.

It was dark as a tomb. 'As our eyes got accustomed to the darkness, we saw [it] was full of German aircraft,' Cooper said. 'Motioning me to go to the right, David went to the left, and we busily placed our bombs on the Stukas and Messerschmitts that were in there for repair.'[2] They were still laying bombs when Seekings hissed a warning. They stiffened again. Two sentries marched past.

They finished placing the charges and moved to the next hangar. Seekings nosed his way into a third, and found about thirty crates of what looked like brand new aero-engines. He set bombs on them and yanked safety-pins.

On the way out they noticed a guardhouse further down the track. The door opened and shut at intervals, transmitting chinks of light, as sentries went in and out. Stirling eased the pin out of a nobbly No. 36 pineapple. 'We'll give them something to remember us by,' he said. He moved silently to the door, and stood poised for a second before kicking it open. 'We saw that the room was crowded with Germans,' Cooper recalled, 'many of whom were asleep. David calmly bowled the grenade across the floor saying, "Share this among you." He slammed the door and jumped clear . . .'[3] The explosion rocked the building.

Stirling later called the grenade attack on the guardhouse 'a silly show of bravado'.[4] If the grenade hadn't exploded, he said, the guards might have had time to save some of the planes. He also confessed that he was not at ease with the action, which seemed to him 'close to murder'.[5] It was almost certainly an impulse animated by his sense of competition with Mayne, and the necessity of convincing his men that he was capable of merciless acts. '[Stirling] was too much of a gentleman,' commented Sgt. Fred White, an L Detachment man who was to become one of the most highly decorated soldiers in the Regiment. 'In our job you needed a killer . . .'[6]

They were still behind the hangars when the first Lewes bomb cracked off inside. They pelted across the road and started to clamber up the escarpment. They had covered about three hundred feet when Stirling complained of a massive migraine. He had a needle in his skull, and felt nauseous. His head was spinning, his peripheral vision had gone haywire.

Stirling's migraine is a possible indicator that he had taken a whopping dose of Benzedrine that night. A highly addictive member of the amphetamine group – 'speed' – the drug kept the men awake, made them more active, but also increased recklessness and clouded reasoning. Benzedrine was on issue to SAS troops, but most weren't aware of how dangerous it could be. The extent of Benzedrine use among wartime SAS troops will never be known for certain, but remains a hidden factor behind many SAS actions. One symptom of the 'let down' after a large dose is intense migraine. It is at least possible that Benzedrine consumption was responsible not only for the crippling migraine Stirling suffered on the Benina operation, but also for what he himself called his 'silly show of bravado' that night.

They plumped down in the scrub to rest and watch the show. Below them, the hangar roofs were blasted off like volcano-plugs, releasing towering gouts of flame and smoke. The heat had set off the 20mm cannons on the Messerschmitt in the first hangar, and tracer bullets were scorching air, creasing the darkness with tramlines of light. The guardhouse was still blazing. The fuel dump suddenly went up in a boiling wedge of brilliant gases. Firefighters were running about like ants, and anti-aircraft guns were walloping blindly into the night. It was, Cooper recalled, 'stupendous', 'a fantastic firework display'.[7] It was difficult to believe that so much chaos had been caused by just three men, and the contents of their knapsacks.

29. 'The lorry kept spluttering to a halt'

A hundred and fifty miles away, north of east across the 'bulge' of Cyrenaica, Aspirant Augustin Jourdan of the Free French SAS detachment was running for his life back to his RV, six miles from Derna West airfield. A couple of hours earlier Jourdan had escaped from his German captors when the truck he had been pulled out of had turned into a fireball.

Jourdan, an ex-French colonial officer in Morocco, had fled from France to Britain when his cadet school had been captured by the Germans. Volunteering for de Gaulle's Free French Forces in London, he had served on missions in Ethiopia and Syria, where he had met his friend, Major Georges Bergé, currently commanding the French SAS detachment. This was Jourdan's first mission with the SAS, and after all the careful planning it had gone seriously wrong.

Jourdan's part in the Malta Convoy op had been the most tricky of all. His targets were two airfields at Derna and one at Mertuba on the eastern end of the Jebel Akhdar massif. As Stirling knew, these aerodromes were sited on a thousand-foot plateau in a bottle-neck on the coastal plain, where a fast run-in by the LRDG was ruled out. Not far behind Axis lines, only a hundred miles from Tobruk, the area was alive with Axis troops.

While Stirling was wondering how to infiltrate these targets, GHQ pointed him in the direction of the Special Interrogation Group – a dozen German-speaking Jews who had fled to Palestine in the 1930s. Most of them had served in 51 Commando, a unique force recruited originally from Jewish and Arab Palestinians, but later filled up with British troops. The commanding officer, SIG, Captain Herbert Buck MC, of 1/3 Punjab Regiment, was a fluent German-speaker who had broken out of an Axis prison-camp and crossed enemy lines masquerading as a German officer. His only prop was an Afrika Korps peaked cap. The ease of his escape brought him an epiphany: a group of commandos trained to carry out sabotage behind Axis lines, disguised as German soldiers. For the Jewish SIG-men it was a risky proposition – capture would mean torture and certain death.

To bring his men up to speed on current army slang, Buck had drafted in two bona-fide non-Jewish Afrika Korps NCOs who had defected to the Allies. Their cover-names were 'Esser' and 'Brueckner' – ex-French Foreign Legionnaires who had fought against the Germans in 1940. Drafted into the German army after the defeat of France, they had been captured by the British and declared themselves anti-Nazi. Brueckner's real name was Heinrich Brockmann – Esser's was Walter Essner.

The plan, put together by Stirling and Buck, was for three five-man groups of Free French SAS under Jourdan to conceal themselves in a convoy of Afrika Korps vehicles, driven and guarded by SIG-men in German uniforms. The SIG would ease them through barriers and checkpoints until they reached Derna and Mertuba airfields. There, at midnight on 12 June, the French would plant their Lewes bombs. They would then beat a retreat and meet up with an LRDG patrol under Captain Alastair Guild of the New Zealand Divisional Cavalry.

The only flaw was that when the convoy left the LRDG base at Siwa on 6 June, they went without the June password. Buck, driving up front in a military version Volkswagen with Afrika Korps TAC signs, hoped they could get by without it. There was also an Opel staff car, but the fifteen Frenchmen were secreted in two trucks, one a German three-tonner, the other a British 30cwt lorry done-up as a 'captured' vehicle, with the Afrika Korps palm-tree and swastika motif.

They reached the drop-off point five days later. The SIG-men donned Afrika Korps uniforms and kit authentic to the last detail – Luger automatics, Schmeisser sub-machine guns, bayonets and 'potato-masher' grenades. Buck wore the uniform of a German private, and the two defectors, Esser and Brueckner, were turned out as Afrika Korps NCOs. The French SAS, dressed in overalls and forage-caps, and carrying .45 calibre Colt automatic pistols and a brace of No.36 Mills grenades each, would from this point dip under blankets and jerrycans in the back of the vehicles.

Next morning they passed the first barrier, manned by Italians. Buck engaged the sentries in conversation and persuaded them to hand over the password. He told them his group was taking the vehicles for repair in Derna. Further on, they passed a checkpoint guarded by German military policemen and oiled the wheels by donating a crate of English beer. They said it was 'spoils of war'.

By 1200 hours they had set up a base six miles from the Derna airfields. Jourdan wanted to recce all the targets, but Buck vetoed a trip to Mertuba as too risky. Instead, Jourdan and Buck were shipped in for a shufti at Derna East and West. They returned excited, having spotted an entire squadron of Messerschmitt 110s and a dozen Stukas.

Jourdan gave the final briefing an hour before last light. Cpl. Jean Tourneret would take four men and hit the Mertuba field. They would travel in one truck with an SIG-man driving, and two others on guard. After setting the charges, they would rally at a point nearby. The remaining SAS were divided into two groups under Cpl. Pierre de Bourmont and Jourdan himself. They would go for Derna East and West in a single truck, driven by Brueckner, accompanied by two other SIG-men, Eliyahu Gottlieb and Peter Hass. Buck would hold the base with the Volkswagen and the remaining 'bogus Germans'.

They split up at 2100 hours. The Derna aerodromes were a fifteen-minute drive away, but from the start Jourdan's truck had engine-trouble. 'The lorry kept spluttering to a halt,' he recalled, 'and Brueckner would get out and spend five minutes with his head under the bonnet.'[1] The tension spiralled. After an hour, Brueckner drew up near Derna West. Hidden under the baggage at the back, Jourdan could hear music from a cinema or a wireless in the hangars. He heard Brueckner tell Hass he was going to the guardroom to ask for a spanner.

Jourdan was wound up after the stop-go journey. Suddenly, he heard the unmistakable crunch of boots on the tarmac. Whipping back the flap, he was grabbed by two Germans and yanked out of the truck. It was surrounded by a platoon of nervous-looking enemy soldiers with Schmeissers. '*Heraus! Aber schnell!*' came the chilling order. The French SAS-men shifted blankets and jerry-cans. They jumped out with their hands up. For a moment they milled around in confusion. Then the truck blew. Tongues of flame licked, shards of twisted metal spewed, black smoke billowed. The Germans hit the deck. For a second, Jourdan didn't know what was going on. Something told him that Hass, the SIG-man left in the truck, had blown himself up rather than face torture. In the same moment he jerked himself free and greased off into the night. Cpl. de Bourmont and his mate followed suit.

Jourdan sprinted like lightning. He made the shadows on the northern rim of the airfield and halted to let de Bourmont catch up. He hung on for ten minutes, gulping air, but de Bourmont and his mate never showed. It took Jourdan two hours to cover the six miles back to the meet-up point, where he found Buck leaning up against the Volkswagen, smoking a cigarette.

Buck was staggered. He had no way of knowing that the entire op had been exposed by Rommel's Rebecca Ring spies in Cairo, and supposed that Brueckner had simply sold them out. That meant the RV was compromised, and they couldn't hold out for stragglers. They poled into the Volkswagen and roared off towards the RV with Alastair Guild's patrol.

30. They crammed down Benzedrine tabs and kept stag

At about the time Jourdan was being jerked out of the truck at Derna, his boss, Georges Bergé, was tromping over lush hillsides towards Prassas airfield, near Heraklion on Crete. There were five other men with him. The going was tough. The team was weighed down with sixty-pound packs of Lewes bombs, time-pencils, detonators, plastic explosives, rations and water. Bergé had served in one of the earliest French parachute units, 601 Compagnie d'Infanterie de l'Air, and had escaped France at Dunkirk. In Britain he had been authorized to raise his own airborne company, and had conducted a number of raids into occupied France. Stirling was later to acknowledge him as one of the co-founders of the SAS.

The three other Free French SAS-men in Bergé's group were Sgt. Jacques Mouhot, a quick-witted Breton, Parachutist Jack Sibard, a former merchant seaman, and Pierre Leostic, who at only fourteen had usurped Johnny Cooper's place as the 'kid' of the SAS. His guide was 2.Lt. Costas Petrakis, Royal Hellenic Army, and his second-in-command twenty-three-year-old Lt. George, the Earl Jellicoe, Coldstream Guards. Son of the late First World War naval hero Admiral John Rushworth Jellicoe, George had returned to the Guards after the disbandment of Layforce, and had been wounded in January during Rommel's push to Gazala. The previous year, while serving with the 8 Commando detachment at Tobruk, he and a fellow officer, Lt. Carol Mather, Welsh Guards, had failed in a brave attempt to put in a two-man raid on Gazala. Jellicoe, to whom Stirling had promised the post of Detachment 2IC, hadn't completed SAS training, but Stirling had assigned him to assist Bergé because he spoke fluent French and had some knowledge of Crete.

At about 0300 hours, while Jourdan and Buck were burning rubber on the way to Guild's position, Mayne and his party skulking near Berka, and Stirling being dragged uphill by his corporals, Bergé and his party approached the barbed-wire fence round Prassas aerodrome. They were inching forward when a sudden movement betrayed them. A sentry croaked in German. There was a muzzle-flash and a round whomped past. They broke up, dropped into the brush, and lay prone, expecting a follow-up. Nothing happened. They regrouped and boxed around the airfield. Approaching from a different angle, they found their way barred by another sentry.

They squatted in the underbrush, and held a whispered conflab. The sentry could be taken out, but that would cost them the element of surprise. The raid was supposed to be synchronized with the strikes in Cyrenaica, and with two other raids on Crete being carried out by SBS *folbot* teams. A quick dekko at his watch, though, told Bergé they had only an hour of darkness left – not enough time to carry out the mission. He decided to pull out to a lying-up place and have another bash the next night.

The Heraklion op, the first SAS seaborne mission, had been planned by Bergé and Jellicoe with the help of the Royal Navy and the Free Greek Navy. The team had been shipped from Alexandria aboard the Greek submarine *Triton* on a five-day voyage. In the early hours of 11 June the SAS made landfall in three inflatable commando-boats at San Barbara creek, about twenty-five miles north of Prassas. While the rest of the team brushed the beach free of tracks, Jellicoe and Mouhot dog-paddled out to sea with the boats, weighted with stones, and scuttled them with their daggers.

An hour after landing they set off, intending to lie up near enough to eyeball their target at first light. This turned out to be a tall order. The country was steep and jagged, and they had overburdened themselves. In addition to Lewes bombs and spare explosive, each man was carrying grenades, a Colt .45 pistol, a Beretta sub-machine gun, a dagger, a compass, maps and aerial photos.

One thing Jellicoe didn't like was the way they were approached several times by Cretan hill-men, in turbans, high boots and sheepskins. The men carried ancient rifles, and some of them greeted the team in English. The SAS blew them off, but by the time the first shards of sunlight turned terracotta among massed terraces of cloud, they had made less than fifteen miles. They ducked into a cave that stank of goat. Petrakis and the parachutists grabbed some shut-eye, but Jellicoe didn't trust the Cretans, and didn't want to be caught napping. He and Bergé crammed down Benzedrine tabs and kept stag. They moved out three and a half hours after last light.

After the first aborted attempt at the airfield on the night of 12/13, they withdrew a few miles south-west of Prassas, locating a cleft in a rock-face that gave them an overview of the aerodrome. It was too exposed to use during daytime, but at last light they counted more than sixty Junkers JU88 bombers parked on the field. Bergé reckoned there were more than there had been the previous night. If they could get them all, it would be the most successful SAS 'bag' to date. It had to be a major jumping-off place for the assault on the Malta convoy. As the shadows lengthened, they checked their weapons and explosives, and prepared to move out for their second try.

31. 'We had finally emulated Paddy Mayne on our own'

Splayed in tussock-grass on Benghazi plain, Mayne and Storie thought they were in the bag. They lay there snuffling dust and grit. The Germans were quartering the ground with the command car rolling at snail's pace beside them. The enemy were a hundred yards away when they stopped and clustered round the vehicle. Suddenly, they leapt into the back. The engine roared, wheels churned gravel. The SAS-men waited until the car was out of sight, then scoped the area. All looked clear. They picked themselves up and continued their march out.

The plain was as rough and wrinkled as antique calfskin – dark veins of sedge, thorn-bush, patches of denuded limestone. It stretched to the foot of the Jebel Akhdar, the Green Mountain, a sixteen-hundred-foot massif of flaking naked scarps, transverse wadis forested by cypress, cork-oak, Aleppo pine and juniper. The foothills were furred in maquis scrub, brilliant yellow flowers, spiky goat-grass. Arab camps were dotted across the plain, melting into the background – black tents of goat's-hair circled by sheep-flocks. Soon, they came across a nest of tents pitched in the lee of the escarpment. The Senussi tribes living on the northern side of the Jebel Akhdar in Cyrenaica were not true Bedouin, but semi-nomadic cultivators and shepherds. The Senussiya was a once-powerful Islamic fundamentalist brotherhood founded in the eighteenth century, whose people had been continuously persecuted, displaced and massacred by the Italians since Libya became an Italian colony in 1912. They hated their colonial masters. Their leader, Grand Senussi Sayid Idriss, was in exile in Egypt. He had thrown in his lot with the British, and had exhorted all members of the Senussi fraternity to assist them.

Some of the Senussi were in the pay of the enemy, so seeking shelter in an Arab camp was a leap of faith. Mayne had got away with it on his March op, though, and decided it was worth the gamble. The tribesmen, in long cloaks and tight headcloths, had the granite-carved faces of sphinxes. They were taciturn until they found out their guests were *Inglezi*. Then they ushered them into a tent, where Mayne was astonished to find Bob Lilley contentedly quaffing bitter tea the colour of drain-water.

Lilley didn't know what had happened to Warburton. They had split up, and just afterwards he'd heard a burst of fire that didn't bode well for his mate. At dawn, he had found himself in a German laager about two miles in diameter. Hiding in a thicket of gorse near a house, he was almost sniffed out by an Alsatian being walked by an Italian girl. When the dog came too near, Lilley thumped it on the nose. Dumping his kit, he set off to walk across the camp, through battalions of enemy soldiers washing, shaving, lining up for breakfast, and buffing their equipment. He was dressed in khaki shorts and a shirt similar to their uniform. No one took any notice of him.

About two miles past the camp, though, he was accosted by an Italian soldier on a bike, who tried to arrest him. 'We were neither of us armed,' Lilley said, 'but he tried to make out I was his prisoner . . . so I had to strangle him. Funny, killing a chap with your bare hands . . . I can still see his white face and dark brown eyes clearly. His cap had toppled off in the struggle so I put it back over his head to make him look more natural.'[1]

About ten miles over the Benghazi plain Lilley stopped at the Senussi camp for a rest. Vehicles were still patrolling the plain looking for the SAS raiders. After a couple of hours in the tent, the Arabs told him there were two soldiers coming towards them. He had a shufti, and recognized Paddy Mayne and Jimmy Storie.[2] The three of them left the Arabs an hour before dusk, padding through esparto grass and thorn-scrub. After dark they broached the escarpment, following well-trodden goat-paths through thick maquis shrub and groves of ilex, arbutus and wild olive. They made the LRDG position next morning to find Stirling, Cooper and Seekings already there. They had arrived the previous morning.

Stirling had recovered from his migraine, thanks to copious quantities of tea laced with rum, supplied by Robin Gurdon's patrol. He listened to Mayne's tale with a wry grin on his face, and couldn't resist the opportunity to crow. 'It's a bit of a change to see my fires lighting up the skies instead of yours, Paddy,' he told Mayne.[3] '[Stirling] was extremely elated,' Cooper recalled. 'That we had finally emulated Paddy Mayne on our own.'[4]

Stirling was so elated, in fact, that he suggested Mayne should come and see 'his fires' for himself. Mayne rose to the challenge, jibing that he had to make sure Stirling 'wasn't exaggerating'.[5] They decided to borrow one of Gurdon's Chevrolets and drive down to Benghazi to 'shoot up some stuff along the road'.[6] Gurdon agreed reluctantly, but pointed out that the idea was rash. The plain was teeming with Germans on the lookout for them.

It was bravado of a kind that would be deprecated in the later SAS. In his reflective mode, Stirling himself deplored this type of action. His main criticism of the French SAS contingent, for instance, was that they were too anxious to 'prove themselves' and erred on the side of 'over-gallantry'. 'We tried to indicate to them that it was rather a disgrace to be a casualty,' he said, 'because after so much training . . . it was very important for them to survive.'[7] In this case, his success on the Benina raid – his first major triumph as a raider – had evidently switched his mind to a different track. Once again, though, the impulse grew out of his need to compete with Mayne. 'It was foolish, of course,' he commented later, 'but that's how [Paddy and I] were.'[8]

All six SAS-men piled into the Chevvy, with an SIG-man called Karl Kahane, a morose Jew who had done twenty years in the German army before emigrating to Palestine. Mayne took the wheel and they careened off the escarpment and skeetered down the steep Regima–Benghazi road with their headlights on. Stirling, in the front passenger seat, kept craning his neck to catch a glimpse of his hangars, hoping they'd still be on fire. He kept assuring Mayne that there were no roadblocks. He was wrong. 'We got about five, six miles and then we saw a red light being swung,' Mayne said. 'That didn't worry us as always before it was only Italians and we['d] shout *tedesco* [German] and drive past. But they were getting wise to us and this time we see a bloody big contraption like a five-barred gate that was mixed up with a mile or so of barbed wire.'[9]

The Italian sentry asked for the password. When Kahane began to harangue him in German, he turned out the guard – a dozen Afrika Korps men with sub-machine guns, under a sergeant major. '[The] sergeant major came up to the truck,' Storie remembered, 'and took a good look at us. Kahane spoke German and said we were on a special mission, but he knew we were British.'[10]

Both Storie and Cooper recalled that at this point, Mayne cocked his Colt .45. 'The German stiffened,' Cooper said, 'the rest of us instantly followed suit with a series of clicks. The German . . . must have realized that he would be the first to be gunned down if he tried to detain us . . . [he] gave the order for the barrier to be removed.'[11]

As it shut behind them, their flesh began to creep. Stirling was acutely aware that the guardhouse where he had lobbed a grenade two nights ago was less than a mile away. There was no way they could get back through the barrier, and now they were in a trap – the message would be passed on by wireless, and every Axis unit in the area would be on the alert for them. Mayne was about to skip off the road when Stirling spotted lights a few hundred yards on. 'It would have been stupid to drive right on to Benghazi,' he said, 'though I have to admit the temptation was there. I was determined . . . that we shouldn't leave without dropping a calling card somewhere.'[12]

Cooper remembered the place as a truck-stop and filling-station that had been occupied by the Italians. 'Some of us jumped out and began fixing bombs on to anything that was of military use,' he said. Stirling recalled only a small petrol-store, where the team 'planted a few bombs for good measure', and some trucks a little further on, where they did the same. 'I seem to remember there was a fire-fight there,' he said.[13]

Storie recalled a more elaborate scenario – a horde of Germans and Italians drinking on the veranda of a café. 'We drew up alongside the café and opened fire,' he said. 'They didn't have time to defend themselves, we just blew everything to bits.'[14] In a letter to his brother, Mayne described 'a lot of tents and trucks and people [and we] . . . started blowing the hell out of them – short, snappy and exhilarating'.[15] The official history records the damage as 'five trucks riddled with MG fire, and "many of the enemy" killed'.[16]

Afterwards, Mayne switched off the headlights and zoomed off the road towards the Wadi Qattara, directed by Stirling, who had taken a compass-bearing. There was only one place where they could cross the wadi to be sure of hitting a route up the escarpment. Mayne suddenly spotted the lights of an enemy vehicle trying to cut them off. He drove like a maniac, outrunning the enemy, plunging down through the wadi. The opposite side was so steep that the men had to jump out and push.

They crested the wadi-side, and were driving steadily along the road up the escarpment, when Bob Lilley suddenly yelled, 'Get out quick! There's a fuse burning.'[17] Cooper smelt it at once, and realized they had twenty seconds. 'I have never left a vehicle more quickly in my whole life,' he said. He vaulted over Mayne, hit the bonnet, and sprinted away. Mayne didn't try to brake. He rolled out of the driving-seat and let the Chevvy travel on, while Stirling flopped out of the other side. The rest flew in all directions off the back. The truck got a few yards before it blatted apart in a luminescent fireball. 'The explosion bowled us all over,' Cooper remembered. 'The truck was blown to kingdom come.'[18]

32. 'The target was a fat and sitting bird'

The previous night, while Mayne, Storie and Lilley were ramping up the Green Mountains, Georges Bergé, George Jellicoe and the three French enlisted men had cut the wire at Prassas. It was a close-run thing – a German patrol actually stalked up on them while they were doing it. They feigned sleep. 'The patrol had a torch,' Jellicoe said, 'and stopped within one foot of my head. A happy snore from one of the Free French satisfied them that we were a party of German drunks!'[1]

After the soldiers had slunk off, they went on cutting. Moments later, though, they heard the patrol coming back. Just then, aircraft zoned over them – two Blenheim bombers fishtailing over the landing-ground, dumping bombs. The bombs whistled down and crunched into buildings wide of the parked planes. They split apart in carnelian sears. Flames licked up. Germans scuttled with fire-extinguishers. Bergé's team used the confusion to slide inside the wire.

The fires lit up their targets, grasshopper-shadows glinting metal. They lay low for an hour to let the furore die down, then shimmied along the lines of planes, easing bombs into place. They counted nineteen Junkers JU88 bombers, two fighters, and a Fieseler Storch spotter. Jellicoe whamped charges on crated aircraft-parts and trucks. He jerked out safety-pins. They had taken care of less than half the planes when the first bomb ripped off in a spurt of black and methyl orange. Wing-parts and glass whiplashed. The aircraft undercarriage buckled and the plane pitched. Dark figures swarmed across the landing-ground.

Bergé and Jellicoe watched the crackling debris, stunned. They had set the time-pencils to two-hour delays, but the Blenheim sortie had cost them over an hour. This was the snag in pressing the time-pencils before sticking the bombs. There was no chance of completing the task. Bergé clocked a troop of soldiers being marched smartly out of the western gate. He and his men fell into step behind them and tramped out unnoticed. They peeled off into the bushes just as the rest of the charges shuddered massively, igniting the bomb dumps – a cauldron of burning gases bubbled, wheezing across the area with battering concussion. Beaming all over his blackened face, Bergé said he was recommending the whole team for the Croix de Guerre. Jellicoe offered his congratulations, but remained convinced that if the RAF raid hadn't intervened they could have bagged the lot. 'The target was a fat and sitting bird,' he commented in his report. 'I feel that the results achieved were not commensurate with the opportunity presented.'²

They backtracked to their cliff, where they picked up Petrakis. The area around Heraklion was relatively open, and their aim was to get out as quickly as possible, and to hike across the spine of the island to the sparsely populated south coast, where the sea could be approached only by a series of coves. Their destination was an inlet near Krotos. Here, they would meet with SBS parties who had raided airfields at Kastelli and Timbaki. All three groups would be extracted by *Porcupine*, a caique piloted by Lt. Cmdr. John Campbell, RNVR.

They spent the next three days trekking across granite hills, through gorges and down tree-strewn valleys, fed and guided by locals. 'Contact with the local population was hard to avoid,' Jellicoe reported, 'and in the end led to betrayal and disaster.'³ On the way, Petrakis went off on a foray and brought back chilling news. As a reprisal for the attack on Prassas, the Germans had shot fifty Cretans at Gazi, just to the west of Heraklion. The number included Tito Georgiadis, a former governor-general, a seventy-year-old priest and a handful of Jewish prisoners. Petrakis said the executions had caused a wave of bad feeling against the British.

On 19 June they found a hide in a narrow gorge under the mountain wall, within two hours of the coast. There they were visited by a villager who offered to bring them food and wine. Bergé was suspicious, and asked Petrakis, who came originally from the local village, if the man could be trusted. Petrakis said he'd been away too long, and couldn't tell. The Cretan disappeared. Bergé sent Jellicoe and Petrakis, disguised as peasants, to the coast. Their task was to make contact with Cretan agents who would be guiding the trawler in.

At last light, Bergé's crew stashed gear into packs and clipped on belts, ready to move. Bergé glanced up and saw three patrols of German soldiers in field-grey greatcoats and angular helmets converging on their hiding-place. He guessed they'd been betrayed. Lifting his Beretta sub-machine gun, he whacked off a burst at the first German, who buckled, with crimson rosettes sprouting from his chest. The enemy broke ranks and dashed for the scrub. The French threw themselves into cover and punched out a volley of gunfire that whanged off the rocks around the enemy and spliffled among the bushes. Fourteen-year-old Pierre Leostic made a break for it, and was swept off his feet by a lick of automatic fire. Bergé couldn't see him, but could hear him moaning. There was another throb of fire, and Leostic suddenly went quiet. The Frenchmen kept shooting until their ammunition was almost finished. After dark they made a final attempt to break out. All of them were wounded and captured.

As the darkness liquefied into rose and blue next morning, Jellicoe turned up at the position. There was no one there. He saw his comrades' kit laid out neatly – too neatly, he thought. When it was fully light, he searched the nearby valleys and ran into two young Cretans in sheepskins, who gesticulated at him in excitement. Jellicoe spoke no Greek, but he got the message. He had to leave – now. He jogged back to the beach, where he hid out with Petrakis and the SBS teams until they were picked up by *Porcupine* on 23 June. Being rowed out to the boat, Jellicoe passed an SOE agent and his radio-op being rowed in. The agent was Patrick Leigh Fermor, a fluent Greek-speaker, who was after the war to become one of Britain's most distinguished travel-writers.

33. 'I suppose you've had a good time then'

Stirling and Mayne made it back to the LRDG base at Siwa on 21 June. The most famous oasis in the Egyptian desert, it lay in a depression of sparkling white salt-flats under the dunes of the Great Sand Sea, encompassing a forest of date-palms and hundreds of sweet-water springs. At LRDG headquarters in the dilapidated hotel, Stirling learned the bitter news of the fall of 'Fortress Tobruk'. Its garrison, the twenty-thousand-strong 2 South African Division, had surrendered to Rommel after a week's siege. Ritchie had pulled the Eighth Army back to Alam Halfa, near Alamein, only sixty miles from Cairo. For Winston Churchill, the war had reached its nadir: 'Defeat is one thing,' he said. 'Disgrace another.'[1]

After their Chevvy had blown up, Stirling's group had tabbed to a Senussi camp, where they were fed by the Arabs until Gurdon found them four days later. When he heard the fate of his truck, he chortled. 'I suppose you've had a good time then,' he said.[2] Lt. Jaquier's section had arrived in Siwa four days earlier. They had lucked out at Barce. The Germans seemed to know they were coming. They had crept to within a few hundred yards of the landing-ground when all its landing-lights suddenly flashed on, dazzling them. They melted into the darkness, blowing a petrol dump as they went. André Zirnheld's section had come in with Mayne and Stirling. They had had better luck on Berka Main landing-ground. Mayne and his section had heard shooting from that direction, but turned out that the French had got the better of the fight – they claimed at least fifteen enemy kills. To Mayne's fury, they had also managed to take out eleven aircraft to his one.

Guild's patrol lurched in a few hours after Stirling's, carrying Jourdan and Buck. Jourdan was in tears. 'I felt very depressed coming back alone,' he said, 'but I was so grateful to Stirling . . . he never doubted my capabilities . . . he gave me the opportunity to create a second French unit.'[3] It turned out later that Jourdan's Mertuba group under Jean Tourneret had all been bagged. Joined by de Bourmont and his mate, they had made the RV near

Mertuba, but next morning found themselves encircled by Germans. There was a ferocious shoot-out. Almost all of them took hits, and some were wounded seriously. According to the official history, Tourneret's group blew no fewer than twenty aircraft before they went down.

Stirling considered the raids a success, but it was difficult to say how many of the planes they had taken out were directly relevant to the Malta convoys. Even the total number of aircraft the SAS and SBS put out of action remains uncertain. Official figures make it around seventy. At different times, Stirling himself made it as few as thirty-seven and as many as seventy-five. The strategic purpose failed. Of the total of seventeen ships that set out for Malta that June, only two got through. All the others were sunk or turned back.

Protecting these convoys from attack was beyond the capacity of the SAS. Many of the ships were crippled by torpedoes from German U-Boats. Others were sunk by aircraft based on Sicily or the Italian mainland, far out of Stirling's reach. The good news was that the two ships that did get through brought enough supplies to keep Malta going for the next two months, until a larger convoy succeeded in reaching port. Stirling maintained that the seventy planes the combined SAS/SBS teams knocked out tipped the balance. 'A lot of the convoy were destroyed,' he said, 'but some got through. [Without our action] there was no way they would have got through. Therefore we regard what we did on [those raids] as saving Malta.'[4]

34. 'Our job was to constantly invent new techniques'

At the end of June Benito Mussolini landed his private plane at Derna, with a transport aircraft carrying a thoroughbred white charger ready for his triumphal entry into Cairo. At No.10 Tonbalat Street 'The Flap' was in progress. RAF bomber squadrons were being evacuated to Palestine, and the Royal Navy's Mediterranean Fleet was weighing anchor at Alexandria. On Wednesday 1 July the acrid fumes of burning paper permeated GHQ ME as secret documents were incinerated – the day would be remembered in military folklore as 'Ash Wednesday'. Neil Ritchie, the 'awfully nice chap' who had assisted the foundation of the SAS, had been bowler-hatted by Auchinleck a week earlier. Like Cunningham, whom he had replaced eight months before, Ritchie had begun to think defensively. 'The Auk' had now assumed direct command of the Eighth Army. G(R) was organizing 'stay behind' parties. Guy Prendergast had moved the LRDG to Kufra on the Sudanese border. Stirling was considering withdrawing as far south as Nairobi.

But not yet. On 3 July almost the entire strength of the SAS – a hundred men – was drawn up in jeeps and trucks on the leafy streets of Garden City. French and British SAS-men, with wings up, were brewing tea on the pavement under the eyes of disapproving Redcaps.

At Peter Stirling's flat near the British Embassy a council of war was in progress. Mayne and Fraser were there, with Cooper and Seekings, Jellicoe, Alston, Jourdan, Zirnheld, Jaquier and a group of recently recruited officers, some of whom had laughed in Stirling's face when he had invited them to join L Detachment a year earlier. One of these was Lt. Carol Mather, Welsh Guards. 'I had to admit that I'd been wrong,' he confessed, 'in effect, I had to eat humble pie in asking to rejoin [Stirling].'[1] With Mather were two friends, twenty-year-old Stephen Hastings, Scots Guards, and Sandy Scratchley, 3 County of London Yeomanry, an Old Harrovian built like a rake-handle, who had been a jockey in civvy-street.

The flat was a riot of chatter, hazy with tobacco smoke. The briefing was late, because Peter Stirling's zealous house-keeper, 'Mo', had hidden the top-secret maps in the bathroom during a tidying-up session, and it had taken some time to retrieve them. Now, while Stirling jabbed 'Mo' reproachfully in the midriff with his pipe, a group of SAS-men poured over the maps, and George

Jellicoe briefed the party on the route they would be taking behind enemy lines. In another corner sat a bevy of demure and rather pretty young ladies, among them Countess Hermione Ranfurly, sipping cocktails as a prelude to visiting the racetrack. 'The *va et viens* between the two groups,' recalled Stephen Hastings, 'added much spice to the proceedings.'[2]

In the few days since Stirling and Mayne had returned from the Malta Convoy ops, there had been a crucial change in SAS capacity. Mayne had suggested to Stirling that he should put in a claim for a consignment of M38 Utility Trucks – Willys Bantam General Purpose vehicles, known as 'GPs' or 'jeeps' – that had just been sent by the US government. Mayne, who had been known to trek as far as fifty miles on his way in and out of targets, and had lost two good men in the process, thought the jeeps would cut down the walking time. The vehicles were tiny in comparison with the LRDG Fords and Chevrolets. They were designed to carry only two men and their equipment, but they had four-wheel drive, which would make them more handy for climbing up and down escarpments.

Stirling managed to 'borrow' fifteen Willys on the wildly optimistic promise that they would be returned intact. He also managed to acquire twenty brand new Ford three-ton trucks. The jeeps and trucks didn't by themselves mean an end to the partnership with the LRDG. Though the SAS had driver-mechanics and navigators of their own, they still relied on Prendergast's boys to guide them in and provide wireless communications. The jeeps had been fitted with sun-compasses, auxiliary fuel-tanks, and coolant-condensers to prevent the engines from overheating – all Ralph Bagnold/ LRDG inventions.

From the RAF, Stirling had picked up a dozen Vickers Type K gas-operated machine guns, stockpiled as spares for the now decommissioned Bombays and Wellesley bombers. The guns had been introduced in 1935, but were already obsolete as aircraft armaments due to the introduction of the powered gun-turret. Ever since Johnny Cooper had used a Type K to break out of the Italian ambush at Bouerat, the SAS had been impressed with the weapon. At a thousand rounds a minute it was the fastest-firing machine gun in the theatre, and for the SAS the ear-splitting racket it made was a psychological advantage. The gun was fed by hundred-round top-mounted pan mags that were cleaner to use than belts, and the ejected cases were snagged in gunnysacks to prevent them blinding the shooter. Its only disadvantage was its tendency to jam in hot weather. Stirling had several of the jeeps fitted with special pintle mountings to hold Vickers in pairs and singles. He set up three on the 'Blitz Buggy'.

Rommel was sixty miles from Alexandria. His advance was blocked by the Eighth Army at Alamein, a position Auchinleck had chosen carefully. It was a thirty-five-mile bottleneck, defended to the north by the sea and to the south by the Qattara Depression, a vast hole in the desert that had itself been an inland sea in prehistoric times, but was now a treacherous area of *mish-mish* sand and saltmarsh. The Auk had come up fighting. The last great battle of his career would be fought, as his biographer put it, 'in some stony pass beneath a torrid unsparing sun, that knows no romance and no illusion'.[3]

Auchinleck intended to hit back on 7 July, to prevent Rommel from boxing him in. The SAS, Stirling told his boys, would strike at five or six landing-grounds on the same night. They would set up a forward operating base at Qarat Tartura, on the very edge of the depression. Their new three-tonners would carry supplies for three weeks. They would stay in the field and bash Rommel's airfields and supply-lines night after night until something gave way.

The convoy roared off that afternoon, cutting through the teeming Bulak quarter and over the bridges of the Gezira. Brought to a halt in the narrow streets, the jeeps were hemmed in by a river of humanity – men in pyjama-cloth tatters, women and urchins, laden camels, trains of donkeys lugging panniers of sand, donkey-carts piled with loaves. Half-starved phantoms leered down on them from galleries of lurching balconies festooned with threadbare rags. The wave of voices, honking horns, braying donkeys, coughing camels and barking dogs was overwhelming.

Everywhere there were cries of '*Backsheesh!*' 'To my . . . ear the constant babble of Arabic had a quality of sustained hysteria,' wrote Stephen Hastings. '. . . What was it to them who marched across their land, made war, lived or died.'[4]

The city gave way to cultivated land. They drove through a straggle of villages, but soon the smells of dung and rotting vegetation passed behind them, giving way to the chalk and flint scent of the desert. The track ran out.

Next day, escorted by a detachment of Military Police, the SAS convoy slipped through Eighth Army lines and hit the Palm Leaf Road – an ancient caravan track running along the north edge of the Qattara Depression. The country on their right flank was a wasteland of rock, lone fangs, sawtooth ridges. To their left, the walls of the great hollow dropped sheer to its floor, a thousand feet below. They linked up with LRDG forward patrols under Captain Robin Gurdon and Lt. Alastair Timpson, Scots Guards, who guided them to Qara, a hamlet on the edge of the depression where a vast block of sandstone protruded out of the desert.

Six SAS parties were tagged to raid airfields at Sidi Barrani, ad-Dhaba, and at two sites sacred to SAS tradition, Baggush and Fuka – now behind Rommel's lines. Mayne and Stirling decided to take on Baggush themselves. Johnny Cooper would be going along without his alter ego, Seekings, whom Stirling had sent to a REME – Royal Electrical & Mechanical Engineers – field workshop to get advice on strengthening the jeeps' springs. As they set off in the Blitz Buggy, a jeep and a three-tonner, Cooper realized that this was the first time Stirling and Mayne had ever carried out a raid together.

It was an eight-hour drive in broad daylight. In the late afternoon, they passed through the remnants of Auchinleck's offensive – burned-out tanks, smoking hulks of trucks and armoured cars. After dark, they left the escort on the Fuka escarpment and descended to the main road. A mile from Baggush they split into two groups. Mayne's six-strong section would trek into the airfield with ten Lewes bombs apiece, while Stirling and two men would set up a roadblock. Intelligence had reported heavy enemy traffic on the Baggush–Fuka road, but they encountered nothing. Stirling guessed that the enemy had been scared off by a British light-artillery column they had sighted earlier, and which had put down two hundred shells on Fuka. He was furious that he hadn't been informed about it by Eighth Army.

Mayne's group sloped off into the shadows, lugging bombs. Stirling and his two men set up shop by the road and waited. The deadline ticked by and there were no whizzbangs from Mayne. They were still clock-watching at 0135 hours, when the sky flared. Cooper heard a kettledrum boom like a peal of dry thunder. 'There they go,' he grinned. More rumbles followed. Stirling counted them off. By the time he had counted twenty-two, the whole skyline was a shimmering aurora borealis of orange and red. Over an hour later Mayne's bulk eased out of the shadows. To Stirling's surprise, he let fly a string of curses. 'The bloody bombs wouldn't work,' he declared. They had counted forty aircraft on the landing-ground, but it had taken them some time to get in because the planes were parked in clusters and were heavily guarded. The really bad news was that half the Lewes bombs hadn't detonated. Mayne found out later that the primers had been put in too early, and had got damp from the lubricant. 'It's enough to break your heart,' he said.

There was a moment's hiatus. Stirling was thinking about the Vickers Ks that were mounted on the jeep and Blitz Buggy, and the fact that they had been designed as aircraft guns. Lewes had drummed the idea of 'strategic damage' into them – it was no good blowing a plane if its parts could be 'cannibalized' – used to refit other damaged aircraft. The machines had to be totalled. Stirling thought that if they could engage the planes at close quarters, the Vickers could rip them to shreds. He decided that they would drive back into the aerodrome and open up with their machine guns.

Stirling was gambling that the airfield garrison would not be expecting to get banjoed again immediately. He was right. They drove the Blitz Buggy and the jeep slowly into the Baggush landing-ground, ten yards apart. No one fired at them. The enemy gunners were constrained by the risk of shooting up their own aircraft. 'Shoot low. Go for the petrol tanks,' was Stirling's only order.

Five Vickers Ks swivelled and rumbled in a terrifying surge of noise. A plane went up, heaving into strangled bits of metal, spewing fire and gasoline fumes. The heat singed the gunners' beards and eyebrows. Stirling and Mayne tooled the accelerators gingerly at fifteen miles an hour as the machine guns ratcheted out armour-piercing incendiaries and tracer. Plane after plane exploded around them until they were moving through a great dark boulevard between walls of dazzling flame. Cooper, manning the forward Vickers on the Blitz Buggy, pumped his way through two hundred-round drums, and was into a third when the weapon jammed.

It took no more than five minutes. Only as they floored gas and sped back into the darkness did the enemy ack-ack guns finally go to work on them. Stirling heard a couple of 20mm shells creasing past him as he drove.

The first joint raid by Stirling and Mayne had been an astounding success. The SAS team had destroyed thirty-seven aircraft, equalling Fraser's record 'bag' at Ajadabiyya in December '41. Stirling knew he had found a new modus operandi for the SAS.

They still had to get away, though. Just after first light, Cooper, in the Blitz Buggy's driving-seat, spotted a pair of CR-42 biplanes hanging low like gnats on the china blue skyline. It was evident they hadn't bagged the entire contingent. Cooper guessed from their line of approach that the planes were homing in on their tracks or had spotted dust trails. Minutes later, he, Stirling and Mayne made an undignified exit from the Blitz Buggy, just before it erupted into flames. Lewes had always stressed the importance of taking out all the aircraft to prevent pursuit. Mayne's attitude was that a raid was like a booze-up – you always paid for it the day after.

At base they learned that the raiding party sent to Sidi Barrani had found nothing, and the al-Dhaba attack had been called off because Intelligence Branch had reported that it was disused. Jellicoe, who had set up a roadblock instead, had taken two German prisoners who told him that this intelligence was mistaken: al-Dhaba was the busiest Axis landing-ground in the area. Stirling was incensed at the lost opportunity. He sent off Jellicoe and a French officer, Aspirant François Martin, with Robin Gurdon's LRDG patrol, to take it out.

Against the advice of the SAS veterans riding with them, Jellicoe, Hastings and Mather pushed on in the face of enemy spotters. The party was strafed and bombed and lost all its vehicles but one. They limped back, nine men clinging on to a single jeep whose radiator they had patched with bits of plastic explosive and kept filled with their own urine. There was more bad news to come: Gurdon had been killed in an air-attack, and Martin had aborted the mission.

Mayne, Fraser and Jourdan hit Fuka on 11 July and another bull's-eye strike by Mayne took out twenty aircraft with Lewes bombs.

On his visit to GHQ in Cairo two days later, Stirling presented a paper to the Director of Military Operations entitled 'New Tactics'. It laid out ideas for massed attacks on airfields by SAS armed jeeps. The current Axis method of defence, he wrote, made it much harder for sabotage teams to destroy planes. A massed onslaught by armed vehicles would wreck the new cluster parking tactics. It would goad the enemy into reinstating perimeter defence, and thus make them more vulnerable to sabotage attacks. In future, he reckoned, the enemy would never know which approach the raiders would use. 'The alternative employment of two methods of attack,' he went on, '. . . either by a small party on foot reaching its objective without being observed, or by a massed attack in vehicles – should leave the enemy hesitating between two methods of defence.'[5]

Stirling's genius as a special-forces commander lay in the elasticity of his intellect: he saw his campaign as an elegant mental dance with the enemy. The Axis response to the first attacks had been to place sentries under each plane: when this hadn't worked, they had put up barbed-wire fences, brought in heavier guards, searchlights, armoured cars. It was staying ahead of these subtle shifts that exercised him. However, the truth in this case is probably that the idea of the massed machine-gun attack came to him in a flash, as an immediate solution to the problem, rather than as a reasoned response to enemy tactics. The 'New Tactics' paper was a prime example of Stirling's rhetoric, and didn't hold up to close analysis. Rather than being torn between two methods of defence, the enemy's logical response would be a belt-and-braces method that would make both SAS modes of attack more difficult.

Stirling was right, though, in varying his approaches. The SAS were not shock troops. It was axiomatic with Stirling that they should never be used as 'cannon fodder'. The Clausewitz style of war – the clash of big battalions battering each other into oblivion with blind bayonet-charges against machine guns and heavy artillery – was exactly the opposite of what he was trying to achieve. When one of the early SAS-men was quizzed about the dangers of parachuting, he rightly answered that it wasn't nearly so dangerous as a bayonet-charge. Twenty thousand casualties in an hour on the first day of the Somme in 1916 were mute testimony to this fact. SAS style was hit-and-run attacks on enemy resources: planes, trucks, railways, supply dumps, communications centres. Surprise was the keynote, and surprise couldn't be maintained by obstinate adherence to the same approach.

In the SAS skills golf bag, demolitions was only a single club. Potentially there were dozens of others. That GHQ classed the SAS as saboteurs made Stirling's blood boil. In their passion for categorization, the staff refused to see that what he had created was a powerful and cost-effective new weapon – a unit of carefully selected and multi-skilled individuals that could gain 'maximum achievement for minimum cost' and could adapt itself to almost any situation. 'I still hadn't succeeded in getting those morons to understand that this was a new form of warfare we were developing,' Stirling said. '... . I don't believe that even Auchinleck ... had wholly grasped the awesome potential of the SAS ...'[6] 'Clearly,' said Johnny Cooper, 'our job was to constantly invent new techniques so that the enemy could never predict our operational methods.'[7]

When Stirling, Mayne and Jellicoe returned to the new forward operating base at Bir al-Quseir, they found the twenty-man party they had left behind cooling their heels in caves, plagued by a million flies. They were on starvation-rations, and down to half a mug of tea per meal. Jellicoe had brought sweets, cigars, pipes, tins of tobacco, last year's glossy magazines, and eau-de-cologne to make up for the lack of washing water. Stirling had brought an armada of new jeeps, fitted with two pairs of Vickers Ks apiece. The following day, Stirling received a message from Major Peter Oldfield of the newly-formed Photo Reconnaissance Wing, pin-pointing the airfield at Sidi Haneish, thirty miles east-south-east of Mersa Matruh, as a forward operating base for enemy Stuka dive-bombers. Stirling decided to hit the aerodrome with a dozen jeeps and a patrol of the LRDG.

He held a dress rehearsal in the desert with twenty jeeps, experimenting with two formations: line abreast to cross the perimeter, and double column to go through the airstrip, the jeeps spaced ten yards apart. The idea was to let rip with a devastating salvo of fire without straying into each other's sights. They practised wheeling right and left, rattling off hundreds of rounds of live ammunition. 'The rehearsal was even more terrifying than the actual attack,' Johnny Cooper said.[8]

The night was bright, with a wedge of moon and wisps of cloud. Stirling had deliberately decided to carry out the raid in moonlight, a thing the SAS had never done before. 'The first attack, at least,' he had written in his paper, 'would have the advantage of surprise.'[9] Mike Sadler, now permanently attached to the SAS, was navigating. The target lay only forty miles away, and Stirling wanted to hit it at 0130 hours sharp, to give them enough darkness to escape.

Descending the escarpment, they passed a chilling reminder of the struggle going on around them – fire-warped tanks encircled by mutilated corpses, huddled in bunches or spread-eagled across the serir, eye-sockets staring sightlessly at the moon.

The LRDG, under Captain Nick Wilder, split off from the SAS patrol, heading north, while the SAS drove east. Shortly,

Wilder's trucks hit a minefield, and one of the Chevrolets was knocked out. Stirling's group had six punctures and was obliged to make detours for boulder-strewn hammadas. Each delay meant halting the entire column. Time dribbled away, tension rose. After three and a half hours, Stirling stopped and marched over to Sadler, his unlit pipe stuck upside down in his mouth. 'Where *is* this bloody airfield then?' he demanded.

'I think it should be about a mile ahead,' Sadler said.

At that moment the desert lit up like a Christmas tree, as the landing-lights of Sidi Haneish went on, no more than a mile away. Stirling jumped. 'I thought we'd been spotted or betrayed again,' he said, 'but it was an aircraft coming in to land. It was perfect for us . . . I hit the accelerator and charged straight for the aircraft.'[10]

About two hundred yards from the perimeter, the jeeps formed into line abreast and stopped. There was a moment's pause. The drivers' hands locked on their steering-wheels, feet tickled accelerators. The gunners froze in firing positions, hearts pounding, eyes peeled. Fingers took pressure on triggers. '*Fire!*' Stirling bellowed. Forty-eight Vickers Ks snarled out in deep-throated unison, in blinding spear-thrusts of blood-red fire at twenty-five thousand rounds a minute. Rounds skimmed the surface, slicing through the defences. The aircraft that had just landed, a Heinkel III, was cut to shreds. Tracer, incendiary and armour-piercing shells stitched a tracery of slashes across its fuselage, and demolished its undercarriage. There was a spatter of return fire from enemy sangars. A broadside silenced it. Axis guards ducked for cover. Dark figures jogged forward to clip the fence with wirecutters, peeling back an entrance.

Engines growled. Bantams wheeled forward, manoeuvring into double column. Vickers Ks rotated right and left as the vehicles passed through the breach. Jim Almonds's jeep, second in the left-hand column, crumped into a tank trap with a bang. Almonds and his two gunners reeled out and hit the deck. Before the landing-lights cut, Stirling clocked the insect forms of the aircraft on the apron – Messerschmitts, Junkers, Stukas and Heinkels.

Guns shuddered, jeeps shook, drumfire tippled in streams of

tracer across the airfield. Stirling egged Cooper and Seekings on as they fired. 'He drove right up the middle of the runway at around twenty mph,' Cooper said, 'and either side of us was an assortment of planes . . . It was like a duck-shoot, just pouring fire into those Junkers and Stukas and watching the bullets tear through the fuselage, and then *bang* – they'd explode.'[11] 'One after another the planes burst into flames,' recalled Carol Mather, in the last jeep. 'Some of the aircraft would only be fifteen yards away, and as I passed them at the end of the column they would glow red and explode with a deafening *phut* and there would be great heat.'[12]

The night was hazy with gas and toxic vapour. Scrap metal flew, shards of glass blew across the sky. Guns jittered, drums emptied, empty cases gunnysacked. Gunners ate smoke and fumes, faces singed by heat, eyes smarting, vision obscured by the nebula of burning gases. They kept on blazing.

Planes crumpled and crashed as their undercarriages were blasted. Fuel and bomb dumps went up, fires crackled, exploding gases roared. Italians and Germans sucked hot gas, coughed, spluttered, puked, reeled in confusion. Mayne saw a pilot lying with his arms over his head, under the wheels of a blazing Heinkel, too terrified to move. The bomber went up a moment after he passed. Gunners blatted rounds into huts and tents. 'There was quite a bit of return fire from the guards,' Cooper recalled, 'but it wasn't very accurate. The burning planes and all the smoke obscured [their] view.'[13]

A green flare bathed the whole conflagration in a ghostly, quasi-electrical light. Stirling had forgotten to fire it to signal the attack, but now it signalled a wheel to the left. The jeeps turned, the gunners kept firing. A single Breda 20mm ack-ack gun had kept up a steady fire on them from the moment they breached the perimeter. Mather didn't notice it until they wheeled. '[We] were swinging round for another visit,' he said, when an ack-ack gun some three hundred yards away opened up on us wildly. Our port side gunners returned fire.'[14]

Hastings, crouching at the wheel of his jeep, heard the ponka-ponka-ponka of the Breda and saw spears of crimson tracer gouging grooves out of the night. He spotted two Germans lying prone, heads and shoulders raised. 'There's two Jerries,' his rear-gunner gasped.

'Well, shoot at them,' Hastings barked. 'Go on, shoot at them.'[15]

Vickers rounds plonked, but the gunner couldn't tell if he'd hit the enemy. Scarlet gashes fleched towards them, knob-sized Breda shells thunked the bonnet. 'I felt something hot pass most uncomfortably close beneath my seat,' Hastings recalled. 'Clang! My face and my gunner's were doused in oil. There was a moment of blindness. I wiped the oil out of my eyes, the jeep swerved violently, hit a bump, recovered itself and miraculously continued.'[16]

In the centre, ex-jockey Sandy Scratchley's gunner, twenty-one-year-old Bombardier John Robson, Royal Artillery, a recent recruit, was struck by a 20mm Breda round that sliced off half his head. He slumped across Scratchley and his forward-gunner. Stirling ordered a halt. The jeeps drew up alongside him. He called for a casualty and ammunition report. Apart from Robson, there were a few grazes and light wounds. Some gunners were out of ammunition, some of the guns had jammed. Almonds and his crew jogged up to report that their jeep had got snagged. 'Oh, bad luck,' Stirling commented. He sent them to join Sadler, whose navigation truck was on standby at the south-east corner of the airfield. 'We'll have one more go over this side of the dispersal area,' he said, '. . . don't fire unless you're certain of getting a target and watch out for those bloody Bredas.'[17]

Mayne stood there fidgeting. Seconds earlier, he had leapt out of his jeep, done a try-scoring dash across the piste to an unharmed Heinkel III, and stuck a Lewes bomb on the wing. It wasn't just for old time's sake. He liked to keep track of his 'bag', which was getting close to the century. Now Stirling had halted the jeeps smack in the blast area, and he had set a short fuse. 'Start up! Start up!' he broke out suddenly. They made it out only an instant before the aircraft blew.

The airfield was brilliant with raging planes and bomb-dumps. On this arm was a row of Rommel's precious JU 52s that hadn't been touched. The ruckle of Vickers started again. 'The noise was appalling,' one of the boys told Malcolm Pleydell later. 'The roar of the aircraft blowing up drowned the din of the machine guns.'[18]

Stirling was concerned about the withdrawal. The attack had gone in late, and first light would be up in only two and a half hours. They wouldn't make it back to base in darkness. It was time to bug out. He looped the wheel and was heading back to the hole in the fence when the jeep spun forty-five degrees and juddered to a halt. Seekings jumped out to investigate and found that a 20mm shell had clunked right through the cylinder head.

At that moment, Scratchley's jeep yammered up beside them, with the dead Robson still lying in the back. Seekings slapped a Lewes bomb on Stirling's jeep. Cooper shifted Robson's corpse and braced Scratchley's rear Vickers. Stirling squeezed into the front by the forward-gunner. The columns were already well ahead. Seekings pressed the time-pencil and vaulted into the jeep by Cooper. 'We roared off the airfield in pursuit,' Cooper recalled. 'The scene of devastation was fantastic. Aircraft exploded all around us and as we left the perimeter our own jeep went up in a ball of flame.'[19] Once out of the airfield they broke up into prearranged groups and made for Bir al-Quseir by different routes.

The attack had taken fifteen minutes and had accounted for thirty-seven aircraft. Some hadn't exploded or caught fire, but even those would need serious repair-work before they could fly again. For Stirling, this raid was the apex of his active career as SAS commander. He would never reach such dizzy heights again. It was also the last successful action carried out by L Detachment. Back in Cairo, wheels were already in motion that would change things for ever.

35. 'Mort au Champ d'Honneur'

At 1600 hours next afternoon, medical officer Malcolm Pleydell, in his cave at Bir al-Quseir, was alerted by a shrill whistle from the sentry. He looked out and saw Paddy Mayne being driven along the edge of the escarpment in a battered jeep, with another follow-ing behind. 'He looked as massive and unconcerned as ever,' Pleydell recalled, 'hunched up and dwarfing both driver and vehicle.'[1] Later Pleydell ran over to Mayne's camp and found him lying full-length by his jeep. He was reading a Penguin paperback, and lazily swiping at flies with a fly-swat. His hands were swollen with desert sores, and the bandages seeped fluid. When Pleydell asked him about the raid, he answered, 'Och, it was quite good crack,' and changed the subject, asking the doctor to dress his hands. Pleydell had just finished treating him when the whistle went off again. He heard the growl of aero-engines, and peeped out from under the tarpaulin covering the cave entrance to see six Stukas reaming over the base at a thousand feet. A brace of Me 109-F fighters was circling around them. 'They looked dark, aggressive, and full of forboding,' Pleydell said.

The SAS sections had withdrawn from Sidi Haneish under a thick blanket of mist. It appeared at first light, lasted an hour, and cut visibility to a few yards. When the mist melted back, Aspirant André Zirnheld, a former philosophy professor, and his mate, Aspirant François Martin, found that they were on the main Qara–Matruh track – an area Stirling had warned them to avoid. Within minutes they heard the scream of Stukas. The sound inflated rapidly into a mesmeric shriek that seemed to petrify the whole landscape. Zirnheld led the two vehicles into the shadow of a cliff, but the Stuka pilots had spotted the dust trail, and the planes yawed in with their sirens blaring and their cannons stuttering. Zirnheld's jeep was hit by a squirt of cannon-fire that spun him out of his seat and slashed open the ligaments of his shoulder. Streaming blood, he tried to run for cover. Another round whacked him in the stomach.

Martin managed to pull him to shelter, but Zirnheld was hanging on to life by a thread. The Stukas made nine attacks before they sheared off into the cobalt sky. Martin and his men loaded Zirnheld into a jeep and continued, but the gut-wound was agony. They halted in a shallow wadi, and Martin went off alone to Bir al-Quseir to bring back Pleydell. By the time the medic arrived, Zirnheld was dead. They buried him at last light, under a crude wooden cross inscribed 'Mort au Champ d'Honneur'. Going through his kit, they came across a crumpled piece of paper, on which he had scrawled his epitaph: 'A Para's Prayer'.

> I do not ask for wealth
> Nor for success . . .
> I want insecurity and disquietude,
> I want turmoil and brawl . . .

Zirnheld had found all he had asked for.

Later that day, Captain Nick Wilder's LRDG patrol reached the forward base, carrying a couple of German prisoners. One of them, a sergeant, was among Rommel's personal flyers. The other, a doctor named Baron Von Lutteroti, belonged to a family Jellicoe had met before the war. Stirling had instructed Wilder's men to give covering fire during the Sidi Haneish attack, but they had been delayed by the minefield, and had laagered up on the north side of the aerodrome to cover the withdrawal.

On the way back, Wilder had fought several skirmishes with German armoured-vehicles. One of his Chevrolets, manned by New Zealand Troopers Keith Tippett and T. B. 'Dobby' Dobson, happened on a Fieseler Storch spotter-plane taking off. They stopped it with a Tommy-gun burst, and picked up the two prisoners before dousing the aircraft with petrol and torching it. Both were recommended for the MM.

Mike Sadler's vehicles came in after dark, with Jim Almonds riding passenger. Almonds's jeep was still stuck in a tank trap at Sidi Haneish. Sadler had stayed near the aerodrome for two hours after the attack to provide a rallying point for anyone who got lost or had mechanical problems. At first light he had taken photographs of the landing-ground to confirm the damage. What amazed Sadler was the way the Germans had got the place working again, putting out fires, dragging hulks away with tractors, so that more planes could land.

On the way back to base, Sadler's group had cleared the mist to find themselves in the middle of a German motorized infantry patrol that seemed to be searching for them. One Afrika Korps soldier had looked straight at them, but evidently hadn't noticed anything wrong. Sadler streaked off into the desert and hid the jeeps between two ridges. Moments later they were buzzed by Stukas that swooped low but turned away, probably mistaking them for part of a German recovery team at work nearby.

Stirling came in on the night of 28 July. With him were Jellicoe, Hastings and six other SAS-men hanging on to a single jeep that was bumping along on four naked wheel-hubs. Jellicoe's own vehicle had given out just before reaching the forward base.

In the morning, Stirling was passed the latest intel by the wireless operator. Axis forces were reported to be scouring the desert like enraged wasps, and he gave orders that the base would be moved next day to a site fifteen miles away. The SAS had been using the current one for three weeks, and had created a converging network of tracks that the enemy were bound to pick up sooner or later.

In the operation debrief, held after breakfast, Stirling was un-characteristically severe with the men. They had wasted ammu-nition. They had shot too high. They had got out of formation. They had engaged aircraft from too long a range. Pleydell said he had never seen Stirling so angry, and wondered what was eating him. The problem might have been initiated by Mayne, who had cocked a snook at the whole 'mass attack' business with his try-scoring sprint to lay a Lewes bomb. Pleydell reported that most of the men, especially the veterans, preferred going in by stealth. Pleydell put this down to egotism. 'With bombs each man could keep a tally of the number of planes which he, personally, had destroyed; there was a healthy rivalry over it.'[2]

Stirling's later explanation for his fury that day, that 'he didn't want the men to get too blasé about the business', is unconvincing. He knew full well that to destroy thirty-seven aircraft it had taken twelve jeeps, forty-eight machine guns, and tens of thousands of rounds of ammunition. He had lost two men dead. This was not exactly what he had planned for the SAS. On one of the first raids, Bill Fraser and four men had destroyed as many aircraft at

Ajadabiyya, using forty Lewes bombs, without a jeep, and without sustaining so much as a graze. The Sidi Haneish op was not the 'maximum achievement for minimum cost' Stirling had raved about.

Yet he was desperate to sell these new tactics to GHQ. He had been struggling for months to convince his bosses that the SAS was more than a bunch of saboteurs. Now, his old hands were pulling the rug out from under him. His defensive attitude is betrayed by the asperity of his concluding remarks at the debrief. 'And don't let me hear any of you say that you could have done better by going in on foot. You couldn't. Get that quite clear in your minds ... There were too many sentry-posts and ground defences about ... you'd never have got anywhere.'[3]

Stirling's plan was to remain at his new forward base for the next three or four weeks to harass Rommel's lines of communication. The SAS would be resupplied by air. He had already made arrangements with Group Captain Bruce Bennett of Combined Ops to have supplies landed by 216 Squadron's Bombays, at an emergency airstrip about ten miles distant. He had requested another thirty jeeps. He and Mayne were planning a series of nightly strikes on soft-skinned vehicles and fuel and water dumps along the main road.

Next day, Stirling sent Stephen Hastings back to locate André Zirnheld's jeep, which had badly-needed spares aboard. Hastings hadn't returned by nightfall, so Stirling dispatched the next raiding party without him – a convoy of eight jeeps split into four parties. The officers included Jourdan, Mather and two new recruits – Lt. Chris Bailey, 4 Hussars, an ex-hotel manager on Cyprus, and Lt. David Russell, Scots Guards, a fluent German-speaker, who had previously done good work with Herbert Buck's SIG. Their orders were to attack dispersed tanks and motor-transport laagers in the enemy's rear areas near the Alamein line.

The patrols expected to find transport pools drawn up five miles to the rear of the enemy positions. They discovered that the Alamein line had stabilized and vehicles were under heavy guard. The only success was scored by Russell, who devised a cunning strategy of his own. Halting his jeep by the main road, he would flag down any German lorry that came along and ask in impeccable German to borrow an air-pump. While the crew were fumbling for the pump, Russell would stick a Lewes bomb with an instantaneous fuse on the chassis, and quickly bug out. Russell's one-man campaign accounted for eight enemy vehicles.

Stirling was now feeling in his element. He was running his own little band of cut-throats from his own hideout in the desert, far from the eyes of GHQ. He envisaged his guerrilla war going on until Rommel was driven back as far as Tunisia, but GHQ had other plans. No sooner had the last raiding party disappeared over the horizon than he was handed a message by the W/T operator, summoning him back to Cairo. He was to come in and bring the entire detachment with him. He was to start preparations for a new job being planned by the Director of Military Operations.

Auchinleck's offensive had ended in stalemate. Rommel couldn't press forward because his supply-lines were stretched to the limit. He needed more tanks and more fuel. An analysis conducted by Auchinleck's brilliant acting Chief-of-Staff, Major General E. 'Chink' Dorman-Smith, indicated that he was dependent for his supplies on three main ports: Benghazi, Tobruk and Mersa Matruh. If there was ever a time to knock out these ports, it was now. Auchinleck's next offensive was projected for mid-September or early October, and in the meantime he intended to throttle Rommel's supply-lines by massive raids on shipping in Benghazi and Tobruk. He would deploy all the special operations forces at his disposal.

Stirling was enraged and refused to come in. He had already told the Directorate of Military Operations that only SAS could plan SAS jobs, and if he was to be put under anyone else's authority, he would reject the order 'under pain of court-martial'.[4] His objections were brushed aside. The reality was that the SAS was dependent on the RAF for resupply. GHQ had instructed 216 Squadron to pick up all SAS personnel not needed to drive the transport back, and to supply only enough food and fuel to get the vehicles to Cairo. Stirling had no choice but to obey orders.

He flew to Cairo at the beginning of August, and discovered that he had been caught in a trap of his own devising. He had always been fixated with Benghazi, especially after his walkabout there last May. He had told an officer of G(R) about an idea he had in mind, to get a naval party into Benghazi harbour, scuttle a ship and block the entrance. All enemy shipping would be trapped inside, and would be sitting ducks for SBS parties with limpet mines.

The G(R) man Stirling told was Lt. Col. John Hasleden, Intelligence Corps, a well-respected figure among G(R) agents and the LRDG. Hasleden, a fluent Arabic-speaker, had been the Egyptian manager for a US cotton-broker before the war, and his journeys on foot behind enemy lines dressed as an Arab were legendary. He had been one of the main instigators of the attempt to assassinate Rommel a year earlier, in which Geoffrey Keyes had been killed. That raid had failed when it was discovered that Rommel was not at home, and there were a few people who were not impressed by the accuracy of Hasleden's intelligence.

Like Stirling, Hasleden had seen the raid as a small-scale affair, involving a dozen of Buck's SIG-men. Instead, the Directorate of Military Ops had run with it, ballooning it into an ambitious scheme to take out both Tobruk and Benghazi in one go. The Benghazi part of the operation, codenamed Bigamy, was to take place on the night of September 13/14. Stirling was instructed to deploy the whole of L Detachment, supplemented by troops from the Middle East Commando and the SBS. He was to take with him a Royal Navy detachment, and two Honey tanks for clearing roadblocks. Stirling's party would be codenamed Force X.

While Force X dealt with Benghazi, Hasleden's Force B would raid Tobruk and Force A – the Sudan Defence Force – would retake Jalo oasis, lost in Rommel's recent push. An LRDG patrol would beat up Barce landing-ground. Reg Seekings felt that it was more like a battalion assault than an SAS raid, and recalled that many of the boys were against it.

Stirling was one of them. He was unhappy about the scale of the task, which reminded him unpleasantly of the sort of Combined

Operations debacles that had ending up wrecking Layforce in '41. Too many men were involved from too many different branches. He maintained later that he was 'bribed' into accepting the plan. GHQ promised him promotion to lieutenant-colonel. If Bigamy was successful, L Detachment would be expanded and have carte blanche to rub out all enemy installations in Cyrenaica. Since Stirling admitted that he didn't trust GHQ's promises, though, it seems unlikely that this was the only reason for his acquiescence.

The planning conference was held at Grey Pillars in early August, and bristled with officers wearing the scarlet gorgets of the general staff. The chairman was Brigadier George Davy, the Director of Military Operations. Arrayed around him were representatives from Q, Supply Branch, and A, Administration Branch. There was an air-vice-marshal and an air-commodore from RAF Intelligence, and top brass from Naval Intelligence. Most were desk-bound officers who had seen no recent action.

Bigamy contradicted one of the three basic SAS principles – the ability to plan its own ops. Stirling was to have under his command two hundred and fourteen men, more than half of whom had no SAS training. He was to have ninety-five vehicles, including forty three-tonners – a massive convoy that would be difficult to conceal. The operation had been planned by people who didn't understand the SAS.

The RAF air-vice-marshal declared that Bigamy wasn't a job for 'colourful individualists', but for disciplined regular troops. Stirling gave him a minus-forty glare. He took exception to the insinuation that his troops weren't disciplined, but agreed it wasn't an SAS job.

The air-vice-marshal added that he didn't believe the SAS had destroyed as many planes as they claimed. Stirling's glare dropped ten degrees. In fact, the RAF-man had probably touched a raw nerve. Though it is unlikely that the SAS deliberately upped their bag, later evidence showed that some of the planes blown up in the early attacks were already out of commission. The Italians craftily pushed damaged aircraft to the periphery of the aerodromes, where they made easier targets for saboteurs, and the fact that they were unserviceable would not have been apparent by night.

Stirling knew this, but answered that the SAS never claimed more than they were certain of. The air-vice-marshal snorted. What was needed for Bigamy, he repeated, was regular troops. Stirling tasted poison. His eyes slitted. He lurched for a heavy glass inkwell on the DMO's desk. Brigadier Davy saw the movement and locked Stirling's eyes. The staff officer on Stirling's right put a hand on his wrist. The air-vice-marshal noticed the movement too, and his eyes widened. He opened his mouth to speak, but he was beaten to it by the air-commodore. 'I understand why you don't consider Bigamy an SAS task, Colonel Stirling,' he cut in, 'but you are the only commander who has actually been inside Benghazi since Rommel retook it.'

Stirling couldn't refute this. The air-commodore had got him, not by bribery, but by suggesting that there was no one else who could do the job. 'The game was lost at that moment,' he admitted. 'I could still have refused and I believe I should have done so . . . I felt that I had lost ground and would appear to be bleating unnecessarily.'[5]

Stirling claimed to have found out later that the air-vice-marshal had a grudge against him. Stirling's friend Brigadier Sir John Marriott had told the RAF-man that Stirling should be awarded the Distinguished Flying Cross, because his pipsqueak unit had knocked out more aircraft than the RAF.

After the meeting, Stirling learned that he had been invited to dinner at the British Embassy. The guests of honour were Winston Churchill, General Smuts, the South African politician, and General Sir Alan Brooke, Chief of the Imperial General Staff. Fitzroy Maclean, now recovered from his injury in the car smash, was also invited. Stirling decided to attend, and try to get into conversation with the Prime Minister. The DMO staff warned him not to mention Bigamy to Churchill – the Prime Minister loved to talk, and was considered a security risk.

Stirling was too junior to sit near Churchill at dinner, but afterwards British Ambassador Sir Miles Lampson called him over and introduced him. The Prime Minister, puffing cigar-smoke, introduced him to General Smuts, and to two British generals who would soon be taking over command from Auchinleck: Harold Alexander, as Commander-in-Chief Middle East, and Bernard Montgomery, as General Officer Commanding the Eighth Army. Although Churchill didn't mention it at the time, Auchinleck had been sacked for losing Tobruk. The Prime Minister said later that he hated dismissing Auchinleck – he felt it was 'like shooting a noble stag'.

Stirling soon saw that his public-relations gamble with Randolph Churchill had paid off. Randolph had praised him to the high heavens and exaggerated SAS exploits. Churchill invited Stirling and Maclean to join him in a stroll round the embassy grounds, where they gave him the lowdown on Bigamy. With an eye on the future, Stirling mentioned that he envisaged a role for the SAS in Europe at a later stage in the war.

Churchill is reputed to have described Stirling to Smuts as 'the mildest mannered man that ever scuttled ship or cut a throat' – a quote from Lord Byron's most famous poem, *Don Juan*. Stirling himself refuted this, but Churchill was certainly impressed enough to send him a request next day for his proposals on improving the coordination of SAS operations.

In response, Stirling wrote a paper proposing that, in future, all special service units, apart from those like G(R), dealing with lone agents, should be amalgamated under the SAS. This included the Middle East Commando, known as 1 Special Service Regiment, which should be disbanded, giving him the pick of its personnel. Control should remain in the hands of the commanding officer – himself. All special operations planning should be carried out by the SAS 'head-shed', not the Directorate of Military Operations. It was an impertinent gambit – an attempted coup d'état for the control of special ops in the Middle East theatre. It would establish the SAS as a real private army without rivals, answerable only to itself.

Stirling and Churchill met again at dinner that night. Stirling poured out his fears that the SAS, being regarded only as a temporary unit, would be quickly disbanded when the North African campaign came to a close. What he needed was permission to constitute the SAS as a Regiment. SAS skills and expertise could then be used to probe 'the soft underbelly of Europe'. Churchill made few comments, but admired the phrase 'soft underbelly of Europe' and asked Stirling if he could use it. Stirling left the meeting a little disappointed, not realizing that Churchill had been bowled over by him and was privately referring to him as 'The Scarlet Pimpernel'. It was the second nickname he had acquired that summer. German radio reports were already calling him 'The Phantom Major'.

36. 'It looks rather that we are expected'

On 10 September, Paddy Mayne and the Force X advance-party ran their jeeps and trucks into the Wadi Gamra, a meandering watercourse cut through the northern scarps of the Jebel Akhdar. The maquis shrub, a fleece of rust-brown and olive-green growing thick as fur around tors of smooth granite, fell away along bare scarp-slopes into the Benghazi plain. Sheep were grazing on the hillsides. Pencil-lines of blue smoke rose above the tents of Senussi shepherds pitched along the gravel wadi-beds. The tribes had migrated here in greater numbers than ever this year to avoid the troubled areas along the coast.

Mayne knew the SAS couldn't avoid being clocked by the Senussi, but he had never yet had a reason to doubt their loyalty. He and his one hundred and eighteen men had just driven sixteen hundred miles across some of the worst desert on earth. They had travelled from Cairo to the LRDG base at Kufra oasis on the Libyan-Sudanese border, and from there across a gap in the Kalansho sand-sea to Cyrenaica. Mayne was confident they hadn't been detected by enemy aircraft.

The wadi was a perfect hiding-place. It led off the main track in a series of twisting angles, opening up into wide, steep-sided basins. The wadi-bed was dotted with thickets of oleander, acacia, ilex, lentisk and wild olive that made ideal camouflage for the vehicles. It took almost an hour to cam-up. After that, Mayne instructed the men to strip and clean the Vickers Ks. The machine guns had been covered in quilts for the desert journey, but the fine dust got in everywhere.

Mayne had Fitzroy Maclean with him. He sent the subaltern to locate a G(R) agent, Captain Bob Melot, who had been dropped by an LRDG patrol on 2 September, and had spent the last eight days lurking in the jebel, dressed as an Arab. Melot and Maclean were to make contact with Alan Lyle-Smythe, an officer of the Inter-Services Liaison Department – a cover name for MI6. Smythe would have intelligence on the situation inside Benghazi.

After inquiring at a Senussi camp, Maclean tracked Melot down to a dry-wash about five miles away, where he was lying up in a cave with his assistant, a deserter from the Italian colonial army now serving with the Libyan Arab Force (LAF). Melot was a fifty-year-old Belgian. A fluent Arabic-speaker, he had been a First World War fighter ace, and manager for a cotton export company in Alexandria between the wars. Taxied in by the LRDG, he had been tramping these wooded hillsides on and off for the past year, moving continuously from cave to cave and camp to camp. He never knew when he would be betrayed, or run into a search-party. He had been lucky so far, but he had learned to be cautious.

Melot obtained his rations mostly from LRDG food-dumps, but the recent German advance had cut into his supply system, and he was starving. Maclean whipped him up a mess of bully beef rissoles fried in oatmeal, from his compo rations. Melot ate ravenously.

Bigamy was due to kick off in three days time. Pouring over the map, though, Melot told Maclean he had a bad feeling about the op. In the past ten days there had been some disturbing troop-movements – small outposts on the edge of the jebel had been reinforced. 'It looks rather that we are expected,' he said. Melot hoped to get more information from the MI6 officer Alan Lyle-Smythe, a bearded Englishman who, in another life, was a professor at the University of Cairo. He trolled around the jebel dressed like an Alpinist, in a checked jacket and hiking-breeches, carrying a knobbly walking stick.

The MI6 agent failed to show at the rendezvous and instead they drank tea with two Arab sheikhs, who expressed their view that there was an uneasiness among the Italians. Melot decided to send his LAF-man into Benghazi to find out what was going on. They escorted him to the edge of the escarpment, where successive grooves had been scored sharply through bare limestone by aeons of rain. Below them the hillside fell away, lush and green under oleanders and cork-oaks. They told him to find out what he could, and bring back with him cigarettes and matches. 'He looked,' Maclean observed, 'singularly unreliable.'[1]

All the next day and night, Melot and Maclean lay under spiky-leafed junipers and wild olives twisted and bent by the prevailing wind. It was dead quiet but for birdsong and the chirp of crickets. Maclean cooked rissoles. The Arab arrived back just after breakfast on 12 September, footsore and exhausted, having trekked more than forty miles. He had brought the cigarettes and matches they had requested, and he had plenty to say. After quizzing him in Arabic and Italian, Melot and Maclean moved him swiftly down to the SAS lying-up place in the Wadi Gamra.

Stirling had arrived earlier that day with the main party. He was confident they hadn't been observed from the air, but the two Honey tanks he had brought with him all the way from Cairo had conked out just north of Kufra. His approach to the jebel had been marred by bad luck. The previous day one of his jeeps had hit a Thermos mine as it crossed the Trig al-'Abd, and its passenger, Lt. Robert Ardley RNR, off HMS *Stag*, had been badly burned. The SAS driver, Cpl. James Webster, Essex Regiment, had leapt down, run round to pull him out, and stepped on another mine. It had blasted the flesh off his leg.

Medical officer Malcolm Pleydell had done what he could for them, but Ardley had third-degree burns, and died that night. This was a blow to Stirling. Ardley had been assistant harbour-master at Benghazi the previous year, and knew the port intimately.

Pleydell performed an emergency amputation on Webster in the blazing sun, 'crude, unskilful work', he commented. 'The dust blew . . . forming a dirty film on the antiseptic solution, coating the instruments and fouling the raw wounds . . .'[2]

At first light Pleydell supervised Ardley's burial, then went to see how Webster was doing. The corporal was lying on a stretcher in the shade of a truck. He was on morphia, but seemed to be recovering. His first inquiry was for Ardley, but Pleydell, who had been a ship's doctor at Dunkirk, knew by experience that the truth would affect his morale. He said that Ardley had been moved further up the wadi to be near the rest of the naval detachment.

Almost a hundred vehicles were now concealed in the olives, junipers and ilexes in the wadi-bed, and along its sides. There were more than two hundred men – SAS, SBS, bluejackets, and recent transfers from Middle East Commando. The place was also full of Senussi Arabs, squatting among the troops in their cloaks, blankets and tight hoods, chattering in fractured Italian, bartering eggs and meat for sugar, salt and cigarettes. At nightfall the MO dropped in on Stirling and Mayne, and found them in a huddle with Melot and his Arab spy, whom Pleydell thought looked 'rather timid'. Melot was translating his report for Stirling. The Arab had spent four hours in Benghazi, chatting to people in the suq, and had stayed the night with his relatives. It was common knowledge, he said, that a British attack was imminent, and some townspeople even seemed to know it would come on 14 September. Five thousand Italian troops were being shifted from al-Abyar, thirty miles distant, and an Afrika Korps battalion encamped to the north-east of the town had been strengthened by Italian infantry. The Arab had passed through a minefield and pillbox positions on his way out, and thought the entire perimeter of the town had been mined. Worse, all ships in port had put out to sea. Only one landing-ground was being used, under heavy guard.

For Stirling, this was depressing news after the sixteen-hundred-mile safari across the Libyan Desert. The SAS couldn't take on troops in division strength, dug in, ready for an attack. 'I suppose this Arab is quite reliable?' he asked Melot.

Melot nodded, and pointed out that if the man were being bribed by the Germans, his obvious ploy would have been to keep quiet and let them walk into a trap, rather than warn them that they were expected.[3]

Stirling instructed the others to keep the news from the enlisted men in case it caused a slump in confidence. He had the wireless operator send a message to GHQ conveying the new intelligence, and asking if there should be a change of plan. Within two hours a message came back: '. . . no great importance is attributed to this information.' The operation was to go ahead as planned.

Stirling must have felt a pang of disquiet at this point. The message from GHQ could be suggesting that it had better data, and that the SAS were *not* expected, or it could be interpreted as saying that he should go ahead with the plan *even though* they were expected. Fitzroy Maclean took it to mean that the Arab's report was false. 'Evidently there was nothing in the rumours we had picked up,' he wrote. 'Melot's Arab had simply been trying . . . to put us off an operation in which he had no wish to take part. We went about our preparations feeling reassured.'[4]

Malcolm Pleydell's reading was different. 'It was evident that the enemy knew of our plans,' he said, 'and were expecting us. We had lost our most powerful card: that of surprise.'[5] Pleydell added that it was on the assumption that the town was ringed with mines that he decided not to accompany the raiding-party. 'I reckoned it would be wiser,' he wrote, 'for the medical post to remain outside the minefield.'[6]

While Maclean insisted that the party was 'reassured', Pleydell wrote that some of them were 'quite thoughtful that evening as they sat round the trucks and considered the possibilities'.[7] Paddy Mayne was even more taciturn than usual. He raised his head from his Penguin only to remark that it 'looked as though there should be some hard scrapping'.[8]

Maclean said that Stirling modified his plan at this juncture, from an assault from several directions at once, to a single approach. 'Our plan was simple,' he wrote. 'The main body . . . would . . . rush the road block and drive full speed down to the harbour, where various targets had been allotted to different parties.'⁹ Carol Mather, though his memoirs were not written down till years afterwards, confirms Maclean's statement. 'As a result of this disquieting news,' he wrote, 'David decided to abandon the plan to enter the town at several different points and concentrate on a surprise attack at an unexpected point to the south of the town.'¹⁰ The official report, though, suggests that Stirling changed his plan later, when he realized that the raid was going in too late.

37. 'Let battle commence'

Next morning the men stripped and buffed the Vickers Ks again. The Lewes bombs were prepared by Captain Bill Cumper, the Cockney demolitions expert, out on his first mission with the SAS. Bombs, grenades and incendiaries were distributed and packed in haversacks. The men were issued with an escape kit. It consisted of a silk map of the Western Desert to be hidden in the battledress lining, a button-compass, Benzedrine tablets, a folding water-bottle, a miniature saw and other gadgets. The men carried Thompsons, pistols, .303 Lee-Enfields, or EY rifles with a grenade-launching capability.

The force was split into two groups. The first, under Bob Melot and Chris Bailey, comprising a dozen men, would knock out an Italian wireless post in a fort overlooking the escarpment. This attack was timed for 1600 hours. Stirling gave Melot orders that the fort was to be overcome within twenty minutes, to stop the Italians warning their base. Melot's group would then meet up with the main assault-group, and Melot would guide them down the escarpment.

The main raid was due to go in after an RAF bombardment, timed for midnight. The men, in jeeps and three-tonners, would concentrate on a single roadblock. Once through it, they would divide into parties, some of them on foot, and go about their assigned tasks. Stirling hadn't rescinded orders concerning the

1. David Stirling. The 'irresponsible and unremarkable soldier' whose vision of a small airborne raiding unit in North Africa created the concept of modern special forces.

2. Blair 'Paddy' Mayne. Mayne was the fighting man whose dazzling performance in combat ensured the continuing existence of the SAS. Mayne ended the war one of only eight men to have won the DSO four times.

3. John Steel 'Jock' Lewes. Lewes was the organizing genius largely responsible for the initial success of SAS raids. Killed in an air-raid after the Nofilia operation, his death was a major blow to L Detachment's morale.

4. Bill Fraser, *left*, is presented to Colonel Gigantes and General Leclerc, *with cane*. Perhaps the most enigmatic of the original SAS officers, Fraser had an intuitive sense of battle. His brilliantly executed raid at Ajadabiyya was a major coup for the SAS.

5. SAS mobile patrol, North Africa, 1942. In this famous image of the wartime SAS, David Stirling poses with a patrol led by a bearded Lt. Edward MacDonald, the ex-sergeant whose performance on Operation Copper impressed Paddy Mayne.

6. Johnny Cooper and Reg Seekings, Cairo, 1942. The two enlisted men who perhaps most personify the exuberant spirit of the wartime SAS, Cooper and Seekings hated each other at first sight, but became inseparable after the second raid on Sirte. Both are seen here wearing L Detachment's short-lived white berets.

7. Mike Sadler. One of the LRDG's star navigators, Sadler had an almost uncanny ability to find his way in the desert by night. He guided many of the early SAS raids, including the assault with armed jeeps on Sidi Haneish.

8. Some early members of L Detachment. *Back left to right,* Rose, Austin, Seekings, Cattell, Johnny Cooper; *front row,* Rhodes, Baker, Badger.

9. Bob Bennett. A mercurial Cockney from London's East End, Bennett was considered the 'steadiest' of the Originals.

10. New Year's Eve at Aghayla, 1942. *Left to right*, Trooper Jeffs, Charlie Cattell, Bob Lilley, Malcolm Pleydell and Johnny Wiseman

11. Bob Melot. A Belgian former air-ace, Melot was a fluent Arabic speaker who worked as a lone agent for the intelligence unit G(R) in Libya, and was seriously wounded while attached to the SAS during the Benghazi raid.

12. Charles 'Pat' Riley. Riley was an unflappable ex-policeman who gained his first patrolling experience with Jock Lewes as one of his celebrated 'Tobruk Four'. He became L Detachment's sergeant-major and training officer, and was later commissioned.

13. George, Earl Jellicoe, *on the right*. Jellicoe was recruited by Stirling as L Detachment's unofficial second-in-command. One of only two survivors of the SAS raid on Heraklion airfield, Crete, he later took command of the Special Boat Squadron.

14. L Detachment sergeants at Kabrit. David Stirling always considered his sergeants the powerhouse of the unit and often relied on their judgement, even in assessing officers. *Squatting front left*, Dave Kershaw; *squatting right*, Reg Seekings; *at the wheel*, Pat Riley; *on bonnet with arm in sling*, Bob Tait; *right*, Johnny Cooper.

15. LRDG Ford truck in the desert: L Detachment scored its first great successes against Axis airfields when ferried in by LRDG patrols. The idea almost certainly came from LRDG commander Lt. Col. Guy Prendergast – an unsung co-creator of the SAS.

16. Ferried to their targets originally by LRDG patrols, the SAS acquired a consignment of jeeps in mid-1942, at the suggestion of Paddy Mayne. The vehicles were designed to carry only two men and their kit, but had 4-wheel drive, and were fitted with sun-compasses, extra fuel-tanks, and radiator-condensers to prevent over-heating.

17. Eighteen men of Bill Fraser's troop, and several civilians, were killed at Termoli when this SAS truck exploded. The truck was thought to have been hit by a German artillery shell, but most casualties may have been caused by the armed anti-tank grenades the SAS were carrying.

18. Paddy Mayne commanded his first defensive action here at Termoli, when 1 SRS, now part of a commando brigade, was joined by a handful of men from 2 SAS. The action was brilliantly successful, but the SRS lost sixty-nine men, killed, wounded, or missing, during the three days of battle.

19. Ian Wellsted, *left*, and Alex Muirhead in France 1944. 'Bertie Wooster' Muirhead, a former medical student, commanded the SRS mortar section in Italy, and fought with A Squadron, 1 SAS, on Operation Houndsworth. Wellsted, an ex-Royal Tank Regiment officer, saw his first action when A Squadron men assisted the Maquis in ambushing a German convoy.

20. Kipling patrol in the Morvan, France, 1944. This photo was taken shortly before Capt. Derrick Harrison's two armed jeeps steamed into the village of Les Ormes, inflicting sixty German casualties, destroying three vehicles and liberating eighteen French hostages. Harrison is in the jeep on the left, his driver L.Cpl. John 'Curly' Hall was killed.

blocking of the harbour. Neither had he covered the possibility that the jeeps might not be able to penetrate the roadblock, despite the fact that he no longer had the two Honey tanks assigned to him for this purpose.

Melot's section left in a jeep and a three-tonner in the early afternoon. The main assault convoy left before last light. The scene was peacefully biblical, with shepherds tending sheep-flocks and smoke rising from Senussi camps. The Arabs waved to them encouragingly as they passed. They halted twice when enemy aircraft appeared, dark specks against a mackerel sky, heavy with cloud. Pleydell was disturbed further by the suspicious fact that the planes didn't come in for a closer look.

Not long before sundown, Pleydell set up a medical aid-post in a small wadi in the outer skirts of the jebel, and waved to the rest of the jeeps as they moved on down the track. The sun faded, and the going became increasingly steep and difficult in the darkness. It was, recalled Mather, in the back of a three-tonner, 'a horrible journey . . . over jagged boulders following the course of a rough track'.[1] The track dwindled and seemed to Maclean, in the leading jeep, to be petering out. The way was littered with sharp boulders that scraped irritatingly against the jeeps' sumps.

During one of the numerous halts, Mather recalled, an SAS-man was spotted scuttling down the wadi. He turned out to be one of Melot's party. He reported that they'd taken the fort, but that Melot, Bailey and Cpl. Doug Laird had been badly injured in the fighting. He couldn't say whether or not the enemy had given the alarm. Jim Almonds, driving one of the jeeps, heard the news, and saw that the mission was in trouble. 'Everyone in the column,' he said, 'realized that the scheme now left far too much to chance.'[2]

Since Melot was no longer available, navigation was handed over to his LAF Arab. Under his guidance, the track entered a steep-sided ravine and ended abruptly in a cul-de-sac. The Arab admitted to Maclean that they were in the wrong wadi. This meant retracing their steps and, for the three-tonners, virtually creating their own route down. 'We had to clear boulders all the way,' wrote Mather, 'build a rough track, and guide each vehicle

down individually.'[3] Mather put the guide's performance down to
'treachery'. The official report suggests, more fairly, that he was
simply incapable of judging what was suitable 'going' for motor-
vehicles.

They were still descending the escarpment when the RAF
bombing-raid went in. It was on schedule. Angling a peep at his
watch, Stirling became conscious that they were badly behind
time. They should have been poised to strike as soon as the
bombers wheeled off back to base, but they hadn't yet made it
down the escarpment. Benghazi was still fifteen miles away.

At the medical post, Pleydell and his drivers heard the bombers
truckling overhead. They climbed up to a high point to watch the
attack, but could make out only twinkles as the bombs struck.
Two hours later, the medical officer was roused from a doze by
the buzz of a jeep engine. One of Melot's party had arrived with
the news that Melot, Bailey and Laird were in a bad way.

Pleydell found Melot twenty minutes later, lying under a great-
coat surrounded by the rest of his section, shivering in the night
air. He had been hit by shrapnel from a grenade, and had multiple
wounds in the leg, thigh and abdomen. His femur was fractured,
and his thigh was peppered with steel fragments. Pleydell was
relieved to find that the stomach-wound was only muscle-deep.
He had lost a lot of blood, and Pleydell administered morphia and
blood-plasma. He loaded him on a stretcher, and shifted him to
the medical post.

Melot's party had concealed their vehicles out of earshot of the
fort and climbed the spur on foot. When challenged by an Italian
sentry, Melot grunted in Italian that they were German troops sent
to relieve the post. They'd almost made it through the door
when the Italians tumbled them, and started shooting and hurling
grenades. Melot was hit in the first seconds, but continued hammering away with his Tommy-gun. The battle was short and
vicious. Three of the Italians were killed, and two captured: one
escaped. The SAS team smashed the wireless gear and bugged out
to their vehicles. On the way, Melot collapsed.

It was 0300 hours by the time Stirling's group made the foot of the jebel. The RAF bombardment had ceased hours before. The jeeps and trucks raced across the plain towards the town, pulling into file along a tarmac road lined with poplar trees. They were almost on top of the roadblock before they saw it – this time there was no sentry and no swinging red light. The column halted. The barrier was a cantilever gate weighted by an oil-barrel filled with earth, and about a hundred and fifty metres further on was another barrier. Stirling saw barbed wire along the sides of the road, and noticed that the soil seemed to have been disturbed. Jim Almonds, further back, felt uneasy. This was a classic place for an ambush. The road was too narrow to turn round without straying into the minefield.

Stirling called forward Bill Cumper, who examined the verges and confirmed it was a minefield. Peering out of his jeep, Almonds saw the two officers talking solemnly, Stirling with his unlit pipe stuck upside down in his mouth, as if discussing a game of bowls. Almonds took a dekko at his watch. It was already 0430 hours and if the attack didn't go in now, they would be caught by daylight on the march out.

Suddenly Stirling beckoned him forward to the head of the column. Almonds's target was the harbour mole, and his crew had the furthest to go. Apart from his front- and rear-gunners, McGinn and Fletcher, Almonds had with him an Arab whose job was to guide him to the harbour. Whether or not this was Melot's LAF-man is not clear. As Almonds drew up near Stirling, the Arab suddenly pivoted himself out of the jeep and raced off into the darkness. Almonds glanced after him open-mouthed, then looked at Stirling. For a moment time seemed frozen. Almonds had a fleeting impression that his CO was completely lost. Then Stirling said, 'Are you all right?'

Almonds nodded 'OK'.

'Right-o,' Stirling said. 'Carry on.'

Cumper opened the catch on the barrier, and the bar flew up. Almonds gunned the engine. Cumper stood out of the way, raised his arm in a mock-Nazi salute and declared, 'Let battle commence!' No one who survived the Bigamy op ever forgot those words.

'Battle did commence good and proper,' Reg Seekings recalled.

No sooner had Cumper finished speaking than machine-gun fire hacked through the night like a mower. Breda 20mm ack-ack guns bumped. There was the chomp of mortar-shells hitting the ground. Small-calibre tracer wonked across the track from snipers concealed in the poplar trees. Rounds slapped into vehicles and sizzled off the road. Reg Seekings, at the gun on one of the forward jeeps, was exchanging a word with Cpl. Anthony Drongin, Scots Guards, when they were caught in a spurt of fire. Drongin was hurled off the jeep and Seekings went down with him. Seekings, miraculously untouched, hoisted up Drongin to find him in agony – a bullet had drilled through his thigh and slashed off his penis.

Almonds drove on past the barrier, roaring towards the second roadblock along a channel lined with barbed wire. A second jeep followed. He braked fast when he saw the barrier was a thick steel chain between two heavy lumps of concrete. The road was bathed in brilliance. Rounds suddenly spritzed out of nowhere. McGinn, on the back, hit the triggers on the twin Vickers, traversing the way ahead with a deadly arc of fire. Almonds realized that the Lewes bombs and limpets would go up any second, and screamed at the gunners to bail out. McGinn and Fletcher launched themselves out of the jeep and tried to claw their way under the barbed wire. Almonds jumped after them. An incendiary shell chugged into the jeep's petrol tank and the vehicle went off like a rocket in a blur of flame. The jeep behind exploded at almost the same time.

Most observers thought that Almonds had gone up with the jeep. Pat Riley clocked him, though. 'I saw Jim sort of collecting himself,' he said, 'and running for it. They had been waiting for us and we had a right old scuffle as we tried to get ourselves out of it as best we could.'[4] Chaos reigned. Two jeeps, driven by Paddy Mayne and Captain Terence 'Jim' Chambers, ex-5 Mahratta Light Infantry, jerked to a halt near the barrier, with their guns slingshotting tracer. The gunners worked through drum after drum, switching drums with burning fingers, jetting out covering fire. 'The jeeps in front directed a withering fire on the enemy guns,'

Mather wrote, 'but they were protected by concrete emplace-ments.'[5] Stirling thought enemy reinforcements would soon be arriving, and knew his party couldn't afford to be caught on the plain in daylight. Reluctantly, he gave the order to withdraw.

Everyone was yelling, gears grating, motors squalling, drivers wrenching steering-wheels. Mayne's and Chambers's gunners drilled rounds into the enemy positions. The two wrecked jeeps beyond the barrier crackled with fire. Trails of gunsmoke wafted through the trees. The jeeps were hemmed in by the poplars, a ditch, the minefield, the drivers trying desperately to turn on a sixpence. A reversing jeep winged Bill Cumper and knocked him down. Seekings laid Drongin in the back of his jeep. A green young officer told Bob Bennett to get rid of the corpse. Drongin opened his eyes and snapped, 'Corporal Drongin to you, sir.' Seekings jumped in and hollered at the driver to back up.

Seconds later he spotted Cumper lumping along on hands and knees, and loaded him in the back of the vehicle. He picked up Mather, who had got separated from his three-tonner. 'Cpl. Drongin was slumped in the back,' Mather remembered, 'shot in the groin. We travelled too fast for the wounded man's comfort, I'm afraid.'[6]

38. 'This is going to be a shaky do'

The first Pleydell knew about the fiasco was when John Olivey's Rhodesian patrol bumped past the medical post on their way back to the Wadi Gamra. They had intended to hit Benina airfield, but had called it off because it was getting light. Only a minute after the patrol vanished into the green-brown draperies of the jebel, an Me 109-F came bowling along above the track at a hundred feet. Pleydell and his team sank into cover and watched it as it hugged the dust trail of the departed Chevrolets. 'We waited in silence,' Pleydell wrote. 'Then it came: the fast crackle of machine-gun fire, sounding hideous and frightening on the chill morning air.'[1]

At the crack of dawn, Chris Bailey had been shifted to the aid-post on a three-tonner. He had been shot in the chest during the assault on the wireless post. Pleydell found only a small entry-wound, but the round had punctured Bailey's lung, and the least exertion had him gasping for air. He had a sucking pneumothorax, and without hospital treatment Pleydell considered the prognosis poor.

For the whole morning the medical officer and his orderly, 'Razor Blade' Johnson, scuttled from bush to bush trying to tend the wounded, watching out for the hawk-shadows that flitted across the wadi. The enemy planes flipped, yawed, machine-gunned the maquis at random. Twice the medics were interrupted in the process of cleaning Melot's wounds, and had to cover the giveaway whiteness of the bandages and cotton wool. Pleydell felt a dreamlike sense of detachment. All morning they heard the tremor of bombs bursting on the escarpment above them, and the far-off shudder of machine guns from the plain below. Pleydell prayed that the rendezvous in the Wadi Gamra hadn't been compromised.

For the SAS raiders, the pursuit had started at first light. By the time the bulk of Stirling's party had reached the foot of the escarpment, the sky was scarlet and gold and the twisted thorn trees were surreal shadows on the frayed edges of the plain. Before sunrise, Axis aircraft had scrambled from local airfields and were raking across the valley after the raiders. 'There were about a dozen [planes] in the air at a time,' Maclean recalled. 'They flew round in a circle, one after another peeling off and swooping down to drop its bombs or fire a long burst from its guns.'[2]

Some of the SAS took shelter at an emergency RV twelve miles out of Benghazi, in a tangle of acacias near a ruined Quranic school. 'We lay all day beneath the thick bushes and trees,' wrote Mather, 'and all day long aircraft buzzed overhead; the CR42s slow, low and dangerous, searching out every bush and tree; the 109s and Macchis faster and not so sharp eyed.'[3]

Maclean was already halfway up the escarpment. Lying in juni-pers and olives near his camouflaged jeep, he looked down on a spectacular panorama – the tilting rust-red and olive tapestry of the Jebel Akhdar, with its flaky ragstone faces, punctuated by grassland, shrub, tangled maquis and forest. Below him lay the plain, from here a vast coarse mat of spiky fibres slashed by roads and tracks, dotted with buildings and trees, and beyond it the walls of Benghazi, hovering over the eerie turquoise of the sea. As he watched, Maclean saw an aircraft strafe a party of Senussi Arabs – men and women making their way with donkeys to the local market.

He saw a spiral of black smoke rising from a three-tonner on the plain. He heard the far-off snap and crackle of small explosions as its ammunition went up. Another lorry, hundreds of feet below, came apart in a white puff. The aircraft were combing the inter-secting wadis on the hillside, passing out of view, then reeling suddenly back. Maclean and his crew would dive into cover again. They couldn't open up with their guns, because it would betray their position to the enemy.

Seekings was in a jeep beetling backwards and forwards across the plain, looking for stragglers. Any vehicles stranded in the open were sitting ducks. Roger Boutinot of the French detachment recalled how his jeep was machine-gunned by an Me 109-F. The crew hurled themselves flat on the gravel floor just as the fighter came in. The jeep whacked apart in flames. 'We had no cover at all,' Boutinot recalled. 'It was all down to luck. You just laid there and hoped you would not be hit.'⁴ Another French team stood their ground and blasted back at an aircraft with their Vickers as it came in to savage their three-tonner. The aircraft took a hit, whistled overhead for two hundred yards and whumped into the ground, disintegrating into a jellyfish-shaped cloud of smoke and flame.

In the afternoon, Pleydell was called to tend Doug Laird, the third of Melot's casualties. He was in agony from an arm smashed in two places, and begged Pleydell to cut it off. At last light Stirling's jeep drew up at the ruined Quranic school. Stirling gave instructions that everyone should make for the lying-up place in Wadi Gamra that night. Up on the escarpment, Pleydell and

Maclean were already moving there with the wounded. They reached the rendezvous at about 0300 hours.

It wasn't until eight hours later that Pleydell was called out to treat Anthony Drongin, who had been ferried up the jebel in the night. The MO found him lying in the sparse shade of a thorn-tree with a forced grin on his face. 'Sorry to have given you so much trouble, sir,' he said. The words almost brought tears to Pleydell's eyes. Drongin, a former commando RSM who had reverted to corporal, had just had his manhood blown away. The fortitude of British enlisted men was incredible, Pleydell thought. He gave the ex-Guardsman an injection of pentothal and started psyching himself up for a harrowing operation – an abdominal incision under conditions of zero sterility.

In the Wadi Gamra, Maclean was lying behind a boulder watching a couple of enemy spotters gyrating, leaving smears of vapour across the velveteen sky. Mayne had chosen the site well, Maclean thought – none of the vehicles was seen. Then, to his horror, he noticed an SAS jeep lumbering up from an adjoining wadi, shrouding the air with dust. He watched helplessly as one of the spotters dipped down to investigate, then spun round and reamed off towards Benghazi.

Maclean wondered if it was possible the pilot hadn't seen them. This thought was quickly dismissed when he peeped out and received a spritz of cannon-fire from the plane's rear-gunner. Flight officer Laurence Pyke, Royal Australian Air Force, who was sharing his refuge, looked at him gravely. 'This,' he said, 'is going to be a shaky do.'[5]

The spotter was back in half an hour, riding point for a wing of fighters and bombers that hung together like a swarm of dark commas. Maclean thought there were between twenty and thirty of them. As they began to troll slowly around the wadi, SAS-men hidden in the junipers opened up with machine guns. Maclean heard the clack-clack-clack of the guns, and saw the blots and trails of smoke from the tracer cutting the air like knife-blades. It had no effect. The aircraft thrummed in low, releasing their payloads and cleaving the bush with their cannons. Quiffs of smoke and dust appeared along the wadi-bed, frozen for a moment like a gallery of giant exclamation marks. The planes came in wave after wave, reeling and striking, saturating the whole wadi with fire. Suddenly a camouflaged three-tonner convulsed in a searing arc of red and black. Then another and another. Watching grimly, Maclean found himself trying to calculate how many vehicles they would need to get back. 'As truck after truck disintegrated before our eyes,' he said, 'it became clear that it would be a tight fit.'[6]

Hidden with the wounded Drongin in the maquis ten miles away, Pleydell saw the aircraft roll and dive, heard the thud of bombs and saw the dark columns of smoke. His team stayed hidden until just before sundown, then laid Drongin in a cam-net and drove him back to the lying-up place. On the way, the MO watched the last enemy plane flying back towards Benina, a dark dragonfly against vast arcades of flame-coloured cloud.

He found the Wadi Gamra full of smoke and the stink of burning oil and rubber. The place was littered with bits of red-hot steel and smouldering kit. Unexploded bombs were stuck nose down in the wadi-bed, and hot jerrycans of petrol lay strewn about, still intact, but swollen to the size of pumpkins from the gas inside. More than twenty vehicles were on fire, including Pleydell's own medical truck. The men were stumbling back from their hiding-places, yelling to each other.

The first officer he saw was Bill Cumper, who escorted him over to the wounded. One of the French officers, Aspirant Germain Guerpillon, was only just alive and died a few minutes later. Another officer, Lt. David Lair, an American who had served with the French Foreign Legion, had been badly injured. A REME fitter, AQMS Arthur Sque, had been shot in the leg. Sque had been particularly unlucky. He had taken leave to accompany the SAS mission at the request of his mate Reg Seekings, but had fallen off a truck on the drive-in and fractured a leg. Left in the open on a stretcher during the attacks that day, he had copped a cannon-shell in the other leg. Another man, Driver Bill Marlow, Royal Army Service Corps, was dead. Considering the intensity of the attack, though, Pleydell thought the casualties weren't as bad as they might have been.[7]

Stirling and Mayne had arrived earlier and were already preparing to move out to Jalo oasis, where they could get resupply from the Sudan Defence Force. In all, more than sixty vehicles had been lost. Petrol, food and water were short. Stirling called Pleydell and told him that the seriously wounded would have to be left behind, as there was no room for them on the transport. Melot and the American officer, Lair, were determined to ride back to Kufra with the column whatever the cost, but the stretcher-cases, Bailey, Sque, Webster and Drongin, would be sent to Benghazi in a jeep driven by a medical orderly under a white flag. Pleydell's three medical orderlies drew lots for the job: an ex-commando medic named Ritchie drew the short straw.

Captain Arthur Duveen was still missing, with sixteen enlisted men. Jim Almonds and his gunners, Fletcher and McGinn, were presumed captured. That night Stirling divided the survivors into three parties, under himself, Mayne and Scratchley. While his group would linger in the vicinity to watch for Duveen's party, the other two would start for Jalo at midnight.

By the time Reg Seekings arrived at the wadi with twelve or thirteen men hanging off his jeep, Mayne's and Scratchley's parties had already gone. He found that Ritchie had laid out a huge red cross in the wadi-bed as an aircraft recognition signal. Seekings collared him and told him to get rid of it. He said that, come first light, the cross would only reveal that there was still activity in the wadi, and would bring in the hunters again.

Lying on his stretcher, Seekings's mate, Sque, overheard the conversation. 'Reg . . . we'll die if we don't get help quick,' he groaned. Seekings apologized, but told him that the wounded were just numbers now. He had to think of the dozen fit men he had with him. He had to get them out to fight another day. 'My pal [Sque] started calling me *sergeant*, then,' Seekings recalled. 'He was disgusted with me. I hated doing it, absolutely hated it. But it was my job.'[8]

Seekings set off and caught up with Mayne's party the following day. By the time they reached Jalo, three days later, six more vehicles had been lost. To cap it all, the SDF had failed to capture the oasis, and was still fighting when Force X arrived. Their presence, though, saved the SAS by providing petrol, water and rations, and preventing the enemy from intercepting them as they withdrew back to Kufra.

39. Talking out of turn over gin-and-tonics

In a list of seven lessons learned from Op Bigamy, GHQ specified that 'Too many people knew of the Benghazi operation and a very much higher sense of security was necessary.'[1] Reg Seekings believed that the cat had been let out of the bag not by SAS personnel, but by desk wallahs from GHQ talking out of turn over gin-and-tonics in Shepheard's bar and other places.

Intelligence files, though, suggest that Op Bigamy was not anticipated: no leak was ever proved. A thorough air reconnaissance of Benghazi prior to the operation had spotted large numbers of Italian troops on the move, as Melot's agent had reported, but concluded that these were units of the newly-arrived Pistoia Division being shifted to the front line. The Arab's report was accurate, but the movements were discounted by GHQ as having no connection with the planned attack.

The main cause of the failure was the time lost in descending the escarpment. This was blamed on Melot's Arab agent, but the real blunder lay in Stirling's failure to send a recce party, to make a thorough survey of the route. He had been relying on Bob Melot to guide them down, when there was always the chance that Melot would be killed or wounded in the attack on the wireless station. That assault itself was a longshot – the chances of being able to capture the fort within twenty minutes, and of preventing the Italian signallers from alerting their base, were not good. Stirling's decision to concentrate on a single roadblock rather than go for an assault from several directions was also a mistake. It meant that one machine-gun post could hold them up: they could not have got through the second barrier, anyway, without using an explosive charge. Bigamy went wrong not because of a security leak, but through a lack of precision and planning by Stirling.

This may be why he 'drew a veil' over it even in his official biography, and, according to Lorna Almonds Windmill, would apologize to her father, Jim Almonds, whenever they saw each other after the war. It might also explain that momentary look of blankness Almonds saw in Stirling's face just before Cumper opened the gate.

The most important 'lesson' learned on the Benghazi raid was one that Stirling's men knew already – it was too big. The SAS concept was to operate in small groups – Bigamy was more like the commando-attacks carried out by Layforce than SAS. It was poor compensation that the simultaneous raid on Tobruk, led by John Hasleden, had fared even worse. Almost all his Force B troops had been captured, and Hasleden had been killed. The navy had lost two destroyers and four motor-torpedo boats.

Bigamy was essentially a failure of the SAS principle of maximum return for minimum cost, but it did divert enemy focus from the front line. Reg Seekings, for one, argued that anything the unit did to keep the rear echelons guessing ought to be considered a success.

40. The Regiment

On 28 September David Stirling marched out of No. 10 Tonbalat Street the commanding officer of the British army's newest regiment, 1 SAS. He had just spent several hours in conclave with Lt. Col. John 'Shan' Hackett, director of General Staff Raiding Forces, G(RF), a new staff cell under the Director of Military Operations. Hackett was now responsible for all military-style special ops.

Stirling had turned up for the meeting with some misgivings. He had always objected to being run by the Director of Military

Operations. He foresaw further cock-ups like Bigamy, planned by staff officers without an inkling of what the SAS was about. To his relief, he found Hackett a kindred spirit, a seasoned soldier who had taken the desk job under protest and who accepted that SAS missions should be chosen by the SAS. 'We saw absolutely eye to eye,' Hackett said later. '. . . [Stirling] was by far the best bloke to choose the targets he would operate most effectively against. We had a very close alliance . . .'[1]

They had discussed the SAS role, particularly in relation to Bernard Montgomery's planned break-out from Alamein, Operation Lightfoot, due to take place on 23–4 October. SAS targets were defined by a list of classic guerrilla tasks, similar to those outlined a generation earlier by T. E. Lawrence: hit and run attacks on railways, locomotives and rolling stock, bridges, roads, supply-dumps, administrative centres, tanks, troops in laager, motor-transport in laager or on the move, land-line communications, headquarters and important officers.

Stirling and Hackett had also worked out an orbat for 1 SAS. It would have an establishment of twenty-nine officers and five hundred and seventy-two men. It would absorb the Special Boat Section, from now on to be known as the Special Boat Squadron, and have the pick of the disbanded Middle East Commando.

The Regiment was to be divided into four combat squadrons. A would be under Paddy Mayne, and B under a new officer, Major Vivian Street, Devonshire Regiment. Street was a staff officer assigned to 'Special Duties', who had been present at the very first conference on L Detachment. He had grown tired of hearing about SAS exploits from the safety of his office, and decided to call in the favours he'd done Stirling over the past year. Mayne's A Squadron included the old operators, while Street's B Squadron was made up mostly of new recruits, with a smattering of vets as NCOs. C Squadron was the Free French detachment, and D, the SBS *folbot* group. There would be three troops to each squadron, and five troops attached to a permanent HQ Squadron at Kabrit, responsible for administration, training, signals, intelligence and light vehicle repair. One recent windfall was a body of a hundred and twenty-one Free Greek troops under their revered commander, Colonel Christodoulos Tzigantes. Tzigantes had re-formed the Greek Sacred Squadron – a unit with a longer history than any other body of troops in the Allied forces. Raised originally in 370BC to defend Thebes against the Spartans, it had been revived a thousand years later, in 1821, to fight the Turks. Tzigantes's third incarnation of the Sacred Squadron, already trained to use *folbots*, would be added to the strength of the SBS.

SAS modus operandi would be stealth if possible, force if neces-sary, and the unit would be capable of approaching its targets by land, sea or air. It would come under the direct control of GHQ via Hackett, though part of it might come under another command for individual missions. Most important for the future, SAS oper-ations were not to be confined to the desert. The unit might be required to operate anywhere in Middle East Command, which included Syria, Palestine and Iraq, East Africa and southern Europe. Squadrons and troops might be organized differently depending on the areas or the type of country they were operating in.

As Stirling passed the pickets at the barrier that day, he had good reason to feel proud of himself. The 'incorrigible' subaltern who may or may not have leapt over the fence sixteen months earlier was now a temporary acting lieutenant-colonel, and had founded one of only a handful of new regiments to be added to the British army's order of battle since his uncle, Simon Fraser, had founded the Lovat Scouts.

This was not a coincidence. The ultimate source of Stirling's success – the knowledge that such a thing was possible – lay in his family tradition. His superiors knew of this tradition, and so gave Stirling more credence than they would probably have allowed him otherwise. That the organization of light raiding forces was considered almost a Stirling family prerogative is illustrated by the fact that a second SAS Regiment had been founded in May, under Stirling's brother, Bill. This can hardly have been a coincidence, either.

To give GHQ its due, it had also sanctioned ideas for 'private armies' from those who had no such antecedents, including Ralph

Bagnold, Herbert Buck, Vladimir 'Popski' Peniakoff and others. It is nevertheless interesting to speculate whether Paddy Mayne or Jock Lewes would have been successful had they set out single-handedly to create the SAS.

If Stirling's family precedent had given him a head start, his network of social contacts had buoyed him at every turn – Ritchie, Marriott, Reid, Randolph Churchill, the 'Silver Circle Club', the Guards mafia. His success was also due to his own personal qualities of rhetoric and empathy, as well as astute politics. His allowing Randolph Churchill to take part in a mission despite being untrained, for instance, had brought him to the attention of the Prime Minister. To Winston Churchill, friend of Lawrence of Arabia, ex-troop commander in the legendary charge of 21 Lancers at Omdurman, Stirling was a man after his own heart.

Stirling's plan, approved by Hackett, was to continue what he had been doing before Bigamy had so rudely interrupted. He would strike along the coast far into the Panzerarmee's back-yard. When Rommel's forces fell back from Alamein, as it was now confidently expected they would, the SAS would cause havoc behind his lines.

Starting in early October, Mayne's A Squadron would set up a forward operating base in the deep Sahara and hit the railway in the Tobruk area, as well as motor transport and landing-grounds. After Montgomery's attack began, A Squadron would go for motor-transport and HQ units. Once Rommel began his withdrawal, the SAS would focus on creating traffic bottlenecks to provide targets for RAF bombing, and on hitting Axis aircraft being leapfrogged to the rear on transit aerodromes. Meanwhile, B Squadron would be under formation at Kabrit, ready to take part in operations by late November.

Recruitment, though, was a headache. Apart from Middle East Commando personnel, Stirling could no longer call on the commando-trained, combat-experienced volunteers who had made up L Detachment. His recruiting NCOs, including Sgt. Jeff Du Vivier, recently awarded the MM for his part in the Ajadabiyya raid, were already tramping round the camps of various regiments, giving talks and asking for volunteers. Du Vivier reported that it was difficult to find them, because battalion commanders weren't ready to let their best men go.

Stirling decided to take the bull by the horns and ask Montgomery for permission to recruit a hundred and fifty combat veterans from the Eighth Army. In early October he turned up at Montgomery's command caravan ten miles from Alamein, with Hackett in support. The SAS star was in the ascendant, and he didn't believe the General Officer Commanding would turn him down.

He was quite wrong. Montgomery, a ruthless martinet and self-publicist, was determined to turn the tide of war once and for all. He was not about to hand over his most seasoned soldiers to a twenty-seven-year-old half-colonel who had just lost a quarter of his force and three-quarters of his vehicles at Benghazi. Lightfoot was the most crucial offensive of the entire campaign.

Stirling and Hackett walked in and saluted. Montgomery glared. 'What do you want?' he demanded. His voice was like a knife, and Stirling's heart sank. Gone was the clubby aura of Ritchie and Auchinleck. 'What, Colonel Stirling,' Monty snapped after listening to his request, 'makes you assume that you can handle these men to greater advantage than myself?'[2] Stirling tried to explain that he needed to bring 1 SAS up to establishment as soon as possible, and training green recruits would take too long. Seasoned veterans could be trained in only a month. 'I find your request arrogant in the extreme,' the GOC concluded. '. . . You failed at Benghazi and you come here asking, no, demanding, the best of my men. In all honesty, Colonel Stirling, I am not inclined to associate myself with failure.'[3] He held up his hand to show that the meeting was at an end.

Stirling couldn't believe that Monty had sent him away with a flea in his ear. He had never been treated like this by a general, not even as a lowly subaltern. Carol Mather, who knew both Montgomery and Stirling and had recently been posted to Monty's HQ as his personal assistant, commented that the GOC felt Stirling had become a law unto himself. 'He considered that Stirling was a spoilt boy,' said Mather, '*Baby Boy*, he used to call him. Others might put up with his gasconading, but Monty would not.'[4] As Mather suggested, Stirling's failure to admit that the GOC had a point, and his sometimes over-belligerent attitude to the 'morons' at GHQ ME, are signs of a side that didn't often show. His patience, tact and ability to gain others' friendship overlay a powerful element of the prima donna. This is probably why Mayne's apparently easy superiority both in leadership and in combat irked him so deeply.

That afternoon, though, after lunching extravagantly at Montgomery's expense, he and Hackett returned to the GOC's caravan to retrieve a document-case and ran into Chief of General Staff, Brigadier Freddie de Guingand. De Guingand, as it happened, was literally 'old school tie' – he had been at Ampleforth with Stirling. He told them that while there was no shifting Montgomery once he had made up his mind, he would put in a good word for the SAS whenever he had the chance. Stirling had to resign himself to recruiting raw material, but he did learn something of value from de Guingand: a tacit admission that an Anglo-American army would soon be opening up a second front in North Africa.

Stirling started putting out feelers and found out that Operation Torch, the Allied landings at Casablanca, Oran and Algiers, would follow Monty's Operation Lightfoot by about two weeks. Stung by the GOC's attitude, he was determined that the new SAS Regiment should make its name before then. By the time he received his formal orders for the next series of operations against Rommel's supply-lines, Paddy Mayne's A Squadron, with Bill Fraser as second-in-command, was already at Kufra oasis poised to strike.

41. 'A one-way ticket with no return'

At 2140 hours on 23 October, five hundred and ninety-two British guns opened up on Axis positions from the Alamein line. Just over an hour later, the blanket bombardment ceased. Montgomery's artillery switched to specific targets. Royal Engineers mine-clearing parties crept out of their trenches, followed by infantry battalions advancing with bayonets fixed, supported by squadrons of Valentine tanks. They encountered savage opposition from Axis troops.

Monty had predicted that Alamein would last thirteen days. He was correct. On the night of 3–4 November patrols of 51 Highland Division probed Axis positions and discovered that the enemy had gone. Rommel was retreating at last, and this time he would not be back. He had lost twenty-five thousand men killed or wounded, thirty thousand captured, eighty-four aircraft, a thousand guns, and four hundred and fifty tanks.

During the last two weeks of October, Mayne's SAS patrols, operating from the Great Sand Sea, blew the railway line in the Tobruk-ad-Dhaba area no less than seven times. So many, in fact, that by the end of the month, he had been requested to desist. The railway would shortly be in British hands and was required to be in working order. Lt. Raymond Shorten, General List, was killed on an attempt to blow the railway at Sidi Barrani, when his patrol was chased by German armoured cars and his jeep overturned in the sand-sea. His navigator, Trooper John Sillito, Staffordshire Yeomanry, a newcomer to the SAS, was stranded in the desert. He made a record-breaking march of two hundred miles back to base in eight days, alone, with one water-bottle and no food. When his water gave out, he was reduced to drinking his own urine. The SAS-men suffered badly from desert sores.

Another newcomer, Irishman Lt. Bill MacDermott, Royal Artillery, grew so frustrated when his charges failed to blow a locomotive that he captured a railway station, taking prisoner three Italians and two Germans. He proceeded to demolish the station before disappearing into the desert. Cpl. Jimmy Storie, Mayne's companion on the second Berka raid, wasn't impressed with Mac-Dermott's proficiency. It was while on patrol with the new officer that he was captured by the Germans, after his jeep was hit by an armour-piercing shell. He blamed the patrol's inexperience. 'What used to happen with the old hands,' he said, 'if you got hit, one of them would swing right round and pick you up – but [these] were new boys.'[1]

For two months Stirling remained behind his own lines, flitting from GHQ to Kabrit, supervising the training of the new recruits. He spent some time in hospital suffering from acute desert sores. Occasionally, as word got round that he was looking for men, he would get walk-ins. One day in October, the doorbell rang at the Stirling flat. Mo, the housekeeper, admitted a gangly-looking major wearing a DSO ribbon on his service dress. The major was thirty-two-year-old Wilfred Thesiger, a distinguished explorer who had fought with Orde Wingate on the Gideon mission in Ethiopia. Thesiger, a fluent Arabic-speaker, had also worked with G(R) in Syria, where he had served for a time as second-in-command of the Druze Legion, a cavalry force raised to fight the Vichy French. He had grown frustrated with G(R). He'd heard that Stirling was about to mount a raid, and wanted to join the SAS.

Stirling had been looking for combat veterans, and here was one ready and willing. Thesiger explained that G(R) had already refused to let him go. The brigadier in command had threatened to put him on a charge for insubordination. '[Stirling] picked up the telephone,' Thesiger remembered, 'and asked for the brigadier. "Colonel Stirling here. I've got Major Thesiger with me. I'm taking him on a forthcoming operation. So please release him at once."'[2] Stirling put the phone down and told Thesiger to get down to Kabrit the same day.

Anglo-American forces landed in Algeria on 8 November. By that time, Montgomery had already chased the Panzerarmee back once again to Aghayla. Just over a week later, Stirling was issued orders to shift his operations beyond Egypt and Cyrenaica, to the Tripoli area. Montgomery was about to go in for the kill.

B Squadron hadn't yet finished its course. Many, like Thesiger, hadn't done their parachute jumps. Stirling knew the squadron was hardly ready, but he felt that they could finalize their training in the field.

They left Kabrit on 20 November in forty jeeps and a dozen three-tonners, led by Stirling. Their destination was Bir Zaltin, a hundred and fifty miles south of Aghayla, where they would rendezvous with Mayne. This time there was to be no sixteen-hundred-mile detour through Kufra. Stirling's convoy drove along the coast-road from Alexandria, passing through the debris of the great battle that had just been fought. The battlefield was strewn with hundreds of wrecked tanks, dismembered guns and the burned-out skeletons of soft-skinned vehicles and aircraft. For days they passed Montgomery's columns moving up to the front – trucks full of infantry, Sherman tanks on transporters, artillery batteries. There was an exhilarating sense of purpose in the air.

The journey, through Tobruk and along the foot of the Jebel Akhdar to Benghazi, was like a fast rerun of SAS history. At Ajadabiyya the convoy left the road and crossed desert flats of sand and gravel without a single tree or clump of grass. The first historic meeting of A and B Squadrons took place at Bir Zaltin on 29 November. 'A Squadron had a quiet self-confidence that was impressive,' Wilfred Thesiger wrote. 'In the past year these men had mastered the desert and learned to use its vast emptiness as their hideout. Many of them had grown up in towns; few of them had been out of England before the war. Yet now they were equally at home among the giant dunes of the Sand Sea or on the limitless gravel flats of the Hammad.'[3]

Mayne's men had made themselves useful by gouging hollows out of the chalky overhangs to hide the vehicles. That evening campfires flickered at the foot of the cliffs. After bully-beef stew, bottles of beer were passed around. Soon, the men were singing 'Lili Marlene'.

Stirling assembled the officers for an O Group. His orders from Shan Hackett were to keep up pressure on a four-hundred-mile stretch of road between Aghayla and Tripoli. The eastern section, from Aghayla to Bouerat, was assigned to A Squadron, probably because the area was already familiar to Mayne. B Squadron was given the more populated, cultivated area between Bouerat and Tripoli. The operation was planned to support Montgomery's next offensive on 13 December.

Each squadron would supply eight patrols. Each patrol would take a forty-mile sector and launch at least three strikes a week. The aim was to make it so hot for Axis motor-transport at night that it would revert to moving by day, presenting clear targets for RAF air-power.

The squadrons split up three days later. Stirling travelled with B Squadron, whose forward operating base would be at Bir Fascia, a Roman cistern forty miles south of Bouerat. It was a four-hundred-mile journey across terrain so bad that it was marked on maps as 'impassable'. Fortunately Stirling had brought with him navigator Mike Sadler, now promoted to lieutenant. Thesiger, who had travelled thousands of miles by camel with Arabs in the Sudan, was highly impressed with Sadler's performance. '[He had] an uncanny aptitude for keeping his direction by night,' he recalled, 'even over ground strewn with rocks, cut up by steep-sided wadis or interspersed with areas of soft sand.'⁴ They arrived at Bir Fascia just as Monty's offensive was kicking off.

Apart from Carol Mather, who had chosen to give up his staff assignment for the new operation, Gordon Alston, the ex-ME Commando Gunner, and François Martin of the Free French, most of the officers were new. These included Thesiger, Major Peter Oldfield, Royal Armoured Corps, Captain the Hon. Pat Hore-Ruthven, Captain P. S. Morris-Keating and Lt. Andrew Hough, all of the Rifle Brigade, Lt. John O'Sullivan, Kings Royal Rifle Corps and Lt. P. J. Maloney, Royal Warwicks. Among the enlisted men there were a few seasoned hands, notably Reg Seekings and Ted Badger, but most were inexperienced, 'good chaps,' said Mather, 'but clueless about the desert.'⁵

Stirling called the officers, allocated their sectors, and showed them air-photographs. 'Right,' he said finally. 'You'd better be off now.'⁶ He intended to go out with Thesiger and Alston's patrol that night for a last bash at the enemy before heading back to Cairo and leaving the squadron with Street. Before he left, Mather buttonholed him about supplies. He pointed out that while they had been ordered to stay in the field for a month, they had rations for only ten days. ' "Oh," replied David rather vaguely,' Mather recalled, ' "you'll just have to live off your fingernails. Forage around and see what you can pick up from the Italian settlements. They're bound to have hams and that kind of thing." ' [7] It gradually began to dawn on Mather that this op was 'a one-way ticket with no return'. [8]

42. They had become invisible

Mather's intuition proved correct. When Stirling came back from Cairo on 7 January, B Squadron had ceased to exist. Of the original officers, all but Thesiger, Alston and Martin had been captured or killed.

Mather's crew had tried motoring through a town with Stirling-like nonchalance, but were instantly identified by Italian colonial *carabinieri*. The Italians followed them to their lying-up place in a cave, where they had attracted a large crowd of local Arabs. Mather and his team fought a gun-battle with their pursuers, then bugged out into the night. They were eventually tracked down, surrounded and captured. The Italians stood them against a wall ready to shoot them, but the execution was called off at the last minute. They were sent to Italy by submarine.

Reg Seekings had gone out with Pat Hore-Ruthven's patrol, and was reported missing. The day Mather was captured, his jeeps took on six Axis vehicles including two tanks. They ran into heavy fire. Hore-Ruthven's right arm was shattered by a 20mm round. Seekings carried him to cover. He was losing blood fast, and Seekings knew he couldn't move him any further. He left him, and hopped on a jeep with the rest of the group. After eluding the enemy for days, they were finally picked up by a patrol of the King's Dragoon Guards on 5 January.

Vivian Street had initially gone into action with the Hore-Ruthven–Seekings patrol, and had enjoyed some success in planting Lewes bombs on twenty Italian lorries. After being spotted and chased by Italian troops later, though, his party headed back to the operating base at Bir Fascia and drove into a squadron of Axis armoured cars. Pulling out hastily, they laid up in a wadi. They were spotted by passing Arabs, who informed the Italians. The enemy encircled them. 'Through my mind flashed the picture of five Englishmen fighting to the death against impossible odds,' Street wrote later, '. . . but a couple of hand-grenades landing near us soon banished these mock heroics, and with the enemy only twenty yards away we were forced to accept the inevitable, and held up our hands in surrender.'[1]

Thesiger and Alston had narrowly evaded capture. For more than a week they went out night after night, shooting up convoys, mining the road, raking camps with furious Vickers fire. Unlike Mather's and Street's groups, they were never challenged, and Thesiger sometimes had the eerie sense that they had become invisible. He began to feel that the spell couldn't hold. 'It seemed inevitable that sooner or later a sentry would identify us,' he wrote, 'and fire a burst into our car. Even if he missed Alston and myself the land mines in the car would probably go up.'[2]

Hiding out near Bir Fascia, they learned on the wireless that the Allied offensive had succeeded. The Eighth Army was advancing towards Sirte. Two days before Christmas, though, while Alston was away getting water, Thesiger had a scare when a section of German armoured cars arrived suddenly and began poking around the area. He spent hours lying in a pit, camouflaged under a blanket, afraid that they'd winkle out the wireless jeep in the bushes nearby. Though the cars rumbled to within a hundred yards of his hiding place, they never found him or the jeep. Alston returned in the afternoon, having heard gunshots, believing that Thesiger had been taken out. It transpired that the shots had been for François Martin, who turned up later. Martin's jeeps had been chased by the same armoured cars, and had only just managed to outrun them.

43. 'Mistakenly overconfident about our security'

Stirling put the loss of B Squadron down to the inexperience of the men, and the more densely populated nature of the country. He felt, though, that the Regiment had achieved its task. 'We certainly succeeded in stopping enemy transport by night for a considerable period,' his official report ran.

Thesiger, Alston and Martin linked up with him at Bir Guedaffia on 12 January. Stirling was looking frail and exhausted, and was suffering badly from frequent migraines and desert sores. Johnny Cooper and Mike Sadler were with him. So was Lt. Bill Mac-Dermott, the Irish Gunner who had lost Jimmy Storie. Stirling's section was accompanied by another A Squadron group under twenty-seven-year-old Lt. Harry Poat, Kings Own Scottish Borderers, an impressive and professional-looking officer who was in fact an ex-tomato-grower from Guernsey. Augustin Jourdan, the sole French survivor of the Derna–Mertuba raid back in June, was also there with most of the Free French detachment.

Montgomery's attack on Tripoli and into Tunisia was due to start in three days. Stirling knew the SAS campaign in the desert was winding down. Although B Squadron hadn't achieved much, Mayne's A Squadron had reduced Axis road-traffic to almost nothing, and had suffered few casualties. It was already back at Kabrit.

Stirling's last scheme in North Africa had four aspects. Poat's section would loop round Tripoli and cause mayhem among the retreating Axis forces as the Eighth Army advanced. Jourdan's group would leapfrog forward into Tunisia and harass communications in the Gabès Gap, the bottleneck created where the Tunisian salt-flats, the Shott al-Jarid, approached the sea. Stirling's party would recce the Mareth Line, a defensive wall built years earlier by the French. They would find out if Rommel was preparing to make a stand there, and if there was a way round. Either Sadler or Cooper would then be sent back as guide for Montgomery's spearhead, 7 Armoured Division. Once in Tunisia, Stirling's orders were to operate under the command of the GOC First Army, Lt. General Kenneth Anderson, in the Gabès–Sousse area.

As commanding officer, there was no necessity for Stirling to make this trip himself. He said later that he wanted to meet up with his brother, Bill, currently commanding 2 SAS Regiment, attached to the advancing Anglo-American forces. His aim, he said, was to discuss with Bill his ideas for creating a third Regiment, and expanding the SAS to brigade status.

Stirling could easily have flown to Algiers. In any case, if his priority was the future of the SAS he would have done better to stay in Cairo. A British officer, Colonel Anthony Head, of Combined Operations, was already on his way there to discuss Eisenhower's request that 1 SAS be sent back to Britain to train for other theatres. Stirling missed Head by four days. His real object in heading the Gabès op seems to have been purely romantic. He wanted to be part of the first Eighth Army unit to link up with the advancing First Army, to be *there* at a moment in history that would never be forgotten.

The forward operating base for the Tunisian op would be Bir Soltan, near Kasr Ghilan oasis on the edge of the vast sand-sea known as the Great Eastern Erg. His party and Jourdan's set off separately on 14 January, having agreed to rally there in about a week. The first part of the drive, across the Hammadat al-Hamra to Ghadames on the Algerian frontier, was a breeze. It was a flat serir of hard-packed sand and fine gravel, where the jeeps could race along at fifty miles an hour. For the first time the SAS was not under threat from enemy aircraft – the only planes they saw were USAF Lightnings. From Ghadames the patrol headed north, along the rim of the Great Eastern Erg, where *mish-mish* and interlocking fish-scale dunes reduced the going to only a few miles a day. They made Bir Soltan eight days later.

The Eighth Army was advancing fast and Stirling didn't want to be overtaken. When Jourdan's group came in he sent them off immediately in eleven vehicles, with orders to pass through the Gabès Gap and blow the Sfax–Gabes railway line. Jourdan was to avoid hitting opportunity targets in the Gap itself until later. The area was thick with enemy troops, and if the French stirred things up prematurely it would make the situation sticky for Stirling's own party.

Jourdan's convoy vanished into the darkness. Martin's section of two trucks followed on as a rearguard. Stirling's group consisted of five jeeps and fourteen men, among them Cooper, Sadler, MacDermott, Reg Redington DCM, an ex-Gunner from Croydon, Charlie Backhouse, ex-Cameron Highlanders, Signaller Ginger Tatton and Sgt. Freddie Taxis, an Arabic-speaking Free Frenchman. They left twelve hours after Jourdan's group, heading for the Mareth Line. Stirling had intended to take Thesiger and Alston with him, but changed his mind when one of his jeeps broke down and he had to exchange it for Thesiger's. Instead, he left them at the base with instructions to await reinforcements.

Stirling's team worked its way around the Mareth Line and drove the same day towards the Shott al-Jarid salt-flats. His orders from Shan Hackett had been to drive across the Shott, outflanking the Gabès Gap. As Reg Seekings was later to prove, the salt-flats could be crossed by motor-vehicle, but only by sticking to known camel-tracks. 'We hit the salt marsh,' Cooper recalled, 'and the first jeep got stuck, so we had to unload it and roll it out. Obviously we weren't going to be able to get across the Shott. Dawn was coming, so David said, "Right, we're going to bluff it" . . . we motored onto the main tarmac road, and went through the Gabès Gap.'[1]

Along the sides of the road the personnel of two Axis armoured divisions were just getting up after a night's bivouac. Stirling told the others not to make eye-contact with them. They should stare straight ahead and pretend the enemy weren't there. They sped along with their accelerators stuck to the floor. Cooper recalled, though, that some of the Germans did look at them curiously. 'Somebody must have recognized us,' he said, 'I mean we had [five] jeeps . . . with all our equipment which [was] so different to theirs . . . anyway, we motored through and nobody challenged us.'[2] Stirling claimed later that they had been identified by an enemy spotter-plane going through the Gap, but no one else remembered seeing it.

For an hour they mixed with Axis convoys moving along the road. After getting clear they turned off into open country, trying to remain halfway between the edge of the Shott and the sea. The area felt foreign after the open Sahara they'd got used to. It was speckled with farms, orchards and patches of cultivation. A crust of low hills about ten miles away glistened quicksilver grey in the sun. They were shattered after their almost non-stop drive from Bir Soltan, and needed to find a lying-up place.

Their aim was to get as far away from the road as possible, but to Sadler's dismay they hit another track that cut through the hills. An hour later they came to a narrow ravine on the left. Stirling thought it looked promising, and gave the order to follow it. It led them to a series of narrow feeder-wadis, where they separated the vehicles and cammed up.

Stirling sent Sadler and Cooper up a ridge nearby to watch for any reaction. Lying sprawled out on the top, they could see the coast-road some miles away across country. Hundreds of Axis vehicles were still moving along it – tiny black shapes like a parade of soldier ants. At about noon they spied two lorries following the track into the hills. The lorries halted below them and Axis troops jumped out. They were wearing blue uniforms of a kind they hadn't seen before, and Cooper couldn't tell if they were Germans or Italians.

Sadler said later that they had finally agreed the troops were Italian. Neither he nor Cooper was worried, though. They thought the enemy had stopped for a rest. Instead of waiting to see if the blue-clad soldiers got back in the trucks and drove off, they left the position. 'I'm sure our judgement was not at its best,' said Sadler, 'we were mistakenly overconfident . . . about our security . . .'[3]

They slithered down the ridge and reported the sighting to Stirling, who didn't renew the watch. Neither did he post sentries. They had covered their tracks carefully, and the jeeps were well camouflaged. The SAS-men rolled out their sleeping-bags. Stirling and MacDermott slept under an overhang near the wireless truck. Stirling's driver, Reg Redington, was already asleep nearby with his boots off and his .45 Smith & Wesson by his head. Cooper, Sadler and Taxis went to doss down at the mouth of the wadi, in front of a camouflaged jeep.

Since the time Stirling and Brough had stumbled over the sleeping sentries at Sirte, Stirling had been lucky on operations. He had acquired an unconscious sense of immunity, akin to Thesiger's feeling when he drove into an enemy camp that the patrol was somehow 'invisible'. Thesiger himself had suspected that his luck would not hold, but Stirling believed that he would continue to get away with it – if he could swan around Italian-occupied Benghazi with a towel around his neck, he could do anything.

He might have taken note of what had happened to B Squadron, and realized that in Tunisia the game was a little different from Cyrenaica and the hyper-arid Libyan desert. Scooting through the Gabès Gap in broad daylight had been risky. It wasn't like passing a convoy at night on the Via Balbia, where the SAS always had the option of vanishing into the Sahara's vastness.

There was also something Stirling didn't know. He had in-structed Jourdan's group to stay quiet as mice until they hit the Sfax–Gabès railway, but the French patrols had had two contacts with the enemy the previous day. Martin's section of two trucks had been chased by Axis armoured cars to Jebel Tebaga, the same area where Stirling's party now lay. One of Martin's trucks had exploded when the bombs it was carrying were hit. Though Martin and his driver had escaped, the three French SAS-men in the truck, Sgts. Castagner and Vacclui, and Cpl. Vaillant, were believed dead. Now, Jourdan's group was lying up not far away, planning to blow the railway that night, but a company of Luftwaffe troops had been assigned to hunt them down. The men in the blue uniforms Cooper and Sadler had seen from the ridge belonged to that company.

In mid-afternoon, Sadler was awoken by the crunch of footsteps. Bleary-eyed, he glanced up from his sleeping-bag and almost jumped out of his skin. Two German troopers were standing over him with Schmeisser sub-machine guns. His weapon was hidden under the jeep's cam-net, and he knew there was nothing he could do. He saw Cooper peering out from his sleeping-bag, looking worried. To their amazement, though, the Germans motioned to them to stay quiet, and continued down the wadi. The moment they were out of sight, Sadler, Cooper and Taxis whipped out of their bags and ran like madmen up the wadi until it petered out, then clambered up into a narrow defile beyond. 'It was a hard run up a hillside,' Sadler said, 'but luckily we managed to get into a little gully among some camel scrub. By now we were absolutely knackered, so we just lay there.'⁴

Cooper remembered seeing Stirling haring off in the opposite direction, but this seems unlikely. The way Stirling recalled it, he and MacDermott had no chance of escape. He was woken up by a yell of '*Raus! Raus!*' and found himself looking down the barrel of a Luger held by a short, thickset German soldier. He and MacDermott put their hands up. They were marched down the wadi with their ten men. At the bottom, they saw Luftwaffe troops massed in company strength.

Stirling remained confident that he would escape, and was aware that the most opportune time was always shortly after capture. That night, at a moment he judged his captors' attention had lapsed, he let out a piercing yell and both he and MacDermott poled off into the darkness. Stirling covered about ten miles, but once again his overconfidence betrayed him. He wasted three hours surveying an airfield for a possible future SAS strike. 'I was a bloody fool,' he commented later. 'I thought I was going to make it back you see.'⁵ The next day, lying up in some acacia scrub, he was seen by an Arab who offered to give him food and water. The Arab led him straight into the arms of the Italians. The story went round later that the CO, 1 SAS, had been sold out for eleven pounds of tea.

Only three months earlier, David Stirling had been flying high. At twenty-seven he had become the founder and commanding officer of a totally new type of Special Service unit. He had been on the verge of expanding it into a brigade – perhaps even of becoming the army's youngest brigadier. It had been a long, hard haul from the clubs and cabarets. Now, his war was over. He would never see active service again.

In two years, Stirling's SAS, at one time down to seventeen men, had destroyed three hundred and twenty Axis aircraft, exercising an influence on the campaign out of all proportion to its size. Between September 1942 and January 1943 it had executed no fewer than forty-three successful raids on Axis lines of communication. The ultimate measure of Stirling's achievement, though, can be gauged from the Desert Fox himself. On 2 February Rommel wrote his wife, Lucy: 'During January, a number of our AA gunners [sic] succeeded in surprising a British column . . . and captured the commander of 1 SAS Regiment, Lt.Col. David Stirling . . . Thus the British lost the very able and adaptable commander of the desert group which had caused us more damage than any other British unit of equal size.'[6]

PART TWO

Europe 1943–5

44. 'It's a bad one this time'

When 16 Panzer Division's counter-attack on Termoli reached fever pitch, Paddy Mayne was shooting billiards in an abandoned palazzo with Bill Fraser, Pat Riley and Phil Gunn, his new medical officer. It was 5 October 1943, and David Stirling had been in the bag eight months.

Termoli was a small port on Italy's Adriatic coast. Set on a promontory, sealed in on three sides by the sea, it was a town of ornate houses tightly packed around a central square, dominated by a cathedral and a medieval castle. Along the sea-front were the remnants of ancient walls that had withstood the Turkish fleet a thousand years earlier. Mayne's squadron had first been billeted in the draughty cells and cloisters of a deserted monastery overlooking the harbour but he had moved his officers to a luxurious palazzo across the road: deep shagpile carpets, comfortable beds, a gramophone – and a billiard table.

From first light, when half a dozen tanks had rumbled towards the Eighth Army's defensive ring north of the town, British units had been pulling back. 6 Royal West Kents and 5 Buffs had retreated in panic, and were digging in along the Termoli–Larino highway. 8 Argyll & Sutherland Highlanders had lost the church and factory they had been ordered to hold at all costs. Men of 56 Recce Regiment had abandoned their brand new armoured cars and Bren-gun carriers. The infantry were so shell-shocked that the CO of 1 Special Service Brigade, John Durnford-Slater, had threatened to have officers and men stood against a wall and shot. One of the few units to hold its ground, 40 (Royal Marine) Commando, had been decimated by 88mm anti-tank shells. The olive grove they had occupied above the town was littered with their mangled dead.

In Termoli, Italian civilians, emboldened by the attack, started dropping grenades and taking pot-shots at British soldiers from their windows. Durnford-Slater called the entire male population together in the piazza and promised mass executions unless these irritations ceased. At 1330 hours, an 88mm round mashed Brigade HQ, killing a staff captain.

While panic reigned and shells were crumping into the streets outside the palazzo, Mayne chalked his cue with Francis Drake-like insouciance. 'He just carried on with the game,' Pat Riley recalled. 'I thought to myself, "Well, if you can do it, chum, I'll do it with you." And we did. We finished the game, and then we went out to get things sorted.'[1]

Mayne ordered every available man – including cooks, bottle-washers, clerks – up to the town cemetery where the eye of the assault was focused. Five captured German trucks were lined up opposite the monastery garden to shift 'Paddy's Boys' to the front. Bill Fraser, commanding No.1 Troop, stopped to give instructions to one of his section commanders, Lt. Johnny Wiseman, a short, stocky, ex-employee of an optical company and former Yeomanry trooper, commissioned in the Duke of Cornwall's Light Infantry. Wiseman's section-sergeant, Reg Seekings, got the men to their feet and ordered them to hop on to the first lorry. Sgt. Bill McNinch, Royal Armoured Corps, an ex-bank manager highly popular in the troop, was already injured in the foot, but had volunteered to drive. He leaned out of the cab and waved as the men moved up. Seekings found the truck already occupied by a section of No.2 Troop. A moment later, Wiseman arrived and told them to get the hell out of it. His own boys piled in. Wiseman jumped into the cab beside McNinch, who started the engine. In the back, Seekings slapped the tailboard shut. A runner from Mayne shouted to Wiseman, who leaned out of the window to talk to him. An Italian family, three or four girls, a twelve-year-old boy, a woman and an old man, who lived across the street, had turned out to watch from their doorway.

Pat Riley, now a lieutenant, was hurrying back towards the palazzo with his batman, who had just told him that Mayne wanted a word. Suddenly, the whole street seemed to shudder, to come apart in rubble and smoke. 'The next thing I knew I was halfway down the street,' Riley recalled, 'lying on my back, laughing like hell. It must have been [the] shock . . .'[2]

Riley never heard the 105mm shell strike, but Reg Seekings did. '[There was] a God Almighty crash and explosion,' he remembered, 'and [a shell] landed right, smack in the truck . . . It blew us to hell.'[3] The first lorry disintegrated. Steel scraps, glass shards, molten rubber shot skywards: blood, flesh, minced body parts spattered walls. Seekings grovelled in the gutter, drenched in blood and bits of other people's warm flesh. He couldn't believe the packet of foot-long, two-pound-apiece No. 76 Hawkins grenades he was carrying hadn't exploded. His was the only pack that hadn't. The runner Wiseman was talking to was spliffed sixty yards through a second-floor window. Only his torso was found. Another man, Sgt. Jock Finlay, Royal Artillery, an ex-auctioneer, was decapitated instantly by spiralling steel, and his head flung into a tangled clump of orange-trees nearby.

Wiseman lolled out of the cab dazed, not a scratch on him. Men staggered about moaning in a pea-soup of dust and smoke. Wiseman's driver, McNinch, still sat at the wheel with bug eyes and a big grin on his face. He was stone dead. A length of tubing had pierced the back of the cab and skewered him right through the abdomen.

Seekings staggered up and blinked red-eyed at a scene like the Devil's kitchen. Bits of human tissue, flayed skin, burned organs, charred hands and feet, crisped intestines, were strewn about the street, festooned from telegraph wires, roofs, the branches of trees. Trucks and walls were greased in blood. Seekings inhaled cordite fumes and the stink of roasted flesh. He saw Sgt. Jock Henderson, Riley's section sergeant, hanging upside down, his chest slit open like a watermelon, his arm hanging off. His ribcage had been sliced open. Seekings could see his lungs pumping and his heart beating. He still had his Tommy-gun clamped across his chest. 'Reg, take the gun off,' Henderson croaked. 'It's hurting me.' Seekings helped him down, and watched white-faced as the man pulled off his own severed arm. 'He said, "It's a bad one this time,"' Seekings recalled. 'I said, "You'll be all right" . . . I knew he wouldn't.'[4]

Henderson called for water. Seekings slithered across a mass of bloody pulp. It had a voice. 'Sergeant, can you get me a drink, please.' Calm as hell. The face had ceased to exist, but Seekings recognized the voice of L.Cpl. Charlie Grant. He gagged as Grant reached across, picked up his dismembered arm and dropped it to one side. For the second time, Seekings saw a man's heart and lungs working close up. He saw another of his section, Alex Skinner MM, Royal Engineers, whose body was crackling, on fire. 'It was the first time I'd seen a body burning,' he remembered, 'and I didn't realize how fast [it could] burn.' Skinner was already dead, but Seekings felt a compulsion to find water to put him out.

He was stepping over more cadavers when he saw the Italian boy from the family across the street, lying on top. His guts were hanging out, swollen up like a pink balloon. To Seekings's horror, the boy suddenly leapt up and started scuttering round in a circle, shrieking. Seekings pulled his Colt .45, caught the boy, and shot him in the head. 'You couldn't let anybody suffer like that,' he said. Among the corpses was another mate, Pte. Titch Davison, Durham Light Infantry. He was also dead, lying on his back, barely recognizable – his nose and jaw had been shattered. When Seekings tried to lift his body out of the way, it fell to pieces. He knew Davison had lied about his age when he had joined up – he reckoned the kid was no more than seventeen.

Lt. Pete Davis, Queens Regiment, commanding No.2 Troop, saw one of the Italian girls sitting dazed in the ruins of her house, while all the rest of her family lay gutted around her in a heap. Looking up, he realized that a lump of flesh hanging from a wire was the scalp of Sgt. Chris O'Dowd, Irish Guards, an SAS veteran. Davis doubled up and hurled vomit.

Corporal David Danger, a bespectacled ex-Royal Signals wireless-op, had been sheltered from the blast by a doorway, and escaped with only a wedge of scrap stuck in his backside. The man next to him hadn't been so lucky – he was peppered with shrapnel in both legs. Bill Fraser had been tossed on top of Pte. Doug Montieth, Devonshire Regiment, by the shock of the explosion. Montieth's uniform was in tatters, but he was relieved to find the blood soaking him wasn't his. Fraser sat in the middle of the road, eyes focused on nowhere, blood globbing from his shoulder. Montieth was unscathed apart from concussion, despite the fact that he had been splattered against a wall so hard that his helmet had been riveted to his skull.

A few yards away Cpl. Spike Kerr sprawled out with his hands over his head, praying loudly to God. David Danger got up and hobbled over to the carnage. He found Pte. Graham Gilmour weaving around drunkenly with his hands across his brows, shrieking, 'My eyes! My eyes!' He had a gash in the head cascading gore, and one eyeball was dangling obscenely by the optic nerve. 'Am I blind?' Gilmour implored him. 'No, you'll be OK,' Danger said, putting his arm around him. Within minutes, Gilmour had recovered himself enough to salute Johnny Wiseman and ask for permission to report to the medical post.

The squadron padre, Captain Robert Lunt, had arrived, and was slapping Spike Kerr's face, assuring him he wasn't going to die. Medical officer Captain Phil Gunn did what he could, concentrating only on those he thought had a chance of pulling through. The boys who had got off lightly dressed wounds for the others. Wiseman stalked dazedly around the casualties, trying to determine how many men he had left in his section. The answer wasn't encouraging. Only Seekings, Gilmour and one other man were still standing. Gilmour was badly injured, and according to Seekings, the third man never spoke to anyone again. Two days later he was found smashing his head against a brick wall, and had to be RTU'd.

Wiseman went off to report to Mayne, whom he found in the palazzo with Squadron Sergeant-Major Johnny Rose. Mayne said Rose had apprised him of 'one or two' casualties. Wiseman answered that he no longer had a section to command. Eighteen had been killed or mortally wounded – the most devastating single mortality the SAS had ever suffered. Although no one mentioned it at the time, most of the casualties may have been caused not by the shell – probably a stray shot – but by the armed Hawkins grenades many of the men were carrying – an embarrassing home goal. Mayne made no comment, but his eyes went deathly cold. He told Wiseman calmly to attach the survivors to his own HQ Troop and get up to the cemetery right away. The enemy was about to break through.

45. 'Will you shoot my brother?'

Termoli wasn't of much strategic importance on its own, but it lay only two miles north of the Biforno river-mouth, and the river was a natural defensive line. Once dug in there, the Germans would be hard to budge.

The Allies had landed on Sicily on 12 July and on the Italian mainland on 9 September, and now the British Eighth and US Fifth armies were steamrolling north, against savage opposition from Field Marshal Albert Kesselring's forces. Although the Italians had surrendered and joined the Allies, and Mussolini had been arrested, Hitler had ordered Kesselring to sell every inch of Italian soil dearly. The Allied planners decided that a *coup de main* seaborne attack by commandos on Termoli would turn the German flank, and render a defence of the Biforno untenable. As it turned out, the assault had taken the Germans completely by surprise.

Surprise was about the only factor in the recipe Stirling would have approved. The rest was Layforce redux – the SAS had been used as shock-troops in exactly the way he and Lewes had deplored. Gone were the three- and four-man groups, the stealth attacks – even the jeeps. Mayne's boys, now designated 1 Special Raiding Squadron (SAS), still wore the sand-coloured beret, para wings and flaming sword badge, but they were part of a thousand-strong Special Service Brigade that included 3 Commando and 40 (Royal Marine) Commando. 1 SRS, numbering two hundred and seven men, had jumped ashore from landing-craft at a beach-head north-west of Termoli in the early hours of 3 October.

It was a dismal night, with a swell on the Adriatic and chiselling rain. At half past three in the morning the thirty-nine-foot LCI (Landing Craft Infantry) carrying the squadron had snagged on a sandbank sixty feet off shore. Bill Fraser judged the water shallow enough to wade through. He jumped into the sea and promptly vanished beneath it. As he was hauled back on board gasping for air, smaller LCA (Landing Craft Assault) were dollied up to ferry the men the final distance. Mayne supervised the transfer with customary coolness.

The Brigade's task was to capture Termoli, but the assault on the town was down to the commandos. Mayne's job was to secure two bridges on the main road, Highway 16, and to link up with elements of the British 11 Infantry Brigade, spearheading 78 Division, advancing from the south. For Mayne it brought back memories of his first action – 11 Commando's assault on the Litani two years earlier.

On shore there was chaos as SRS-men mingled with commandos, rallied by the Brigade Major, Brian Franks, Middlesex Yeomanry, the ex-manager of London's Hyde Park Hotel. It was still drizzling and the ground beyond the beach was slippery under their rubber-soled boots.

At five thirty that morning, B Section of No. 3 Troop 1 SRS, under twenty-two-year-old Lt. John Tonkin, Royal Northumberland Fusiliers, made first contact with the enemy. Advancing to a bridge on the road, they bagged three German prisoners, then spotted a slow-moving convoy of five enemy trucks. Tonkin's three-inch-mortar team lobbed a salvo of bombs at the convoy. The first truck belched flame; glass and scrap-metal blew. Germans staggered out coughing smoke and Tonkin's Bren-gunners sickled them down – an officer was killed, another injured. Germans scattered and made off. Three of them dropped their rifles and reached for the sky. As Tonkin's section regrouped, his flankers spied a German platoon hovering in the shadows. The SRS Bren-gunners went to ground and dusted the enemy with .303 rounds so thickly that they broke and ran, carrying the wounded with them.

The rain had stopped, and now the blackness was scored with strands of blurry light. Tonkin's men tabbed it into a long valley, where they saw dark figures lining the ridges above them. For a moment the SRS-men thought they had encountered 11 Brigade. Then the men on the heights rattled fire at them. A field-gun throbbed. Shells coughed and thumped. Rounds riffed around them from behind, and Tonkin realized they had been boxed. They had walked into a trap rigged by battle-hardened German troops of 1 Parachute Division – veterans of the drop on Crete. 'Every man for himself!' Tonkin screeched.

There was no easy way out of the box. L. Cpl. Joe Fassam, Royal Artillery, hurtled out of the ditch he had been sheltering in, searing away with his Tommy-gun. Enemy fire whacked him down. Six of his mates made use of the diversion to break out of the valley, lugging with them the three prisoners they had picked up earlier. Two lay in the bush until the shooting died down. Tonkin himself leopard-crawled through the undergrowth right into the muzzle of a German paratrooper's Schmeisser. He and twenty-two of his men were captured.

Captain Bob Melot, now recovered from his grenade wounds at Benghazi, was with a group from Captain Ted Lepine's A Section, moving up fast towards Tonkin's position. On the way they slammed into a group of German paratroopers who had gone to ground in an abandoned farm. There was a violent contact. Melot got walloped in the chest by a 9mm Luger round, while the section staff-sergeant, Fred 'Nobby' Clarke, Royal Engineers, was sent crashing by a plug of shrapnel in the skull.

Clarke got up with blood guttering down his face and continued to urge the men forward. Sgt. Bob 'Buttercup' Goldsmith, Royal Sussex Regiment, hauled Melot away. Pte. Eddie Ralphs, South Lancashire Regiment, hefted his Bren across exposed ground and rolled into cover. He splayed the bipod, lifted the stock to his shoulder. He got a German in the sights, pinched metal, belted out a double-tap. Cartridge cases flew. The enemy soldier dropped.

Ralphs lined up on another. While Goldsmith lugged Melot to safety, Ralphs drilled at least nine Germans, killing four and wounding the others.

The A Section men skirmished forward, rousting the Germans from the farm, taking nine prisoners. By 0800 hours they had closed on the bridge Tonkin had occupied earlier, but found no sign of Tonkin's men apart from scattered equipment. Here, they met up with some of Bill Fraser's No.1 Troop, who had reached the second bridge too late – the enemy had already blown it. This hadn't pleased the hard-nosed Reg Seekings, who felt the Intelligence boys should have known about it: they had been boasting about the accuracy of their information. Earlier, trawling through a slime-filled ditch at the side of Highway 16, with Johnny Wiseman's section, Seekings had sighted a German tracked motor-cycle dragging a 105mm recoil-less field-gun. Seekings remembered that about twenty Germans were hanging on to the vehicle and trailer. His section opened up suddenly, killing all but two. The survivors ran a little way, then turned to fight. Wiseman's men cut one down. As the other brought his weapon up, Seekings plugged him.

Around the bend Wiseman's section came up against another stubborn company of German paras in a farmhouse. They were well dug in, and Wiseman guessed it was going to be a tough nut to crack. He sent a wireless message to Mayne requesting the three-inch mortar detachment commanded by Captain Alec Muirhead, a tall, slim officer with a laid-back manner, commonly referred to as 'Bertie Wooster'. By the time Muirhead's 'tubes' arrived, Reg Seekings had shimmied to within sixty yards of the buildings carrying a wireless set, as forward fire-controller. Once the tubes were assembled, Seekings stood up and told Muirhead over the net, 'Aim on me plus twenty-five and you'll be spot on.' Seconds later a flight of mortar bombs hoiked over Seekings's head and ramped into the farm. White smoke puffed, fire crackled, masonry and fractured tiles flew. Volley after volley followed, racking the buildings. When the Germans finally white-flagged, almost every one of them was carrying multiple shrapnel-wounds.

These Jerry paras didn't surrender unless they were all dead or wounded, Seekings observed. He recalled that the prisoners were wearing cuff-bands commemorating the Crete operation, of which they seemed immensely proud.

A gigantic major, uniform limp with blood, pointed to a lieutenant prone on a stretcher. The man was dying in torment, with his intestines flopping out. 'Will you shoot my brother?' the major asked Wiseman, who spoke some German. Wiseman turned to Sgt. Fred 'Chalky' White, Loyal Regiment, an ex-professional footballer who had joined L Detachment from the Middle East Commando the previous year.

'Leave it to me,' White said.

The sergeant put a .45 calibre Smith & Wesson round through the lieutenant's head at hard contact range. 'The major just blinked,' Seekings recalled.

Wiseman reported the bag to Mayne, with HQ Troop at a road-junction half a mile away. Mayne told Wiseman to withdraw and bring his prisoners back to the schoolhouse in Termoli. The commandos had taken the town with a hundred German dead and a hundred and fifty captured. They had advanced so quickly, the German battle-group occupying the port hadn't even had time to destroy its secret documents. 'You've done your job,' Mayne said. 'We've got the town and we're holding it.'

The commandos had thrown a hard perimeter around Termoli, and before sunset most of Mayne's troops had been relieved by the Lancashire Fusiliers, scouting ahead of 11 Brigade, the land-based half of 78 Division. The other half – 36 Infantry Brigade – was about to be landed by sea, and would take over the defence of the town next morning. The SRS retired to the monastery on the waterfront. Only one section of No. 2 Troop, under Lt. Pete Davis, remained out: Davis had lost wireless comms with Mayne and hadn't received the order to withdraw.

The cost of the day's fighting for the squadron had been one dead, three wounded, and twenty-three missing. The SRS had taken out twenty-three enemy killed, seventeen wounded, and thirty-nine captured.

This was the fourth action Mayne's SRS had carried out since the invasion of Italy had kicked off three months earlier. On 10 July they had landed at Capo Murro de Porco, on Sicily's eastern coast, with orders to take and destroy a coastal battery in support of Lt. General Dempsey's 13 Corps landing. The Murro de Porco action, described later by Dempsey as 'a brilliant operation, brilliantly planned and brilliantly carried out', had dispelled any doubts about Paddy Mayne's qualities of leadership.

In seventeen hours, the SRS boys had silenced not one but three batteries, captured four hundred and fifty prisoners, and taken out more than two hundred Italian soldiers. The following day the squadron was landed on a beach at the nearby town of Augusta – the first opposed daylight landing of the war. They captured the town, drove the Italians out and secured vast quantities of stores and equipment. For these two actions, Mayne was awarded his second DSO. 'It was Major Mayne's courage, determination, and superb leadership,' his citation ran, 'which proved the key to success.'[1] 'Have you heard they have given me a bar to my DSO?' Mayne wrote home. 'Still managing to bluff them.'[2] Both Captain Harry Poat and Lt. Johnny Wiseman won the MC, and Reg Seekings the DCM.

In a third landing, at Bagnara, on the 'Toe of Italy', on 4 September, the SRS took the town and secured a bridgehead for the advance of the Eighth Army.

Mayne was perfectly aware that, in Stirling's eyes, these ops would have amounted to a misuse of the unit. Stirling commented years later that SRS actions in Italy weren't strictly SAS, but admitted that Mayne had handled them brilliantly. The formation of the Special Raiding Section (SAS) was a compromise Mayne had reached with GHQ ME back in March. Without it, 1 SAS might already have been history.

46. 'Paddy Mayne was the man'

Stirling was officially confirmed missing in action on St Valentine's Day, 1943. Long before then, Johnny Cooper, Mike Sadler and Freddie Taxis had become the first Eighth Army troops to link up with the First Army, but hardly in the glorious way Stirling had imagined. Filthy, bearded and dishevelled after their three-day march from the Tebagu hills, they were treated by the Americans as spies. 'They just would not believe we'd come from the Eighth Army,' Cooper said. 'I don't even think half of them knew where the Eighth Army was, anyway.'[1]

Stirling's loss threw Kabrit into turmoil. It wasn't clear till then just how much of a one-man show the Regiment had been. Stirling's brilliance lay in his suppleness, his penchant for out-foxing the enemy on a blow-by-blow basis. His aversion to writing down orders, instructions and SOPs (Standard Operating Procedures) meant a hiatus in continuity – even the dispositions of SAS units were in his head. When Captain Harry Poat, the ex-Guernsey tomato-grower, turned up with his patrol at Kabrit that January, fresh from his Tripoli ops, nobody knew who he was.

Stirling had often been urged to nominate an understudy, but hadn't got round to it, because he'd never expected to be captured. George Jellicoe was theoretically second-in-command, but had been in Britain since the Sidi Haneish op, nursing an injured knee. He only got back in January, and was hardly up to scratch with the admin. In any case, despite his background, no one seemed to consider Jellicoe of sufficient calibre to take Stirling's place. 'David's capture is regarded as a great blow here,' wrote Peter Stirling to his mother, 'as there is literally no one of the same stature and prestige to replace him.'[2]

Stirling commented later that the 'fossilized shit' looked on his sudden removal as a heaven-sent opportunity to 'regularize' the SAS. They neglected to consider the fact, he said, that no ordinary officer could command the unit, nor use it effectively. To the rank-and-file, Paddy Mayne was the only man who could do it.

The army wasn't a democracy, but since the men had the option of RTU, their opinion mattered. 'Nobody ever thought of Jellicoe or anybody like that becoming CO of the SAS,' said Reg Seekings. 'It was Paddy Mayne. Paddy Mayne was the man . . .'[3]

Like many of the other 'Originals', though, Seekings doubted that Mayne had the social connections to swing it. 'We wondered if [Mayne] could weather the storm,' he said. To some it looked like curtains. Even Bob Bennett, whom Mayne considered one of the 'steadiest' of the Originals, believed the unit would be disbanded. Bennett agreed that Mayne was the man, but wasn't sure he'd make an effective CO without Stirling to keep an eye on him. Stirling himself maintained that Mayne, while inspired in the field, didn't have the sense of military politics necessary for overall command.

Lt. Pete Davis, Queens Regiment, like most new recruits, thought the SAS had been held together only by Stirling's personality, and that without him it would founder. Johnny Cooper had been as close to Stirling as any of the enlisted men. His assessment was that 1 SAS had reached the end of the road.

It may not have helped that, some time in January, Mayne got himself arrested in Cairo. The story was that, incensed by GHQ's refusal to allow him to fly back to Britain after the sudden death of his father, he 'went on the rampage', hunting for BBC correspondent Richard Dimbleby, intending to beat him up. In the course of his fruitless search, Mayne is supposed to have wrecked half a dozen restaurants and finally laid out a Provost Marshal and a squad of Redcaps on the steps of Shepheard's Hotel. He was arrested and thrown into the cells, but was released the following day when the Provost received a message from GHQ, stating that this officer was 'too valuable to be reduced to the ranks'.

The 'half-dozen restaurants' and the 'squad of Redcaps' story is undoubtedly an exaggeration. Another version is that Mayne had a disagreement with six large Australians – Stephen Hastings recalled that the incident happened much earlier, before Mayne's father died. If it did occur, it must have been before 24 January, because on this date Mayne led most of A Squadron to the Cedars, the Middle East Skiing School in the Lebanon, to retrain for mountain warfare in the Caucasus. While they were there, Major Vivian Street, commanding B Squadron, returned to Kabrit and was appointed acting Commanding Officer, 1 SAS Regiment.

After being captured on the coast-road operation in December, Street had been one of seven prisoners to miraculously escape from an Italian submarine after it had been depth-charged by a Royal Navy destroyer. He didn't retain command for long. Within three weeks it had been handed over to an outsider, Lt. Col. Henry 'Kid' Cator, Royal Scots Greys. It was Cator who presided over the partition of 1 SAS.

47. 'Those bloody fools back at HQ will one day tell me who I'm talking to'

For Mayne, Cator was hardly an ideal choice. Though he was famous for raising No.1 Palestinian Company of the Auxiliary Pioneer Corps – a unit in which Palestinian Jews and Arabs served side by side – his success was largely built on his social connections. Cator was the Queen's brother-in-law – a great asset when he was lobbying to convert his three hundred Palestinian labourers into 51 (Middle East) Commando. 'I had tea with the King and Queen,' he wrote, '. . . I had . . . a real heart-to-heart with the King about the Palestinians. He said he would see [Colonial Secretary] Lord Lloyd.'[1]

Cator, a friend and comrade of the late Geoffrey Keyes VC, who had kicked Mayne out of 11 Commando, didn't believe the Ulsterman was made of the 'right stuff' to command a regiment. Like almost everyone else, he also underestimated Mayne's ability to fight his corner. During a series of meetings with Col. Anthony Head of Combined Ops and the DMO in March, however, Mayne put forward an impressive case for retaining 1 SAS. He argued that it would be a mistake to disband a unit with such high morale – a morale that was partly the result of the distinct identity engendered by its unique training and ethos. The SAS were multi-skilled, para-trained, and capable as no other unit bar the LRDG of penetration for long periods behind enemy lines.

At the same time, Mayne knew there would have to be a compromise. The work of the SAS in North Africa was almost done. The focus of fighting in the near future would not, it was now admitted, be the Caucasus, but in the Mediterranean – the Balkans and Italy – the 'soft underbelly of Europe'. At the Casablanca Conference in January, Winston Churchill had agreed with US President Franklin D. Roosevelt that the invasion of northern Europe would not be ready for another year. Before then, the Allies would invade first Sicily, then mainland Italy. This action, the High Command correctly predicted, would topple Mussolini's regime, and divert Hitler's legions, which would be forced to occupy the country.

Seaborne ops were obviously the key to the invasion of Mediterranean Europe. With a dense local population to consider, there would be little scope for the type of deep-penetration raids the SAS had carried out hundreds of miles across uninhabited desert. It was agreed that for guerrilla methods to succeed, the country must either be sparsely inhabited or home to a sympathetic population. Even the unit's brief forays in Tripolitania and Tunisia had demonstrated this. Mayne was obliged to accept that if the SAS were to continue, it would have to revert to a commando role. He considered this a temporary measure. He never sold out Stirling's and Lewes's original concept, resisting pressure to rechristen the unit 'No.1 Commando'. He believed that when the time was ripe, 1 SAS Regiment would once more emerge as the British army's guerrilla force par excellence.

If Mayne had been hoping to gain command of the Regiment, though, he was disappointed. Instead, on 19 March, 1 SAS was split into two groups, 1 Special Raiding Squadron (SAS) under Mayne, and 1 Special Boat Section (SAS) under Jellicoe. While the SRS would be a commando unit, the SBS would retain the *folbot* role, and would absorb the Greek Sacred Squadron. The French SAS detachment was to be returned to national command, joining two existing French parachute battalions that would eventually become 3 and 4 SAS. Command of the twin SAS raiding units would be given to Henry Cator, who would remain at GHQ ME with the title Commander HQ Raiding Forces. Fortunately for Mayne – and possibly for the SAS – Cator would have only an administrative role. SAS units would come under the orders of the general officer commanding the theatre in which they were operating.

The bulk of SRS personnel would come from A Squadron, which returned to Kabrit from Lebanon in February. On their first day back, Mayne told the assembled squadron they were about to start a new and intensive retraining course. They would be divided into Nos. 1, 2 and 3 Troops, respectively under Bill Fraser, Harry Poat and Captain David Barnby, East Yorkshire Regiment. Instead of hand-picking personnel, Mayne reverted to the old commando system of choosing the officers and senior NCOs and letting them pick their own men.

Bob Melot, long since transferred to the SAS from G(R), was appointed Intelligence Officer. Bill Fraser was still in the desert, commanding the last SAS forays in Tunisia, harassing Rommel's lines of communication with mixed patrols of A Squadron, French and Greek detachments. When he returned on 20 April, he found that he had under his command most of the surviving Originals – Reg Seekings, Charlie Cattell, Bob Bennett, 'Lofty' Baker, Bob Lilley, Dave Kershaw, Jimmy Brough, Frank Rhodes, as well as post-Squatter men such as Ted Badger, Chris O'Dowd, Fred White and others. Johnny Rose was promoted Squadron Sergeant Major, and Pat Riley appointed commander of C Section, No.1 Troop, on his return from the Officer Cadet Training Unit on 27 April. No.1 Troop, a repository of all the skills and experience the SAS had acquired since its inception, was regarded as the elite. Nos. 2 and 3 Troops were made up of survivors of B Squadron, and new recruits.

Noticeably absent were Johnny Cooper and Mike Sadler – both of whom Stirling had commissioned in the field. Cooper, who had been joined by Reg Seekings at Constantine, Algeria, in

February, had found it hard to accept that Stirling would not be coming back. For days, he and Seekings tried to get permission to parachute into Italy and extract their CO from whatever camp he was in. The plan was scotched by HQ, and the pair of them did penance on a couple of missions with Popski's Private Army, a sabotage unit commanded by an Arabic-speaking white Russian, Vladimir Peniakoff. They admired Popski as a character, but weren't impressed by his team. Cooper was now on his way for officer-training at OCTU, and would miss the Italian ops. Mike Sadler was currently attached to 1 New Zealand Division as guide and navigator in Tunisia, a job that would ultimately land him in hospital with stress-related stomach ulcers.

The war in North Africa officially came to an end on 12 May. The following day, Lt. General Miles Dempsey, newly-appointed GOC 13 Corps, Eighth Army, visited the SRS boot-camp at Az-Zib ('The Penis') on the coast of northern Palestine. The camp – a few huts and a cinema surrounded by tents – stood on wasteland where a stream poured into the Mediterranean, near the village of Nahariyya. Dempsey, later to become the SRS's favourite general, told the squadron that they would be under his command for the forthcoming invasion of Sicily.

Dempsey got off on the wrong foot, though, when he talked down to the assembled unit in the camp cinema, as if they were green troops. Reg Seekings, for one, who had been on almost every major SAS operation since the beginning, was no more amused than he had been with Jock Lewes's 'yellow streak' speech. As he marched the men out in silence, he saw Mayne whispering in Dempsey's ear. The general suddenly stiffened and ordered Seekings to bring the 'gentlemen' back in again. Once they had sat down, he apologized. 'I've been giving you all that tripe . . .' he said, 'when you've had more D-Days than I'll ever have . . . Those bloody fools back at HQ will one day tell me who I'm talking to, and stop me making a bloody fool of myself.'[2]

Dempsey watched a night training demonstration and stayed the night. The squadron had been working all out for six weeks, following a commando-style course designed by Mayne himself.

One of its keynotes was that whatever a man's rank or experience, he would relearn basic military skills from lesson 1:01. 'Nothing was taken for granted,' said Lt. Derrick Harrison, Cheshire Regiment, commanding C section, No. 2 Troop. 'What can be learned can be forgotten, so we started from scratch . . . It was this thoroughness that accounted in great measure for the success of our . . . operations to come.'[3]

Twice-daily callisthenics sessions under the acerbic tongue of CSM Gus Glaze, Army Physical Training Corps, punctuated instruction in map-reading, compass navigation, field-craft, weapon-training, bayonet practice and shooting. The men stripped and assembled Lee-Enfield rifles, Thompsons and Bren-guns until they knew them better than their own faces.[4] In the new theatre there would be no jeeps or LRDG Fords to ferry them in, no mounted Vickers machine guns, no Sidi Haneish style blitzes with thousands of rounds of ammunition. The Bren light machine gun had to do the job of the Vickers, with a maximum of three hundred rounds, in ten magazines. At five hundred rounds a minute, the Bren had only about half the rate of fire of a Vickers K, but it was light and highly accurate. Mayne, a stickler for ammo-conservation, and a marksman with the Bren himself, trained the men to fire in single shots rather than bursts.

The squadron would still require demolitions skills. The uninitiated were introduced to the mysteries of the Lewes bomb and the time-pencil by demolitions guru Captain Bill Cumper, and a section of Sappers he now had under him. To give the unit a heavier punch, though, it was assigned a support detachment of three-inch mortars, under the command of Lt. Alec Muirhead. Muirhead, ex-Royal Worcesters, a former Cambridge University medical student, knew nothing about mortars, and, as it turned out, neither did most of the forty men who volunteered for his detachment from the Infantry Base Depot at Geneifa. They soon mastered the skills so well, though, that they could assemble the tubes and fire the first round in twenty seconds. Muirhead discovered a natural gift for estimating ranges, but also had one narrow escape when he mistakenly directed the detachment's fire on to his own position. Like the Sappers, and a Royal Signals wireless unit also appended to the SRS, the mortar group would be broken down into three sections, attached one per troop.

The SRS fired most Axis small-arms until they knew them as intimately as their own weapons. Many preferred the German Schmeisser to the Tommy-gun. On foot behind enemy lines, the ammunition they could carry would soon be exhausted, and this skill would provide them with an almost endless source of resupply. Pistol shooting wasn't neglected. The men were sent in sections to Jerusalem to undergo the new Grant-Taylor close-quarter battle-shooting course.

Overland marches in full equipment and rock-climbing were crucial aspects of the seaborne-assault role. The men practised cliff scaling with assault-ladders and ropes, and with only hands and feet, carrying equipment and weapons, first by day, then by night. They also endured gruelling bashes in full kit in the arid hills of north Palestine, culminating in a forty-mile drag from Lake Tiberias to the sea. This exercise, to become a model for future SAS selection courses, had a twenty-four-hour time limit, and was carried out partly in the blazing heat of the day and partly by night.

Although the SAS hadn't done an operational drop since Squatter, and the SRS would not jump at all on the Italian campaign, it retained its parachuting skills. The days of makeshift equipment, though, were over. Recruits were now sent to the new parachute school at Ramat David near Jerusalem, where they were trained by full-time airborne forces instructors. More vital for their new commando role was landing-craft drill that began in Haifa harbour under the tutelage of the Royal Navy, in early May.

That they were being primed for 'stormtrooper' tasks quite different from the 'sneaky pete' primary role of the SAS was evident from the fact that they no longer wore camouflage. Gone was the dust-coloured kit that had so often saved them in the desert by making them indistinguishable from the enemy. Now, they wore blue shirts, with shorts, crepe-soled boots and white socks. Stealth was being sacrificed for sharp, fast penetration: the men had to be easily distinguishable to prevent them getting into blue-on-blues.

The training stretched the men to the limits of their endurance. Mayne demonstrated that he could be an accomplished training officer when his heart was in it. He also showed himself an unexpectedly ruthless martinet. He exerted such tight discipline that the 'colourful individualist' reputation that had flourished under Stirling was soon dispelled. 'Unlike some who take on this specialized and highly dangerous job,' Dempsey commented, 'you maintain a standard of discipline and cleanliness which is good to see.'[5]

That afternoon, Dempsey watched the men firing Axis weapons and took part in an exercise in which they snaked on their bellies across the beach while machine-gunners pumped out live ball ammunition over their heads. In the evening he watched a mock assault on a pillbox in the hills, preceded by a cliff-climb, and the descent of a fifty-foot embankment on ropes. The general said later that he had been very impressed, and that the SRS 'took its training very seriously'.[6] So seriously, in fact, that at the end of their six weeks in Palestine the men felt they were ready to tackle anything.

It was Dempsey who informed them that they had been tagged to take out a coastal defence battery on Sicily, in support of his 13 Corps landing by sea and glider. Though they weren't told the date or name of the target, they were shown sketches and aerial photos, and from the day after Dempsey's visit began to train on a lifesize mock-up of the Capo Murro de Porco battery. Covered by Muirhead's mortars, they practised the attack over and over until they knew the target better than they knew their own quarters. On 4 July, after a month in the Red Sea on landing craft, rehearsing all their training drills, they embarked on *Ulster Monarch* for the invasion of Sicily.

48. 'The best crowd he had ever had under his command'

The cemetery at Termoli was being whapped by 88mm anti-tank rounds from the German position six hundred yards away, on a ridge overlooking the main road. 'Moaning Minnie' rockets, sixty at a time, were shrieking over the walls and tombstones, detonating in cascades of stone-chips and debris. One man of Pete Davis's section who had survived the earlier truck-blast lay curled up in a foetal position, sobbing. His nerves were shot. Nobody sympathized, but Davis's men were disturbed, especially after the carnage they had just seen outside the monastery. All day, British infantry units famous for doggedness had been running scared. Paddy Mayne's cool settled Davis's men, though. He told them calmly to take cover behind the cemetery walls and knock holes in them as firing-slits. He appeared completely unruffled by the hellfire. Reg Seekings noted that Mayne always seemed in total control of himself. When things turned noisy, he became cooler and cooler.

Forty minutes after sunset, in splicing rain, three tanks clanked down the railway line on Mayne's right flank. They were heading straight for the positions occupied by a hundred men cobbled together under Harry Poat, from 1 SRS, the commandos, and Brigade HQ's cooks and runners. Some of the men started to think it was curtains. They'd fought on doggedly till now, but their Bren-guns were no match for tanks.

Poat's rag-tag squad had been reinforced by twenty men of 2 SAS, commanded by Major Roy Farran, ex-3 Dragoon Guards, a wry-humoured Irishman who had been ordered into Termoli to set up a base for future operations behind enemy lines. This was the first time 1 and 2 SAS had fought shoulder to shoulder. Farran's D Squadron detachment had arrived in jeeps with the spearhead of 78 Brigade on 3 October, to be joined by another small 2 SAS group who had sailed into the harbour in caiques and a schooner. Lurking in the basement of Brigade HQ under heavy shellfire earlier, Farran had been gripped by Major Sandy Scratchley, the beanpole ex-Yeomanry officer and former jockey, now attached to 2 SAS. Scratchley had tongue-lashed Farran for sitting around while Termoli was falling around their ears. Now, the 2 SAS group lay on a ridge overlooking a goods yard on the railway line with a three-inch mortar and six Bren-guns trained on the approaching tanks.

Poat screamed, '*Fire!*' A dozen Brens ruptured the night with ear-splitting double-taps. 'Number-Twos' fingered rounds into mags with cool precision. Poat's single anti-tank gun burped smoke. 57 mm shells blowtorched air. Wet clods and stones whistled. Bomb fragments lufted a spume of mist over the tanks. Tank cannons sprattled. Behind the gunners, Bob Melot was goading them on, his chest strapped up where he'd been hit two days before. Persuaded with some effort by Mayne to get treatment at the medical post, he had later discharged himself and come back to the front.

Arthur Thompson and his mate Trooper Davie Orr, RAC, ramped hell-for-leather across open ground to the monastery to get an ammo-resupply. Rain slashed down. Cannon-rounds blimped and whiffed past their ears. Soon they splashed back, biceps straining, sledding five weighty boxes of .303 ball roped together by the handles. Tank shells sawed air. Earth, stones, shrapnel ripped and splattered. A building near the railway station blazed up in raw sienna and black. Reg Seekings's kid brother, Ronnie, ex-Cambridgeshires, now serving with 1 SRS, was so close to the tanks he got his face singed by a muzzle blast. Melot supervised the switching of red-hot Bren-barrels and the refilling of mags. SRS-men man-handled two more six-pounder AT guns through the mud and set them up on Farran's ridge. It was no easy task. The six-pounders, firing 57mm HE, incendiary or armour-piercing shells, weighed over a ton, but had a range of two thousand yards. The SAS laid the guns, and fired. Basso profundo booms thundered. Shells squealed overhead, thumped, guffed smoke. Iron splinters gouged and heaved. The tanks rotated guns and went into reverse, gears grinding, scuddering backwards along the tracks through mud and pools.

The SRS-men could hardly believe it. Arthur Thompson thought that if the Jerries had known it was just the SRS holding the line, nothing would have stopped them. A foray by enemy half-tracks followed, but was turned back at six hundred yards by some concentrated firing from 2 SAS. 'The fighting on 5 October was an all-out attack on Termoli through the cemetery and down the railway line,' the official Brigade diary ran. 'It seems that the enemy lacked the commitment to advance through fear of being cut off. The attack was abandoned when the threat to the town was greatest.'[1]

But it wasn't over yet. Shells whinged overhead all night. In a railway station building, a blood-smeared surgical team fished for slugs and sutured wounds on an improvised operating-table. Poat's men fell asleep in pounding rain, their coats stuck to their backs. Lt. Derrick Harrison and his crew of No. 2 Troop slept in a station hut on doors they ripped off their hinges. At first light, they went to join the defenders on the fifty-foot cliff overlooking the station yard. Two hundred yards away, a ridge sloped up before them, with the walled cemetery on the left and the railway and the beach to the right. 2 SAS lay in front of a farmhouse on the far left, past the cemetery.

It was still raining, and the SRS-men struggled to scoop slit-trenches and foxholes out of the waterlogged ground. Mayne directed, his face grim. 'We came here to take this place,' he told the men. 'We've taken it and we're staying. What we have, we hold on to.'[2] It was the first defensive action he had ever fought. A brace of Me 109-Fs appeared, curving in from the sea for a strafing run. They broke off when a squadron of RAF Spitfires creamed out of low cloud towards them. Mayne received news that the Irish Brigade had landed, and would soon be moving up to relieve them. 'Sure, you'll see some fighting now,' he grinned.

The enemy came at 0500 hours on a wave of wheedling mortar bombs and 88mm A/T shells frying air, figures in blue greatcoats, angular helmets and jackboots, hefting Schmeissers. The SRS were well dug in, and the Germans ran into a wall of lead from thirty Brens they had put together in the night. The Brens tap-tapped, flailing fire. The Germans took hits and fell sprawling in the mud. The attack faltered. Most didn't get anywhere near the SRS trenches, but even those who did were battered back by .303 rounds fired point-blank. Germans staggered, streaked with blood, uniforms smouldering from the close-quarter shots. Mortar shells crimped wide into the engine sheds. 'I'm sure we inflicted heavy casualties . . .' Roy Farran said. 'The range was so short we couldn't fail to hit a man advancing in an upright position.'[3]

The Germans withdrew, but came again and again. 88mm shells screwed and burst, spraying iron fragments across the SRS positions. Sgt. 'Buttercup' Joe Goldsmith sprinted through the station with a gasper hanging from his mouth, and plonked his Bren down in the best field of fire he could see. He didn't realize until after he had started shooting that he had set up shop by a five-hundred-gallon fuel-tank. He fought his corner the whole morning, aware that one stray round would blow him to hell and back.

At 1000 hours a forest of enemy mortar fire sprouted up in front of SRS trenches, the bomb-bursts leaping down the slope like wildfire. Captain Sandy Wilson's section of No. 1 Troop lay in the eye of the barrage. Wilson, ex-Gordon Highlanders, was blasting off rounds from a six-pounder AT gun under a haystack with his No. 2, L.Cpl. Bob Sherzinger, Royal Artillery, when a rain of mortar bombs forked down and sheered grapeshot across them. Most of Wilson's men were hit. The haystack blazed up and collapsed. Wilson and Sherzinger were trapped under the bales and suffocated. The only man unscathed was Sgt. Duncan MacLennon, 56 Reconaissance Regiment, who pulled every one of his wounded comrades to safety before returning to the position and ripping off at the encroaching Germans with his Bren.

The same foray forced the section led by the ex-L Detachment man, the barrel-chested Sgt. Fred 'Chalky' White, to pull out. Regretting his move, White skirmished back alone to the position he had just vacated under covering fire. Charging like a bull, with shrapnel grooving the ground and enemy rounds zipping past like flies, he retook his old spot. When the blue-coated enemy came haring out of cover down the slope towards him, he held them off single-handedly for two hours.

The attack was so ferocious that Mayne, with Davis's section, had to pull out of the cemetery and dig in fifty yards away. '[The Germans] got themselves firmly established in the cemetery,' Harrison said, 'and sniping started from the tombs.'[4] The shooters were spotted by a tank crew manning one of the four Shermans of 3 County of London Yeomanry, that had rumbled up in support. '[The Sherman] scored a beautiful direct hit on the dome in the cemetery,' Farran recalled, 'and the green marble disintegrated like the atom [bomb] at Bikini. Everyone cheered loudly.'[5]

The Germans dove into a bunch of railway buildings and started slinging mortar shells and chugging machine-gun fire. Pat Riley's section hit them with an anti-tank gun. Six-pound shells scored air and mashed brick. Whiffs of smoke polyped the walls. The Germans ran.

Muirhead's mortars were silent. Ammunition was out. Cpl. Bob Lowson, Liverpool Scottish, hammered a truck into Termoli to hunt down more bombs. He found an ammo dump of the West Kents and buttonholed the RSM in charge. Instead of giving instant help, the RSM demanded, 'Have you got anyone to fire them?'

'Of course I have,' Lowson snapped. 'Just give me the rounds.'

He hefted crates on to the truck and bulleted back to Muirhead's position. While the bombs were broken out, he went back for more. Muirhead's mortar-men sighted tubes, slipped bombs, ducked. Bombs wheezed. Bombs crashed and split, shock-waving the enemy. Muirhead's team pitched bomb after bomb, loading and ducking like lunatics, till the barrels were steaming and the base-plates were hammered into the earth by the recoil. Bombs honked and greased the enemy with scrap and fire. The Germans wilted. Not long after noon, Derrick Harrison left his position and moved to the top of the railway embankment. He could see all the way down the railway to the dunes on the beach, where heads in Gothic helmets were bobbing up and down. He lay behind his Bren and began to take pot-shots.

About two hours later, Harrison clocked movement in the

goods yard and realized it was the point battalion of the Irish Brigade arriving in jeeps. By three o'clock, the Brigade was sweeping past his position with bayonets fixed, while Mayne's boys and 2 SAS rammed out massive covering fire. Roy Farran didn't realize how many the enemy were until they came out of cover. 'Several hundred figures in blue overcoats began to double back,' he said, 'tacking this way and that to avoid our bullets . . . I think [they] must have been surprised at our firepower for we'd conserved ammunition carefully until this last moment.'[6]

The mortars stopped firing. The crews sat back, exhausted. One by one the Brens went silent. By 1500 hours, the only Germans they could see were dead ones. The battle was over. Termoli had been held.

It was, though, Mayne thought as he walked quietly back to his palazzo, the costliest action an SAS unit had ever fought. His squadron had taken more attrition than any other at Termoli, including the commandos. In three days 1 SRS had lost sixty-nine men, killed, wounded, and missing – exactly a third of the two hundred and seven who had come ashore. When racked up together with the previous three ops in Italy, the SRS was down about fifty per cent on its original strength.

The men had fought brilliantly. Mayne could be forgiven for basking in the reflection that he had been entirely vindicated as a commander, against all those who thought him incapable of it. He, an ex-solicitor and non-career officer, had trained them, commanded them, and moulded them into the finest fighting unit in the British army. 'Paddy Mayne was fantastic,' Seekings said. Miles Dempsey, who had been in Termoli during the battle, would later tell the squadron that in all his military career he had never before met a unit in which he had such confidence.

'The Unit has done smashingly well,' Mayne wrote Malcolm Pleydell later, 'General Dempsey . . . paid us what I imagine were the highest compliments paid to any unit . . . he said we were the best crowd he had ever had under his command. I think he is right too; the lads have done well!'[7] They had done well: the fighting had been magnificent, but it had not been SAS.

The same thought crossed Reg Seekings's mind when he got back to the monastery, to find the bloody, rotting flesh of his comrades still lying in the alley where the shell had hit their truck. They had lain there untouched for two days and the stink was appalling. The tragedy of it, staved off by the adrenalin-high of the battle, hit him all at once. These highly skilled men had, he thought, been squandered by staff wallahs who had no idea what they were doing.

That evening the remains were collected. Padre Bob Lunt wrapped each bundle in a blanket, while L.Cpl. Sid Payne, RAC, supervised the digging of graves in the nearby garden. 'Into the gathering dusk,' said Lt. Pete Davis, 'the silent crowd of men emerged from their billets, with heads bared and softened tread . . . in a quiet voice the padre read the service.'[8]

49. Never quite lived up to its promise

Termoli was 1 SRS's last action. By 12 October the squadron was in Molfetta, near Bari. John Tonkin turned up there six days later, having escaped from his German captors. Tonkin had been wined and dined by the GOC 1 Airborne Division, General Heidrich, and had been warned obliquely about a secret order from Hitler that all British commandos should be 'ruthlessly destroyed by German troops', even if they surrendered. How much Tonkin passed on, or even believed, about Hitler's notorious *Kommando-befehl* is unknown. In any case, it was far from the minds of the SRS that winter. They rested at Molfetta until the last week in November, and Mayne 'celebrated' in customary fashion. He got drunk. He trashed the mess. He ripped out railings from a balcony. He gave the officers permission to have a party with local girls, then, after downing a bottle of whisky, ordered the girls to leave and booted the officers through the door. He splattered medical officer Phil Gunn against a wall, injuring his shoulder.

From Molfetta the squadron returned to North Africa by landing ship, not to Kabrit, but to the 2 SAS camp at Philippeville, forty miles north of Constantine, in Algeria. The camp had been largely vacated by 2 SAS, which was now based at Noci in Italy. It was a huddle of tents pitched in a grove of cork-oaks between the beach and dense maquis scrub that hid a malarial salt marsh. Beyond the scrub, forested hills rose to a height of a thousand feet, their knobbly peaks stretching across the skyline like knuckles.

After David Stirling had gone in the bag in January, it had looked as if his mantle would be inherited by his elder brother, William Stirling, Scots Guards, commanding 2 SAS. While 1 SAS's days had then looked numbered, 2 SAS's star was in the ascendant: it had seemed then that it would be the keeper of the SAS flame. Bill Stirling had some things in common with David. He was tall, he had a warm personality, he got on well with the men, and he drove motorcars with reckless disregard for anyone's safety. He was more intellectual and less gung-ho than his younger brother – not lacking in bravery, but an organizer rather than a have-a-go patrol leader in the field. He never attained David's legendary status.

Bill had been at the Stirling flat in Cairo when David had first broached the SAS idea, and was thus privy to it from the beginning. Like David, he was a commando officer, having served as commander of 62 Commando, or Small Scale Raiding Force, a unit raised originally to conduct *coup de main* raids for the Special Operations Executive. 62 Commando was sent to Algeria after the Torch landings, but, like Layforce earlier, had been disbanded for lack of a role. Bill Stirling managed to get authorization to raise 2 SAS from its ashes. To ensure that its training was as rigorous as that of 1 SAS, he borrowed ex-jockey Capt. Sandy Scratchley and one of his brother's best NCOs, Sgt. 'Honest Dave' Kershaw, on a temporary basis. The training matched the course at Kabrit – infantry skills, PT, demolitions, Axis weapons, route-marches and parachuting, which was run at a parachute school in Morocco. Final selection for 2 SAS depended on the ability to run to the top of a nearby six-hundred-foot hill and back in sixty minutes. Failures were RTU'd.

2 SAS was based round a hard core of ex-62 Commando men, and a few experienced hands such as Scratchley, twice-wounded tank veteran Roy Farran, Major Geoffrey Appleyard, ex-7 Commando, who had helped train 62 Commando and had starred in its raid on Guernsey, and Captain Philip Pinckney, ex-12 Commando, who had served with the British-based Special Boat Section. Despite this, though, most of its personnel lacked both commando training and combat experience.

It was never to achieve the cachet of 1 SAS. In Italy it had been outdone and outshone by 1 SRS's dazzling actions. Mayne had proved everyone, including David Stirling, wrong about his command capabilities, and established 1 SRS as the top special forces mob in the British army. If 2 SAS had never quite lived up to its promise, it was mainly because many of the tasks it was handed were pointless or badly planned by outsiders. Attempts to operate in jeeps in Tunisia proved ineffective because of the cultivated and heavily populated environment. A scheme to destroy a radar station on the Italian island of Lampedusa was thwarted when Italian defenders heard the SAS-men coming and blitzed fire on them as they made the beach. A recce of another island, Pantelleria, turned sour when the SAS team accidentally dropped the prisoner they had grabbed as an informant down a cliff. The raiders had to abort the mission. Op Marigold, a joint 2 SAS/SBS raid to snatch a prisoner from Sardinia, went wrong when one of the marauders dropped his rifle and alerted defenders on the beach. The SAS-men scrambled back to their submarine empty-handed.

The problem was not that Bill Stirling had failed to grasp his brother's concept of the SAS as a strategic force operating behind enemy lines in small parties. In fact, Bill suggested to HQ Allied Forces that 2 SAS should be dropped in up to a hundred and forty small packets on Sicily and the Italian mainland, before and during the invasion. They could soften up German lines of communication prior to Allied landings. They could wreak havoc as the Allies pushed forward. Supplied with jeeps landed in gliders, they could keep up the pressure indefinitely.

Instead, the High Command assigned A Squadron, 2 SAS, under

Sandy Scratchley to capture a lighthouse at Capo Passero on Sicily, with gun emplacements threatening the Allied landings. The light-house was captured without any resistance from the Italians, but scarcely proved a fit target for the unit.

Two groups of Geoffrey Appleyard's B Squadron were dropped in northern Sicily to bump roads and convoys, cut telephone wires, disrupt the Catania–Messina railway and hit the German HQ near Enna. The mission achieved nothing of significance. There was no rehearsal, and the men hadn't been trained in regrouping on the drop-zone. In a landing ominously reminiscent of Squatter, equipment containers went astray and wireless sets were smashed, putting the raiders out of comms with HQ. The aircraft carrying Squadron OC Appleyard vanished on the way back to base. The second drop was spotted, and the stick commander captured. 'The value of damage and disorganisation inflicted on the enemy,' the official report ran, 'was not proportionate to the number of men, amount of equipment and planes used.'[1]

In September a composite squadron of 2 SAS was deployed at Taranto to carry out recce patrols and hit opportunity targets ahead of the Allied push – a role that could have been better performed by a light armoured-car unit. A jeep-mounted group from D Squadron, commanded by Roy Farran, shot up German convoys, linked up with Canadian forces, became involved in street-fighting, and pushed up to Bari, where it was assigned the task of rounding up escaped Allied prisoners. Only fifty were scooped up. 'The military return for the use of sixty-one men . . . was not justified,' the report read, 'when they could have been employed on more important sabotage duties.'[2] Finally, Farran and a small group were sent to Termoli to examine the possibilities of carrying out deep infiltration missions behind German lines. It was during this job that they encountered Mayne's SRS, and were caught up in the defence of Termoli.

Meanwhile, two seven-man sticks of 2 SAS parachutists had jumped into the La Spezia–Genoa area of north Italy to hit railways being used to ferry supplies to German forces. This mission, Oper-ation Speedwell, was at least a classic use of SAS troops, and was successful in derailing trains and cutting the railway. Too few men were dropped, though, to make a major impact, and casualties were high. Bill Stirling, who had been pushing for a larger deployment from the start, burned. 'I submit that examination should be made,' he wrote to AFHQ, 'into why, aircraft and personnel being available, an effective force was not sent against German lines of communication in northern Italy, so that when similar opportunity occurs in future, advantage may be taken of it.'[3]

In late October, 2 SAS finally got lucky when four parties landed by motor-torpedo boat, led by Farran, managed to cut the Ancona–Pescara railway seventeen times, and to mine the main road. A follow-up operation in December, Op Sleepy Lad, led by Sandy Scratchley, succeeded once again in cutting the railway and disrupting road traffic, but was marred when the Royal Navy failed to make the extraction. The SAS-men managed to escape by commandeering a fishing-boat.

2 SAS would remain in Italy for another four months, but Mayne's squadron was earmarked for Blighty. On Boxing Day 1 SRS sailed from Algiers on SS *Otranto*. Mayne himself had flown back weeks earlier. Lt. Johnny Cooper, now returned from OCTU, and Lt. Mike Sadler, recovered from his stomach ulcers, had been flown to Scotland. Sadler's task was to set up an SAS intelligence section, while Cooper's was to prepare a camp for the unit at Mauchline in Ayrshire. Mayne had landed to find that there was no longer any talk of disbanding the SAS. On the contrary, with effect from 7 January 1944, the reputed 'social misfit' Major Paddy Mayne would become Lieutenant-Colonel Blair Robert Mayne, DSO and bar, Commanding Officer, 1 Special Air Service Regiment.

50. 'We don't think about you at all'

There was a new wave of optimism in Britain. The Germans had been turned back at Stalingrad, the US had joined the Allies, Rommel had been pushed out of North Africa, Italy had been invaded and the Italians had surrendered. The Russians were advancing from the east, rolling up lost towns one by one. The Germans were still fighting in southern Europe, but the divisions engaged there were pinned down and couldn't be released for other fronts. When the Allies unleashed Operation Overlord, the invasion of France, scheduled for 1 May, Hitler's forces would find themselves trapped between a rock and a hard place.

France provided the right conditions for guerrilla warfare. It was a country with an oppressed population, occupied by a foreign power. The Special Operations Executive, formed about the same time as the commandos, had been exploiting these conditions for four years. The SOE worked through the Maquis – the French Resistance – using French-speaking agents, men and women, some ex-forces, others civilians, to organize propaganda and sabotage. Unlike the SAS, the SOE was not military – its goals were mainly political, and it was run by the Ministry of Economic Warfare. At the beginning of the year, though, SOE chief Major General Colin Gubbins suddenly started putting his operatives into uniform. 'You can bet your life,' wrote Sandy Scratchley, 'that he did this because he was windy of the potential of the SAS.'[1]

If this was the case, Gubbins's worries were well founded. On 7 January, the day Mayne was promoted half-colonel, 1 Special Air Service Brigade was formed. It was a recognition of the value of military-type special forces outfits – not only the SAS itself, but also the commandos, the Airborne, the SBS, Orde Wingate's Chindits, and the LRDG. Commanded by Brigadier Roderick 'Rory' McLeod, Royal Artillery, the Brigade was made up of five units – 1 SAS, under Mayne, 2 SAS under Bill Stirling, 3 and 4 SAS, French parachute battalions, and 5 SAS, a Belgian unit of squadron strength. Exactly two years earlier, in January 1942, the SAS had been down to only seventeen men. It would soon number two and a half thousand.

In January 'Mayne's Boys' docked at Greenock in teeming rain. Mayne was there to greet them. He announced that everyone would get a month's home leave, a rail warrant, and a hundred pounds. When they returned, on 4 February, they were directed not to Mauchline, where Johnny Cooper had originally been instructed to set up camp, but to Darvel, a village in Ayrshire. It lay about ten miles from 1 SAS Brigade Main HQ at Sorn Castle, where Rory McLeod had set up shop. Brigade Tactical HQ would be at Moor Park at Rickmansworth, on the outskirts of London.

The SAS Brigade was officially part of the Army Air Corps for administrative purposes. For operations, though, it belonged to Lt. General Frederick 'Boy' Browning's 1 Airborne Corps, itself part of Montgomery's 21 Army Group. The invasion of France would be in part a needle-match between two old adversaries: Erwin Rommel commanded the German armies in France.

From the start, there was jealousy between the Airborne and the SAS that would outlive the war. 'Although few of the Airborne people had much in the way of operational experience,' Johnny Cooper said, 'they tended to look down on us as poor country cousins and thought that their professionalism overshadowed our private army outlook.'[2]

At the suggestion of his wife, novelist Daphne du Maurier, Browning had introduced a maroon-red beret for the Airborne, together with sleeve-flashes depicting Bellerophon riding Pegasus. As the SAS was now 'Airborne', Browning decreed that the Regiment should ditch its sand-coloured beret in favour of the 'maroon machine'. Mayne was not amused, but since the order only applied once the existing beret had worn out, he continued to wear his original beret, and made sure it lasted. He told his men that, once in the field, they could stuff their maroon berets in their kit and don their 'real' headgear.

The SAS retained its flaming sword badge, but the men wore Pegasus on their sleeves. They fought a desperate battle to retain the honour of wearing wings above the left breast-pocket, instead of on the sleeve like Airborne troops. These might seem trifling points to outsiders, but as Mayne and Stirling had always recognized, they were vital to SAS identity. Rivalry was inevitable. Both units were para-trained *corps d'élites* with a sense of being 'men apart', bonded by the mystique of shared hardship. Their ideologies, though, were quite different. Airborne units were trained to fight in platoons and companies, honed to work as closely interdependent teams, and encouraged to develop an aggressive 'do-or-die' spirit. Anyone who didn't wear the 'maroon machine' was an inferior 'crap hat'. They were geared to sharp, ferocious actions, and equipped to operate independently for a limited period. 'The Paras are arguably the best-trained shock-troops in the world,' admitted a later SAS veteran Ken Connor, 'with an inbuilt self-belief that they are better than anyone else in this type of action.'[3] They were also considered expendable. The Allied planning staff estimated that only fifty per cent of its para-troops, and thirty per cent of its glider-borne troops, would survive the first operation on D-Day. When General Eisenhower left the camp of his crack 101 Airborne Division after a pre-invasion pep-talk, he was seen to be in tears.

Despite its title and origins, the SAS had ceased to be purely a parachute unit after Squatter. Parachuting was only one means of delivery, and its methods of operation were distinct from those of the Airborne. Airborne battalions dropped on or near their targets, often in full sight of the enemy, on the theory that casualties sustained in the air would be less than those suffered if the troops had to fight their way to their objective. SAS drops were carried out in secrecy some distance behind enemy lines.

Though the SAS had proved at Termoli and elsewhere that it could operate as a regular unit, and fight defensively, the collective ethos wasn't its main impulse. SAS-men were selected for individual initiative, and were trained to operate in small groups behind enemy lines for long periods. Its modus operandi was 'stealth if possible, force if necessary' – it wasn't geared to big, stand-up battles, but to hit-and-run tactics.

The appointment of Roderick McLeod as SAS Brigadier was not greeted with universal enthusiasm. The SAS regarded McLeod as an outsider, though in fact they could have fared worse. A former Staff College instructor with a deep interest in clandestine warfare, he fought the SAS corner tenaciously, and attempted to preserve the purity of its approach.

At Darvel, 1 SAS was housed in disused spinning mills, with the officers billeted in private houses, and the officers' mess located in the Turf Hotel. The training-ground for the Brigade would be in the nearby Cunninghame Hills, where SAS veterans of the desert and Italy reacquainted themselves with the misery of snow, rain and biting winds. 'We thought it was tough dealing with extremes of heat,' said one desert veteran. 'It was a treat compared to those bloody windswept moors.'[4] They trained mostly in the dark, navigating by compass, carrying steel-framed Bergen ruck-sacks full of sandbags, with 'thunderflash' charges in their webbing. After gruelling treks over mist-shrouded moors, through peat-bogs, and across gushing streams, they would set their thunder-flashes on roads, bridges or a railway spur line specially assigned to them by the railway company. They would melt back into the mists before the charges went off. 'Like this,' wrote Derrick Harrison, 'we learned to make our way with unerring accuracy to places that were little more than pinpoints on the map.'[5]

They learned how to locate underground telephone and tele-graph cables and destroy junction-boxes, to short-circuit telephone communications using fusewire. On one occasion a group of SAS trainees used this technique with great success on a Scottish village. A householder who tried to call the fire brigade couldn't get through, and his house burned down.

SOE agents were hauled in to brief them on the French Resist-ance – the Maquis – who would be their eyes, ears and support groups on the ground. Maquis bands were not homogeneous. The FTP – Francs-tireurs et Partisans – was a communist organization that had been in action since the German invasion of Russia. The

Armée Secrète (AS) was mostly made up of former French soldiers, and was training to go into action after the Allied invasion. After D-Day all resistance was supposed to be unified under a single body, the FFI – Forces Françaises de L'Intérieure – but the SAS were warned to expect friction between the different groups, who were suspicious of each other's political motives.

The boys were advised to be circumspect about the French natives they turned to for help. The poor were more likely to be sympathetic than the middle classes; the old, with their memories of the First World War, were better bets than the young. The Maquis was riddled with moles and informers, some acting out of misguided patriotism, others, such as the dreaded Milice – the French Gestapo – were fully paid-up Nazi stooges. In the field they should never relax until they were certain who their friends were.

Mayne had spent his first few weeks back home on an intensive recruiting drive, selecting men for both 1 and 2 SAS. Though he had managed to poach a few from the Airborne divisions, and obtained a handful from his parent regiment, the Royal Ulster Rifles, the largest single group – more than three hundred in all – came from the Auxiliary Units of the British Resistance Organisation. These were regular soldiers trained to fight as guerrillas in 'stay behind' parties, should Britain be invaded by the Germans. Their training was deemed appropriate for an SAS role, and they were invited to volunteer for the Brigade.

Mayne selected recruits according to his own subjective ideal of what an SAS soldier should be. He didn't like men who were too full of themselves. He had a reputation for being able to size a man up immediately, and once told Derrick Harrison that he carried a blueprint of the typical SAS-man in his head. 'No one fits it exactly,' he said, 'but when I look at a man and listen to him, he must come close to it.'[6] Harrison extrapolated from this that Mayne's values included a high standard of mental and physical stamina, intelligence, teamwork, versatility and confidence without rashness. These were more or less Stirling's values, too, although he had laid more emphasis on individual initiative than teamwork. For now, though, Mayne admitted, in a letter dated 17 March, that some of the men he had recruited fell short of the qualities he was looking for.

Of Mayne's five squadron commanders, only one – the Officer Commanding D Squadron, Major Ian Fenwick – came from the Auxiliary Units. The others – Bill Fraser, Tony Marsh, Ted Lepine and Tom Langton – had served previously with the SAS.

Mayne was keen on making use of the reservoir of experience among the senior NCOs. One day in February, he called Reg Seekings to the Turf Hotel and showed him a list of non-coms he was recommending for a commission. Seekings's name was on top of the list. Although his best mate, Cooper, was now an officer, and despite being one of the most decorated men in the Regiment, Seekings turned it down. It was all very well for Stirling to talk about a 'classless' unit, but in practice most officers still came from the upper echelons of society, and however distinguished in battle, Seekings knew he could never really be one of them.

Instead, Mayne offered him the post of Squadron Sergeant-Major of the elite A Squadron, and Seekings accepted. He was in good company. Mayne's RSM was Johnny Rose, the man who'd fixed the Blitz Buggy during Stirling's walkabout in Benghazi. SSM B Squadron was Cyril Feebury, ex-Coldstream Guards, ex-8 Commando, a former SBS-man who'd distinguished himself on the Rommel Raid in Libya. C Squadron's SSM was another 'Original', Bob Lilley – the man who'd killed an Italian bare-handed near Benghazi, before joining up with Mayne.

A parachute training school had been set up at Prestwick, where all ranks had to undergo a refresher-course of four jumps. Bombays were now out of service, and in future SAS units would jump from Stirling, Halifax and Albemarle bombers, most of them incorporating a hatchway in the base of the fuselage. SOPs had improved since Squatter. The parachutist now carried his main weapon with him in a special sleeve strapped to the leg, rather than packed in a separate container.

The standard issue .45 calibre Smith & Wesson revolver the SAS had hefted on earlier missions had been replaced by the .45

Colt automatic. The Colt was heavy and inaccurate, and SAS troops came to prefer the less freely available 9mm Browning GP35, which would be so highly favoured by post-war SAS anti-terrorist teams. The Tommy-gun was still around, but had been supplemented by the 'baked bean can' 9mm parabellum Sten-gun, and the superior but limited-issue Patchett 9mm. The No.36 Mills grenade 'pineapple' was used side by side with the Lewes bomb and the No.82 'Gammon' bomb – a kilo of plastic explosive in a canvas bag connected to a fuse that exploded on impact, capable of damaging armoured vehicles.

Seven-inch Sykes-Fairburn stiletto fighting knives, manufactured by Wilkinsons, were issued for 'silent killing'. The SAS never liked this weapon much, because it was impractical, and blew their cover if they were captured. A bayonet was better, because it had multiple uses, and was standard issue to all units. In practice, 'silent killing' was a messier and more difficult business than it appeared in the movies, usually requiring at least two men to carry it out efficiently. The 'fighting knife' was mostly used for preparing food, and even then was of less value than the unromantic clasp-knife.

The .303 Lee-Enfield Mark IV had been replaced by the US-made .30 calibre Winchester M1-A1 carbine. At only three kilos, the carbine was half the weight of a Lee-Enfield, and ideal for paratroops. Though not so accurate, and lacking the range of the Mark IV, it had a semi-automatic capability and could produce a higher rate of fire. Its rounds were only half the weight of .303 rounds, meaning that the shooter could carry more.

Separate containers were still deployed for explosives, wireless sets, petrol, spare water and rations, but all personal kit was stowed in a canvas Bergen rucksack with an external steel frame and the new jungle-green '44 pattern webbing. As well as a more easily accessible water-bottle, with a fitted lightweight steel mug, the new webbing incorporated ammo pouches slung lower than the old '37 pattern, which tended to prevent the soldier from lying flat. Heavy 'Compo' rations had been supplemented by twenty-four-hour ration-packs in cardboard containers that could be packed easily into the webbing. The rations consisted of tinned sardines, cheese and meat dripping, oatmeal blocks, meat blocks, soup cubes, tea, biscuits, sweets and chocolate. A new and highly efficient solid-fuel Hexamine cooker had also been developed.

For parachuting, the gear was stuffed in a cylindrical container known as a 'leg-bag'. The bag rested on the leg during the exit, but was held in place by a couple of hooks that were released after the canopy developed. The bag dropped and dangled below the parachutist at the end of a fifteen-foot cord, attached to his harness. This system took the weight off the parachutist as he hit the ground, and also increased his stability in the air. The main drawback was that the leg-bags tended to get snagged on the edge of the hatchway as the men went out.

All parachute troops wore rubber-soled boots and a specially designed dennison smock with a leg-strap to prevent it flying up during the descent. They were also issued with a dome-shaped helmet with a chin-pad, to replace the old broad-brimmed helmet whose design went back to 1914. Much of this new generation of 'airborne' gear would be retained for decades after the war.

2 SAS under Bill Stirling returned from Italy on 17 March and was established at Monkton, near Prestwick. 3 SAS, originally 3 Battalion d'Infanterie de l'Air, under Commandant Pierre Chateau-Jobert, had been raised in Algiers mainly from Vichy French soldiers. It was stationed at Auchinleck, twenty miles south of Darvel. Its sister battalion, 4 SAS, formerly 1 Battalion d'Infanterie de l'Air, under its one-armed veteran CO, Commandant Pierre Bourgoin, was established at Galston, five miles west of Darvel. 4 SAS was recruited from pro-Gaullist troops, so relations between the two battalions were strained – it was said that they hated each other worse than the enemy.

Intra-brigade rivalry wasn't confined to the French. Mayne's 1 SAS saw itself as a cut above the less experienced, Johnny-come-lately 2 SAS. When Roy Farran asked Mayne if it was true that his battalion looked down on 2 SAS, Mayne told him, 'No, we don't. We don't think about you at all.'[7]

Competition filtered down to squadron level and below.

A Squadron, the direct heir of L Detachment, thought of itself as the crème de la crème, and this continued in the latter days of the war, when its Officer Commanding, Bill Fraser, its troop commanders, Cooper, Wiseman and Muirhead, its SSM, Seekings, and many of its senior NCOs – Jeff Du Vivier, Fred White, Bob Tait, Jimmy Brough and others – were desert or SRS veterans. Inter-squadron jealousy was another trait that would continue after the war's end. 'As the squadrons took shape,' wrote Johnny Cooper, 'a rivalry was born which has continued through the history of the SAS via Malaya, Oman, Borneo, and even the Falklands.'[8]

Even within the squadrons there was a new axis of distinction between the 'old operatives' and the recent recruits. Men who had been there from Day One, like Seekings, were worth their weight in gold because, as Derrick Harrison, now a troop-commander in C Squadron, pointed out, there was no manual of SAS operating procedures. 'Everything had been developed in the light of experience,' he wrote, 'and from our mistakes. The whole fund of knowledge of this type of work lay in the minds of the "old operatives".'[9]

51. 'We just picked up our rucksacks and left'

SHAEF – Supreme Headquarters Allied Expeditionary Force – under General Dwight D. Eisenhower, had been planning the invasion of France for the past year. By March, though, the role of the SAS Brigade still hadn't been worked out. When Mayne was finally issued with Operation Order No.2 on 29 March, outlining the SAS job on Overlord, he saw at once that it was a kamikaze mission. Dropped behind the coastal strip of Normandy between the Cotentin peninsula and Dieppe, up to thirty-six hours before the D-Day landings, the SAS was to form a defensive line and stop three German panzer divisions from reinforcing the front. Not only would such an action throw all SAS skills to the wind, it would involve a fight to the death, or at least end in devastating casualties. 'The [plan was] to drop the SAS not behind enemy lines but between his front line infantry and his armour,' David Stirling commented. 'It would have been bloody suicidal . . . It would have been quite ineffective and marvellous opportunities would have been totally missed.'[1] It also contradicted the policy of Montgomery's 21 Army Group, that no SAS troops were to be inserted into the area prior to D-Day, for security reasons.

It was Bill Stirling who rose to the challenge. Primed by his argument with HQ Allied Forces over operations in Italy the previous year, Stirling drafted a letter to Browning, demanding a return to the strategic principles on which his brother had founded the unit. His model was the classic pre-Alamein campaign David had waged against Rommel in North Africa before and after the Benghazi debacle, when SAS raiders had operated from a forward base behind enemy lines. SAS units, Bill Stirling said, should parachute in behind the German front and set up bases, from where they would sally forth on foot or in jeeps and hit enemy lines of communication. Most SAS officers agreed with Stirling. 'It was ridiculous to think that scattered parties of parachutists could do anything much to delay the arrival of panzer divisions,' wrote Roy Farran. '. . . Far better to employ us further inland where we might operate for months.'[2]

As Operation Order No.2 was still subject to amendment, though, Stirling delayed sending the letter. On 8 May Browning himself wrote the Chief of Staff, 21 Army Group, suggesting that, because of the delay in the formation, equipping and training of 1 SAS Brigade, its role should be shifted to harassing enemy lines of communication and assisting resistance groups in delaying the advance of panzer divisions.

This seemed to be all that Stirling wanted, but he sent his letter anyway. Whether he resigned voluntarily or was bowler-hatted by Browning remains unknown, but from this point he vanished from the scene. Farran considered resigning, and was convinced that had he done so most 2 SAS officers would have followed suit. But Stirling asked him to stay and work under his replacement, Major

Brian Franks, Middlesex Yeomanry, who had served with Layforce and with the Commando Brigade in Italy. Like McLeod, Franks was an outsider, but he was widely respected by the SAS. '[Franks] proved to be one of the best commanding officers one could wish for,' said Farran.[3] He would become one of the three men upon whom the post-war survival of the SAS depended, and would be considered by David Stirling one of the five other 'fathers' of the Regiment.

It seemed on the surface that Bill Stirling had sacrificed his command for nothing. The SAS role still hadn't been officially defined, though, and his stand probably influenced the final decision. According to Reg Seekings, Mayne stood aloof from the wrangling, commenting only that the command were 'having disagreements'.

David Stirling claimed later to have played a role in the debate by getting a letter to his brother from his prison camp, urging him to refuse to allow 2 SAS Regiment to be used in semi-tactical roles. Stirling said later that his brother had to make a stand, because Mayne wasn't au fait with the top brass. David believed that Bill had sacrificed himself, not only for 2 SAS but for the other regiments as well.

On 28 May, after days of wrangling, Browning issued Operation Order No.1 – apparently in reverse sequence – stating that the SAS role during the invasion of France would be to set up bases in the German rear and undertake a programme of sabotage that would inflict crippling damage on their lines of communication. The actual areas of operation were selected by the Commander, SAS, and the initial points of focus would be Operation Loyton, in the Vosges, Operation Houndsworth, based in the Morvan mountains, west of Dijon, and Operation Bulbasket, in the Vienne, east of Poitiers. Operation Gain, in the Orléans gap, south of Paris, was added at the last moment. These ops would be only four of a total of forty-three SAS missions that were planned in France, incorporating all five regiments.

Most of the ops would follow similar lines. A recce party of one or two officers would be parachuted in to make contact with the local Maquis, via a Jedburgh Team – one of eighty-six units run jointly by the Special Operations Executive and the US Office of Strategic Services (OSS). 'Jeds' – usually consisting of a French officer and a British or American officer or NCO, and a wireless operator – were tasked to help arm, organize and assist the local Maquis, to carry out acts of sabotage, and to provide a link between the partisans and the SAS.

Once contacts with the Maquis were established, an SAS 'Main Recce' party would follow, then a 'Base Party', consisting of the operation commander and a troop of signallers. They would set up a signals-base and a drop-zone, where the main party could be parachuted in, followed by parachutages of supplies, ammunition, jeeps, mortars, folding 'airborne' bicycles, and even six-pounder anti-tank guns.

A system of parachuting heavy equipment – 'heavy drop' – had been developed. Jeeps were slung under the open bomb-doors of an Albemarle, packed into a wooden cradle, with collapsing air-tanks beneath to absorb the impact on landing. The jeep was partly dismantled, with steering-wheel, petrol tanks, and other components packed separately. It was parachuted down on four static-line canopies.

Operating from bases within the specified area, SAS patrols would move out and hit German lines of communication, initially railways, later roads and any other targets that came up. Though some parties would start out with specific objectives, once in the field targets would be left to the discretion of the commander. The jeeps would allow SAS parties to operate far from their bases, which always ran the risk of being compromised by Maquis moles, or 'Dee-Effed' – 'Direction-Found' – by triangulation on their wireless signals.

At the end of May, under hush-hush conditions, small groups began to vanish from Darvel. Taking only their Bergens, so as not to reveal that a major movement was in progress, they reappeared at Fairford, otherwise known as 'The Cage', a secure transit-camp in Gloucestershire, where the SAS parties would be briefed for operations. It was sited on an airfield used by the RAF's

38 Squadron, a new air unit raised and trained for special forces work. Once the SAS had heard the details, they were kept under strict quarantine. 'Fairford was like a concentration camp,' Reg Seekings commented, 'surrounded by barbed wire, watch-towers, machine-guns, searchlights. It took three security checks to go and have a shower, and that was under armed guard.'⁴

On 1 June Mike Sadler turned up at Fairford with a three-tonner and, without any explanation, singled out four officers to accompany him to London. They included Ian Wellsted and John Stewart of A Squadron, and John Tonkin and Richard Crisp of B Squadron. Twenty-three-year-old Tonkin, who had been captured at Termoli and escaped, was the most seasoned of the four. Born in Singapore, he had been brought up on the Isle of Man and had a degree in civil engineering from Bristol University. He was to lead the advance-party for Op Bulbasket, with his oppo Richard Crisp, a Sandhurst-trained officer of the North Irish Horse, who had yet to see action.

In London they were joined by an SOE security major who told them that they were not to stray from his sight. If any of them needed to answer the call of nature, they would all go together. Sadler took them to the operational flat of the Special Operations Executive at 46 Devonshire Close, where they spent most of the next two days studying mug-shots of their SOE contacts and learning codes. Tonkin and Crisp were then shifted to SAS Brigade HQ at Moor Park, where they received their final briefing.

They didn't return to Fairford, but spent their last hours at Hassell's Hall, near Sandy in Bedfordshire – the SOE dispatching centre – where they packed their Bergens and received final instructions. Paddy Mayne made a final appearance to wish them luck. 5 June passed featurelessly watching films and doing jig-saw puzzles. 'We just couldn't realize the invasion was to start that night,' Tonkin said. '. . . At 2000 hours the cars came for us, so we just picked up our rucksacks, waved goodbye to the others and left.'⁵

52. The biggest airborne assault in history

In the early hours of 6 June, more than twenty-three thousand Allied troops dropped out of the sky over Normandy, on parachutes and in gliders – the biggest airborne assault in history. They were accompanied by thirteen hundred RAF bombers that reamed over German shore defences, pounding them in wave after wave. At 0550 hours guns thundered fire from Allied warships standing offshore, sounding like the rhythmic boom of a million giant kettledrums. First light fell on a vast armada of transport vessels crammed with troops and weaponry. By sunup, a hundred and thirty thousand Allied soldiers, mostly Canadian, American and British, were scrambling ashore on beaches Omaha, Utah, Gold, Juno and Sword, stretching fifty miles along the Normandy coast.

Among the first Allied parachutists to drop over France were Tonkin and Crisp, with Jedburgh Team Hugh, led by Capt. Bill Crawshay. Five hours before the amphibious landings, the Tonkin stick jumped 'blind' – without a reception committee – into the Brenne marshes, east of Poitiers. Tonkin's job was to locate a base and drop-zone for Bulbasket – an operation tasked to hit German lines of communication from the south of France to the Overlord beaches. The group landed safely and was joined by Capt. André Maingard, an agent of the SOE's F Section, codenamed 'Samuel'. Maingard was astonished to discover that the invasion had begun.

'Samuel' helped Tonkin and Crisp locate a DZ for the parachutage of nine more SAS-men under Lt. Tomos Stephens, and five tons of supplies, that night. Stephens, a short, feisty Welshman, ex-South Wales Borderers, had been captured in North Africa, where he'd met Tonkin in a rehabilitation camp, and later volunteered for the SAS. Shortly after the Stephens stick arrived, Tonkin received intelligence from the Maquis that no fewer than eleven German tanker-trains were hidden on sidings in the forest near Châtellerault. The fuel was earmarked for 2 Waffen-SS Panzer Division, Das Reich.

It seemed too good to be true, and at first Tonkin didn't believe it. He sent Tomos Stephens, dressed in the flannels and flat cap of a French worker, on a close target recce. When Stephens returned saying he had crawled right up to the tankers, though, Tonkin was euphoric. Das Reich was one of Rommel's major reserve units – with fifteen thousand men and two hundred tanks, it was twice as large as any other Wehrmacht Panzer Division. It was reckoned to be only three days away from the front. If Bulbasket could take out the fuel bowsers, it would delay Das Reich's arrival at the beach-head by hours.

Two-and-a-half hours after Tonkin's Bulbasket stick touched down, another SAS op, Titanic-4, went in over the Cotentin peninsula, between the US beach-heads, Omaha and Utah. A six-man group from 1 SAS, under Lts. Harry 'Chick' Fowles and Fred 'Puddle' Poole, it was a throwback to the dummy SAS brigade created by Dudley Clarke. Equipped with Lewes bombs, Very flare-pistols and noisemakers, the team was part of a scheme that included landing straw-man parachutists fitted with small-arms simulators, sand-filled weapons-containers and flare-pitching 'pin-tail' bombs. The aim was to convince the Germans that Allied paratroops were dropping south of the town of Carentan, deflect-ing their attention from real DZs to the north and east, where the US 101 and 82 Airborne Divisions were shortly to be inserted.

The drop went pear-shaped when the SAS-men lost their real weapons-containers, and had to go to ground. After hiding out for a month they were located, surrounded and captured by German paras. They remained prisoners for the rest of the war. Titanic succeeded in distracting a German battalion from the beach-head, but many of the US paratroopers missed their DZs and were scattered. Some drowned in lakes and rivers, others came down among the enemy and were taken prisoner or killed.

Around the time Titanic-4 was inserted, sixteen men of 4 SAS, under Lts. Henri Deplante and Pierre Marienne, jumped over Vannes, in Brittany. They were the advance party for Op Dingson, an attempt to raise the local Maquis in revolt against the Germans. The Deplante-Marienne stick were spotted by German Feldpolizei – three were bagged and one killed. The survivors managed to guide in a main party a hundred and fifty strong, who mustered a group of three thousand Maquis. Ill-equipped to fight a major battle, though, they were obliged to split up when the Germans moved against them in strength twelve days later.

A second operation by 4 SAS, Samwest, was inserted at the same time as Dingson. Consisting of a hundred and forty-five men, including thirty local partisans, the op went awry when the Maquis, from rival groups, began fighting between themselves. Some of the SAS-men, overjoyed to be on native soil again, started visiting local restaurants and were eventually tumbled. The Germans ambushed their base, killing thirty-two SAS-men. Although the op's original purpose failed, thirty men of 4 SAS remained in the area for weeks, organizing local resistance.

53. 'Saboteurs surprised at a rendezvous and shot'

Mike Sadler peered out into the night as the fields of France passed under him like a moonlit ocean. It was 0145 hours on 5 July. A month had passed since the D-Day landings, but Rommel's Fifth and Seventh Armies were still holding on in Normandy. Minutes earlier, the Stirling bomber Sadler was riding had quivered as she hit an air pocket. 'There's another aircraft about,' the pilot observed. Lying full-length in the greenhouse-like forward-dome, Sadler felt suddenly vulnerable. Now he was keeping his eyes peeled for bandits, as well as the torch-flashes of the Maquis reception party lurking in the woods somewhere below. There was no sign of anything – the moonlit river went on and on.

Sadler felt the plane's engines doppler-out as the pilot skewed into the drop-zone area near La Ferté-Alais, thirty miles due south of Paris. He could at least take solace in the fact that he would not be jumping tonight. He was along as an observer, and to get a whiff of the sharp end. His regular job, as Assistant Intelligence Officer, 1 SAS, was briefing SAS parties going into action. It seemed a very long time since the day when Corporal Sadler, trainee navigator, had guided David Stirling and Paddy Mayne to L Detachment's first successful strike at Sirte-Tamet.

The twelve-man stick Sadler's aircraft was carrying were all D Squadron, 1 SAS. Commanded by six-foot-two Captain Patrick Garstin, Royal Ulster Rifles, all but one were newcomers. The exception was L. Cpl. Tom 'Ginger' Jones, Argyll & Sutherland Highlanders, an ex-miner who had fought with L Detachment and 1 SRS. Three of the stick, Troopers William Young, Joseph Walker and Thomas Barker, were also from Mayne's Royal Ulster Rifles contingent. Another, L.Cpl. Serge Vaculik, was a Czech-born Free Frenchman who had served with 4 SAS, but had been posted to 1 SAS as a linguist. Most of the others, Lt. Jean 'Johnny' Wiehe, an RE from Mauritius, Sgt. Thomas Varey, L.Cpl. Howard Lutton and Troopers Norman, Morrison and Castelow, had volunteered for 1 SAS from the Auxiliary Units. Sadler thought the men seemed jittery.

The Garstin stick were reinforcements for Op Gain, whose first elements had gone in on June 14/15, and set up an operating base in the forest of Fontainebleau. Gain's commander, Major Ian Fenwick, King's Royal Rifle Corps, Officer Commanding D Squadron, had collected orders two days before the drop, instructing him to blow all double-track railways connecting with the Overlord beach-heads via Orléans, Tours, Le Mans and Argentan, as well as any single-track lines crossing the region.

Fenwick, a well-known *Punch* cartoonist with a reputation for eccentricity, had endured a quiet war as a regional Intelligence ofiicer for the Auxiliary Units. His lack of combat experience, though, was balanced by that of his resourceful squadron sergeant-major, 'Gentleman Jim' Almonds, double MM and L Detachment Original, whom Pat Riley had last clocked near Benghazi leaping from a jeep. Almonds had escaped from an Italian prison-camp, and on arrival in Britain had immediately been requested by Mayne, and promoted Squadron Sergeant–Major, D Squadron.

Almonds was not the only Original to have rejoined SAS ranks. Among the other escapees were his friend Trooper Jim Blakeney, one of the famous 'Tobruk Four', 'Great Escaper' Cpl. Dougie Arnold, and Cpl. Roy Davies, once Jock Lewes's batman, who had jumped on the first fateful drop at Fuka. All three had been bagged on Squatter. Operating at first on foot, later in jeeps heavy-dropped to them, sometimes trekking twenty-five miles or more in and out of target-areas, the Fenwick group had cut the Orléans–Pithiviers line repeatedly in the past three weeks. Almonds and Fenwick had banjoed trains with jeep-mounted Vickers Ks.

Sadler saw three lights flash up, spaced a hundred yards apart. Ten yards to the right of the last light, a torch blipped out the morse letter 'B'. The pilot read the code and brought the Stirling round for the final approach. In the cabin, the SAS parachutists were already at action stations, gear on, hooked up, braced to drop through the hatchway in the middle of the floor.

The green light stabbed. The dispatcher yelled. '*Go!*' One by one, Garstin's men slipped into the hatchway and flopped into the night. In the forward-dome, Sadler couldn't see the stick going out, but a split second after '*Go!*' he saw the unmistakable flash of small-arms fire from the DZ. He caught his breath. The drop had been compromised – and by someone who knew the recognition code. The pilot was already putting the aircraft into a tight turn and heading back home. Sadler knew there was nothing they could do.

A moment later a Messerschmitt 110 darted out of the shadows like a manta-ray, cannons gashing the night with lines of 20mm tracer. Rounds greased the Stirling's cabin, punching through the skin and blipping out the other side. The pilot wrenched the column, going into a switchback evasion routine, bucking, dodging, flipping and rolling. The German held on doggedly, hugging his tail, thumping fire. The pilot heaved the stick forward, taking the plane into a headlong plummet, spindling through cloud. In the dome, Sadler thought the wings were going to fall off.

Hanging from his lift webs, Pat Garstin heard rounds buzzing from the DZ. He saw muzzle-flashes and realized they'd been compromised. His leg-bag hit dirt, and he braced himself for ground-rush. He smacked soft soil, ankles and knees together, let his calves give and went into a roll. He screwed and pressed his harness-release. He came up to see canopies jellyfishing around him, and others going down in woods to the south-east. Men in civvies oiled out of the shadows towards them, shouting, 'Vive La France!' Garstin wasn't taken in. He went for his MI carbine and cocked it. Light-machine-gun fire popped out of the darkness. L. Cpl. Howard Lutton was hit. Trooper Tom Barker was wounded. Lt. Johnny Weihe took a slug in the spine. Garstin felt kicks in the neck and arm and bit the turf, squirting blood.

Nine of Garstin's stick were captured, four wounded. Morrison, Norman and Castelow, the last out of the aircraft, had landed in woods and escaped the cordon. The location of the drop-zone had been leaked by a traitor in the local Maquis, and the Germans had themselves set up the DZ lights. In fact, SOE's F Section circuit in this area had been penetrated the previous year, and was now run from Berlin. Similar leaks had been responsible for the capture of several SOE teams dropped into the area. The reception committee had been organized by Sturmbannführer Hans-Joseph Kieffer, an ex-police inspector from Karlsruhe, commander of the local Funkabwehr, or Signals Counter-Intelligence – a Section of the Sipo-SD. They hadn't been expecting to capture SAS-men. Kieffer's tip-off had only mentioned a resupply drop.

The prisoners were rushed to Paris before sunset, and the wounded sent to hospital, where Lutton died. The rest were held in a converted hotel in the Place des Etats Unis, then taken to Kieffer's HQ in the Avenue Foch. Kieffer saw them briefly, then handed them over to his Funkabwehr interrogators. Ginger Jones, the ex- L Detachment man, was cuffed with his hands behind him. Every time he gave an answer his interrogator didn't like, a man behind his chair back-handed him viciously. L. Cpl. Serge Vaculik was beaten twice. His cover story was that he was 'Martin', a French Canadian from Quebec. The Germans didn't swallow it. They called him a terrorist. They told him he was going to be shot.

According to some accounts, all the SAS-men were informed separately that they would be executed, but they didn't believe it.

It was against the Geneva Convention to execute prisoners in uniform – they might be saboteurs, but they weren't spies. They were thrown back into a cell in their 'hotel'. Days went past and nothing happened. There would be sudden, violent interrogations, and spells of 'punishment', handcuffed in darkness.

On 8 August, almost five weeks after their capture, the Sipo-SD guards brought them a pile of ragged civilian clothing and told them to put it on. The story was that they were going to be exchanged for German prisoners in Switzerland. Ginger Jones was sceptical. He told Vaculik he couldn't see why they needed civvies to be exchanged. Vaculik agreed that the story didn't hang together – one of the guards had told him that their uniforms were being taken away to be washed. Vaculik told Garstin that he had a bad feeling about the new move, and suggested they make a break for it. Garstin, whose wounds hadn't healed, was so weak he could hardly stand up. He said they should be patient – he reckoned that they were going to be repatriated.

The Germans bullied and cajoled them into parting with their uniforms. At 0100 hours next day the Garstin stick donned ill-fitting and down-at-heel civvy togs, and were shoved, handcuffed, into a waiting truck. The truck joined a convoy of fifteen or more other vehicles heading north. Among their guards were an English-speaking SD-man named Alfred Von Kapri, and Karl Haug, a fifty-year-old ex-First World War soldier, who had been part of the group that had captured the SAS-men back in July. The party was commanded by SS-Hauptsturmführer Richard Schnur. All three worked for the Funkabwehr under Kieffer.

At sunrise the truck came to a halt, and the men were turfed out to find themselves on the edge of a forest near Beauvais in the Somme. Jones spotted another truck parked some distance into the trees. Vaculik asked Von Kapri in French if they were going to be shot. 'Yes, of course,' he replied.

Schnur, in the uniform of the Sipo-SD, ordered the guards to march the SAS-men a hundred metres into the trees, where they came across a small clearing. Here they were lined up elbow to elbow facing a squad of six Germans armed with sub-machine guns, about ten yards away. Garstin had to be propped up by Ginger Jones. Schnur drew a document from his pocket and read it aloud, while Von Kapri translated. 'On the orders of the Führer . . . you know that saboteurs are punished with the death penalty,' he droned, 'in accordance with the rules of warfare.'

'We haven't even been given a trial,' Garstin gasped. 'My God, we're going to be shot!'

The two survivors claimed afterwards that Garstin had arranged for the whole stick to make a break for it on the word 'shot'. Whatever the case, at that moment Serge Vaculik charged shrieking towards the firing-squad. He was followed closely by Ginger Jones and Tom Varey. Haug claimed later that he never opened fire. Schnur said that he was too busy putting the paper back in his pocket to shoot. One of the guards – perhaps Von Kapri – riddled the helpless Garstin with 9mm bullets from behind. The other three Ulstermen were blasted, one of them on the run. Germans chased Jones, Varey and Vaculik thirty metres into the wood, ratcheting off rounds as they ran. Jones tripped and fell, but the SD-men thought he had been hit and ran straight over him.

Jones waited until they were all out of sight, then lifted his head to scope the area. He saw four bloody corpses, and realized suddenly how the scene might be construed – four dead Britons in civilian clothes, shot in the back, as if trying to escape. They had been tricked into forsaking their uniforms so that they could be shot as absconding spies. Jones didn't linger. He jumped over a fence and vanished into the forest, emerging into a cornfield, where he went to ground.

When Schnur returned half an hour later and found Jones's body gone, he had a fit of hysterics. He was perfectly aware that he was contravening the Geneva Convention, and might one day be executed as a war criminal. The last thing he needed was living witnesses. He blamed Haug for letting the SAS-men get away. The guards fanned out into a line and began scouring the wood again. They had covered about five hundred yards when they spotted a prisoner – Tom Varey – sprinting through the trees. As he crouched behind a pile of wood, an SD-man named Otto

Ilgenfritz shouted, 'Halt – stand up!' When he did so, Ilgenfritz plugged him from thirty yards.

The Germans were convinced that Jones's cadaver had been spirited away by the Maquis, and that only Vaculik remained at large. Later, they carted the five corpses to a Luftwaffe unit in a nearby village, asking for help to search for the remaining man. Schnur informed the officer in charge that the dead were 'saboteurs who had been surprised at a rendezvous and shot'.

The Garstin stick weren't the first SAS-men to die as a result of the *Kommandobefehl*, the notorious 'Commando Order', of which John Tonkin had heard rumours at Termoli the previous year. The order stated that Allied commandos should not be afforded the rights of ordinary prisoners of war, and should be killed on sight, even if they tried to surrender.

How much the SAS knew of the danger at this stage is uncertain. SAS-men bagged in North Africa after the order was issued had been spared because Rommel rejected it as dishonourable. The fate of 2 SAS soldiers murdered by the Nazis after their capture in Italy was still unknown. They were listed 'missing in action.' Jim Almonds claimed that the SAS knew by June that if they were caught they would be shot. It is unlikely this was official, because Jedburgh teams going into action as late as July were informed that, since they were in uniform, they were protected by international law.

In March a subaltern of 2 SAS, Jimmy Hughes, reached the UK, having escaped from a German prison-camp. He repeated to 2 SAS Intelligence Officer Major Eric Barkworth what a sympathetic German officer had told him about the *Kommandobefehl*. Barkworth was worried, and passed Hughes's report on to HQ 1 Airborne Corps. They concluded that such rumours were mere 'interrogation technique'. The fact that some missing SAS-men hadn't been reported killed or captured by the enemy in Italy, they said, was a ploy to prevent the Allies from ascertaining the success of their missions.

54. 'For the life of me I couldn't think what all the noise was about'

In the early hours of 3 July, two days before the Garstin stick was inserted, John Tonkin returned to Bulbasket base in the forest of Verrières. Tonkin and his driver had spent the night scouting for a new base location – he had good reason to believe that the old one had been compromised. He didn't notice anything amiss as he unrolled his sleeping-bag among his comrades. He had posted no sentries, and set no booby-traps. All seemed peaceful. He never dreamed that he had been allowed to pass through a cordon of SS Panzer Grenadiers, Sipo-SD troops and SS anti-partisan forces, four hundred and fifty strong, who had moved into place at last light the previous day.

Since D-Day, Tonkin's party had cut the railway twice, and derailed a goods train. His greatest success, though, had been the destruction of Das Reich's fuel-tankers. After Tomos Stephen's recce, he had relayed the coordinates of the hidden trains to Moor Park. The reaction had been swift. On the night of 11 June, an Allied Mosquito squadron had swooped over the hidden siding in three waves, demolishing the trains with five-hundred-pounder bombs and cannon-fire. It was a brilliant coup.

Shortly, though, Tonkin had taken a parachutage of four jeeps and had shifted his base to the Verrières forest, about twenty-five miles from Poitiers. Here, things had started to go wrong. On 28 June two NCOs, Sgt. Douglas Eccles, Welsh Guards, and Cpl. Kenneth Bateman, Wiltshire Regiment – both ex-1 SRS – failed to return from a mission to blow points in a railway marshalling yard at St Bénoît. The jeep driver came back without them, and reported hearing no gunfire. Tonkin should have assumed they'd been bagged, and that his base was exposed. Instead of moving out, though, he stayed put.

Three days later, two Frenchmen were led into the camp by Trooper John Fielding, an ex-Auxiliary Units soldier, who had spotted them pushing a punctured motorcycle and sidecar along a nearby road. The men claimed to belong to the Maquis. A long interrogation failed to confirm their identity, but still the SAS let them go. They were almost certainly spies of the pro-German Milice – the French Gestapo.

Two more disquieting incidents happened that day. First, look-outs reported an unidentified vehicle drifting back and forth along the roads around the forest. Then, a Maquis group hustled in a man who claimed to be a US fighter pilot, Lt. Lincoln Bundy, whose Mustang P-51 had been taken out by ack-ack fire. Though Bundy eventually turned out to be kosher, Tonkins received no positive ID from Moor Park.

These episodes together added up to a case for scrapping the camp, and in fact Tonkin did order his men to move out to an alternative site, in the Bois de Cartes. When the well at the new location turned out to be dry, though, he decided to move back to the old site. He reasoned that since it was now four days since Bateman and Eccles had disappeared, they either hadn't cracked or were already dead. This reasoning was faulty. In fact, the two SRS veterans had been tortured by Sipo-SD and had broken that same day, disclosing the location of the base. The following day, while Tonkin had finally gone to look for a new camp, German troops encircled the area. They brought with them mortars, artillery, and heavy machine-guns.

At first light two Maquisards who had spent the night with their girlfriends in Verrières ran into a German sentry in the woods. He opened fire. One of the Frenchmen, Marcel Weber, took a bad hit in the thigh. The German party heard the gunfire and assumed it was the signal to attack. The B Squadron men awoke to the tremor of mortar shells churning the forest floor. 'For the life of me I couldn't think what all the noise was about,' said one of the survivors, Lt. Peter Weaver, ex-Dorset Auxiliary Units. 'Then I realised, Christ, we're being mortared!'[1]

SAS-men and Maquisards, pale-faced, wide-eyed, wrestled free of sleeping-bags, rammed on boots, groped for carbines and escape-belts. Spandau rounds whiplashed the campsite, kicking dirt, whiffling leaves, thunking trees. Half-dressed men rolled for cover.

Shells quivered, roils of earth blew, bullets whirred and seared, smoke spiralled. Bits of shrapnel smacked into Troopers Joe Ogg and John Williams as they tried to dress. They spasmed, lashing blood. Medic Cpl. Bill Allan crawled over to them, ripping open shell-dressings, his bloody fingers probing their wounds.

Sgt John Holmes, Royal Armoured Corps, an SRS and desert veteran, yelled at Troopers Bob Guard, Ed Richardson and Tom Cummings to take up all-round defence. Two minutes later, Marcel Weber clawed through underbrush towards them, ghost-faced, his thigh pulsing blood. 'The Boche are coming!' he croaked.

Tomos Stephens pulled Weber into cover and two SAS-men braced him, half-carrying him towards John Tonkin's position. Rounds clittered and sissed past them, but no Germans appeared. A minute later, Pete Weaver had twenty-seven SAS-men stood-to in defensive positions. Stephens monkey-ran back to Holmes. 'Every man for himself,' he hissed.

Most of the men followed Weaver, Stephens and Richard Crisp south. They ran into a firewall, shifting closer, bullets drubbing past their ears, sprattling dirt. They wheeled away from it. They scrammed south-west through trees. They cut across a road and ducked south-east, straight towards a mortar battery. Shells hacked and split, foliage flamed, bullets ticktacked. They raced back the way they'd come. More rounds blistered them. A 9mm slug blagged Richard Crisp's thigh. Blood gouted. The men milled, trapped on all sides. 'Come with me, or stay where you are,' Weaver said. 'I'm not ordering you to do anything. It's your choice.'

John Holmes's party split off, rushed down a slope to a stream, hit a bridge. Trooper Vic White crouched and let rip covering fire with his carbine, slatting .30 rounds. Holmes told him to pull out. White said he'd be there in a minute. Holmes and his party sprinted across open ground towards another limb of woodland. Cpl. John Kinnivane stopped, winded. Holmes and three others hit the trees and crept into cover. White and Kinnivane never made it.

Pete Weaver hared off into the trees with Stephens, who was doubled over with stomach cramps. They were running south, yellow corn gaping in brilliant sunlight through gaps in the forest. Stephens told Weaver the cramps were agony. He had to stop. 'For Christ's sake!' Weaver spat. 'They're here!'

Stephens told him to go on. He cut back into the woods. Minutes later rounds slapped his thigh, hurling him off his feet. SS-men in field-grey skulked out of the trees. Stephens put his hands up, his thigh blebbing blood. An SS-man swung his rifle, crunched his skull. Stephens rolled over. A German put the muzzle of his rifle against his head. He shot him point-blank.

Weaver ran into the corn. He dropped on all fours. He animal-crawled through wheat-stalks, bellying and scrabbling along. Others followed. Halfway across, Weaver staggered to his feet. Shells wheezed and plumped, columns of smoke sprouted. There were screams behind him, as Trooper Pascoe was scythed by shrapnel. The others wheeled again, running through corn. Weaver ran the other way, out of the field, across grassland towards another spur of forest. Four SS-men swarmed after him, crashing through corn-stalks. The forest seemed miles away. Gunshots beheaded wheat and grated grass. Weaver dropped over a stile, beelined for a bramble-patch, crawled in, lay still. A moment later SS-men spurted past and disappeared.

John Tonkin crashed through undergrowth with Cpl. Rideout and Troopers Keeble and MacNair. He stopped short when he remembered he hadn't secured the cipher books. He went back for them. The camp was seething with SS-men, helping themselves from SAS ration-packs. Tonkin crawled up and stuck time-pencils on PE blocks. He came so close to the Germans that discarded chocolate wrappers fell on his head.

Medic Bill Allan had stayed with the wounded Ogg and Williams, and had been taken prisoner. Cpl. Pascoe was dragged up, half-comatose, blood-drenched. The Germans bundled the wounded into a truck and sent them to Hôtel de Dieu hospital in Poitiers. Six of the Maquis had been captured. The SS handcuffed them, kicked them to the side of a road, and mowed them down in cold blood. They moved the cadavers to Verrières, half a mile away, and dumped them in the village square. They hung up

Tomos Stephens's body for the villagers to see. Some witnesses said that Stephens was still conscious, and that the SS-men bludgeoned him to death in front of them.

Twenty-eight other SAS-men had been captured. Together with the US pilot, Bundy, they were taken to the German army Feldkommandatur in Poitiers, shoved in cells and interrogated. The army tried to hand them over to Sipo-SD, who didn't want them. Hitler's *Kommandobefehl* hung over them, but no one wanted to take responsibility.

In the end, the buck was passed to Oberleutnant Vogt of 80 Corps, a former priest. Vogt recced a site in the St Sauvant forest, twenty miles south of Poitiers, where he ordered three pits dug beside a track. Just before first light on 7 July, while the Garstin stick were being interrogated in Paris, thirty-one men were lined up by the track, with their hands cuffed behind them. Their number included US pilot Bundy, Eccles and Bateman, who had been tortured into revealing the location, and Bob Bennett's best mate, SAS Original 'Lofty' Baker. A firing-squad faced them. Weapons clacked. Vogt snapped the order to fire. The Germans blubbed out 9mm shells at close range, cutting down the helpless men. The bodies sprawled, still cuffed. The Germans scooted around giving *coups de grâce* with pistols. They yanked the dog-tags off the corpses, dumped them in the pits and shovelled dirt over them. Six days later, in the Poitiers hospital, the three wounded – Ogg, Williams and Pascoe – were murdered by morphine overdose.

On 5 July John Tonkin, Pete Weaver, John Holmes and five others met up at an emergency RV at a small farm near their former base. All of them escaped. Tonkin would not discover the fate of the Bulbasket crew until January 1945, when their bodies were unearthed by local villagers.

55. 'A marvellous killing-ground'

The Morvan was a region of rolling wooded hills in the middle of Burgundy, lying on the north-eastern rim of the Massif Central, between the Loire and the Saône. It was an ideal hideout for Op Houndsworth, a scheme run by Bill Fraser, whose aim was to cut the railway line between Paris and Lyon, and the Le Creusot–Nevers line to the south. One of the most backward regions of France, the Morvan was sparsely inhabited, with few villages or farms. Its main industry was logging – its dense forests supplied firewood and charcoal for Paris and Dijon.

Paddy Mayne was inserted into the Morvan on the night of 8 August, with his batman Cpl. Tommy Corps, Mike Sadler and a Jed officer. As there was no RAF dispatcher on board, they had to dispatch themselves. Earlier, during take-off at RAF Northolt, their aircraft had spun laterally and caught fire. None of the stick had been hurt.

Mayne took some satisfaction in reporting to Moor Park later that it had been 'a superb drop'. He had jumped in his formal service-dress uniform complete with medal ribbons, with a wind-up gramophone and records in his leg-bag. He had worn the uniform, he said, to outdo Bill Fraser, whom he'd heard was in the habit of wearing his Gordon Highlanders kilt to 'impress the locals'.

Ex-Yeomanry trooper Capt. Johnny Wiseman, whose section had been wiped out at Termoli, was on the DZ to meet them. He escorted Mayne to the camp of Capt. Alex Muirhead, his former mortar officer in Italy. In the morning they motored to Fraser's base, up twisting hairpins that led them deeper into the hills and forest. When the cars could go no farther, they cammed them up in the trees, and trekked two and a half miles on foot along a valley that climbed at right-angles from the village of Mazignen. The main Houndsworth base lay in a forest clearing, by a stream – a cluster of tents crudely constructed from hanging parachute canopies, covered by a large tarpaulin against the incessant rain. A couple of lopsided huts were the cookhouse, presided over by self-appointed chef, ex-L Detachment NCO Sgt. Cornelius McGinn.

Fraser came to greet Mayne, looking pale and tired. Mayne and Sadler sprawled on sleeping-bags in his tent, where they were joined by Major Bob Melot, who had been inserted twelve days earlier, and the chaplain, Captain Fraser McLuskey. The padre thought Mayne looked happy to be back in the field. 'He'd had to stay at base for the first month or six weeks,' he observed, 'but he'd been fretting to get into action himself – this was his life.' McLuskey felt that Mayne was a man who could only live to the full in the open air. 'He looked awkward in the mess, or anywhere indoors,' he added. 'Outside, all his awkwardness fell away.'[1]

Mayne told Fraser that he had only decided to drop to Houndsworth at the last minute. His plan had been to visit Ian Fenwick with Gain in the Orléans forest, sixty miles further north. The previous day he had signalled Fenwick for drop-zone coordinates. Fenwick had sent them, but then advised him to cancel the drop. Moor Park had subsequently lost comms with Gain, and Mayne was worried that the op had been compromised. Fraser couldn't help him, as none of the SAS teams was in direct contact.

Fraser gave Mayne a sitrep on the Houndsworth operation. Fraser was now the single most experienced operator in the SAS apart from Mayne himself, and the animosity between them had long since vanished. No one cared if he was gay. His squadron sergeant-major, the blunt-spoken Reg Seekings, said that he used to think that Fraser was 'scared' before an operation, and felt he had to keep an eye on him. He had stopped doing that a long time ago. Now, he rated him as one of the best soldiers he had ever known.

Padre McLuskey noticed a certain similarity between Fraser and Mayne, despite the fact that Mayne was by far the more powerful personality. They had, he thought, the same gift for making the necessary decision instantly. 'Both had the same intuitive knowledge of where to go and what to do when there was trouble,' he commented. 'Both appeared to be careless at times, but each had a feel for the essential . . . with Bill and Paddy I was never inclined to worry . . . when it came to soldiering in their own type of warfare, they had a good deal in common.'[2] It might have been this similarity that had prevented Mayne from making Fraser second-in-command of the Regiment. The honour had gone to Capt. Harry Poat, the ex-tomato-grower from Guernsey.

Houndsworth had been in place since D-Day, when its recce party, under Lts. Ian Wellsted and Ian Stuart, had dropped in with Jedburgh Team Harry. The advance party had been inserted four days later. Apart from Fraser himself and a couple of other SAS Originals, Cooper and Seekings, the advance group consisted of fourteen signallers of F Squadron GHQ Liaison Regiment, known as Phantom.

The SAS had its own organic W/T ops, but the Phantoms were there to ensure close comms with TAC HQ at Moor Park. Phantom used MCR 1 sets powered by a hand-generator. While one man turned the wheel, the operator transmitted by TG – Morse code – with a one-time pad to encrypt messages. Some men were issued with an individual Jedset, the eighteen-inch-long receiver-component of the MCR 1, with a thirty-six-hour battery. The Jedset was designed so that the men could tune into the BBC Forces Network, known as 'Sabu', and receive simple instructions in code allotted to their call-signs. It was not, their instructors had warned them fiercely, 'for listening to Vera Lynn'. SAS units were also equipped with an S-Phone, a walkie-talkie with a ten-mile range for ground-to-air contact, and a Eureka beacon – a six-kilo portable homing system for drop-zones, with a fifty-mile range. As a last resort, the teams had a pair of homing pigeons, trained to carry messages encrypted on rice paper in capsules on their legs.

Three more Houndsworth sticks under Johnny Wiseman, Alex Muirhead and Scotsman Lt. Leslie Cairns, an ex-Gunner, took off on 17 June. All three aircraft missed the DZ. The first two turned back, but Cairns's plane vanished and his sixteen-man stick was lost.

Wiseman and Muirhead tried again four days later, together with a third stick commanded by Captain Roy Bradford, an ex-Devon

Auxiliary Units officer, and accompanied by the Regiment's medical officer, Captain Mike McReady, and padre Fraser McLuskey.
The drops suffered two casualties – SAS vet, ex-ME Commando
man Sgt. Fred 'Chalky' White crashed through the roof of a farm
and was paralysed, and Trooper Bill Burgess broke a leg. Fraser
told Mayne that his A Squadron boys had bumped the railway no
fewer than twenty-two times. Before the first consignment of
jeeps was dropped, though, his squads had operated with the local
Maquis cell, Bernard, hitting German troops and convoys.

On 24 June, a seven-man troop under Alex Muirhead, with
fifteen partisans, had laid an ambush on the road between the
Morvan's chief town, Château-Chinon, and Montsauche Les-
Settons. The ambush-party included Cooper, Wellsted, L.Cpl.
John 'Nobby' Noble, Royal Army Service Corps, L.Cpl. Frank
'Silvo' Sylvester, Wiltshire Regiment, Trooper Pete Middleton
and a Yugoslav-born Free French sergeant named Zellic, attached
from 3 SAS as a linguist.

Muirhead chose the ambush-site carefully. 'The place selected
was an excellent one,' Cooper recalled, 'as there was a gentle
incline which meant that large lorries would have to change gear
and slow down. On the western side there was deep forest and on
the opposite side of the road, open fields.'³ There was a blind bend
a little further along the road. Beyond it, Wellsted, an ex-Royal
Tank Regiment officer whom Mayne had poached from the Airborne, stretched piano wire from tree to tree to decapitate motorcyclists outriding the convoy.

The 'bomber' group, led by Maquis mechanic 'Roger', armed
with Gammon bombs, concealed themselves behind a pile of cut
pit-props where a logging track hit the road. The rest of the
Maquis, under their chief, 'Bernard', fanned out in the forest either
side. Cooper, Zellic, Noble, Middleton and Muirhead sited two
Bren-guns on the slope overlooking the junction. It was, said
Cooper, 'a marvellous killing-ground'.⁴

The convoy came into view at about 1640 hours, led, as
expected, by a motorcyclist, followed by a couple of three-tonners,
two civilian cars, and a light armoured vehicle bringing up the

rear. There were at least fifty soldiers in the trucks, most of them 'Grey' Russians – ex-Soviet Red Army prisoners who had volunteered for service with the Wehrmacht. To the SAS-men and the Maquis, they were all Boche.

Wellsted and Sylvester were proned-out in undergrowth with face-veils over them, waiting patiently to behead their motorcyclist. Wellsted heard a heavy truck change gear on the incline. An instant later, he recalled, there came the 'hellish melody of chattering Brens' as the gun-groups opened fire, followed by the 'unmistakable roar of a [Gammon] bomb'.[5]

The way Cooper remembered it, the moment the first lorry drew abreast of the timber-pile, two Gammon bombs sailed over the top. One hit the truck's bonnet, the other the rear, crammed with enemy troops. The bombs cracked apart and blowtorched flame. The engine blazed up, smoke billowed, windscreen-glass slewed. Germans screamed, dropped weapons, sucked fumes. Charred bodies squirmed, burning men hit the road smoking and twitching. Bren-guns tattooed from up on the slope. Maquis rifles spattered.

The second lorry, fifty yards behind, stopped dead. The civilian cars were riddled with shot. Bodies sprawled out. The light armoured vehicle did a U-turn and scooted off. The motorcyclist outrider swerved, wobbled and turned back. Germans scuttled across the road, dodging fire, one group shifting a Spandau machine gun. Bren-fire stitched patterns across their backs. Germans slumped into the ditch, where enfilade-fire jiggered them. Bodies jerked crazily, limbs squelched, frothing blood. 'It was pandemonium . . .' Cooper recalled. 'Many were killed by fire from the Maquis as they fled across the road . . . it was a massacre.'[6]

Wellsted and Sylvester, M1 carbines in their hands, wormed up through the ditch to see the first truck blazing. 'The bodies of the men in the cab lolled grotesquely in their seats,' Wellsted recalled. 'It was the first time I'd seen a dead man, but I found myself strangely unmoved.'[7] Hot cartridges in the burning trucks popped like corks. Ricochets whinged through the trees, spiffling leaves, grooving bark.

The Spandau crew had made the forest and set up the gun. Spandau rounds burped across the road. An enemy soldier was immolated on the cab of the first truck, writhing and wailing. Wellsted, Middleton and Sylvester clumped Colt .45 rounds at him till he fell silent. Middleton snapped off carbine shots at helmets popping up from the ditch. Wellsted whaled No. 36 pineapples. The Bren-gunners moved out of position to clear the ditches. Nobby Noble hunkered down on the verge, thumped a Bren-burst at a Boche corporal in a thicket, shattering his arm. 'My shooting was good that day,' he commented. 'I was awake.'[8] A German jumped out of the ditch and darted across the road. Sylvester bopped him with a carbine-tap from the hip.

Maquis swarmed out of the woods, picked up German weapons, yanked off dead Germans' boots. One of the partisans had been drilled through the forehead – the only casualty among the ambushers. Someone shouted to the enemy in the ditch to come out with their hands up. No one came. They were all dead or too badly wounded to move. French hostages, serving with the Maquis, had been prisoners in the cars – a middle-aged man covered in blood, a white-faced youth, an old man who complained his rescuers had wrecked his motorbike, which had been in the truck. The Maquis laid the wounded man on a wooden gate and dollied him off. The others followed.

Three German prisoners had been taken. Thirty-two were dead. Muirhead didn't know if the motorcyclist had given the alarm, and ordered the SAS-men to pull out before back-up arrived. 'We made off as quickly as possible,' Cooper recalled.

Next day, German reinforcements moved in. They torched La Verrerie, a farm near the ambush-site, and set ablaze the villages of Montsauche and Planchez, shooting dead two protesters. That afternoon, Maquisards jogged into the SAS camp near Vieux-Dun just as Padre McLuskey was holding communion, and begged Fraser for help. The Maquis medical post in a château near the village of Vermot had been bumped by 'Grey Russians'. Sgt. Fred White, still paralysed, had been in the hospital at the time, and was woken by a blitz of Spandau MG34 rounds that ripped up his headboard. The Maquis medical staff had managed to dolly-out the stretcher cases, under covering fire from the local partisans. The Maquis were soon sent reeling by a mortar barrage, and melted into the forest, where the Germans were reluctant to follow. Instead, the enemy trashed and burned the château.

Fraser agreed to help. At 1900 hours that night, in torrential rain, the SAS set out in two groups – one under Fraser, the other under Johnny Wiseman – to take the pressure off the partisans. After two hours' trekking through dripping woods, Reg Seekings, lead-scout with Wiseman's group, crawled up to a road. He found himself face to face with a German machine-gunner only fifteen yards away. Much to Wisemen's later amusement, Seekings snapped his head back and yelled, 'Look! Enemy!'

He commented later that turning his head saved his life, because at that moment the enemy gunner fired and instead of hitting him square in the face, the bullet lodged between his spine and skull. He was spared further attrition, because the German machine gun jammed. The gunner lobbed two grenades that burst either side of him, but left him untouched. He tried to lift his carbine, but found his arm wouldn't move. He was pulled out by Sgt. Jack Terry, DCM, Royal Artillery, ex-SRS, a distinguished combat veteran, and one of three survivors of the commando mission to assassinate Rommel. 'I felt as if I was in an underground river,' Seekings said. 'No pain. Going like the clappers in this river, a raging torrent, but silent, going like the hammers of hell.'[9]

The rest of the troop went to ground in the woods, and bugged out under covering Bren-fire from L. Cpl. David 'Pringle' Gibb, Royal Armoured Corps. While Seekings was dragged back to camp, Wiseman withdrew the group to a low hill, where they lurked until after dark.

Seekings had used up another of his nine lives – a 9mm slug was jammed in his neck, but hadn't done any permanent damage. A Maquis doctor tended him that night while the chaplain shone a torch. 'Probe as he might,' McLuskey wrote, 'the doctor couldn't get hold of [the bullet].' Seekings had to be moved by stretcher next morning, but was on his feet again within a few days.

The round wasn't finally removed until he returned to the UK.

Meanwhile, Fraser's own party had approached Vermot and spotted a 'Grey Russian' battle-group, fifty strong, forming up in column of threes in the street. It was a perfect target. Fraser set up his pair of Brens silently on a hill overlooking the village. One of his gunners was his Squadron Quarter Master Sergeant Duncan MacLennon, the man who had distinguished himself at Termoli by pulling to safety all the other members of his section. The gunners flipped and slid sights. Fraser ordered, '*Fire!*' The Brens clattered with the sustained blip-blip of double-taps. The effect was devastating. 'The fire of . . . well-handled Bren-guns was poured down on [the enemy],' Ian Wellsted recalled, '. . . all was disorder. Cries of the wounded and hoarse orders mingled with the wild racket of the Brens, and in the narrow streets there was little chance to get any cover, or put up an adequate reply . . .'[10] Fraser commented that the Bren-gunners 'had a field day' – of the fifty enemy, only ten escaped unhurt.

All night a battle raged in the woods around the SAS camp, and in the morning the Germans attacked with renewed vigour, obliging Fraser to pull his squadron out to a fallback base. Though the enemy discovered the deserted Maquis HQ, they failed to locate the abandoned Houndsworth camp. Frustrated, they returned to Vermot, where they looted and burned down every house, beat or shot six men, and raped a fourteen-year-old girl. They then moved on east to the larger village of Dun-les-Places, where they hanged the local priest from his own church tower, lined up men and boys and machine-gunned twenty-seven of them, dumped the corpses in the square and dismembered them with grenades. They then looted the houses, and set fire to them.

Despite the repercussions, Fraser considered his actions a success. Not only had they taken out a hundred and fifty of the enemy, they had also dissuaded the Germans from pursuing the Maquis into the forests: they were never to attempt it again. The presence of SAS troops in the area had also remained unsuspected by German command.

Houndsworth's first consignment of jeeps was dropped on

5 July. One of Fraser's men, Cpl. Eric Adamson, had been crushed when his jeep rolled, suffering a double fracture of the pelvis and severe damage to the urethra. The jeep was a write-off, but the other four had been put to good use in bumping roads and railways further afield. Fraser's men cut the railway. They derailed six trains. They wrecked three locomotives and fifty wagons. They brought traffic on some roads to a standstill. They destroyed two gazogene – synthetic petrol – plants. Alex Muirhead and Johnny Cooper mortared a plant at Autun. They fingered targets for the RAF. Sgt. Jeff Du Vivier, Fraser's old mate from the Ajadabiyya raid, led a foray on folding 'airborne bicycles'.

The only major setback Houndsworth had suffered was when Capt. Roy Bradford's jeep ran into a German convoy near Lucy-sur-Yonne, and Bradford was killed in a shoot-out, together with his REME mechanic, Craftsman Bill Devine. His gunner, Sgt. Fred White, now recovered from his paralysis, took rounds in the shoulder, hands and leg, and later had three fingers amputated. A Free Frenchman in the jeep, Jacques Morvillier, was injured in the arm. The only member of the party to escape unhurt, Sgt. Cornelius 'Maggie' McGinn, Gordon Highlanders, managed to lead the two wounded men to safety. He was later awarded the MM.

Resupply and reinforcement drops kept coming. Jeeps were heavy-dropped. AT guns were parachuted in. Containers landed and were dragged away by bullock-cart. By the end of July, Fraser's command consisted of a hundred and forty-four men, nine jeeps, and two six-pounder anti-tank guns.

56. 'Thank you, Madame, but I intend to attack them'

Mayne was impressed. Houndsworth had scored more consistently than any other op, and suffered few casualties. He couldn't tell Fraser the real reason he had been inserted. In Normandy, Rommel was hanging on by a thread. His men were fighting doggedly, but couldn't hold out much longer against the massive air-power the Allies had unleashed. Every attack was preceded by a devastating air-strike by the British 2 Tactical Air Force, or the US 8 and 9 Air Forces. Rommel was short of guns, and the Luftwaffe was noticeable by its absence. The Germans had already lost the best part of a hundred thousand men. Even Hitler was worried. 'In the east,' he announced, 'the vastness of space will . . . permit a loss of territory . . . without suffering a mortal blow to Germany's chance of survival. Not so in the west! If the enemy here succeeds . . . consequences of staggering proportions will follow in a short time.'

Allied command was expecting a breakthrough by mid-August, and was preparing a surprise for Rommel. When his Panzer divisions started to withdraw, they would find the 'Orléans Gap', south of Paris, blocked by a huge US and British Airborne force that had parachuted in behind them. Elements of both 1 and 2 SAS would be deployed as the patrol unit for this op, Transfigure, under the direct command of Mayne. Three troops of C Squadron, under Major Tony Marsh, and one troop of C Squadron, 2 SAS, under Major Roy Farran, with twenty jeeps each, would be landed by Airspeed Horsa gliders on the edge of the Rambouillet forest, not far from the Gain position.

Mayne had intended to jump to Gain to check out the situation there as a recce for Transfigure. This was why Fenwick's silence bothered him. Sadler and his chief, Melot, both knew about Transfigure. Melot had been inserted with a secret mission of his own – to recce a drop-zone in the Merry-Vaux forest for Op Kipling, a C Squadron recce-party under Derrick Harrison, tasked to prepare the way for one of the SAS glider-borne groups outriding the Airborne drop.

Mayne told Fraser he wanted to go and investigate Gain himself, despite the risk. He left the same day, with Sadler and Melot, in three jeeps. While Sadler travelled independently, Mayne escorted Melot as far as Toucy, ten miles west of Auxerre. They left him there with a jeep and a crew that included his Intelligence Sergeant, Duncan Ridler, and his W/T op, Sgt. David Danger, both SAS veterans of Italy and the desert. By nightfall, Mayne had reached the Gain base near Chambon-la-Forêt, where he made contact with Jim Almonds and acting commander Captain Michael 'Jock' Riding, an Auxiliary Units officer. He learned with a shock that Ian Fenwick had been killed only the previous day.

Riding reported that on the day Mayne had asked for DZ coordinates, their base had been banjoed by the Germans. By chance, Fenwick, Riding and Almonds had all been at the second base, sorting out the site for Mayne's insertion. It was a hot Sunday afternoon. The Gain camp was occupied by Riding's troop, who were chugging petrol into their jeeps, chocking carbine magazines, priming Lewes bombs, greasing weapons. There were no forward pickets out. They had been occupying this base for a month, and they knew it was too long. What they didn't know was that the Germans had triangulated the location from intercepted wireless signals. Riding's men were encircled by hundreds of troops.

Fenwick's first base in the Fontainebleau forest had been hit back in June. On an attempt to blow locomotive sheds and a railway turntable at Bellegarde in early July, Fenwick and Almonds had walked into a German ambush. They managed to vanish into the darkness without casualties, but Fenwick had been forced to relocate for the second time. Since then, his men had been making use of their jeeps, ranging far into the countryside, bumping isolated vehicles on the roads in the Orléans Gap. By the end of the month, though, Fenwick had started to hear whispers that his camp might be compromised again, and had dispersed his men to three separate locations. Only he, Almonds, and Riding's troop remained at the old base.

The first the SAS-men knew of the attack was when mortar rounds crunched into the trees. Machine-gun fire blipped. Field-grey figures popped up amid dapples of shade. The SAS-men grabbed escape-kits and went to ground in all-round defence. Any German who showed himself got greased. They held the enemy off skilfully for seven hours, slipping away one by one. Soon after dark, the Germans were lobbing mortar-bombs into a space that was completely devoid of SAS-men. Not a single man or vehicle was lost.

Almonds and Riding had both heard gunfire and made their way to the base separately. Riding and his signals NCO, Sgt. Bunfield, managed to creep to the wireless jeep and manoeuvre it through the German cordon. Almonds, narrowly avoiding German machine-gun positions, arrived at the camp to find it deserted. He headed for the prearranged emergency RV, where he met up with Riding just before first light. Together, they drove back and retrieved Almonds's jeep.

Fenwick, still at the second base, had no news of the situation. Next morning he motored into the village of Nancray-sur-Rimarde, where he made contact with the Maquis. Their intelligence was that Almonds and Riding were both dead, and that all the jeeps had been lost. Fenwick decided to go and see if he could pick up any survivors. He set off in a jeep driven by Cpl. Simon Duffy, with Sgt. Frank Dunkley, Royal Tank Regiment, as rear-gunner on the Vickers K, and two Frenchmen, L. Cpl. Menginou, a linguist attached from 4 SAS, and a Free French sergeant working with the Maquis. On the way, the jeep was identified by the pilot of a Fieseler Storch spotter-plane. The Germans set up an ambush on a T-junction outside Chambon-la Forêt – the village closest to the base.

Earlier, the Germans, furious that the SAS troop had eluded them, had rounded up the men and boys of Chambon and thrown them into the local church. They told the mayor of the village that unless he revealed the location of the SAS, all the hostages would be shot. The women fled. Outside the village one of them ran into Fenwick's jeep, and flagged it down. The woman told Fenwick about the plight of the men, and that the Boche were expecting him. She begged him to turn back. Whether Fenwick underestimated the threat, was set on revenge for his reportedly dead comrades or was incensed by the enemy's treatment of civilians, will never be known. 'Thank you, Madame,' he answered, 'but I intend to attack them.'[1]

Fenwick roared towards the first German machine-gun post with his Vickers K blazing. Miraculously the jeep got past, only to run into a wall of fire from a second position. A 20mm round smashed into Fenwick's forehead, killing him instantly. The same burst killed Menginou and the French sergeant. Duffy was hit by a slug that sliced open his jaw, and the jeep careened off the road, crashing into a tree. The Germans closed in and pulled Frank Dunkley out of the wreckage. Duffy flickered into consciousness to see the sergeant being marched away, his face covered in blood. He was never seen alive again.

57. 'My wife will be furious if I get myself killed today'

Mayne appointed Riding commander of Gain in Fenwick's place, but instructed him to lie low for the next few days. He sent parties to watch the Orléans–Pithiviers and Orléans–Montarges roads. The first two parties brought back good intelligence, but a third, consisting of Troopers Long and Morton, failed to return. The two SAS-men finally tramped into camp twenty-four hours late, to report that the jeep sent to extract them, manned by Troopers John Ion and Leslie Packman, had been bumped by a company of about forty Germans. They had heard gunshots while making for the rendezvous at first light, and had seen the jeep abandoned in the road. They weren't sure whether Ion and Packman were still alive.

In fact, the two SAS-men had been hustled to a château at Chilleurs-aux-Bois, where they were tortured by the SS and shot in the back of the head. Their hands were cut off. Jim Almonds realized what had happened when he visited the deserted château a few days later and found a lock of Ion's distinctive blond hair. When their graves were opened weeks afterwards, a third decomposed body was found with them – possibly that of Frank Dunkley, who had suffered the same fate.

Mayne terminated Gain three days after Ion and Packman vanished. The Fenwick group had lost eleven men killed or missing, but had cut the railway sixteen times, destroyed two locomotives and fifty-six trucks, and derailed two trains. After Mayne and Sadler left, Almonds and Riding were picked up by the advancing Americans, who accused them of being spies. They were taken in front of the General Officer Commanding the US Third Army, George Patton, who told them, 'If you're Brits, you'll be OK, if not, you'll be shot.' They were back in Britain by the end of August.

While Mayne and Sadler were with Gain, Bob Melot had signalled Moor Park that the DZ in Merry-Vaux forest was ready. The Op Kipling recce party – Capt. Derrick Harrison and five men of C Squadron – dropped the following night. Harrison and his mates had adopted a new way of jumping – with their leg-bags hitched high across their chests. There were no problems on exit, but Harrison's hand was caught in the uncoiling rope when he jettisoned his bag, and his middle finger was broken.

Melot was waiting for them on the DZ with partisans from Maquis Chevrier, a well-disciplined unit mostly made up of ex-regular French soldiers. Within minutes of landing, Melot and a plump, dark-haired Maquis girl had splinted Harrison's broken finger with a lightweight file from his own escape kit. In the next few days, another eighteen men and five jeeps arrived.

Melot's instructions from Mayne were to ensure that the Maquis kept quiet in the lead-up to Transfigure. This proved difficult, because he was unable to reveal details of the forthcoming oper-ation. On 18 August, though, everything changed. Melot got word from Moor Park that Transfigure had been cancelled. The Americans had broken through at the Cotentin peninsula, render-ing the Airborne plan obsolete. As Harrison's jeeps passed through local villages over the next days, the SAS-men were taken for liberators, fêted and garlanded by the villagers. After running unexpectedly into the forward battalion of the US 4 Armoured Division, they loaded up with 'K Rations'. They returned to the Kipling base at Merry-Vaux on 22 August. Bob Melot was astonished to hear that the Americans had arrived.

That afternoon, Harrison's second-in-command, Lt. Stewart Richardson, Royal Tank Regiment, discovered that one of the pintle-mounts for his rear Vickers K was cracked. He asked Harrison if he could drive to the neighbouring village of Aillant to get it welded. Harrison agreed, but decided to accompany him in a second jeep. Stewart's driver was Trooper Tony Brearton, another ex-RTR-man, and Harrison took with him L.Cpl. John 'Curly' Hall, Yorkshire Hussars, who had been with him at Termoli. The fifth man was an interpreter, Fauchois, attached from 4 SAS.

They roared out of the forest purlieus into the cultivated land – a flat patchwork quilt of blond wheat-fields and green trees in majestic leaf. Scanning the way ahead, Harrison noticed a guff of black smoke hanging over the village of Les Ormes, not far away. As they moved forward, the pall of smoke grew thicker. Harrison stopped at a crossroads a hundred yards from the village and heard the distinct chuckle of small-arms fire. Seconds later, an old lady wobbled up the track from the village on a bicycle, tears streaming down her face. She told Fauchois that the 'Boche' had occupied the village and were torching it. She was on her way to alert the Maquis in Aillant. When Harrison inquired how many Boche there were, she answered that there might be two or three hundred. 'Too many for you, Monsieur,' she said.

Harrison told her that they would inform the Maquis, but after she had gone, he realized that by the time the partisans arrived, it would be too late to save the village. The SAS-men held a quick powwow. 'I say attack,' said Fauchois. 'We'll have the element of surprise,' Harrison said, 'and should be able to shoot our way out of anything we meet. The odds are something like fifty-to-one but I hope they'll get such a shock that we'll pull it off.' The others agreed.[1]

Harrison gripped the front twin-Vickers. Hall gunned gas. The two jeeps fried rubber, spooned dirt, shrieked into the village square with Union Jacks up. A Waffen SS officer in field-grey stood in the road, pistol in hand. Harrison saw his eyes go big with shock, and squeezed twin-triggers. The Vickers K rasped, the German lurched and fell. The pistol clattered into the gutter. Harrison took in houses, an orchard, a church, a truck, two staff cars, a bunch of Boche in field-grey. He stood up in his seat, pulled iron, traversing the Germans. Twin-Vickers streaked, incendiary rounds socked metal, chugged petrol tanks. Cars and trucks threw up steel shards, spurls of flame and smoke. Germans twitched, lurched, spattered blood, dropped Schmeissers, hurdled through smoke, and clawed for cover. 'Many of them died in those first few seconds in front of the church,' Harrison said, 'lit by the flickering flames of the burning vehicles.'[2]

Harrison screamed at Hall to reverse, but the jeep caromed on. It stopped smack in the middle of the square, thirty yards from the church. The Germans were recovering. Schmeissers and rifles chirred out from cover, rounds scraping air. There were German faces at the windows of a nearby high building.

Harrison dekkoed Hall and saw his driver face-down on the steering-wheel, pulsing blood. He toed the starter. The engine was dead. He squeezed twin-triggers again. Nothing happened. Both guns were jammed. He pivoted into the back of the jeep, grabbed the Bren. It popped a burst and stuck hard. German rounds wheezed, spiked bodywork. He vaulted to the single Vickers on the driver's side, double-tapped. The gun bleared flame twice and stopped. 'A dud jeep and three jammed guns,' Harrison thought. 'Hell, what a mess!'[3]

He had almost forgotten Richardson, until he realized that covering fire was whomping over his shoulder. He flashed a glance, saw the other jeep halted by a wall, took in the twin-Vickers yomping, Richardson cracking .45 calibre rounds from his Colt at the Germans in the windows. He grabbed his M1 carbine and pumped off fifteen .30 calibre slugs at the enemy. He switched mags painfully with his splinted hand, and fired again. 'I fired whenever I saw movement,' he said. 'A German made a dash for safety. I fired from the hip and he pitched forward on to his face.'[4]

He lugged Hall's body from the jeep, dragged him to the centre of the square. A shooter appeared in a doorway to his right. He fired one-handed, slapped the enemy back. He kept on dragging Hall's body as 9mm bullets rasped and croaked around him. He saw brilliant tracer-trails like lightning streaks homing in, dancing like a boxer as if he could dodge them. 'Look out!' someone bawled in English. 'The orchard on your left!'

Harrison saw Germans doubling towards him through the trees. He sprinted for the orchard wall, crouched down, sprayed fire. He ran back to the jeep. He saw Fauchois trying to hump Hall's body to the second jeep, and yelled at the Frenchman to stop. Skulking behind the jeep, he lobbed off more rounds. Suddenly it came to him that it was his wedding anniversary. 'Lord, my wife will be furious if I get myself killed today of all days,' he thought.

His hand kicked, spurted blood. He had taken a hit. The Germans saw it and buzzed thick fire. The covering tattoo behind him faltered. He told himself to keep shooting. He fumbled for a mag with his bloody hand and clicked it in place shakily. The carbine was slick with his blood. He shot at a German who had emerged from the orchard. The carbine jammed. The German's rifle clacked. A slug zipped his knuckles.

He felt for the butt of his Colt .45. It wasn't there. He wrangled the bloody mag out of the carbine. More German rounds whipped and clanked. He ejected cartridges, cleared the stoppage, got the fresh mag in. He lifted the carbine. A jeep engine growled behind him. 'Dash for it!' someone screamed. He turned and played hopscotch towards the other jeep, still whacking off .30 calibre rounds. He made the jeep. It was already moving as he jumped for it. Hands helped him in. The motor shrieked. Jeep wheels screwed, roiling dust. At the rear Vickers, Fauchois sent a goodbye tattoo splurging across the square. Tony Brearton stamped gas, the jeep spurted forward, careened round a bend, plunged into trees.

Back at Kipling base in Merry-Vaux, Harrison reported to Melot that Hall was dead. After dark, Richardson led a recce back to Les Ormes. He returned with the news that the Germans had skedaddled. Harrison's patrol had come on the SS-men in the act of executing twenty villagers. The first two had been shot a moment before they had whaled into the square, but the other eighteen had run for it when the SAS started shooting. Richardson had seen Hall's body, placed in a coffin by the locals, next to their two dead hostages. He was able to report that during their action that day they had snagged a truck and two cars, and sixty enemy dead and wounded. Harrison was feeling bad about Hall, who had been with him ever since he had first joined 1 SAS in North Africa. 'The news [Richardson] brought back gave us some consolation,' he wrote.[5]

There was no time to rest. That night a villager rushed into the camp to say that a big convoy was making a beeline for Kipling base. Two jeeps went out to set up an ambush. Back at camp, with both hands bandaged, Harrison waited for gunfire in vain. To his surprise, the two jeeps returned with a string of vehicles behind them. Moments later, Harrison found himself face to face with Major Tony Marsh, Duke of Cornwall's Light Infantry, C Squadron's OC. 'Hello Harry. Hear you've been getting yourself in a mess,' Marsh said. Harrison was surprised – he'd thought Transfigure was off. Marsh confirmed that it had been cancelled. Instead of being inserted by glider, he'd begged a ride on a fleet of US Dakotas. His men had driven through American lines from Orléans, and had bumped a German column on the way.

Four days later, Marsh instructed Harrison to drive back to Orléans, pick up the rest of C Squadron, and guide them to Kipling base. As he passed through a local village, Harrison's jeep almost collided with a black Citroën. The car stopped, and out stepped Paddy Mayne, who invited him into one of the houses for lunch and a chat. Marsh and Melot joined them there later.

Since leaving Gain, Mayne had been weaving in and out of Allied lines, visiting SAS operations. Harrison had last seen his commanding officer at Fairford, but found that his experience under fire had changed his perspective. 'When I first met [Mayne] he was Zeus. He was a god,' said Harrison, '. . . [Now] he was just one of the gods . . . Zeus on earth.'[6]

58. 'Why don't we just fuck off quietly because we're not going to do any good here'

Another 'Zeus on earth' was Field Marshal Erwin Rommel. The British had tried and failed to take him out in Libya in 1941. They tried again in July 1944, when Gaff, a six-man unit of 2 SAS, was inserted between Chartres and Rambouillet, tasked to infiltrate the château Rommel was using at La Roche-Guyon, west of Paris. Their orders were to kidnap or kill him. The Gaff commander, Lt. Jack 'Ramon' Lee, was a Franco-American who had served with 62 Commando. One of his men was English, but the other four were attached from 3 SAS, and, like Lee himself, ex-Foreign Legionnaires.

The intel on Rommel's location was sound. It had come from Bill Fraser at Houndsworth via his Maquis contacts. Fraser was desperate to have a crack at Rommel himself, but was overruled by Rory McLeod, who insisted that the op should be launched from the UK by 2 SAS. Like the earlier 11 Commando attempt, though, Gaff was redundant before it started. Eight days earlier, Rommel had suffered a fractured skull when his car crashed during a strafing run by RAF Spitfires on the Vimoutiers road. He would never see active service again.

Six days after Harrison's shoot-out in Les Ormes, Mayne arrived back at Fraser's camp in the Morvan, with Marsh and Melot. He told Fraser that the Allied front line was now fluid. The Normandy break-out had been successful. Three days earlier, Paris had been liberated. Orléans had also been taken, and Kipling was enveloped by the advancing Allied cohorts. Mayne proposed to move Marsh's C Squadron boys to the Morvan, and pull Fraser's A Squadron out. They had done a superb job – Houndsworth was the most successful of SAS ops in France – but they had been in the field for three months and Mayne reckoned they needed a rest. German divisions were streaming towards the frontier. There would be less scope for SAS dirty-work as the Allies advanced, and C Squadron would convert to a counter-intelligence role, in Holland and

Belgium, once the front line had passed them by. All other 1 SAS
teams would be extracted.

Next day Marsh returned to Kipling base, where he met Derrick
Harrison, who had guided in two dozen jeeps carrying the main
C Squadron party. Five hours later they were in the deep wooded
valleys of the Morvan. Marsh set up his own camp, a mile and a
half from Brassy. On 1 September he dispatched two jeeps under
Lt. Peter 'Monty' Goddard to bring back a trailer of three-inch
mortar bombs, damaged and left behind the previous day.

Goddard, an ex-Royal Army Pay Corps officer and former
chartered accountant, had never been in action before, but was
keen to have a bash at the Hun. Because of his lack of experience,
Marsh sent with him his veteran squadron sergeant-major, Bob
Lilley, and another SAS veteran, Sgt. Bob Lowson, the man who
had ferried mortar bombs for Muirhead at Termoli. The fourth
man was Trooper 'Titch' Howes.

That night, Harrison and Marsh were woken up by the groan
of a jeep engine. Big Bob Lilley loped out of the shadows, squatted
down with them, and lit a cigarette. He said that Goddard had
been killed. At Tannay, they'd been having a quiet lunch in a café
with some Maquis, when artillery fire had started up nearby. A
German column was, said Lilley, 'leathering shite out of this
chateau on the hill' – a Maquis base. Goddard agreed to help the
partisans ambush the German column. The plan was that the
Maquis would attack from the front, while the SAS crew hit
the enemy from the rear. Lilley was with Howe in the leading jeep
when they turned a bend and saw the column stretching away in
front of them. The last enemy vehicle was a truck carrying a 3.7cm
flak gun.

Shells whooshed and crumped into the distant building.
Goddard's jeep pulled up alongside him, and the ex-accountant
announced that he was going to capture the gun. Lilley scanned
the column, and saw no sign of the Maquis. 'Look, sir,' he said,
'why don't we just fuck off quietly because we're not going to do
any good here.'[1]

Goddard insisted. He pulled on a pair of leather gloves, and hoiked the single Vickers K from the driver's side of Lilley's jeep. 'You cover me,' he told the sergeant-major. Lilley unclipped the Bren from behind his seat, and lay prone on the verge. He popped off covering fire. Goddard sprinted down a ditch, his Vickers cackling, manically spliffing tracer. Lilley whacked bursts. The Germans clocked Goddard, and enfiladed him before he had got within a hundred yards. Lilley said he'd been hit so many times his body was carved to shreds. 'I suppose I should have gone and got myself killed but I didn't want to,' he said later. 'I'd given up trying to be heroic by that stage. It was terrible, a waste of life.'[2]

Goddard had ignored the 'old operator's' advice, and got whacked out. Though Goddard received no posthumous decoration, his action demonstrated that the standard of SAS recruits had been diluted in the desperate quest to fill the ranks. Goddard, like Ian Fenwick, had broken Mayne's axiom of confidence without rashness.

Brian Franks thought that some of the new SAS recruits shouldn't have been there at all. 'They were either so scared as to be useless or so confident that they were extremely careless,' he wrote. 'Most of these men . . . were clearly not of the right type and hadn't had sufficient training . . . the experienced men were good and could almost always be guaranteed to get away with it.'[3]

The Germans were fighting their way back home, with US divisions in hot pursuit. The SAS job was almost done. On 7 September, Frederick Browning broadcast a message to SAS troops, declaring that they had done more to hasten the destruction of the German Fifth and Seventh Armies than any other single effort in the army. 'To say that you have done your job well is to put it mildly,' he said. 'You have done magnificently.'[4] For his command and coordination of SAS ops, Paddy Mayne was awarded his third DSO, and the Croix de Guerre with palm. 'It was entirely due to Lt. Col. Mayne's fine leadership and example,' ran the citation, 'and his utter disregard of danger, that the unit was able to achieve such striking successes.'[5]

Some 2 SAS ops would stay in the field until October. One of these was Loyton, commanded by Brian Franks himself. The Loyton advance party had gone in on 1 September, with the intention of harassing the retreating German columns in the Vosges area until the Americans arrived. Franks later claimed fifteen enemy vehicles destroyed, one train derailed, and fifty Germans killed – a poor return for the hundred SAS-men involved. Loyton was an ambitious strategic operation that might have worked had it not been sent in too late. As it was, Franks lost two men killed and twenty-eight captured, all of whom were murdered in cold blood by the Germans. The inhabitants of the town of Moussey, who had offered every possible assistance to the SAS, suffered heavy reprisals. Over two hundred of them were herded into concentration camps from which most did not return.

Loyton would not be extracted until 19 October. By then Houndsworth was long over. Leaving their jeeps for Marsh's crew, the A Squadron boys had hared off towards Orléans in a motley convoy of requisitioned civilian cars powered by gasogene. Using side roads they dodged through the German lines. 'The first indication of Allied troops,' Johnny Cooper wrote, 'was an American military policeman on point duty . . . the MP was dumbfounded and let us through.'[6]

At the airbase, the Houndsworth team found a squadron of USAF Liberators disgorging tons of flour for the people of Paris. Reg Seekings, the 9mm round still lodged in his neck, went off to see the base commander, who turned out to be a Texan weapons enthusiast. Seekings offered him a Bren-gun in return for places on the Liberators going back to the UK. The USAF-man said they could hitch a ride on the aircraft leaving the next morning.

They took off through galleries of cloud and watched the sun strobing the French countryside beneath them. Ian Wellsted was shocked at the devastation he saw – villages bombed and shelled to rubble, the frames of wrecked aircraft amid patches of burnt sienna, reminding him of 'moths that had singed their wings at a candle's flame'.[7] The battlefields of France gave way to the deep azure of the Channel, then to the cliffs of England – green meadows, dwarf cows, toy houses. 'How beautiful it looked in the sun, and how peaceful,' Wellsted wrote. '. . . It was good to be back in English skies.'[8]

59. 'In the face of enemy machine-gun fire'

On the morning of 9 April 1945, Paddy Mayne's signaller, David Danger, received an urgent wireless message. It came from Cpl. Eddie Ralphs, the man who had scragged nine Germans at Termoli with his Bren. Ralphs was pinned down in a ditch with other B Squadron men, and his OC, Major Dick Bond, had just been shot dead by a German sniper. 'Paddy almost blew up,' recalled Billy Hull, Royal Ulster Rifles, Mayne's driver. '[He] just kept saying, "Poor Dick, poor Dick".'[1]

They were crossing the flatlands of north Germany, wooded fens, criss-crossed with ditches and canals, that made tough going for their newly-armoured jeeps. Heading for the city of Oldenburg en route to the U-Boat docks at Wilhelmshaven, B and C Squadrons, 1 SAS, were pathfinding on the left flank of 4 Canadian Armoured Division, whose tanks were rumbling far behind. The SAS had taken over from an armoured recce squadron the previous day. For the German ops, they had left their SAS insignia behind. They were disguised in black berets with Royal Tank Regiment badges, and had even been issued with RTR paybooks. By now, the fate of the missing Bulbasket men was suspected, and the murder of the Garstin stick known from the survivors, Jones and Vaculik. The SAS knew what would happen to them if they were captured, and their identity revealed.

It was full daylight, and for the past few minutes the squadrons had been travelling in echelon, bunched closer together than they should have been. They had been hunting for a way across the next canal, and Dick Bond's men had found a bridge intact at a village called Borgerwald. They hadn't been expecting a contact.

Briefing the SAS-men that morning, Intelligence Officer Major Mike Blackman had informed them that 'there would be next to no opposition, except from the German equivalent of the Home Guard'.[2] Most of the men were inexperienced newcomers, and regarded the job of supporting an armoured division as 'a swan'. Derrick Harrison, with Tony Marsh's C Squadron, knew it wasn't real SAS work, but at least it was a job. 'We were satisfied,' he said, 'if a little perturbed. Our "mechanised mess tins" were poor substitutes for the armoured cars we were relieving.'[3]

Mayne was aware that there could be German strongpoints on the road, and had warned the men to keep their eyes peeled. Many of the newcomers had never seen him in action, though, and considered him far gone in drink, and 'over the hill' at twenty-nine. Derrick Harrison surmised that there might be trouble from the Hitler Youth. Neither he nor Mayne knew they were up against their old foes from Termoli, the crack 1 Parachute Division.

Mayne stood up and scanned the landscape over the armoured farings that were now standard fittings on SAS jeeps. He could see the B Squadron vehicles halted at a crossroads at the bottom of the valley through which the canal ran. The road was a narrow track leading between a cluster of buildings. On the left-hand side was a barn, and on the right a nest of two houses forming a protective 'L' shape, with the upstroke of the 'L' at right-angles to the road. Beyond the two houses was a dense copse of trees. He kicked out Danger, and Hull hit the accelerator. Jeep wheels mangled tread as the vehicle raced towards the village. Harrison, whose C Squadron jeeps were halted on the side of the road looking down on Borgerwald, saw Mayne flash past.

Since Loyton had been pulled out of France the previous October, all five SAS Regiments had been largely unemployed. The exception was 3 Squadron, 2 SAS, under Roy Farran, which had been sent to carry out Ops Galia and Tombola – partisan missions in northern Italy. The Italian jobs had tied down large numbers of German troops, but on the northern front there were few opportunities for SAS operations. The war had settled down to static fighting in Holland and on the German border, punctuated only by Hitler's desperate and unsuccessful Ardennes offensive in December.

In January, Brigadier J. M. 'Mad Mike' Calvert, Royal Engineers, had taken over the running of 3, 4 and 5 SAS. A military thinker of genius, Calvert's ideas were far ahead of their time. His paper *The Operations of Small Forces Behind Enemy Lines* had led to the setting up of the Auxiliary Units, many of whose soldiers were now fighting with the SAS. In March, when Rory McLeod was moved to India, Calvert was appointed Brigadier 1 SAS Brigade. Despite the fact that he was the army's top expert on guerrilla warfare, and had done a superlative job as 2IC of Orde Wingate's legendary Chindits in the rain-forests of Burma, the SAS considered him as much an 'outsider' as McLeod.

Calvert himself foresaw a role for the SAS in East Asia, and Churchill had allowed him to make preliminary plans. The same idea had occurred to David Stirling, now incarcerated in Colditz Castle, who had conceived the Chung-King Project – a three-part scheme proposing the deployment of an SAS Brigade to prepare the way for a US invasion of Japan. Meanwhile, though, Hitler still had to be dealt with. Calvert had been searching for any acceptable job for the SAS Brigade in the Dutch-German theatre, and had agreed to a number of operations, none of them classic SAS tasks.

In March, Frankforce – a squadron each from 1 and 2 SAS, under Brian Franks – had crossed the Rhine on amphibious Buffaloes. Their mission, Archway, was to scout deep into Germany ahead of Montgomery's 21 Army Group. The innovative Amherst, which had gone in on 8 April, had involved a blind drop on radar in zero visibility by seven hundred men of 3 and 4 SAS over the Groningen, Coevorden and Zwolle areas of northern Holland. Equipped for only seventy-two hours in the field, the SAS-men were to harry the Germans, prevent the destruction of eighteen bridges, secure the airfield at Steenwijk, provide intelligence, and recce the routes for 2 Canadian Corps. Larkswood, a task involving three hundred men of 5 (Belgian) SAS, was running parallel with Mayne's. A single squadron of 2 SAS would drop near the Zuyder

Zee and capture the key bridges over the Apeldoorn canal – a mission codenamed Keystone.

Mayne's operation, Howard, with a hundred and eighty men of 1 SAS, had begun on 6 April when his force had left Tilbury with forty jeeps. At Canadian Army HQ near Nijmegen, Mayne had been briefed by Mike Calvert, who informed him that 5 SAS would be taking the left flank on 4 Armoured Division's advance, while his B and C Squadrons took the right. The Mayne group had concentrated at Meppen, and crossed the Rhine at Emmerich the next day.

At Borgerwald, Mayne found his B Squadron men squatting by their jeeps in front of the L-shaped nest of houses. There was a constant tick-tack of rounds from the enemy, but it was coming from the house hidden behind the L's upstroke, which stood in the shooters' line of fire. About a hundred yards away, the three point-jeeps stood abandoned. The acting commander, Tim Iredale, confirmed that OC Dick Bond was dead. He told Mayne that the three leading jeeps had been banjoed suddenly from enemy positions on the right.

Lt. Phillip Schlee, who had been with the scout party, said later that they had been whopped by Spandau-fire and rockets fired from Panzerfausts – the German equivalent of the bazooka – as they passed between the second house and the wood. The gunner in the first jeep, Sgt. Schofield, had taken hits in both thighs. The third jeep's gunner had also been wounded. Schlee was in the middle jeep, with Eddie Ralphs on the rear Vickers. Ralphs spritzed .303 tracer at the enemy. The others rattled off with Brens and Tommy-guns. 'Eventually,' Schlee said, '[we] got out of our jeeps . . . and took to the ditch with the wounded.'[4] They were still pinned down there by enemy fire.

Iredale told Mayne that Dick Bond had attempted to reach Schlee's position by crawling down the ditch, but had found his way blocked by a drainpipe. It was while attempting to creep over the pipe that a German sniper had potted him clean through the forehead. Lt. John Scott, an ex-ranker field-commissioned by Mayne in France the previous year, had then sent Bond's driver,

Trooper Mike Lewis – a Czech-born Jew whose real name was Mikhael Levinsohn – to have another go. 'He was small and I thought he would be able to climb through the drainage pipe,' Scott said. Instead, Lewis, like Bond, tried to crawl over the pipe. The same shooter took him out with an identical head-shot. 'I felt very bad about it,' said Scott, 'since I was the one who ordered him in there. He was a brave man.'[5] The jeeps had been ambushed so suddenly that no one in Iredale's group could estimate the enemy's strength.

Mayne doubled forward to the first house, to find out if it presented any threat. It didn't. Scott and his boys had pumped the roof full of lead minutes earlier, and a German family had evacuated it under a white flag. Mayne sauntered to his jeep, unhooked the Bren, pulled back the cocking lever. He filled his smock with magazines, and nodded to Hull to follow him with his Thompson. Hull sensed that Mayne was in 'one of his silent rages'. This may have been because he had been pally with Bond, an Auxiliary Units officer who had taken over B Squadron recently. More likely, though, it was exasperation at the indecisiveness of his new men. 'We were all pretty clueless,' admitted one of them, Lt. David Surrey-Dane, ex-4 Para. 'We hadn't much idea of this type of forward reconnaissance work.'[6]

While Mayne edged around the first house, hugging the wall, Hull went inside to find a vantage point for covering fire. He slipped upstairs and found a window overlooking the second house. He blipped .45 calibre bursts. There was an instant answer. 'The bastards opened up on me,' he said, '. . . bullets were ricocheting off the walls and ceiling, and in seconds the ceiling was set on fire by tracers.'[7]

At the same moment, Mayne stepped out of cover, his Bren held at the shoulder like a rifle. He tick-ticked short bursts. Tracer whaled vapour trails. Rounds spat back at him, chiselling brickwork. Although the official report said that Mayne took out all the enemy in the house, it is probable that it was occupied only by the sniper who had potted Bond and Lewis. He lifted the Bren, sighted it, and blew him away. The main threat, he saw, came from machine-gunners and the Panzerfaust shooters in the wood.

He called up one of Iredale's jeeps to give covering fire, ramped back to the B Squadron men, and asked for a volunteer. The first taker was Lt. John Scott. They climbed into a jeep. Mayne braced the steering-wheel. Scott gripped the Vickers and heaved back the cocking-handles. Mayne hit the starter. The Willys motor revved, and the jeep shot forward. The second they were past the covering vehicle, Scott swivelled the gun at the second house, and squeezed iron. Rounds blatted and lashed, whipping off the walls. '*The woods!*' Mayne hollered. '*Fire at the woods!*' Scott angled the gun at the trees, pulled metal, boosted fire. Smoke trails curved into the copse. A rocket hissed past them, gobbing smoke. Spandau rounds creaked, stripped air, clunked steel. Mayne's car streaked past the abandoned jeeps. Scott banked the Vickers and snapped rounds. Mayne yelled at Schlee's men in the ditch that he'd pick them up on the next run.

Mayne braked, wrenched the steering-wheel. Scott ducked into the seat next to him, grasping the Browning on the passenger's side. Mayne speared the accelerator. Scott spliffed .50 calibre ball. The jeep rushed past the wood back to the first house, and wheeled again. Three times Mayne surged through the tunnel of enemy fire, while Scott saturated the place with rounds. Panzerfaust rockets had stopped coming. The machine-gun fire dwindled, then died. Finally, Mayne braked the jeep opposite the drainage pipe where Bond's and Lewis's bodies lay sprawled. He jumped out, pitched over to the ditch and started hoisting the wounded out. Scott wellied fire into the place where the enemy had been. 'By the time Paddy got our men out of the ditch, things were quiet,' he recalled. 'We retreated down the road some three miles, where we buried Dick Bond and Trooper Lewis at the side of a farmhouse.'[8]

The new recruits, who had thought Mayne was 'over the hill', were dumbstruck at the sheer audacity of the deed. For his action at Borgerwald, he would be awarded his fourth DSO. The officers who wrote the citation, Derrick Harrison and Ian Blackman, though, were not happy with the result. They had put him in for the Victoria Cross.

John Scott, who, despite his bravery that day, received no award, said later that the citation was inaccurate. First of all, Scott himself was not named – and in fact, though a 'rear gunner' is mentioned, the citation does read as if Mayne had been doing the shooting himself. Second, the report states that Mayne rescued the stranded men 'in the face of enemy machine-gun fire'. Scott was clear that there was no enemy fire at the time he stopped the jeep. To have attempted to pull out the wounded under direct fire from only yards away would have been suicidal, and Mayne was always a calculating soldier. According to another witness, David Surrey-Dane, the phrase 'in the face of enemy machine-gun fire' was added to present a better case for Mayne's being awarded the VC. 'I think they tried to make it something more Hollywood style,' Scott said.[9]

This was entirely unnecessary. The Borgerwald action was a splendid feat of arms, even without the added phrase, and the suppression of Scott's part in the affair. That Mayne deserved the VC, not once, but many times over, is incontestable. As it happened, Mayne himself wasn't entirely happy with his fourth DSO. He told Surrey-Dane that he would rather have had the more modest MC.

60. He couldn't believe that he'd actually survived

Bill Fraser's A Squadron had crossed the Rhine at Wesel with Brian Franks's Frankforce almost a fortnight earlier. Two days after the crossing they ran into a party of Canadian parachutists pinned down in a wood by a Spandau machine gun. Fraser hit dead ground, and his jeeps popped up on the machine-gunners' left flank, only thirty yards away. The Spandau cranked towards them and blitzed Fraser in the point-jeep. A bullet smashed into his hand and his jeep somersaulted out of control. Fraser survived.

Alex Muirhead's troop wheeled their jeeps right, Vickers Ks clattering a deadly broadside. The Spandau went silent, all the gunners dead or badly wounded. 'We blasted hell out of them,' Reg Seekings recalled. He spotted an arm waving and weaved up to the machine-gun nest to find a German sergeant shot in the thigh. 'You can imagine what a mess he was in,' he said. 'Bone everywhere. I got him out, but he died about half an hour later.' Before Seekings left the position, though, a fifteen-year-old boy popped up clutching a pair of potato-masher grenades. Seekings bawled at him in German to throw them down. He was just about to zap the kid, when he dropped the bombs. The German command-post surrendered moments later, and an officer told Seekings that if he had shot the boy, they would have fought to the death.

Lying up in a farmhouse at Schermbeck the following day, Harry Poat informed Ian Wellsted he'd been promoted squadron commander – Fraser had been casevaced to a field hospital. He didn't want to go: he couldn't accept that after surviving North Africa, Italy and France, by the skin of his teeth, he wouldn't be in at the kill. When they set off that day, Seekings found himself saddled with a W/T operator named Perkins, who up to then had been with John Tonkin. Tonkin had asked to swap him for Seekings's operator, Neil McMillan, because Perkins had threatened to punch him. When Perkins jumped into Seekings's jeep, the SSM told him, 'One squeak out of you and I'll flatten you for bloody good.'

Seekings's rear-gunner, Tpr. Jock McKenzie, Cameron Highlanders, was another 'character'. In Italy he had tried it on with the daughter of an Italian family he and Seekings had been billeted with. When Seekings had warned him off, he had threatened to kill him in his sleep. The girl's mother had asked Seekings how he dared go to bed. He told her that Mac wouldn't risk harming him: he needed him too much.

The 1 SAS contingent of Archway, mostly Fraser's A Squadron, and Tonkin's D Squadron, had split up with the 2 SAS party the previous day. While 2 SAS was heading for Munster with 6 Independent Guards Armoured Brigade, the 1 SAS crew were forging ahead of 8 Battalion, the Parachute Regiment, and the Inns of Court Regiment – a light armoured unit – making for Ostrich and Rhade. They were in a convoy of a dozen jeeps led by two Dingo armoured cars. Just past Ostrich they were following a road running between tall trees when a German stuck his head up out of a ditch and let rip with a Panzerfaust. The rocket hooshed, struck the leading Dingo, welted flame. Small-arms fire shuddered out of the bush, and from a barn further on. The jeep ahead of Seekings's, driven by Trooper Dixie Deane, jiggered forward past the flaming Dingo. Deane's gunner sprattled Vickers fire at the barn up ahead. Seekings hit the accelerator, and the jeep lurched. Behind him, Sgt. Cornelius 'Maggie' McGinn, who had survived the attack on Roy Bradford's jeep on Houndsworth, reversed his vehicle with rounds clanking against his armoured farings. McGinn rolled out of his seat into the wood. Further back, Sgt. Jeff Du Vivier and his oppo, Trooper 'Digger' Weller, had unpacked a two-inch mortar. Seekings heard shells whooping over his head, stonking the barn. Ian Wellsted and Jack Terry were skirmishing towards the building on foot, carbines tack-tacking.

As his jeep shot through the wall of incoming, Seekings's rear-gunner, Jock McKenzie, was hit. Seekings passed the barn and stopped. He pulled Mac under the jeep and searched him. He couldn't find any wound. 'Get back behind that gun,' he roared.

'I'm hit,' Mac pleaded. 'I'm bleeding to death. I know it.'

'I'm also hit, sir!' Perkins yelped suddenly. Seekings glanced up at his W/T op and his eyes widened. A row of seven or eight entry wounds was stitched all the way down Perkins's left arm, at neat one-and-a-half-inch intervals.

Seekings lifted McKenzie back on to the seat, and noticed that his battledress was drenched in blood. He ripped away the sleeve and found that Mac's armpit had been blown out by an explosive bullet. His face was as white as chalk. Seekings broke open two shell-dressings, shoved them in the bloody hole, and told Mac to put pressure on them.

Seekings remembered passing an Airborne first-aid post earlier, and knew he had to get the men back there. Perkins lay drooped over the rear guns. Seekings sat Mac in the front. 'What can you do to man those guns?' he demanded. As he accelerated Mac fired the forward Vickers one-handed, screaming '*You bastards!*' Gritting his teeth with pain, Perkins managed to get off a burst or two from the rear gun. When Seekings pulled up at the first-aid post, the Airborne medical officer told him that if he had arrived a few minutes later, Mac would have bled to death. Seekings suddenly recalled his remark to his Italian landlady, and grinned.

The Archway team fought on day after day into the heart of Germany, hitting machine-gun posts, running into ambushes, taking prisoners, whacking out SS troops, Hitler Youth, German Home Guard. Tpr. John Glyde, Royal Artillery, was almost de-capitated when his jeep was hit by a Panzerfaust rocket. L Detachment Original and prison-camp escapee Cpl. Jim Blakeney was taken out by an armoured car, while running from his blazing jeep. Jock Lewes's former batman, Tpr. Roy Davies, Welsh Guards, was badly wounded when his jeep was hit. Tpr. Dougie Fergusson, Highland Light Infantry, another ex-L Detachment man, was shot trying to rescue him. Ian Wellsted was wounded in both legs. Jeff Du Vivier copped a 20mm round in the calf, while ripping off his Vickers at an armoured car.

They passed through Nienburg. They passed through Neustadt. At Celle they found the bodies of two thousand concentration-camp victims – men, women, children – slaughtered by panicking Germans on the platforms of the railway station. At Bergen-Belsen they came across a camp eight miles square, where sixty thousand people had been packed into accommodation intended for only fifteen thousand. Typhoid was rampant, and the Allies had agreed to a three-day truce: fighting would result in the escape of the inmates, and the spread of the disease to Allied and German lines alike. After being inoculated, the SAS-men were sent into Belsen to find out what medical attention was needed. They were the first British troops into the concentration-camp.

Many were hardened fighters, but none expected what they saw that day. 'I will never forget my first sight of the inmates,' Johnny Cooper wrote. 'Ostensibly they were human beings, but to me [they] were just walking skeletons . . . we . . . discovered a whole series of communal graves, consisting of trenches about a hundred yards long and twenty feet deep, which were being steadily filled with naked, skeletal bodies . . .'[1]

One of the strangest aspects of the SAS visit to Belsen was that German guards and Hungarian and Romanian auxiliaries continued to shoot and torture prisoners, even though they knew British soldiers were in the camp. Intelligence Sergeant Duncan Ridler saw a group of living scarecrows feasting on what looked like a six-foot-high pile of potato-peelings. As he watched, a Romanian auxiliary shot a woman dead. Cooper realized that his mate Reg Seekings was working himself up into a frenzy. 'I could see that he was on the verge of pulling out his pistol,' Cooper said, 'and shooting the first German guard he came across.' Despite apocryphal stories, though, no guards were shot that day. The truce was observed. Instead, all the Romanians were arrested. Seekings contented himself with grabbing a guard and beating him to a pulp with his fists. 'As long as I live I will never forget the Germans who perpetrated such acts,' wrote Cooper. 'Although I was only twenty-one at the time, I had been in action for three years and was no stranger to violent death. What I saw in that camp, however, defies adequate description, and those scenes will stay with me forever.'[2]

On 3 May Mayne's two units, now amalgamated as a composite squadron under Tony Marsh, were north of Oldenburg when they were ordered to withdraw from the front and RV with the other SAS squadrons at Poperinghe, on the Franco-Belgian border. The same day, three armoured jeeps carrying Johnny Cooper, Reg Seekings, Jack Terry and other A Squadron men snailed along the docks of Kiel, the first Allied troops into the town.

Cooper and Seekings had set off at first light from their lying-up place in a farmhouse near Lübeck, sixty miles to the south. All along the road, Germans had come out waving white flags. About six miles out of Kiel, Cooper's jeep was halted by two German generals with their hands up. They told him that they had five hundred officers and NCOs under their command, who wanted to surrender. Cooper had little choice but to agree. The Germans marched forward one at a time, laid their weapons on the jeeps' bonnets, and saluted formally – not one of them, Cooper noted, attempted a 'Heil Hitler'. At first, Cooper found the whole thing 'a laugh', but it started to become embarrassing when it dawned on him that his tiny force couldn't possibly guard the prisoners. In the end, he told the senior general that his men would have to stay put until the main force arrived, and motored on towards the town.

Cooper wasn't aware that in entering Kiel they had driven across an armistice line. Brian Franks had sent a wireless message earlier warning him to stay out of the town, but he hadn't received it. The SAS jeeps halted outside the town hall, where Cooper graciously accepted the surrender of the Deputy Mayor. He, Seekings and Terry sauntered into the building and started smashing anything that sported a swastika or a portrait of Hitler. '[We] were in the mayor's office, having a right old time . . .' he recalled, 'when the following signal reached us: "Cooper of 1 Troop, get out. Get back to your original positions. You are well over the armistice line and this might upset the armistice agreement."'[3] Cooper acknowledged the signal. He and his men hopped quickly into their jeeps and beat a hasty retreat. As they roared back past their five hundred astonished prisoners of war, they waved them a cheery goodbye.

A week later Reg Seekings was sitting in a roadside café just outside Brussels when a young woman rushed in. 'The war is over,' she said.

'I've heard that one before,' Seekings replied.

'No, it's true,' she insisted. 'Your Prime Minister, Mr Churchill, is speaking now.' Seekings jogged into the nearby garage where there was a wireless tuned to the BBC. He heard Winston

Churchill declare that the armistice had been signed. The first feeling that came over him was one of astonishment. When he considered all he'd been through since jumping with Mayne's stick on Squatter, he couldn't believe that he'd actually survived.

61. 'In peacetime a man born to battle has to change his ways'

On 8 October 1945, 1 SAS paraded for the last time. The disbandment ceremony took place at Hylands Park, near Chelmsford – the 1 SAS base since the previous November. 2 SAS were disbanded the same day at their base at Colchester. 'The whole Regiment was drawn up, squadron by squadron, in front of the main house,' wrote Johnny Cooper. '. . . It was a very tragic day.'[1] Mayne was conspicuous, not only by his size, but because he was the only man present wearing the sand-coloured beret of desert days.

The SAS Regiment had come a long way from the *Case for the retention of a limited number of special service troops, for employment as parachutists* that David Stirling had scribbled out in his hospital bed. Yet his three basic principles – surprise, the deployment of small parties and the economical use of manpower – had remained unchanged, despite the various ways in which the wartime regiments had been misused. The SAS had established a unique modus operandi, neither as an Airborne commando-style raiding force, nor as an SOE-type group of secret agents operating with partisans, but as a military force capable of establishing bases behind enemy lines and launching continual raids for long periods. It had also established three ideal principles of action: command at the highest level, intelligence at the highest level, and the right to plan its own operations.

On 21 September, 5 SAS had been formally handed over to the Belgian government. A week later the two French regiments reverted to the French. The order to stand down 1 and 2 SAS had been issued on 4 October. The night before the disbandment, the 1 SAS boys held a wild party in Hylands House, the two-centuries-old manor that served as the officers' mess. It was the culmination of several days of revels, during which, at one point, Harry Poat and Johnny Cooper had drunkenly telephoned Prime Minister Clement Attlee's office and told his private secretary, 'If you cut our bacon ration, we'll cut a slice off your arse!'[2]

The high-point, though, came when Mayne drove a jeep up the central staircase of the hall, round two right-angled bends, through a pair of oak doors, and on to the landing. The house's owner and occupier, the long-suffering and amenable Mrs Hanbury, heiress of the Truman, Hanbury & Buxton brewing company, regarded Mayne with much affection. That night, though, she decided a line had been crossed. 'Now, Paddy, that's quite enough of that,' she said. 'You're keeping me awake. It's time you all got to bed.'[3] Despite the best efforts of the Regiment's star drivers, the jeep was stuck there. It had to be dismantled and brought down piece by piece.

In the early hours of 8 October, Mayne drew himself up, and told the men, 'I want everyone on parade, properly turned out at 8 a.m.' 'Everyone had to forget their hangovers quick,' said ex-SSM, now Captain, Jim Almonds, whom Mayne had commissioned in the field, 'get smartened up and get outside.'[4] Mike Calvert, who took the salute that morning, had had personal experience of Mayne's belligerence. During the SAS's last job, Op Apostle − overseeing the surrender of three hundred thousand German troops in Norway − Calvert had brought him down with a rugby tackle in the mess. Mayne, who had been haranguing SAS Brigade Major Esmond Baring at the time, picked himself up, seized his commanding officer with giant's hands and hurled him over his shoulder. Calvert's head came into sharp contact with the fender of the nearby fireplace, and he got up with two black eyes.

Since March − two months before the German surrender − Calvert had been working doggedly to find a new role for the Regiment. His initial objective, to deploy SAS troops in the Far East, had been supported by David Stirling, who had been released from Colditz in April. Stirling had relived old times by bringing Fitzroy Maclean MP to lunch with Winston Churchill, the man who had started it all with his 'bands of brothers' memo back in 1940. Churchill had been voted out of office that July.

Stirling's proposal was to form a new SAS brigade from three elements: 2 SAS, an American Regiment made up of ex-Office of Strategic Services men, and another consisting of released prisoners of war. Curiously, perhaps, Mayne's 1 SAS played no part in his scheme. Clearly, Stirling retained a degree of the old competitiveness. While he had endured a frustrating two years as a prisoner of war, Mayne had taken the SAS to new heights of excellence, and had emerged one of only eight men to have won the DSO four times. What Stirling might have achieved had he not been captured would forever remain open to conjecture.

Before his political defeat, Churchill had encouraged Stirling's Far East scheme, as he had encouraged Calvert, but this time his support may have been disingenuous. He had known all along about the Manhattan Project, and the likelihood that the war against Japan would be won by atomic strikes, rather than by ground troops. The SAS had even begun training for a job in Asia, but with the devastation of Nagasaki and Hiroshima in August, all bets were off.

The Regiment's days were not quite over, though. A small group of SAS-men, including Bob Bennett, were sent to Greece attached to the Military Reparations Committee, and spent another four years wearing the flaming sword. Rumours that they became involved in the civil war have never been confirmed. There was also the matter of the murder of SAS troops on Gain, Bulbasket, Loyton and other ops, to be dealt with. Brian Franks, who felt a personal commitment to his dead Loyton comrades, was determined to find out who was responsible. The previous May, Franks had sent a team to France, under his IO Major Eric Barkworth, to trace all the SAS-men still missing in action. This group would develop into the SAS War Crimes Team, which would bring several Nazis to court, and remain in operation for another four years.

Calvert had suggested to the Chief of the Imperial General Staff, Field Marshal Sir Alan Brooke, that the War Office should make a study of wartime special forces operations, so that the usefulness of these units could be assessed. On 13 August the Director of Air Warfare, Major General K. N. Crawford, issued a memo arguing that 'the Special Air Service Regiment has proved its value in the present war and it is considered that it should be retained in some form in the post-war army'.[5]

This conclusion was a triumph, not so much for Calvert or even Stirling, as for Blair Mayne. Too modest a man to claim that he had been a founder of the Regiment – though Stirling would later accept him as 'co-founder' – the SAS owed more to him than any other individual alive. It was Mayne who had rescued L Detachment with his classic strike at Tamet; it was Mayne who had proved its efficiency by personally bagging almost a hundred aircraft; it was Mayne's A Squadron that had saved the unit's reputation on the coast-road ops; it was Mayne whose compromise had rescued it from disbandment; it was Mayne's outstanding organization and command of the SRS that had led to the formation of the SAS Brigade, and the superb performance of Mayne's 1 SAS in France and Germany that had led directly to the recommendation that its skills should be preserved after the war.

Mayne didn't found the SAS, perhaps, but in a very real way he was the man who made the Regiment, the man without whom it might easily have vanished into obscurity, like the short-lived 'Popski's Private Army'. Even Stirling acknowledged this. '[Mayne's] achievements in battle and his superb leadership of the Regiment,' he wrote, 'undoubtedly made inevitable the establishment of the SAS as a permanent part of the British Defence Forces.'[6] Original Ernie Bond, captured on Squatter, put it more concisely. 'A lot of the SAS's strength was down to Mayne – the way he worked.'

As Mayne saluted Calvert that morning, though, it must have seemed to him that the dark days were just beginning. The articulate Calvert, more similar to Mayne than either would have admitted, probably voiced the thoughts of both, when he wrote, 'I was a fighting man. The fact remains that in peacetime a man born to battle has to change his ways, and this I had to face.'[7] Calvert was a professional soldier, Mayne was not. Yet the idea of returning to the law didn't attract him. 'The more I think of being a solicitor again,' he had written his mother earlier, 'the less I like it.'[8] For Mayne, as for many of these SAS-men, peacetime held little promise. They had gone in search of the dynamic, and in the SAS they had found it to the full. They would never find it again. 'The end of the war was for me an anti-climax,' said Johnny Cooper. 'I had experienced many theatres of war and had enjoyed the solid comradeship with so many of my friends in the SAS, especially Reg Seekings.'[9]

Seekings himself put it more bluntly. 'It [was] like the bottom dropping out of the world,' he admitted. 'You were lost.'[10]

The RSM called the men to attention for the general salute. Four hundred hands snapped to maroon-red berets. Then the men of 1 Special Air Service Regiment turned sharply, and marched out of history, into legend.

PART THREE

Small Wars and Revolutions
1947–80

62. 'The standard jungle-drills must have come out'

Below him the rain-forest canopy stretched unbroken to every horizon, like the green baize of a billiard table. Lt. Johnny Cooper dropped towards it, fighting to stay conscious, desperately trying to steer his 'X' type parachute with his right hand. He knew something was badly wrong. His helmet was missing, his left arm numb, and his neck felt as if it had been doused with acid.

Seconds earlier, Cooper had jumped from an RAF Dakota over the Betong Gap in Malaya's Selangor state, the last in a stick of three parachutists taking part in a 'tree-jumping' experiment. The jumper in front of him, Major Peter Walls, had hit the doorframe and stumbled back. Cooper gave him a push with his left hand, without noticing that his arm had become entangled in the other man's static-line. When Walls's parachute developed, the line snapped Cooper's arm like a twig, wrenching off his helmet and whiplashing his neck with friction-burns.

The jungle was riding up to meet him at breakneck speed. 'I crashed into the top of the foliage,' he recalled, 'slithered through many branches and finally came to rest with my canopy well and truly hooked up.'[1] Scanning downwards, he realized with a shock that he was dangling two hundred feet above the jungle floor, with a giant thicket of bamboo directly beneath him. The bamboo-tubes looked like a nest of sharpened stakes. A wave of pain from his smashed arm overwhelmed him. He passed out.

Later it felt as if he'd dreamt it all – that he was still back in the desert with David Stirling and Reg Seekings. In fact, it was May 1952. Six years had passed since the disbandment of the SAS Brigade, and the Cold War was in full swing. Cooper was serving in Malaya as a troop commander in a brand new unit – 22 SAS.

He wasn't sure how long he'd hung there. It seemed hours

before he heard a voice shouting, 'I've got Cooper. He's up here.' Dragging himself out of the fog of pain, he glanced down. With a surge of gratitude, he realized that the voice belonged to Sgt. Roger 'Olly' Levet, Royal Horse Guards, his troop-sergeant. He made out more figures in bush-hats and jungle-green fatigues working slowly through the dense undergrowth. Soon, his entire troop was gathered in the bamboo beneath his feet.

For a few moments there was a stand-off, as Cooper and his troop eyeballed each other, two hundred feet apart. No one knew what to do. Cooper had been in plenty of tight corners, but never one quite like this. He tried to ignore the excruciating throb in his arm, and to remember the drill he'd been taught for the infant art of 'tree-jumping'. Attached to his harness he had a hundred-and-fifty-foot rope, knotted at eighteen-inch intervals, which he was supposed to secure to a branch to let himself down to the forest floor. Since the two trees he was snagged on were more than thirty feet apart, though, he realized that the chances of carrying out that particular drill, one-handed, were precisely zero. The other alternative was to cut himself free. This was also a definite no-no. If the fall didn't kill him, he would almost certainly be impaled on the razor-sharp bamboo. Soon, though, he was relieved of the necessity of making a decision by the Regiment's medical officer, Captain Freddie Brunton, who had just arrived on the scene. Brunton shouted to him to let down his scaling rope, so that he could send up a canteen of water. While Cooper was tugging up the canteen, Brunton shimmied up the nearest tree with climbing irons. He told Cooper to swallow one of the Benzedrine tabs he'd been issued with, to prevent him passing out again. Cooper chugged water greedily and crammed down four Bennies.

Brunton hammered a piton into his tree-trunk and secured Cooper's scaling rope to it. He told Cooper to cut himself loose. Cooper severed his lift-webs and plunged sixty feet before the rope pulled him up. He swung like a pendulum, narrowly missing the tree. The MO told the men to let him drop. Cooper tumbled the last fifteen feet, landed smack on Olly Levet, and passed out. When he came round again, the MO was giving him a morphine shot.

Cooper remembered nothing about the march-out, but Levet told him later that, despite his injury, he'd taken charge of the troop, given instructions to the lead-scout, and ordered the men to take up covering positions as they crossed a fast-flowing torrent. 'The standard jungle-drills must have come out,' Cooper said, 'despite the effect of Benzedrine and morphine.'[2]

By the time he arrived at the Kinrara Military Hospital in Kuala Lumpur by ambulance, several hours later, he had downed a quart of Tiger beer on top of the speed and morphine and was as high as a kite. He waltzed into the Emergency Room, swinging his mauled arm, only to be whizzed straight into surgery. The surgeon, Major Steele, told him later that his arm had been fractured in three places, and had suffered severe nerve-damage from the wrenching action of the static-line. The jury was out as to whether he'd ever again be able to use the limb properly. This was a shock to the twenty-nine-year-old Cooper, who had been commissioned for the second time in the regular army only six months earlier, having finally decided that he wasn't cut out for civilian life.

63. 'Scope for tremendous development'

During his wartime officer cadet training, Cooper had been told that his parent unit, the Scots Guards, wouldn't take him back as an officer. The Guards didn't accept 'field commissionees' or officers who'd once been Guardsmen. Despite two world wars, the old mystique still obtained. On the demise of the SAS, therefore, Cooper soldiered on with an 'adopted' parent unit, 6 Green Howards, mostly in Cyprus, until it was demobilized two years later.

After demob he returned to his old firm, Vickers & Wheelers, as a trainee wool-buyer, but he missed the SAS and especially his oppo, Reg Seekings. That summer, though, he heard through the grapevine that the Regiment had been revived as a Territorial Army mob. It was designated 21 SAS (Artists), and was based at Duke's Road, Euston, in London, commanded by wartime veteran

Lt. Col. Brian Franks. Cooper wrote Franks immediately, and was offered a TA commission.

The catchment area of 21 SAS was the south-east of England, but Franks had also created a 'phantom' SAS troop at Wetherby, Yorkshire, attached to 10 (Yorkshire) Airborne Battalion. Since Cooper was working in nearby Bradford, Franks asked him to take command of the troop, which was almost entirely composed of wartime SAS-men. 21 SAS (Artists) was the creation of Brian Franks and 'Mad Mike' Calvert. The Crawford memo had concluded that the SAS should be retained 'in some form' after the war, a decision confirmed in a year-long study by the War Office's Directorate of Technical Investigation, to which Calvert had made a major contribution. The DTI affirmed that the wartime SAS had shown it could achieve results out of all proportion to its size. Although the full potential of SAS-type outfits was not yet known, the report ran, there was 'scope for tremendous development'.

As a result of the DTI report, 21 SAS (Artists) was established by Royal Warrant on 8 July 1947. Its curious designation came from a reversal of the numerals of the two British wartime Regiments, 1 and 2 SAS. The 'Artists' component derived from the 'Artists' Rifles' – a battalion of the Middlesex Regiment raised in 1859, when Britain was thought to be in danger of invasion by the French. Founded by an art student, whose name, by coincidence, was Edward Sterling, its ranks were drawn partly from the London artistic community. 'Originals' included such figures as William Morris, Holman Hunt, J. E. Millais, G. F. Watts and Lord Leighton. Though the threat of invasion never materialized, the Artists' Rifles was added to the British army's orbat. It fought with distinction in the First World War, winning no fewer than eight VCs and fifty-six DSOs.

During the Second World War, the Artists' had been used as an Officer Cadet Training Unit. It was also searching for a role in the post-war world, and Franks suggested an amalgamation. Recruiting began in August 1947, and by the following year 21 SAS (Artists) was almost two hundred strong, its ranks including fifty-nine men who had fought with the wartime SAS or other special forces units. At the same time, Franks was instrumental in creating the SAS Regimental Association, chaired by David Stirling, with Blair Mayne as vice-chairman, and the 'Z Reserve' – a register of ex-SAS-men ready to volunteer for special forces work in the event of general mobilization.

One casualty of the amalgamation was the 'flaming sword' cap-badge, in post-war years more often referred to as the 'winged dagger'. 21 SAS wore Boy Browning's maroon beret with the Pegasus arm-flash, but had acquired the Artists' Rifles' 'Mars and Minerva' cap-badge. The Regiment was organized along the lines of the wartime SAS. Equipped with Austin Champ utility vehicles, it was trained for long-range penetration and reconnaissance in Norway and the Middle East. Though it was divided into four combat or 'sabre' squadrons and an HQ squadron, Franks empha-sized that squadrons and troops were only administrative units. The new SAS, like the old, would fight in whatever numbers or formations the job required. Franks, originally a signaller, also formed the first SAS signals squadron, and had the precocious idea that the Regiment should include specialist units such as 'boat troop' and 'mountain troop'. This concept never took off in 21 SAS, but was later to become a feature of the regular Regiment.

Franks had bigger fish to fry than simply raising a TA Regiment. He pushed the War Office to grant the SAS Regiment a Corps Warrant, which would give it the status of a specialist arm of the British army. This would mean that 21 SAS (Artists) would be a cadre from which other SAS units could be raised in future – a flexible resource with almost infinite possibilities.

The Corps Warrant was ratified by a Joint Staff Memorandum in July 1950. A month earlier, the first major post-war flap had broken out, in Korea, where a multinational United Nations 'Blue Beret' force had been deployed for the first time. Under the auspices of 21 SAS, Franks authorized the raising of a new sub-unit to operate as jeep-borne long-range patrols behind North Korean lines. Volunteers included ex-wartime SAS-men like Bob Bennett, and 2 SAS vets Alastair McGregor DSO, MC and Jock Easton, all three of whom had served with the Reparations Committee in

Greece. It also included volunteers without wartime experience who had passed selection for 21 SAS. Designated M Independent Squadron, it was mustered at the Airborne Forces Depot in Aldershot under another distinguished 2 SAS officer, Major Tony Greville-Bell, DSO. Before deploying to Korea, though, the commander of United Nations forces there, General McArthur, decided that it was no longer required. Instead, the squadron was diverted to Malaya, where six months earlier 'Mad Mike' Calvert had raised the Malayan Scouts.

64. A force that would 'live, move, and have its being in the jungle'

From the dizzy heights of brigadier, Calvert had plummeted in rank to major after the war. He had spent the immediate post-war period becoming, in his own words, 'a true staff wallah'. To the uninitiated he seemed more of a staff officer than a sharp-end warrior – his intellect was formidable, but at first glance he didn't look the soldierly type. Barrel-chested and corpulent, he tended to waddle, possessing what one comrade described as 'a simian grace'.

To those who knew him, though, Calvert was a legend. A Sapper officer, fluent in Cantonese, he had graduated from Cambridge, where he had studied mechanical engineering, won a double-blue for water-sports, and boxed heavyweight for the university and the army. He had won thirteen decorations during the war, including two DSOs. Under the controversial Orde Wingate, Calvert had spent three of the war years commanding 77 Chindit Brigade in the jungles of Burma, where he had acquired a reputation as an inspirational leader of outstanding bravery. The 'experts' had then believed it impossible for British troops to outfight the Japanese in the jungle: the Chindits had proved them wrong.

In January 1950 Calvert was summoned to Malaya, where a Communist insurrection had broken out two years earlier. A thousand men and women had been killed, and the war – officially termed an 'Emergency' for insurance reasons – was tying down forty thousand British and colonial troops, and seventy-five thousand full-time and part-time police. Hidden in their jungle strongholds, the Communist Terrorists – CTs – seemed invincible. Calvert was tasked by the Commander-in-Chief Far East, General Sir John Harding, to find a way of rooting them out.

It was a classic Mao Tse-tung guerrilla campaign, orchestrated by the remarkable Chin Peng, secretary-general of the Communist Party of Malaya, to jerk his former British comrades out of what he called their 'gin-and-tonic stupor'. The prize would be some of the richest rubber plantations and tin-mines in the world. Chin Peng, OBE, had fought alongside British stay-behind parties of the SOE-style Force 136 during the war, as commander of the Malayan Peoples' Anti-Japanese Army. His four-thousand-strong guerrilla band, almost all ethnic Chinese, had learned to live and fight in the dense rain-forest that covered nine-tenths of the country.

Redesignated the Malayan Races Liberation Army, the force consisted of anti-British 'Killer Units' with jungle hideouts in almost every state of the Federation. They already had a source of arms – three thousand weapons had been dropped to them by the British during the war, which had been greased carefully and cached in the jungle. The MRLA drew support from among more than half a million Chinese squatters living in kampongs on the forest fringes, who, with disaffected city workers, rubber cultivators and tin-miners, formed the 'proletarian pool' in which the terrorist 'fish' could swim. In the jungle the Communists were parasites on some hundred thousand aborigines, commonly known as 'Sakai'.

The insurrection kicked off on 16 June 1948 with the murder of Arthur Walker, manager of the Ladang Elphil rubber-estate in Perak, shot in his office by a trio of Chinese who arrived on bicycles. The same day a Chinese gang tied up John Allison, manager of the neighbouring Sungei Siput plantation, and his assistant, Ian Christian, and drilled them both with .45mm rounds from a Tommy-gun. The Malayan Emergency was declared two days later.

Calvert spent six months studying the problem. He travelled thirty thousand miles, met everyone, saw everything. He went on patrol with soldiers and police. He measured them against the abilities of his wartime Chindits, and found them wanting. Instead of patrolling, British troops were taught to hack their way through the bush in a straight line, 'making a lot of noise and achieving very little'. They knew nothing of navigation, less of tracking, and did not have the patience to lie in ambush. One Guards commander told him that he didn't consider it the job of his men 'to chase bare-arsed niggers around South-East Asia'.[1] Worst of all, many had an instinctive fear of the jungle.

Medical Corps wisdom currently held that British soldiers could not remain in the jungle for more than two weeks. Calvert's Chindits had been able to stay there indefinitely. Like his friend, ex-Force 136 fighter Freddie Spencer Chapman, author of the celebrated book *The Jungle is Neutral*, Calvert believed that mental rather than physical toughness was the key to survival in these conditions.[2] He conceived of a special force that would possess this mental toughness to a high degree – that would 'live, move, and have its being in the jungle, like the guerrillas'.[3] Given leave to raise his special force in July, he named it the Malayan Scouts (SAS).

65. 'The Special Air Service, at last, was back in the regular army'

The Malayan Scouts was raised for the Emergency, and was not intended to outlive it. Calvert saw the Scouts as the prototype for other short-term SAS units that could be formed for a specific task in a specific geographical environment – desert, mountains, snow – and easily disbanded. Bitterly opposed to the break-up of the SAS Brigade five years earlier, he originally wanted to call the new unit the 'Special Air Service'. When this was turned down, he'd suggested the 'Pacific Rangers'. This was also vetoed: Rangers were the US version of the commandos, and the unit was not to operate in the Pacific. Raised within a month of the issue of the SAS Corps Warrant, the Malayan Scouts was part of the SAS Regiment, along with 21 SAS (Artists), and a small Regimental HQ.

Calvert recruited A Squadron, Malayan Scouts (SAS), from British units serving in Malaya. Volunteers were accepted on 'the Chindit principle' that any infantryman with the right training could be deployed on special operations. This non-elitist approach had worked against the Japanese in Burma. Unlike the SAS, though, the Chindits had fought in big battalions, where the weak links were covered by the strong. The Malayan Emergency was a different kind of war – a war of counter-insurgency, involving small numbers and tiny formations. The Chindit principle failed in Malaya, because SAS-style patrols of three or four men could not afford weak links. Recruited without selection, the Malayan Scouts quickly began to suffer not only a collapse of discipline, but also an appallingly low standard of military skills.

When Tony Greville-Bell's independent squadron from 21 SAS, now renamed B Squadron, Malayan Scouts – poled up at Calvert's base at Kota Tinggi in Johore Bahru the following January, they were shocked at the behaviour of A Squadron. The local recruits were dirty, bearded, indisciplined, drunken – and much worse, careless in weapon-handling. 'It was a hell of a problem,' said the new squadron's sergeant-major, 'Original' Bob Bennett. 'We had pretty good discipline in [B] Squadron, and it made things difficult all round when I was making my guys shave and do all the normal things soldiers do in camp, while A Squadron seemed to do just as they pleased . . . We soon heard the stories of Calvert's boozing and the wild parties that went on when the lads were out of the jungle.'[1]

The A Squadron boys sneered at Bennett, pointing out that this wasn't the desert. Many of the 'normal things soldiers do in camp', like shaving, were counter-productive in the jungle. But they missed the point. Bennett wasn't advocating 'wooden-top' discipline on operations, only smartness while back in camp – a quality

of which both Stirling and Mayne had approved. Calvert's Intelligence Officer, John Woodhouse, agreed: 'I couldn't see that it
mattered if a man was bearded or not in the jungle,' he said, 'but
I did recognize the importance of looking tidy when you were
not on operations and within a base area.'[2]

Some of the A Squadron men were excellent soldiers, and would
become veterans of the Regiment, but others had joined the Scouts
for 'a swan'. Calvert himself admitted that local commanders had
taken the opportunity to unload their undesirables on him. Some
came directly from military prisons – he had even recruited a dozen
deserters from the French Foreign Legion, who had jumped ship
en route to French Indo-China. Some, perhaps a minority, were
useless, and would, in Woodhouse's words, 'probably have been
useless in any Regiment'.[3]

The first A Squadron operation-cum-training exercise, in the
Ipoh area of Perak, was a washout. The troops moved through the
jungle like tourists on an afternoon stroll, dumping litter, lighting
huge fires, chatting noisily, handling their weapons with careless
abandon. Battle discipline was non-existent, standard operating
procedures were conspicuous by their absence and navigation
abysmal – most of the men had never seen a map, and in any
case, the ones they had were air-charts with vast areas designated
'obscured by clouds'. Some of the men felt claustrophobic in the
dense jungle, others couldn't remain in ambush positions for
more than a few hours. Unsurprisingly, they had no contact with
the terrorists, which only increased the sense of boredom. By the
end of the op, according to John Woodhouse, the squadron had
virtually fallen apart.

This failure didn't bother Calvert, who had a 'Darwinian'
approach to training. Any man who wasn't up to it, he thought,
would soon be weeded out by the hardship of living in the jungle.
The Malayan Scouts didn't need selection. Jungle ops *were* the
selection: if you survived, you were in.

The indiscipline of the troops off ops, though, stemmed directly
from his own cavalier attitude – Calvert had never been hot on
parade-ground regulations, and didn't approve of soldiers being

'dressed up like a tailor's dummy'. Stirling's early stipulation that discipline in camp should be as stiff as that of the Brigade of Guards hadn't lasted, but had given way to a culture of self-discipline inherited by the B Squadron boys. Calvert later admitted that A Squadron's unruliness was his own fault. 'In my defence,' he wrote, 'I must say I had so much to do that some minor problems escaped me. I was serving three different generals . . . I attended high level meetings while still having to attend to people brought up in front of me for the loss of a pair of boots or something . . .'⁴

Calvert was also reaping the harvest of his war years in a blend of tropical diseases that were now scourging his bloodstream, which, with a drinker's self-delusion, he had always maintained a good daily dose of liquor would keep at bay. He had even recruited fellow heavy boozers as officers, on the bizarre principle that if they could stand a hangover they could put up with the discomforts of the jungle. Fighting a rearguard action against alcoholism, he was also struggling to hide another secret: his homosexuality, which in the British army of the day was still the ultimate stigma.

Calvert's heroes were officers who were loved by their men. His punishments for what might otherwise have been court-martial offences often consisted of verbal admonitions, on his long-held but dubious belief that soldiers who misbehaved often turned out to be good fighters when the chips were down. 'This to me was always Calvert's weakness,' said Woodhouse. 'He didn't appreciate the importance of good discipline. There is little doubt that the outbreaks of offences resulting from ill-discipline can be laid at Calvert's door.'⁵

The wild drinking that Bennett and the other B Squadron men had heard about when they arrived was no mere rumour. Calvert's perilous attempt to rugby-tackle Paddy Mayne wasn't the most reckless act he was capable of when smashed. On one occasion he booby-trapped the latrines at a nearby Australian RAF base. On another, occasioned by the visit of an Indian general, he hurled a grenade into a pig-wallow, causing the officer to throw himself flat in mud and pig-manure. Woodhouse confessed later that the other officers knew morale was heading for a precipice, but just stood by and watched. 'We were aware of the problems . . .' he said, 'but Calvert dominated us in a way which is rather hard to explain now.'[6]

By the time B Squadron had arrived, the A Squadron boys had completed their training 'on the hoof' in the rain-forest, and now considered themselves the jungle experts. To them, the B Squadron men seemed rigid and aloof. Though some of these veterans had seen hard fighting – more SAS-men had been scragged in three days at Termoli than would be lost in the whole eight years of the Malaya crisis – the younger A Squadron men scoffed at them. Their attitude was similar to that of the young Stirling and Lewes to the 'old sweats' of the First World War. B Squadron were proud of their medals and para-wings hard-won on wartime operations. A Squadron, who hadn't even done their jumps, quickly dubbed them 'Big Time Bravo'. Woodhouse commented later that A Squadron wasn't irredeemable. It had some bad apples, he said, but its best men had 'the immense unshakable physical endurance and determination of young British soldiers at their best'.[7]

They had at least proved Calvert right in his assertion that British soldiers could survive long periods in the jungle. An A squadron patrol under Lt. Mike Sinclair-Hill had remained in the ulu for a hundred and three days. They had also had the Scouts' first contacts with the Communists. The first kill was made by Trooper Bill Anderson, almost by accident. 'We got into a river and I was about up to my knees,' Anderson recalled, 'and I suddenly saw this figure who appeared from a bush. He jumped up like a jack-in-the-box. I just turned and shot him. I worked that bolt three times, I remember.'[8]

Sinclair-Hill's patrol had seen casualties: one Scout killed in action, a police officer and a Chinese auxiliary accompanying patrols shot dead, and four SAS-men missing. Three of them turned out to have taken refuge in a village on the coast, when one of their number was wounded. The fourth, Trooper John O'Leary, Royal Artillery, had been left behind by his patrol. Finding his way to an aborigine longhouse, he was hacked to death by the natives, at the instigation of the Communists.

21. 'Gentleman' Jim Almonds, *front left*, with Gain patrol in the Orleans Forest, 1944. One of Jock Lewes's 'Tobruk Four', Almonds was a talented engineer who constructed most of the parachute training equipment at Kabrit. Captured on the Benghazi raid, he escaped in time to join 1 SAS for post D-Day ops in Europe.

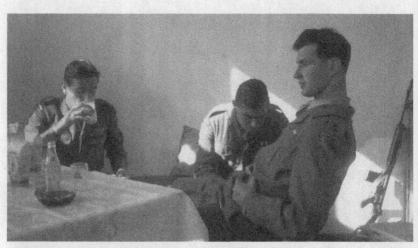

22. Johnny Cooper, Johnny Watts and Tony Jeapes, *c.* 1960. With SAS experience spanning two decades behind him, Cooper is on the eve of departure, while both Watts and Jeapes will go on to command 22 SAS, and will retire generals.

23. John Woodhouse instructs recruits in Malaya. A quiet, reserved man, Woodhouse was a superb training officer, and one of the best commanders 22 SAS ever had.

24. J. M. 'Mad Mike' Calvert. A guerrilla genius, Calvert's influence on the development of the modern SAS has been underrated. Asked to devise a strategy to flush out Communist insurgents in Malaya, he envisaged a force that would 'live, move, and have its being in the jungle, like the terrorists'. Originally named the Malayan Scouts, the force became 22 SAS.

25. Johnny Cooper, *right*, in Malaya. Having fought throughout the war with L Detachment and 1 SAS, Cooper later sought a commission with 22 SAS. He served as a squadron commander in both Malaya and Oman.

26. Sgt. Hanna with parachute harness, Malaya. 'Tree jumping' in Malaya was a legacy of B Squadron's drop in the Bellum Valley, when most of the sticks landed accidentally in forest. Casualty-projection was only 1.3 per cent, but any injuries sustained were likely to be serious.

27. Helicopter in Malaya. The Malayan Emergency saw the first use of helicopters by the SAS, mainly on search and rescue missions. Patrols used marker-balloons to guide the aircraft to gaps in the jungle-canopy, but disliked calling in helis on operations because of the risk of compromise.

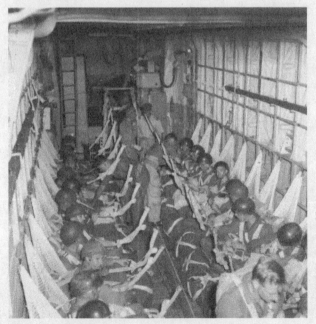

28. B Squadron, 22 SAS, before a jump in Malaya. In the early days of 22 SAS, 'Big Time Bravo' was the only parachute-trained squadron, as most of its personnel had come from 21 SAS (Artists') or had served in special forces during the war.

29. SAS Patrol in Malaya. Calvert's concept was to insert whole squadrons into the jungle, where they would fan out in small patrols from a central base, re-supplied by air. The squadrons would remain in the jungle for up to three months, developing the 'ground feel' crucial to anti-guerrilla ops.

30. Wadi Maidan, Jebel Akhdar, Oman. The Jebel Akhdar assault was the first deployment of 22 SAS outside Malaya, and was crucial to the long-term establishment of the Regiment. Originally asked for a handful of SAS-men, CO Tony Deane-Drummond eventually brought in both A and D Squadrons, a total of eighty sabre personnel.

31. Sabrina or the 'Twin Tits', on Jebel Akhdar. Johnny Cooper's A Squadron launched an impressive assault on this natural defensive position on the northern side of the Jebel, led by Tony Jeapes and Ian Patterson. The attack was a feint to distract the rebels from the real assault, which was to go in further south.

32. Tanuf Slab, Jebel Akhdar, Oman. Considered impregnable by locals, the Jebel Akhdar was a convoluted landscape of ridges, peaks and perpendicular slabs, reaching a height of over 19,000 feet. The final assault by the SAS required a ten-hour non-stop climb carrying loads of fifty kilos, to be made at night in complete silence, under constant threat of attack.

33. Johnny Watts, *in front*, and Peter de la Billière on Jebel Akhdar, Oman. A party of twenty-two men of D Squadron, led by Watts and de la Billière, made the summit just as dawn was breaking. The exhausted troops went quickly into all-round defence, but the expected counter-attack failed to materialize.

34. Alf 'Geordie' Tasker, the Radfan, Aden. One of a nine man A Squadron patrol led by Captain Robin Edwards, Tasker was pinned down with his men on Jebel Ashqab by hundreds of local tribesmen. They made a fighting withdrawal by night, after Edwards and radio-operator Nick Warburton were killed; their severed heads were later put on display in Ta'izz.

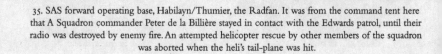

35. SAS forward operating base, Habilayn/Thumier, the Radfan. It was from the command tent here that A Squadron commander Peter de la Billière stayed in contact with the Edwards patrol, until their radio was destroyed by enemy fire. An attempted helicopter rescue by other members of the squadron was aborted when the heli's tail-plane was hit.

The aborigine problem was one Calvert had considered carefully. He knew that while some of the aborigines sympathized with the CTs, others had been coerced into helping them by threats and atrocities. To smash the Communists, he believed, the Scouts would first have to undermine their ties with the jungle-folk. Calvert's initial report had recommended a 'hearts and minds' campaign to bring the aborigines on board. He had also proposed translocating the half-million-plus Chinese squatters on the forest fringes to rob the Communists of their main support. Both of these proposals had been adopted by the new Director of Operations, General Sir Harold Briggs, whose celebrated 'Briggs Plan' was the blueprint for British success in the Emergency.

After the murder of O'Leary, A Squadron was naturally wary of the 'abos', but on their first ops they had made a start on the 'hearts and minds' battle by operating basic jungle clinics. There were few trained medics among them as yet, but a handful of soldiers had acquired a rudimentary grasp of medical skills. The clinics were little more than distribution centres for penicillin – in great demand among the Sakai as a treatment for yaws, a common skin disease – but they were a foot in the longhouse door. A Squadron men also made the first use of inflatables for river patrols, and of helicopters for resupply.

Within days of their arrival, B Squadron was thrown into the rain-forest on Calvert's sink or swim principle. There was almost no one to train them, and Int. Officer John Woodhouse took on the training himself. The first requirement was to be able to live and move in the jungle for weeks, in small patrols, without noise, without leaving traces, constantly on the alert for the enemy. 'In the three months I was with [B Squadron],' he recalled, '. . . I did establish the rudiments of battle-discipline. We got away from the rather slap-happy way A Squadron had gone round the jungle.'⁹

Woodhouse was a quiet, reserved officer, lean, gangly and unimpressive-looking at first sight, with what the SAS came to call 'a Bergen stoop'. Like Jock Lewes, though, he was a superb and unorthodox training-officer. When one man had a 'negligent discharge' with his weapon, for instance, Woodhouse made him walk around with a primed grenade in his hand for the next forty-eight hours. Once, when fired on by one of his own sentries in the jungle, he put the man on a charge – for missing. When a later recruit – Peter de la Billière – stumbled across his trip-flares for the third time, Woodhouse loaded the flares with plastic explosive, 'to help him concentrate'.[10]

Woodhouse was a Second World War veteran who had won the MC during the Italian campaign. Despite his public school education, he had joined the Devon & Dorset Regiment as a private, and had been promoted from the ranks. He was soon a platoon commander in 1 East Surrey Regiment, and had seen action in Tunisia and Sicily. Although he had no SAS experience, he was more versed in patrol work than most. He had commanded an infantry patrol-unit that had acquired some special forces functions, including the snatching of prisoners as informants, and long-range reconnaissance patrols.

Woodhouse was also a fluent Russian-speaker, and had worked as a liaison-officer with Soviet forces at the end of the war. His last job before volunteering for the Malayan Scouts was G3 Intelligence with 40 Infantry Division in Hong Kong. He had joined Calvert on the understanding that he would be given command of a combat unit, but on arrival in Malaya had found himself appointed the Scouts' Intelligence Officer. Despite this apparent double-dealing, and his resentment of Calvert's continual criticism, Woodhouse retained an enormous respect for his new CO's intellect. '[Calvert] had that spark of genius . . . that a soldier is lucky to see at close quarters once in his career,' he commented. '. . . He had the moral courage and tactical sense to match three-man patrols against gangs much bigger . . . he . . . made the Regiment, and it reflected his faults as well as his virtues.'[11]

At the end of March, A and B Squadrons were joined by a third – C Squadron, a hundred volunteers Calvert had recruited in Rhodesia. Its chief was Captain Peter Walls, later to be General Officer Commanding the Rhodesian army. The Rhodesians were physically tough, well educated and idealistic. Their Achilles heel, as far as Calvert was concerned, was their inability to make friends with the aborigines, coupled with their susceptibility to jungle diseases, which seemed to hit them more severely than any of the British squadrons. The Rhodesians were followed a few months later by a second contingent from the UK – D Squadron – made up of untrained volunteers from the Airborne Forces Depot. Though neither C nor D had undergone a selection course, they were happily without the discipline problems of the A Squadron men.

B Squadron boss Tony Greville-Bell agonized over the discipline situation. He complained to Calvert. Calvert fobbed him off. He had never really got on with Greville-Bell, who he thought was under the impression that he 'had come to take over from me'. In the end, Greville-Bell complained to C-in-C John Harding. By military custom, this was a major faux pas, and Harding, another vet of the Italian campaign, who'd had three fingers shot off in Sicily, called him to a meeting in Kuala Lumpur. Whatever Greville-Bell had been expecting, Harding handed out what he described as 'the biggest bollocking I have ever had in my life'.[12] He had transgressed the ultimate military taboo: an officer does not go over the head of his immediate superior. Greville-Bell had compounded the offence by sending a screed to the second-in-command of 21 SAS, Major 'Leo' Hart, who had been SAS Brigade Major at the end of the war, suggesting that B Squadron should operate under its own command. After his 'bollocking' by Harding, Greville-Bell was given the elbow from the Malayan Scouts, and in his own words 'treated like a criminal'. Posted to a series of military 'Siberias', he eventually resigned.

But Greville-Bell's reproaches had hit the bull's-eye. Despite closing ranks, the 'head-shed' knew it. In London, Leo Hart was openly admitting that the SAS Regiment would be glad to see the back of Calvert and his half-baked Scouts. Their reputation had gone from bad to worse, and other units in the theatre were showing them open contempt. Hart was protective of the Regiment's name, and didn't want to see it go down the sewer over Calvert's roughneck army.

Calvert's days were numbered. Even the men noticed that he looked ill and unhappy. 'We'd see him totally drunk all the time in our mess,' said Mike Sinclair-Hill. 'Then, one day, I found him unconscious on the floor in his room. I tried slapping him and throwing water, but he was just totally dead.'[13]

On 8 June, Director of Operations General Sir Harold Briggs arrived for 'discussions'. He held a number of private interviews with Calvert, who, at a cocktail party that night, seemed devoid of his customary exuberance. Next morning, he told Woodhouse that he was going into hospital and would be sent home. Woodhouse was dismayed. He couldn't imagine anyone capable of both putting the administration in order and maintaining and improving Calvert's tactics in the field. The Scouts' disbandment was already being predicted by its detractors, and he was worried that, with 'Mad Mike' out of the way, their hopes would quickly be fulfilled. 'You can't go, sir,' he protested. 'Who will take over command?'

'I must go. They'll make me go,' Calvert said. 'You chaps must carry on.'[14]

Later that day, Calvert was admitted to Kinrara Military Hospital with 'hepatomegaly of unknown origin' – enlargement of the liver, a well-known product both of alcoholism and of malaria. The official line was that he was invalided out as a result of a 'cocktail of exotic diseases', but this was almost certainly a cover-up. The 'medical grounds' pretext was a tried and tested military anti-scandal formula – Auchinleck had used it when sacking Cunningham during Crusader. When Woodhouse visited Calvert in hospital to say goodbye three days later, he showed no symptoms of the 'exotic diseases' he was supposed to be suffering from. 'Remember, I expect a lot from you, John,' were Calvert's last words to him.

Calvert was flown to hospital in Singapore, and then on to London. By October, though, he had recovered sufficiently to be posted to Hanover, as OC Royal Engineers, with the British Army of the Rhine. It was here that Calvert heard good news from Malaya. 'The designation "Malayan Scouts" had been dropped,' he wrote, 'and the unit renamed 22 SAS Regiment. The Special Air Service, at last, was back in the regular army.'[15]

David Stirling omitted Calvert's name from the select list of men whom he considered his co-founders of the SAS, though he did admit that Calvert had played a vital part in the development of the Regiment. John Woodhouse, who was later to become an almost legendary commanding officer of 22 SAS, and whose name *was* on Stirling's list, said that he had learned all he knew about counter-insurgency from Calvert. He added that Calvert had ana-lysed the whole Malayan scenario with stunning prescience, and had outlined future SAS principles – three- or four-man patrols, medical aid to the local population, and, most important of all, the idea of a counter-guerrilla force establishing bases in the deep jungle, and staying there. Calvert had come up with these ideas long before anyone else thought of them.

The creation of 22 SAS was to be 'Mad Mike's' last great achievement. Within a year he would be charged with 'committing or attempting to commit acts of gross indecency' with certain German youths. He was court-martialled, found guilty, and drummed out of the army.

66. 'Like a bunch of grapes hanging out of his slacks'

Calvert's replacement was Lt. Col. John 'Tod' Sloane, Argyll & Sutherland Highlanders, a conventional line-infantry officer with a no-nonsense attitude. He'd been sent in to clean up the Malayan Scouts and he intended to do so. Calvert's non-existent admin was to be put on a firm footing. The Regiment was to be whipped into shape. Sloane's first action was to pull all four squadrons out for six weeks' rest and retraining in Singapore. During that time, Sloane ruthlessly RTU'd the cowboys, bar soldiers and misfits, and persuaded some first-rate men not to leave. One of these was Major Dare Newell, an A Squadron officer who had worked for SOE in the Balkans and fought the Japanese in the Malayan jungle with Force 136. Newell was later to play a major role in preserving 22 SAS. Together as a unit for the first time in their history, squadrons previously at each other's throats began to feel the unfamiliar stirrings of *esprit de corps*.

When Sloane moved the Regiment to its new base at Sungei Besi at the end of January it was no longer the Malayan Scouts, but a new regular army formation, 22 SAS – its designation following in sequence from 21 SAS (Artists'). The switch in title had been instigated mainly for recruitment purposes, and coincided with a change of tour-length from eighteen months to two years. It was felt that volunteers would be more ready to join if the designation didn't suggest that the unit would operate only in Malaya. The new Regiment would remain junior to its Territorial equivalent, 21 SAS, and despite the change, its future was not yet secure. It was still not listed on the British army's order of battle.

One prop to the new *esprit* was the common cap-badge the squadrons now shared. B Squadron had turned up wearing the Artists' Rifles 'Mars and Minerva' insignia, but A Squadron still wore the badges of their parent units. All squadrons now wore Bob Tait's wartime 'flaming sword' badge and 'Who Dares Wins' motto with the Airborne maroon-red beret.

While in Singapore the squadrons had started training for a new operation, to kick off in February. Meanwhile, Johnny Cooper had arrived from the UK. Cooper had served as a subaltern in 21 SAS for four years, but his future had been decided when he attended the Regiment's first annual camp at Okehampton in Devon. 'The camp turned into a splendid reunion, and the atmosphere was wonderful,' he wrote. 'The problem was that this happy fortnight upset me for my future life as a civilian. I had great doubts about what I was doing and whether it was all worthwhile.'[1] It had taken him some time to finally decide, but two months after Mike Calvert had arrived in Germany he applied for a short-service commission with the newly designated 22 SAS.

Cooper was appointed OC 8 Troop, B Squadron, and spent his first weeks on jungle orientation. Once the civilized surroundings of the rubber-estates fell away, he found himself in an alternative dimension. He'd experienced the majesty of the Sahara, and had fought in the woods of the Morvan, but had never seen anything quite like this. The primary rain-forest was a dark cathedral of staggering vastness, where the trunks of gigantic trees rose, smooth and black, scarlet and scaly, ash-grey and crusted green, as perfect and straight as columns, up to a canopy so dense that it cut out the sky. Giant lianas as thick as a man's thigh coiled round the great tree-boles or drooped from the branches like pythons. The forest bed was a carpet of rotted leaves and saplings, from which extended a dense growth of bamboo, rhododendron, rattan, thorn-bush, and the whip-like 'wait-a-bit' *nante sikkit* thorn.

At first, navigation in this labyrinth seemed impossible. A man could rarely see more than ten yards – it was difficult to judge distance, and there were no landmarks. Straight line marching was frustrated by thickets, precipices, rock-outcrops, swamps and meandering rivers that switched back on themselves in continuous hairpins. Going varied with the terrain. It was easier in primary jungle than secondary, but in places it might take eight hours to cover a mile on the map.

The forest abounded with unpleasant surprises. There were malarial mosquitoes, sand-flies with a sting that caused nettle-rash, bees that killed by suffocation, wasps with an allergenic chemical that bloated the flesh, hornets so aggressive they buzz-bombed anything that moved, red ants, hairy caterpillars, fever-laden ticks, centipedes, scorpions and venomous snakes that might rear up suddenly on the track. There were also larger animals – elephant, tiger, water-buffalo, bush pig, and even rhino. The most hated creatures of all were the leeches that could creep inside a man's clothes or through his boot-eyelets. Some were poisonous, others – the swamp-dwelling bull- or tiger-leech – could suck half a pint of blood at a go.

After the Communists, Cooper commented, leeches were their number one adversary. 'You couldn't feel them,' he wrote, 'but as they slowly sucked blood, they enlarged into horrible black swollen lumps.'[2] They had an alarming propensity for homing in on a man's private parts. It wasn't unknown for a leech to crawl down the urethra and expand inside, from where it could only be dislodged by surgery. Trooper Don 'Lofty' Large, an ex-Gloster who had fought the Chinese at the heroic battle of the Imjin River in Korea, once claimed to have seen eleven leeches clinging to the end of a comrade's penis. 'It looked like a bunch of grapes hanging out of his slacks,' he wrote. 'When he pulled them off he bled like a stuck pig.'³ Leech-bites could develop into ulcers that needed twice-daily dousing with antiseptic, and took weeks to heal up.

The majority of SAS casualties, though, came from jungle diseases. Malaria-carrying anopheles mosquitoes were more of a problem on the inhabited jungle fringes than in the deep forest. To contract malaria could be an RTU offence, because the SAS were under orders to take daily doses of the newly-developed prophylactic, Paludrine. A common hazard was leptospirosis or 'lepto' – a virus carried in the urine of rats, which could be passed on in water through a leech-bite and was potentially fatal.

There were no seasons in the rain-forest but the monsoon. It was almost always hot and wet. Tropical rain fell like a knife, often continuing without a break for seventy-two hours. The wet was a burden an SAS-man had to carry – it soaked his clothes and his equipment, doubling the weight, rotting the material within days. Stitches fell to pieces. Boots lost their soles. Wet clothes chafed the skin, making it agony to continue. Mildew could sprout between first and last light.

The patrol carried .30 M1 carbines familiar to Cooper from his days in France and Germany, and a Bren-gun. Lead-scouts were equipped with 'pump-guns' – 12-bore pump-action shotguns with deadly 9-ball ammunition. As Bill Anderson had discovered on the unit's first contact, encounters with the enemy were blink-of-the-eye affairs, and with visibility down to as little as five yards, a pump-gun with its scattershot pattern was frequently a better bet than a high-velocity rifle. Later on, both the M1 and the Bren would be replaced by the 7.62mm FN, the Belgian-made proto-type of the standard-issue self-loading rifle, or SLR. Unlike the later model, the FN could be fired fully-automatic.

Movement in the rain-forest was a far cry from Jock Lewes's treks in the open desert. The men carried Bergens weighing between thirty and forty kilos, packed with up to twenty-eight days' rations on top of ammunition, grenades, poncho, hammock, field-dressings, lightweight sleeping-bag, parachute-cord for lashings, spare clothes and plimsolls, and specialized equipment such as radio batteries and explosives. In addition there was belt-kit, including a parang – a sixteen-inch jungle knife – water-bottles, mess-tins and Hexamine cookers.

They had to lug these weights across a jungle floor that was a maze of deadfall, clambering over tree-trunks, skidding along slimy surfaces or crawling underneath. They marched through endless mud-swaths, where roots and vines tripped them and 'wait-a-bit' thorn clutched at them, where leeches wiggled on leaves ready to attach themselves, where ants marched in long files, where centipedes, spiders and beetles swarmed. All these obstacles and more had to be covered in dead silence – commands were given by hand-signal. Progress was grindingly slow, and the senses were engaged all the time. The ears and nose worked as hard as the eyes. The enemy could be lurking unseen only metres away. The CTs were hot on ambushes, and left home-made booby-traps of spike-filled pits covered in foliage. The sound of voices, the odours of fire or cooking, carried long distance, and could give life-or-death warning of the enemy's proximity. Every ten minutes or hundred metres, the patrol would freeze and listen, absorbing the ocean of sensations around them.

The rate of movement depended on the terrain, which was anything but uniform. On level ground, following a track, the patrol might make two kilometres an hour. Crossing undulating ground, one kilometre was good going. In dense undergrowth, they would be lucky to cover five hundred metres. In bamboo thickets, where they had to hack a path, it might take all morning to cover the same distance.

Some regions of Malaya were mountainous, involving arduous climbs, mostly up slopes slippery with mud. Coming down was worse than going up because the patrol had to steady themselves by grabbing hold of vines and creepers that lacerated the hands. Where possible, Cooper learned, it was more tactical for the patrol to contour around slopes than tramp over the top.

In the valleys there were streams and rivers to be crossed. The men breasted them in turn, while the others took up all-round defence. Sometimes the streams were shallow enough to be forded. If not, they could be traversed by swimming with the aid of a pair of trousers knotted and filled with air, or by a fixed line of rotan – a jungle creeper. If the river was in full spate, this experience could be sobering. 'When my turn came to put my faith in that rotan,' wrote Lofty Large, describing his first river-crossing, '. . . I was bloody terrified. The river was a raging torrent . . . the water did its best to tear me loose, but it didn't break.'⁴

The ability to navigate came through trial and error. Tracks existed, but the SAS avoided them if possible because of the risk of ambush. Animal trails were teeming with leeches. The patrol followed contours, using hilltops and river junctions as fixed points. With the sun almost continuously out of sight, navigation wasn't a precise process but a rough and ready estimate that could be honed to an instinct.

Iban trackers had been brought in from Sarawak to assist a short-lived patrol unit – Ferret Force – made up of ex-Chindits, Force 136-men and Malayan police. The unit had enjoyed some minor successes, but was part-time, and unable to remain in the rain-forest for long periods. On the disbandment of Ferret Force the Ibans had joined the SAS, and it was from these tattooed headhunters that they had begun to learn the art of tracking. The Ibans would eventually form their own unit, the Sarawak Rangers. Some SAS-men became so skilled that they outstripped their teachers, and several, like Bob Turnbull and 'Whispering Leaf' Hague, would become legendary.

The Ibans taught them that any human encounter with the jungle resulted in 'sign' – it was virtually impossible to move there without leaving traces. Spoor could be divided into 'top sign' and 'ground sign' – the dividing line being ankle-height. On the ground, the tracker looked out for footprints, minute mud-splashes on stones and vegetation, bruised grass-stalks, broken twigs, up-ended leaves, weeping roots, disturbed insects, disturbed water, urine traces and faeces. Above ankle-level, he watched for marks of cutting, bruising and scratching on trees, imprints on the moss of tree-roots, the absence of spider-webs, the changes in the colour of vegetation. A good tracker could not only follow a trail but discern how many people had passed, how long before, how fast they were travelling, what food they had eaten, and, often, who they were. Aborigine footprints, for instance, were splay-toed, whereas the CTs when walking barefoot left the bunch-toed prints of those brought up wearing shoes.

Unlike the desert, where most marching had been done at night, nocturnal movement in the jungle was near-impossible except in swamp, or under bright moonlight. The darkness fell with startling rapidity, and the forest became a bedlam of surreal noises – fire-alarms, bicycle bells, clashing cymbals, dentists' drills, bugles, grinding brakes, fishing-reels, echoing snarls. The place was so electric with sound and movement that newcomers could rarely sleep. One of the worst hazards was deadfall – massive branches that snapped off trees during the night, crushing anyone camping beneath them. An entire tree fell within earshot at least every thirty-six hours. There was no way of predicting it, nor of avoiding it. Men could only lie awake, tense and fearful, straining for the sound of ripping deadwood and hoping it wouldn't happen to them.

Calvert's object had been to create a force that would be, as he put it, 'the antibody injected into the system, that would seek out and destroy the malarial germ'. His method of 'injection' was to deploy a squadron by road, boat or helicopter to the insertion-point. From there, the squadron would infiltrate the tactical area on foot, carrying supplies, and set up a base maintained by one troop under the OC, with a signaller. Comms would be established by voice-radio, a fifteen-kilo transmitter requiring a dozen five-kilo batteries to keep it going for a month. The transmitter broadcast using ground-wave and the signal was often blocked by mountains and atmospheric conditions. The Regiment was working on Morse-transmitting, with the help of some Australian signallers. 'Telegraph' sets were smaller, lighter, and used sky-wave frequencies that bounced signals off the ionosphere. Antennae were wire coils, and signallers had to learn formulas for setting up various lengths and configurations. Some SAS-men even used bows and arrows to get the antennae up into the highest trees.

Signals had always been the SAS's Achilles heel. In the early days the Regiment had used LRDG operators, and had later relied on Phantom. In coming years, signals would become so revered in the SAS that radio-sets would be regarded as sacred objects, and radio-operators as the 'shamans' of the SAS tribe. In the early days, patrols were out of contact until they returned to base, but as technology and technique improved, radios would filter down first to troop, and later to patrol level.

There were still no trained patrol medics. Some SAS-men had acquired medical skills from an enthusiastic RAMC orderly attached to HQ Squadron, inevitably nicknamed 'Doc'. The importance of patrol-level medics soon became apparent from the difficulties of casevacing wounded or injured men from the jungle. Anyone who went down would have to be carried a long distance – a tough job in these conditions. A helicopter landing-zone had to be carved out of the forest, with great effort and long delay, and the helicopter's descent would almost certainly compromise the patrol's position. The more injuries or wounds that could be treated on the ground, the less risk to the patrol.

Slowly, from these beginnings, the four-man patrol concept would emerge, with each man a specialist – medic, demolitions-man, signaller or linguist. Later, to qualify for skills pay, every SAS-man in a combat or 'sabre' squadron would be required to pass an annual skills test, with one skill at 'advanced' and the others at 'basic' level. This meant that each man in the patrol was 'cross-trained' to take over another's job if necessary.

From the squadron-base, three troops, notionally of sixteen, but generally, in practice, of no more than a dozen men, would move out to the furthest limit of the tactical area, and establish satellite-bases. The troop would fragment into three- or four-man patrols who would go out for several days at a time. Although every troop was supposed to be led by an officer, many were commanded by sergeants, corporals and even troopers. Every NCO now joining the SAS dropped rank to trooper, which meant that many SAS troopers were ex-sergeants and corporals with leadership experience. It was during these days in Malaya that the SAS tradition of putting skill before formal rank was established. 'There were two corporals in [my] troop,' Lofty Large recalled, 'and one of them was troop commander, I was never sure which . . . No one worried about rank, the only thing of importance was the ability to get the job done.'[5]

A basic jungle skill was the building of a basha – a shelter consisting of a pile of deadwood or a hammock for a bed, covered with a waterproof poncho, slung between trees. In the patrol base, the bashas would be strung tactically around a hillock or high ground, each with its own own stand-to area for all-round defence, constructed of bulletproof timber. There would be one sentry by night. The patrol was stood-to before last light and remained rock still for an hour. The patrol was stood-down by a hand-clap. They slept wearing plimsolls, with their weapons in their parachute-silk 'zoot suits' or sleeping-bags, and were stood-to again by a double hand-clap before first light.

Patrol discipline was already improving when Cooper arrived. Litter was burned, buried or carried. Weapons were hefted without slings, which could snag on vegetation, and always carried in the 'ready' position. Every man knew his immediate action on contact, his field of fire, procedure on the halt, emergency RVs, sentry-drills, the necessity to maintain silence. Ambushes were becoming more efficient. Mike Calvert had taught that in a jungle ambush only the first two or three of the enemy got bumped. He had shown the men how to make 'daisy-chains' of grenades strung together with instantaneous fuse, that could be laid along the track. When the enemy scout was sighted, the string of pineapples would be detonated, taking out guerrillas further down the line. This system only required two men on stag at a time. One ambush, run by Sgt. Bill 'Gloom' Ross, ex-Green Howards, remained in place for thirty-two days, and finally bagged two CT couriers bearing letters from which valuable intelligence was gleaned. Other ambushes stayed in place for up to sixty days.

Woodhouse, who believed that booby-traps were the best weapon against terrorists, had his patrols rig up trip-wires attached to grenade daisy-chains on every main track they found. His men would seek out abandoned CT camps and wire them up, knowing that the guerrillas almost always returned. The patrol would bury three-inch mortar bombs in the area, attaching them to pressure-switches that would close a circuit when trodden on. The traps would be inspected from a distance every ten to twenty days. Booby-traps could backfire on the patrols, though, and after several blue-on-blues, Sloane outlawed them.

Calvert had trained the men in snap-shooting using air-rifles and fencing-masks – one man lying in wait while two others stalked him. The air-pellets didn't penetrate the skin but they stung painfully, adding extra incentive to the exercise. These drills proved highly useful in a milieu where a split-second decision meant life or death.

The Regiment's first MM was earned by Sgt. Bob Turnbull of D Squadron, an ex-Gunner from Middlesbrough, legendary for his tracking skills, and the beau idéal of the jungle soldier. Turnbull's patrol, with an Iban tracker named Anak Kayan, once trailed a group of Communists for five days through the forest, alternately losing sign and picking it up again. Finally, after a continuous slog of twelve kilometres, they spotted a sentry in a bamboo thicket. Though he couldn't see it, Turnbull deduced that there was an enemy camp nearby.

Turnbull and Anak Kayan reckoned the group they'd been dogging consisted of five men, but there could have been many more in the camp. They knew they could take out the sentry easily, but this would only give the others a chance to escape. There were no easy approaches to the camp, except along the track, so Turnbull decided to lay up. He was expecting a rainstorm, and thought it would cover his patrol's advance.

The rain started at about 1615 hours, slashing into the vegetation. The enemy sentry moved, but Turnbull didn't know if he'd retired or had gone to relieve himself. Taking a chance, he crept into the sentry's post, with his patrol spaced at five-metre intervals behind him. Crouching in the undergrowth, Turnbull heard voices muttering in Chinese, from beyond a low bank. He motioned the patrol into line abreast. When they were in position, he signalled the attack.

The patrol topped the bank, and clocked seven men – four CTs and three aborigines. Two of the terrorists had their weapons stripped, and were cleaning them. Turnbull's pump-gun snarled four times. Three of the terrorists jerked like puppets and flew backwards, landing in bloody, mutilated heaps. A fourth lurched towards the bamboo thickets, streaming blood and rainwater. The other three SAS-men clattered rounds, snapping him down, while the aborigines stared, open-mouthed. The patrol cleared the camp – a dicey job where enemy could be skulking only a metre away – but found no more CTs. They uncovered documents, radio components, a pistol and a Sten-gun. Before he died, the wounded terrorist told them that a patrol of five CTs had moved out only two days before.

In the initial contact, only Turnbull had fired. He had taken out all four terrorists with .12-bore 9-ball rounds boosted off with incredible speed and accuracy. It was not the last time his snap-shooting skills would be called on. He later tracked down a guerrilla chief called Ah Tuck, notorious for carrying a cocked Sten-gun. Running across him in the forest, Turnbull beat Ah Tuck to the draw, and shot him dead. Another time, posted tail-end-charlie on a patrol led by an officer, Turnbull whacked out a terrorist over the patrol-leader's shoulder, before the officer had even released his safety-catch.

On another occasion, Johnny Cooper's troop sergeant, Olly Levet, demonstrated the superiority of the pump-gun over the M1 carbine in jungle conditions. Levet was with his signaller near their troop-base on a steep hillside when they heard movement in the bamboo thickets further up the slope. They slid into ambush positions. Levet told his oppo to drop the enemy lead-scout as soon as he appeared. He would kayo the rest with 9-ball. Moments later, a guerrilla nosed through the bamboo. The signaller's carbine snapped out. A slim .30 bullet whipped into him but didn't put him down. Levet lamped 9-ball, whaling the guerrilla off his feet, then welted off eight pumps into the bush behind him. When the smoke cleared, the two SAS-men wove forward to inspect the damage. In the bamboo they found three terrorists ripped to bloody rags by pump-gun rounds.

The only aspect of jungle movement Johnny Cooper found unpleasant was through mangrove swamps. Here, beyond the jungle canopy, the patrol had to move in blazing sunlight, either wading up to the waist in slimy ooze, or hopping from root to root along the mangroves, an exhausting exercise that skinned the arches of the feet. There was nowhere to sleep at night but in a hammock slung from fragile roots that might easily snap, pitching the sleeper into the water. The swamps were full of giant bull-leeches that not only sucked huge amounts of blood but whose bites stung painfully. Swamp-water was infected with 'lepto' and leech-bites gave the virus an easy access point. Sloshing through the dark water was dangerously noisy and incredibly slow, even by jungle standards. 'Before my initiation there,' Cooper wrote, 'I found it hard to believe that it could take one hour to cover five hundred yards.'[6]

In spite of this, Cooper found his first experience in the rain-forest satisfying – he never felt claustrophobic or nervous of creepy-crawlies. Like others, he'd started out with a sense of detachment that gave away imperceptibly to a feeling of absorption. The true lesson of the ulu was to acquire what the SAS called 'ground feel' – the ability to blend into the forest, to become one with the environment instead of separate from it. Far from being hostile, Cooper found the jungle cool and tranquil – a place where a man could make himself at home.

67. The worst going he ever experienced in Malaya

Within a year, four hundred thousand squatters on the jungle fringes had been resettled by British troops. Though moved forcibly, most found their new circumstances more favourable than the old. They were given new houses and land of their own, and eventually provided with schools and medical facilities. At the same time, stiff measures were adopted to prevent any contact with the terrorists.

Denied access to Chinese squatters, the Communists started growing their own crops and forcing local Malays to provide them with food. While the Regiment was in Singapore, intel had come in from ex-CTs that a hundred guerrillas of the MRLA's 12 Regiment had installed themselves at Kampong Sepor in the Belum valley, on the Thailand–Malaya frontier. They had blistered on to the Malay villagers, and were cultivating paddy-fields on the banks of the Sungei Belum.

B, C and D Squadrons, 22 SAS, were tasked to take out the terrorist base. While C and D would tab in across the mountainous spine of Malaya, B Squadron would be inserted by parachute on the paddy-fields. It would be the first operational jump since the war. The SAS would be part of a battle-group that included Royal Marines, Gurkhas and Malayan Police.

The ex-21 SAS-men of 'Big Time Bravo' were the only trained parachutists in the Regiment, but most hadn't jumped since Overlord. Rough training facilities were cobbled together at Changi airport in Singapore, which would shortly blossom into a new parachute school.

The op – designated 'Helsby' – kicked off almost as soon as the Regiment returned to the field after its sojourn in Singapore. B was scheduled to drop from RAF Dakotas on 8 February 1952. The other two squadrons, under John Woodhouse, set out in three-tonners from Kota Bahru at the beginning of the month. They were hoping to reach Batu Melintang in the central mountains before saddling up their Bergens. Heavy rains had barred the roads, though, and the men had to debus two days short of the drop-off point. This meant beetling on at a tremendous tack to reach the tactical area before B Squadron was inserted.

The squadrons had grown accustomed to the slow pace of movement in the cool shade of the great forest trees. This was commando-style battle-marching in double-time, with full equipment and a week's provisions, across five-thousand-foot mountains, grilled by the sun. After twenty miles the tracks ran out. The men found themselves scrambling up hillsides so steep and slick with mud that they had to use hands as well as feet. They slid and slipped down impossible slopes, tracked along treacherous stream-beds, or slashed their way with parangs through bamboo thickets. Woodhouse, who was often to be found carrying a straggler's Bergen as well as his own, was determined to reach the RV on time, or die in the attempt. He admitted, though, that this was the worst going he ever experienced in Malaya.

The squadrons tramped on for five days to reach the Sungei Belum. On the way, Woodhouse got word that the B Squadron drop was to be postponed a day, which gave him a small respite. On the morning of 9 February, C Squadron hit the Sungei Belum opposite the DZ to find that it had been swollen by recent rains into a forty-metre-wide surge of brown froth. Woodhouse ordered the men to construct bamboo rafts, while Lt. Mike Pearman volunteered to swim across towing a line. He bellyflopped in, and was whisked away by the current. Woodhouse reeled him back on the line, fearing he would drown. Pearman was furious. 'You bloody nearly drowned me yourself pulling me in like that,' he spluttered. He plunged in for another try. This time he reached the opposite bank, far downstream, and fixed the rope to a tree. Once the rafts were ready, it took only an hour to get the squadron across.

In the meantime, D Squadron had lost the way, and emerged from the forest a day's march east of the CT base at Kampong Sepor. This effectively ruled them out of the initial stage of the operation.

The three Dakotas carrying B Squadron, under Alastair

McGregor, had taken off from Butterworth on the coast at about 1300 hours. The drop had been scheduled shortly after first light, but had been delayed by rain and cloud over the mountains. Now the weather looked bad again, and the pilots were about to turn back a second time when there was a brief window. The Dakotas creamed in over the DZ two hours after noon, riding a fast tail-wind, dumping scaled-down dummy parachutists to assess drift. They were escorted by a flight of RAF Brigand light bombers, ready to hammer any flak coming up from the ground. The wind was dicey and the DZ a postcard rice-paddy on the river-bank, hemmed in by forest. The sticks went out anyway. Fifty-four olive-green fluted silk cupolas ballooned across the sky. All but four of the SAS-men missed the drop-zone and ended up in the trees. Most canopies were caught up in branches. Three men were slightly injured, but all managed to let themselves down to the ground on their knotted ropes. It was later said by some that the 'tree jump' was deliberate: in fact, it was an accident caused by the bad weather and the fast tail-wind.

Helsby proved an anti-climax. There were CTs around, but not in the numbers anticipated. C Squadron got bumped as it braced Kampong Sepor, and the Rhodesians fractured into four-man patrols to pursue their attackers. The patrols came back empty-handed: the MRLA had melted away across the Thai border. McGregor's men took one badly wounded prisoner, who told them before he died that he was a courier from Thailand, proving, as suspected, that there were cross-border contacts. The only SAS casualty was a D Squadron man, hit in the backside as he squatted to relieve himself. Following orders from the C-in-C, the SAS and other units evacuated all the civilians from the area, and set fire to their crops to deny them to the terrorists. Without establishing a patrol-base in the region, though, little of long-term value could be achieved. In fact, the guerrillas were back inside two months.

The operation's one major legacy was the 'tree-jumping' idea. The success of the freak drop convinced the SAS 'Head-shed' that in future it would be more reliable to jump directly into the forest canopy than on a cleared DZ. Since the parachute would almost certainly be snagged, it was safer than landing on ground obstacles like tree-trunks and bamboo. All that was needed was a more efficient method of getting down. That May, B Squadron boss Alastair McGregor roped Peter Walls, Johnny Cooper and other officers and NCOs into a tree-jumping experiment over primary jungle. It was as a result of this experiment that Johnny Cooper very nearly lost the use of his arm.

68. 'The Regiment had got something. You could sense it from the moment you arrived'

Despite being told in hospital that the idea of returning to active duty was 'just a pipe-dream', Cooper's arm mended. He was a captain again within a year, and soon boss of a newly rehashed D Squadron. Most of the early Airborne forces volunteers had gone. The new squadron was raised from local recruits and assembled around an original troop of fifteen, who, under Cooper's command, trained the recruits from scratch. Their real training, though, consisted of being thrown in at the deep end in 'Mad Mike' style, on a one-hundred-and-twenty-two-day patrol in the deep jungle of Pahang. Cooper's orders were to recce the area for the construction of a jungle fort, Fort Brooke – one of many that were being installed to protect the aborigines and keep them out of the clutches of the CTs.

Lt. Col. Oliver Brooke replaced Tod Sloane as commanding officer in '53. He was an old acquaintance of Cooper's from his time as boss of the SAS 'phantom troop', when Brooke commanded 10 (Yorkshire) Airborne Battalion. Under Brooke, 'hearts and minds' became buzz words. The concept had not been Calvert's invention, but a lesson learned from Mao Tse-tung, who had ordered his Red Army to make friends with the Chinese peasants and treat them well. Mao had been rewarded by their support – the single most crucial factor in his success. By now, many SAS-men had picked up Malay – a lingua franca among the forest-dwellers – and were able to communicate with them. Others had become proficient as patrol medics, and 'jungle-clinics' were more extensive. The linguists and the medics worked together, treating cuts, bruises and broken bones, as well as complaints such as yaws, tinea, malaria and tuberculosis. Slowly the soldiers began to penetrate aboriginal culture, learning their customs, taboos, beliefs and humour, sometimes sitting crosslegged in their long-houses for hours, listening with Job-like patience to their chattering, picking up crucial titbits of information.

It was a difficult and painstaking process. The aborigines frequently passed intel to the Communists and played both sides, so contacts with them always held a degree of risk. Unlike both the terrorists and the Malay troops, though, the SAS never molested aborigine women. They employed the men as porters and labourers for the construction of jungle forts, and always paid them for their work.

Little by little, 22 SAS was developing a technique of winning over the local population, running parallel with their aggressive fighting patrols. Some of the troops were unable to cross the line – in the case of C Squadron (Rhodesian) it was due to a cultural prejudice. The Rhodesians returned home early on, but retained their identity as C Squadron until the establishment of majority rule twenty-eight years later. C Squadron still remains vacant in the 22 SAS orbat.[1]

'Hearts and minds' was, if anything, even more debilitating than pure patrolling. By the time Cooper's squadron had handed Fort Brooke over to a police platoon, and was fished out of the ulu by helicopter, half of the eighty-strong unit had already been casevaced with fatigue, malaria or leptospirosis. One of Cooper's patrols, under Lt. Bruce Murray, had smashed up the local Communist gang, killing some and chasing others out of the tactical area. Cooper had also lost two men, Cpl. 'Digger' Bancroft and Tpr. Willis, in a CT ambush. On extraction, Cooper received a personal message from Brooke, congratulating him on 'a really splendid effort'.[2]

The character of 22 SAS was changing. During his first year as

CO, Oliver Brooke had sustained a broken back in a tree jump, and was casevaced to Blighty, crippled for life. His replacement, Lt. Col. George Lea, another ex-10 (Yorkshire) Airborne commander, inherited a regiment that had improved in every way since Calvert's day. Squadron patrols were now setting up bases and remaining in the jungle for three months at a time, just as Calvert had envisaged. Adminstration was efficient. Most of the dross had been filtered out and discipline had returned. 'The Regiment had got something,' Lea wrote later. 'You could sense it from the moment you arrived.'

Under Lea, Cooper was in turn Operations Officer and OC B Squadron. John Woodhouse had left the Regiment around the time of Cooper's accident, to take up a posting with a TA infantry battalion in the UK. He had turned up in Britain not knowing if he would ever serve with 22 SAS again, but holding the conviction that, while Calvert's tactics were a certain blueprint for success in Malaya, his 'Chindit policy' had caused most of the Regiment's teething problems.

Before taking up his TA posting, Woodhouse was given temporary command of some SAS Z Reservists in annual training at Otley in Yorkshire, under the auspices of 21 SAS. This two-week stint in the company of ex-wartime SAS-men changed Woodhouse's life. 'It was their example,' he wrote, 'which inspired me to spend as much of the rest of my military career as possible in the service of the SAS.'[3]

Woodhouse was later assigned to take charge of a group of SAS volunteers languishing at the Airborne Forces Depot in Aldershot, and was asked to plan a selection course for them. Given no support from the Airborne, he organized everything single-handedly and took the group off by train to Snowdonia, where he ran a course geared to training in navigation and battle tactics under stress. The course was rudimentary, and lasted only ten days, but established the principle upon which the Regiment's future excellence would be built. Afterwards, Woodhouse, who had gone down with recurrent malaria while conducting the course, wrote a report on the necessity of selection weighed against his early experience with the

Malayan Scouts. He sent it to the Colonel-Commandant of the SAS Regiment, General Sir Miles Dempsey, a supporter of the unit since the days when Mayne's SRS had been under his command.

Woodhouse's memo laid the foundation for a permanent Selection in Snowdonia, later transferred to the Brecon Beacons in south Wales. The process received a major fillip two years later when another ex-Malayan Scouts officer, Major E. C. 'Dare' Newell, was assigned the post of SAS Regimental Headquarters Major – a key link between the War Office and the SAS Regiment. He set about improving recruitment and selection, and the integration of common principles between the two existing regiments. To this end, he started a system by which, after a squadron operation in Malaya, regular NCOs would be cross-posted to 21 SAS as Permanent Staff Instructors – PSIs.

Though the survival of 22 SAS was still by no means assured, Newell was able to spearhead a 'Whitehall campaign' lobbying for its continued existence. He was so successful in defending SAS interests that David Stirling would later refer to him as 'Mr SAS himself'. Stirling would also call John Woodhouse '[the man] who restored to the SAS its original philosophy'. This was not quite justified: as Woodhouse indicated, the 'original philosophy' had never been lost among members of the Z Reserve and the Territorial units. Yet it was Woodhouse, more than any other individual, perhaps, who moulded the future character of the regular Regiment.

After a four-year absence, Woodhouse returned to Malaya and took command of D Squadron. The same year, the Regiment expanded in strength to five hundred and sixty men, in an HQ squadron and five sabre squadrons. In addition to A, B and D, there were new squadrons from New Zealand and the Parachute Regiment. The 'old operators' criticized the way the paras worked – more infantry-style than SAS – and the Kiwis' tendency to fall sick. Both, according to Lea, 'did [22 SAS] more good than many of the old hands were prepared to admit at the time'.[4]

The most significant event of the Emergency also took place while Lea was in the hot-seat. In 1957, Malaya was granted independence within the British Commonwealth. The carpet was abruptly whipped from under the MRLA, and many of the guerrillas surrendered. Ching Peng and his politburo, who had tried unsuccessfully to sue for peace, fled to Thailand. Though many terrorists remained obstinately in the jungle, their numbers had wilted to less than two thousand.

SAS operations began to wind down, as the British government handed over responsibility to the Malayan authorities. By the end of the year, the New Zealand and Parachute Regiment squadrons had departed. At the same time, Lea was succeeded as commanding officer by Lt. Col. Anthony Deane-Drummond, DSO, MC, another old Airborne hand. A month later, Johnny Cooper returned from a recruiting-drive in the UK, and was given command of A Squadron – his third stint as a sabre squadron boss.

69. 'He was a coward and had surrendered to save his skin'

Tony Deane-Drummond was a tall, sandy-haired man, with a slightly intimidating manner. His nickname was 'The Cupboard', after the time he'd hidden in a cupboard for thirteen days, in a house occupied by German troops. He had taken part in the first British parachute operation – the celebrated Tragino Aqueduct raid in Italy – as an officer of 11 SAS Battalion, a commando force that had no connection with Stirling's SAS. He had fought with the Parachute Brigade at Arnhem, and had been captured and escaped twice.

Deane-Drummond arrived in Sungei Besi with only one cloud on his horizon. A desk-wallah in the War Office had warned him that 22 SAS might only just last out his tour of duty. 'Your chaps have been quite superb in the jungle,' the officer said, 'but I can't see a task for them away from the trees.'[1] Deane-Drummond, who had been graded A1 fit only a month earlier, having been previously diagnosed with terminal cancer, appreciated that the army couldn't afford a specialist mob for jungle-fighting. He decided that his long-term goal would be to demonstrate that 22 SAS was more than a bunch of 'Jungle-Jims'.

The new CO acquired a few days' experience with D Squadron, whose boss, Major Johnny Watts, ex-Royal Ulster Rifles, had recently taken over from John Woodhouse. He then returned to base, where B Squadron, under Major Harry Thompson, had just come out of the ulu. Thompson was despondent. On the recent op he had found plenty of abandoned CT camps, but no terrorists. He was afraid they'd been scared off. 'Don't worry, Harry,' Deane-Drummond told him. 'Intelligence reports a complete CT gang in your next area of jungle.'[2]

Thompson was anxious to hear the details, but Deane-Drummond wouldn't tell him until he was ready. Nicknamed 'Skinhead' by his men, Thompson, ex-Royal Highland Fusiliers, was a six-footer with a bald pate and a fringe of red hair, quick-tempered and liable to lash out at his subordinates, but dedicated to the SAS. He had passed the newly revamped Selection in the Brecon Beacons, run personally by Dare Newell, a year earlier. One of his current troop commanders, Captain Peter de la Billière, had been on the same course. Thompson and de la Billière were very different characters. While de la Billière was quiet and reserved, Thompson was an extrovert, and something of a showman.

Thompson had to wait a week before Deane-Drummond briefed him on the new operation. His squadron was to enter the Telek Anson swamp, thirty miles north-west of Kuala Lumpur, where the last group of terrorists in the area was hiding out. The group's leader was a high-ranking officer of the MRLA, named Ah Hoi. He was known as 'Baby Killer', because he had once murdered the wife of an informer in front of her assembled village by cutting out her unborn baby with a parang. Thompson's objective was to snatch or take out Ah Hoi and his twenty guerrillas.

Thompson was leery that the CTs would move out of the area just as he suspected they had done on his last op. He decided that the squadron would go in by parachute. They would drop into the trees near the headwaters of the Sungei Tengi, a river that wound its way through the swamp to the coast. The guerrillas, whose base was thought to be in the middle of the swamp, wouldn't expect them to come from inland.

Deane-Drummond appreciated the boldness of Thompson's scheme, but had some reservations. He knew tree-jumping had its dangers. Though a recent study had concluded that casualties were relatively low – only 1.3 per cent – they tended to be serious, requiring immediate casevac. A helicopter casevac wouldn't halt the operation, but it might compromise Thompson's carefully thought-out approach. Deane-Drummond guessed that the parachute idea had its origin in what he called Thompson's 'relish for the spectacular', but he didn't try to interfere with the plan. He simply hoped it would come off.

Statistics showed that there was a seventy-four per cent probability of a jumper's parachute getting caught up in a tree, but B Squadron spent much of the next week on synthetic training, just to make sure they could steer their chutes into the forest canopy. They were to jump from two RAF Beverleys – the first time these aircraft had been used for parachuting. The planes would make one run only, and would drop to parachuting speed soon after take-off, so no one on the ground would hear the engines shift tone as they came in over the DZ. After the sticks had gone out, they would continue into the distance as if they were on a regular flight.

Seventy men of B Squadron mustered on the airstrip at 0500 hours on a humid morning in February. They fitted their X-type parachutes in the dark, and clipped their heavy Bergens to the harness, while the Beverleys' engines warmed up. They stalked silently to the aircraft with the stink of aviation fuel in their nostrils. The leg-bag technique developed at the end of the war had been modified for tree-jumping. The men carried their kit, including three weeks' rations, in their Bergens, strapped in canvas sheets. On exit this bundle or 'container' would be dropped immediately beneath their feet, and would protect their legs as they crashed through the forest. Their 7.62mm FN rifles were strapped on their chests in a 'valise' for immediate access on landing, and they carried two-hundred-foot coils of webbing with 'bikini' clasps at the end, enabling them to sashay down from the trees.

There was silence as the planes groaned up to dropping altitude. The squadron was apprehensive. They knew the statistics were favourable, but were also aware that their former commander, Oliver Brooke, would spend the rest of his life in a wheelchair as a result of a tree-drop. The flight lasted thirty minutes. Braced against the door, the RAF dispatcher yelled, 'Stand up!' The boys heaved themselves out of the nets and began fitting their containers. They checked each other's chutes and static-lines, and the dispatcher worked his way down the sticks for a final check, slapping each man on the shoulder as he passed. Back at his post, the RAF-man bawled, 'Action stations!'

The men shuffled into position and froze, all muscles tense. Nobody spoke. This was the moment of truth. From here there was no turning back. For trained parachutists, the green light constituted an order to jump. To refuse meant disobeying a direct order, and certain RTU. 'Red on' gave them four seconds. The blood drained out of their faces. Everything went quiet. Time stopped. Nothing existed but that yawning door. The green light flashed. The dispatcher screamed, '*Go!*' The sticks stomped up to the door. The men flipped out into the sky.

As Captain Peter de la Billière's canopy snapped open, he saw light thickening in the distance. The forest looked like a turbulent grey-green sea. He assessed his drift and heaved on his lift-webs, feeling the Bergen beneath his feet pulling on his canopy. In seconds he was breaking the surface of the forest. 'With a sudden rush I shot through the leaves and branches,' he recalled, 'and came to a stop with a tremendous jerk. My chute had lodged securely.'[3]

Everywhere, men were shimmying down to the forest floor on webbing straps. On the ground, Harry Thompson discovered that there was a casualty. Trooper Jerry Mulcahy's canopy had snagged, but the branch had snapped, and he'd pitched two hundred feet, landing on a tree-root. His back was broken. Some of his ribs had been fractured and had punctured his lungs. Blood dribbled from

Mulcahy's mouth. His head, shaven by his mates as a prank during a wild party the previous night, gleamed ominously white. He was paralysed and in agony. As a medic shot him up with morphine, Thompson had his operator radio base for immediate casevac by chopper.

It was now about 0700 hours. At Sungei Besi, Tony Deane-Drummond was tuned into the squadron frequency. He knew the sticks were in, but had expected some delay before they assembled on the DZ. When the casevac request came through, his heart sank. This was exactly what he'd feared. He detailed his medical officer to go in, and asked the RAF for a helicopter. As it whirled off, Thompson relayed good news. There was a natural clearing in the forest only a hundred metres from the DZ, where lightning had knocked down trees. Thompson's men were sending up an orange marker-balloon for the heli pilot.

Against SOPs, the pilot let down almost vertically into the clearing. Thompson watched the aircraft descend. She hovered, clattering, rotors razoring undergrowth, grating foliage, sucking leaves into air-intakes. The MO pitched out, making a beeline for Mulcahy's stretcher. The whirlybird wheezed out of the hole, rotors gyrating, slashing more foliage. She did a circuit and shuddered in again. Mulcahy was hefted aboard. The chopper lifted off through a double helix of flying leaves. Sixty-nine survivors saddled Bergens, checked weapons, sidled off silently into the forest towards the Tengi River. Thompson had to assume the insertion had been comped.

Going was tough. They made only twelve hundred metres that day. Thompson set up a squadron base near the Sungei Tengi and established comms. Next day the squadron split into troops and trekked off to make satellite bases. Every troop carried a radio, and at the evening halt encoded sitreps went through to squadron and Regiment HQs. The radio ops got on the net every morning at sunup to check that the troop's orders were still valid.

De la Billière's troop waded through swamp for three days. It was 'a hellish environment in which to live and move ... The leeches were unspeakable,' he recalled. At first the water was only ankle deep but it was soon up to the knees. Occasionally one of the patrol would sink up to his armpits. Getting drenched in swamp-water didn't faze anyone, though. Humidity was a hundred per cent, and almost every afternoon saw a tropical deluge. The men were wet through all the time, with rain, swamp-water or sweat.

De la Billière had been in Malaya just over a year, and had got to know his 6 Troop well on jungle patrols. His biggest challenge had been earning the men's respect. He was twenty-two. They were mostly older, and they were 'Big Time Bravo': they knew it all. Woodhouse's brief had informed him that there were no bad soldiers, only bad officers, and that he had the best soldiers in the world under his command. If he issued orders infantry-style, he knew he'd soon lose control. In the jungle there was no one else to run to, no guardhouse, no provost-sergeant. The only thing he had on them was that he'd seen action in the Korean war and they hadn't. He called them by their surnames. They called him 'Boss'. When he insisted on following SOPs they smirked. They thought he was a typical infantry officer. In the end, he came to the same conclusion Jock Lewes had come to. He would do anything they did, and more – patrolling, setting ambushes or fetching water. Any difference of opinion would be sorted out by Chinese Parliament.

This tradition had always existed in the SAS, but it had been actively encouraged by Tod Sloane, who had introduced 'criticism sessions' where everyone could put forward his point of view. Some SAS-men thought the system useful, others didn't. The hard-nosed Peter Ratcliffe felt that such discussions were a waste of time, simply confusing the issue, and allowing waverers to be negative. It was not the case that the opinion of the greenest trooper was equal to that of a senior NCO or officer commanding: as Tony Jeapes later pointed out, it was simply a method of eliciting constructive ideas that the commander might be able to use, but had generally thought of already.

In Stirling's day, the wider gulf in economic and educational background between officers and men meant that there had been greater deference to the 'officer class'. Wartime officers had still retained a modicum of the almost mystical aura of the aristocracy, which is why enlisted men found it difficult to accept officers commissioned from their own ranks. That deference was now melting away as 'other ranks' became more independent-minded: this was what Stirling meant when he talked about a modern SAS-man being 'more ready to fight his corner'. In the post-war world, the 'magical' gulf between officers and men had vanished. De la Billière's troop-sergeant, Lawrence Smith, soon told him if he disagreed with his proposals and why, but did it in a charming way. Another of his NCOs, Cpl. 'Tanky' Smith – an ex-Royal Tank Regiment man – was less charming. 'If he disagreed with me, he said so without mincing his words,' de la Billière recalled, 'and usually followed up with a couple of verbal punches, just to make sure I'd got the message.'[4]

The descendant of a French Huguenot family, de la Billière had lost his father – a Royal Navy surgeon – at the age of seven, when his ship, *Fiji*, was sunk by the Luftwaffe. He had attended Harrow, but hadn't shone as a student and left school with no qualifications. His ambition had been to join the Merchant Navy, but he'd failed the fitness test on colour-blindness. At the age of seventeen he'd decided instead to join the SAS – a unit of which he'd heard 'exciting rumours'. Enlisting as a private in the King's Shropshire Light Infantry as the first phase of his plan, he was soon selected for officer cadet training and was commissioned in the Durham Light Infantry. A man who made it his policy to avoid direct confrontation if possible, his one lesson from combat in Korea had been 'when someone is out to kill you, you had better get him first'.[5]

After three days in the swamp, de la Billière concluded that not even the guerrillas could endure these conditions. He moved his troop to drier ground along the river-bank, where it soon became clear his hunch had been right. Lawrence Smith picked up sign left by CT hockey-boots, and the patrol tracked the enemy through ten-foot-high swatches of lalang, or sword-grass, where they'd cut a path. The lalang was even worse going than the swamp – scratching hands, ripping clothing to shreds. After a while, though, they came across the remains of recently used camps, marked by piles of shells from freshwater terrapins the enemy had cooked and snaffled.

This information was vital. When de la Billière relayed the news to Thompson, the OC thought it confirmed that the terrorists had seen the casevac. They were bugging out downriver, fast. Thompson deployed his other two troops to cut them off ten miles downstream from where de la Billière had found sign.

The NCO commanding one of the troops, Sgt. 'Bosun' Sandilands, had decided to move by night. It was an unorthodox strategy, made possible by the low height of the mangrove trees and the bright moonlight. Sandilands thought the night-sounds would cover his patrol's approach, and at the same time he might pick up voices or the smell of cooking-fires. One afternoon, setting out early to cross a wide expanse of swamp, he clocked movement among some mangrove trees about seventy metres away. From hiding-places among the roots, his patrol spotted two CTs. They were tying hooks to fishing-lines, and had their rifles by their sides.

Sandilands thought the range was too great to be certain of a kill, but there was no obvious way to close it without being seen. He had the idea of approaching them using a drifting log as cover. His men detached a floating trunk from among the mangrove roots. Sandilands and his oppo crouched behind it and began to crawl through the water, pushing it in front of them. Moving steadily, they closed the gap. The guerrillas gave no sign of having spotted them, but Sandilands was aware that it would soon be dark and didn't want to lose the chance of a kill. About fifty metres from the enemy, he gave the sign to open fire. The pair blasted 7.62mm rounds. Bullets whined and whacked, grooving water. One of the enemy went down. The other streaked off into the twilight. Sandilands and his mate didn't follow up. Knowing it would be dark in minutes, they waded back to the patrol and strung their hammocks in the mangroves for the night. At first light they crossed the water, examined the corpse, and followed the tracks of the survivor eight kilometres to an abandoned terrorist camp.

Harry Thompson heard Sandilands's report, and became certain that Ah Hoi was still in the area. He drew his troops in a ring around the swamp, and called for back-up from police and infantry units. He began to squeeze. As the patrols moved in, he shifted his squadron base to some paddy-fields near a village on the jungle fringes. Deane-Drummond choppered in with Malayan Special Branch officers. They waited. 'At last the break came,' Deane-Drummond recalled. 'Out of the undergrowth beside one of the paddy-fields stepped a girl barely four foot six inches tall . . . she said her name was Ah Niet, and she had Ah Hoi's terms of surrender.'[6]

Deane-Drummond had a Special Branch officer tell Ah Niet there would be no 'terms', except those extended to all surrendering CTs. If Ah Hoi refused, the RAF would blitz his camp with bombs within forty-eight hours. This was a bluff – the SAS had no idea where the camp was – but Ah Niet swallowed it. She vanished back into the forest. That night, Thompson watched a caravan of lights coming towards him, as Ah Niet led a miserable file of ex-guerrillas to his post. One of them was 'Baby Killer' Ah Hoi, dressed in a woman's silk jacket and straw hat. 'Even at this stage . . . he ranted on and said that the Communists would win in the end,' said Deane-Drummond. 'Like all bullies, he was a coward and had surrendered to save his skin.'[7]

Sandilands was awarded the MM for his work, and de la Billière received a Mention in Dispatches. Despite this, though, Thompson told Deane-Drummond that he wanted de la Billière RTU'd. They had disagreed over the deployment of his patrol's bashas. John Woodhouse had laid down that in a troop-base bashas should be distributed 'tactically not comfortably', but de la Billière's old hands had persuaded him that this was pointless – it was impossible for the terrorists to approach a camp in thick jungle by night without being heard. They preferred a more 'sociable' layout with the bashas grouped together. According to Ian 'Tanky' Smith, Thompson arrived at their base one day in a foul mood, and criticized the arrangement. De la Billière defended it. Thompson, Smith said, lost his rag and told them, 'Right, I'm going to RTU the pair of you!'[8]

This might have been the end of de la Billière in the SAS.

Deane-Drummond, mindful of Thompson's tendency to explode, though, refused to RTU him. He was aware, as de la Billière was, that Woodhouse's stipulations were guidelines, not orders. Instead, he moved de la Billière to HQ Squadron and later posted him quietly to Johnny Watts's D Squadron, where, said Deane-Drummond, he subsequently performed 'brilliantly' in every job assigned to him. Harry Thompson would die in a helicopter crash in Borneo. De la Billière would become the Regiment's commanding officer, Director, SAS Group, and – thanks to the Iranian Embassy siege – the most famous SAS officer of his time.

70. 'There will be nothing left for my squadron at this rate'

Johnny Cooper, the callow young Guardsman who had jumped with Jock Lewes on Op Squatter, was now a thirty-six-year-old major and the most experienced SAS warrior in the business. While B Squadron was chasing Ah Hoi in Telek Anson, Cooper's A Squadron was operating south of Ipoh on Op Ginger, in support of the Commonwealth Brigade. In two months Cooper's boys made half a dozen kills. Harry Thompson sent a message asking him to go easy. 'There will be nothing left for my squadron at this rate,' he said.[1] That August, Deane-Drummond was flown in with brigade-commander Freddie Brooke to congratulate Cooper personally.

When the heli touched down, Cooper ushered the two senior officers over to the bole of a tree, where a corpse lay wrapped in a poncho. This was a seventh CT they'd taken out – only that morning. Cooper ordered a brew. While his guests sipped tea from giant half-litre mugs, he described how the other CTs had been bagged – all of them by superb shooting from his patrols.

The first pair had been slotted by Trooper O'Brien of 3 Troop, who, with an Iban tracker, had been staking out a rebel staging-post. It was a bamboo platform on stilts with a thatched roof that had been located by the troop boss, Captain Muir Walker, a six-foot Scotsman with wild red hair known to the officers as 'Red Rory' and to the troops as 'Black Abdul'. Walker had packed its floor full of plastic explosive.

Walker wired the PE to an igniter and had his men take up ambush positions. Two men at a time were on stag with the igniter, with the rest a hundred metres to the rear. They lay in wait in teeming rain for fourteen days. They didn't smoke or cook. They conversed in signs and whispers, and crawled into the bush to relieve themselves. O'Brien was on stag when four Communists entered the post. He pressed the igniter, hoping to blow them to smithereens. Nothing happened, and O'Brien concluded that the rain had rendered the wiring useless. Unable to warn the rest of the troop for fear of alerting the enemy, he picked up his FN rifle and drew a bead on the entrance. When two of the guerrillas climbed out, he pulled iron. The FN barked twice. The men hit forest humus and wet leaves. The others lurched out of the back of the shelter and whipped off into the jungle. Walker ascertained later that one of the dead was a VIP – district committee secretary Ah Poy. He was a major bag.

A couple of weeks later, two more guerrillas were taken out by L. Cpl. Jimmy Ladner, Royal Artillery. Ladner was lead-scout on a patrol commanded by his squadron sergeant-major, T. W. 'Jesse' James. The patrol, returning to its base after a day's trek, was three hundred metres short of camp. Ladner clocked bamboo shoots lying on the track that he hadn't noticed on the way out. He halted and placed his hand across his face. It was a signal to James, behind him, that there was someone around. The patrol froze. Ladner, wide-eyed, saw a flash of khaki ten metres away. For an agonizing instant he held fire. He thought it might be one of the aborigines, who sometimes wore military-style shirts. The next thing he clocked was a red star. Ladner whoffed a shot from his pump-gun. As he fired, he spotted a second Communist. With blurring speed, he pumped and fired again. The lethal 9-ball shot whacked off the second man's arm at the elbow and hurled it fifteen metres down the track. Ladner knew he'd been a hair's breadth from annihilation. He received one of the half-dozen MMs awarded to the Regiment in Malaya. He said later that his real reward was staying alive.

The last pair of guerrillas had been taken out by 'Jesse' James himself. 'He left my HQ on a short exercise patrol,' Cooper recalled. 'Rounding a [bend] on a jungle track he came face to face with two CTs walking towards him. His reflexes were so quick that his carbine was up to his shoulder and both men were shot dead before they could themselves open fire.'[2] Cooper was proud of the men's performance. He knew SOPs still weren't perfect – the men were in too much of a hurry, too competitive, and occasionally lacking the modesty David Stirling had considered a cardinal virtue. Still, things had come a long way since 'Mad Mike' days.

Ginger was Cooper's last successful operation in Malaya. This wasn't through any fault of his own, but simply because by that summer most of the Communists had surrendered or were about to. Cooper acquired several new officers, including his second-in-command, Captain Warwick Deacon, a noted mountaineer, and Captain Tony Jeapes, Devon & Dorset Regiment, another future commanding officer of 22 SAS, who would end his career a major-general. A Squadron were sent to patrol the Thai frontier. They spent weeks quartering the jungle, and even patrolled the Sungei Perak river in motorized dugouts, but found only deserted CT camps. In December, Cooper received instructions to pull his squadron out – a tall order, because all available helicopters were grounded. Instead, he had his men construct rafts and float down-river to base, getting in only twenty-four hours later than they would have done by chopper. At Sungei Besi, Deane-Drummond told Cooper he had a week to retrain and re-equip for immediate reassignment in the Middle East.

71. 'Condition their frame of mind to the extent where negotiations will be successful'

When A Squadron arrived at Bait al-Faluj, five miles from Muscat, in January 1959, they didn't even know where they were. Most had never heard of Muscat and Oman, the large sultanate lying on the south-eastern corner of the Arabian peninsula. Ruled by the reactionary Sultan Sa'id bin Taimur, it was the 'land that time forgot' – a country that boasted no roads, schools or hospitals, no electricity grid and no private cars. Inhabited by a galaxy of small tribes, both settled and nomadic, life went on there as it had for centuries, at the pace of the camel, the donkey and the sailing-dhow.

Five years earlier, the British-controlled Iraq Petroleum Company had identified potential oil-bearing strata in the Fahud area of north-western Oman, from aerial photographs. The IPC prospecting-team had been hampered in its attempt to reach the spot by the hostility of interior tribes, owing allegiance not to the Sultan in Muscat, but to the Imam of Oman, Ghalib bin 'Ali, in Nizwa. The Sultan deployed his British-officered armed forces and wrested Nizwa from the Imam's control. The IPC team completed its task, and the first exploratory shaft was sunk at Fahud two years later. The oil-rig was delivered by air, courtesy of the RAF.

The Imam's brother, Talib, raised a small force of Omani exiles and with the backing of the Saudis, and a nod and a wink from the USA, returned to Oman. He planned to take back the interior, and its oil, in the name of his brother. Talib's trump card was the support of Sulayman bin Himyar, chief of the Bani Riyam tribe – the most powerful sheikh in the region. Ghalib, Talib and Sulayman were now holed up with their rebel force in the Jebel Akhdar, or 'Green Mountain' – the central massif a four-hundred-mile-long mountain-chain that stretched from the Indian Ocean to the Persian Gulf.

The presence of the rebels was a threat to the drilling operations, and to the stability of the Sultanate. The SAS brief was to scale the Jebel Akhdar and take out the three chiefs, or, in Deane-Drummond's words, 'to give [their] followers really bloody noses . . . [and] . . . condition their frame of mind to the extent where negotiations will be successful'.[1] The locals considered the Jebel Akhdar impregnable. About fifty miles long and thirty square miles in area, it reached a height of nine thousand nine hundred feet – a convoluted Martian landscape of lurching ridges, hammered peaks and sheer-sided wadis, riddled with caves, overhangs and perpendicular slabs like giant steps. The jebel had never been explored or mapped by Europeans. Johnny Cooper's ex-comrade, former 1 SAS officer Wilfred Thesiger, had attempted to get in a decade earlier, but had been sent on his way by Sulayman bin Himyar. Ordered arrested by the Imam, Thesiger had narrowly escaped with his life.

The Green Mountain didn't appear to live up to its name, except on the central plateau, where there were orchards and forests, and running streams all year round. It was bitterly cold in winter, when temperatures plummeted to freezing and snow was not unknown. There could be savage rainstorms, but on still days the heat was overpowering, with the sunlight reverberating back from the metallic rocks, and the surface too hot to touch.

The Directorate of Military Operations in London had toyed with the idea of dropping a British parachute brigade on the plateau, but Tony Deane-Drummond thought this plan a non-starter. The drop would result in up to twenty per cent casualties, and the massive resupply operation required would be impossible to keep secret. Deane-Drummond was aware that the world had entered the 'media age' – instant radio and television coverage made military movements difficult to conceal. And secrecy was of the essence, because the Suez crisis two years earlier had made the British persona non grata in the Middle East, especially with the Americans, who were jealous of their commercial activities in the Gulf.

Directorate of Military Operations counter-insurgency expert Major Frank Kitson suggested that Arabic-speaking Englishmen should go in disguised as tribesmen, with the SAS in a supporting role. British intelligence officers on the ground had pointed out that it would be impossible for Europeans to pass themselves off as natives in this country. The Arabs didn't miss a trick, and could tell even which tribe a man belonged to from over a mile away. The other strategy – air-strikes – had proved ineffective. RAF Venoms and Shackletons had strafed and bombed the plateau, but had found targeting impossible without observers to vector them in.

D Squadron, under Major Johnny Watts, had been patrolling the massif since November. Watts, a dark, eccentric-looking man with a humorous expression and a roll-up eternally dangling from the corner of his mouth, had orders to carry out offensive recces of all possible routes up the mountain, and to take out enemy pickets. The principal human target was Talib bin 'Ali, who was reckoned to be the rebel commander. Watts's base was at the village of Tanuf on the western side of the massif, from where Captain 'Red Rory' Walker, transferred from A Squadron as Watts's second-in-command, had recced up to a pass known as Aqbat adh-Dhuffar, at about seven thousand feet. He had set up a forward operating base at a position named 'Cassino', facing a twin-peaked ridge christened 'Sabrina' or the 'Twin Tits' after a pinup girl of the day. Sabrina was a natural defensive position. Connected to the Aqbat by a narrow rock bridge a mile long and only a hundred metres wide, with sheer drops on both sides, it was easy for the enemy to defend, and impossible to avoid. It was at this stage that Watts realized that a second SAS squadron was going to be needed if they were to broach the plateau.

Deane-Drummond agreed, but he'd already pushed the boat out asking for one. The original proposal had been for 'a few SAS volunteers'. To the CO, the request had been the break he'd been waiting for. Four months earlier, he'd been notified that the Regiment would be returning to the UK that spring, where it would be downsized to a skeleton force. Without an immediate task, it would have to compete with 21 SAS, and a new TA Regiment soon to be raised in the north of Britain, 23 SAS. These two Regiments were to be groomed for a major special forces role with NATO. If 22 was to survive, it would have to find itself a separate role: what Deane-Drummond had in mind was a 'fireman force' that could be trained to work in small units in any country, at short notice, in complete secrecy. The Jebel Akhdar operation would be its test-mission, and was therefore make or break for 22 SAS. To succeed they had to have another squadron. There were six hundred well-armed rebels on the plateau, and the sabre personnel of D Squadron alone numbered only forty men.

On 30 November, a five-man patrol under Sgt. Herbie Hawkins was banjoed near Cassino by fifty Arabs who slipped down from Sabrina under the cover of a ferocious gale. The rebels came on the patrol out of every wrinkle and fissure in the rocks, supported by the tack-tack of Bren-gun fire. Hawkins's patrol held off until the enemy were within a hundred and fifty metres, then squeezed metal. Their FNs crackled, pumping deadly 7.62mm rimfire. Bullets juked and fizzed off rock. Fragments geezed. Brens clittered. The wind wailed. Arabs tumbled. Hawkins's men stopped at least a dozen rebels in their tracks with concentrated shooting. When darkness fell they made a skirmishing retreat. The incident would go down in SAS folklore as the 'Battle of Hawkins' Hump'.

The same night, two troops under Peter de la Billière bumped a gallery of caves further south, where they suspected Talib might be hanging out. They hit the caves with a rocket-launcher and a Browning machine gun. Rockets hooshed and shivered, blowing brilliant flame and grey smoke. The Browning chunked. Bullets sizzed. De la Billière was expecting the rebels to bug out, but they stood their ground. They clacked cocking handles. They popped .303 rounds. They hoiked bombs from a two-and-a-half-inch mortar. Mortar shells creased air, spliffing iron coils and rock splinters. 'The richochets were prodigious,' de la Billière recalled, 'bullets whanged and whined . . . and chips of rocks flew. All at once we were in trouble.'[2]

The SAS-men were saved by a strafing-run of RAF Venoms that honed in with cannon sprattling. Venom engines droned. Cannon shells boomed and crunched round the caves. The SAS made a fighting withdrawal. They'd suffered no casualties but cuts from flying rock shreds. Intel reports later suggested that they'd taken out twenty enemy dead, and though they'd missed Talib, the chief was reportedly 'shaken' by the attack.

The SAS, too, had learned a lesson about the enemy – the 'adoo'. 'They are a much tougher crowd than [we] thought,' Watts wrote Deane-Drummond, by now back in Malaya.[3] The CO was becoming concerned. Patrolling was one thing, but a general assault on the plateau would certainly need another squadron. It wasn't until 29 December that the War Office gave its approval. Cooper's boys had been deployed as a result.

Meanwhile, 'Red Rory' Walker had decided to show the Arabs once more that they hadn't got much to be cocky about. On Christmas Eve his men stonked rebel positions with three-inch mortars. 16 and 17 Troops moved out to attack Sabrina. They shimmied up the left 'tit' on ropes, ramped into the Arab position, and in an all-night gun-battle drove them off the peaks. At first light on Christmas Day, Walker pulled his men back to the forward base. He'd shown the rebels that they had a more formidable enemy than the Sultan's Armed Forces. By January, D Squadron had notched up forty adoo kills. They'd sustained only one casualty – Cpl. 'Duke' Swindells, who'd won the MM in Malaya. Swindells had allowed himself to become skylined on a ridge, and had been taken down by a sniper.

That, Deane-Drummond told Cooper's squadron during their initial briefing at Bait al-Faluj, underlined the difficulties of fighting here. Swindells was a good soldier in Malaya, where there were no ridges to be skylined on, and where visibility was down to ten or twenty metres. Here in the arid mountains there was no cover, and men could be clocked miles away. Added to this, the hill-tribesmen were superb shots. The 'hard core' were armed with .303 Lee-Enfield Mark IVs – probably the most accurate service-rifle ever made. Hawk-eyed, brave and hardy, the Arabs came from a culture where men carried rifles from childhood. They'd inherited a tradition of inter-tribal warfare and vendetta that went back millennia. 'Do not underestimate the rebels,' Deane-Drummond warned Cooper's crew. '. . . Their minor tactics, and use of ground are both excellent.'⁴ Deane-Drummond said that five-sixths of the adoo were local tribesmen from the Bani Riyam and the Bani Hinna tribes. About a hundred were Omani exiles who had been trained in Saudi-Arabia. There were about ten Saudi 'advisers'. The arms and equipment had been supplied by the US military mission in Saudi-Arabia. They were sustained and provisioned by about five thousand civilians living in villages on the plateau.

Deane-Drummond's plan was a return to the old Stirling key-notes of surprise and the economic use of force. The main rebel strongholds were the villages of Habib, Saiq and Sharaijah, on the southern edge of the plateau. D Squadron's recces confirmed that the best way of approaching them would be from the village of Kamah, south of Tanuf, on an unguarded route that led up a steep mountain face known as 'Ambition'. This would take them up to Habib, at seven thousand feet.

Cooper's squadron had only five days to acclimatize. While they were at Bait al-Faluj, Deane-Drummond took Watts and Cooper on an air-recce over the proposed route. From the spotter aircraft, Deane-Drummond noticed that Ambition was joined to the plateau by a narrow neck that, if defended, would put the kibosh on the assault. Instead he chose a slightly more westerly route that would involve scaling a slab named 'Vincent'. From here he hoped to find a short-cut across a natural 'causeway' from a hump named 'Pyramid', cutting directly across two wadis to the wall of the plateau. They would scale the last leg up to a point known as 'Beercan', a stone's throw from Habib. The route was convoluted – not a straight climb, but a succession of ups and downs taking them over steep rocky slabs and up sheer cliffs. Boulder-strewn screes would be tough going at night, and in places a slip would mean plummeting down thousands of feet.

The SAS would have to be at Beercan before first light, at about 0645 hours. The climb had to be completed in a single night, with the men carrying immense loads of ammunition, rations and water. The squadrons would be assigned ten donkeys apiece for their .50 Brownings and ammunition. Once on top, the SAS would take a resupply drop from the RAF. If the squadrons failed to make the DZ, or the drop went astray, there was a fallback logistics-plan. Supplies would be hauled up the jebel on a caravan of a hundred donkeys that had been imported specially from Somalia.

One well-placed picket with a machine gun could make mince-meat of the assault-party – and there were thought to be four main sites where pickets could halt the advance. Deane-Drummond knew that a diversion would be essential to make Talib shift his watchdogs to cover the Aqbat adh-Dhuffar and Tanuf areas to the north.

This was where Cooper's A Squadron came in. The day before the main assault, Cooper would relieve de la Billière's troops now holding the forward base near Cassino, and launch a major attack on Sabrina. D Squadron patrols would mount feints on the two-thousand-foot slab above Tanuf. RAF Venoms would concentrate their strafing runs on the northern area. Deane-Drummond hoped Talib would be convinced that the assault was coming that way. Leaving one troop on the Aqbat adh-Dhuffar to carry on the deception, the rest of A Squadron would RV with D Squadron at Tanuf and would be motored round to the foot of Vincent, where they would begin the real ascent. The assault would go in at the next full moon – 25/6 January.

They would have a dismounted troop of the Life Guards and local troops from the Northern Frontier Force and Trucial Oman Scouts as back-up, plus six hundred levies from the pro-Sultan Abiriyeen and Bani Ruwaha tribes. The sabre personnel of the two SAS squadrons amounted to only eighty men. Colonel David Smiley, the ex-SOE man who commanded the Sultan's Armed Forces, told Deane-Drummond privately that he doubted the SAS could do it. The final assault required a ten-hour non-stop climb carrying loads of up to fifty kilos, to be made in complete silence and under constant threat of attack. The general consensus was that at least two battalions of trained mountain troops would be needed to carry out the operation. 'The Cupboard' was determined to prove them wrong.

72. 'We had done it in the nick of time'

For two days it rained heavily on the jebel. Dry-washes became raging torrents, and the head of the massif was wrapped in cloud. Deane-Drummond scanned the met reports, and postponed the assault until the night of 26 January. Three days before D Day, though, the clouds drifted off south, and sunlight burst through them in probing laser beams. The air smelt clean and new.

In the early hours of 25/6 January, three troops of Cooper's A Squadron slipped out of a wadi under the apron of Sabrina to scale the 'Twin Tits'. A fourth troop covered them with Bren-guns. The moon had ballooned into a cloudless sky soon after dark, bathing the whole surreal edifice of the mountain in pale gold. As the men made their way cautiously up the slope, though, not a squeak was heard from the rebels. Reaching the summit forty minutes later, Captain Tony Jeapes, leading the right-hand assault-group, found out why. The enemy positions had been blitzed by Shackletons and Venoms earlier that day and the enemy had retired to a fallback position. Jeapes also found that his radio op couldn't get comms, and shot off a white Very flare to let Cooper know they'd cleared the ridge. A moment later, Bren and Lee-Enfield fire rippled out of the night from enemy sangars fifty metres away.

Jeapes led his troop up to high ground behind the left 'tit' and wreaked fire down on the Arabs below. The SAS-men walloped Energa grenades from the muzzles of their rifles. They whaled No.36 pineapples. They moved forward and down, belting out FN and Bren fire. Rebel rounds whipped and shrieked. Grenades thunked and shrilled, cascading spurts of orange fire. The SAS-men skirmished, double-tapping, weaving, jogging, rolling and firing. Trooper Wright, boosting hip-fire from his Bren, took a grenade fragment in the thigh and skittered over, blagging blood. Energas smacked stone and erupted in dark blots, splattering rock-chips. Arabs beetled out of sangars and ran for it. 'There was one very brave Arab standing there throwing grenades,' Jeapes remembered. 'Three of us fired and couldn't hit him. We charged using a Bren-gun. Bullets were pinging off the rocks. I got as far as the outcrop he was standing on, waited till he threw the grenade, and shot him.'[1]

The six-foot-five Jeapes leapt over the wall of a sangar. An Arab in a dishdasha and headcloth popped up with a rifle in his hands, and squeezed metal. The weapon misfired. Before Jeapes could shoot, Cpl. Slater blasted the rebel, who did a high-dive off the rocks into a fifty-foot chasm.

The SAS cleared the area and found the sangars were empty. Three of the enemy were dead, and probably the fourth, who'd nosedived over the precipice. Blood smears told them that up to five more had been hit and dragged off by their comrades along a wadi behind the sangars. Jeapes's squad wheeled right to cover an attack by Ian Patterson's troop on the opposite 'tit', but the opposition had faded away. The rebels had pulled out. By 1400 hours, Wright had been casevaced by Sycamore helicopter, and the whole squadron was back with Cooper at Cassino. Three troops got ready to move back down to Tanuf under the cover of night. 4 Troop would stay on the pass to launch another diversionary attack.

It took them fourteen hours to reach base. They were so shattered after their engagement that few made it without stopping. They'd gone a full day and a night without sleep – it was the hardest trek Jeapes remembered. They had a few donkeys with them and at one point had to lift them down an eight-foot drop. It was the first time Jeapes had ever heard SAS soldiers saying they'd had enough. 'Our march down to Tanuf was mighty tough,' admitted Cooper. 'We were bloody glad to get in.'[2] Deane-Drummond was there to meet them, with Johnny Watts, whose D squadron had been patrolling aggressively on the Tanuf slab for most of the day. Deane-Drummond was delighted with Cooper's performance, and told the men they couldn't have done better. He was confident Talib would draw his pickets back to Sabrina. The A Squadron boys hit the sack, remembering that what they'd done was only a feint. The real job was to come that night.

Deane-Drummond had two more tricks up his sleeve to distract the enemy. The previous evening, before the donkey-trains left for Kamah, he'd called the chief 'donkey wallopers' and inquired about watering-conditions up the Wadi Tanuf, giving the impression that the assault would go in from the north. 'They were told not to tell anyone on pain of death,' commented Don 'Lofty' Large, with D Squadron. 'So we knew the enemy would know within minutes.'[3]

The other ruse came just before dark, when the CO had all the men jump aboard fifteen three-tonners and ordered the convoy to drive north, away from the starting-point at Kamah. The trucks bounced and jolted along the rough track around the jebel, in plain view of Talib's watchers. At last light, the lorries halted and turned back the way they'd come, hotfooting it with lights off towards the start-point.

The assault started at 2030 hours, the men tabbing off in file up the eight-thousand-foot Vincent, the first stepping stone to the plateau. The climb was 'blind' – no one had done it before. They had studied air-photos and two SAS-men had made a recce from the desert, but Deane-Drummond was aware that there were a lot of unanswered questions. The most pressing ones were whether their ruses had worked, and if they'd be able to cross the 'causeway' between the wadis.

D Squadron led the way with de la Billière's troop on point, preceded by a two-man scouting party. A Squadron followed, led by Johnny Cooper himself, with Deane-Drummond's HQ, and the donkey-train carrying their radios, bringing up the rear. The rocks had sponged up the day's heat, and even two hours after sunset the air was still hot. Sweat poured off them. They were tramping straight up the mountainside, lugging loads varying between forty and fifty kilos. According to de la Billière, who'd lain awake all day psyching himself up for the effort, the first hour was the worst. 'So steep was the face of the slab,' he wrote, 'that some of the squadron couldn't stand the pace and fell back.'[4]

According to the official report, the A Squadron troop left at Cassino put in their diversionary attack just as the main party started their climb. Deane-Drummond, though, recalled hearing gunshots about three and a half hours later, just as he reached Vincent. Apart from that, all was quiet. They encountered no pickets, but passed two abandoned enemy sangars. They staggered and stumbled on up the unrelenting mountain for a solid seven hours without a halt. The going was harder than expected. The rocks that had looked so smooth to Cooper from the air were ragged screes that slowed progress to a crawl. The aerial photographs hadn't revealed the twenty-foot sheer-sided wadis that had to be worked around, with agonizing delays. Lofty Large thought they were making too much noise. 'There is no way a man can climb over loose rocks and shale, heave himself up rock slabs,' he wrote, '. . . in almost total darkness with a heavy load . . . and be both fast and quiet.'[5]

By about midnight Cooper's squadron had taken up fire positions on Vincent, from where they would cover D Squadron's advance. They were still exhausted from their battle the previous night, and their almost non-stop descent to Tanuf. Getting off the slab down fifty-foot broken cliffs proved more of an obstacle than anticipated, and it took D Squadron another four hours to reach the edge of Pyramid, where a two-hundred-foot precipice plunged down to 'the causeway' that had been seen from aerial photos. Johnny Watts deployed one of his four troops on Pyramid to support the next leg. In the lead, de la Billière's scouts started looking for a way down the cliffs. Deane-Drummond's HQ party moved up behind Watts, whose three leading troops were bunched together by the cliff edge.

Deane-Drummond was worried. It was now 0500 hours, which gave them an hour and a half to get up to Beercan before first light. The troops were already shattered. 'Men began to collapse in their tracks,' said Lofty Large. 'I saw two fall flat on their faces, unconscious before they hit the ground.'[6] De la Billière's scouts came hurrying back to report that they'd found the place where the track descended the cliff, but they'd also come across a .50 heavy machine gun mounted on a tripod at the mouth of a cave. It was loaded with belts of armour-piercing, ready to fire, and was set up so as to command the crucial bottleneck.

Watts guessed that the crew was asleep somewhere nearby, and detached a troop to take them out. They would have to wait till first light, though, so as not to compromise the advance. 'We couldn't knock out the machine-gun crew,' said de la Billière, 'without making a noise that would advertise our presence to half the [jebel].'[7] They would have to slip past the position quietly. Time was dripping away, and Deane-Drummond advised Watts to have his two remaining troops drop their Bergens, leave them with the detached troop, and make the rest of the climb with only weapons and belt-kit.

There were twenty-two men in the final assault party. After they'd jettisoned their Bergens, they felt light enough to take off. Led by Watts and de la Billière, they slunk past the gun, worked their way down the cliff, and dropped about five hundred feet into the Wadi Sumait. Dark rock steeples towered menacingly above them, and they were glad to know that the D Squadron troop on Pyramid was covering them. Deane-Drummond's party followed closely behind, still carrying their Bergens. From the top of the wadi, the CO could see the advance party above him as they moved up the final six hundred feet in a desperate race against time. He glanced east, and noticed that there was already a faint gash of crimson on the skyline.

It was getting light by the time de la Billière's men came in sight of the end. They could feel their energy draining away. Despite having no Bergens, every step was agony. 'Suddenly we came over one more ridge,' de la Billière wrote, 'and saw . . . [that] the slope eased off into a rough rocky plateau.'[8] They had arrived. Watts and de la Billière collapsed behind a rock, reflecting that they were the first foreigners to ascend the Jebel Akhdar in a thousand years. Watts pulled himself out of his torpor and sent the men off in pairs in all-round defence, telling them to die at their posts if need be.[9]

Not far below, Deane-Drummond heard 'the sweet music of aircraft engines', and looked up in the thickening light to see three RAF Valettas coming in for the supply-drop, right on schedule. On the top, Watts realized suddenly that he'd left his smoke grenades in his Bergen, and that the pilots wouldn't make the drop unless they saw smoke. He had his men set fire to a square of flannelette soaked in gun oil, and ignite some green bushes. A column of white smoke guffed out in the clear dawn air. The Valettas banked gracefully and zoomed in low. Fifteen seconds later, a bevy of pink fluted domes blossomed out of the sky. 'It was the best possible welcome we could have had,' said Deane-Drummond, 'and we had done it in the nick of time.'[10]

When the CO's party crested the plateau at seven o'clock, the expected attack hadn't arrived. As the sun climbed further, it became clear to Deane-Drummond that there were no rebels in the vicinity. His deception plans had worked perfectly. They had taken the plateau.

The third D Squadron troop was up an hour after the HQ party, too late for Johnny Watts, who delivered a 'bollocking' to the troop officer. The subaltern countered that they'd had to stop to take out the machine-gun crew at the crack of dawn. After Watts's party had descended into the Wadi Sumait, they'd divided up and scoured the caves around the gun, lowering themselves down the cliff on a fixed rope. A two-man team, 'George' and 'Alex', were climbing down to a lower cave, when one of the Arabs emerged, clocked Alex on the rope, and pot-shotted him with a .303. The Arab missed, but Alex was stuck there like a monkey on a stick until his comrade finally blotted the rebel. Alex landed on the ledge, pinned a No.36, and lobbed it underarm into the cave. An ear-splitting blam chased out a whoff of smoke. Alex wasn't happy with George. He said his mate had waited till the very last moment to whack the Arab, just to give him a hard time.

When Watts argued that it shouldn't have taken so long to deal with a three-man MG crew, the subaltern pointed out that the action had alerted another rebel gun-crew, and enemy rounds had started blipping and pinging around his troop. Arab snipers posted on the Ambition feature woke up and belatedly realized the jebel was under attack. RAF Venoms wheeled in and rocketed them, unsuccessfully.

Cooper's A Squadron, relieved by the Northern Frontier Force, set off to the plateau at mid-morning but were held back by snipers engaging them from half a kilometre away. By bad luck, a stray round hit the Bergen carried by Trooper Carter and set off an Energa grenade. It went up in a fireflash that mortally injured Carter, and sprayed Troopers Hamer and Bembridge with shrapnel. All three men were dollied out by choppers, whirling in perilously under fire from enemy mortars. Carter and Bembridge died, but Hamer survived. Cooper detailed a troop to knock out the snipers and machine-gun post, but they weren't silenced until 1430 hours. By then, Cooper's advance party was already on the plateau with Deane-Drummond. The D Squadron troop left on Pyramid didn't set off until 1500 hours, after being relieved by the Life Guards.

The leaders of the rebellion – Talib, Ghalib and Sulayman – were never found. It turned out that the chiefs had taken the air resupply-drop for reinforcements, and had fled to Saudi-Arabia on camels with sixty tribesmen. The rebellion had been nipped in the bud: a small party of SAS-men, most of whom had seen service only in the Malayan jungle, had captured a mountain that had remained impregnable for a thousand years. The oil companies were delighted. A multibillion-barrel oilfield was struck at Fahud in 1964.

73. 'A great success as a bloody idiot'

A and D Squadrons stayed in Oman until March, when Cooper moved them back to the UK to join the rest of the Regiment at its new base, Merebrook Camp, near Malvern – a disused wartime emergency hospital. The three sabre squadrons were immediately reduced in strength to three troops each – a total of no more than seventy sabre personnel. At a staff conference that Christmas, Deane-Drummond told the assembled officers that 22 SAS was shortly to be transferred to Bradbury Lines at Hereford, where a Junior Leaders' camp had become vacant. The bad news was that they were to be further downsized to an HQ and two sabre squadrons – A and D. B Squadron was to be disbanded. Many officers were surplus to requirements, and would be RTU'd. Johnny Cooper was offered a desk job at the War Office.

Cooper was the only Original left in 22 SAS – Bob Lilley had served with the Regiment for a time, but had now departed. Bob Bennett was serving as RSM with 21 SAS. Cooper had dedicated the best part of twenty years to the Regiment, and was its most experienced soldier. When the medals had been handed out for the Jebel Akhdar op, though, Watts, de la Billière and Jeapes had all been awarded MCs, and Deane-Drummond his second DSO. Cooper had been left out. At thirty-nine, he wasn't beyond the pale of operational employment. He deserved to be Regimental 2IC or commanding officer, yet there was no longer a place for him in the Regiment. Cooper decided that they could keep their 'desk-wallah' appointment. He left 22 SAS within a month, and was soon in command of C Company, the Northern Frontier Regiment, in Oman. Deane-Drummond left shortly afterwards, handing over to Lt. Col. Dare Wilson. He went off to command 44 Airborne Brigade.

Bradbury Lines proved the perfect base for the Regiment. Hereford itself was a sleepy, picturesque town strategically placed for training in the Black Mountains and the Brecon Beacons, just across the Welsh border. It was big enough to provide most amenities, and small enough for SAS-men and their families to become part of the community. The barracks had been built in the 1930s, and consisted of wooden huts in configurations known as 'spiders', set in meticulously maintained grounds and gardens. The offices, including the 'Blue Room' or briefing room, and the 'Kremlin' – the Intelligence and Planning centre – were sited in a block overlooking the rarely-used parade ground, the centrepiece of which was the famous clock tower, which was to become a monument to fallen comrades. It was on the clock tower that James Elroy Flecker's famous lines from *Hassan* were inscribed:

> We are the pilgrims, master; we shall go
> Always a little further; it may be
> Beyond the last blue mountain barred with snow,
> Across that angry or that glimmering sea . . .

'The pilgrims' was a tribute to the dead rather than the living members of the Regiment – those who had 'failed to beat the clock'. Many would be buried in the cemetery of St Martin's church in Hereford – another regimental monument.

Over the next four years, 22 SAS settled into its new base and went about the business of transforming itself into a professional special forces unit. The keyword was flexibility. SAS-men must be multi-skilled on several levels, cross-trained so as to be able to take over each other's jobs instantly. On a troop level, they must be prepared to fight in any environment, and to arrive by land, sea and air. Dare Wilson set up a training wing, a repository of all SAS skills. Every man would be a swimmer, a driver and a parachutist, and would be trained in combat survival, escape and evasion, resistance to interrogation, battlecraft, close-quarter battle shooting, foreign weapons and jungle warfare. Every man would attain either advanced or basic level in signals, medical skills or demolitions, and some would acquire languages, including German, Arabic, Malay, Thai and Swahili.

Brian Franks's concept of specialized troops was also taken on board. At first the idea was to have one speciality in each of the two sabre squadrons – a 'mountain troop' in A Squadron, and an 'amphibious troop' in D Squadron. A year later, it was decided to duplicate the specialist troops in both squadrons. In each, there would be four specialities. The 'Boat Troop' would be trained in the use of *folbots*, Gemini inflatables, ship and submarine landings and sub-aqua techniques. The 'Mobility Troop' would specialize in operations by Land Rover for the European and desert theatres, with advanced driving and repair and recovery skills. They would also be trained in astro-navigation and desert navigation techniques developed by the LRDG. The 'Mountain Troop' would become experts in mountain warfare, rock and cliff-climbing, skiing and snow survival. The 'Air Troop' would be trained to jump in small sticks from six thousand feet. Later, they would develop HALO – high-altitude, low-opening – drops, and would be inserted from civil aircraft from up to thirty-five thousand feet, breathing from oxygen cylinders.

SAS missions might require high security, but the existence of the Regiment was not secret. Until the late sixties it openly paraded in uniform. Even afterwards, its existence was never denied, and its deployment was publicized when convenient as a political tool by the government. Though the Jebel Akhdar campaign had been under wraps at the time of its execution, a report was given to the press three months later. This was an example of the careful manipulation of the media, the use of which as a psychological weapon had been part of the SAS role from the very start, when Stirling's operations at Kabrit were filmed and shown in cinemas world-wide. In SAS ops, the unit's 'mystique' was always the hidden fourth dimension.

In the UK, the unit had to come to terms with the fact that the Special Air Service Regiment was more than just 22 SAS. There were two other Regiments, 21 SAS (Artists) and 23 SAS. 21 now had sabre squadrons in London, Portsmouth and Hitchin. 23 SAS, with its HQ in Birmingham, had sabre squadrons in Leeds, Tyneside and Glasgow. 23, formed in 1959, had an even more curious pedigree than 21 SAS. It was descended from MI9 – the wartime escape and evasion division, responsible for setting up 'rat-lines' to extract downed aircrew and escaped prisoners. After the war it had become a territorial unit, Intelligence School 9 (IS9), later known as the Reserve Reconnaissance Unit.

In the year 22 SAS settled at Hereford, the War Office issued a directive laying out the Regiments' various roles. The directive defined three characteristics of the SAS as a whole: the ability to operate for extended periods in small numbers in enemy-controlled territory; the ability to be moved by unorthodox means such as parachute or small craft; the ability to operate in extremes of climate and terrain. The three types of operations it was suited for were intelligence gathering, operations in cooperation with guerrilla forces and raids.

The directive also laid down SAS roles in various war scenarios – limited, cold and global wars. 22 SAS had a capability for counter-guerrilla ops in desert, snow, mountain and jungle, in limited and cold war. In global war it would operate as an intelligence-gathering unit for 1 British Corps on the Rhine. 21 and 23 SAS had no role in cold or limited war, but in global war would be available within forty-eight hours to act as 1 BR Corps' main 'Corps Patrol Unit' (CPU) or intelligence-gathering force, with particular reference to enemy nuclear systems.

21 and 23 SAS developed a new role in Europe, where, in the event of a Soviet advance, six-man patrols would lay-up in subterranean nuke-proof hides, observing enemy forces passing over their positions and relaying intel back to UK Base by 'tele-graph'. The NATO plan was to hold off until the Soviet divisions became bottlenecked at the river Weser, then hit them with nuclear strikes. Due to their role, 21 and 23 lacked the troop specializations of 22, but were as highly trained as 22 SAS in the other standard SAS skills.

When Peter de la Billière was posted to 21 SAS as adjutant the same year, he quickly found out that there was 'an unpleasant amount of antipathy . . . between the regulars and territorials of the SAS. The regulars looked down on the part-timers as amateurs, and tried to unload poor instructors on them.'[1] The regulars' main beef, de la Billière said, was that the territorials were 'unorthodox' – a curious criticism in a unit that was founded on unorthodoxy. In fact, the regulars' attitude sprang mostly from a kind of jealousy – that a man could be both, say, a highly-paid solicitor *and* an SAS trooper, seemed to challenge the superiority of those who could only do one job at a time. De la Billière acknowledged that TA personnel were 'the cream of society', and dismissed the notion of 'amateurism' as nonsense. Unorthodoxy was a virtue, and though it was obvious that standards could not be the same when people were soldiering in addition to their 'day jobs', he found TA standards high. He was determined to change this attitude, and later, as CO of 22 SAS, he made it a rule that no one could advance past the rank of sergeant without a successful tour with 21 or 23. 'People began to see that the territorial SAS were first class,' he wrote, 'and enhanced the reputation of the whole Regiment in a special way of their own.'[2]

The TA units were superior to 22 SAS in one sense: all their officers came up through the ranks. This was a tradition that 21 SAS had adopted from the Artists' Rifles and passed on to 23 SAS. In the early days, many ex-wartime SAS officers had reverted to trooper to serve in 21 SAS. These two Regiments remain the only units in the British army that do not have an officers' mess: they became the true embodiment of Stirling's ideal of a 'classless SAS'.

The regular Regiment fell short, because it was hampered by problems endemic to the professional officer. Good officers existed, certainly, but they were reluctant to join the SAS because it offered poor career prospects. Those who did volunteer often lacked the tact, flexibility, imagination and open-mindedness required for low-intensity operations. The fact was that such personalities were rare among army officers anyway, for the simple reason that – as psychologist Norman Dixon has demonstrated – men with these characteristics rarely seek military command.

22 SAS might have emulated the TA Regiments and followed Stirling's precedent of commissioning NCOs from the ranks. Although some ex-sergeants did make squadron commander, they had to be commissioned in their parent units before 22 SAS would accept them. Eventually, a system of promoting NCOs was introduced, but since they were debarred from service in sabre squadrons, the changes were self-defeating – a commission became more a reward for service than an advantage to the Regiment. Feudal taboos died hard, even in 22 SAS.

In spite of this, regular officers who became SAS squadron commanders were generally excellent. Troop-commanders, as Lofty Large pointed out, were 'a different kettle of fish'. 'Mostly they were too young and inexperienced to be expected to cope with handling an SAS troop on operations,' he said. '. . . The good ones tried not to get in the way . . . some, like Rory Walker . . . were brilliant and great to work with . . . but there were others.'[3]

John Woodhouse had the sagacity to recognize the existence of this problem, and encouraged junior officers to forget their Sandhurst-conditioned 'us-and-them' ideas and observe the principles Jock Lewes had deduced after the first fortnight of training L Detachment. 'In the SAS, as an officer, particularly in your first year or two,' Woodhouse wrote to one of his troop-commanders, 'you have got to prove your enthusiasm, your superiority in physical endurance, and your SAS skills to your men ... in the SAS you will never get the devoted support of your troops until you have proved to them by your personal example that you will never spare yourself physically or in any other way ...'[4]

Many young officers found it hard to deal with SAS vets who lacked deference, were opinionated, self-reliant, critical and ready, as Large put it, to 'tell [them] to go away in best Trog's English'.[5] He described one subaltern with eighteen months' service who claimed his troop was making too much noise on night ops. He tried to lecture them on techniques of night-movement – a subject covered on boot-camp training in every military unit. Most of Large's troop had a decade of experience behind them, much of it on ops, and some had been battlecraft instructors. 'This particular child tried to impress us with his great superior knowledge ...' Large commented. 'He was a great success as a bloody idiot ... his ... cock-ups in the man-management department made him (and us) the laughing stock of the whole squadron.'[6]

The SAS was, almost by definition, a unit of individuals capable of thinking for themselves. This concept, a quiet but devastating revolution in military outlook, had originated in the wartime commandos, but had really flowered in the SAS. SAS-men were selected for this very quality – the ability to operate without orders, and without traditional military discipline. Inevitably, the Regiment became a unit where the dominant values were those of the other ranks, where officers needed to prove themselves to the men rather than vice versa.

Stirling himself had recognized, almost from the beginning, that the real dynamo of the SAS was the 'sergeants' mess'. He had occasionally let in officers through the back door because he owed them favours, or because they might be able to do him one, but had otherwise relied on his sergeants to assess their quality. If senior NCOs like Almonds, Rose, Seekings or Kershaw didn't like them, they were out.

This tradition continued in 22 SAS. 'A false notion exists,'

wrote Ken Connor, '. . . that [the officers] were in command of
the Regiment. The truth is that it was run by the NCOs.'[7] In the
early 1960s, the majority of troop commanders were sergeants. If
a troop officer existed, he was just one of four patrol commanders
– the others might be corporals or even troopers. The idea that he
might be dispensable or even an impediment to the good functioning of the Regiment was, as Connor has pointed out, 'not one
that was ever going to be popular with the average army officer'.[8]

In the early sixties an exchange programme was initiated with
7 Special Forces Group in the USA. Malaya had been a triumph
for small formations, high quality manpower and minimum force,
but Stirling's small-is-beautiful – the-man-is-the-Regiment – concept didn't go down well in America, where big equalled best, and
where the man was considered subordinate to the machine. US
Special Forces bore little resemblance to the SAS. The 'Green
Berets' was basically an airborne group trained along the lines of
the Parachute Regiment. The main difference was that US Special
Forces soldiers were linguists, many of them immigrants, and were
groomed to train foreign nationals, and for large-scale 'hearts and
minds' missions. Even in the USA they were often referred to as
the 'Peace Corps in uniform'.

The first Green Berets officer to be seconded to 22 SAS was
Captain 'Charging Charlie' Beckwith. He was assigned to A
Squadron, commanded by Major Peter Walter MC, ex-Royal
Lincolns, a former sergeant who'd distinguished himself in Malaya.
His SSM was Sergeant-Major Bill 'Gloom' Ross MM, another
Malaya legend.

For Beckwith, it was a revelation. His experience, which included
a tour on the Thai border in Malaya, left him a changed man. 'I felt
I had captured a new world,' he wrote. 'The American army not
only needed a Special Forces capability, but an SAS one.'[9] Against
entrenched opposition from his own authorities, Beckwith went
on to found and command Detachment Delta, or Delta Force,
the SAS Regiment's US counterpart. Delta Force, like the New
Zealand SAS Squadron and the Australian SAS Regiment, was
thus another, though 'unofficial', member of the 'SAS Family'.

74. 'A battle for a man's mind and a test of his will to win'

When Charlie Beckwith arrived at Bradbury Lines, he had no idea how the SAS assessed, selected and trained its soldiers. His first impression was that the Regiment was 'a group of roughnecks'. He soon found out that 'no one gives you anything in the SAS. You have to earn it.'[1] Selection, established by John Woodhouse before the US Special Forces was even founded, was the source of its excellence. 'A great deal of rubbish has been written about Selection,' wrote Major Peter Ratcliffe, former Para and ex-RSM of 22 SAS, 'much of it by people who passed and want to make themselves out, wrongly, to be supermen. For although it is the toughest human proving ground in the world, Selection is not just about muscle and brawn, or even sheer endurance. It is a battle for a man's mind and a test of his will to win.'[2]

No one has ever put it better than that, except perhaps Rudyard Kipling, whose poem 'If' has frequently been used, suitably modified, to psych-up Selection candidates:

> If you can force your heart, and nerve, and sinew
> To serve your turn long after they are gone,
> And carry on when there is nothing in you
> Except the will, which says to you 'Hold on',
> If you can fill the unforgiving minute
> With sixty-seconds' worth of distance run,
> Then yours is the earth, and everything that's in it,
> And what is more, you'll be SAS, my son.

John Woodhouse's Selection course lasted ten days and was geared to conditions in Malaya. He was looking for soldiers who could react instantly to a contact even when mentally and physically exhausted. 'It's all very well being able to march, and get from A to B,' Woodhouse said, 'but we had to be extremely alert for possible contacts with terrorists at any moment, and if you're tired and your senses are dulled, you may be no good at that side of it.'[3] Physical fitness was essential, but you could be very fit and still fail Selection. The SAS was not in the business of recruiting supermen. In a sense the physical torture candidates had to endure was a sideshow, a means of reducing them to a state where their mental qualities would shine through. The SAS wanted individuals who didn't need orders, who could make their own decisions, override exhaustion and apply sound judgement even in extreme and hostile conditions. As another 22 SAS vet, Nick Downie, put it, 'The whole SAS way of life is in the mind. It's nothing whatever to do with being a physical superman.'[4]

Woodhouse's Selection was taken over by Dare Newell's 'two men and a dog' SAS Selection Detachment, which moved the course from Snowdonia to the Brecon Beacons – a range of hills whose highest peak was Pen-y-Fan, at three thousand feet. The Beacons enjoyed some of the worst and least predictable weather conditions in the British Isles. In the 1970s and 80s so many Selection candidates suffered from hypothermia – some fatally – that the Training Wing had to introduce marker-panels to be carried on Bergens, and later a SARBE search-and-rescue-beacon.

SAS Selection has changed in detail over the years, but the object remains the same: to select men able to keep functioning mentally when beyond their normal limits of endurance. Despite Mayne's assertion that he could spot a potential SAS-man at a glance, attempts by military psychologists to pinpoint an 'SAS type' failed. There is no SAS type. Among SAS-men there are plenty of physical giants like Mayne himself, but it was soon observed on Selection that some of the strongest and fittest soldiers were the first to go down.

Ken Connor, ex-Parachute Regiment, one of the longest-serving veterans of 22 SAS, passed Selection in 1963. He found himself among the 'smallest and least experienced' of the candidates; 'they were all bigger, stronger, taller, sun-tanned and as fit as fleas,' he recalled. Connor was astonished when, on the very first test – a nine-mile run in boots and PT-kit – twenty or thirty of them dropped out. 'You get blokes turning up and they're six-foot and built like brick shit-houses,' said 'Mac', another 22 SAS vet. 'And you think Jesus Christ, what am I doing here? . . . Then after a week . . . some of these big guys, they're gone. It's not size that counts . . . you've got to be fit, obviously, but it's what's in your head.'[5] Jimmy Ladner, Royal Artillery, who won the MM in Malaya, passed Selection in 1957. He had a simi-lar experience. 'I was only five-foot-seven-and-a-half,' he said, '. . . and . . . it seemed . . . to me the [other candidates] were all massive people . . . I started singing *Onward Christian Soldiers* on the hard parts, and I started passing all these big chaps who I was very scared of.'[6]

Out on the stark hills, gymnastic or athletic ability didn't count for much. As Lofty Large pointed out, there was only one way of training for carrying a Bergen, and that was carrying a Bergen. He noticed that many super-fit candidates from the Army Physical Training Corps went down in the first few days. 'My theory is that they'd never really been knackered before in their lives,' he commented. 'Whereas being smashed out of our minds with fatigue was the norm for us lesser mortals.'[7]

SAS Selection has been popularized, some would say trivialized, by Reality TV shows, but the real thing remains distinct. One of the elements missing from the simulation is the all-important aspect of motivation. What drives all successful Selection candidates is the desire to win the buff-coloured beret: more than anything else in the world, you have to want to be in. Selection is also the great leveller. Despite later claims, L Detachment had never really undergone selection. It had maintained high standards because its recruits were all trained commandos, but in later years, especially in Europe, standards had fallen. Stirling himself sometimes recruited officers on the old-school-tie basis. Since Woodhouse's days, though – with one small hiccup – there has been no 'back door' to the SAS. No SAS soldier who wants to serve in a sabre-squadron, regular or TA, no matter what his rank or connections, can circum-vent Selection. Pass or fail is purely on merit.

The regular Selection course that evolved from the Woodhouse prototype lasted four weeks for regulars: for TA units the process was spread over a number of weekends, with a solid two weeks in the final phase. For regulars and TA the real 'test phase' lasted five days. The early Selections were run from the Para Battle School at Dering Lines in Brecon, and later directly from Bradbury Lines. For the TA, the final phase was based at Sennybridge Camp in mid-Wales. Lofty Large, who spent two years as a PSI on the Training Wing of 23 SAS, pointed out that TA Selection wasn't an easy option. 'Selection courses for 23 SAS . . . were very hard,' he said, 'and the pass rate was the same as for 22 SAS, ten per cent . . . 23 SAS has remained a well-selected SAS unit.'[8]

Anyone could join the TA SAS from civvy-street, although many successful recruits were ex-regular soldiers. 22 SAS candidates had to have served for three years in another military unit or in the TA SAS, and to have at least three years left to serve. About sixty per cent of successful candidates came from the Parachute Regiment. Such was the rivalry between the two units that Paras who failed SAS Selection were in for stick when they got back home. In the eyes of the Airborne, they had failed twice: once in forsaking the 'maroon machine', and again for failing to show that every Para was as good as an SAS-man any day. Para Selection – 'P' Company – though more team-oriented, was extreme, and prepared candidates well for SAS Selection. 'Their own training has fitted paratroopers to being pushed harder and harder,' wrote Peter Ratcliffe, 'and as often as not when other men drop out, the Paras are still there, rock solid and reliable.'[9] Of the eleven candidates who passed Ratcliffe's Selection in 1972, six came from the Parachute Regiment. In Robin Horsfall's Selection seven years later, five out of the nine successful candidates were ex-Paras, one a Royal Marine, and three from line infantry battalions.

Candidates weren't told what to expect. No one woke them up, made sure they were at the right place at the right time, or inspected them to ascertain whether they had the correct kit. It was all up to them. If the truck left without them, it was tough luck. 'The message was clear,' said Ken Connor. 'There would be no checks . . . no one to hold your hand . . . If you weren't there it was because you didn't want to be there . . . so pack your kit and piss off.'[10]

In the early days the course kicked off with a series of 'sickeners', designed to weed out 'passengers'. For Lofty Large, who passed Selection in 1957, it was running round the assault-course at Dering Lines, so many times that he lost count. 'It was a piece of cake for the first ten times around,' he recalled, '. . . then I began to notice it a bit . . . At the end I was . . . completely smashed. Some had already dropped. We were told that was just a warm up.'[11] For Peter de la Billière, who had passed Selection the previous year, it was doubling up and down the slope at the back of the camp. 'After the first two ascents and descents, my breakfast . . . came to rest on the hillside,' he remembered. '. . . Dimly I saw that there was method in this apparently senseless slogging up and down . . . it was eliminating a few scroungers and others who had under-estimated the task.'[12] The 'sickener' exercises were dropped later, and replaced by a standard battle-fitness speed march, though with very similar results.

The preparation phase also included exhausting PT sessions, weapon-training, map-reading and navigation instruction, followed by arduous practical tests in the hills. By the time the test-phase arrived, numbers were whittled down to only the serious contenders. What they had in front of them was five days of successively harder marches over the mountains in all weathers, carrying weapons, belt kit weighing about fifteen kilos, and Bergens weighing up to thirty kilos. The weights increased every day, and all the marches were against the clock. Among them was a 'point-to-point' speed march known as 'the Fan Dance' – a triple traverse of the highest point, Pen-y-Fan, whose summit was almost vertical, from three different directions, in six hours. The others were self-navigating exercises on which candidates had to choose their own route and find their way by compass. The marches purposely involved steep climbs and descents, and the use of roads and bridges was forbidden on pain of failure. Some of the treks were partly at night, and were made much harder by the weather conditions – usually candidates would have to ford streams or even fast-flowing rivers. Candidates had to remain alert throughout the trek, carrying their rifles at the ready. The weight in their Bergens had to remain constant, and might be weighed at any time.

The marches were divided into 'legs' with specified RVs that were quite often hard to find and sited at the most inaccessible points. They couldn't be missed out, because there was a member of the Directing Staff – DS – at each location to check candidates off and give them the grid reference of the next RV. Candidates would have to find the reference on the map and point to it with a stalk of grass before being allowed to continue.

During the course the DS would encourage candidates to give up, and play mind-games with them. Lofty Large remembered being pressed to have a beer at a pub he passed on the way, and candidates would frequently be pushed to accept a lift in a three-tonner – a one-way journey that ended on Platform 5 at Hereford station. Often they'd be unexpectedly handed a twenty-litre jerrycan of water to carry – as Brummy Stokes, another future RSM of 22 SAS, discovered, the water was stained red and couldn't be tipped out. They might even have to hand over their Bergens and find another way of carrying their kit.

Frequently they would arrive at a checkpoint to be given a task of mental arithmetic to solve, or a grid reference that had to be memorized: their last RV of the day might turn out to be that reference. Peter Ratcliffe recalled reaching the final RV of one trek in teeming rain, and climbing exhausted into a three-tonner. The moment the candidates had settled in, the DS ordered them to get off and hike another twenty klicks (kilometres). They had marched only about four hundred metres when the staff told them they'd been conned: the exercise really was over. By that time at least one of their number had dropped out, unable to face another twenty-kilometre tab.

It was in the course of these marches, alone, cold, soaked through, desperately following a compass across streams, clambering up hillsides through fog or lashing winds, that the candidate discovered whether he really wanted to 'be SAS'. 'Operating at or beyond my normal limit,' Peter de la Billière wrote, 'I was plagued by the constant worry that in the rain, mist and darkness, I might not be able to find the next rendezvous . . . My morale sunk to its lowest ebb. I was on the verge of asking myself . . . whether this whole endeavour really was for me.'[13] Ken Connor, whose navigation wasn't his strongest point, suffered similar moments of doubt. 'Often I thought that it was only me against the world,' he said. 'There were lots of times on the marches [when I thought] is this really worth the effort?'[14]

The successive marches slowly took their toll – many candidates developed blisters; almost all had shoulder- and back-sores where the Bergen straps had cut into their flesh. The object was to wear them down gradually by attrition. For those who decided it *was* worth it, the last 'Endurance March', known as the 'Long Drag', was a killer. It was forty-six miles alone carrying a thirty-kilo pack, in perhaps twenty hours, starting at midnight. Candidates weren't told the actual deadline, which the DS adjusted according to the season: there were two selections a year, summer and winter. 'Winter Selection was . . . much harder than the summer course,' wrote Robin Horsfall, 'because of the terrible mountain weather.'[15] Summer or winter, no one who survived the Long Drag ever re-membered it as being a walkover: Peter Ratcliffe described it as 'gut-twisting', while another 22 SAS vet, Barry Davies, called it 'a real bitch'. For most, it would remain a nodal point of their lives.

Those who finished the Long Drag in time knew that they'd passed the test-phase – they were 'almost' in the Regiment. They still had to pass a combat survival and resistance to interrogation exercise. 'Combat survival' was preceded by training from SAS instructors, and civilians including gamekeepers and Home Office experts, on setting snares, rigging gill-nets, slaughtering and but-chering animals and birds, starting fires and cooking in extreme conditions, and the identification of edible or useful plants. They were also given lectures on dog-evasion by Royal Army Veterinary Corps officers. Candidates were then strip-searched and sent off alone, at night, in a wilderness area in Wales, with orders to evade the infantry battalion sent to track them down – the hunters usually had tracker dogs. Most candidates were caught, tied up, blindfolded, thrown into a vehicle and dumped at an 'interrogation centre'. The few that weren't caught had orders to give themselves up at a certain time. The longer the candidate remained at large, the shorter his confinement in the 'interrogation' phase.

This lasted up to forty-eight hours, and consisted mainly of long periods of sensory deprivation, standing against a wall in 'maximum stress' position, on fingertips and toes, with a sack over the head. Candidates were manhandled, kicked, rammed into walls and obstacles, humiliated by being urinated on, or even stripped naked in front of women and verbally abused. Occasionally there would be accidents, including broken bones, but some early ploys, including manacling candidates blindfold to a railway line in front of an apparently oncoming locomotive, were soon ruined when word of the bluff spread through the grapevine.

Periodically, candidates would be marched into an interrogation room, where the sack would be whipped off their heads and they would be questioned by a man in a foreign army uniform – in actual fact an officer of the specialist Joint Services Interrogation Wing. A candidate was permitted to give his name, rank, number and date of birth. Any other utterance – even a simple 'yes' or 'no' – resulted in automatic failure.

Some successful SAS-men thought the resistance to interrogation course unrealistic in the sense that it was only a pale imitation of the treatment an SAS soldier could expect as a real prisoner. This is undoubtedly the case, yet the RTI course, like Selection itself, had a function quite apart from the practical one – it was a unique initiation ritual, as vital and as life-changing as the Sun Dance Ceremony of the old plains Indians.

Later, an extra phase of Selection was brought in for regular candidates – 'Jungle Selection' – in which potential SAS-men relived the Regiment's experience in Malaya. This phase lasted five weeks, and usually took place in Belize or Brunei. After two weeks of lectures on jungle warfare and survival, followed by daily exercises, candidates were placed in four-man patrols and sent off into the bush. The jungle phase had a social aspect. 'Most of the tests undertaken in the tropics were designed to put each small team under intense pressure,' wrote Robin Horsfall; 'staff could see whether students were able to control their tempers and do their share of the work.'[16]

The emphasis on 'personality and character' in Selection started under the command of Peter de la Billière, who felt that the physical standards of Selection had become almost impossibly demanding, and that the procedure might exclude those who were not at their best under test conditions: 'This is where the personal judgement . . . of a Commanding Officer can play an important role,' he wrote.

The danger of the personality-oriented approach was that it allowed a subjective element to creep back into what had originally been as objective a test as it was possible to design. Dare Newell had declared that Selection was 'designed rather to find the individualist with a sense of self-discipline than the man who is primarily a good member of a team'.[17] De la Billière's 'relaxation' was a return to Paddy Mayne's dictum that he 'had a blueprint of the ideal SAS man in his head'. The 'Commanding Officer's judgement' could only ever be subjective – de la Billière himself praised John Woodhouse for his ability to perceive that 'the judgement of personalities was subjective, and always needed a double check'.[18] If Selection was subject ultimately to the 'CO's judgement', then the inevitable outcome would be a unit consisting purely of men whom the Commanding Officer liked.

This opened a dangerous avenue back to the old 'people-like-us-he's-a-good-chap' type of elitism that had been the hallmark of the crack units of Victorian times. 'They [the SAS] do not want people who are emotionally stable,' wrote Peter Watson, author of the classic study of the psychological aspects of soldiering, *War on the Mind*. 'Instead they want forthright individuals who are hard to fool and not dependent on orders.'[19]

Despite carping from various sources that Selection standards have gone down or up since its inception, though, the pass-rate has remained fairly constant, at around ten per cent – both for TA and regular SAS. Following the publicity surrounding the Iranian

Embassy siege, 21 SAS (Artists) was inundated with candidates, so many of whom turned up armed with knives and other offensive weapons that the Regiment had to hire civilian security-men to frisk them. Of the one hundred and twenty volunteers who presented themselves at Chelsea Barracks in the weeks after the siege, most were blown off by a few circuits round the drill-square. Only eleven passed the course.

This was exactly the same proportion who had passed Peter Ratcliffe's regular course eight years ealier. 'One hundred and twenty men had started out on Selection,' he recalled. 'Eleven of us had got through. And I was one of them. I was in the SAS. Although I was careful not to let anyone see it, it was the proudest moment of my life. It remains so to this day.'[20]

75. 'When fighting for your life, you've got to enjoy it'

At about 1100 hours on the morning of 30 April 1964, Major Peter de la Billière logged an urgent radio message in his ops tent at Thumier, sixty miles north of Aden, in south-western Arabia. It came from Captain Robin Edwards, whose nine-man patrol was scrimmed up in two stone sangars under the peak of Jebel Ashqab, about six miles to the north-east. Edwards's patrol had just taken out an Arab goatherd of the Qutaybi tribe, who had wandered near their position. He'd been blotted with a single shot.

Herders were a hazard that had plagued SAS ops in the desert ever since Bill Fraser's patrol had gone for Ajadabiyya. One of the amazing things about Arabia, de la Billière commented, was that if you halted even for a few minutes in an apparently desolate spot, someone – usually a herder – would pop up. 'It was simply not worth being spotted,' he said.[1] In the earlier case, Fraser had let the shepherd go. Edwards's decision to shoot the tribesman was, said SAS vet Ken Connor, 'questionable . . . from both a moral and a tactical point of view'.[2]

The shot quickly roused armed warriors in the village of Shi'b Taym, a cluster of mud-brick buildings below them, only a thousand paces away. Soon a knot of bearded men in white dishdashas and looped headcloths, carrying .303 Lee-Enfields and curved daggers in their belts, gathered around the body. They evidently thought the goatherd had been killed by an accidental discharge. They were soon persuaded otherwise, when 7.62mm rounds started slatting down on them. Several took hits. The rest scattered into the rocks.

De la Billière hadn't seen Edwards's lying-up place, but was aware it was wide open. He kicked himself for not having spent time helping the troop officer to select a better one before the op. To the patrol, the place had looked good in darkness, but first light had revealed that it was ten metres below the highest ridge on the jebel, and within easy small-arms range. Both de la Billière and Edwards knew that once the Arabs got up to the ridge, they could drop fire down into the sangars. It would be as easy as potting ducks on a pond. De la Billière also knew that Edwards was out of range of the Royal Horse Artillery battery near his post. After considering it for a minute, he phoned the RAF Air Support Officer, Squadron Leader Roy Bowie, and asked for a team of Hawker Hunter fighter-bombers, based at Aden, to be put on stand-by.

Edwards's patrol had ducked out of Saracen armoured-personnel carriers three miles inside enemy territory not long after last light the previous day. The APCs had been shot up on the way, and had kept enemy heads down with .50 Brownings mounted on their turrets. The SAS had piled out unnoticed under covering fire. Their mission was to tab into the Radfan hills, sixty miles north of Aden city, and reach a position in the Wadi Taym, codenamed 'Rice Bowl'. The SAS half troop were pathfinding for an op by the Paras and Royal Marines, whose target was the Danaba basin, a cultivated area in the Wadi Taym. At Rice Bowl they would secure a DZ for a drop by a Para company, and mark it with an Aldis lamp.

The march in, up the Wadi Thabwa, had looked easy enough,

but given the conditions the target was probably too far for the
patrol to have made comfortably by first light. That was the first
mistake. The situation had been made worse, though, by the
fact that Tpr. Nick Warburton, the patrol signaller, was suffering
from food poisoning. Warburton, an energetic ex-National Service
Sapper, had been OK before the op. He tramped on doggedly
with severe stomach-cramps, lugging his twenty-kilo A41 voice-
radio, but was soon left behind. The patrol had to stop twice to
let him catch up.

Though the Wadi Thabwa cut directly through the hills to the
target area, Edwards had decided to slog up its sides and broach
the four-thousand-foot Jebel Ashqab, a diamond-faceted hogsback
dominating the south side of the wadi. From here, in daylight,
'Rice Bowl' and an adjacent feature, 'Cap Badge', would be clearly
visible. Hitting a ridge at 0200 hours, Edwards located two ancient
stone sangars that seemed like an ideal defensive position. These
sangars were testimony to the tribal wars and vendettas that had
raged across these hills since time immemorial. It probably seemed
to the patrol unlikely that the hillmen, skilled in the use of ground,
would have sited them in a place open to dropping fire from
above. This was the second mistake.

Edwards, ex-Somerset & Cornwall Light Infantry, a broad-
shouldered, good-natured Cornishman from Padstow, was on his
first mission with the Regiment. He was legendary, though, for
having fought his way back to fitness after a bout of polio that had
struck him immediately after he'd passed Selection. He was a close
friend of de la Billière, who'd been back with 22 SAS since January
as A Squadron boss, after his stint as adjutant, 21 SAS, and a
two-year tour in Aden attached to the Federal Regular Army.

Trouble in south-western Arabia had flared up in 1962, when a
Soviet-backed military coup toppled the traditional ruler of North
Yemen, the Imam al-Badr. The revolutionary government was
aided by the USSR's proxy, the nationalist Egyptian president,
Gamal 'Abd an-Nasser. Egyptian troops and aircraft had been
deployed. Since then, the Imam's supporters had been waging a
guerrilla campaign, funded by the Saudis, abetted by a certain

Major Johnny Cooper, ex-Sultan of Oman's Armed Forces, and a group of serving and ex-SAS-men. This 'blanket' campaign was organized by no less a personage than David Stirling, and coordinated by Lt.Col. Jim Johnson, commanding officer, 21 SAS.

Aden was one of Britain's oldest colonies. Adopted in 1839 as a coaling-station on the sea-lane to India, it was also of strategic importance on the Bab al-Mandab – the 'door' to the Red Sea. In the early sixties Britain had stitched together a Federation of more than two dozen Sheikhdoms extending inland over an area of about a hundred thousand square miles of mountain and desert. The Arab nationalists in North Yemen, though, were intent on exporting the civil war to the British-controlled Federation, both through the hill tribes of the Radfan, and the folk of Aden city itself. An emergency had been declared that December, but Britain had lost the 'hearts and minds' of the locals from the start by announcing that she would vacate the area within two years. The hill tribes could hardly be expected to show loyalty to a power that was soon to abandon them.

De la Billière had arrived in Aden in April to conduct a recce for A Squadron, which was earmarked for a desert training exercise there. On discovering that a combined group of British and Federation forces – Radforce – was about to launch an op against dissident tribesmen in the Radfan, though, de la Billière importuned the local C-in-C, Lt. Gen. Sir Charles Harington, to give the SAS a part in it. Radforce included 3 Para and 45 Commando, but had no deep-penetration troops. De la Billière suggested deploying SAS patrols to secure DZs, vector in air-strikes, direct artillery-fire, and supply intel on enemy movements.

Harington leapt at the chance. All that was left was for de la Billière to persuade his commanding officer, Lt. Col. John Woodhouse, who had taken over the hot-seat in 22 SAS a year earlier, that the training ex should be scrapped in favour of a live operation. Woodhouse didn't need much persuading. He was constantly on the alert for new jobs. A Squadron arrived on 22 April and was at the forward operating base at Thumier within eighteen hours.

This was de la Billière's first op as squadron commander, and he found it unexpectedly frustrating. He saw his tours with 22 SAS as a chance to get to the sharp end, but as officer commanding, his task was to coordinate patrols from the forward operating base rather than leading from the front. He confessed that this presented him with a dilemma. 'I hated sending other people into danger while I sat back in relative comfort and safety,' he wrote.[3] It was only when the Regiment's 2IC, forty-one-year-old Second World War vet Major Mike Wingate-Gray, Black Watch, arrived at Thumier that de la Billière had felt justified in heading patrols.

Patrols went out for four to five days. Conditions were even harsher than de la Billière remembered from his time on the Jebel Akhdar five years earlier, and certainly much worse than in Malaya. In daytime, the sun napalmed them. Air temperatures often clocked fifty Celsius, and the naked rocks mopped up heat, nudging the surface up to eighty Celsius – hot enough to scorch bare flesh or fry an egg. There was no open water, and SAS-men carried only two litres each, plus a plastic container with an extra four litres per patrol. That gave the men a total of three litres for the entire period, when the minimum body requirement in these climes was at least eight litres daily. 'Even with every precaution taken,' de la Billière admitted, 'we finished patrols in a state of utter exhaustion.'[4]

Now, de la Billière was back behind a radio set in the ops centre, grokking the situation in the jebel. Within two hours of the first shot, Qutaybi tribesmen had crawled up to the ridge overlooking the sangars and located the SAS position. They'd started wellying pot-shots at the patrol; .303 rounds droned, whining off rock, grooving stone. Every time an SAS-man poked his nose out, a slug fractured granite, spattering fragments in his face. Almost everyone had been jagged, but as yet there weren't any serious wounds. The SAS replied only when they clocked a good target. They carried a hundred and twenty rounds apiece, and two hundred for the Bren, and were trained to scrooge their ammo. The Arabs fired and dodged, using the ground expertly. It was hard to get a clear shot.

De la Billière knew that these Arabs were hard fighters. Like the Jebel Akhdar folk, they'd been raised in a milieu of constant eye-for-an-eye feuds. In Arab culture there were two kinds of tribes: 'warrior' tribes (*Qabayil*) and 'weak' tribes (*Du'af*). The Qutaybi were *Qabayil*, and proud of it – to them, courage and endurance were cardinal virtues. De la Billière knew they would close in on the nine-man patrol sooner or later, and when they did there'd be a massacre. He decided to call in the Hunters.

Eight minutes later, Edwards and his men scoped the aircraft trail-blazing vapour fumes. Signaller Nick Warburton was patched through to Roy Bowie at Thumier, who was talking the pilots in. The patrol watched rockets reefing down into the ridge, erupting in splatters of white smoke and debris. The sharp tang of cordite pillioned the scorched-stone smell of the hills. The Hunters worked in duck-and-drake pairs, fastballing over the position for fifteen or twenty minutes at a time. They plunged into strafing mode. 20mm cannon zipped ladders of dirt and rock splinters across the hills. Flint-dust whiffled up and drifted. The planes skimmed in so low that their 20mm brass shell-cases creased the boys' heads. When they peeled off, heading back to Aden, they'd be replaced by another pair. Between noon and sunset successive pairs whammed off a hundred and twenty-seven rockets, and scattergunned seven thousand rounds of twenty-mil.

The Hunters had swept the Arabs off the high ground, but de la Billière was grimly aware that the shield would go down at last light. He knew the Arabs knew it too. Sunset was the time they liked to attack. In the ops tent, Mike Wingate-Gray was sifting through schemes to extract the boys before dark. There was no shortage of volunteers for rescue missions, but Wingate-Gray wanted a clean extraction with no casualties. A Wessex chopper went in with another A Squadron troop to try to pull the patrol out. The heli stuttered back to the FOB with .303 rounds punched through its rear rotor and petrol-tank. The RHA gun-battery lobbed twenty-five-pound shells along the approaches to the position, without much effect.

At about 1630 hours, L. Cpl. Paddy Baker got zonked in the

leg with .303 rounds as he adjusted position. 'I'm hit!' he hollered. The patrol medic whaled extra field dressings at him. Baker caught them and lapped them on with gritted teeth, trying desperately to stay out of sight. Arab lead churned overhead, scorched air, butterflied off hard ground. Baker thanked his lucky stars the Arabs were using do-it-yourself ammo that lacked the hitting-power of standard ball. Bullets were still bullets, though, and he'd copped two of them. As he worked the dressings on, his blood pooled on the hotplate stones.

Two Arabs were flanking in on them from cover. Sgt. Alf 'Geordie' Tasker, a beefy redhead with a walrus moustache, poked the muzzle of the Bren their way, pulled metal, double-tapped. Rounds thumped. Crimson whorls licked white dishdashas. Arabs rolled. Baker ripped covering rounds to dissuade any other heroes. The enemy stayed in cover, ricky-ticking shots.

The sun's fire was cooking out slowly, but the hills still after-glowed with heat. Edwards scoped the shadows ballooning, the grooves in the jewel-faceted ridgebacks thickening purple. The whole area was now looped in a pool of shadow from the high ridges. The Hunter strikes were losing effect. The enemy had been increasing in dribs and drabs all day, and Edwards guessed they were massing for an assault.

As the last fighter-bombers hauled off into the pink towards the coast, Edwards told his patrol to prepare to move. They would evacuate the position in darkness, using fire-and-movement. Four men would bob out of the sangars into the rocks and the rest would drop into the wadi under covering salvos. Edwards told signaller Nick Warburton to let the OC know they were moving.

At Thumier, de la Billière rogered the message, then heard the radio fizz. There was no answering call. He thumbed the pressal, reciting the patrol's call-sign like a mantra. Static warped in from the void. He hoped it was a technical hitch, but that seemed a shaky bet, because Warburton had been coming through loud and clear all day. He looked up to see the drained faces of Wingate-Gray and his SSM, Lawrence Smith. They were all aware of the most likely scenario – that the enemy had overrun the position.

On the hill, Edwards realized Warburton hadn't moved in half a minute. He crawled over, and found the signaller straddled over the radio set with a slug in his head. The set had been shattered, which meant they were out of comms: they were on their own. The SAS-men filled mags, clipped them in place, checked gas-plugs, pumped 7.62mm rounds into chambers, psyched up for take-off. Enemy rounds fried oxygen, whizzed and belled off stones. Edwards inquired if everyone had taken their Paludrin. Big Geordie Tasker snorted, wondering whether Edwards was serious. If they got out of this, a bout of malaria would be small beer.

The sun sank and faded into cherry and mauve, its fire absorbed by the cloak of night. The moon wasn't yet up. Edwards had arranged an artillery barrage to cover the withdrawal. When the darkness was full, he croaked the order to move. Half the team sneaked out of cover, threw themselves into rocks and blimped bullets. Tasker worked the Bren, boosting tracer at adoo shooters behind the boulders fifty metres away. As the other half of the team speedballed to the wadi, Edwards timbered over, struck in the head. He was dead before he hit the downslope. The others dogged into cover, punched fire. Muzzle-flashes flacked. The four men left on the hill streaked after them, as Arab fire thrashed empty sangars. Twenty-five-pound shells from the far-off Horse Artillery yawed through darkness, smashed into the position, volcanoed up in the night. The seven survivors of the Edwards patrol monkey-jogged down the wadi, clambered silently up the side, found the goat-track on top, and patrolled back towards base.

At 0500 hours, de la Billière jerked up from the camp-bed he'd taken a snooze on two hours earlier, and asked for news. There wasn't any. He and Wingate-Gray gulped tea and hung on the radio till blocks of wan light dropped through the door gap, when the set suddenly bristled. They sat up. Three men of Edwards's patrol had been picked up by armoured cars only a klick from the base. They grabbed weapons, piled into a Land Rover, and shot off to investigate.

The men turned out to be Paddy Baker, Geordie Tasker and a

third man. Baker said that they'd got within sight of base two hours before first light, but had held off in case the sentries opened up. Edwards and Warburton were dead. The other four were probably somewhere behind. He told the officers that they'd dogged the goat-track along the lip of the wadi in case the adoo tried to cut them off, but the whole withdrawal had been weird. After moonrise, they'd seen enemy where there weren't any, heard sounds, mixed up boulders for tents. Baker had hobbled along behind the rest with another trooper who'd taken a hit, bugged by a feeling someone was following them. They dropped into the rocks and clocked moonlight on a white dishdasha. They let the Arab come almost abreast before they took him out, bopping twenty rounds apiece at three more shadows tagging behind him. Baker had kept on squeezing the trigger after his mag was empty, so light-headed from blood-loss he wondered why his weapon wouldn't work.

The other four members of the patrol came in during the day. De la Billière was shattered by the loss of his friend Edwards, and blamed himself for the fiasco. He knew he'd rushed the boys into the job without considering all the possibilities, and was so plagued by remorse and guilt that he had to stalk off into the desert and sit on his own for a while. The survivors didn't seem weighed down by grief, though. 'When fighting for your life with a fifty-fifty chance, you've got to enjoy it,' said Alf Tasker. 'It was a good day.'

As a result of the contact, the parachute drop was scrapped and the op postponed. Later, a whole brigade was sent in to do the same job. The bodies of Edwards and Warburton were decapitated and their heads exhibited on stakes in the North Yemeni town of Ta'izz. Two days later, Maj. Gen. J. H. Cubbon, GOC Middle-East, informed the press. De la Billière was furious – the families of the dead men hadn't been notified, and didn't even know they were abroad, although Cubbon was not to know this.

The SAS continued patrolling the Radfan till the end of the month, but Wingate-Gray didn't think the job a good use of their skills. There was no 'hearts and minds' element, and the Parachute

Regiment could do short-range patrolling just as well. Besides, A Squadron was needed to relieve D Squadron in Borneo, where 22 SAS had been operating for the past two years.

76. 'I think we should expect to fight to the death for this'

The 'Confrontation' in Borneo had grown out of the conflicting aspirations of Malaya's President Tunku 'Abd ar-Rahman, and the President of Indonesia, Ahmad Sukarno. The world's third largest island, Borneo was mostly jungle, river and mountain, but was divided into three small states and one large one. The large one, Kalimantan, occupied three-quarters of the island's land-mass, and was part of Sukarno's Indonesia. Of the smaller ones, two – Sarawak and Sabah – were British colonies, and the third, the Sultanate of Brunei, a British Protectorate. Sukarno wanted to make them part of his expanding empire, while all three were potential members of the budding Federation of Malaysia, being fashioned by Tunku 'Abd ar-Rahman.

A Sukarno-inspired revolt against the Sultan of Brunei in December 1962 had been put down by British troops from Singapore. The rebels, driven across the border into Kalimantan, continued to receive Indonesian support. Sukarno had openly declared his hostility to the Malaysian Federation. He was convinced that the people of northern Borneo supported him, and in the case of the minority races – Chinese, Dayaks, and some jungle aborigines, including Ibans and Muruts – he was correct. There were even elements among the majority Malay population who favoured an Indonesian state over a western-oriented Malaysia.

The task of British Director of Operations Major-General Walter Walker was to guard the frontier with Kalimantan and maintain internal order. Walker, an outspoken ex-Gurkha, knew of 22 SAS from Malaya, and wanted to deploy the Regiment as an airborne quick-reaction force capable of tree-jumping. Commanding officer John Woodhouse had reservations about tree-jumping, and told Walker his boys would be wasted as a back-up unit. They were jungle-trained, and could operate independently in the ulu for months on end. They had the medical skills for a 'hearts and minds' campaign, and many of them spoke Malay.

Woodhouse talked Walker into employing an SAS squadron as an early-warning force along the border. They would operate in troops and two- to four-man patrols, hang out with the forest tribes, including their old friends the Ibans, talking Malay, learning local dialects, working their barefoot-doctor routine, employing the headhunters as scouts and spies. They would deploy their new lightweight patrol radios, hugging skywaves, tapping out Morse. Walker could hold the rest of his forces in mobile reserve, move in when the SAS gave the alarm.

A Squadron arrived covertly in Singapore in January 1963, under the designation 'Layforce 136', and was flown to Brunei. They were in the jungle within forty-eight hours, and spent the next four months watchdogging a seven-hundred-mile slice of border south of Brunei. They were too thin on the ground to patrol it all, but used the jungle tribes – Ibans, Muruts and Kelabits – as their eyes and ears. By the time they were relieved by D Squadron in April, it seemed that the danger of cross-border attacks had diminished. Walker was reined in. The US were fighting a war in Vietnam, and a 'Vietnamization' of all south-east Asia looked imminent. British forces would be more valuable in Singapore. Then, just as Walker was about to depart, news came through that Indonesian troops had crossed the border and bumped a police-station at Tebudu, in Sarawak, killing one policeman, wounding two more, and rifling the armoury. More cross-border raids were expected.

The Tebudu incident changed everything. British commitment was stepped up, and helicopters were deployed. John Woodhouse moved HQ staff to Brunei and set up his head-shed in a villa near the Sultan's palace, nicknamed 'The Haunted House'. Tension notched up several degrees in September, when the Federation of Malaysia was proclaimed. In Jakarta a mob stormed the British

Embassy, where the military attaché – ex-22 SAS officer Muir 'Red Rory' Walker – marched up and down outside through a shower of brickbats, wearing an SAS beret and playing the bagpipes. Walker's action cocked a regal snook at the crowds, but didn't stop the Embassy from being razed to the ground.

Within days of the proclamation, Sukarno ordered his regulars to launch cross-border raids and establish 'liberated zones' in north Borneo. In December a hundred Indonesian troops killed twenty-seven men of the Malay Regiment asleep in a longhouse at Kalabakan, on the Sarawak border. SAS patrols sent to trail them guided in infantry companies that took out all but four of the invaders.

De la Billière's A Squadron arrived in Brunei for its second tour only weeks after the Edwards Patrol shoot-out in the Radfan. The squadron's blood was up. Three months earlier, an A Squadron signaller, Tpr. James 'Paddy' Condon, had been murdered in cold blood by Indonesian soldiers. Condon, an Irish ex-Para from Tipperary, on loan to D Squadron, had been in a four-man patrol sent covertly across the Kalimantan frontier in response to a series of incursions by Indonesian troops.

On 13 March, Condon's patrol – commanded by Sgt. 'Smokey' Richardson – encountered a much larger enemy force. In the firefight, Condon was separated from the rest, wounded badly in the groin, and captured. The Indonesians interrogated and tortured him, then shot him dead. De la Billière, whose recent experience in Aden had shown him how deeply the death of a comrade could affect a closely-knit unit like the SAS, took pains to restrain his men's fury. Jungle patrolling required a calm, cautious approach. 'Given the close relationships which exist within the SAS,' he wrote, 'such anger was inevitable . . . [but] . . . it could be dangerous if it ran out of control.'[1] The boys eventually found out the name of the Indonesian sergeant who'd topped Condon, and paid Iban headhunters to do what they did best.

The Kelabits, who inhabited the three-thousand-foot Kelabit Highlands on the Sarawak border, were enthusiastic SAS supporters and frequently offered patrol members their women as wives. Despite their readiness to lop off Indonesian heads, though, the Ibans were still uncommitted to the Federation, and de la Billière was aware that they might decapitate SAS-men with equal abandon. He reckoned it was still too dangerous for an SAS patrol to sleep in an Iban longhouse. A settlement would be approached warily – a scout would be sent ahead to scope the place out for lurking Indos. The patrol would then enter the village and chat to the tribespeople, offering instant medical aid for toothache or broken bones. They would remain no more than half an hour, so no one had time to warn the nearest Indo unit, and would make sure they put a long distance between themselves and the village before sunset.

The patrols would elicit the needs of the village and provide them promptly. In some cases they set up small provision-stores, trawling for information as they doled out cut-price sugar and flour. Some SAS troopers improvised stills for *tapei* – rice wine – from their Bergen frames, and one sergeant, 'Gypsy' Smith, built a hydro-electric generator for a village out of radio-spares and a bicycle-lamp dynamo. The SAS also established the 'Step Up' system, calling in helicopters full of Gurkha stand-by troops within minutes, to impress the natives. 'By such means,' de la Billière wrote, 'we gradually won the Ibans round.'[2]

There were frequent contacts. The Indonesian invaders operated in company strength, and John Woodhouse had prescribed an SOP known as 'shoot-and-scoot'. Most contacts in the jungle were head-on. The object was to lay down instantaneous accurate fire, and bug out immediately. The patrol had to avoid an extended shoot-out at all costs.

One of the trouble-spots was the Long Pa Sia Bulge, a mountain region on the frontiers of Sabah and Sarawak, assigned to de la Billière's 4 Troop, under Sgt. Maurice Tudor. By August, after three months of intensive patrolling, de la Billière judged the area clear of Indos, and pulled Tudor out by chopper to attend a Malay language course. Tudor's patrol – four men now commanded by L. Cpl. Roger Blackman, including Troopers Billy White and 'Jimmy Green', and an officer attached from the Australian SAS

Regiment, Lt. Geoff Skardon, made their way through the forest back to their pick-up point at Moming.

Two days after Tudor had been lifted out, Blackman's radio-op, 'Jimmy Green', copped a message from the 1/2 Gurkhas, reporting that gunshots had been heard from the area of the main track into Kalimantan, along the Moming river. The patrol hadn't heard anything, but went to check it out. They walked smack into a platoon-strength ambush. Billy White was lead-scout. The first he knew about it was when he came round a tree and almost knocked over an Indo soldier cooking lunch. The Indo was kneeling, and White slotted him at hard-contact range downwards through the shoulder. The high-velocity 5.56mm Armalite slug bored through his body and emerged from his rear-end in a mash of blood and flesh. The Indo froze in a kneeling position, stone dead.

Blackman, five metres behind White, shrieked, 'Get out!' Blackman and 'Green' dumped their Bergens and skidded into the bush. The jungle erupted with fire. Bullets bluebottled, clenched up humus and muck. White took a round in the thigh that sliced through the femoral artery. Bone chips flew. Blood geysered in yard-long spritzes. 'I'm hit!' he screamed.

Skardon, who'd been tail-end-charlie, flipped off his Bergen and fast-tracked up to his comrade, yanking him into the cover of the tree. Indo bullets needle-tracked bark, squiffed foliage, horneted past Skardon's ears. White was deathly pale. The hole in his thigh was billiard-ball sized. Blood splurged, drenching Skardon's OGs. Skardon heaved White ten metres back into a depression. Indo slugs snapped in, spliffed mud, snapped branches. 'I think we've had it, Chalky,' Skardon said.

'I know, skipper,' White said. 'Thanks for trying.'

They were White's last words. Skardon realized that the gushes of blood had fizzled out. White was already dead, but Skardon wouldn't accept it. 'Come on, Chalky,' he grunted. 'I'm going to carry you.' Skardon lumped White to another pit, just as exposed. He laid him down. He smacked his face until it dawned on him that White wasn't coming round. By the time he'd let go, five Indos had broken cover and were scuttling towards him, trying to cut off his escape. Skardon whapped his SLR to his shoulder, eyesighted in, jerked iron, punked off three rounds. He pulled back, flanked into a stream between high banks, splotched through dark water. Thorn spikes gouged him, snagged his belt. Skardon flicked it off, ramped up the bank and dove into dense jungle. When he stumbled into the RV at Landing Point 1, where Tudor had been choppered out two days earlier, 'Green' and Blackman had been there two hours. Next morning, after debrief, the three of them went back into the ulu with a Gurkha company to collect White's body. The Indo soldier White had whacked out was still kneeling behind his tree, and not far away they found ambush positions of thirty enemy, littered with dumped shell-cases. White was there, just where Skardon had left him. 'Never experienced anything like that before,' Blackman commented, 'basha-up with a chap . . . then next day wrap him in a poncho and bundle him into a helicopter; affects you more than you like to admit.'[3]

The fact that Skardon hadn't 'scooted' but had gone to pull White out, putting his own life in danger, became a bone of contention in de la Billière's squadron, and the subject of numerous Chinese parliaments. SOPs were in place for good reason, but abandoning a wounded comrade went against the very cement of soldierly honour. A Squadron SSM, Lawrence Smith, a man whose experience and judgement, de la Billière said, 'he could rely on completely',[4] declared that while 'shoot-and-scoot' was a sound tactic, he would have ignored it to save a mate. Finally, John Woodhouse came up with a pronouncement that did him credit: '. . . morale demands . . . an order that if a man is known to have fallen, the patrol will remain in the close vicinity,' he wrote, 'until either they see for certain that he is dead, or they recover him alive. I think we should expect to fight to the death for this.'[5]

77. 'One of the most efficient uses of military force in the history of the world'

They were stalking through the rain-forest over a thousand metres inside Kalimantan, making for the River Sekayan, where they would bump longboats ferrying Indonesian forces. It was a four-man patrol of D Squadron, three of whom were new to Borneo. The patrol-boss was nine-year SAS vet Sgt. Edward 'Geordie' Lillico, the lead-scout Tpr. Ian Thomson, an ex-miner from Fife.

The patrol had separated from the rest of the half-troop earlier, and had dumped Bergens with them. They carried only belt-kit, but still they moved with a grinding slowness, careful not to disturb a grass-stalk or damage a single leaf. Thomson was carrying a 5.56mm US-made M16 Armalite rifle. Though it had only half the effective range of the SLR, it was a good weapon for a lead-scout because of its fast rate of fire. The others had standard-issue 7.62mm SLRs. Thomson navigated and picked the route through the undergrowth, remaining as far ahead of the patrol as the limit of visibility. As Roger Blackman's patrol had found out six months earlier, the lead-scout was the man most likely to get whacked. The others had to make sure they wouldn't be taken down in the same burst of fire, or by the same mine or booby-trap. The 'shoot-and-scoot' SOP still obtained. Now the SAS were operating in a foreign country the British weren't even officially at war with, it was even more important to avoid casualties.

It was February 1965, and D Squadron, under Major Roger Woodiwiss, Devon & Dorset Regiment, was on its fourth tour in Borneo. Indonesian incursions were escalating. At a conference in Tokyo, President Sukarno had declared that Indonesian troops had every right to be in northern Borneo, as the Malaysian Federation didn't exist. Since the start of A Squadron's tour the previous year, there'd been a change in British policy in the Confrontation. Harold Wilson's Labour government had been elected, but despite its commitment to pulling out 'East of Suez', Defence Secretary

Denis Healey had proved himself a hawk. He authorized Director of Operations Walter Walker to allow his forces to penetrate Kalimantan on aggressive ops, designated 'Claret'. At last, the SAS was to take the war to the enemy, though the existence of 'Claret' was secret. 'I couldn't tell the world about it,' Healey said. 'So I had to keep it from Parliament.' At first a maximum distance of three thousand metres was allowed, later extended to ten thousand.

There'd been other changes too. John Woodhouse had left the Regiment a few weeks earlier and been replaced by his former second-in-command, Mike Wingate-Gray. D Squadron had just taken over from B Squadron under Major Johnny Watts. The squadron originally formed from 21 SAS, which had vanished after the Jebel Akhdar op, had been re-established to bring the Regiment up to strength. The pressure on 22 SAS had also been relieved by the deployment of two companies of the Parachute Regiment – the Guards Independent Company and C Company, 2 Para, both of which were to be trained up to SAS standards.

This was the Lillico patrol's second trip across the frontier in two days. The previous day they'd come across an abandoned guerrilla camp only fifteen hundred metres from the border. The camp, a jungle-shanty of dilapidated bashas, looked as if it hadn't been used in six months, but Lillico wanted to have an extra shufti before they moved on to the river. Returning to the same place twice was against another Woodhouse SOP, but SOPs were guidelines, not orders, and the place might yield interesting data.

There was a mass of bamboo on the approach to the camp. This was hard going, because bamboo could make a racket if trodden on. Thomson was only six metres from the camp when he paused behind bamboo fronds to scope it out. The rest of the patrol froze. They watched, they listened, they waited. The shelters were scattered through the bamboo, at the base of the great jungle trees. There was a rock outcrop and a stream, but to Thomson, nothing had changed since yesterday.

Thomson eased out of cover, and the world blew apart. Automatic fire gobbled air, rounds scattergunned, yocking up dirt, snarfing leaves, clipping in from all sides. Thomson took hits in the left thigh that splintered the thigh-bone and hurled him behind a rock. He tried to grapple himself up, but couldn't make it. He couldn't feel his leg, and blood was spouting into his eyes. He clocked an Indo trooper sitting up two metres away, with a bolt-action rifle – not much more than a kid. His eyes were wide and his mouth was going like a beached fish. Thomson groped for his weapon, stabbed it the kid's way, carved a burst across his torso.

Rounds were still incoming, snarking soil, smacking leaves. Thomson had copped the same wound that had taken out Billy White of A Squadron the previous year: his femoral artery was punctured. His leg wasn't in the right place, and blood was whaling from his thigh in long squirts. He clamped his jaws and leopard-crawled into a bamboo clump, his dud leg sliding, globbing blood. His shattered thigh-bone crepitated. He made the brush, ripped the rag off his head, bound it tight until the bleeding stopped. He grabbed the morphine syrette from round his neck, jabbed muscle, squeezed plastic. Then he realized that the patrol commander, Geordie Lillico, was proned out not five metres away, white as a ghost and sodden with blood.

Lillico had taken a slug through the thigh that had gouged the sciatic nerve but missed the artery. On exit it had pulped one entire cheek of his arse. He couldn't stand. When Ian Thomson hopped up to investigate with his leg tourniqueted, Lillico opened his eyes. Thomson clocked movement, and saw an Indo step out from behind a tree. He whamped a 5.56mm double tap and the Indo capsized. Enemy fire was starbursting out of the jungle and Lillico already had his SLR braced. The weapon pumped twice. Brass cases pinged. Bat shadows flitted. Acrid fumes wafted. Silence lulled.

Lillico had seen Thomson on his feet, and thought he was sound. He told him to get back to the emergency RV and bring up the rest of the patrol. Thomson didn't argue, even though he knew he couldn't walk, and the meet-up point was over a klick away. Thomson bellied through the bamboo on elbows and one knee, with the jagged bone-ends of his femur crunching. As he crawled off, Lillico clocked three Indos lurking, and sighted-in, squeezed steel. 7.62mm rounds gnashed, and Lillico saw impact and blood-spray. Two Indos spudsacked, the other vanished. Lillico hugged his gunstock, ready to fry anything that moved. Nothing did, so he tore open field-dressings, whopped them on his wounds. He mainlined morphine. He didn't feel pain. He felt mystical and at peace with the world.

The patrol's two tailenders hadn't been hit in the initial contact. Following SOP they'd bugged out back to the emergency rendez-vous. The other patrol had heard the contact and had already tapped out a warning to Roger Woodiwiss's ops room. When the two survivors reported Lillico and Thomson missing, Woodiwiss tasked the RAF with immediate chopper search-and-rescue. He requested the local company of 6 Gurkha Rifles as back-up.

The six SAS-men at the RV had two choices. They could scour the jungle for Thomson and Lillico themselves, or they could go for the Gurkhas, three hours' march away at Sain, and guide them in. The crucial factor was enemy strength. The two survivors thought the Indos were probably a company. The consensus was to go for Gurkha back-up.

Before dark, Lillico managed to drag himself five hundred metres through thick belukar undergrowth and into a pig-rut under a fallen trunk. The light was beginning to mush. Lillico heard the thump of heli-blades above him. He knew the chopper pilot wouldn't locate him in this dense brush, and was too bombed to remember he was carrying a SARBE search-and-rescue beacon.

Night came and nightsong enveloped him. Lillico dipped out. When he came round in the morning, six Indos were scattered through the bush within a radius of thirty metres, searching for him. One of them shimmied up a tree and perched on a fork, scoping the area. For a second Lillico's eyes locked the climber's, and he thought the Indo had spotted him. Just then, he heard the skittering of a chopper. This time he remembered the SARBE, but knew he couldn't activate it. The heli was a small Whirlwind, and if she came in low, the Indos would shoot her down. He lay there rigid until the enemy left. After a while he heard gunshots and his heart jerked. He thought they'd bagged Thomson.

Ian Thomson was splayed out by a stream near the emergency RV about fifteen hundred metres away with his Armalite smoking. He'd lain up in a pig-hole all night, slackening off the tourniquet to prevent gangrene. Thomson was patrol medic and carried the medical pack. There were twenty syrettes of morphine in the pack, and he'd been squidging the stuff in on the hour. At first light he'd started scuffing through bush on his elbows. It took him the whole day to make the RV, where he found the rest of the patrol had split. His and Lillico's Bergens were still there. He found a full water-bottle, chugged down liquid, puked it back up. He sledded his body to a stream for more. That was when he heard heli-blades looping. He was still high as the moon, and he thought the chopper was the enemy. He whaled off bursts at her through the forest canopy. The rounds never went anywhere near the heli, and the pilot, Flying Officer Dave Collinson, didn't hear them, but only a hundred metres away a Gurkha lead-scout did. When he glided suddenly out of the foliage, Thomson already had his rifle zeroed-in. The Gurkha patrol had donned their bush-hats inside out so that the scarlet head-bands showed. It was the gash of red that stopped Thomson from blotting him.

Above them, Dave Collinson was on his eighteenth pass when the Gurkha signaller came through with the message that Thomson had been found. He dipped the Whirlwind down towards the canopy with the winch-motor churning, but this was primary jungle, and the trees towered up to two hundred feet. They were just too tall for him to get the whirlybird in low enough for the winch-cable. He told the Gurkhas they'd have to find a clearing where he could get in lower.

That day, Lillico scooped himself two hundred metres uphill to a ridge, where he thought the RAF search-and-rescue boys would have more chance of seeing him. It was a marathon, and by the time he'd topped the rise he was feeling faint again. Not long before last light, the squiffing of chopper-blades hacked into his consciousness. He activated the SARBE. Collinson picked it up almost at once, and homed in. His winch-man spotted Lillico and the winch-cable spigoted down. Minutes later, Lillico had the strop round him and was being winched up into the Whirlwind, dropping his precious SLR on the way.

Lillico won the MM for his grit. Thomson, who was pulled out next day, was awarded an MID. Thomson recovered, but with one leg shorter than the other, and was never fit for active service again. Lillico recovered and soldiered on. Thomson never forgot the look on the young Indo's face in the split second before he shot him. Lillico never quite forgave himself for losing his rifle. When de la Billière's squadron took over from Woodiwiss the following month, they heard about the Lillico patrol and were highly impressed. De la Billière called it 'one of the most extraordinary feats of survival known even to the SAS'.[1]

Although 'Claret' had been authorized the previous year, it was Woodiwiss's D Squadron who'd begun deep penetration in earnest. De la Billière now discovered that bigger patrols were needed to take on the Indos, and increased numbers to troop strength. The SAS were back in their old long-range raiding mode – hitting enemy forces on the river or on a track, photographing enemy installations, even tapping Indo phone-lines. De la Billière still felt the urge to lead from the front – a practice that Woodhouse had frowned on as 'hogging the limelight' or 'gong hunting'. 'Troop operations are for troop commanders,' he'd written de la Billière the previous year, 'not you or me.'[2]

In September, though, de la Billière accompanied a patrol led by Sgt. Maurice Tudor to hit Indo shipping on the Aya Hitam river, but took care to stay in the background. 'For me there was the irritation of not being in control,' de la Billière wrote, 'since I was merely a guest or passenger – of having different ideas about how things should be done, and of being obliged to suppress them.'[3] When Tudor's troop moved to the riverbank, de la Billière remained behind to guard their Bergens with his radio-operator, Cpl. Geordie Low.

Low and de la Billière were busy enciphering and tapping off messages when they heard the pop and clatter of small-arms fire from the river. It lasted two minutes. Moments later, Tudor's men burst out of the undergrowth, grunting that the enemy were after them. They'd bumped two longboats, sunk one and run the other aground, taking out sixteen Indos. The bad news was that the boats had been followed up by two more. They'd immediately put in at the bank, and the crews were already in hot pursuit. The men saddled up their packs. De la Billière and Low crammed the radio-gear into a Bergen. As the eighteen SAS-men legged it through the ulu, the Indos started lobbing three-inch mortar shells. 'It is no fun being mortared in the jungle,' de la Billière recalled, 'as bombs detonate in the tree-tops, and hurl shrapnel downwards.'[4] By sunset they had outrun their pursuers.

A Squadron was relieved by B a month later, and de la Billière returned to Blighty with a bar to his MC. Whether Woodhouse considered his activities 'gong-hunting' is unknown: the 'co-founder of the modern SAS' had long since left the army, and had taken up a post with David Stirling's 'rent-a-fighter' company, Watchguard International. De la Billière had lost twenty-five per cent of his Squadron in casualties during his two tours in Borneo.

Though B Squadron had some contacts, theirs was the last active SAS tour in Borneo. That December Sukarno was toppled by a military coup and replaced by General Suharto, who, in May the following year, opened negotiations with Malaysia. Cross-border raids continued sporadically as Suharto manoeuvred for concessions, but during its last tour, D Squadron had no brushes with the opposition. The Borneo Confrontation was over, with the loss of only a hundred and thirty-four British servicemen – as Denis Healey commented, 'about the same number of people that are killed on the roads on a Bank Holiday weekend'.

Healey considered Borneo the greatest triumph of his administration. It was a victory for the Stirling–Lewes concept of tiny units operating with maximum efficiency, for the Calvert–Woodhouse principle of hearts and minds, and a final vindication of the conviction that the man is mightier than the machine. 'The Americans tried to win the Vietnam war by bombing,' Healey commented, 'and millions were killed, and they lost.' The Borneo campaign, he said, was 'one of the most efficient uses of military force in the history of the world'.[5]

78. 'The covert and clandestine actions for which it is world famous'

When Major Peter de la Billière arrived back at Bradbury Lines in 1969, after four years of staff work, he found the same neat lawns and 'spider' barracks, but the Regiment itself much changed. In the 'Kremlin' – the Intelligence and Planning cell – he encountered his new commanding officer and old squadron boss, Lt. Col. Johnny Watts, as craggy as ever, and with the eternal roll-up hanging from his mouth. Watts told him that since Borneo and Aden had fizzled out, the Regiment was having to 'sell itself' to the military establishment – winkling out jobs here and there. As second-in-command it was de la Billière's job to locate suitable assignments.

22 SAS was now part of a new command structure. The post that Dare Newell had occupied as HQ Major had always been intended to form the nucleus of a higher command, and this was now in place, with a Director, SAS Group – currently Brigadier Fergus Semple. The Brigadier commanded 21, 22, 23 SAS, and the newly-formed 63 SAS Signals Squadron (TA). The SAS Group was based at Duke of York's Barracks in King's Road, Chelsea. Although the TA regiments were smaller than the regular unit, 'Group' was good for business. It meant more posts for senior NCOs and officers as permanent staff: sergeant-instructors, training-majors, adjutants. There were now, for instance, three possible slots for regular lieutenant-colonels, and three for regular regimental sergeant-majors.

22 SAS had expanded back almost to its Malaya level, with four regular sabre squadrons and a new 'R' or 'Reserve' squadron. 'R' Squadron was a TA unit based in Hereford, whose personnel were 'weekend soldiers' but trained alongside the regulars with a view to providing individual replacements when needed. The other new squadron was 'G', formed around a nucleus of men from the Guards Independent Parachute Company. The Guards Para, the pathfinder company of 16 Parachute Brigade, was already an anomaly – a unit of the Parachute Regiment wearing Para Reg

insignia, made up entirely of Guardsmen. Now it was to be converted lock, stock and barrel to SAS.

Some of the old hands weren't happy about the addition of G Squadron. The designation itself – 'G' for 'Guards', when the logical title would have been 'E' Squadron – suggested that it was somehow 'different'. It was sponsored by the Household Division, and since all of its men came from one source, it formed a sort of unit-within-a-unit that to many SAS-men looked suspiciously like a 'takeover' by the old elite.

What really infuriated the vets was the fact that the Guards' Para boys got in through the supposedly non-existent 'back door', doing a specially modified form of Selection, designed to ensure that most of them passed. This was a betrayal of the first principle of the SAS concept – of an elite based purely on merit. 'If you impose the most rigorous demands on those wishing to join the SAS,' said Ken Connor, 'you maintain the highest standards within it. Once you start making exceptions – like G Squadron . . . you cannot maintain or regain those former standards.'[1] Though it quickly became obvious that the squadron's manpower couldn't be supplied entirely from the Brigade of Guards, and it grew as heterogeneous as the other squadrons, the readiness of the head-shed to grant 'privileged status' wasn't easily forgotten.

In the early sixties the British army had ceased to be a conscript force, and had turned professional. Outside the portals of Bradbury Lines, the post-colonial world that had given birth to 22 SAS was quietly vanishing. The post-war generation was coming of age. The 1960s had seen the USA bogged down in Vietnam, peace rallies, 'Ban the Bomb', the Hippies, the Beatles, LSD. Towards the end of the decade, the pacifists had given way to militant urban terrorist groups – the Provisional IRA, the Baader-Meinhof gang, the Red Brigades, ETA, the Red Army, the PLO, the PFLP. In 1969, three Palestinian terrorists were arrested attempting to hijack a Boeing 707 at Zurich, Switzerland. It was the overture and beginners of the new age. During the following year alone, the US State Department recorded three hundred cases of terrorism world-wide.

The sun had set on the British Empire, and wars of decolonialization were on the wane. In the UK the main military focus was on Europe and the Soviet threat, but though 22 SAS had a role in NATO in the event of total war, it had been outshone in that sphere by 21 and 23 SAS. The TA might train only at weekends and in holidays, but they trained for a single purpose, and their signallers and spotters were second to none. They frequently thrashed 22 SAS in NATO competitions. This might have caused ex-21 SAS Adjutant de la Billière a wry smile, but it didn't go down well with those chauvinistic regulars who thought of the TA as 'amateurs'.

Three years earlier, outgoing commanding officer Lt. Col. Mike Wingate-Gray had suggested a number of alternative roles for 22 SAS in the event of total war, including long-range penetration, raids and reconnaissance behind enemy lines, and the raising, training and direction of guerrillas. Just how many such opportunities there would be in a Europe devastated by nuclear blasts was debatable. After performing their observation tasks, 21 and 23 SAS were trained to don their nuclear-biological-and-chemical-warfare suits, respirators and rubber overshoes, and beat a hasty retreat.

Wingate-Gray had also suggested a short list of roles that were more suited to the new era. These included bodyguarding and VIP protection – techniques that had been under development by 22 SAS since the early 60s, in the specialist Bodyguard Cell. New roles, though, included on the one hand 'the support of police Special Branch operations' and on the other, industrial sabotage and 'blanket' or black-cell operations. These jobs had one common factor – they would be covert, and would require the efficient use of concealed arms – pistols and perhaps mini-sub-machine guns. The key was the development of close-quarter battle shooting techniques.

22 SAS had gained its first experience of covert urban ops on Operation Nina, in Aden. The 'brains' behind these so-called 'Keeni-Meeni' actions was counter-insurgency guru Frank Kitson – a future Chief of the General Staff – who had cut his teeth on the Mau Mau 'pseudo-gangs' in Kenya. During the Mau Mau

emergency, white policemen, dressed African-style with faces blackened, accompanied teams of 'turned' ex-terrorists into the bush. The technique worked. Kitson's plan to try the same thing on the Jebel Akhdar op had been vetoed, but it proved effective on the streets of Aden, where SAS-men disguised as Arabs or Africans wandered the alleys of the Crater District with pistols under their robes, ready to hit opportunity targets.

For Keeni-Meeni ops – Kitson borrowed the term from a Swahili phrase suggesting the movement of a snake in the grass – the Regiment drafted in some of the dozen Fijian SAS-men it had recruited in the early 60s, as well as its star Arabic-speakers, and troopers with dark complexions. The effect, augmented by stage make-up, turned out to be so convincing that when one operator was arrested by a British infantry unit, his cover was never blown and he was released with compliments on his 'excellent English'. The Keeni-Meeni teams even deployed a man made up as a blonde-haired European woman, who trolled around offering an easy target, with a group of watchers trailing 'her'. There was no body-armour available, and the female impersonator's life rested firmly on the speed of 'her' colleagues.

On another occasion, a covert SAS team in a battered minibus dogged a uniformed 'decoy' squad in a Land Rover in the hostile district of Sheikh Othman. An Arab poled out of an alley suddenly and lobbed a grenade, which whacked apart, injuring one of the decoys in the arm. The SAS team bagged both the grenade-thrower and his back-up man, but were painfully aware they'd been a split second too late.

The Keeni-Meenies showed that the old Grant-Taylor close-quarter battle shooting system – taught to the SAS during the war – wasn't effective where perfect timing was required. Grant Taylor, a US Office of Strategic Services officer, had taught aiming by squaring the torso on to the target and firing from the waist. In the late sixties, though, an SAS team came up with the 'SAS Method' – a homegrown technique that was more mobile and fluid. Instead of shooting from the waist, the shooter used the pistol at arm's length, as an extension of the index finger, pointing at a target. The team also developed a self-defence technique aimed at clearing a space wide enough to draw the weapon.

The SAS Method was based on fitness, strength and agility, and was so simple it could be acquired in a fortnight. The shooter would first aim to distract the opponent by a punch or kick to the face, groin or shin, or by the use of an improvised weapon such as a pen, coin or key, jabbed in the eye or kidney, or a spurt of fire from a cigarette-lighter. When a clearance of at least a foot had been acquired, the shooter would draw his pistol from a shoulder- or waist-holster, and fire a double-tap, to make sure that, once engaged, the target stayed down. However, the SAS were trained never to escalate the conflict. They would only draw pistols in response to a deadly threat, but once the weapon was drawn, would shoot to kill. The pistol, usually a 'High Power' 9mm Browning, was specially modified to the hand of the individual user, whether left- or right-handed. It was carried under a shirt with press-stud fastenings that would pop open immediately, later with Velcro. Waistband holsters were concealed under a civilian jacket specially weighed down by fishing-weights, to prevent it from flapping open and revealing the weapon.

The prosaic character of the Browning pistol was itself the perfect expression of the no-frills SAS approach – the weapon was solid and reliable rather than 'hi-tec', and used ammunition that was readily available. The weapon was not the crucial element in the process – it was next to useless in the hands of a shooter lacking the kind of mental toughness looked for in SAS Selection. The Regiment disliked the US approach to bodyguarding – large numbers of obviously huge, gum-chewing bodybuilders in dark glasses. Once guards could be identified by the opponent, it didn't really matter how many there were – as the assassination of John F. Kennedy had aptly demonstrated. The 'grey man', hidden in a crowd, unseen by the enemy, was worth ten obvious guards – the SAS emphasis on concealment and understatement was an expression of the British character, and a reflection of the prime SAS conviction that the 'Regiment was the man', not the technology.

The 'SAS Method' was practised at the 'Killing House' – a new type of CQB range at Bradbury Lines, whose prototype D Squadron had built of sandbags at Nanyuki in Kenya, during a training exercise there. Designed on a piece of graph-paper and constructed by a local builder, the £30,000 the house cost proved to be a sterling investment.[2] The Killing House consisted of a number of rooms through which shooters would proceed, taking on targets as they popped up. Some targets would be engaged in the dark, others would involve jumping over obstacles, rolling and coming up into a firing position – a loose martial-arts stance with one foot forward and the other trailing. Some targets would require the shooter to change magazines or clear stoppages. The new close-quarter battle techniques didn't create the urban SAS role which had already been suggested in Wingate-Gray's paper, but the innovations took it off the drawing-board and made it a practical possibility. 'Almost overnight,' wrote Connor, 'it made possible the change from a purely military force into a unit capable of carrying out all the covert and clandestine actions for which it is world famous.'[3]

79. 'Fifteen hundred *pistolas*'

On Remembrance Sunday, 1969, twenty-eight years after the foundation of L Detachment, D Squadron, 22 SAS, paraded at Newtownards, Northern Ireland, in full uniform, to salute the memory of the man who'd done so much to shape the Regiment – Lt. Col. Blair 'Paddy' Mayne. Mayne had lived to see the foundation of 22 SAS, though his life after the war had been a let-down. He had worked briefly for the British Antarctic Survey, together with John Tonkin and Mike Sadler, but had been hampered by the back injury he'd sustained in the war, possibly as early as Squatter. He had been appointed Secretary of the Northern Ireland Law Society, but had never succeeded in exorcizing his demons. He had never married and had lurched from one booze-up to the next, frequently involved in brawls that had at least once landed him in jail.

Mayne and Stirling met several times after the war, but Mayne had never got on with the aristocratic types in Stirling's circle. Neither Mayne nor Stirling had shown much interest in the SAS Association, of which they were the principal officers, but had left the work largely to Brian Franks. Mayne died on 14 December 1955 when he crashed his Riley sports car into a stationary lorry, on his way back from a drinking session.

Paddy Mayne wasn't the most tragic peacetime casualty among SAS Originals. The 'unsung hero' of L Detachment, Bill Fraser, whose strike at Ajadabiyya had done much to establish the unit's reputation, and who had fought his way through the entire war, had long since been dishonourably discharged from the army, and had ended his days a destitute alcoholic living on the streets.

D Squadron was not in Northern Ireland for purely ceremonial duties. Civil rights marches, demanding justice and equality for the minority Catholic population, had become prevalent in the past year. That August, a Protestant-Loyalist backlash drove a mob from the Protestant heartland of Belfast's Shankill road into the Catholic Falls Road area. The Royal Ulster Constabulary not only failed to protect the Catholics, but colluded in the disorder, opening fire on Divis Flats in the Falls, and killing a nine-year-old boy. In Armagh, on the border with the Republic of Ireland, the RUC paramilitary reserve, the notorious B Specials, shot dead twenty-nine-year-old John Gallagher. There were riots in Dungannon and the Bogside area of Londonderry.

Six thousand British troops were deployed initially to do the job the RUC had failed to do, and were welcomed by Catholic communities. Though there had already been a split between the traditional or 'Official' Irish Republican Army (OIRA), who favoured a peaceful settlement of nationalist grievances, and the 'new' or 'Provisional' IRA (PIRA), who supported a strong-arm solution, nationalist terrorists were conspicuous by their silence. Behind the scenes, the Provisionals had infiltrated the civil rights movement, and were the backbone of Catholic defence committees. They came out of the closet the following year, when relations between the British army and Catholic communities soured, after the introduction of the Falls Road curfew. It was then that PIRA decided to target British troops.

D Squadron had been deployed in the Province ostensibly to run a 'training exercise', but in practice to prevent gun-running by Loyalist paramilitaries. After laying a wreath on Mayne's grave, and firing a salute, they put a watch on Belfast Lough and began monitoring radio chatter from ships entering the harbour. At one stage they picked up a message from an Argentinian ship carrying 'fifteen hundred *pistolas*' and boarded the vessel, to discover to their great embarrassment that *pistola* meant a side of beef.

While the Regiment was making its first inroads into urban warfare, 2IC de la Billière was scouring the world for new jobs. One area of focus was the Persian Gulf, threatened by the presence of a Soviet-backed state in the People's Democratic Republic of the Yemen, which had filled the vacuum created by Britain's withdrawal from Aden. South Yemen's next-door neighbour was the Sultanate of Oman, still ruled by the same reactionary Sultan, Sa'id bin Taimur, for whom the Regiment had put down a rebellion a decade earlier. The SAS had maintained an interest in the Sultanate ever since.

80. 'Purely for training purposes'

In March 1970 a swarthy-looking man with long dark hair, and a roll-up hanging from the side of his mouth, turned up at Sharjah, a small Sheikhdom in the Gulf. The man's name was 'Mr Smith', and though his journey officially ended there, he continued overland to Muscat, where he sought a meeting with the Sultan of Oman, Sa'id bin Taimur. 'Mr Smith' was Lt. Col. Johnny Watts, commanding officer of 22 SAS Regiment, and he had come to make bin Taimur a proposal.

Salalah, capital of Dhofar – Oman's southernmost province –

lay six hundred and twenty-five miles away from Muscat by road. There had been trouble in the region for the past eight years. The Sultan, who'd built a rambling palace on the beach at Salalah, regarded Dhofar as a sort of personal fief, although the idea that the local tribes had ever really been his 'subjects' was a fiction. In fact, his writ had never extended far beyond the coastal plain. The people of Dhofar – cattle-rearing hillmen, camel-riding Bedu, townsmen and fishermen – had been marginalized for centuries. In the early sixties, though, it had begun to dawn on them that while their neighbours were growing affluent, they remained in poverty. They revolted against the Sultan's rule, forming an organization called the Dhofar Liberation Front.

In the mid-sixties, the DLF was 'hijacked' by the Yemen-based Marxist Popular Front for the Liberation of the Occupied Arab Gulf (MPFLOAG) – an organization sponsored by the Soviet Union, China and Iraq. Dhofari tribesmen were trained in the Yemen by Soviet military advisers, and sent to the USSR or China for political indoctrination. The insurgency had become an international affair: if the Sultanate of Muscat and Oman fell to the Communists, then the oil-rich Gulf States, Kuwait, and even Saudi-Arabia might well go down like dominoes.

Within four years Chinese-backed insurgents were in possession of all Dhofar but the coastal plain, and were closing in on Salalah. In particular, they controlled the 'Midway Road' to northern Oman across the Dhofar mountains – the only land-communication with Muscat. The Sultan's armed forces and his Baluch mercenaries recruited from Pakistan – both British-officered – had proved incapable of fighting the guerrillas in their mountain heartland. They had developed a 'Jebel Akhdar' syndrome – the belief that the jebel was impregnable, especially in the rainy season.

The situation in Dhofar was looking critical, but Watts had drawn up a plan to retrieve it. He offered bin Taimur the use of 22 SAS to set up a 'hearts and minds' campaign to win over the Dhofar people, and to train loyal Dhofaris as anti-guerrilla fighters. The Sultan had never been strong on hearts and minds, and baulked

36. Billy White, *left*. Lead scout on the four-man Blackman patrol in Borneo, White came face to face with an Indonesian soldier. He shot the enemy, but was hit in the thigh by rounds from a platoon-strength ambush. White bled to death, but the rest of the patrol escaped.

37. Edward 'Geordie' Lillico. Investigating an Indonesian camp across the Kalimantan border, Lillico's D Squadron patrol ran into a heavy ambush. Both Lillico and his lead scout, Ian Thomson, were badly injured. Thomson managed to crawl back to the ERV, while Lillico dragged himself through the jungle for a night and a day, narrowly evading enemy troops.

38. Helicopter flying over Borneo: the SAS campaign here in the 1960s was a victory for the concept of tiny units operating with maximum efficiency and the principle of hearts and minds. As Denis Healey commented, 'one of the most efficient uses of military force in the history of the world'.

39. Tony Jeapes in Dhofar. Jeapes, OC D Squadron during its first tour in Dhofar, had the idea of raising a thousand surrendered Jebali tribesmen to spearhead the campaign against rebels in the hills.

40. 'Lab' Labalaba, hero of Mirbat. When the tiny SAS team at Mirbat, Dhofar, came under sudden assault, Labalaba kept up uninterrupted fire from a field-gun until shot dead.

41. SAS patrol searching the scrub, Dhofar hills. The 'Jebel' in Dhofar proved unexpectedly difficult terrain.

42. Mirbat, Dhofar. The battle-ground seen from the mortar-pit beneath the BATT house. Several members of the SAS team had to cross this open ground to reach the gun-pit, to the left of the fort, where Labalaba manned the artillery-piece.

43. SAS patrol withdrawing across Jarbib, Dhofar. The first attempt to occupy the Dhofar hills was cut short after twelve days, with the SAS-men suffering from exhaustion and dehydration. Having shown the rebels that the SAS could operate in their territory, though, the operation was considered a success.

44. Peter Ratcliffe in Dhofar. An ex-Para who joined the army to escape a humdrum life in Salford. Ratcliffe would later become RSM of 22 SAS, and the only SAS NCO ever to relieve a squadron OC of his command in the field.

45. Simba position, Qamar mountains, Dhofar. Peter Ratcliffe's 'Green Five' sangar here came under enemy fire from mortars and Katyusha rockets on successive days, killing two of his patrol, and wounding others.

46. The Iranian Embassy siege. Red Team leader sustains burns to his legs from blazing curtains while abseiling down to a rear window. As he swings away from the flames, the SAS-men on the roof are initially unable to cut him free, in case he misses the balcony and plummets fifteen feet to the ground.

47. The Iranian Embassy siege. Executed in the full glare of TV cameras, Operation Nimrod lasted only eleven minutes, but gave the SAS instant celebrity. Previously little known, the Regiment was to become a household name and to spawn imitators in almost every country in the world.

48. Pebble Island, Falklands War. D Squadron, 22 SAS scored a spectacular success here when they destroyed Argentinian aircraft, including ground-attack Pucaras – the first raid of its kind since L Detachment days.

49. Royal Navy Sea King helicopter, Falklands War. The crash of a Sea King while cross-decking from *Intrepid*, resulted in the death of twenty members of D and G Squadrons, 22 SAS and support elements. The death-toll included eight senior NCOs, among them two squadron sergeants-major, the most devastating single loss the Regiment had sustained since the Second World War.

50. SAS mobile patrol, Gulf War. For the Regiment, the Gulf War marked a return to their early role of desert raiders. Equipped with 'pinkies' – Land Rover 110s – fitted with Browning machine-guns, GPMGs and Milan missiles, backed up by Unimogs and dirt-bikes, one hundred and twenty-eight men of A and D Squadrons, 22 SAS, were sent across the Iraq border on deep-penetration ops.

51. 'Saddam could go swivel'. Peter Ratcliffe, RSM, 22 SAS, holds a meeting in the Wadi Tubal in Iraq, at the height of the Gulf War, to discuss new furniture and fittings for the sergeants' mess. The event is both a calculated expression of professional coolness, and a gesture of disdain at Saddam Hussain's regime.

52. Candidate for 23 SAS Regiment (TA) on selection, Brecon Beacons. SAS selection has been called 'the toughest human proving ground in the world'. Not a trial of physical strength, athletic prowess, or even pure endurance, it is rather 'a battle for a man's mind and a test of his will to win'. The pass-rate for all three SAS regiments is about ten per cent.

53. The aftermath of the Loughgall ambush, Northern Ireland. Acting on a tip-off, the SAS Ulster squad lay in wait for Provisional IRA men planning to destroy the RUC station here with a bomb carried on a JCB digger. Opening fire only after the bomb had been set off, the SAS scored the British Army's greatest ever success against PIRA.

54. 21 SAS Regiment (Artists) (TA) on parade at the Royal Academy of Arts, London, in honour of their Artists Rifles forebears.

55. 'We are the pilgrims, master . . .' The clock tower at the SAS base in Hereford, engraved with the famous lines from Flecker's *Hassan*, is a monument to fallen SAS comrades, and to the everlasting honour of the Regiment.

at the idea of arming his subjects. Watts's carefully prepared pitch fell through.

British Consul-General in Oman David Crawford, Political Resident Geoffrey Arthur, and Oman Defence Secretary Col. Hugh Oldham had to face the unpalatable fact that the one certain assurance of Communist victory was the continued rule of Sa'id bin Taimur. They plotted to overthrow him. They had an asset in Sheikh Braik bin Hamud, son of the Wali – the Governor – of Salalah, and another potential asset in bin Taimur's only son, Qabus, a Sandhurst-trained officer who had been under virtual house-arrest for the past seven years. They agreed that Qabus would be asked to replace his father.

Through an enterprising intelligence officer of the Sultan's armed forces, Tim Landon, they discovered that Qabus had shared a room at Sandhurst with an officer currently serving in 22 SAS. This officer visited Qabus in the name of old acquaintance, and put the scheme to him. Qabus accepted. On 23 July 1970 the Sultan's armed forces threw a cordon round the palace at Salalah, where the Sultan was sojourning. A small team recruited from the Trucial Oman Scouts, the SAF, the British Army Training Section and 22 SAS, led by Tim Landon and Sheikh Braik, entered the palace. The Sultan and his bodyguard were waiting for them, and immediately opened fire, killing a sentry and wounding Sheikh Braik. The salvo was abruptly cut short when bin Taimur shot himself in the foot. The Sultan was flown to Britain the same day, given medical treatment, and took up residence in the Dorchester hotel. Within a week, Qabus had announced sweeping changes. The people of Salalah danced in the street.

A few days later, a five-man SAS-team arrived in Oman as the new Sultan's bodyguard, headed by the officer who had been his Sandhurst room-mate. Watts also sent his 2IC, Peter de la Billière, to Muscat to discuss the deployment of 22 SAS in Dhofar. By early September, the first troop of fifteen SAS-men under Captain Keith Farnes, an ex-Para, had arrived at Salalah. Designated the British Army Training Teams – BATT – they established an HQ at Umm al-Gawarif, and four-man sub-bases at the fishing ports of Taqa and Mirbat. Farnes started discreet work on a plan for the defence of Salalah, and the eventual defeat of rebel forces – Operation Storm.

As it happened, this was a propitious time for a Borneo-style campaign in southern Oman. The DLF had never aimed to change the social order, but the MPFLOAG Communists had outlawed the practice of Islam and started wreaking savage reprisals against any who resisted: they abducted children for indoctrination; they blinded men with hot irons; they cut off noses. When resistance continued, MPFLOAG attempted to disarm the DLF. One group of two dozen tribesmen, led by local DLF under-boss Salim Muba-rak, fought back. On 12 September, Salim led his men down from the mountains and surrendered to Qabus.

One of the problems of fighting in Dhofar was the unusual nature of the terrain. The Salalah plain – the Jarbib – was locked in by a horseshoe-shaped massif, twenty-five miles long and seven miles wide, with both sides closing in on the sea. The central area of the massif, the Qarra Mountains, was a thousand feet lower than the three-thousand-foot 'shoulders', and this configuration acted as a windtrap, snagging the Indian monsoon from June to September. During monsoon season, Jebel Qarra lay shrouded under a blanket of water-vapour – the only patch on the entire coast of southern Arabia that had regular rainfall. Here, deep clefts and sheer valleys bristled with dense shrubbery as thick as a jungle, and water cut down ancient wadis into deep pools dappled by reeds and ferns, forested in sycamore, acacia, myrtle and jasmine. The monsoon gave the advantage to the guerrillas, because the pea-soup mist meant that ground forces had to operate without air-cover or artillery support. The Sultan's air force had only one helicopter and two 'Skyvan' transport aircraft, and resupply had to be effected by camel-train.

The hill tribesmen, collectively known as the Jebali, were of a distinct character from the camel-rearing Bedu of the Najd – the gravel plains beyond the mountains, bordering on the vast dune-sea of the Empty Quarter. Prickly, suspicious, avaricious and fierce, they spoke ancient Himyaritic languages rather than Arabic, wore their hair in tight ringlets bound with strips of leather, herded dwarf cattle, and dwelt in caves and thatched stone huts. The dominant tribe of the region was the Qarra, to one of whose sub-groups, the Bayt Ma'ashini, most of Salim Mubarak's crew belonged. If the SAS could induce men like these – born and bred in the jebel – to fight against their old comrades, it could turn the tide.

This was a ploy straight out of the 'Kitson counter-insurgency manual', but the idea of recruiting SEPs – 'Surrendered Enemy Personnel' – as combat teams rather than as guides or scouts was down to Major Tony Jeapes, MC, victor of the Sabrina diversion on Jebel Akhdar eleven years earlier. Jeapes had recently returned from the Devons & Dorsets to command D Squadron, 22 SAS.

Landing in Dhofar hot on the heels of Farnes's troop, Jeapes interviewed Salim Mubarak at Umm al-Gawarif, over sweet, milky British army tea. He found the ex-rebel impressive. Salim told Jeapes that he knew the mountains like the palm of his hand – especially the eastern area, of which he'd been the DLF second-in-command. It transpired that Salim had been trained in China, and knew the techniques of psychological warfare even better than Jeapes did. Not only did he suggest ways of inducing more DLF-men to defect, he also said that if the SAS could provide the weapons and training, he could raise a 'Firgat' (correctly *firga*: a 'band', 'team' or 'company') that would 'grow until it was a thousand strong and . . . would sweep the jebel from end to end'. He said that he would call his team the 'Firgat as-Salahadin', after the great Kurdish fighter against the Crusaders.

A week later Jeapes flew to Muscat, where he put the idea of raising *firag* (the British anglicized the plural to 'Firgats') to the commander of the Sultan's armed forces, Brigadier John Graham. He proposed raising a thousand Jebali, equipping them with 7.62mm FN rifles and providing them with proper training and support. At first, Graham seemed hostile. He suggested that if 'support' meant General Purpose Machine Guns and mortars, the Firgats might hand the weapons over to the insurgents. He asked how they would manage radio communications, when many of the Jebali didn't even speak Arabic. Jeapes replied that the SAS would have to handle comms and support themselves – an impossible task, he admitted, for a team of only troop strength. He would need to deploy the whole of D Squadron. Jeapes thought Graham was about to give him the brush-off, when suddenly the Brigadier grinned, and said, 'Don't worry. I was being Devil's advocate. I like it. I like it.'[1]

The recruitment of local Dhofaris was one aspect of a 'Five Fronts' plan Johnny Watts had drawn up prior to the coup d'état. The emphasis of the scheme, though, remained on convincing the population that they would get a better deal under Qabus than under the Communists. Watts's agenda encompassed the setting up of an intelligence cell to collect data and run ops to demoralize the rebels, the establishment of a psy-ops team to persuade DLF fighters to defect, the provison of medical and veterinary assistance, and a civil aid programme that would include water-drilling, road-building and sanitation.

One limitation on aggressive actions was the need to prevent SAS casualties. Watts's last words to Jeapes before he left Hereford were, 'Whatever you do, you must not have casualties . . . Because if you do that will be it – finished. We will be withdrawn.'[2] At this stage, the Regiment's presence in Dhofar was secret – SAS teams were officially posted to Sharjah. The Ministry of Defence hadn't yet even permitted the deployment of SAS patrols in tactical areas, and Watts didn't want his men being shipped out with suspicious gunshot wounds, and awkward questions asked. Not until December did an MOD spokesman admit that the Regiment was in Dhofar, and then announced it was there 'purely for training purposes'.[3]

By the following February, over two hundred ex-DLF fighters had come in. These included men from the notoriously prickly Bait Kathir, some of whom were camel-nomads rather than hillmen and spoke Arabic as a mother-tongue. The Bait Kathir Firqat was mustered under legendary sharpshooter Musallim bin Tafl, who had accompanied explorer and ex-SAS-man Wilfred Thesiger on his first crossing of the Empty Quarter. By then, Salim Mubarak's

Firgat as-Salahadin was completing its training at Mirbat – a small town forty miles east of Salalah. Its instructors were D Squadron's 'Boat Troop' under Captain Ian Crooke, ex-King's Own Scottish Borderers, an irascible twenty-five-year-old Scotsman.

To get along with the Firgat-men, the SAS had to reach across a wide cultural gulf. First of all, it was difficult for the SAS, whose allegiance was to Squadron and Regiment, to grasp how SEPs could turn so readily on their former mates. For the Jebali, changing sides wasn't a moral problem, as their first loyalty lay always with their family and tribe, not with the MPFLOAG fighters. Similarly, while the SAS hierarchy was a rank-structure imposed from outside, the Jebali saw themselves as individuals entitled to make their own decisions. Their chiefs were 'the first among equals' who held authority by mutual consent. If individuals disagreed with their sheikh's decisions, they would simply turn to another.

Their attitude to fighting was equally hard to fathom. The hillmen and Bedu lived by the cult of reputation, and in battle they considered the idea of concealment – 'hiding from the enemy' – something of a disgrace. Since fighting was to them more of a sport than a deadly struggle for survival, they tended to fight hard, but withdraw when they felt like taking a rest. Since they considered that they were in the hands of God, they took what the SAS considered to be unnecessary risks, and were improvident with food and water. They would ask the BATT teams boldly for anything they wanted, and didn't believe it was necessary to show gratitude.

Despite this gap in perspective, the Firgats and the SAS developed a mutual respect. The Arabs were tough and courageous warriors, and could move incredibly fast in the local terrain, though they had a cultural prejudice against carrying heavy loads. The BATT-teams developed a modus operandi using the Firgats as fast-moving scouts, while the SAS were the workhorses, lugging the heavy weapons and radios in their Bergens. 'The Jebali Arabs . . . were . . . extremely loyal to people they accepted,' wrote Tpr. Brummie Stokes, ex-Green Jackets, an SAS Arabic-speaker attached to the Firgat. 'We, of course, were all "infidels" . . . but that apart, appeared all right in their eyes; they mucked in with the rest of us.'[4]

By the end of the month, Ian Crooke thought the thirty-two-man Firgat as-Salahadin ready for its first operation. Jeapes was aware that the first op had to be a success, and planned an attack from the sea on the village of Sudh, about twenty miles along the coast from Mirbat. Intel had indicated that the adoo were gathering there in strength. The Firgat landed by motorized boom on 23/4 February, supported by two SAS troops, to find there were no adoo in the town. A half-hearted 'counter-attack' by a pair of rebels that night was cut abruptly short when an SAS team demolished the enemy position with missiles from an 84mm Carl-Gustav rocket-launcher.

The Sudh operation paved the way for a more ambitious task – a show of strength on the jebel to encourage other DLF-men to defect, and to demonstrate that the mountains weren't impregnable. Before this could be put into effect, though, Salim Mubarak was diagnosed with angina pectoris by SAS medic Tpr. Nick Downie, ex-21 SAS, a former fourth-year medical student. Despite Downie's expertise, Jeapes refused to believe it. When Salim died in his sleep the same night, the Firgat-men immediately suspected he'd been poisoned, and only just stopped short of opening fire on their SAS trainers.

On 13 March two SAS troops under Ian Crooke, and two Firgats of about sixty men under a new chief, Mohammad Sa'id, toiled three thousand feet up the shoulder of the Jebel above Mirbat, by night. The force occupied a point on the plateau named the 'Eagle's Nest', and waited for the adoo's response. When nothing happened after three days, they moved across the plateau to a water source at Tawi Atair, engaging a three-man picket on the way, and wiping them out. The adoo retaliated by stonking their position with a 60mm mortar. Crooke had a three-inch mortar flown in by heli, and his men started lobbing mortar-bombs back.

One infuriating factor was that while the SAS had been supplied with sub-standard bombs, some of them made in India, the guerrillas were using the best British-made product. '. . . There are some people in Britain willing to sell anything to anybody in return for a fast buck,' wrote Peter Ratcliffe;' . . . there are too many influential figures with their fingers in the till, for there to be any chance of mere soldiers getting the trade . . . stopped.'[5]

The water at Tawi Atair was three hundred feet down, and proved impossible to get at. Dehydration became a more perilous threat than the DLF. Though a second Firgat group moved up to relieve them, killing half a dozen rebels on the way, moisture-loss became so severe that Jeapes decided to pull the troops out after twelve days. 'The soldiers were willing to go on,' he wrote, 'but their lined and gaunt faces betrayed the effects of lack of water and lack of sleep.'[6] Ian Crooke's condition horrified the OC – he was suffering not only from dehydration but also from hepatitis. Despite having cut the op short, Jeapes considered it a success. They had shown the adoo that they could operate on the jebel, had taken out nine enemy dead, and encouraged more defections from the DLF.

The next move was to establish a firm foothold on the plateau. Op Jaguar was put in after the monsoon that year, when Jeapes's D Squadron had been replaced by A and G Squadrons. The largest operation mounted so far, it consisted of a hundred SAS-men and three hundred Firgats, supported by two hundred and fifty men of the Sultan's Armed Forces. Jaguar was a major victory for the government – the rebels were pushed back into the deep wadis on the jebel. Although marred by the Firgats' refusal to fight throughout the fasting month of Ramadan – a development that exasperated Johnny Watts – the combined forces established two permanent bases in the hills, at Jibjat and Madinat al-Haq. They also set up a defensive line – the 'Leopard Line' – to prevent the movement of arms to the guerrillas from the Yemen. By the end of the op, SAS and Firgats had taken possession of most of the eastern jebel, including the Midway Road.

81. 'Jesus wept!'

When he heard the first mortar-bombs chafing the sky over Mirbat, coughing up smoke and debris among the mud-brick houses, Cpl. 'Lab' Labalaba ramped across rocky ground to the gendarmes' fort. He hurled himself into the gun-pit under its walls, where an Omani artilleryman, Walid Khamis, was manning an ancient twenty-five-pounder field-gun. Labalaba, ex-Irish Rangers, one of a dozen Fijians in the Regiment, grabbed an HE shell. As Walid snapped open the breech, Labalaba slid the round home with massive hands. The two men ducked as the shell whoffed out, gouging a brilliant yellow gash through the greyness of first light.

The shell caromed into the escarpment about six hundred metres away, slapping stone, firebursting in a starfish of flame and debris. As soon as the smoke cleared, rebel soldiers popped up from the dark slopes, trolling casually towards the perimeter wire, and Labalaba realized that Mirbat was under attack.

It was 19 July 1972, bang in the middle of the monsoon, and the sky was a gunmetal haze of dribbling cloud. The adoo had used the cover of the monsoon to collect in numbers on the jebel, for an unheard-of frontal assault. Stung by the SAS–Firgat successes of the last six months, especially Jaguar, they were determined to make a spectacular show. Their intention was to capture the town, kill the Wali, make a propaganda speech, and melt back into the hills.

Mirbat was a small fishing port standing on a blunt headland on a curve in the Dhofar coast. Forty miles from Salalah, and a stone's throw from the ancient ruins at Samhuram, it was a pale imitation of the great trading civilization that had existed here two thousand years earlier, when Dhofar was the main supplier of frankincense, a priceless commodity used in religious ceremonies. It was the peculiar nature of Dhofar's geography that provided the almost unique conditions for the cultivation of frankincense trees. Frank-incense still grew on the northern downslopes of the jebel, where the mountains gave way to the great gravel flats of the Nejd.

The town itself was a warren of mud-brick buildings sited on the southern side of a shallow wadi. On the northern side, near the beach, stood the Wali's fort, occupied by a squad of gendarmes, looming over a dog's-leg of market stalls. Slightly behind it stood the BATT-house – an oblong building with high sealed windows and walls pickled like beef jerky by sun and salt. The BATT house had been the headquarters of the SAS training team in Mirbat since the Regiment's first arrival in Dhofar. About five hundred metres away to the north-east, across undulating ground littered with egg-shaped boulders, the main fort stood on a hump, dominating the ground around it. The building was a medieval-style redoubt with double doors and an octagonal tower, also occupied by gendarmes. The gun-pit lay under the eaves of the fort, about forty metres short of the wire perimeter fence that ran all the way around the town.

Minutes before Labalaba had reached the pit, two hundred and fifty rebels had overrun the eight-man picket of gendarmes on Jebel 'Ali – a high ridge about six hundred metres north of the wire. Their plan had been for a sneak attack, but the gendarmes had spotted them. A single shot had blown their silent approach, and instead they rushed the position with a Shoagin machine gun crackling and Kalashnikov AK47s tracklining fire.

In minutes four gendarmes were dead, and the others skeetering for their lives. A thousand paces away to the north, on the slopes of Jebel Samhan, half-a-dozen rebel mortar-crews punked bombs. Tube muzzles flared. Bombs slashed damp sky across two-thousand-metre parabolas, cannonading into hard ground and soft mud buildings in Mirbat town.

Half a klick to the south-west of Labalaba's position, on the roof of the rambling BATT-house, Captain Mike Kealy and his crew heard the thump, saw the spurt of flame from the gun-pit. They clocked muzzle-flak from the direction of Jebel 'Ali, heard the clack of small-arms fire, heard enemy mortar-shells shilling over and chundering in. Tracer blickered out of the half-light, riddling sandbags, whiplashing sand. An 84mm anti-tank rocket rasped air, howled overhead.

For a second, BATT-boss Kealy couldn't get his head round the scene. A twenty-seven-year-old former Queens Regiment officer from Farnborough, he'd been with the Regiment only a year, and this was his first taste of action. His first thought was that the Firgat he'd sent out two days ago had come in, and got into a blue-on-blue shooting-match with the guard. He was quickly put right when his radio-op, Tpr. 'Tak' Takavesi – another Fijian – reported that the forty-strong Firgat was still out on the coastal plain. This told Kealy two things. First, that they were about to get bumped by a large and well-supported rebel force. Second, that, since there were few 'Firgat-men' in town, its defence was down to his eight-man SAS-team and about thirty poorly-trained Omani gendarmes.

Kealy heard nearby gumfs of fire, and took a moment to click that Tpr. Harris was letting rip with the team's own three-inch mortar in the sangar below. Bombs dopplered towards the ridge. Concussions kettledrummed at two-second intervals. An instant later the General Purpose Machine-Gun and the half-inch Browning dug into sandbagged positions on the roof, ruckled fire. Behind the Gimpie, Tpr. Pete Wignall hooked steel, high-angled 7.62mm tracer. On the Browning, Tpr. Roger Chapman cracked off rounds. Brass cases chinged on roof boards. Cordite fumes lufted. The Gimpie brattled drumfire. The Browning throbbed.

At the gun-pit, the shroud of enemy gunfire was shifting closer, slugs splotching shoffs of sand around Labalaba and Walid. The rebels weren't yet on the perimeter wire, but they soon would be. Two gendarmes in the ammo-pit behind them were belting rounds through the fence. One of them was hit and snapped off his feet. The other stopped firing. Labalaba boosted another round into the breech. Walid grunted, staggered, hurled blood. Labalaba saw him go down out of the corner of his eye, but whamped the shell into the chamber, locked it closed, fired the gun. The round sledgehammered out, whoofing smoke as the barrel jerked back. Labalaba yokked the breech open, ejected the case, grabbed another shell. AK47 rounds mosquitoed, scalloping sandbags. Labalaba felt a smacking punch to the jaw, and went reeling. He blacked out for a second, and when he came round his chin didn't seem to be there any more, and his face was gushing blood.

On the BATT-house roof, Tak Takavesi glanced up from the radio, and told Kealy that Lab had just been chinned, but was all right. Tak asked permission to go and help his oppo. Kealy nodded, and told him to take medical kit. A minute later, the big Fijian burst out of the BATT-house doors, SLR in hand, and started swerving across the rocky ground. Chapman and Wignall worked frantic covering fire. The light was coming on, probing feebly through the film of drizzle. The SAS-men could see the fort and the ground beyond the wire, but the wall of Jebel Samhan was invisible two kilometres away. To the west, Kealy saw the bottle-green waters of the Arabian sea licking an ivory beach. The SAS-men watched, bated-breathed, as the rugby-playing Fijian danced and wove, miraculously dodging 7.62mm short rounds hacking stone chips around his ankles. A minute later he was in the gun-pit and out of sight.

Cpl. Bob Bradshaw, crouching behind the sandbags with his Armalite, pointed beyond the wire, where a score of figures had glommed out of the haze and were mooching towards the perimeter. The figures broke into a run, Kalashnikovs thwacking rounds. Roger Chapman cut loose fragments of fire, his gun-barrel fizzling in the rain. Kealy saw tracer flexing through the wire, shrapnelling ground, spinning in richochets. The adoo kept coming.

At the fort gun-pit, Lab was jamming another round into the gun with his jaw siling blood from under the field-dressing he'd slapped on it. The bullet had lopped half his jawbone, and he was in agony, but he kept on working, locking the breech, pounding off rounds point-blank at the wire, ker-blooming fire and smoke. Walid was curled foetus-like in a pool of blood, ashen-faced. Tak squatted against sandbags, lamping rounds at attackers nearing the wire. Lab heard missiles cropping air. The fort shuddered, dust and smoke volcanoed, small-arms salvoes clacketed, shellbursts torched scarlet and orange. Grit and debris splattered them.

On the BATT-house roof, Kealy and his men were scoping

the fort open-mouthed. For a minute it seemed to have vanished in a pyre of smoke. Kealy was certain the main attack would be directed there, and ordered Wignall to switch the Gimpie to cover it, while the rest of the team hooked fire at the attackers. The desert beyond the wire was now jumping with adoo, who had pinpointed the BATT-house as the main source of fire. Machine-gun and AK47 rounds skittered into the sangars, but no one was hit. Wignall, snapping-in bursts from the Gimpie, called for more ammo. Kealy, Cpl. Reynolds and Tpr. Tommy Tobin monkeyed down the bamboo ladder to the courtyard, formed a chain, hoisted up ammo-boxes.

Wignall saw rebels clambering up the wire, hand over hand. Bradshaw clocked a rebel officer in khakis braced on the other side, cool as a cucumber, urging his men on, waving his AK47. Bradshaw sighted-in, pinched off a shot, missed, fired again. On the third shot the officer went down. Other rebels had jumped from the top of the wire and were inside the compound, reeling towards the fort. Chapman traversed the Browning, palpitated fire. He hit one in the leg, another smack in the head. Kealy and Bradshaw potted Arabs climbing the wire. One went limp and hung there, another pitchforked forward, snagged by the legs.

Kealy had sent a contact report to Salalah earlier, but realized they needed a chopper casevac for Lab, and air-support. He knew that the Sultan's Air Force Strikemasters couldn't fly in this mist, but wanted to alert them in case there should be a window later. He safety-catched his Armalite, and slid down the wet ladder into the yard. He braced the long-distance radio, got comms with Salalah. Up on the roof, Bradshaw was trying to talk to Tak or Lab in the gun-pit, but got no response.

When Kealy climbed back on the roof, Bradshaw told him there was radio silence from the gun-pit. Kealy looked worried, and said he was going to find out what had happened there. As he belted up, Bradshaw and Chapman followed suit. Kealy stopped them, saying he would go alone. For a moment enemy fire was forgotten, and a blazing argument raged. Finally, Kealy agreed to take Tommy Tobin, who was a medic. Bradshaw pointed out that Kealy was still wearing flip-flops. 'You won't get far in those,' he said.

Kealy yanked on desert boots, and found Tobin waiting for him outside, with Harris, who was adjusting mortar-sights in the ground-level sangar. There was a lull in the shooting, and Kealy reckoned the enemy were bringing up more ammo. Still, instead of going straight across to the fort as Tak had done, he decided they'd work their way round through the wadi. It was shallow and wouldn't give much cover, but it was better than nothing.

While they were still running up the wadi, Roger Chapman saw a heli riding in on sea-mist, and realized it must be the casevac-flight. He stuffed red and green flares into his belt, left the house, and sprinted two hundred metres to the helipad near the sea. The adoo were still holding fire, and Chapman judged it safe for the chopper to come in. He lobbed a green flare, watched green smoke-coils rearing like fingers. Then, just as the aircraft drifted in, there was a reprise of fire – 12.7mm Shaogin rounds whipped up dirt across the helipad. Chapman grabbed a red flare and chucked it. The heli hived off in the nick of time, angling back across the bare water.

Kealy and Tobin hadn't seen the helicopter come in. When the enemy started shooting again they were still trotting up the wadi. Adoo rounds seared air, chocked up sand, and they flung themselves down. They started pepperpotting forward, one man humping fire, the other jogging and zigzagging, lurching into cover. They made it to the fort without a scratch. Tobin slithered into the gun-pit by Lab, Kealy dived into the ammo-pit behind. He saw the dead gendarme. The other was pressed against the sandbags, eyes bugged out, too terrified to move.

Tobin found that Tak had been wounded three times, and was losing blood, but still shooting. Lab was blood-smeared and gimlet-eyed but remained on his feet. Tobin judged Walid the worst off, and rigged up a drip, jagged a needle into his arm. Lab shimmied across into the ammo-pit to report to Kealy. His big face looked shapeless and his mouth was clogged with blood. He mumbled through the shell-dressing, telling Kealy that Tak had been hit. A bomb lumped into the rim of the pit and zapped apart, whopping them both against the sandbags. Grit fragments lacerated their skin. Enemy rounds clicked and rasped over them. They jabbed their weapons over the parapet, pitapatted double-taps. The enemy were through the wire on the right, rushing the fort. Lab crawled back to the gun, traversed it right, ramped off a shell. The gun thundershocked fire, the barrel jerked back. Lab worked like a madman, ejected the shell-case, loaded another, rammed shut the breech. A round whizzed into his skull, and he tottered and treed over the gun carriage.

Behind him, Kealy thought the final assault was coming. A grenade splatted nearby. He jerked up, saw an Arab drawing a bead on him. He slingshotted Armalite rounds at point-blank range. The Arab hit the wall of the fort, leaving a smear of blood. Another guerrilla edged in from behind the angle in the wall, and Kealy's Armalite burped again. Shell-cases sang. Stone chips zipped. The Arab vanished.

In the gun-pit, Tobin shifted Lab's body off the gun and pulled the firing lever. A twenty-five-pound shell spitfired, smoke whoffed. Tobin ratcheted the breech-handle, dropped the hot case, laid another shell, fired again. Enemy bullets zizzed into the pit. A 7.62mm slug sliced off Tobin's jaw, sawed bone-chips, spritzed blood. Kealy saw him go down, and stopped shooting. He grabbed the radio, knowing his only option was to bring both machine guns and the mortar to bear on the gun-pit.

At the BATT-house, Bradshaw had good news – he'd just got through to Salalah, and learned that the Strikemasters were coming in despite the low cloud. He heard Kealy's voice crackle on the short-range radio headset, rogered his orders to swing both guns to covering fire, and told him that the aircraft were on their way. Bradshaw instructed Chapman and Wignall to zero-in near Kealy's position, then lit off down the ladder to talk to Harris in the mortar-pit. He knew that at five hundred metres the fort was too near for the mortar's maximum elevation, and the only way was to lift it manually. He grabbed the big tube, cradled the bipod between his thighs, bent backwards until he judged the angle right. Harris slipped a bomb, and the mortar bopped. Bradshaw took the recoil braced back against the sandbags. The bomb whistled, scraped air.

Kealy heard it bump earth a few metres ahead of him, clocked a V-shaped whoosh of rock and dust, and ducked. He heard Browning and Gimpie rounds ravage dirt, shaving sandbags. Just then another grenade plopped down next to him, and Kealy pressed against the side, waiting for shrapnel to gouge his body. It never happened: the grenade failed to explode. Hardly able to believe it, Kealy popped up to spliff the thrower, and felt a slug part his hair. That was twice in seconds he'd narrowly escaped getting stitched.

Chapman was scoping the sea, and saw a Strikemaster scoring in under cloud-cover. He tuned to air-force wavelength on the SARBE, and started talking the pilot in on the fort. In the ammo-pit, Kealy heard the blast of aircraft engines, and cannon-fire wedging. He whipped the recognition-panel from his belt, laid it over the corpse of the gendarme. A dark shadow flitted over him. A second Strikemaster followed up, rolling in at roof height with cannons spitting, riddling adoo. The enemy stopped shooting and legged it to the nearest cover – the same wadi Kealy had run up. The first aircraft banked over the wadi and pitched a five-hundred-kilo bomb. Kealy couldn't see the action from his position, but at the BATT-house the boys saw the bomb drop, heard the crunch, saw dark smoke bell up and ochre sand pancake down.

Bradshaw took the Sarbe from Chapman and directed the aircraft to the picket-post on Jebel 'Ali. The Strikemasters flipped and reeled, lapped in for another run, straight on the jebel. The adoo stayed put, blattered out machine-gun and automatic fire. Adoo tracer tracked air, punched fuselage, but the planes didn't shift a centimetre. Cannon-fire gnashed, twenty-mil shells chewed dirt, notched stones, etched adoo flesh. The Strikemasters bellied up and wheeled back under the mist towards Salalah.

It was 0800 hours. At Umm al-Gawarif, men of G Squadron were mustering after breakfast ready to test-fire weapons. They'd only arrived from the UK that morning, and most of the senior NCOs and troop officers were up in the jebel, relieving B Squadron pickets. The group left for the test-firing numbered only twenty-three, but had with them almost all the squadron's General Purpose Machine-Guns, and four M79 grenade-launchers. Before they moved to the range, though, the Squadron OC, Major Alistair Morrison, was handed a signal from the emergency ops-centre set up at Salalah airfield. The group was needed urgently to relieve the team at Mirbat. Morrison told them to forget the test-firing. They would shift at once to the airfield, where three helis were waiting to lift them. They would go into action in two ten-man groups, deploying all the GPMGs.

At Mirbat, the pressure was off the fort and the gun-pit. Fire was still popping out from Jebel 'Ali, but the enemy were mostly back behind the wire. Kealy had time to tend the wounded – he wasn't a medic, but Tak talked him through. Labalaba was past help. Tobin and Walid were dying. Takavesi was plastered in blood, but still on his feet. Kealy remembered that there was a Land Rover inside the fort, and told Tak to crawl over to the gate and get the gendarmes to open up, so they could use the vehicle to move the casualties out. It was a dicey move, as they didn't know if the gendarmes still held it – the wall might have been breached on the opposite side, and the place full of adoo. When Tak called out to the gendarmes in Arabic to open, they refused. They thought it was an adoo trick.

Kealy paced down to the wadi to find out if any of the rebels had survived the bombing. While he was there, the helis carrying the G Squadron troop slooped in, wheels skimming the sea. They scooped across the beach, droning over the landing zone like giant wasps. The G Squadron men bobbed out, going straight into action, skirmishing forward, one group moving, the other firing, hashing out an overwhelming volume of ordnance from their nine Gimpies. They juggernauted into five adoo holding a ridge by the Wali's house, near the beach, spurling a weft of fire. The Arabs took hits, keeled over, snuffled dust and grit. They fell back. On the opposite side of the gendarmes' fort, beyond the wire, the handful of Firgat-men left in the town were inching in on the enemy, who were now caught in a pincer between two advancing forces. Minutes later, the whirlybirds whipped in again, landing a platoon of the Northern Frontier Regiment. Soon the rebels were in full retreat.

Kealy, shattered, and black with blood and dirt, was by now in the fort. He'd at last persuaded the gendarmes to open the door, only to find that the Land Rover had been battered by shrapnel, and was useless. As he was talking to the gendarme officer, the first G Squadron trooper arrived at the gun-pit with a Gimpie slung over his shoulders. He surveyed the carnage, saw Tobin, Walid and Tak stretched out in sand soggy with blood, the dead gendarme, the dead Labalaba, the slug-sheared sandbags, the field-gun smattered with blood, the piles of spent cases. He ate the smells of blood, dust and gunsmoke. 'Jesus wept!' he said.

A casevac heli swept in to pick up the wounded as Kealy crossed the wire and recced forward to Jebel 'Ali to see if he could spot the Firgat troop that had been out on the plain. He felt responsible for them, as he'd sent them out to follow a rebel patrol seen crossing the area two days earlier. Visibility was still down to three hundred metres, and he saw no sign of them.

He sprinted back across the perimeter, and returned to the BATT-house to find that the G Squadron men had laid out thirty-eight adoo bodies. The SAS had lost Labalaba and Tobin dead, and Takavesi badly wounded. The Sultan's Armed Forces had lost two killed and one seriously hurt. Kealy discovered later that the enemy patrol reported two days earlier had been a feint. He'd fallen into the trap by sending out the Firgat after it. In fact his SEPs ran into the retreating rebels on their way back to Mirbat, and lost four men killed.

The defence of Mirbat was the most significant defensive action the SAS Regiment had fought since Termoli, a generation earlier. It changed the course of the Oman campaign. The adoo had been hoping for a tit-for-tat show of force to counter the success of Jaguar, and had failed spectacularly. The tide of the battle had been turned by the Strikemasters, arriving just at the crucial moment when the gun-pit was on the point of being overrun by the adoo. It was consolidated by the arrival of G Squadron. Neither of these factors can detract from the sheer professionalism and grit of the BATT-team in Mirbat, who had fought to the death.

Kealy was awarded the first DSO the Regiment had won since the Jebel Akhdar, a dozen years before. Tobin was awarded a posthumous DCM, and Bradshaw an MM. These awards had been well and truly deserved, but Labalaba received only a posthumous MID, when, as almost everyone in the Regiment recognized, he deserved the VC.

The final death-toll among the enemy was reckoned to be over eighty, and the DLF/MPFLOAG cause was seriously weakened. The rebels began to lose control of the hill tribes so badly that they were obliged to resort to terror. This had the effect of pushing the fence-sitters into the hands of the government. In August and September 1972, a record number of former-DLF fighters surrendered to Sultan Qabus.

82. 'Close with the terrorists and kill them'

On Friday 8 September, three months after the battle at Mirbat, Lt. Col. Peter de la Billière was about to quit Bradbury Lines for the weekend when the telephone rang in his office. On the line was Major-General Bill Scotter, Director of Military Operations. Scotter told him that he had just had a call from Prime Minister Edward Heath, who'd asked about the army's capacity for handling terrorism. The inquiry had been sparked off by an incident that had occurred three days earlier – the murder of eleven Israeli athletes by Black September guerrillas in Munich, during the Olympic Games. The massacre, which had also resulted in the deaths of five Arabs and a German policeman, had ruthlessly exposed the inadequacy of civil police to deal with determined terrorists armed with automatic weapons. It had initiated similar queries in almost every country in Europe.

De la Billière, who had taken command of 22 SAS from Johnny Watts the previous January, already had a plan for this contingency.

One of his first actions as commanding officer had been to commission a young troop-officer, Capt. Andrew Massey, to write a proposal for setting up a counter-terrorist force. De la Billière thought Massey's plan fitted the bill, but the paper had vanished quietly into the maw of the Ministry of Defence. Now, Scotter wanted to know how long it would take to develop the unit Massey had proposed.

De la Billière's first question was how much cash would be available. The DMO astonished him by saying that money was no object – a phrase de la Billière had scarcely if ever heard uttered previously in relation to the British army. He was so taken aback that he told Scotter the force would be ready in five weeks.

The estimate was not as ambitious as it sounded. 22 SAS had already created a counter-revolutionary warfare (CRW) cell, though it currently consisted of only one officer, responsible for monitoring terrorism world-wide. The Regiment had been practising VIP protection and bodyguard techniques for years, and had covered most of the groundwork needed for anti-terrorist duties. In May, some of these skills had been put into action on a joint SAS/SBS mission. A team had dropped by parachute into the Atlantic ocean, to search the liner *QE2*, in response to an anonymous telephone call claiming she'd been rigged with explosives. The call turned out to be a hoax, but the exercise provided valuable experience. The Regiment was already geared to terrorist ops: all that was required was the necessary organization and transport.

The project was designated 'Op Pagoda'. De la Billière put it in the hands of Massey, who selected twenty SAS-men from all four sabre-squadrons, and housed them together in a separate block at Bradbury Lines, on constant stand-by. They were supplied with four Range Rovers straight off the production line, and four black Austins. Known initially as the 'Special Projects' team, they were trained in hostage-rescue drills in the Killing House, where the new focus was on distinguishing hostage from kidnapper, and taking out multiple opponents. The team practised for hours every day with live ammunition until they were capable of operating in all conceivable circumstances. 'Our aim was to instil so much precision and drill into them,' de la Billière said, 'that in emergencies the chances of emotion and fear influencing their judgement was reduced to a minimum.'[1]

The prototype team was ready in the five weeks de la Billière had requested, but no one was really satisfied with the result. Sgt. Ken Connor, who was brought in by Massey to improve standards, felt that many of the techniques already acquired on bodyguard and VIP training had been ignored. Under Massey and Connor, the team was reduced to a sixteen-man troop. They were equipped with black overalls, without body-armour, and wore their 9mm Browning pistols in standard belts. Technology was kept deliberately simple, on the 'Spartan's sword' principle – that the key to success was high-level training rather than hi-tech kit.[2] Shortly, the Special Projects team was placed under the counter-revolutionary warfare cell, which was expanded by four NCOs and charged with the further development of anti-terrorist methods.

Anti-terrorist operations were broken down into phases. The first necessity was gaining entry into the building, ship, train, aircraft or bus. Remington shotguns were acquired to blow off locks or hinges, and plastic-explosive 'frame-charges' developed for blowing in doors and windows. The CRW cell also went to work, Jock Lewes style, on a 'stun-grenade' that would be powerful enough to disorient terrorists without wounding or killing hostages. The final product, developed by the British army's nuclear-biological-and-chemical warfare establishment at Porton Down, was a six-inch by three-inch 'flashbang' made up of magnesium particles and fulminate of mercury. The bomb wouldn't harm hostages, but delivered a tremendous detonation and a fifty-thousand-watt flash. Later models were designed to detonate six times in succession.

Gas would play a major role in hostage-type scenarios. Like all British soldiers, the SAS were already trained in operating in CS and CR gas environments, but worked on improving their resistance without respirators. The Pagoda team was issued with the US-made Ingram M10/11, and later the Heckler & Koch MP5, which fired from a fixed bolt position, and could be dropped or bashed without going off. Porton Down also developed a special anti-terrorist bullet that would lodge in the enemy's body rather than passing through it and killing a hostage.

As commanding officer, it was de la Billière's job to sell the new CRW concept, not only to VIPs, but also to the police. The SAS might be highly trained, but they lacked police powers. The police would retain primacy in any terrorist situation, and the SAS couldn't be called in unless the chief police officer on the ground requested their assistance directly from the Home Secretary.

One of de la Billière's first actions was to invite senior police officers to Bradbury Lines to see the anti-terrorist team in action, and to work out ways of operating in concert. From these early visits there developed a regular two-day seminar for senior police officers. 'There were a thousand and one details to be tied up,' de la Billière recalled. 'We had to be able to communicate with the police efficiently by radio, and, at the ordinary human level, to get to know our opposite numbers.'[3]

The association with the police eventually blossomed into monthly joint exercises, controlled at high-level from COBR – the Cabinet Office Briefing Room – sited in a subterranean vault beneath Whitehall, where a junior cabinet minister would preside over representatives of the various services, military and civil. One vital command innovation was that during a terrorist threat, the Director, SAS, would sit on the Cabinet Office Committee with the Prime Minister and Home Secretary, in place of the army's Chief of the General Staff.

The SP team – eventually redesignated the Anti-Terrorist team – wasn't entirely secret. From the start, it entertained visiting VIPs, who would take the part of 'principals' or 'hostages' in live firing exercises in the Killing House. Over the next three years, it worked out a modus operandi. If a terrorist incident occurred, the team would be recalled to camp on a bleeper device with a thirty-mile range. After a briefing by the team-leader, they would move fast to the scene of the incident in Range Rovers, which were fitted with strengthened chassis and anti-roll bars. If the site was more than three hours' driving away, the team would be moved by helicopter or Hercules C130 transport aircraft. On arriving at the target area, they divided into a 'method of entry' squad, who would deal with locks, doors and windows, a back-up squad, consisting of trained snipers, who would secure the perimeter, and an assault squad, who would enter the tactical area. The ultimate aim was to secure the release of the hostages, not take out the terrorists, though there was always an Immediate Action plan should they start killing hostages. 'The IA plan would be very simple,' wrote an early member of the SP team, Barry Davies, 'close with the terrorists as quickly as possible, and kill them.'[4]

83. 'Not a very pretty sight!'

Sgt. Peter 'Billy' Ratcliffe didn't hear the mortar-bomb that killed his mate Tpr. Chris Hennessy and wounded two others. The adoo were using straight high-explosive bombs that made hardly any noise until an instant before impact. Ratcliffe, on his third tour in Dhofar, knew it was no use throwing yourself down – if the bomb was near enough you'd be vaporized just the same. Ratcliffe was a career soldier whose life had begun the day he'd joined the Parachute Regiment. Born in the slums of Salford, the son of a bread-delivery man, he had enlisted to escape from a broken home and numerous run-ins with the police. In the Airborne Forces Depot he'd passed out champion recruit. Now he was a senior NCO in the world's top special forces unit, 'a far cry,' he wrote,' . . . from the snotty-nosed kid who had grown up in abject poverty . . . with a more than even chance of ending up in jail'.[1]

He had been filling sandbags about twenty-five metres from the main sangar when the bomb struck. One moment he was watching three men shovelling sand, the next they were all bowled flat by the blast. Ratcliffe staggered back to the sangar to find that Hennessy had been shredded – his guts and bits of his flesh were smeared across the rocks. The mortar-bomb had grooved down his torso, hit the deck and blattered apart, scattering body parts up to sixty feet. Next to what was left of Hennessy's body, the signaller lay squirming and shrieking in shock and pain. He'd been right next to Hennessy when the bomb clumped, and had taken shrapnel fragments all over – his face, legs, chest and arms looked as if they'd been flayed. His skin was a moonscape of raw flesh. Later, it was the smell that Ratcliffe remembered. 'The smell of fresh blood and splashed-about entrails is much stronger than most people could possibly imagine,' he wrote, 'and it is not only extremely unpleasant but also extremely unsettling . . . [it's] something you never ever get used to.'[2]

Ratcliffe grabbed the medical pack and broke it open, trying to staunch the signaller's worst wounds with one hand while he fished for a morphine syrette with the other. At that moment he clocked the third man, Tpr. 'Killer' Denis, who was sprawled out inside the sangar. He was huddled against the stone wall, stark naked but for his boots and socks. For some reason the blast had shagged off his uniform, but left him unhurt except for a peppering of shrapnel in the backside. Ratcliffe stared at Denis for a second, and then felt his body quaking with laughter. An instant later, he was almost rolling around, roaring with mirth. 'Fuck me, Denis,' he grunted. 'That's not a very pretty sight!'

Denis exploded, both of them bellowing and snorting until the tears streamed down their cheeks, their howls of glee fusing with the signaller's shrieks. Ratcliffe reflected later that anyone listening to the noise would have thought they'd taken leave of their senses. It was no disrespect to the dead Hennessy or the wounded signaller: Ratcliffe later realized the explosion of laughter was caused by the after-effects of shock.

In was October 1975, and D Squadron was on its last tour in Dhofar. The war was almost over – all but fifty or sixty adoo had evacuated the jebel and withdrawn back across the border. Ratcliffe and his patrol were manning the 'Green Five' sangar at Simba in the Qamar mountains – a two-kilometre square redoubt of bunkers and machine-gun posts on the arid western end of the Dhofar range, overlooking the coastal settlement of Hauf. From these crags, the Arabian sea looked like finely tempered ultramarine glass, the buildings of Hauf like clay models, the roads like dark pencil-lines. D Squadron's main task was to watch and eventually cut the supply-route that ran within a mile of their position, along which the enemy moved camel-trains laden with weapons to the last knots of resistance on the mountains.

Hauf currently belonged to Yemen, but was traditionally part of Dhofar, and Sultan Qabus had claimed it back. His main offensive was due at the end of the monsoon, but the previous day Ratcliffe and his mates from D Squadron had watched a preliminary assault on the town by Hawker Hunters of the Sultan's Air Force, and a bombardment by the Sultan's artillery.

Ratcliffe's troop on Simba had worked as forward air-controllers, vectoring the jets in. Not a single bomb missed its target. The bombing and a ten-hour barrage from five-and-a-half-inch guns had made the rebels hopping mad. The next day they'd opened up on Simba with 81mm mortars and Russian-made Katyusha rocket-launchers, from four kilometres away. By luck or good-shooting they'd managed to lob a bomb right on to Green Five.

Chris Hennessy's body and the two wounded men were choppered out that night, and replaced a couple of days later by two more – a fresh-faced trooper called 'Ginge' and another named 'Ian' – like Ratcliffe, an ex-Para. When they arrived, Ratcliffe and three other men from his troop were still filling sandbags, trying to strengthen the sangar. The replacements hadn't been there more than ten minutes when the position was hit by a pair of Katyusha rockets.

Unlike the mortar bombs, you could hear the Katyushas twanging two seconds before they hit. One of the rockets whamped into the rocks about two hundred metres away, and erupted in a blotch of fire. Ratcliffe heard the second whining in, and realized it was heading for the sangar, where the two replacements were just dumping their Bergens. 'Incoming!' he screeched. The two men scooted in opposite directions – Ginge straight into the missile's trajectory. To Ratcliffe it looked as if an invisible hand had scooped him up and dashed him against the wall. By the time the bomb exploded, Ginge was already dead from the impact.[3]

Like Hennessy, Ginge had been ripped apart by the explosion. Ratcliffe's immediate reaction was the feeling that he wanted to grab his weapon, rush down into the hills and slaughter any adoo he came across. He had the strength to control himself, though, knowing that he'd never find the rebels – even if he tasked a chopper to seek them out, it would be shot down. All he and his mates could do was wait for the big offensive.

Between November and December that year two hundred and twenty-two adoo surrendered to the Sultan – a record number, more even than during the amnesty three years earlier. Defensive lines, with wire and minefields, were set up, and by January the supply-line from Hauf was finally cut. On the jebel, mopping-up operations revealed huge arms caches and complete field hospitals set up inside caves. At last, after fourteen years of conflict, and centuries of neglect, Dhofar was declared safe for civil development. 22 SAS had suffered a dozen dead and many wounded, but no one in the outside world even knew they'd been fighting there.

Peter Ratcliffe, who'd seen two of his comrades blown to pieces within forty-eight hours, felt that the experience had changed him. After this there would be nothing war could throw at him that he couldn't handle.

84. 'Al Capone gangsterism'

The Anti-Terrorist team was first sent into action under de la Billière's successor as commanding officer Lt. Col. Tony Jeapes – one of the architects of SAS success in the Dhofar campaign. Jeapes had taken over in early 1974. By then, the Pagoda team had grown to a full squadron. Rather than having a permanent specialist unit, the SAS head-shed had decided to rotate squadrons through the role in turn – this system meant that every man in the Regiment would acquire counter-terrorist training and experience, and the constant turnover would ensure that the squad didn't get stale.

Within a year the SP team was called out on its first mission – an aircraft hijacking at Manchester. The hijacker, an Iranian, demanded to be flown to Paris. The Pagoda team suggested flying him to Stansted, where they had the plane talked down by a French air traffic controller and posted men on the ground in the uniforms of French police. When the aircraft came in, they stormed aboard, took the Iranian down, and bundled him out. It turned out that his pistol was a replica.

That winter, a Provisional IRA unit that had been active in London for months tried to assassinate ex-Prime Minister Edward Heath by placing a bomb under his car. The bomb failed to go off, and was spotted by a taxi-driver who pulled into Heath's parking-space as he drove out. Only days later, the same four men – Tom O'Connell, Edward Butler, Henry Duggan and Hugh Doherty – bombed Scott's restaurant in Mayfair, killing two customers and injuring a dozen more. Angered by the fact that the restaurant had promptly reopened, the gang made the mistake of hitting the place again in December, opening fire on it with a 9mm Sten-gun from the window of a stolen Ford Cortina.

Unfortunately for them, the restaurant was under observation by a couple of plainclothes police officers, who immediately jumped into a cab and ordered the driver to give chase. They trailed the vehicle into Balcombe Street, a cul-de-sac near Marylebone Station, where the terrorists abandoned the car and broke into a flat owned by John Matthews and his wife, whom they took hostage. The street was quickly cordoned off by armed police. The SAS Special Projects team was called in.

The siege went on for six days. As it happened, the chief police negotiator had been involved in SAS operations before most of the SP squad were even born. He was Assistant Commissioner Ernest Bond, formerly Sgt. Ernie Bond of L Detachment, who had served under David Stirling in 8 Commando and had been on the ill-fated Bombay flown by Charlie West, shot down on Operation Squatter. Bond believed that the PIRA-men holed up in the Matthews' flat were responsible for forty bombings and fifteen murders, and wanted to capture them alive. His opportunity came when the terrorists heard a BBC radio announcement that the SAS team was poised to strike. They surrendered the same day.

Though the Balcombe Street siege ended without violence, it sparked off a new wave of terror in Northern Ireland. On 19 December, three Catholics were gunned down by Loyalists in a bar at Silverbridge, County Armagh. Two weeks later, the Provisional IRA bombed a bar at Gifford, County Down, killing three Protestants. At Whitecross, Loyalists slaughtered five Catholic members of the Socialist and Democratic Labour Party. The following day, a band of twenty Provos stopped a bus carrying Protestant linen-workers from Bessbrook, at Kingsmills Junction. The workers were dragged out, lined up in the road and mown down with sub-machine guns. Ten were shot to pieces; the eleventh was badly wounded, but survived.

The 'Kingsmills Massacre' – condemned by Northern Ireland Secretary Merlyn Rees as 'Al Capone gangsterism' – was one of the most vicious mass-murders of the Troubles. It provoked outrage from Loyalist politicians, who demanded that Prime Minister Harold Wilson take immediate steps to deal with the escalating violence, especially in the border area, where the Provisional IRA was out of control. Within forty-eight hours of the Kingsmills incident, Wilson had announced that the SAS would be deployed on patrol and surveillance duties in South Armagh.

85. 'Never a happy hunting-ground'

Around noon on 7 January 1976, the second-in-command of 22 SAS, Major 'G', was enjoying a quiet drink in the Cross Keys pub in King's Road, Chelsea, when he heard Wilson's announcement on televison. He gulped down his drink and hurried back to SAS Group Headquarters in nearby Duke of York's Barracks, where his phone shortly buzzed. It was the Director, SAS, Brigadier Johnny Watts, who inquired if he'd heard the report on TV and if he knew anything about the deployment of the SAS in Northern Ireland. Major 'G', temporarily in command of the Regiment while the CO was wrapping up in Dhofar, confessed that he didn't.

He was not alone. Watts was soon carpeted at the Ministry of Defence, where an irate Chief of the General Staff, General Sir Michael Carver, virtually accused him of going over his head to get the SAS sent into action in Armagh. In fact, Watts was no more in the Prime Minister's loop than anyone else in the MoD. His real concern was that 22 SAS simply didn't have the men to meet Wilson's pledge. Of the Regiment's four squadrons, one was still in Dhofar, another on a key NATO exercise in Europe, a third on Pagoda duties, and the fourth, D Squadron, dispersed on courses and small-group missions all over the world. Though the press speculated that the number of SAS-men sent to Northern Ireland was in the hundreds, the initial party consisted of only eleven sabre personnel, mostly instructors from the Training Wing, or men on convalescent leave after being wounded in Oman.

The SAS party was allotted quarters at Bessbrook Mill, a British army base since the early 70s, currently the HQ of the local battalion, 1 Royal Scots. A former linen-mill, it was a solid, castle-like structure with watchtowers, anti-mortar screens and a helipad, set in the rolling green meadows and undulating gorse-covered moors of South Armagh. Nearby Bessbrook village was a Quaker enclave in a largely Catholic border area that was known as 'Bandit Country'. The Provisional IRA units in the area were the most ruthless in the Province, and had to date taken out forty-nine British soldiers, the majority by radio-controlled bombs. They hadn't suffered a single casualty.

The SAS planned to change all that. They drew up a list of eleven top PIRA chiefs in South Armagh, planning to hunt them down and arrest them if possible, or shoot them if necessary. On the surface, their task didn't seem far removed from the counter-insurgency work the SAS had done in Malaya, Borneo and Dhofar.

In practice, the crucial 'hearts and minds' element was missing. They had won over Ibans and Muruts in Borneo, and Jebalis in Oman, but the Catholic population of Armagh nursed a hatred of British forces that had become ingrained in their culture over generations.

On the other hand, SAS patrols couldn't adopt the aggressive fighting tactics that had served them so well in jungle and desert. In Borneo they had hit the enemy across the Indonesian frontier, but here they were not allowed to enter the Republic of Ireland – the natural resort of any terrorist under pursuit. They were also restricted to the same rules of engagement as any other British unit in the Province. They could open fire only if they had reason to believe a person was about to endanger life and there was no other means of stopping them, or if they had just killed or injured someone and there was no other way of making an arrest. Even then, shooting was only permissible after a warning.

It was months before the SAS contingent built up to squadron strength. Some of the men came hot-foot from Dhofar, and lacked any special training for the Northern Ireland situation. 'They came from the jebel and wadis of an Arabian kingdom where open warfare existed,' Major 'G' commented, 'and on to the streets of the United Kingdom, full of political and military restrictions and limitations. They had gone from one extreme to the other.'[1]

From the start, the Regiment was caught in a knot of conflicting expectations. Their deployment had been accompanied by a blaze of media hype, including a twelve-minute BBC documentary showing SAS-men in training at Hereford. Hardliners saw the unit as a 'death-squad' brought in as a final resort to teach the terrorists a lesson they wouldn't forget. Some even believed that the SAS shouldn't be confined to the rules of engagement, and should be immune from prosecution. At the same time, the SAS was subject to closer-than-usual scrutiny by civil rights watchers and radicals, who regarded it as a fox let loose in the chicken-coop. 'Is South Armagh so short of terrorist gangs . . . that it needs a new one to be imported?' wrote journalist Claud Cockburn in the *Irish Times*. '. . . The SAS became famous during World War II and their deeds were treated as heroic rather than reprehensible. All such actions are applauded in an acknowledged war by people who find them horrifying or illegitimate unless a genuine war is going on. Now the Government is in the awkward position of . . . denying that it is waging war and yet defending the use of forces such as the SAS.'2

The Prime Minister's statement specified that the Regiment would operate 'in uniform' and carry the standard weapons issued to the British army. The rest of the army greeted their arrival with suspicion and resentment: the deployment of the SAS carried the implication that orthodox strategy had failed. Yet the Regiment was expected to clean up 'Bandit Country' following the same rules that had led to the problems in the first place. The SAS attitude was that they could either play it their way or go home.

At first the troop patrolled the rolling gorse-covered downs, woods and meadows, wearing camouflage and carrying Bergens. They set up covert hides in hedgerows or copses, watching the movement of suspects in villages or isolated farmhouses, lugging in all their equipment. They manned the hides for up to ten days, without cooking or smoking, bagging excrement, peeing into plastic containers, talking in whispers. That they didn't intend to confine themselves to this role, though, became evident when, within weeks of their insertion, they arrested Sean McKenna, a PIRA-man believed responsible for two attempted murders, two bomb-blasts, kidnapping and possession of firearms.

In the early hours of 12 March, twenty-two-year-old McKenna was roused from sleep by two men wearing civilian jackets over combat trousers who had entered his house through a window and kicked in his bedroom door. One of them held a Browning 9mm pistol to his head and explained that if he put up a struggle or refused to come with them, he would immediately be 'stitched'.

Outside the house, the intruders were joined by a third man with a Sterling sub-machine gun. Though the men were evidently British soldiers, McKenna's house lay at Edentubber near Dundalk, in the Republic of Ireland, about a quarter of a mile south of the border, where the British had no jurisdiction. McKenna was escorted over the border and taken to Bessbrook RUC station, eventually receiving a twenty-five-year sentence for his offences. The official story was that he'd been arrested wandering about, drunk, in a field on the British side.

The SAS were able to pick up McKenna because they had access to intelligence of a higher grade than that provided by the local battalion. Major 'G' had been aware from the outset that the conditions under which they were supposed to function violated two of the three key principles of SAS operations: command at the highest level and intelligence at the highest level. In Armagh the SAS came under the commanding officer of 1 Royal Scots, and was limited to the intel provided by the battalion's intelligence officer. It was to circumvent this that Capt. Robert Nairac was brought in.

Nairac, whose murder by the IRA a year later would become a cause célèbre, was not and had never been an SAS officer. Since the Regiment's first tour in Ulster, small groups of SAS-men had been working in the Province, mainly assigned intelligence duties. In late 1973 the SAS had helped set up a new undercover squad known as the Army Surveillance Unit – later 14 Intelligence Company. The unit had been developed from the SAS Northern Ireland cell by Captain Julian 'Tony' Ball, an ex-Parachute Regiment private who'd been commissioned in the Kings Own Scottish Borderers after serving in the ranks of 22 SAS. Another brainchild of Frank Kitson, lately commanding 39 Brigade in Belfast, the Unit had been created in recognition of the fact that SAS-men couldn't pass themselves off as natives of Northern Ireland. As one ex-SAS commanding officer commented, at close quarters, even in plain-clothes, they tended to stand out.

In effect, the Army Surveillance Unit was an 'SAS' squad raised for a specific environment, of the type envisaged years ago by Mike Calvert when creating the Malayan Scouts. Within a decade it would have become a fully-fledged member of the UK Special Forces Group. It recruited men – and eventually women – from other army units, and put them through a special selection. Designed and run by SAS staff, the course was highly demanding but without the long marches and heavy Bergens of SAS Selection proper. The Unit operated in three detachments, each assigned to the area covered by one of the three PIRA 'Brigades', and in its role of undercover surveillance it was highly successful.

Nairac had worked closely with Tony Ball in setting up the unit that later became '14 Int.' but according to witnesses never actually served with it. When the D Squadron troop was posted to Bessbrook, he was back with the Grenadier Guards in Britain. 'G' requested him specifically to act as liaison officer between the SAS and the RUC Special Branch. 'Nairac was invaluable to us,' he wrote, 'in knowing . . . routes to Special Branch . . . They gave us the help that did enable us to apprehend five of the eleven top names on our list within two or three months. That was still with our eleven men . . .'[3]

The second terrorist Nairac fingered was Peter Cleary, a staff captain of PIRA's 1 Battalion in Armagh. Cleary had already been arrested by British forces and had since fled to the Republic, where he'd been given a three-year suspended sentence for firearms possession. In February, masked men in civilian clothes turned up at Cleary's house in Belleek, on the northern side of the border, looking for him. They claimed to be Provisional IRA-men, but Cleary's family tumbled them from their English accents, and believed they were SAS.

In April, after three soldiers of 1 Royal Scots were blown up by a landmine in Belleek, the SAS found out from Nairac that Cleary was in the habit of visiting his fiancée, Shirley Hulme, in his sister's house at Tievecrum, fifty metres north of the frontier. An SAS team staked out the house for three days, cammed up in a ditch nearby. At 1700 hours on the third day they spotted Cleary approaching the house, but stayed put until they were sniffed out by dogs, and clocked by a curious member of the family who shone a torch into the ditch. One of the SAS-men fired a shot in the air, and they closed in on the house. Cleary was identified by a man in civilian clothes – probably Nairac. They dragged the PIRA-man off to a field nearby, to await the arrival of a helicopter. Less than an hour after leaving the house, Cleary was dead.

According to SAS witnesses, all but one of the patrol went off to put down landing lights for the chopper, leaving Cleary alone with a single guard – an officer – armed with an SLR. Just as the heli approached, Cleary suddenly leapt at his minder and tried to grab the weapon. The SAS officer opened fire at hard-contact range, blamming off three shots. Cleary dropped dead at his feet.

The shooting of Peter Cleary caused the first furore of the Regiment's sojourn in Ulster. His family claimed that the SAS had beaten him up in a barn before pulling him off to the field, from where, only ten minutes later, they'd heard gunshots. The SAS said that Cleary had attempted to escape at the house, obliging them to restrain him by force, and that fifty-five minutes elapsed between quitting the house and the shooting incident. For many, Cleary's death only confirmed that the SAS was operating as a 'murder squad'. 'Shot resisting arrest' seemed an obvious euphemism for deliberate execution.

Major 'G' admitted that some of the D Squadron boys arrived in Northern Ireland from Dhofar with a 'hard-nosed attitude', but pointed out that Cleary was too vital a resource to be shot out of hand. 'In a tactical sense it was our loss too,' he said. 'It was the last thing we wanted.'[4]

Very soon, though, the Cleary shooting was eclipsed by a scandal that brought into question the Regiment's very competence. It began on 5 May, when two soldiers of D Squadron were halted by officers of the Garda Siochana – the Irish police – seven hundred metres across the frontier, in an unmarked Triumph 2000. The driver, Tpr. John Lawson, was wearing a brown pullover and a white shirt, and carrying a Browning 9mm pistol. The passenger, Cpl. Illisoni Ligari, a six-foot-two Fijian nicknamed 'Horse', who had taken part in Keeni-Meeni ops in Aden, was wearing a white overcoat. He was carrying a loaded Sterling sub-machine gun on his knees, hidden under a map.

The men had crossed the border on the Newry–Dundalk road at about 2240 hours at a point code-named 'Hotel One', apparently unaware that there was a concealed checkpoint a little further on. When flagged down by Sgt. Patrick McLoughlin and Garda

Murray, who were covered by a platoon of Irish soldiers, Lawson said they'd made a map-reading error. McLoughlin informed them that they'd brought firearms across the border illegally, and that he was arresting them under Section 30 of the Offences against the State Act. They were escorted to the Garda station at Omeath.

Less than an hour later, McLoughlin and Murray stopped a Hillman Avenger and a Vauxhall Victor crossing the border at the same point. The cars were carrying another half-dozen D Squadron men, two of whom wore camouflage gear, the rest civvies. One man carried a sawn-off Remington shotgun, and the others Browning pistols or Sterlings. The driver of the first car, thirty-two-year-old Tpr. Vincent Thompson, told the police that they were looking for their two mates, who hadn't reported in.

McLoughlin replied that their comrades were in custody, and inquired how they'd come to cross an international border. Thompson said that they must have taken a wrong turn. When the sergeant ordered them to hand over their weapons, their senior rank, thirty-four-year-old Staff Sgt. Malcolm Rees, ex-3 Para, instructed the men not to comply. It was only when the cars were surrounded by Irish troops that the SAS-men finally submitted. They appeared in court in Dublin the following day, and were released on £40,000 bail.

They were flown back to Bessbrook by chopper, where D Squadron's OC, Major Brian Baty, MM, a former corporal commissioned in the Argyll & Sutherland Highlanders, ordered them straight to Aldergrove to be interrogated by the army's Special Investigation Department. The other men in the troop protested that they shouldn't be treated like criminals, but Baty was unsympathetic and ignored them, creating a near-mutiny. It was only when Director SAS Johnny Watts and the Regiment's CO flew out to Bessbrook that the situation calmed down. Watts and the colonel told the group that if the men were put on trial, they would both resign.

In fact, the SAS-men were caught in a cleft stick. If they admitted that they'd been ordered into the Irish Republic on a mission, it could cause a major breach in diplomatic relations. The only possible alternative was to persist in the 'map-reading error' scenario, which would hold them up to public ridicule.

The episode set off the biggest press-bonanza yet. Some British newspapers were disgusted with the Garda, who they said could easily have turned a blind eye and sent the SAS back. The *Sunday Times* linked the incident with the human rights case being brought against the British government by the Irish in the European Court at Strasbourg, over alleged torture of IRA suspects. The *Guardian* called it a 'border pantomime'. The IRA hailed it as an indication that British troops were involved in clandestine activities within the Republic.

What the SAS were actually doing on the wrong side of the border has never been explained. The whisper in SAS circles was that it really was a map-reading error, but the indignation of the other D Squadron men at their OC's asperity suggests that the teams were acting under orders: it has been said that they were hunting for a group of Irish National Liberation Front prisoners who had just escaped from Long Kesh.

At the trial in Dublin a year later, Major Brian Baty told the court that he'd given orders for 'a surveillance party' to be mounted that night, but that SAS personnel were subject to the same rules as the rest of the army – that is, they were forbidden to cross the border. In the event, the 'map-reading error' story was accepted, and the court fined them £100 each. Neither Watts nor the commanding officer resigned. The real damage, though, was already done. 'If that's the elite then what the fuck must the rest of us be like?' wrote Lt. Anthony Clarke, whose battalion, 3 Para, took over from 1 Royal Scots at Bessbrook that April. 'Cowboys the lot of them; there are some guys I've recognized who failed our selection . . . so how did they get in the SAS? I wouldn't give them the time of day . . . They are a joke.'[5]

Though South Armagh was much quieter at the end of the first SAS tour, it was mainly because the bulk of the terrorists had simply moved out – a phenomenon familiar to the SAS from their time in Malaya. Many vets of Borneo and Dhofar couldn't come to terms with the legal niceties involved every time they squeezed a trigger. Just as Johnny Cooper had done sixteen years earlier, some sought greener pastures as contract soldiers in the Middle East, or with the burgeoning private security industry. Looked at from the inside, the first deployment of the SAS in Northern Ireland had not been a great success. 'It was never a happy hunting-ground for the Regiment,' Major 'G' said. 'It wasn't our scene.'[6]

86. 'What the SAS are employed to do'

When Peter de la Billière took over from Johnny Watts as Director, SAS, at the end of 1978, the Regiment's reputation was at an all-time low. In Northern Ireland, the catalogue of errors that had begun with the arrest of the eight D Squadron men had continued on subsequent tours with the apparent flouting of the rules of engagement, and the shooting of innocent civilians. Each case had been turned into political capital by the Provisional IRA.

De la Billière's first problem was to deal with a court-case brought against Cpl. Alan Bohan and Tpr. Ron Temperley for the killing of sixteen-year-old John Boyle at Dunloy, in County Antrim, that July. It was the first time SAS-men had been charged with murder. The two soldiers were part of a four-man patrol staking out an arms-cache in a graveyard. Concealed under a fallen tombstone, the hoard consisted of an Armalite rifle, a pistol, an incendiary bomb, a combat jacket and a face-mask, wrapped in a plastic bag. At mid-morning on 10 July, a teenage boy named John Boyle approached the hiding-place. According to the soldiers, he took the Armalite from the cache and pointed it at them. Believing that Boyle was about to open fire, they shot him four times, killing him instantly.

The problem, it turned out, was that the victim, John Boyle, was the person who'd reported the existence of the weapons in the first place. He had come across them while exploring the graveyard the previous day, and had immediately told his father, Cornelius, a local farm-labourer. After examining the cache for himself, Cornelius had phoned the police at Ballymoney, who had dispatched Detective Constable George Millar to inspect it. Millar had passed on the intel to the army, and the SAS team had been tasked to keep it under observation.

De la Billière had no doubt that his men had acted in good faith, and believed their story that the boy had pointed the gun at them. He was sensitive, he said, to the terrible responsibility placed on soldiers in life or death situations in Northern Ireland, and was convinced that John Boyle knew about the weapons because he was a low-grade operative of the IRA. In reality, no connection was ever found between any of the Boyle family and the Provisionals. In his eagerness to be seen as loyal to his men, de la Billière also ignored the fact that it was through John Boyle that the find had been reported to the police.

The original autopsy had suggested that Boyle had been shot in the back, but de la Billière asked for a second examination, which disproved the allegation. Boyle had probably returned to the place simply because he was curious about the guns he'd found. The most likely scenario was that he'd lifted the rifle from the bag and stood up, facing the hidden soldiers. Seeing the rifle in his hands, the SAS-men thought the rules of engagement fulfilled, and shot him. As it turned out, they had not been in any danger, since though fitted with a magazine, the Armalite wasn't loaded. Evidently John Boyle had neither the means nor the intention of shooting them, though Bohan and Temperley didn't necessarily know this at the time.

The judge, Ulster Chief Justice Lord Lowry, dismissed Bohan's statement that Boyle had pointed the rifle at the soldiers as 'self-justificatory and untrue'. While Temperley testified that the RUC had told them during the briefing that the cache had been discovered by 'a ten-year-old boy', this was denied by DC Millar, who insisted he'd made clear that the information had come from a family 'with children between the ages of ten and twenty-four'. When asked why this didn't appear in his written statement, Millar said that his original testimony had been altered by the Director of Public Prosecutions, and that he'd signed the final document on the assumption that this part had been 'omitted for legal reasons'. Finally, Lowry acquitted the two SAS-men of homicide, but criticized Sgt. Bohan as 'an untrustworthy witness'. It was clear that in the SAS story facts had been 'modified' to suit the circumstances, and, no matter how well-intentioned, that the two men had killed an innocent schoolboy.

In court, Bohan had lost his temper when the prosecution suggested that he'd been ordered to 'shoot the person who approached the cache because he was likely to be a terrorist'. It was not a question of 'orders' but of mental attitude. The SAS were geared to fast, aggressive action when they saw lethal weapons in other people's hands. This solution had served them well snap-shooting at Communists in the jungle, but it was not right for Northern Ireland.

De la Billière pointed out that if Boyle *had* been an armed terrorist the two soldiers might now be dead instead of him, and if they'd allowed him to escape they would have been accused of incompetence. This was true, but didn't negate the fact that soldiers are always obliged to make moral decisions on the legitimacy of their targets. Even in Malaya, Borneo or Oman, where the Regiment had operated outside the law, the killing of non-combatants wouldn't have been any more acceptable. Lofty Large, who, in Borneo, had refrained from ambushing an Indonesian longboat because it carried women and possibly children, never regretted his decision, despite discovering later that he'd missed an important target. 'Neither I nor any man in the British army had ever intentionally made war upon women and children,' he wrote. 'I saw no reason to change.'[1] Later, in the Falklands conflict, Sgt. Peter Ratcliffe would vow to get rid of a corporal who'd opened fire on civilians, telling him, 'anybody would think we're a gang of psychopaths'.

Despite the controversy surrounding D Squadron's first emergency deployment in South Armagh, though, the Regiment was judged too good a resource to dispense with. The use of the SAS fitted in with the shift of emphasis from visible 'Green Army' patrols to undercover tactics, which the new GOC, Lieutenant

General Tim Creasy, believed would cut down army casualties. It was also in line with the policy of 'police primacy' – giving a higher profile to RUC units. From now on, the four squadrons of 22 SAS would rotate through the Northern Ireland role on four-to-six-month tours, but would be spread throughout the whole Province. There would be troops in Bessbrook, London-derry and Belfast, and a fourth in reserve under the orders of the Commander Land Forces.

The first major operation the SAS set up in Belfast, a month before the John Boyle incident, also involved the death of an innocent bystander. Through an informer, the RUC learned that a four-man PIRA Active Service Unit was planning to fire-bomb a Post Office depot in Belfast's Ballysillan Road. The police knew the target, and the direction from which the terrorists would approach, but not the exact time of the attack. An SAS team was tasked to stake out the depot, together with police Special Branch and Special Patrol Group officers.

On the night of 20 June, the IRA-men – William Mailey, Denis Brown, James Mulvenna and a fourth whose name is unknown – commandeered a blue Mazda estate car from the Shamrock Club in the Ardoyne. They collected their incendiaries – webbing haver-sacks wrapped in rubber, each with a container of petrol, a primer, a timing-device, a detonator and a metal bracket. They parked the car in a side road near the Post Office depot and, leaving the fourth man at the wheel, stalked off to set up their bombs. The depot consisted of a building and a large compound for Post Office vans, with petrol-storage tanks containing thousands of gallons of fuel. Once ignited, the petrol would form a fireball that would blitz the houses nearby with burning gases and debris. The compound was surrounded by an eight-foot-high wire fence.

An SAS observer had been sited in a house looking directly down the 'Loney' – an alley that ran along the fence. There were several other SAS-men concealed in the compound, 'cut-off' parties at the ends of the alley, and a two-man 'reaction team' hidden in bushes nearby. At least one armed policeman formed part of the ambush group. The SAS had already been lying in wait for almost a week, and, according to one of them, Sgt. Barry Davies, the operator in the observation-post was fed up, and entertaining doubts about Special Branch intel. At about midnight that night, though, he saw three men marching boldly down the alley, almost touching the fence. 'Before he could raise the alarm,' Davies recalled, 'one of the figures moved his arm – the first bomb was already arching its way towards the target.'[2]

According to another SAS-man, Tpr. 'Scott Graham', an ex-Para, there were four terrorists, wearing tartan scarves and carrying haversacks. The first bomber hurled a pack over the fence. 'It landed with quite a thud,' Scott recalled.[3] He remembered that the men then halted, and laid the other haversacks on the ground. One of them, he said, 'seemed to have taken out a pair of wire-cutters and began slicing his way through the steel fencing'.[4] Scott and his oppo withdrew quietly from their post, making their way round the buildings.

Scott claimed that the two of them had moved silently to within about twenty metres of the group when one of the bombers looked up. Sensing that they'd been clocked, Scott bawled, 'Halt! Army!' Three of the men greased off down the alley, while the fourth stood his ground 'and seemed to be going for a gun'.[5] Scott yelled, 'Fire!' and the two men thrummed automatic fire from their Heckler & Koch MP5s. They advanced at a walk, spraying rounds. 'Each time we emptied our magazines we pushed home another and continued firing,' Scott said, 'as the men ran in every direction, trying to escape the hail of gunfire.'[6]

Three of the bombers crumpled – the fourth continued running, and Scott wasn't sure if he'd been hit or not. A moment later, the fleeing terrorist was confronted by one of the SAS-men in a 'cut-off' position, whose weapon had jammed. The soldier smashed the butt of his rifle into the bomber's head, breaking his neck. Meanwhile, Scott and his mate walked up to the proned-out terrorists to check that they were dead. Scott recalled that by this time the place was already jammed with police vehicles and 'hundreds of police officers'.[7]

Davies mentions only three terrorists. According to him, the two-man 'reaction team' jumped out of cover. They confronted the bombers, 'two of whom were about to throw satchel-bombs'. One of the SAS-men rattled 9mm bursts from his MP5, dropping the pair of them. The third sprinted off down the alley, but the shooter stopped him with another torrent of rounds. The second SAS-man pumped off a magazine from his SLR, and just as he stopped shooting, two more men appeared at the end of the alley. The first SAS-man shouted a warning. One of the new arrivals dropped with his hands over his head, but the other tried to get away. The SAS-man fired a fourth time, killing him. Both Scott and Davies claim to have been present on the operation, but there are serious discrepancies in their accounts, and neither account is consistent with the statement issued by Army Headquarters at Lisburn shortly after the incident. Neither do they tally with the testimonies given by unnamed SAS-men at the inquest – presumably including both of them. The official press-release claimed that the 'four' terrorists were killed 'in an exchange of fire' – suggesting that the IRA were carrying firearms. This was not the case: no guns were recovered and the forensic evidence showed no sign that they'd handled firearms.

At the inquest, though, the SAS claimed that they'd 'heard gunshots' or had 'thought they were under fire'. Davies suggested that the terrorists were shot because they had thrown or were about to throw 'satchel-bombs'. This can't have been the case if, as Scott says, three of the bombs were at that time on the ground. In any case, the bombs the IRA were carrying were incendiaries designed not to be thrown like grenades or gammon-bombs, but to be hooked on guttering or window-frames and detonated by a timer. This was the technique the IRA had used about three months earlier when blowing up the La Mon House restaurant in County Down, killing a dozen customers. Scott didn't seem sure whether the bombers had cut through the fence, and failed to answer the question as to why they should do so if the bombs were designed to be thrown.

Neither was he definite about the number of terrorists involved. He initially mentioned 'three or four men', but thereafter continually referred to 'four men'. He described how three bombers were shot, and another taken down with a blow to the head from a rifle-butt, but also admitted that 'one of the bastards escaped' – a total of five.

It is the case that four men were killed in the incident, but only three of them were bombers. The fourth was William Hanna, a passer-by walking back from the Mountainview Club in the Shankill Road with his friend David Graham. Both Hanna and Graham were Protestants, and had no connection with the terrorists. The fourth bona fide IRA-man, whom Davies says remained in the car, escaped.

Davies claims that Hanna was killed trying to get away, and Scott says he was 'hit by a ricochet'. At the inquest, though, soldiers 'A', 'B' and 'C' – one of whom must have been Scott – stated that Hanna was still alive when they approached him and 'made a twisting movement as if to draw a weapon'. Two of them then pumped bullets into his body until he lay still.

David Graham testified at the inquest that he and Hanna had been walking along deep in conversation, when they were fired on 'without warning'. He immediately fell on his face and rolled into the bushes nearby. It is probable that Hanna was hit in this first burst. Since Davies himself admitted that there was a cover-up, his insistence that a clear warning was given has to be regarded with caution.

Even though the SAS had killed a helpless bystander, the army considered the Ballysillan Post Office job a coup. No one expressed regret over the death of William Hanna, indeed, Davies, writing years later, said, 'Had [Hanna] . . . remained still after the challenge, he would be alive today,' as if the fault lay with the innocent victim. Far from apologizing, the army even resorted to the disgraceful tactic of trying to smear Hanna by claiming he was a Loyalist paramilitary – an accusation that, even if true, was completely irrelevant.

There can be little doubt that in the Ballysillan case, the SAS ignored the rules of engagement and opened fire on men they knew to be terrorists, killing a member of the public in the process. Scott expressed the sentiments of SAS-men on the ground perfectly when he complained that the politicians made the Regiment fight the IRA with 'one hand tied behind their backs'. 'If the authorities had given the SAS a free rein,' he commented, '. . . we could have finished off the IRA years before. But we weren't allowed to fight the way we could have done, with no rules. We had to keep to the . . . stupid "yellow card", and were never permitted to take the initiative . . . The IRA could play as dirty as they wanted while we had to play by the bloody rules.'[8]

Despite the army's satisfaction with the outcome, the RUC was not happy. Deputy Chief Constable Jack Hermon was so incensed that he told Commander Land Forces, Major-General Dick Trant, he didn't want any further 'shoot-outs' on the streets of the capital. The Ballysillan job put the lid on aggressive SAS actions in Belfast for a decade.

Undercover ops continued outside the capital, however, with further controversy. In September, only weeks after the Boyle incident, SAS-men shot dead a twenty-three-year-old Protestant civil servant named James Taylor, who was out pigeon-shooting with two friends near Lough Neagh. Once again, Taylor had no link to any terrorist organization, and on this occasion he clearly had been shot in the back.

This was also the case with Patrick Duffy, whom the SAS killed two months later. Duffy, a PIRA quartermaster, entered a house in Londonderry known to hold a cache of firearms, which was being watched by an SAS team. He was later proved to have been shot twelve times in the back. The claim by SAS witnesses that he had spun round and made a movement suggesting that he was about to draw a weapon was discounted by forensic evidence.

By the end of 1978 the SAS had killed ten people in Northern Ireland, three of them innocent. Every case had been a peach for anti-government propaganda and had confirmed the public view of the Regiment as an execution-squad. Even Cornelius Boyle, father of the dead John Boyle, said later that he held no bitterness against the Regiment for killing his son, because 'this is what the SAS are employed to do'.[9]

Questions were asked about the moral legitimacy of waiting until terrorists were in a position to threaten the public before taking counter-measures – measures that frequently ended in the death of the very people the SAS were supposed to be there to protect. In practical terms this was easy to answer: even if the SAS knew about an impending PIRA operation from an informer, the rules of evidence required that terrorists were caught in the act. Whether securing a conviction was more important than preventing an act of terrorism, though, was another moot point.

By the end of the decade, aggressive undercover ops had gone out of favour. The new emphasis was on long-term surveillance, and the painstaking collection of evidence to secure convictions. SAS commitment in the Province was scaled down. Instead of squadrons being rotated through the Ulster role, a permanent squad of twenty men, the 'Ulster Troop', was created, at first drawn from whichever squadron was on Anti-Terrorist duty, later independent. At the same time, the Army Surveillance Unit – 14 Intelligence Company – was enlarged and combined with the 'Ulster Troop' in the joint 'Intelligence & Security Group', which came under the command of an SAS officer. From now on, 14 Int. operatives and SAS-men were able to act together.

For Director SAS de la Billière, Northern Ireland had proved something of a nemesis. The 'finest fighting regiment in the world' had been exposed, in the eyes of the public, as a bunch of sinister killers who were unashamedly capable of taking out innocent teenagers, and weren't even competent to navigate their way round country roads.

In an unprecedented letter to the *Daily Telegraph* in March 1979, following the false allegation that an SAS sergeant had raped the wife of a police surgeon in Ulster, de la Billière wrote testily, 'I am disturbed at the increasing tendency to report on the SAS as if it were some secret undercover organization. In fact it is a corps of the British army, subject to both military and civil law in exactly the same way as any other corps.'[10] Within a little over twelve months, though, the Regiment's name was to be redeemed, and the SAS pitchforked to celebrity, when six terrorists of the Democratic Front for the Liberation of Arabistan siezed the Iranian Embassy in London's Princes Gate.

PART FOUR

Black Ops and Green Ops 1980–91

87. 'Blind or not, we're going in'

In the Kremlin at Bradbury Lines, Major John Moss, ex-9 (Parachute) Field Squadron, Royal Engineers, currently OC B Squadron, 22 SAS, was handed a disturbing signal. It had come bouncing off a satellite from a patrol signaller almost nine thousand miles away, on the most southerly point of the American continent, Tierra del Fuego. The signaller, Mick Gibbons, Gordon Highlanders, was part of an eight-man B Squadron patrol that had been sent to recce an airfield at Rio Grande, on the Argentine side of the peninsula. It was the base for five Super Etendard fighter-bombers of the Argentine air force, armed with deadly Exocet missiles.

It was 18 May 1982, two years after the Regiment's apotheosis at the Iranian Embassy in London. The war in the Falkland Islands had broken out seven weeks earlier, and B Squadron was due to embark on one of the most daring SAS schemes of the post-war era. They were to be transported in a pair of Hercules C130s to Rio Grande, where they would crash-land on the runway. The SAS-men would fast-ramp out in armed Land Rovers and on foot, and chop up the Super Etendards and their Exocet payloads with rockets and machine-gun fire.

Early that morning, an advance patrol under Captain Andrew 'M', Royal Hampshire Regiment, had landed near an isolated farmhouse twenty kilometres north of Rio Grande in a Royal Navy Sea King helicopter. 'M''s unit carried demolitions equipment and LAW 66mm rocket-launchers, and had the capacity to knock-out the Argentine hardware if the opportunity arose. Otherwise, they would put in a covert OP, observe the airbase, and vector in the main party.

The Sea King, of 846 Naval Air Squadron, had lurched horizontally off the deck of the Royal Navy carrier *Invincible* after dark the previous night. *Invincible*, one of two carriers of the Royal Navy Task Force, had steamed to within five hundred miles of the target, escorted by the frigate *Brilliant*. She had then turned round and headed back to the Falkland Islands, where she had put in a diversionary bombardment on the capital, Port Stanley.

The Sea King had been stripped down to bare essentials to allow for extra fuel-tanks. Even with these modifications, she had only just enough fuel to reach the tactical area and hop across the border into neutral Chile. Once there, she would be ditched and the crew would go into escape and evasion mode. Originally, a D Squadron NCO, Peter Ratcliffe, had been tasked to stay with the aircrew and lead them out, but this idea had been scrapped in the need to keep the payload down to the minimum.

The aircraft flew low over the sea in blackout conditions, ducking long-range radar pickets. Her pilot, Lt. Richard Hutchings, a slim, moustachioed officer of the Royal Marines, was flying in unfamiliar passive night-goggles. Before the heli came in over the coast, her Omega warning system started bleeping, telling Hutchings that she'd been painted by enemy radar. For the SAS patrol sitting on the floor behind, tension spiralled. Hutchings took the aircraft down so low that her wheels were almost touching the sea. The Omega's bleep faded, but moments later co-pilot Lt. Alan Bennett spotted the momentary distant flash of a signal flare. The Sea King passed over dry land, banked behind hills, and dropped into radar dead-ground.

When the pilot put the heli down at the preselected landing-zone, two SAS-men, Tpr. Gwynne Evans and Cpl. Mick Gibbons, jumped out and crouched on the desolate pampas in their white Arctic warfare suits, ready to go. Suddenly, Captain 'M' whistled his men back inside. He'd spotted a second signal flare in the distance, and believed the insertion had been compromised. He told the pilot to fly them across the border into Chile. 'I'm sorry,' he told his patrol. 'It's Chile after all.'

'Chilly! It's fucking freezing,' Taff Evans replied.

The patrol was finally dropped on the tundra about twenty miles west of the Chile–Argentine border. They set up their bashas, and tapped out a message reporting the mission aborted. Less than an hour later, Hutchings ditched the Sea King in a coastal lake, ten miles south of the Chilean town of Punta Arenas. The plan had been to submerge the heli to escape detection, but though the crew punched holes in her fuselage, she refused to sink. They had to leave her half-submerged, and head for civilization.

Nine thousand miles away, in Hereford, John Moss was dismayed to learn that the recce mission had failed. This meant that his main party would be going in blind. If the op had been compromised, it could also mean that the Argentines would be on the alert for a raid. The chances of success, already slim, would be much reduced.

The proposed op was balanced on a political tightrope. It would be the first British operation against mainland Argentina, and if the Argentinian government got wind of it, it would provide rich propaganda capital. US President Ronald Reagan had warned Prime Minister Margaret Thatcher not to extend the war to the continent itself. The suspicion that this caveat had been ignored might be enough to rob her of the fragile support of both the USA and the European Community. The mission would require the tacit agreement of Chile, which wasn't keen on being accused by its Argentine neighbour of assisting the United Kingdom.

The Falkland Islands had been occupied by a two-and-a-half-thousand-man group of Argentine marines and special forces on 2 April, in an attempt by Argentina's dictator, General Leopoldo Galtieri, to boost the popularity of his military junta. A British dependency since 1833, the country consisted of two main islands – East and West Falkland – and a hundred smaller ones. Treeless, windswept moorlands, the islands were inhabited by about two thousand Britons, mostly sheep-farmers, and defended by a Royal Marines detachment seventy-nine strong. The Marines made a heroic stand at Government House in Port Stanley, but after twelve hours the Governor, Rex Hunt, ordered them to surrender. Galtieri moved in a ten-thousand-man garrison, equipped with heavy artillery, helicopters, light armoured vehicles and Pucara ground-attack aircraft. The following day, Argentine forces occupied South Georgia, another British dependency about eight hundred miles south of east.

The SAS hadn't fought regular forces on this scale since the Second World War. For the unit that had just become famous as the counter-terrorist force par excellence, a return to 'Green Ops' was something of a surprise. Commanding officer Mike Rose had put D Squadron and half of G on standby as soon as news of the invasion had come through. They joined the British Task Force in mid-Atlantic on 13 April.

The plan for the Rio Grande raid was seen as a way of short-circuiting the war by taking out the Argentines' most deadly weapons. In early May, a single Exocet strike had reduced the Type 42 air-defence destroyer *Sheffield* to a smouldering wreck, with the loss of twenty men killed and two dozen injured – the first Royal Navy destroyer sunk in action since the Second World War. Although it was thought that the Argentines had only three Exocets left, it was enough to take out the Task Force's vital carriers, *Hermes* and *Invincible*. The plan also caused disagreement within the Regiment.

The Rio Grande target was defended by at least thirteen hundred crack Argentine marines, as well equipped as the SAS. It was guarded by advanced radar systems, and its ground defences included SAMs – surface-to-air missiles. The transports would be operating at the extreme limit of their range, and would have to be dumped during the mission. Since there would be only two aircraft, a single strike by an enemy missile would knock out half the raiding force in one go. There was no real deception plan, apart from the idea that the pilots would talk to Argentine air-controllers in Spanish.

The day he received the 'mission aborted' signal from Tierra del Fuego, John Moss mustered B Squadron in the Interest Room at Bradbury Lines. He told them that if Mikado was successful, it could save the Task Force hundreds of casualties. 'Blind or not, we're going in,' he said. 'Our country is at war and we're needed.'[1]

Not everyone was convinced. The SAS had always had a healthy regard for probability curves, and a week of rehearsals on remote airfields in the UK had suggested that the chances of succeeding were less than fifty-fifty. Enemy radar pickets would give their air defences at least a six-minute warning. So in their view, with the element of surprise missing, the odds were that the two Hercules would be taken down before they got anywhere near the target, and the squadron totalled. Apart from being contrary to every principle in the SAS book, and a sheer waste of its expertise, such *coup de main* raids were the province of shock troops like the Paras.

Many members of the squadron felt that there was a better way of doing it. The whole weight of SAS tradition was against rigidly imposed 'do-or-die' schemes. The Regiment had always encouraged lateral thinking. After the abort signal had come in, John Moss had attempted to switch the plan to a long-range infiltration across the Chilean border, or at least to insert a second recce party, but his idea was vetoed.

Some of the Regiment – and not all of them enlisted men – were strongly critical of the plan which had the approval of de la Billière.

Part of the problem may have been that, after the embassy job had rocketed the SAS to stardom, two distinct Regiments had emerged – the 'real' SAS, and the SAS of the public imagination. This schizophrenia was a common experience for media celebrities, but for a military unit it was a double-edged sword. The 'mythological' SAS was peopled with gods and heroes, the real SAS with flesh-and-blood human beings. While the Regiment's super-hero image was a valuable psychological weapon, no SAS-man – and especially no SAS commander – could afford to confuse the Regiment's imaginary capacities with its actual ones. Therein lay the road to disaster. 'The important thing to remember,' wrote Peter Ratcliffe sagely, 'is that the Regiment is not infallible . . . its soldiers are not immune to getting things wrong, especially in the confusion of war.'[2]

On the night of 19 May Robin Horsfall said goodbye to his eight-months-pregnant wife, Heather, on the steps of their Hereford home, knowing that there was a more-than-even chance that he'd never see her again. When he arrived at Bradbury Lines to help load the kit on the three-tonners, he discovered that one of the squadron's most respected NCOs, Staff Sergeant Jake W. – a veteran of Aden, Borneo and Dhofar – had already resigned over the Mikado issue. Jake had advised Moss that the best-case scenario would be high casualties, the worst, obliteration. Failure would mean more than the loss of good men: it would be a huge propaganda victory for the enemy.

The news of Jake's resignation spread like wildfire. When de la Billière turned up to see the squadron off, he was astonished to find the atmosphere cool. 'I had never known such a lack of enthusiasm,' he wrote. 'Throughout my career the SAS had invariably reacted like hounds to a fox the moment they scented conflict.'[3] De la Billière was exasperated. Due to misleading staff reports, he'd been under the impression that the squadron was delighted with the job. He'd stuck his neck out persuading the Cabinet Office and the Task Force command to allow the SAS this opportunity. A change of plan or a cancellation now would be highly embarrassing. He divined – or thought he divined – that the unit's lack of zeal was down to OC John Moss.

At RAF Lyneham, waiting for the VC-10s that would take the unit on the first leg of their journey – to Ascension Island in the Atlantic – the squadron heard that Moss wouldn't be coming with them. At midnight, de la Billière had summarily RTU'd him for his negative attitude, and replaced him with the Regiment's 2IC, Major Ian Crooke, the ex-KOSB officer who'd served under Tony Jeapes during the first tour in Dhofar.

Moss had always intended to carry out his orders. He had simply contested the effectiveness of de la Billière's plan.

Though de la Billière later harangued B Squadron over their attitude, and suggested obliquely that it had been 'a near mutiny', there was never any question of insubordination. A call by one NCO to support Jake by offering to resign was ignored by the rest of the boys, even those who sympathized. Some called Jake a 'coward'. Others, like Horsfall, appreciated that he'd shown great moral courage, but weren't prepared to emulate him. 'It wasn't

the Army, or Queen and country, or even my mates I went for,'
he wrote, 'it was for me . . . to prove I was every bit as good as
the rest of them.'[4]

On 20 May the ditched Sea King helicopter, half sunk in the lake
near Punta Arenas, was discovered by a local forester, who reported
it to the Chilean *carabineiros*. They promptly buried the evidence,
but located the crew, who were flown to Santiago. In a press
conference there at the British Embassy, Hutchings declared that
the heli had been on a routine reconnaissance flight when she
experienced engine trouble, and was unable to return to her ship.
He had therefore sought refuge in the nearest neutral country.

In fact, the Argentine forces in Rio Grande had detected her
approach, recognized her as hostile, and suspected that she had
dropped an SAS team. The following day, twelve hundred Marines
had swept the area on foot and in armoured personnel carriers.
Meanwhile, Captain 'M''s patrol had managed to make the escape
rendezvous, from where they were flown to Santiago and hidden
in safe-houses until the end of the war.

88. 'Eleven, repeat eleven aircraft. Believed real'

The day before B Squadron arrived on Ascension, Sgt. Peter
Ratcliffe jumped off a Sea King on to the deck of the assault-ship
Intrepid, sailing with the British Task Force off the Falkland Islands.
It was 2130 hours, and darkness was falling. A withering icy wind
blasted across the heaving, ash-grey sea. The previous day, the
Royal Navy assault force had steamed in from Ascension to link
up with the carrier group. With them, on the landing-ship *Fearless*,
came Lt. Col. Mike Rose and the 22 SAS Battle HQ. Most of the
G Squadron personnel were holed up in covert hides on shore,
observing enemy movements. The rest, with the bulk of D Squadron, had spent the afternoon trans-shipping equipment from the

carrier *Hermes*, in preparation for the planned landing by the Parachute Regiment and the Royal Marine Commandos at San Carlos Bay on East Falkland, due to kick off in three days. Ratcliffe's D Squadron had been earmarked for a diversionary attack on the Argentine garrison at Darwin and Goose Green, to precede the landings.

The two ships were about a mile apart, and the Sea Kings, cross-decking men and stores, took about five minutes to make the trip. Most of the kit had already been transferred and stood like a mini-mountain range on *Intrepid*'s deck. Ratcliffe had chosen to take the penultimate flight, as he guessed the last one would be crowded. When his chopper cleared the deck, the last flight was hovering about seventy-five metres away. Suddenly, Ratcliffe heard one of his mates yell, 'She's gone down!' Instantly, alarm klaxons wailed and the ship's tannoy blared, 'Crash teams, action stations!'

It was said later that the Sea King had been hit by a big seabird – possibly a storm-petrel, with a six-foot wing-span. Survivors remembered hearing a bang before the heli ditched. There were thirty men on board when she smashed into the waves, and only eight of them got out alive. The Sea King crumpled on impact, and the tail-section sheared off. The pilot and co-pilot punched out the cockpit doors and pitched themselves into an automatically inflated dinghy. In the hold, most of the SAS-men were trapped as the freezing water gushed in. One managed to inflate his life-jacket, which shot him out through the jagged gap where the tail had been. A few others got out through the main door, bursting up through the surface to cling on to the pilot's dinghy.

The water was only one degree above freezing – so cold that by the time they were picked up, they were already slipping away with hypothermia. The Sea King had long since vanished into the deeps of the South Atlantic, taking with her twenty-two men, including twenty members of D and G Squadrons, and support elements. The death-toll included eight senior NCOs, with years of accumulated experience, among them two squadron sergeants-major. In one blow, more SAS-men had been killed than in Borneo and Dhofar put together – the most devastating single loss the Regiment had sustained since the Second World War. 'It was,' commented Ratcliffe, 'a horrible way to die.'[1]

D Squadron had been the first SAS unit to go into action in the Falklands conflict, on Operation 'Paraquat' – the re-taking of South Georgia. On 21 April Capt. John Hamilton's 19 Troop had been inserted on the island's Fortuna glacier, but ran into a fifty-mile-an-hour blizzard. After taking five hours to cover half a klick, Hamilton had to request extraction. Of the three Wessex helicopters sent to lift them out, two crashed in the appalling conditions.

Four days later, though, a seventy-five-man assault force of SAS, SBS and Royal Marines landed on South Georgia, at Grytviken, a British Antarctic Survey station of white-walled houses and tin-roofed stores, nestling under vast granite tors veined in ice and snow. Backed up by a naval barrage from *Antrim* and *Plymouth*, they captured the base without a single casualty on either side. D Squadron SSM Lawrence Gallagher tore down the Argentinian flag and raised the Union Jack. Gallagher would be lost in the Sea King crash.

Now, as the frozen survivors were ferried on board *Hermes*, Ratcliffe saw the accident as divine retribution for the startling coup they'd brought off only three days before. 'Whether it comes within hours or days,' he wrote, 'there is always a payback time.'[2] The victory was the D Squadron raid on Pebble Island off the northern coast of West Falkland, the base for a squadron of Argentine ground-attack Pucara aircraft. The Pucaras would present a serious threat to British forces during the planned landing at San Carlos Bay.

The first phase of the op was an infiltration by two four-man patrols of D Squadron's Boat Troop, dropped by Sea King choppers on West Falkland on the night of 11/12 May. Equipped with collapsible seventeen-and-a-half-foot Klepper canoes – a modern rubber-skinned version of the *folbot* – they trekked by night to the point nearest to Pebble Island, assembled the canoes, and paddled across the straits. While one patrol remained with the boats, four men led by troop-officer Captain 'Ted' crawled across boggy turf and through elephant grass to within sight of the airstrip. The patrol lay almost motionless in the grass for two days. At 1100 hours on 15 May, SAS battle HQ on *Fearless* copped a coded message from Boat Troop's signaller. 'Eleven, repeat eleven aircraft. Believed real. Squadron attack tonight.'[3]

When the Sea Kings ferrying the forty-five-man D Squadron raiding party touched down on Pebble Island, Captain 'Ted' was there to guide them to the target. Mobility Troop was to execute the raid, while Air Troop would hold off the Argentine garrison and Mountain Troop would stay in reserve. The original plan had been to wipe out the one-hundred-and-fourteen-strong enemy force in the area, as well as taking out the aircraft. The insertion had gone in late, though, due to weather conditions, and there was only time to hit the airfield.

The operation was commanded personally by D Squadron boss Major Cedric Delves, an introverted officer of the Devons & Dorsets. With the raiders was a team of forward fire-controllers from 29 Commando Regiment, Royal Artillery, whose task was to direct the twin 115mm naval guns on the destroyer *Glamorgan,* standing offshore. *Glamorgan* was covered from air-attack by the frigate *Broadsword,* and *Hermes* carried the helis that would make the extraction.

The SAS-men were cammed up and raring to go. They toted M-16 rifles, with three spare mags taped to the stock, and up to four hundred 7.62mm rounds apiece for the GPMGs. The commando gunners carried a three-inch mortar, and every SAS-man lugged two mortar-bombs, one high explosive, one white phosphorus. A few had with them LAW 66mm rocket-launchers, and the demolitions men had plastic explosives charges, modern equivalents of the Second World War Lewes bombs. As they set off across the bleak moorland, adrenalin surged through them.

For Ratcliffe's Mobility Troop, the adrenalin rush quickly began to cool when they lost contact with Mountain Troop ahead of them. Instead of moving tactically, Delves had set up a cracking pace, at times breaking into a run, leaping over walls and obstacles. The raid was deadlined for 0700 hours. If the squadron failed to make it back to the RV on time, they'd be stranded – the Sea Kings wouldn't be able to extract them, because carrier *Hermes* would have steamed out of range.

When Mobility Troop reached the target area they discovered that, because of the delay, their prominent role had been usurped by Mountain Troop under Captain John Hamilton. Navigation was the most basic of SAS skills: members of the troop were disgusted with themselves for having got lost on a small island.

The aircraft were dispersed widely across the runway. At seven o'clock precisely, directed by Captain Chris Brown of the commando artillery, the guns of *Glamorgan* grumbled out of the darkness. 115mm shells caterwauled, guzzled air, scranched into the Argentine positions, spasmed apart in dazzling strokes. One shell scored a direct hit on the fuel-dump – thousands of litres of aviation-fuel blastwaved out in crimson and orange shrouds.

The commandos' mortar popped, sowing the sky with spurts of white phosphorus that illuminated the area like a *son et lumière* show. Dark figures scurried in among the planes, two teams of seven men, spattering fuselage with Gimpie bursts, crouching to loose off 66mm LAW missiles that zonked into wings and tail-planes, or gouged slabs of tarmac off the runway. There was little return fire – the enemy seemed to be keeping their heads down. Two plucky Argentine soldiers took pot-shots at the raiders, but were cut down by Gimpie fire. In the eerie light of the white phos, one of the raiders was astonished to see two SAS sergeants lamping into each other with their fists – a long-standing feud had finally erupted in the least apposite of places.

The demolition teams darted forward to deal with the Pucaras; the aircraft's wings stood so high that the SAS-men had to climb on each other's shoulders to get at them. Troop officer John Hamilton and demo-man Tpr. Ray 'Paddy' Ryan, ex-Royal Green Jackets, accounted for two of the aircraft. Ryan, who earned the nickname 'Pucara Paddy' on the raid, would be lost when the Sea King went down.

Delves had given Hamilton only fifteen minutes to complete the task, but by the time forty-five minutes had elapsed, he was beginning to think he would never get the men back. Suddenly they came hurtling off the airstrip with the aircraft crepitating gas and flame behind them. A final shot from *Glamorgan* smashed into the ammo-dump, convulsing in a shock-wave. One of the men was hit in the leg by shrapnel. As Staff Sgt. Currass, an ex-RAMC medic, knelt to slap a field-dressing on the wound, the enemy set off a landmine that splatted turf and stones, hurling Cpl. Paul Bunker, ex-Royal Army Ordnance Corps, three metres into the air. Bunker hit the deck with only concussion, and was dragged off by his mates. Both Currass and Bunker would go down with the Sea King.

The squadron regrouped at the mortar-pit in all-round defence, then withdrew back to the LZ. At nine-thirty four Sea Kings chattered out of the night, and the raiders were aboard within half a minute. They were back on *Hermes* ten minutes after first light. The SAS had destroyed six Pucaras and five other aircraft. 'There was now nothing left to interfere with the British landings at San Carlos Bay,' Ratcliffe commented. 'The mission had been an enormous success.'[4]

89. 'Long nosed kamikazes'

On 21 May two battalions of the Parachute Regiment and three Royal Marine Commandos waded ashore at two beach-heads on San Carlos Bay. The previous night, D Squadron 22 SAS had tabbed across East Falkland to launch a barrage on the Argentine garrison at Darwin, to distract them from the landings next morning. Once in position, the SAS laid down so much flak from rifles, GP machine guns, Milan anti-tank missiles and three-inch mortars that the Argentines were convinced they were under attack by a full battalion, rather than just forty men.[1]

Next morning, while the Commandos and Paras were establishing their beach-heads, D Squadron was preparing to withdraw when an enemy Pucara came in low over the sea in a strafing run.

As the aircraft roared overhead, Tpr. 'Kel', ex-New Zealand SAS, sighted up with a Stinger missile-launcher and let rip. The missile streaked after the aircraft, pierced her through the tail, and emerged the other side. The pilot ejected. The Pucara exploded in mid-air. As the troop watched the remains of the plane whiplash into the hills and disintegrate in smoke and debris, the men cheered. This was the first time any of them had seen a Stinger in action. A US-made heat-seeker missile, its existence was still classified. It had been acquired for the Regiment by a couple of SAS NCOs, through their contacts with Delta Force. The missiles had been parachuted into the sea with one of only two SAS-men trained to operate them, Staff Sgt. Paddy O'Connor, Irish Guards. O'Connor had been lost in the Sea King crash.

Unfortunately the current operator, 'Kel', hadn't been trained to use the system. He'd picked up the basics from the manual but had forgotten that after firing, the launcher had to be recharged with compressed gas. When more Pucaras honed in over the squadron, he sighted up again. His next two rounds flew only twenty metres, blowing up so near to the SAS-men that they had to dive for cover. The Stinger missiles were worth fifty thousand pounds apiece, and Kel's troop officer quickly ordered him to stop shooting.

Later that day, while D Squadron was tramping back to San Carlos Bay, one troop of B Squadron parachuted from Hercules C130s into the Atlantic, in dry-suits. Picked up in Gemini inflatables and transferred to *Intrepid*, they were destined to replace the D Squadron men lost in the Sea King accident. The rest of B were still on Ascension, awaiting the order to embark on Op Mikado. They'd become so frustrated with their on-off orders that some of them had taken to wearing false noses and headbands with the words 'long nosed kamikazes', inscribed in Japanese. Eventually, though, Mikado was scrapped, either because of the discovery of the ditched Sea King or because the RAF considered it impossible: it is known that one RAF pilot assigned to the mission suffered a nervous breakdown. In any case, much of the feared damage had already been done. By 25 May the Task Force had lost four more ships to the Argentine Air Force – battleships *Ardent, Antelope* and *Coventry*, and the cargo-ship *Atlantic Conveyor.*

G Squadron patrols had taken a low-profile but immensely important part in the campaign, observing enemy movements from covert locations on the islands. One patrol, led by Sgt. Scott Graham, who had been involved in the Ballysillan operation in Belfast, moved their observation-post every night, carrying fifty kilos of equipment, rations and ammunition.

The main problem was finding cover on the bleak moors of East Falkland, where there were no trees, bushes or natural depressions, and where under the soggy surface turf the ground was as hard as rock. Moving into position before first light, they dug fifteen-inch-deep shell-scrapes and covered them with chicken-wire, camouflaged with grass and heather. Inside these 'coffins' they could hardly move for fear of upsetting their camouflage – any disturbance in the ground might be spotted by enemy heli-copters. They ate dry rations, and hardly spoke, even in whispers. The ground was freezing, and as their food became depleted, the men began to suffer from hypothermia and trench foot.

Scott's patrol finally took up a position on a rise three miles from the main Argentine garrison at Goose Green. They dug a lying-up place on the lee-side of the hill, and a camouflaged OP on the crest, from where they could watch the base. They worked in twelve-hour stags, estimating enemy strengths, logging their activities, pinpointing the positions of storage-tanks, clocking the movements of vehicles and helicopters. By night, they would transmit the intel back to SAS Battle HQ on *Fearless,* in encoded messages. The data proved vital to the coming battle.

Another G patrol reported that the high ground covering the approaches to Port Stanley was poorly defended. This included a fourteen-hundred-foot hill called Mount Kent, on the route from the British beach-head to the capital. On *Fearless,* Mike Rose relayed the report to 42 Commando boss Lt. Col. Nick Vaux, and suggested that the Marines should take the hill. Vaux agreed. The SAS would go in ahead of them and secure the area.

Rose already had a D Squadron advance-party on the ground.

When the rest of the squadron was flown in by Sea King two days later, though, they were mistakenly landed over twelve miles from the target. They had to be extracted, and were dropped in the Mount Kent area on 28 May, just as 2 Para were going into action at Goose Green, winning their legendary victory against the Argentine garrison.

On reaching the summit of the hill, the SAS party found that the defenders had cleared out in a hurry. They had dumped all their equipment, apart from weapons and ammunition. One company of 42 Commando was landed by Chinook helicopter three days later, with a 105mm field-gun. They secured the heights overlooking Port Stanley, for the main assault-force's advance.

A fortnight later, on 13 June, the SAS launched its last major operation: a seaborne assault on Port Stanley harbour by troops from D and G Squadrons and half a dozen SBS-men, headed by Delves. The attack, in four rigid raider boats, was intended as a diversion for an assault by 2 Para on Wireless Ridge, overlooking the bay. It went wrong when the boats were caught in searchlights from an Argentine hospital-ship in the harbour and were hit by a massive volume of fire from the shore. The raiders turned tail and zipped off into the darkness. They took only three slight casualties, but all the boats were written off.

The following day, Mike Rose received a signal from the head-quarters of the Argentine commander, General Menendez. He was ready to discuss surrender terms. Rose flew to Port Stanley in a Gazelle helicopter with his signaller and interpreter, but the pilot landed them in the wrong place. The three men were obliged to make their way through a quarter of a mile of Argentine defences, manned by nervous enemy troops, before reaching Government House. That night, though, Menendez signed the surrender in the presence of British Commander, Land Forces, Major-General Jeremy Moore, Royal Marines.

By the end of June, the squadrons had returned to Bradbury Lines, in a mood curiously devoid of jubilation. The loss of so many men in the Sea King disaster had affected everyone, and for the Regiment, the worst of it was that they hadn't died in action.

'It seemed so cruel that they should have been killed in a helicopter crash,' Scott Graham commented. 'We all expect to lose one or two men on active service, but not twenty, snatched like that, their lives somehow wasted.'[2]

The dismal homecoming was made worse by an aura of recrimination. B Squadron felt they hadn't been properly deployed, and had spent most of their time hanging around. The patrol sent to Tierra del Fuego had achieved nothing but the loss of a helicopter. The patrol-boss, Captain 'M', had resigned his commission after being hauled in front of a board of inquiry. Though most of the men didn't know the full story, some felt his performance had been tantamount to cowardice.

D Squadron was criticized for its attempt to land on the Fortuna glacier on South Georgia, despite warnings about weather conditions – an action that resulted in the loss of two helicopters. D was also condemned for attempting a seaborne landing in Gemini inflatables, during which the engines of three of the craft failed. Two of the boats had been washed away, and the SAS-men had survived only by the skin of their teeth. The Gemini engines were known to be unreliable, but the unit's real mistake, it was alleged, had been in trying to show off their boat-skills, when the Royal Navy could have landed them directly. The aborted raid on Port Stanley was also condemned for exposing the men to risk without any strategic advantage.

The SAS was lionized in the press, but underneath the media hype the Regiment knew that things hadn't gone as smoothly as they should have done. Apart from the G Squadron surveillance ops, this war had been a reversal in the trend that had taken them away from the 'traditional' SAS role and increasingly into counter-insurgency and anti-terrorist operations. Hardly anyone currently serving in the SAS had fought this kind of war previously. They'd become unaccustomed to the turmoil and chaos that is an inevitable outcome of conflict on such a scale. Units had got lost, had been landed in the wrong place, had suffered a horrific air accident, had been swept away to sea in unreliable boats, had shot-up civilians, had made some poor decisions over the execution of operations; senior NCOs had indulged in fisticuffs in sight of the enemy. These were the realities of war, but they didn't correspond to the conduct of the imaginary, idealized SAS that had been created in public consciousness.

Another factor that made the Falklands different was that there was no Regimental debrief. 'The debrief is a crucial relief valve,' wrote Ken Connor. 'Once all the problems have been aired, you can put them behind you and get on with improving, evolving and changing your training to prevent any repetition of mistakes in the future.'[3] The Regiment had scored some outstanding victories: the raid on Pebble Island, the capture of South Georgia, the diversionary attack on Darwin and the G Squadron surveillance patrols. A number of decorations had been awarded: a DSO for D Squadron OC Cedric Delves, two MMs, and three MCs – including a posthumous one for Captain John Hamilton, who had led the Pebble Island raid but had been killed on 10 June.

The feeling of gloom reached its nadir at a Regimental get-together at the Pal-Udr-Inn Club – the NAAFI – at Bradbury Lines, when Brigadier Peter de la Billière rose to deliver his final address to 22 SAS. He was stepping down as Director, and wanted to make some observations on the conduct of the recent campaign. After going over the Regiment's successes, and cracking a few jokes no one laughed at, he turned to the subject that had evidently been preoccupying him: B Squadron's 'quasi-mutiny'. 'He roundly denounced us,' said Robin Horsfall, 'as unwilling to do the job he had asked us to do.'[4]

There was dead silence in the room. The effect on men who had just gone through the most extensive conflict the British army had fought since Korea was not dissimilar to that of Jock Lewes's notorious 'yellow streak a yard wide' speech to L Detachment, forty years earlier. 'The hatred in the room was tangible,' Horsfall recalled. '. . . I wanted to stand up and tell him to piss off: we had been willing to go from day one . . . We had tried to improve a ridiculous plan and had been denied by an arrogance that bordered on stupidity.'[5]

De la Billière then proceeded to relate to the assembled Regiment the parable of Major Ian Fenwick, who had been killed driving into an ambush he'd been warned about, on Operation Gain in 1944. It was a singularly ill-chosen example: Fenwick's action had not only been suicidal, it had also been influenced by faulty intelligence. It had gone against the very core of the Regiment's values. Paddy Mayne had talked about 'courage without rashness': David Stirling himself had said that to be a casualty was 'a disgrace'.

De la Billière's tale was an astonishing display of condescension for an officer who'd spent much of his career in the Regiment, to men selected for their ability to think for themselves. They started to wonder if it was a joke. Some began to titter. The laughter grew in volume, and by the time he'd reached the part where Fenwick said, 'Thank you, Madame, but I intend to attack them,' and was shot in the head as he drove through the ambush, the whole Regiment was roaring with mirth. 'Here was this man,' said Horsfall, 'trying to convince us that we too should have been that stupid.'[6] Despite orders from the RSM to desist, they continued to hoot with laughter until de la Billière left the rostrum. He stalked out of the room, with derision ringing in his ears. 'We'd had our moment,' Horsfall commented. 'The SAS had laughed DLB out of the door.'[7]

90. 'A bloody milestone in the struggle for freedom'

For almost a decade after the Falklands conflict, the main concerns of 22 SAS were anti-terrorist duties, and operations in Northern Ireland. In 1987 the Regiment scored the British army's greatest ever triumph against the Provisional IRA, at Loughgall in County Armagh.

Loughgall had the reputation of being the best-kept village in the Province. The birthplace of the Orange order, it had a population of only three hundred and fifty and was centred on a single main street, at the base of a steep hill that ran down from the

Church of St Luke's. One side of the main street was bordered by a football field, opposite which there was an RUC station – a single two-storey building ringed by a high mortar-fence. The police-post was operated on a part-time basis by a sergeant and five constables, who on Friday evenings closed up shop at 1840 hours.

At forty minutes past closing-time on Friday 8 May it was still light, and the village was full of the scent of apple blossom from the acres of orchards that surrounded it. Twenty-one-year-old Declan Arthurs, the son of a mechanical-plant contractor, drove a JCB excavator down the main street. Next to the driver rode twenty-nine-year-old Gerard O'Callaghan and twenty-four-year-old Tony Gormley, both of them hefting firearms. On the JCB's bucket lay an oil drum containing two hundred pounds of Semtex, wired with two forty-second fuses.

The JCB was shadowed by a blue Toyota Hiace van carrying five other men, armed with assault-rifles. All eight were volunteers of the Provisional IRA's crack East Tyrone unit. Their intention was to drive the excavator into the fence surrounding the RUC station, and detonate the charge.

The East Tyrone Brigade had been active against the security forces for a decade, and had been so successful it was nicknamed the 'A Team'. Two years back it had captured the RUC station at Ballygawley, shooting dead two RUC constables and demolishing the place with a bomb. A year ago it had blown up the police-post at the Birches, Armagh, with an explosive-charge carried in the shovel of a digger. The strike on Loughgall would be a carbon copy of the Birches attack.

They had hijacked the JCB from a farmer named Peter Mackle earlier that evening, and a group of them was still holding his family hostage to prevent them from informing the police. They didn't know that the police were already aware of the operation, from a source very close to them, and were waiting in ambush. With them were twenty men of 22 SAS.

For the SAS, this op was a crucial chance to make a 'clean kill'. No attempt would be made to arrest the subjects. The SAS boss

– one of the two staff-sergeants who ran the Ulster Troop – had even stationed men inside the vacant police-station together with police personnel from the HQ Mobile Support Unit, so that it could be claimed that the terrorists were threatening life, thus satisfying the rules of engagement. Other SAS-men were concealed around the building, and in a copse of trees at an oblique angle on the opposite side of the road. There were SAS 'cut-off' groups at both ends of the village, but no attempt had been made to seal off the tactical area, in case PIRA got wind of the trap.

The Ulster Troop had been reinforced by fifteen men of G Squadron, currently assigned anti-terrorist duties at Hereford. They were armed with two 7.62mm GP machine guns, Armalite M16s and Heckler & Koch G3 assault-rifles. They had been lying silently in cover for the past two days.

At the controls of the JCB, Arthurs noticed nothing amiss. He made one pass through the village. Everything seemed quiet. Behind a hedge, fifty metres away, Sgt. Scott Graham eased forward the safety-catch on his GPMG. 'I could see the driver,' he remembered, '. . . and standing either side of him were two men dressed in dark boiler-suits, their faces covered with masks. They were both carrying what I presumed were rifles.'[1]

On his second run, Arthurs rammed the vehicle into the fence. There was a crash of tangled steel – the fence buckled but didn't break. The digger failed to break through, but the charge was powerful enough to damage the target even from this distance. As the three men leapt down, the Toyota Hiace van overtook them and jerked to a halt in front. Three IRA-men jumped out of the back doors and sighted-up their assault-rifles on the station. Among them was the operation commander, thirty-year-old Patrick Kelly, from Dungannon.

Tony Gormley crouched over the JCB's bucket, igniting the two fuses with a Zippo lighter. Then he, O'Callaghan and Arthurs sprinted towards the group around the van. At that moment, gunshots seethed across the road from the SAS-men hidden in the copse, and from the others near the station. Rounds slewed along the tarmac, palpitated into the JCB, drumfired into the van's bodywork. Arthurs tried to take cover behind the van. The other two turned and darted in the opposite direction.

Arthurs was hit in the head and body from both sides, and slumped across the tarmac in a shower of blood. Kelly was zapped in the torso, and slap though the temple. He fell against the driver's door, leaving a daub of gore, his rifle clanging on the road. The van-driver, nineteen-year-old Seamus Donelly from Aughnaskea, stomped gas, but was hit by slugs that slashed through the door and window. He lurched out of the cab and staggered across the road seeping blood. He clambered over the locked gate of the football pitch, and had managed to totter ten metres through the field when he was shot down.

Padraig McKearney and James Lynagh, the men who had planned the attack, were in the back of the van with two other PIRA operators. Despite the fact that they were wearing flak-jackets, they were all cut to bloody shreds by a tattoo of rounds that punched through the vehicle's thin sides.

Seconds later, the two-hundred-pound charge in the JCB kerauned in a blast-wave that lifted the RUC station's roof clean off and demolished the building's nearest wall. Debris splattered fifty metres. The JCB came apart in shards of hot steel – one of its rear wheels whirled across the road and plumped down on the football pitch.

Gormley made twenty metres before gunfire took him down. O'Callaghan, still carrying his assault-rifle, popped a round or two, and was peppered back and front as he crossed the road. He bit the tarmac seventy metres from where the bomb had gone up.

The shooting went on for five minutes and the SAS-men fired twelve hundred rounds. When it stopped, there was a deathly silence. Then some of the SAS-men hopped out of cover and moved forward cautiously to examine the bodies, while their partners covered them. According to Scott Graham, all eight PIRA men were dead with multiple wounds. Whether this is entirely true is questionable: Arthurs was found to have a wound from a shot that had been fired downwards through the top of his skull, and O'Callahan had been shot behind the ear.

A hundred and thirty metres along the road, up the hill towards the church, two more men had been shot. They were two brothers, Oliver and Anthony Hughes, who'd driven into town in their white Citroën, completely unaware that anything was going on there. As they came over the hill, they heard the bomb go off. At the wheel, thirty-six-year-old Anthony Hughes, a father of three, stopped the car and rammed the gear into reverse. 'There was a heavy burst of gunfire from behind us,' Oliver Hughes recalled. 'I heard the back window of the car smash and at the same time heard Anthony shout . . . I felt a sharp pain in my back and a burning in my stomach. I lost consciousness.'[2]

The Hughes brothers were not members of the IRA, and had no links with any terrorist organization. They had taken a short-cut through the village on their way from dropping off the daughter of a friend at an orchard nearby. Though it was later claimed that they had been 'caught in crossfire', forensic evidence proved that the car had been hit by fifty rounds fired from the back – in fact from an SAS cut-off group in the garden of a house only ten metres away. The SAS said that they believed the brothers were about to open fire, and thought they were IRA-men because they were wearing blue boiler-suits like the others. Actually, they were wearing the suits because they'd spent the day repairing a lorry drive-shaft. Anthony Hughes had been killed instantly. Oliver survived, despite two rounds through the back that collapsed a lung, one in the shoulder, and another in the head.

The Loughall incident was the greatest single victory the British army had scored against the IRA since the Irish War of Independence in the 1920s. The Intelligence and Security Group had known about it long in advance. The PIRA unit's explosives cache near Coalisland had been under twenty-four-hour surveillance by the covert Special Branch unit, E4A. Once again, though, an SAS 'clean kill' had been marred by the death of an innocent civilian.

In Republican west Belfast, the Loughgall killings sparked off the worst rioting for years. Hundreds of youths took to the streets and began lobbing petrol bombs at the police, who dispersed them with salvoes of rubber bullets. There were disturbances and protests all over the Province, and the funerals of the eight 'martyrs' were turned into paramilitary parades. 'Loughgall will become the tombstone for British policy in Ireland,' announced Sinn Fein leader Gerry Adams, 'and a bloody milestone in the struggle for freedom, justice and peace.'³

The veiled threat implied by Adams's words was taken seriously by British intelligence. It was clear that sooner or later PIRA would go for a massive revenge-killing against British forces. The only questions were where and when.

91. 'Unholy priesthood of violence'

That November, radio-tecs in Gibraltar picked up a powerful radio pulse on a military frequency, emanating from an unknown source in Spain. For the past two years, Ministry of Defence technicians had been involved in a deadly competition with PIRA in the field of radio-controlled bombs. From relatively simple devices used to control model boats and aeroplanes, PIRA bomb-makers had progressed to transmitters that armed explosive devices by coded signals, and couldn't be jammed by army blocking frequencies. By 1985 they had discovered the 'white band' – an area of the electronic spectrum where military 'inhibitors' couldn't operate. The unidentified pulse detected in Gibraltar set alarm bells ringing, and the British Embassy in Madrid asked the Spanish police to keep their eyes open for terrorist suspects.

On 5 November, three days before a PIRA bomb in Enniskillen killed eleven civilians and injured sixty, police at Málaga airport on Spain's Costa del Sol spotted a PIRA operator named Daniel McCann. The thirty-year-old commander of the Provisionals' Clonard battalion, in west Belfast's Lower Falls area, McCann was a butcher's assistant and former hospital employee who was suspected of killing two off-duty RUC detectives the previous August, in a bar near Belfast docks. He was travelling on a false passport in the name of Robert Wilfred Reilly.

Spanish detectives followed McCann discreetly to the seaside resort of Torremolinos, where he met with two other suspects, a man travelling in the name of Brendan Coyne, and a woman whose stolen passport bore the name of Mary Parkin. Coyne was Sean Savage, a twenty-three-year-old PIRA bomb-maker from west Belfast. The identity of 'Mary Parkin' remains unknown.

British intelligence suspected that PIRA was planning a bomb attack on British forces in Gibraltar. An assessment suggested that the most likely target would be the public changing-of-the-guard ceremony, which took place on Tuesdays in Gibraltar's Main Street. Specifically, the best place for a bomb would be the assembly point for the band of 1 Royal Anglian Regiment, currently on garrison-duty on the Rock.

On 3 March an attractive Catholic woman whose passport gave her name as 'Katherine Smith' flew from Dublin to Brussels, and on to Madrid and Málaga the following day. 'Smith' was thirty-one-year-old Mairead Farrell, from Andersonstown in west Belfast, who had already served a ten-year prison stretch for planting a bomb in the Conway Hotel. The same evening, Daniel McCann and Sean Savage arrived in Málaga on a flight from Paris, and met up with Farrell at the airport. They booked into a hotel in Torremolinos.

In the morning, a man calling himself John Oakes hired a red Ford Fiesta from a car-hire company in Torremolinos. The same day, Oakes drove the car to Valencia, where he picked up a hundred and forty pounds of Semtex explosive. The Semtex may have been brought in by a PIRA back-up team: two PIRA suspects, a man and a woman, had been clocked at Valencia in February.

At about 2200 hours the same day, Saturday 5 March, Mairead Farrell hired a white Ford Fiesta in Torremolinos in the name of Katherine Smith. Farrell drove the car to Marbella and parked it in the basement car park of a building called the Edificio Marbeland. Before first light on Sunday morning, the red Ford Fiesta hired by John Oakes pulled up in the car park, with the Semtex on board. It was transferred to the white Fiesta.

A third car – a white Renault 5 – had been hired in Torremolinos on Saturday morning. This car was eventually parked in Gibraltar, in the area where the changing-of-the-guard ceremony was to take place the following Tuesday. Whether it entered Gibraltar on Saturday or Sunday, and whether driven by Sean Savage or John Oakes, is disputed. The official British line was that Sean Savage was seen parking the car in the Plaza in Gibraltar at about 1250 hours on Sunday 6 March.

An MI5 surveillance team made a positive ID of Savage, and watched him lean on the Renault for a few moments. They observed him fiddling about with something inside the vehicle that they couldn't see. Savage appeared to have entered Gibraltar unnoticed, but one Spanish police officer alleged later that the Renault had been shadowed by their anti-terrorist squad, who informed the British that they were ninety per cent sure it wasn't carrying a bomb. On Sunday afternoon at about 1430 hours, Farrell and McCann crossed the border into Gibraltar on foot, having left the red Fiesta in a car park at La Linea, two miles away. The Semtex was still in the white Fiesta at Marbella.

On Saturday, a twelve-man SAS team from the Pagoda squad flew into Gibraltar. Their deployment had been sanctioned personally by Prime Minister Margaret Thatcher in late February, on the strength of a top-secret report from the Joint Intelligence Committee. The report was the result of a four-month-long surveillance operation by MI5, concluding that a PIRA active-service unit was planning to bomb the changing-of-the-guard parade in Gibraltar on 8 March.

The SAS were briefed by their troop commander, 'Gonzo' – later referred to as 'Soldier E' – on the basis of intel passed to him by an MI5 Northern Ireland expert, 'Mr O'. Gonzo told the boys that one or more of the terrorists would be armed, and that at least one of them would be carrying a remote-control button to activate the bomb. The SAS were to observe the normal rules of engagement: the terrorists were to be arrested if possible, shot if there was any likelihood of a threat to themselves or to the public. The SAS groups were supported by MI5 watchers, and by teams of armed local Special Branch officers. 'Our orders were clear,' one officer commented later, '[the terrorists] were to be arrested, or, if necessary, shot.'[1]

MI5 officers had made Farrell and McCann as they crossed the frontier. Farrell was carrying a leather handbag. McCann wore a white shirt and grey slacks. The MI5 team passed the news of their arrival to the SAS force commander, Soldier 'F', in the hastily established SAS ops room. Authority was officially handed over to 'F' by the Gibraltar Commissioner of Police, Joseph Canepa.

The SAS assault-team consisted of only four men, divided into pairs. They were dressed in jeans and bomber-jackets, and carried 9mm Browning Hi-Power pistols in their back waistbands. The Brownings' magazines held twelve rounds, and each man had three spare magazines in his pockets. They were each equipped with a concealed radio – one of the pair was tuned into the surveillance network, the other to the ops room. Before deploying, the SAS teams were told that a bomb had been planted in the area of the assembly point.

McCann and Farrell met up with Savage near the parked Renault. When the watchers reported they'd moved away, and were roaming around the city centre, the police-chief reclaimed authority from the SAS. Shortly, though, the three suspects returned to the vicinity of the car. One of the MI5 surveillance team, 'H', recalled that they exchanged a joke and moved off with smiles on their faces. 'It was a chilling moment,' he commented later. 'I felt that these were evil people who were prepared to spill blood.'[2]

The three terrorists were walking back in the direction of the Spanish border. As the watchers tailed them, a bomb disposal expert attached to the SAS, 'Soldier G', did a recce of the Renault to assess whether it might contain a bomb. He didn't notice any displacement of the suspension such as would be caused by a big explosive charge. One known PIRA method, though, was to use a 'blocking car', put in to reserve the parking-space for the vehicle carrying the explosives, which would be brought in at the last moment. However, the intelligence brief had stated that on this operation there would be no blocking car.

'G' also knew that a lighter charge – up to thirty pounds of Semtex – wouldn't cause any noticeable displacement. Such a bomb would still be capable of doing terrible damage: if detonated during the parade, it would not only take out the fifty soldiers involved, but in all probability would kill and injure scores of onlookers. The casualty projection was around three hundred. For 'G', though, the tipping point was the radio-aerial in the centre of the Renault's roof. While the car was fairly new, the aerial appeared old. 'G' told the police that the car was 'suspicious'. This gave the Commissioner of Police, Joseph Canepa, grounds to arrest the terrorists on suspicion of conspiracy to murder. He handed authority back to the SAS for the final time.

It became clear afterwards that the three terrorists were walking back to the border because their mission was complete. None of them was armed, none of them carried a 'button', and there was no bomb in the Renault. The parade wasn't due for another forty-eight hours, and they had evidently entered Gibraltar on a reconnaissance operation. They were wary of surveillance, though: MI5 personnel noted that they continually looked around and glanced in the wing-mirrors of cars as they passed. McCann and Farrell walked in front; Savage trailed behind.

They wandered up Winston Churchill Avenue, a double-carriageway leading towards Spain, with a large flat-block and a Shell petrol-station on the right-hand side. Before reaching the Shell station, they halted for a few moments to chat. Then Savage turned back towards the town centre, possibly intending to pick up the car.

The first SAS-team – Soldiers 'A' and 'B' – were already trailing the terrorists. Savage walked directly towards them and actually bumped one of the SAS-men with his shoulder as he passed. The new development bothered them, as they thought Savage might be going back to detonate the bomb. Leaving him for the second team following behind them, they closed in on Farrell and McCann.

As the two SAS-men moved in, McCann looked straight at Soldier 'A'. Their eyes locked. The smile on McCann's face was wiped off in an instant, and 'A' knew he *knew*. 'The look on McCann's face, the alertness, the awareness of him,' 'A' recalled, 'he looked at me, then all of a sudden his right arm, right elbow, actually moved across the front of his body ... At that stage I thought he was definitely going for the button.'³ The SAS-man was already drawing his pistol. He said later that he intended to shout 'Stop!' but wasn't aware whether the word came out or not. He flipped the safety, squeezed the trigger, fired a round into McCann's back, the 9mm slug smacking through his ribs and blipping out from his chest. In a split-second blur, 'A' saw Farrell make a move towards her handbag and shot her in the face. As McCann tottered, 'A' pumped another round into his body.

'A''s partner, Soldier 'B', standing in the road on his left, said later that he'd heard 'A' make a garbled shout, and registered gunshots. He didn't have time to see whether they came from the terrorists or his mate. He spotted only Farrell's movement towards her handbag and believed she was going for the 'button'. He slipped out his Browning and shot her twice in the back as she reeled forward from A's bullet. The rounds pulped her heart and smashed her spine. He switched fire to McCann and shot him in the jaw and head. As Farrell sprawled on the path, he shot her again: he couldn't see her hands and thought there was still a chance she might activate the bomb. Three of his rounds missed, and slapped into petrol-pumps in the Shell station in front of him.

At that moment a police siren wailed and a police car skidded up beside them. The car was driven by Inspector Revagliatte of the Gibraltar police, who was unconnected with the operation. 'A' and 'B' had already donned black berets for quick identification. They jumped into the car and were whisked off to the Ops room to report to their boss.

Later, some eye-witnesses claimed that the siren had gone off before the SAS-men opened fire, and it was this that made Farrell and McCann turn sharply. Certainly it was the almost simultaneous noise of the siren and the gunshots that caused Sean Savage to whirl round on SAS-men 'C' and 'D', about a hundred and thirty metres away. Savage had just hung a left off Winston Churchill

Avenue into a tree-lined boulevard when he heard the shots, spun round and went into a crouching stance. As 'C' yelled a warning, Savage made a movement towards his hips. 'I fired,' 'C' said later. 'I kept on firing until I was sure he had gone down and was no longer a threat . . .'[4] As 'D' grabbed his pistol, a woman on a bicycle suddenly swept between him and Savage. He shoved her out of the way and fired nine rounds into the bomber's body. The 9mm bullets fractured his skull, broke an arm and a leg, and punctured a hand. Savage was later found to have taken sixteen bullets, and sustained twenty-seven wounds.

The SAS and MI5 teams were back in the UK by nightfall. By then, the government had already released a statement claiming that a bomb had been found in Gibraltar, and that three suspects had been killed by the police. This deliberate disinformation – following the principle that the first statement is the definitive one, and subsequently difficult to refute – was confirmed by a Ministry of Defence spokesman the following morning, alleging that a large bomb had been defused.

The revelation of the truth created a furore that hadn't been seen since the Iranian Embassy siege. This time, though, the SAS were cast in the role of villains. There had been no bomb and no 'gun-battle' – eye-witnesses alleged that the SAS had shot the terrorists as they were surrendering, or 'executed' them as they lay helpless on the ground. The fact that they'd been allowed to enter Gibraltar even though under surveillance was seen as a deliberate plot to take them out. 'The evidence,' said human rights researcher Father Raymond Murray, 'suggests the intention was always to shoot the members of the IRA team.'[5]

The government responded by claiming that British intelligence hadn't known which members of PIRA would be involved in the incident, and that they had not been under surveillance because the Spanish anti-terrorist police had lost them shortly after they arrived at Málaga. The Spanish later retorted that they had not lost the suspects: in fact, they had shadowed them all the way to the border. Margaret Thatcher's statement that 'those who live by the bomb and the gun and those who support them cannot in all circumstances be accorded . . . the same rights as everyone else' was less than helpful, suggesting as it did that the three unarmed terrorists really had been executed.

The spectre of the SAS as a death-squad once again raised its head, as people began to recall the controversy over the deaths of John Boyle and William Hanna. Paddy McGrory, a lawyer representing the victims' families, whose knowledge of the SAS derived mainly from his acquaintance with the late Blair Mayne, described the SAS shooters as 'members of an unholy priesthood of violence'.[6]

The idea that the SAS had been sent in to execute the three PIRA terrorists is as unlikely as the allegation that the Pagoda team had been ordered to kill the Arab hostage-takers during the Iranian Embassy siege. The SAS-teams were working on the intel supplied in their briefing: that there was a bomb, and that the terrorists were liable to detonate it with a button device. Faced with making a lightning decision, they took the most secure path. To have desisted could have resulted in the deaths of scores of civilians, while a mistake in the opposite direction would result in the deaths of known terrorists. This was regrettable, but to the shooters, the lesser of two evils. Once they opened fire, they were trained to keep on shooting until they were a hundred per cent certain that no such device could be operated.

The apparent 'setting up' of the terrorists also caused controversy. The British army had learned long ago in Northern Ireland, though, that failing to catch bombers in the act too often resulted in their walking free. If they had allowed the Spanish authorities to arrest the PIRA trio, or had picked them up at the border, they would probably have been released through lack of evidence. Once they were in Gibraltar, though, they could not be allowed back into Spain, where they could have set off the presumed bomb by radio-control.

The death of McCann, Farrell and Savage was not the most advantageous outcome from the intelligence point of view. It meant that MI5 were unable to locate the explosives immediately, or identify and pick up the PIRA back-up team – including the mysterious 'John Oakes' and 'Mary Parkin'. It also created three more martyrs for the Republican cause. Nevertheless, given the intelligence, the SAS made the only reasonable choice. The coroner agreed. At the inquest in September the verdict was nine to two in favour of lawful killing. At the European Commission in Strasbourg there was an eleven to six verdict that the SAS had not used unnecessary force.

92. Sow fears in the mind of the enemy

Sir David Stirling died on 5 November 1990 after collapsing at a London clinic. The same evening, his coffin was laid in a chapel of St James's Catholic Church, where the Director, UK Special Forces, draped it with the Union Jack and set on top Stirling's decorations: his DSO, his recently acquired Knight Bachelor, and an SAS beret. Shortly before his death, Stirling had made arrangements to meet a friend to discuss a wide range of security issues, including the need to start covert operations against Iraqi President Saddam Hussein. He was to miss by a few months the first deployment of the SAS in its original desert role since the Second World War.

Three months earlier, Saddam Hussein had invaded Kuwait with a hundred thousand troops and twelve hundred tanks. His pretext for the invasion was the allegation that Kuwait had been pumping crude oil from the Ramallah field, whose ownership was disputed, and that the tiny but fabulously rich desert princedom had originally belonged to Iraq. He also claimed that the Kuwaitis had contravened an OPEC agreement by overproducing oil, costing Iraq fourteen million dollars in lost revenues.

The real origin of Saddam's dispute with Kuwait lay in the eight-year war his country had fought with neighbouring Iran, ostensibly over her monopoly of the Shatt al-Arab waterway. The war had been conducted in bloody Somme-style offensives against trenches and machine guns, in which the attackers had been mown down like sheep. Both sides had used chemical weapons and long-range missiles, but Iran had made the mistake of targeting Kuwaiti oil-tankers in the Gulf, bringing down on her the wrath of the USA. Reviled by world opinion, and denied access to foreign arms, Iran was obliged to sue for peace. Though Saddam crowed over the masses of armour and artillery his forces had captured, it had been a pyrrhic victory – almost two million people had died, and not an inch of ground had been gained. Kuwait had supported Iraq during the war and made her extensive loans. When the princedom's rulers asked for repayment, Saddam replied by occupying Kuwait.

The invasion was denounced by the UN Security Council, which immediately declared a trade embargo against Iraq. Within a fortnight, the spearhead brigade of the US 82 Airborne Division had landed in Saudi-Arabia to secure the nation's oil reserves. The first phase of operations by Coalition troops – Desert Shield – was defensive: to protect Saudi-Arabia against invasion, and to gain time for a massive concentration of men and materiel from thirty-two countries, including Britain, France, Italy, Egypt, Syria, Qatar, Oman, the United Arab Emirates and Bahrain, as well as Saudi-Arabia and the USA. Saddam continued to build up his forces, however, and by November the Coalition was facing no fewer than twenty-six Iraqi divisions, comprising four hundred and fifty thousand men. At the end of the month, the UN Security Council authorized the use of force if the Iraqis failed to withdraw from Kuwait by 15 January.

General 'Stormin' Norman' Schwarzkopf, Commander-in-Chief of Coalition forces, had devised a counter-offensive based on air-power. Wave after wave of Allied bombers would hit strategic targets, cut the command infrastructure and gain control of the skies. When this had been achieved, the air force would turn its attention to the Iraqi army, pounding its artillery, armour and static defences, until the morale of Saddam's troops had been worn down. Only then would Coalition ground-forces go in for the kill.

At first, 22 SAS had found its nose pushed out of joint for lack of a suitable role. The obvious job – reconnaissance on the Kuwait frontier – had been bagged by the US 5 Special Forces Group and the US Marines. The only task available was the rescue of sixteen hundred British hostages held in Iraq and Kuwait. A team briefed to plan a hostage-rescue operation, though, calculated that it would require a force of brigade-strength – more than three times the manpower of all three SAS regiments combined. It would also result in more casualties than the number of hostages released. In December the plan was scrapped when Saddam released the hostages anyway.

D and G Squadrons had been on standby for the Gulf since August, while A Squadron was in Columbia, training local troops to fight the drug barons. B Squadron held down the SP role. G Squadron was sent to the UAE to brush up on desert warfare, but returned to the UK just before Christmas to take over Pagoda duties. A, B and D Squadrons were deployed in the Gulf by 2 January.

There was still no official role for them: C-in-C Schwarzkopf was not a believer in special forces. His campaign would be fought with aircraft and missiles, backed up by armoured divisions and motorized infantry: what the hell could special forces do, he inquired, that a Stealth fighter could not? The Regiment had an ally in the GOC British Forces in the Gulf, Lt. General Sir Peter de la Billière, who had postponed his retirement to take up the job. De la Billière had served in a number of administrative posts since stepping down as Director, SAS after the Falklands, but saw himself as an operational commander, and was determined to have one last bite of the cherry.

Despite having no official sanction, de la Billière instructed the Regiment's head-shed to start devising plans for deep-penetration raids behind Iraqi lines, to be ready by the UN deadline on 15 January. It was only a couple of days before the deadline that de la Billière was able to win Schwarzkopf over, with a formal presentation using maps and graphics. The SAS task, he explained, would be to 'cut roads and create diversions which would draw

Iraqi forces away from the main front and sow fears in the mind of the enemy that some major operation was brewing on his right flank'.[1] It was a return to the classic 'golden era' of SAS operations in North Africa under Stirling and Mayne.

The SAS group had been reorganized in the past decade, and was now UK Special Forces, with a director and deputy-director. It comprised 21, 22 and 23 SAS Regiments, the Royal Marines' Special Boat Service, 63 SAS Signals Squadron and the Intelligence & Security Group, known as 14 Intelligence Company. The three regular SAS sabre squadrons deployed in the Gulf had been reinforced by a troop from R Squadron, and were supported by the SBS and RAF special forces air squadrons – a total of more than five hundred men.

The first Coalition sorties went in on 17 January, when two Iraqi early-warning radar installations on the Saudi-Arabian border were taken out by a dozen Apache helicopters of the US 101 Airborne Division, using laser-guided Hellfire missiles. The Apaches were followed by a squadron of F-15 fighters tasked to skewer the nearest Iraqi air-defence command centre, opening up a brace of blind corridors through which thousands of Coalition bombers would swarm, to hit two hundred and forty strategic targets all over Iraq.

While Coalition air-strikes continued, A and D Squadrons and half of B Squadron were transferred from their HQ in the United Arab Emirates by Hercules C130s to their forward operating base at al-Jauf in Saudi-Arabia, south of the Iraq frontier. The squadrons were equipped with 'pinkies' – Land Rover 110s, fitted with Browning machine guns, GPMGs and Milan missiles, backed up by Unimogs and dirt-bikes. The hundred and twenty-eight men of A and D Squadrons were divided into four half-squadron mobile groups. They were ready to launch their deep-penetration raids as ordered, but wondered if there was really any place for them in this hi-tech circus.[2]

The mobile groups were already crossing the border when it became clear that they were needed after all. At 0300 hours on 18 January the Iraqis fired seven Scud missiles at Israel, followed later by another three. The Scuds caused few casualties, but succeeded in riling Israeli Prime Minister Yitzhak Shamir, enough to declare that he was sending a hundred aircraft across Saudi-Arabian airspace to bomb Iraq and launching a commando assault. For Schwarzkopf, this was a nightmare scenario. Israeli intervention would cause irreparable damage to the Coalition. Schwarzkopf was obliged to divert a third of his aircraft from their main task, to take out the Scuds.

The Scud was a dinosaur in military terms. Designed by the Russians a generation earlier, it had a speed of five thousand kilometres an hour and flew at an altitude of thirty kilometres. The missiles had been imported by Saddam Hussein during the Iran–Iraq war, and their range extended by cannibalizing parts, to give the weapons the capability of reaching Tehran. Though this had been at the price of reducing the power of its warheads, Scuds had still succeeded in causing at least eight thousand casualties during the war.

President George Bush assured Shamir that evening that all known Scud sites had been blitzed, but the Scuds kept coming. Most of those aimed at Israel had been fired not from permanent sites, but from mobile transporter-erector launchers (TELs) in western Iraq. The Iraqis proved skilful at hiding these launchers, so that not even the most advanced surveillance equipment could trace them. Locating mobile Scud-launchers was a job for the Mark I human eyeball – a task tailor-made for the SAS.

The A and D Squadron mobile patrols received orders to track down Scuds and destroy them if possible, or vector-in strike aircraft. The half of B Squadron left at al-Jauf were given a different task. They would be dropped in the desert of western Iraq to set up covert observation-points on three major roads – known in SAS terminology as main supply-routes (MSRs) – and report the movement of Scud erector-launchers. The B Squadron boys would divide into three eight-man 'road-watch' patrols and go in by RAF Chinook helicopter.

93. 'If it comes to a firefight it could well save your arse'

One of the first things Peter Ratcliffe noticed at al-Jauf was the cold. The 'Green Slime' – the intelligence boys – had told them it would be like a spring day in England, but it was more like the Arctic. Polar winds thrashed unfettered across the Iraqi desert, and night temperatures plumped to freezing. The men hadn't come equipped for Arctic warfare – some of them hadn't even brought sleeping-bags. Ratcliffe, appointed Regimental Sergeant-Major, 22 SAS only a fortnight earlier, pushed the RQMS to search the local souks for sheepskin coats.

The SAS forward base was a new but as yet unused civil airport about a hundred and fifty miles south of the Iraqi frontier, where Coalition jets were forever screeching in and taking off. The ops room had been set up in the baggage-reclaim hall of the terminal building, using the carousels as desks. It was crammed with radio-equipment, computer terminals, satellite-link decoders and an enormous wall-chart showing the dispositions of SAS units. The four mobile half-squadrons ordered into Iraq to hunt Scuds were represented by four stickers. On the morning of 22 January, Ratcliffe noticed that one of the stickers still hadn't been moved across the border. It was the A Squadron patrol tagged Alpha One Zero, commanded by the squadron boss, Major 'Graham' – an SBS officer both Ratcliffe and the commanding officer had reservations about. At the briefing, Graham had seemed ill at ease and lacking in confidence.

Two days earlier, Graham had reported from the field that his way was blocked by a berm – a man-made barrier of sand. The berm stretched almost all the way along the border, and the other half-squadrons had crossed it without trouble. The RSM wondered what was so special about the berm in Graham's area. 'My gut feeling, which began to grow stronger as I stared at that little sticker on the map,' Ratcliffe said, 'was that Alpha One Zero was in no particular hurry to join the war.'[1]

He was distracted by the entrance of the commanding officer, Lt. Col. 'J', who was in a foul temper. He told the RSM that he'd just had an unsatisfactory chat with the sergeant in charge of one of the three B Squadron patrols assigned to the road-watch operation: Bravo Two Zero. Against his advice, Sgt. 'Andy McNab', or 'M', had refused to take a 'dinky' – a short-wheelbase Land Rover 90. The patrol had held a Chinese parliament and decided to go in on foot. They had an enormous amount of gear for digging and camouflaging a hide, all of which would have to be jettisoned if they got bumped. With a Land Rover they at least stood a chance of getting out of a contact. Without a vehicle they'd be stuck. 'J' asked Ratcliffe to go and 'knock some sense' into McNab.

The RSM found the patrol gathered among alps of kit – 5.56mm M16 rifles with underslung M204 40mm grenade-launchers, Minimi light machine guns, ammunition-boxes, LAW 66mm anti-tank rocket-launchers, M204 grenades, L2 hand-grenades, white phos grenades, claymore mines, jerrycans, Bergens, shovels, communications-gear, poles and gunnysacks packed with camouflage-nets, thermal sheeting and hundreds of empty sandbags. It looked as if they intended to lug everything but the kitchen sink. Ratcliffe's belief was that an SAS patrol should be as light on its feet as possible. He saw at once that they were taking too much.

He buttonholed McNab. 'I'm strongly advising you to take a vehicle,' he said. 'If it comes to a firefight it could well save your arse. So take the Boss's and my advice and don't be a fool.'

The RSM could tell from the sergeant's expression that he wasn't having any. 'No way,' McNab said. 'We don't need it and we're not taking it. It's a sure fire way of getting compromised.'[2]

One member of the patrol chipped in that it would be like going into action with an albatross round their necks. Another, Cpl. 'Chris Ryan', said that there'd be nowhere to hide it. Ratcliffe knew they were judging the terrain from satellite pictures, which showed elevation but not depression – there would almost certainly be places where they could stash the vehicle. In the Second World War, 1 SAS and the LRDG had cammed-up in landscapes that looked completely empty. Ryan commented later that in fact they'd read the satellite images upside down, and mistaken low ground for high.

McNab wouldn't shift on the Land Rover issue, or on the question of equipment. Ratcliffe reckoned they would be carrying loads of seventy-five or eighty kilos each – nearly three times what a candidate carried on Selection. It would be as if each of them was hefting an extra man on his back. The RSM gave them about a dozen paces. He could have ordered them to take a dinky, but he knew that this would be counter-productive. The patrol would follow orders, but would then act like prima donnas – perhaps even getting comped purposely, so they could say, 'I told you so.' It was the custom in the SAS that the final decision was left to the man commanding on the ground, whatever his rank. Ratcliffe accepted that there was nothing he could do, and returned to his CO in the same foul mood 'J' had been in when he'd first stalked into the ops room.

The three B Squadron patrols went into action that night in two RAF Chinooks. In the end, only one of them, Bravo One Nine, took dinkies. The third group, Bravo Three Zero, was extracted immediately. The patrol-boss took a shufti at the place he was supposed to put in his OP – a uniformly flat gravel plain – and realized a hide would stick out like 'balls on a bulldog'. He aborted the mission.

Bravo Two Zero had been assigned the most northerly MSR, not a tarmac road but a desert track running along the edge of a low escarpment. Their plan was to land about twelve klicks from the place where the road kinked as it descended the high ground. They would set up a covert OP close to the road and watch for the movement of Scuds. The patrol had been tasked to stay in the field for ten days, and even if they clocked one Scud in that time, it would be priceless intel. They would transmit the details on the SATCOM gear they had with them, to alert fighter-bombers on stand-by twenty-four seven.

Bravo Two Zero was an eight-man patrol – six B squadron men and two from A Squadron. One of the A Squadron boys was the patrol 2IC, Sgt. Vince Phillips, an ex-Royal Army Ordnance Corps specialist who'd done time in both the Parachute and the Commando Brigades. A long-legged marathon-runner, thirty-six years of age, Phillips was nearing the end of his service and was married with two young girls. The other A Squadron man had been with the Regiment only a few weeks. This was 'Mike Coburn' – a twenty-six-year-old New Zealander from Auckland who'd served previously in the New Zealand SAS. Two of the patrol were ex-Paras. L.Cpl. 'Dinger' was a vet of 22 SAS who'd served in the Falklands, a married man with two daughters, and a big smoker and drinker with a reputation for wildness. Tpr. Steven 'Legs' Lane was a more recent arrival – a tall, wiry, reserved man, his role was patrol signaller. The patrol medic, twenty-nine-year-old Geordie 'Ryan', came from Tyneside. Married with one child, he had joined the Regiment from 23 SAS. The two remaining men were physical opposites: twenty-four-year-old Tpr. Bob Consiglio, an ex-Marine from an Anglo-Sicilian family, was small but powerful – the others joked that when carrying his pack he looked from behind like a Bergen with legs. 'Mal' was a giant who'd lived in Australia, but had served with the Rhodesian army.

The patrol commander, Andy McNab, was a thirty-four-year-old Cockney of part-Greek descent, brought up by foster-parents. He'd joined the army as a boy soldier to escape a life of petty crime. An ex-Royal Green Jacket, he'd been awarded the MM in Northern Ireland for taking out one terrorist and wounding another.

The Chinook carrying Bravo Two Zero went in at an altitude of only thirty metres to dodge the radar shield. There was one drama on the way when she was painted by enemy radar probes. She went into evasion mode, blowing chaff, losing altitude, banking and yawing. Inside, there was chaos. The loadmasters bawled at each other over the din of the rotors, and trod on the feet of the SAS team in the cabin. The heli finally put them down after a two-hour flight, at a point around three hundred kilometres north of the border. The patrol ramped out into the desert night.

Lying on the side of a wadi under a full moon and a sky

ponderous with stars, Mike Coburn checked his Magellan GPS unit and realized that the RAF 'crabs' must have landed them in the wrong place. They were only two kilometres short of the site they'd chosen to put in their OP, when they should have been twelve kilometres south of it. According to Ryan, though, it wasn't a mistake. He said that the team had talked the RAF pilot into putting them down nearer the target. McNab was aware that with their vast loads they wouldn't make it from the original drop-off point to the lying-up place before first light. Moving tactically with packs weighing eighty kilos or more, they couldn't cover more than five hundred metres an hour: twelve kilometres would have taken them twenty-four hours. The bad news was that there was what appeared to be a small village on a knoll no more than six hundred metres away. It shouldn't have been there: it wasn't marked on the map.

The 'village' was a temporary settlement – a nest of rambling wood houses and tents standing among stone-pines and mesquite bush, with a rusted water-tower full of holes. It was the home of Abbas bin Fadhil, head of an extended family of the Buhayat – a shepherd tribe of the Iraq desert. Abbas heard the Chinook come in, and recognized the thump and swish of a twin-engined heli. He was familiar with the sound, because he'd done a dozen years in the Iraqi special forces, including eight years in the Iran–Iraq war, reaching the rank of sergeant-major. He'd been wounded several times, and still had two bullets in his body. He had finally been invalided out with multiple wounds in the ankle that had left him crippled. Now he was a sheep-farmer with a gammy foot, but ironically, he'd had more combat experience than all the members of Bravo Two Zero put together.

There was no electricity in the settlement, and no TV, but Abbas was aware that the country was at war. He had no way of knowing whether the chopper he'd heard belonged to enemy or friendly forces, but he sent his ten-year-old nephew, Adil, off to the nearest military post to inform them anyway.

Meanwhile, the patrol had located a lying-up place in a wadi about half a klick from Abbas's settlement. It was a cul-de-sac only a few hundred metres south of the road, a steep-sided ravine, not large, but with a slight overhang and a seven-foot boulder on one side, behind which they could all hide if necessary. Though the LUP was less than a mile and a half from the place they'd been landed, it took over two hours to get there with their Bergens. While four men prepared the place, setting up Claymore and Elsie mines, or stood sentry, the other four went back for the gunny-sacks. Once they'd been brought in, one man kept watch while the others tried to get some shut-eye. It was harder than they'd expected: most had only bivvy-bags, and the night air was freezing.

The original idea had been to dig a hide, line it with sandbags, and cover it with thermal sheeting, to prevent imaging-devices locating them by body-heat. The problem was that the ground was rocky – there was no sand at all. Not only could they not dig a hide, they couldn't fill the sandbags either. This meant that half of the kit they'd lugged with them was useless. They'd practised digging the OP in the Empty Quarter of the United Arab Emirates – the world's largest sand-desert. The 'Green Slime' hadn't told them that the desert of Iraq is predominantly stony, covered with a shallow skin of heavy clay in places, but with hardly any sand.

The second problem became apparent the next morning at first light, when McNab and Ryan clocked an Iraqi S60 anti-aircraft battery on the top of the escarpment overlooking the road. It was less than a kilometre away, and was manned by at least a dozen Iraqi soldiers. That shouldn't have been there, either.

The morning was so cold that Coburn crept off to do a few exercises to get the circulation going. On his way down the wadi, McNab stopped him and asked him if he could help Lane on the radio. Coburn thought this odd, since Lane was a first-class signal-ler, but it quickly transpired that he'd failed to get comms with the forward base. The radio was a PRC 319 set with a burst capacity. This meant that the signaller tapped in an encoded mes-sage, which was recorded and transmitted in a micro-second burst, too fast for enemy direction-finding gear. The 319 worked through a wire dipole antenna that bounced signals off the ionosphere via a relay station in Cyprus, to the forward operating base at al-Jauf.

Lane told Coburn he'd checked the set carefully. There seemed to be nothing wrong with it. He was picking up static, which suggested it was working, but there should have been homing transmissions in Morse-code coming in on the frequencies he'd been given, and there weren't any. Coburn worked methodically through a mental troubleshooting manual. He gave up half an hour later, confused. The radio had a self-testing mechanism, and if the set was faulty, it would have shown up on the electronic message screen. The only other possibilities were that the transmitting station had been taken out, or that they'd been given the wrong frequencies.

In the course of the morning, every man in the patrol had a go at fixing the set. No one succeeded. About noon, McNab called them together for a conflab: the loss of comms was a serious business. Phillips reminded him that they had SATCOM, but McNab countered that they'd been instructed to use it only for Scud sightings or life-and-death emergencies. SATCOM left a massive signals 'footprint' and multiplied their chances of being compromised.

There was a lost-comms drill. If nothing was heard from the patrol by noon next day, the chopper would return to the drop-off point to deliver a new radio, or to extract them. The dilemma here was that they didn't know which drop-off point the heli would use – the 'official' one, or the one where they'd actually been landed.

If they hadn't got through to base by midday, they would move out at last light. They'd shift everything to the 'official' drop-off point, then two of them would come back to the actual landing-place, so they could cover both. McNab wasn't giving up. After they'd sorted out the signals glitch, they'd get relocated somewhere else. The patrol spent the day watching the road. There was hardly any movement – only the occasional Bedouin pick-up greasing along in a dust-tail.

Adil, the boy Abbas bin Fadhil had sent to the military post, had come back hours later saying that the army thought the helicopter they'd heard was one of theirs. That afternoon, Adil took the family's sheep out to graze near the settlement. One of his animals wandered over the lip of the ravine in which the patrol was hiding.

The SAS-men had been alerted to the approach of Adil and his flock by the sound of sheep-bells tinkling. They saw one of the sheep as it came over the lip of the wadi – not being accustomed to lean Arab sheep, most of them thought it was a goat, although Abbas's people had no goats. They also heard Adil's voice as he called to the flock, and reckoned they were about to be made. They hurled pebbles at the animal until it retreated. To their great relief the herdsboy didn't come any closer.

That night, McNab led a four-man patrol out to recce the area and ascertain the exact position of the road. They boxed round a couple of encampments, but weren't certain whether they were civilian or military. Forced to retreat by barking dogs, they returned to the ravine.

94. 'High possibility compromise'

At al-Jauf next morning, Peter Ratcliffe was heading to the ops room when the commanding officer came charging out and almost bumped into him. The RSM saw at once that 'J' was hopping mad, and thought he could guess why. Alpha One Zero was still hovering around the frontier, unable to cross the berm. 'J' had lost patience, and had decided to send in another second-in-command to stiffen up the patrol. As he had no spare officers, he asked the RSM if he'd be prepared to go. Ratcliffe was astonished but delighted to get this unexpected chance to do some real fighting. 'What time am I going in?' he asked.

By noon, Bravo Two Zero had been in the field for about thirty-six hours without making contact, and in the COMCEN, the SAS yeoman of signals asked the ops officer if he wanted to initiate lost-comms procedure. The officer was concerned, but couldn't send a chopper. All the Chinooks were tasked up for the next forty-eight hours, resupplying the mobile patrols. Half an hour later, the yeoman returned looking sheepish. He told the ops officer that one of his operators had noticed an anomaly on the frequency-prediction charts for the area. They didn't match the frequencies given to Bravo Two Zero, which were those assigned for Kuwait. When the officer asked what this meant, the yeoman answered that it meant Bravo Two Zero had the wrong frequencies: they hadn't got a hope of getting comms with the ones they'd been given.

In the LUP, McNab confirmed the decision to pull out that night to the emergency RV twelve klicks to the south. He was confident that the Chinook would come in on schedule. He told Bob Consiglio and Mike Coburn to rig up the SATCOM equipment in case there was anything for them on the net. As they were assembling the satellite-dish, Steve Lane suddenly whispered that he'd picked up a fractured message on the emergency guard-net. He reckoned that he should be able to transmit back, but it was against SOPs except in emergencies, because of the risk of getting dee-effed. McNab told him to forget SOP and to transmit the patrol's location statistics, the position of the enemy anti-aircraft battery, and the intel that they were moving to the emergency RV that night. Lane tapped the message off, but received no confirmation. Coburn was just trying a radio-check on the SAT-COM when McNab grabbed his arm. Everyone froze. They heard the jingle of sheep-bells coming towards them. Vince Phillips crept down from the sentry-position, hissing that it was the same herdsboy again, but this time he was moving directly towards them.

What happened next was a replay of the SAS patrol versus herdsboy scenario that had first been acted out just under fifty years ago, when Bill Fraser's patrol had been lying up on their way to hit Ajadabiyya. Then, it had been Arthur Phillips who was said to have been spotted; this time it was his namesake Vince Phillips. Ryan later claimed that Phillips admitted he'd made eye-contact with the boy. Coburn wrote that the shepherd was singing as he approached the wadi, but stopped abruptly as if he'd noticed something. Within a few seconds, though, the boy had resumed his singing and continued as if nothing had happened. The whole patrol had squeezed behind the standing boulder before the herder came into view, but none of them was certain if he'd clocked them or not.

McNab had to assume they'd been spotted. He told Lane to get on the guard-net and send the message, 'High possibility compromise. Request relocation or exfil.' In fact, questioned a decade later, Abbas's nephew, Adil, admitted he'd been herding sheep in the area on that day, but had noticed nothing unusual.

It was icy, with a chilling wind lashing off the desert. Abbas bin Fadhil thought there was snow coming, and was worried about the fuel in his loader freezing up. Fuel was very hard to come by at the time. That afternoon he decided to park the vehicle in the adjacent wadi, out of the wind. It was only a few minutes' drive from the house, and he knew that at the end of the wadi there was a sheltered place. What he didn't know was that it was now occupied by Bravo Two Zero.

Abbas drove the loader right up to the end of the wadi. As he turned the slight bend, he saw two armed men peering at him from among the rocks, one on his left, near the standing boulder, and another on the higher ground to his right. 'They were wearing camouflage jackets and shamaghs over their faces,' he recalled, 'and I had no idea who they were. They could have been Iraqi commandos, or special troops of the intelligence service, or even crashed enemy pilots.'[1] Abbas tried to avoid eye-contact, and hastily turned the loader round. He trolled off back to the house.

The SAS patrol had heard the loader coming and assumed it was a tank or armoured personnel carrier. They extended their LAW 66mm anti-tank weapons ready to take it out. When it came into view, McNab saw that it was just 'an idiot pottering about on a digger', and relaxed, thinking – quite rightly – that it was there innocently. Ryan was convinced that the driver had come to look for them after being alerted by the shepherd-boy, but Coburn clearly recalled the look of shock on Abbas's face.

At the settlement, Abbas hobbled into the house and unpacked his AK47 rifle. His father, a seventy-year-old named Fadhil, asked what he was doing. Abbas told him he'd seen strangers in the wadi. 'I don't know who they are,' he said, 'but I'm going to find out.'[2] The old man declared that he would come, and got out his rifle – a five-shot, bolt-action Brno. They were joined by Abbas's younger brother, Hayil, who had also served in Iraqi special forces. He was also armed with a Kalashnikov AK47. Together, the three of them made their way back to the wadi on foot.

In the lying-up place the team was frantically packing away radio equipment, chugging water, stuffing themselves with Mars bars. Now they were certain they'd been compromised, and the only choice was to clear out pronto. They would ditch all the OP equipment and anything they couldn't carry. It would soon be dusk, and within the hour they'd have the cover of night. They buried the Claymore mines, and were soon pacing back down the dry-wash with their Bergens on and their weapons at the ready.

Abbas and his brother stood about five metres above them on the edge of the wadi as they came down. The Arabs held their weapons close by their sides so the strangers wouldn't see them. They were all masked with shamaghs, and Abbas still didn't know for sure they were foreigners. Up to now, they hadn't made any aggressive moves. If it came to a firefight, Abbas knew, he and his family were at a disadvantage. There were only three of them – one an old man, and himself, crippled. He wanted to be sure of his ground before taking any action. As the patrol padded down the water course, the Arabs paralleled them along the wadi side.

Further down, the walls of the wadi fell away, and flattened out into a basin about six hundred metres wide. The point where the patrol had been dropped lay to the south. To the east lay Abbas's settlement, clearly visible from here, and to the west the desert stretched away in galleries of serrated humpbacked ridges. The Arabs took up a position on the eastern side of the basin, and waited for the patrol to emerge.

The SAS were strung out. Coburn, who was near the back, didn't remember seeing the Arabs, who were hidden from him by the wadi wall. Ryan did see them. He described them as being clad in ankle-length white dishdashas, dark overcoats and red shamaghs. As he emerged from the wadi he waved to them, hoping the SAS would be taken for Iraqis. Coburn recalled that he saw someone ahead waving, but couldn't see who he was waving at. Abbas replied by firing two shots over the patrol's heads – a traditional Arab warning when encountering an unidentified party in the desert. The 'friendly' answer was to refrain from shooting back, and throw sand or dust in the air.

The SAS didn't know this. They went into an instinctive contact drill, diving, rolling and bringing their weapons into action. There wasn't much to shoot at, as Abbas and his two companions were by now lying headlong in the grass. 'Immediately they went down,' Abbas recalled, 'and they started shooting back at us, so of course we knew they were enemies.'

McNab turned the gun-battle between the Arabs and the eight-man SAS patrol into a 'Rambo' style Hollywood epic, with the patrol charging huge numbers of enemy, grenades being flung into armoured cars and Iraqis lolling out of windows dead. In fact it lasted only five minutes. The Woodhouse 'shoot and scoot' SOP still obtained, and the patrol's priority was to get out of the contact like a flash, not take on enemy machine guns. Acording to three members of the patrol, the Iraqi battery on the slope two kilometres away started belting 40mm shells at them. Abbas later denied they opened fire, and claimed that he hadn't alerted the gunners before returning with his rifle. At that stage he didn't know if the men in the wadi were friends or foes.

During those few minutes, some members of the patrol claimed to have seen Iraqi troops advancing towards them, but their accounts do not agree on details. Some saw armoured personnel-carriers, others didn't. Ryan saw a tipper-truck, no one else did. It will never be known exactly what happened and the extent to which a battle was fought with troops (as opposed to civilians).

95. 'No pain, only shock'

The patrol regrouped. They decided to head south to the drop-off point. Free of their Bergens, they raced across the desert, covering the distance before midnight. They lay there in the blasting wind for two hours, but the heli didn't arrive. They concluded she wasn't coming. They couldn't stay, and they didn't want to head south towards Saudi-Arabia: that was the way the enemy would expect them to go. The OC B Squadron had advised them to make for Syria. It was nearer, but McNab knew they'd never make it directly across the desert: they weren't carrying enough water. The only place they could be sure of getting water was the Euphrates. That route would be risky – the Euphrates valley was densely populated, and crawling with enemy troops and installations. The alternative was dying of thirst.

The main problem was that McNab hadn't filed this plan with the ops officer, so any search and rescue mission would be looking in the wrong place.

McNab put together a rough deception scheme. They'd march due west for a while, then wheel north and hit the same road they had been watching from the LUP. He reckoned the enemy wouldn't expect them to double back. North of the road there was a stretch of flat desert, then another road heading west to Krabilah, the border post.

They started about 0100 hours, tabbing into a wind so cold that it seemed to slice through their smocks. T. E. Lawrence, who had fought in this desert with the Bedouin in the First World War, said that nothing could be more debilitating than the north wind. '[It] cut open the skin,' he wrote, 'fingers lost power and sense of feel: cheeks shivered like dead leaves until they could shiver no more, then bound up muscles in a witless ache.'

It was a shock for all of them when big Mal, the ex-Rhodesian army man, collapsed from dehydration. He was the only one wearing thermal underwear. Despite sub-zero wind-chill, he'd sweated so much that his body was drained of moisture. Ryan revived him with rehydration salts dissolved in a water-bottle. Mal managed to get up and McNab put him with Ryan and Phillips at the front of the patrol. Not long afterwards, they descended a falaise into a deep wadi running roughly north. McNab, near the back of the file, heard the roar of aero-engines. He reckoned they were Coalition jets, and stopped to try to contact the pilots on TACBE – a ground-to-air radio-beacon with a range of seventy kilometres. He got a garbled response from an American flier, but there was no confirmation that his text had gone through. By the time he'd put the TACBE back in its pouch with stiff, frozen fingers, three of the patrol had vanished into the night. Ryan was in the lead, carrying the patrol's only night-sight, followed by Phillips and Mal. None of them noticed they'd separated from the rest until they reached the MSR. Mal was still weak, and Phillips had been hobbling along for hours in agony from an injury he'd sustained during the contact. The weather conditions were atrocious, and getting worse. There was a telltale lightness over the eastern horizon, which meant they'd soon have to go to ground. They staggered on for another ten klicks, until they stumbled on what Ryan took to be a 'tank berm': it was actually a rainwater-harvesting hollow dug out by the local Bedouin.

They lay up near the 'berm' for most of the day. They couldn't believe how cold it was. Soon after first light, it began to rain. The rain was followed by sleet. Ryan dozed off and woke with a feeling of pins and needles in his cheeks, and his limbs quaking uncontrollably. He was covered in a thin layer of snow. It was actually snowing in the desert.

In fact, snow was common here in winter. T. E. Lawrence wrote about it in *Seven Pillars of Wisdom* – the most famous book ever penned on warfare in this desert. It seemed that none of the intelligence staff had ever read it – certainly the SAS patrols hadn't been informed. By the time they set out into the blizzard at last light, all three were hovering on the edge of hallucination. Phillips was incoherent. He staggered, dragging behind the others. At one point he screamed that his hands had turned black. He was wearing black leather gloves. Ryan told him to put his hands in his pockets and tramp on. Within an hour he'd gone down. Ryan and Mal were so disoriented they didn't realize he was missing until it was too late.

Phillips's body was found the next day by a Bedouin named Mohammad – a relative of Abbas bin Fadhil. He was crossing this stretch of desert in his pick-up when he saw something black lying on the surface. It was Phillips. Mohammad searched his clothing, and found a Browning pistol and a pair of mini-binoculars, which he kept. He lifted the cadaver into the back of his pick-up and shipped it to the police-station in nearby al-Haqlaniyya. He returned to the area with some relatives to hunt for the others whose tracks he'd clocked near Phillips's corpse. The authorities were now aware that the soldiers involved in the firefight two days earlier were heading north.

Lying up to the north-west, McNab's section had also been tormented by the snow. 'I had known cold before, in the Arctic,' he recalled, 'but nothing like this. This was lying in a freezer cabinet, feeling your body heat slowly slip away.'[1] They tried cuddling up for warmth, but by mid-afternoon they were desperate. McNab decided that if they didn't move they'd all be dead by last light. They pressed on into the whiteout for the rest of the afternoon, and long into the night. By dawn on 26 January they had struck the route from al-Haqlaniyya to Krabilah – an asphalt road about five metres wide.

Resting up not far from the road, they had more bad luck. They were spotted by an old shepherd, who came over to talk to them. After he'd gone, they moved their location about fifteen hundred metres, but just before last light they clocked two three-tonners pulling up near the point where they'd made contact with the old man. They estimated that the lorries were carrying thirty to forty troops. McNab was certain the Iraqis were searching for them, and that they'd been alerted by the shepherd. He didn't realize Phillips was dead, and that his body had been found that morning.

The Syrian border lay a hundred and twenty kilometres to the west. McNab knew they might not survive another night in these conditions, and decided to hijack a vehicle. The plan was simple.

McNab and Consiglio were both swarthy and might be taken for Iraqis, especially with shamaghs wrapped round their faces. Consiglio would pretend to be injured, and McNab would stumble on to the road, half-carrying him, and flag down a car.

There were few vehicles on the road. When one appeared suddenly, McNab dragged a moaning Consiglio on to the hardtop. As the lights approached, he waved his arms frantically. The car slowed down. The other three leapt out of the ditch, and jabbed weapons at the driver and passengers.

Accounts differ as to how many people were in the car. All agree, though, that among them was a man in uniform, who shrieked that he was a Christian and showed them a Madonna icon. He was Adnan Badawi from Mosul, serving in the local gendarmerie. McNab and Coburn both maintained that the vehicle was 'a New York yellow cab'. Adnan, who had no reason to lie over the issue, revealed that it was a white Crown Toyota taxi.

The SAS herded the driver and passengers into the ditch. Adnan was so evidently intimidated that McNab thought he might be of some use to them. He bundled him back in. The five SAS-men piled in with him, and as they luxuriated in the sudden warmth McNab drove towards Krabilah.

About forty minutes passed. Most of the patrol were dozing off when they hit a vehicle checkpoint. It was manned by armed police. There was a tailback of vehicles extending about seven hundred metres, and McNab stopped. Dinger stepped out and popped the bonnet in case anyone got suspicious. McNab told Adnan they would bypass the checkpoint on foot. He instructed him to drive through and meet them on the other side. Consiglio snorted that he'd 'dob them in' as soon as they disappeared. Coburn felt they should have slotted him, but not even he wanted to shoot Adnan in cold blood. Instead, they jogged off into the desert.

That evening, an Iraqi police sergeant named Ahmad was on duty at the main police-station in Krabilah town when Adnan slunk in, pale-faced. He was terrified that he'd be accused of abetting the enemy. He told Ahmad he'd been kidnapped by five Brit commandos. He'd reported them at the checkpoint, but the police had sent him on here. Ahmad collected seven or eight comrades. They drove back. An air-raid alert was on – the road was chock-a-block with cars going like the clappers with their headlights off. About three klicks from the checkpoint Ahmad clocked two men in camouflage gear on the side of the road – one playing possum, the other flashing a torch at cars zipping past. 'Is that them?' he asked Adnan.

The Christian nodded. 'That's exactly what they did with us,' he said.

Ahmad drove on to the barriers. He rounded up about thirty armed men – regular police and militia – and seven vehicles. He led the convoy back to the point where he'd seen the two enemy soldiers. When the Iraqis roared up, the SAS were still trying to stop a car. McNab saw them coming. 'We were spotted from the road,' he wrote, '. . . vehicles came screaming along and blokes jumped out firing . . . All we could do was run.'[2] They went to ground in a dip four hundred metres away. They returned fire. 'They only fired a few shots,' Ahmad remembered, 'and we fired a salvo. It went on for about ten minutes. By that time they'd gone silent and we thought we might have hit them, but we weren't sure, so we . . . worked our way round in a big circle. When we got there, though, there was no one. They'd got away.'[3]

The SAS patrol passed within a hundred metres of the Iraqis as they bugged out. They melted into the shadows, heard the crump and splat of S60 ack-ack guns battling an air-attack. 'The ground shook with the ferocity of the artillery bombardment,' Coburn recalled, 'a great umbrella of red tracer reaching up into the Iraqi sky searching desperately for the hated bombers.'[4]

The air-raid was a useful diversion. The locals kept their heads down. The patrol scooted across the road, making for the Euphrates. They moved slowly through a warren of mud-built houses, through frozen slush to the water's edge. They dipped water-bottles into icy meltwater. The Euphrates roared. McNab considered crossing, but dismissed the idea as crazy. The river was in full spate and half a kilometre wide. In their state of rag-order, he'd give them ten minutes.

Coburn's GPS racked up ten kilometres to the border. They decided to push along the river-bank as a patrol, navigating on a communications mast standing on the frontier. Its red warning lights blinked, enticing them. They were only about two kilometres away when fire stoved into them out of dark groves on their left. AK47 rounds screeched and zipped. McNab and Coburn hit the deck, clocked muzzle-flashes, heard the punking of Bob Consiglio's Minimi on their left flank. Tracer spilt out of the shadows in long sequences of green and orange. Coburn splayed the bipod on his Minimi, spliffed a burst. McNab vanished into a gully. Coburn's weapon clunked dead – a stoppage. There was no time to clear it. He rolled, grabbed an M16 mag from his pouch, snagged it into the housing, braced the cocking lever. He drummed off the whole mag then crawled to the gully after McNab and threw himself in freezing mud.

Consiglio had been swallowed up by the night. None of his mates ever saw him again. Exactly what happened to him after the first contact has never been established. It seems likely he advanced through the bush and got caught in another contact. He held the Iraqis off until his ammo expired, then hugged a track at a right-angle to the Euphrates, perhaps intending to cross. He ran smack into a group of seven militiamen hidden in a copse of trees. 'We saw this man running towards us,' said one of them, Subhi, a local lawyer. 'We shouted out a warning . . . and he turned as if to go back. We opened fire. Some bullets hit him and he fell down on the track. We opened fire again. One of the rounds must have struck a grenade he had in his equipment, because it exploded and continued to burn, and all the time he was screaming words in English. He might have been trying to surrender, but . . . we weren't sure. [It] went on for about fifteen minutes and then stopped.'[5] They didn't approach the body until light, when the police arrived. Bob Consiglio was dead. He'd been shot in the mouth, and his chest was badly charred by a phosphorus grenade.

Lane and Dinger were at the patrol's tail-end when enemy fire blatted out. They whipped back ragged starflashes in the night. They edged nearer the river bank, lagged into black water. The cold cut them like a razor blade. The current was so vicious it tore the weapons from their hands. They found a boat and tried to detach its mooring-chain. It wouldn't budge. They dog-paddled until they reached a sandbank, crept ashore, clocked a bridge a stone's throw away with guards patrolling. They lay shivering, gasping for breath. Dinger found a chunk of polystyrene and broke it up. They stuffed the bits inside their smocks for buoyancy. They slid into the ice-river again, headed for the opposite bank – an island called Rummani. Lane was wheezing breath, gulping water. The cold had drained the energy out of him. He was going down. Dinger collared him, fought the current, hefted him to the shore, heaved him on to dry land. He spotted a mud-brick hut, housing a pump engine. He dragged him inside, but Lane struggled to get back into the river. Dinger heated water with his last Hexamine block. He held hot water to his oppo's mouth. Lane knocked it aside snarling.

When light spanned up through chinks in the roof, Dinger pulled Lane outside, hoping the sun would warm him. He was rambling. His skin was frozen; his eyes had gone opaque. He pulled him back inside again. A few minutes later a bolt on the outside of the door rammed shut – someone had locked them inside.

Dinger was torn between looking after his mate and escape. In a last burst of energy, he managed to smash through the roof. He limped off into the palm-trees and vegetation by the river-bank. Soon he was surrounded by civilians and captured. He was tied up and taken across to the mainland on a tractor-drawn cart. He saw them bringing Lane's body in on a stretcher. He was certain his mate was dead.

While Dinger and Lane were breasting the river, Coburn and McNab were belly-lurching across the bed of a wadi by the river, passing close enough to Iraqi police to see their faces. When they crept over the opposite side, they were hit with a splurge of fire from a cordon. McNab darted off in the opposite direction. Coburn tried to worm through a tomato field. He'd run out of ammo, and ditched his weapon. He was armed only with a bayonet. Ahmad, the Iraqi police sergeant who had supervised the deployment near the checkpoint, was in command of the police section dug in five metres away. 'Suddenly a man came crawling over the lip of the wadi towards us,' he recalled, 'and we shouted at him to stop. He didn't, so we opened fire . . . He screamed out something in English. I ordered the men to stop firing and I went over to him, followed by some others. He was badly wounded in the leg and arm and blood was pouring out.'[6]

'There was no pain, only shock,' Coburn remembered, 'as if someone had taken a sledgehammer to my ankle and smashed it into a million little pieces. I was certain I had just lost my right foot . . . then the pain hit, totally possessing my mind, body and soul.'[7] He was lugged to a Toyota Land Cruiser, and taken to the local barracks for interrogation.

McNab was snaking back through sludge and gloom downriver. He found a wide expanse of mud, located an irrigation pipe, inched inside. He stayed there for the rest of the night. In the morning he was clocked by a labourer clearing irrigation ditches. The man wasn't even aware there'd been trouble the previous night, but reported the sighting to a police-post. The police poled up in a Land Cruiser and closed in. They jerked McNab out, tied his hands behind his back, and threw him in the back of the Land Cruiser. At the local barracks, the first thing McNab saw was Dinger, still alive, his head bloated to the size of a football.

Phillips, Lane and Consiglio were dead, Coburn badly wounded, McNab and Dinger captured. The same day – 26 January – Ryan and Mal split up.

They'd survived the snowstorm. Revived by the sun next morning, they'd crossed the same road on which the rest of the patrol had hijacked the taxi, and a railway line north of it. Near the town of Anah they ran into a shepherd who appeared to be slightly handicapped, and wasn't aware there was a war going on. Mal went off to his cottage with him, hoping to find a vehicle, while Ryan waited in a wadi. At the cottage four hours' march away, Mal spoke to a man in a Toyota pick-up who alerted the police in Anah. Mal was surrounded and captured. His claim to have shot three Iraqis before running out of ammo was denied by local police, who reported that his weapon was still loaded when he was brought to the station.

Ryan waited for Mal until last light, then struck out for the border alone. A week later he crossed into Syria, having walked for seven days and eight nights, on only two packets of biscuits and water. His lone marathon was one of the longest solo escape-marches in SAS history, almost equalling that of John Sillito in the Sahara in 1942. He had covered a hundred and eighty-six miles.

96. 'The right bloke to have around if it's action you're looking for'

As McNab's men raced nearer Krabilah in the hijacked Toyota, an RAF Chinook and a US helicopter fitted with thermal imaging equipment searched the area of the original drop-off point. It was still believed that Bravo Two Zero was making for Saudi-Arabia. No trace of them was found.

Meanwhile, Alpha One Zero half-squadron, under SBS-major Graham, had crossed the border via a checkpoint and had almost immediately got into a contact with the Iraqis. The patrol was laagered up for the day, with its vehicles under cam-nets, when an Iraqi Gaz jeep materialized out of the desert. Two Iraqi officers jumped down and headed for the laager. The first lifted a net and found Sgt. 'Cameron Spence', ex-Queens Regiment, and his A Squadron crew, with their weapons sighted-in. 'I had a moment to register the look of blank surprise on the Iraqi's face as he came under the cam-net,' Spence recalled, '. . . fired, quick double-tap – *ba-bam* – and he went down. As he fell his body was hit by at least six more rounds . . . he pirouetted in a macabre death-dance before hitting the dirt, face down.'[1]

The second officer was treed by a salvo that ruptured his rib-cage and slashed off the side of his head. Spence lamped forward to the twitching body of the first officer and hauled it over, searching for grenades or hidden weapons. Two men closed in on the Gaz vehicle and fished out another Iraqi officer, squealing and struggling. They threw him on the ground and cracked him with a rifle-butt until he shut up. A map found on one of the enemy suggested they were encircled by an entire Iraqi artillery regiment. They had fired between twenty and thirty rounds, and anyone within two klicks would have heard the shots. The odds were that the enemy was already homing in on them. The priority was to move out – fast.

OC Major Graham seemed hesitant. His instructions were to move north into his designated area of operation. Instead, Graham ordered the patrol back south. It was the wrong decision. '. . . I don't think he was scared so much as gripped by an inability to be decisive,' Spence commented. 'He didn't like being deep inside Iraq. It was alien to him and the way he'd been trained . . . right from the start he was the wrong guy for the job.' They moved out within thirty minutes, taking the Gaz jeep, the prisoner, and the two bodies with them.

Back in the ops room at al-Jouf, Lt. Col. 'J' 's delight over the Regiment's first reported contact soon turned sour when he found out that Graham was withdrawing. 'I thought the CO, who was always ultra-cool, was going to explode,' said RSM Peter Ratcliffe. 'This time he completely lost his rag, and his comments about Alpha One Zero and its commander . . . didn't make pretty listening.' 'J' told the RSM he was sending him in next day to relieve Graham of his command. Ratcliffe wondered if he'd heard right. The only instance he knew of a squadron commander being relieved of his command was the case of John Moss in the Falklands war. But that was at Hereford, before the squadron had gone into action. Never before in the history of the SAS had a squadron commander been relieved in the field and replaced by a non-commissioned officer.

After a moment's thought, Ratcliffe saw sense in the proposal. The original idea, to send him as 2IC, wouldn't have worked, as his advice would have been overruled. As he boarded the Chinook next day rigged up for a war he'd never expected to see at the sharp end, the CO put his arm round his shoulders and bawled over the roar of the engine, 'What I have done is a first. What it won't stand is a major contact in the first twenty-four hours.'

Ratcliffe lit off the Chinook's tail-ramp into deep-freeze cold. The wind knifed him through his duvet-jacket. The patrol that turned up to meet the chopper were almost blue – and they'd layered themselves with every stitch of clothing they had, including NBC suits. When they saw the ankle-length sheepskin coats the RSM had brought, it felt like Christmas. As they helped the crabs unload the stores, Ratcliffe sent one of the men for the officer commanding.

Ratcliffe knew the next few minutes would be SAS history in the making, and he had turned the scene over in his mind again and again. He thought there was a possibility that Graham might resist, and had primed two senior NCOs accompanying the heli to restrain him if necessary. All the same, it wasn't every day an RSM took over a major's squadron, and Ratcliffe hadn't been looking forward to the confrontation. When Graham appeared, the RSM said nothing except 'I'm sorry,' and handed him a letter from the CO. 'You are to hand over your command to the RSM,' it read. 'He can take whatever action is necessary to ensure that you leave your present location.'[2] 'When he'd finished [reading] he looked up,' the RSM recalled, 'his face working with some powerful emotion . . . then he walked away.'[3] He needn't have worried. Graham behaved impeccably. He fetched his kit, said goodbye to his 2IC, and got on board the chopper alongside the Iraqi prisoner. 'The worst part of my job was over,' Ratcliffe said.

Within minutes off taking over, the RSM had ordered the patrol back north and demolished any defiance from the men. He told Graham's 2IC, Staff Sergeant 'Pat', that he was now patrol commander. He was there to give the orders, and the 2IC was there to take them: when he wanted suggestions he'd ask for them.

The patrol covered fifty kilometres that night – roughly the distance they had withdrawn earlier. At the bivvy, Ratcliffe gave orders to burn the Gaz jeep and the corpses. He gathered the half-squadron, and told them there would be no more pissing about: they were here to hit the enemy and that was what he intended to do. When he'd finished he stuck his chin out, daring anyone silently to challenge him. No one did. The post of Regimental Sergeant-Major was virtually sacred: Ratcliffe was the most experienced soldier in the British army's most elite Regiment. He was no physical giant, but the boy from the Salford slums who'd been champion recruit in the Paras had the qualities of a Paddy Mayne. He had the same sureness of touch, the same calculating disregard for danger. Even the doubters were fired-up. '[Ratcliffe] isn't your master tactician,' Cameron Spence commented, 'but he's the right bloke to have around if it's action you're looking for.'[4]

97. 'Shut the fuck up and keep shooting!'

Two D Squadron patrols had been roaming the Iraqi desert since 20 January, hunting for Scuds. The search was frustratingly slow. Travelling at night, you could pass within a thousand yards of a launch-site without clocking it. The desert was hard going. The 110 Land Rovers jiggered and bounced over the pebbledash surface. They often made only twenty kilometres an hour. The wind lashed the SAS crews across the Land Rovers' unshielded frames.

They moved in convoy — seven or eight pinkies followed by a Mercedes Benz Unimog support vehicle, with three outriders on Cannon motorcycles. The motorcyclists acted as forward scouts and couriers, carrying word-of-mouth messages between wagons, while the patrol observed radio silence. The drivers wore passive night-goggles, and the pinkies' lights were taped over. The wagons carried winches, sand-channels, MIRA thermal-imagers that could locate troops and vehicles in low visibility, and Trimkit GPS systems for navigation. They were armed with a smorgasbord of weapons, including twin- and single-mounted GP machine guns, 0.5 inch Brownings, Mk19 40mm grenade-launchers and Milan wire-guided missiles, clamped to their roll-bars. The Brownings could pump out a thousand rounds a minute, and engage the enemy up to fifteen hundred metres away. The Milan missile was capable of taking out a main battle tank at two kilometres, and the Mk19 was handy against soft-skinned vehicles. The SAS crews had M16 Armalites, some with M203 grenade-launchers, and Minimi light machine guns. The tiny columns packed the punch of a small army.

The night Ratcliffe joined Alpha One Zero, most of D Squadron's units were cammed-up in a wadi near a motorway designated MSR2. They were in the 'Iron Triangle' – an area of western Iraq criss-crossed by Iraqi early warning and communications towers, buzzing with enemy troops and crammed with Scud launch-sites. At first light, the men of 17 Troop woke to find that they were within a stone's throw of a Scud microwave control-tower. It was uncomfortably close, but they couldn't move until nightfall. That morning, two Iraqi soldiers came sauntering along the wadi. One of them stopped abruptly and pointed at the nearest cam-net. A burst of half-inch slugs from a Browning gouged open his chest.

Instantly the SAS came under riveting fire from forty Iraqi infantrymen concealed on a ridge a hundred and fifty metres away. At the same time, the Troop's sentry on an adjacent ridge was bumped by a full Iraqi platoon. They came on determinedly, pepperpotting, whaling 7.62mm short rounds from their Kalashnikovs. Support-fire from Shoagin machine guns chunked off the rocks, whizzed and creased air around him. The sentry yelled for support. Three SAS-men ramped up with Minimis and a bagful of L2 and white phos grenades. Two of them hit dirt, tracked muzzles across the Iraqi advance, tick-tocked taps. The third man pulled pins, pitched grenades. Bombs split, oscillated shingle and dust, spun shrapnel waves, severed limps, sent Iraqis twisting in bloody parcels down the slope. Some lay horrifically shredded, blubbering and moaning. At least two rolled into cover and went on shooting.

The SAS-men on the wagons trocked covering shots, blazing off spears of fire from mounted twin-Gimpies and Brownings. They fired so fast their cam-nets were ripped to ribbons. L.Cpl. Taff Powell, rattling double-Gimpies from the back of a pinkie, got plunked through the guts. Blood pumped. Taff sealed the entry-wound with a palm and went on shooting with his right hand. 'I'm hit in the legs!' he yelled confusingly. Not realizing how badly he was hurt, another shooter on the wagon shrieked, 'Shut the fuck up and keep shooting!'

One trooper shished 40mm grenades from an Mk19 launcher. The bombs pivoted into the Iraqi fire-group, pintailed steel sprays. The Iraqis withdrew. The pinkies' engines fired. The four men from the sentry position raced down to join them. The wounded Taff was hoisted on to the Unimog, where the medic stuck a drip in his arm. The convoy roared out of the wadi towards the motorway, guns still raging. The front-gunner on the lead wagon saw two white jeeps veering towards them, full of Iraqi troops. He swung Gimpies, pinched triggers, stitched both jeeps with ladders of two hundred link. 7.62mm rounds notched bodywork, webbed windscreens, hit meat. The jeeps stopped, drivers and passengers obliterated.

The pinkies howled on to the hardtop, and formed up, engines idling. The last wagon and the Unimog had been left behind. Seven men were absent, including the wounded Taff. The missing wagon suddenly caromed up in a belch of black smoke, tossing an axle and wheels into the air. A pinky went back for the crews, but the driver saw only the burning wreck and the Unimog gutted. He fast-tracked to the rest. The wagons burned rubber down the highway, looped cross-country to the emergency RV. The crews hung on there for twenty-four hours, but the lost men never arrived.

In fact, they were already en route to the border. After the others had bugged out, they jumped on one of the Iraqi jeeps shot up minutes before. Evading the blitz from the ridge, they drove through a tunnel under the road and emerged on the opposite carriageway. The other crews had seen the vehicle pass too far away to register that their comrades were on it.

They hammered the jeep until it clapped out, then started tabbing. The wounded Taff refused to be carried, and staggered on. After forty-eight hours, though, the rest of the patrol knew he'd peg if they didn't get transport. They held up the next truck that came along, shot the driver in the arm and administered medical treatment. Then they drove his truck into the desert, where it soon conked out. On foot again, they made a Bedouin camp and persuaded one of the tribesmen to sell his lorry, pooling the twenty gold 'escape' sovereigns each man had been issued for emergencies. By the time they made the Saudi-Arabian border after five days on the run, Taff was comatose. Only emergency surgery saved his life.

After leaving the ERV, the rest of the patrol stayed in the field. In early February they located a column of Scud erector-launchers and escort vehicles in the Wadi Amiq, nicknamed 'Scud Alley'. They hid up and waited till the column got under way after last light, then painted it with laser target-designators. Two waves of F-15 fighter-bombers pitched out of the night, searing the convoy with bombs and cannon-fire. The fuel went up in a balloon of napalm that fried the crews. The SAS took out more vehicles with Milan rockets.

Another D squadron patrol, Delta Two Zero, laser-painted another couple of Scuds for an air-strike, then wrecked a Scud control centre and a nearby OP, taking out thirteen of the enemy.

On 8 February Peter Ratcliffe's Alpha One Zero patrol carried out a stealth attack on another microwave Scud-control station, Victor Two. Part of a large complex sited on the main Baghdad– Amman road, it was defended by two concrete bunkers. The plan was to sabotage the switch-gear in underground silos.

This was a raid in L Detachment style. A team of five demo- litions-men led by Ratcliffe himself would enter the main com- pound, covered by crews of three wagons in the lee of a high berm, about two hundred metres south of the road. A Milan missile on a fourth pinky would slam the right guard-bunker the moment the charges went up. The left bunker would be taken out by a team with a LAW 66mm rocket-launcher. The only sign of the enemy as they approached was two three-ton lorries parked by the road, slightly to the south of the installation. They appeared to be deserted.

Ratcliffe and his team penetrated the complex through a gap in the wall, and were amazed to find themselves in a labyrinth of twisted steel and shattered concrete. Ratcliffe clicked that the place had been hit by Coalition bombers, and was furious he hadn't been told. The switch-gear silos were already in ruins, but the control tower was still functioning. Ratcliffe told his chief demo-man, an ex-Para called 'Mugger', to blow the tower instead. Mugger said he'd prepared the charges for switch-gear, not steel-cutting: they weren't the right tool for the job. Ratcliffe insisted. Mugger clamped charges on three of the mast's legs and added extra plastic explosive.

Mugger and his two assistants set the charges and primed them with two-minute delays. While they were doing it, the team assigned to take out the left-hand bunker was spotted by a driver who'd been asleep in one of the trucks. Patrol boss 'Major Peter' squiffed three starflashes from his M16. The driver hit the deck with three slugs in his belly, but the gunshots alerted the sentries in the bunkers, who returned fire. A Milan missile shooshed into the right bunker, slapped concrete, detonated in catherine-wheel arcs of flame. The LAW shooter on Peter's team was about to blast the left bunker, when another Iraqi driver leapt on his back and tried to throttle him. The shooter's mate rushed across and clumped the Iraqi with a rifle-butt.

Four of Ratcliffe's team had already taken cover on the other side of the wall. Ratcliffe and Mugger were about to dip through the gap when they heard Peter's shots and the blam of the Milan missile, followed by a cacophony of fire. AK47 ball sizzed off the wall: tracer looped-the-loop in rococo patterns. Ratcliffe knew they were stuck. Outside, the world's biggest firefight was going on; inside they would be stitched by their own charges in ninety seconds. There was no choice: they had to run out into the enemy fire.

The two of them ducked through the hole and joined the others. They spread out in line abreast and made a dash across the road towards the berm two hundred metres away. 'I swear not even the finest line-up ever made it from one end of the rugby pitch to the other at the speed we travelled that night,' Ratcliffe recalled. They were still running when the charges went up one after the other. Ratcliffe didn't stop to check if the tower was still standing. Rounds were zinging around his head, hiking up dust round his feet. He registered that the right bunker was in flames.

They made the wagons unscathed, and were about to get back in the vehicles when they were spritzed by rifle and machine-gun fire from enemy on top of the berm. Two bullets holed Mugger's shirt, and Ratcliffe felt one whamp over his head. He saw with horror that they were sitting ducks. The SAS gunners elevated Brownings, twin-Gimpies, and Mk19 grenade-launchers. Guns shuddered. Welts of brilliance torpedoed the berm. Grenades wheezed and popped. The SAS drivers started up. The men skipped aboard. A swerving wagon sent Ratcliffe flying, hurled his M16 out of his hand. He tottered to his feet, was about to go hunt his weapon, when the driver yelled, 'Jump on or we're fucking going without you!' As the Land Rover bumped into the desert with enemy bullets still grooving its chassis, Ratcliffe recalled that his twenty gold 'escape' sovereigns were hidden in the butt of his rifle.

Despite shaky intel, the raid had gone like clockwork – there were zero casualties. Two motorcyclists the RSM dispatched the following morning confirmed that the mast was down. At the lying-up place, Ratcliffe zipped off a blunt 'mission accomplished' message, lit a gasper and inhaled deeply. 'We had done the business,' he said, 'and got out with all our personnel and all our vehicles intact.'[1] For his bravery and leadership, Ratcliffe would later be awarded the DCM.

98. 'The SAS had some new curtains to choose. Saddam could go swivel'

Next day, Ratcliffe copped orders to move south and find an area where all four half-squadron patrols could rendezvous. A resupply mission was overdue, but there were no Chinooks available to bring out desperately needed fuel, rations and water. Instead Lt. Col. 'J' had decided to send the supplies overland in a convoy of three-tonners, escorted by the spare B Squadron men in six pinkies. Ratcliffe located a perfect site in the Wadi Tubal – a sealed-off ravine that could take seventy vehicles and was invisible to anyone more than a few metres from the lip. Delta One Bravo came in later, reporting the loss of their seven men. They weren't aware that they were on the run.

The news from the other half of A Squadron was also bad. The day after Ratcliffe had hit the microwave station, a two-wagon patrol of Alpha Three Zero, led by the SSM 'Barry', had driven into a trap near a communications centre. The enemy had let them come in, encircled them, bumped them from the rear. They had managed to get one of the wagons out, but Barry's driver reversed into a ditch, and the pinky ended up with two wheels spinning free. Barry took rounds in the thigh, groin and legs. The two others hauled him behind an anthill. With slugs shaving air around them, they went into a fighting withdrawal, one man heaving the wounded SSM, the other giving covering fire. They made about two hundred metres from the crashed wagon, when the Iraqis started closing in. Barry had been slipping in and out of consciousness, but came round and clicked what was going on. He ordered them to bug out. He said he would hold the enemy off. 'Me against a few dozen Iraqis is pretty fair odds,' he gasped.

One of the men offered to give him a *coup de grâce*. Barry thanked him, but said he'd take his chance: he was a fluent Arabic-speaker, and thought he might be able to talk the enemy into sparing him. The others weren't convinced. They'd heard the stories about Iraqi brutality. They went off reluctantly, but considered him a dead man. The pair escaped under Barry's covering fire, and made the RV with the rest of the half-squadron. In fact, Barry survived. It took the Iraqis a day to find him, and instead of finishing him off, they hoisted him on to a stretcher. Though he was as harshly interrogated as the other prisoners, he was also given expert surgery by a British-trained Iraqi doctor. He was later awarded the MC – one of only two ever doled out to non-commissioned officers of 22 SAS.

Ratcliffe's patrol was assigned to relieve Delta Three Bravo in the 'Iron Triangle', but returned to the Wadi Tubal two days later to find that the resupply convoy had arrived, with fuel, ammunition, stores, fresh food and cigarettes. Tubal now held three full SAS sabre-squadrons, plus R Squadron reserves and HQ personnel: the largest gathering of SAS-men in the field since A and B Squadrons, 1 SAS, encountered at Bir Zaltin in 1942. Ratcliffe celebrated the occasion by holding a historic meeting of the Sergeants' Mess. The senior NCOs thought they were coming for an operations-briefing. When the RSM started to ask for ideas for the summer ball, and whether the mess could afford a new suite and curtains, some of them thought he'd finally flipped. 'Disbelief. Anger. Laughter. Hysteria,' Sgt. 'Serious' Spence wrote. 'It took most of the rest of the afternoon to stop crapping our-selves.'[1] It was only later that they began to see what Ratcliffe was getting at. This display of British bureaucracy at its most footling was cocking the ultimate snook at Saddam Hussein's 'Mother of all Battles'. As Spence wrote, 'The SAS had some new curtains to choose. Saddam could go swivel.'[2]

On 23 February the squadrons were ordered to return to al-Jauf. The Coaltion's land offensive had started up, and the SAS was no longer needed. The Regiment hadn't prevented the Iraqis from firing Scuds at Israel, but from the time they entered the field, the number of launches had fallen by 50 per cent. They had done the business. The withdrawal was marred by the death of L.Cpl. 'Shug' Denbury, of Alpha Three Zero, killed in a contact two days before the SAS pulled out.

99. 'More than a Regiment'

The Squadrons returned to Hereford in March 1991, just four months short of fifty years since Lieutenant David Stirling had hopped over the barrier at GHQ, Cairo, with his badly-penned proposal for a new type of parachute force. Since then, the SAS Regiment had come full circle, from desert raiders to sea-commandos, to guerrilla fighters, to counter-insurgency troops, anti-terrorist squads, long-range reconnaissance patrols, seaborne assault troops and back to desert raiders once more.

Back in 1941, before the SAS carried out its first raid, Jock Lewes experienced a vision of remarkable prescience. He saw that the SAS concept would not be limited by the personalities of the dreamer, the thinker and the fighter who created it, but would live on in the imagination of others, long after the Originals had passed away. '[It] cannot now die,' he wrote, '. . . it is alive and will live gloriously . . . it has caught hold on life.'[1] Within fifty years of its foundation, the SAS idea had opened up a whole new approach to warfare. Special forces existed in almost every nation on earth. These new elites were the ultimate answer to the massed citizen-armies of the First and Second World Wars – a return to the specialized, highly trained, professional warriors of feudal times: the new Samurai.

The Gulf war was a watershed for the SAS. Bursting into international consciousness just over a decade earlier, during the Iranian Embassy siege, its popularity reached unprecedented heights. The war was followed by a spate of sensational books by SAS soldiers that for the first time revealed details of its operational methods. There had been SAS books before, but what was notable about the new crop was that they pandered to the public 'tabloid' conception of the Regiment as a force of supermen.

David Stirling had not lived to see the SAS fight in the Gulf. He would have been proud of their achievements, but probably wouldn't have recognized the bravura style of the post-war publications. He had always extolled modesty as a prime virtue, and said that it was an SAS tradition 'never to be heard in public boasting about our Regiment's past or present perfomances'.

Some felt that the Regiment's accomplishments in the Gulf had actually left much to be desired. In the North Africa campaign during the Second World War, Wilfred Thesiger wrote that A Squadron, 1 SAS, had a 'quiet confidence' that he thought derived from the fact that they had 'mastered the desert and learned to use it as their hideout'. They had what a later generation of SAS-men would call 'ground feel' – a sense of being at home in the extreme conditions of the desert wastes. The post-war SAS had developed 'ground feel' in Malaya, Borneo, Oman and other theatres. It was lacking in the Gulf, where, as Peter Ratcliffe himself admitted, the men felt 'uneasy'. Mike Coburn wrote that he had done so much of his training in the jungle, that in the desert he felt dangerously exposed. This was a far cry from Mike Calvert's concept of a force that would be as comfortable in its surroundings as the natives. Many of the bad decisions made on SAS ops in the Gulf war were due to this lack of 'feel' for the environment.

This wasn't entirely the Regiment's fault. They had trained for desert warfare in areas that were geographically very different from the desert of Iraq. There was also a failure of intelligence. The British had records of fighting in this region going back two centuries, yet they were ignored. Ryan's assertion that the unit's original E & E plan had been to 'jog to the border wearing shorts and running shoes' showed an alarming lack of touch with reality.

The SAS 'did the business' in the Gulf, but there was also a sense in which it was out of place. This was partly because its soldiers were children of a more automated world, and had been brought up with less contact with the environment than their predecessors. It was at least partly, though, because the 'imaginary SAS' of public perception had begun to seep inexorably into the way some SAS soldiers saw themselves.

Ken Connor felt that the Regiment's headlong ascent to celebrity status had attracted recruits who were mainly interested in its 'macho image' – a tendency that, he believed, had been borne out by the events of the Gulf war and its aftermath. 'The Regiment that I knew and served with,' he wrote, 'has effectively been disbanded . . .'[2] Connor's view is extreme, but Stirling himself observed obliquely in his speech commemorating the opening of Stirling Lines, in 1984, that celebrity brought with it certain hazards. He warned the assembly that the SAS must never regard itself as a *corps d'élite*. 'Down that road,' he said, 'would lie the corruption of all our values. A substantial dash of humility, along with an ever-active sense of humour, must continue to save us from succumbing to that danger. Only then can we be sure of consolidating the foundation of these splendid new lines, and shielding the spirit of integrity of those setting out from here on their exacting tasks.'[3]

It was a timely warning. Stirling confessed that he felt fit to burst with pride at what his small Detachment had become, but he also took the opportunity to note that he had never regarded himself the sole founder of the SAS. He said that the Regiment had been co-created by five other individuals – Jock Lewes, Paddy Mayne, Georges Bergé, Brian Franks and John Woodhouse. He added a list of those he thought had made major contributions to the development of the SAS, including Johnny Cooper, Reg Seekings, Bob Bennett, Jim Almonds, Pat Riley, George Jellicoe and Fitzroy Maclean, of L Detachment; Roy Farran of 2 SAS; Ian Lapraik of the SBS; Eddie Blondeel of 5 SAS; Christodoulos Tzigantes of the Greek Sacred Squadron; Mike Calvert of the Malayan Scouts; Johnny Watts, Dare Newell, Peter de la Billière, Tanky Smith and Geordie Lillico of 22 SAS. He said that to mention everyone who'd played a part in the SAS story would have meant calling almost the entire roll of past and present members.

In fifty years, the SAS Regiment had indeed come a long way from its roots, yet had remained unchanged in its conviction that a great fighting unit is made, not by technology, but by the quality of the men who comprise it. 'Our Regiment,' said David Stirling, 'has a special magic in generating for itself an intense loyalty in all who have served it. Indeed we are more than a Regiment – we are a family.'[4]

Epilogue

The lives of Vince Phillips, Steven 'Legs' Lane and Robert Consiglio were commemorated at a memorial service at St Martin's church, Hereford, a week after the squadrons returned from the Gulf. They were buried with full military honours, among the graves of fallen comrades who, like them, had not 'beaten the clock'. The pallbearers and firing party were turned out in immaculate service-dress with sand-coloured berets and SAS wings. WOI Peter Ratcliffe DCM, marching solemnly behind Phillips's coffin, could not help overhearing Vince's two young daughters sobbing. Ratcliffe, the archetype SAS warrior, maintained the mask essential to the sacred post of Regimental Sergeant-Major. He could not show how moved he was.

These men, and the thousands of others who have served in the SAS, from every conceivable background and nationality, were not the supermen of public imagination. Such beings, as T. E. Lawrence said, do not exist. What made them distinct was not muscle and brawn nor super-powers, but commitment and courage, the will to carry on when there was nothing left, the spirit to dare all to win all, for the everlasting honour of the Regiment.

The pallbearers came to a halt by the graves. As the coffins were lowered in, the firing party presented arms with crisp movements. The RSM and officers saluted. A bugler played the last post. In a quiet voice, the padre read the service.

Bibliography

Primary Sources

Asher, Michael, *Shoot to Kill: A soldier's journey through violence*, London, 1990.

Ballinger, Adam, *The Quiet Soldier: On selection with 21 SAS*, London, 1992.

Beaumont, Roger A., *Military Elites*, Indianapolis, 1974.

Beckwith, Charlie A., *Delta Force – the Army's Elite Counter-Terrorist Unit*, San Diego, 1983.

Byrne, J. V., *The General Salutes a Soldier: With the SAS and Commandos in World War Two*, London, 1986.

Calvert, Michael, *Fighting Mad: One man's guerrilla war*, London, 1964.

Chin Peng, *My Side of History: Recollections of the guerrilla leader who waged a 12-year war against the British in the jungles of Malaya*, Singapore, 2003.

Close, Roy, *In Action with the SAS: A soldier's odyssey from Dunkirk to Berlin*, Barnsley, 2005.

Coburn, Mike, *Soldier Five: The real truth about the Bravo Two Zero mission*, Edinburgh, 2004.

Cooper, Johnny, *One of the Originals: The Story of a Founder Member of the SAS*, London, 1991.

Curtis, Mike, *CQB: Close Quarter Battle*, London, 1997.

Davies, Barry, *Joining the SAS: How to get in and what it's like*, London, 1998.

Davies, Barry, *SAS: Shadow Warriors of the 21st Century: The SAS Anti-Terrorist Team*, Staplehurst, 2002.

Deane-Drummond, A. J., *Arrows of Fortune*, London, 1992.

De la Billière, Peter, *Storm Command – a personal account of the Gulf war*, London, 1992.

De la Billière, Peter, *Looking for Trouble: SAS to Gulf Command*, London, 1995.

Durnford-Slater, John, *Commando: Memoirs of a fighting commando in World War Two*, London, 1953.

Eppler, John, trans. S. Seago, *Operation Condor: Rommel's Spy*, [Paris, 1974] London, 1977.

Graham, Scott, *Shoot To Kill: The true story of an SAS hero's love for an IRA killer*, London, 2002.

Hastings, Stephen, *The Drums of Memory: An autobiography*, London, 1994.

Hoe, Alan, *David Stirling: The Authorized Biography of the Creator of the SAS*, London, 1992.

Horsfall, Robin, *Fighting Scared*, London, 2002.

Hunter, Gaz, *The Shooting Gallery: The elite within the elite: one man's secret wars*, London, 1998.

James, Malcolm (Malcolm Pleydell), *Born of the Desert*, London, 1945.

Jeapes, Tony, *SAS Secret War: Operation Storm in the Middle East*, London, 1996.

Kennedy Shaw, W. B., *Long Range Desert Group: World War II action in North Africa*, London, 1945.

Large, Lofty, *Soldier Against the Odds: From Korean war to SAS*, Edinburgh, 1999.

Liddell-Hart, B. H. (ed.), trans. Paul Findlay, *The Rommel Papers*, London, 1954.

Lloyd-Owen, David, *Providence Their Guide: The Long Range Desert Group 1940–45*, London, 1980.

Maclean, Fitzroy, *Eastern Approaches*, London, 1949.

Mather, Carol, *When the Grass Stops Growing*, London, 1997.

McAleese, Peter, *No Mean Soldier: The story of the ultimate soldier in the SAS and other forces*, London, 1993.

McNab, Andy, *Bravo Two Zero: The true story of an SAS patrol behind enemy lines in Iraq*, London, 1993.

Moorehead, Alan, *African Trilogy: The desert war 1940–1943*, London, 1944.

Mortimer, Gavin, *Stirling's Men – the inside history of the SAS in World War II*, London, 2004.

Ratcliffe, Peter, with Botham, Noel, and Hitchen, Brian, *Eye of the Storm: Twenty-five Years in Action with the SAS*, London, 2000.

Rennie, James, *The Operators: On the streets with Britain's most secret service*, Barnsley, 2004.

Ryan, Chris, *The One That Got Away*, London, 1995.

Spence, Cameron, *Sabre Squadron*, London, 1997.

Spencer Chapman, Frederick, *The Jungle is Neutral*, London, 1949.

Stevens, Gordon, *The Originals: The secret history of the birth of the SAS in their own words*, London, 2005.

Stokes, Brummie, *Soldiers and Sherpas: A taste for adventure*, London, 1988.

Thesiger, Wilfred, *Arabian Sands*, London, 1959.

Thesiger, Wilfred, *A Life of My Choice*, London, 1987.

Timpson, Alastair, with Gibson-Watt, Andrew, *In Rommel's Backyard: A memoir of the Long Range Desert Group*, Barnsley, 2000.

Wellsted, Ian, *SAS with the Maquis: In action with the French resistance June–September 1944*, London, 1994.

Secondary Sources

Almonds Windmill, Lorna, *Gentleman Jim: The wartime story of a founder of the SAS & special forces*, London, 2001.

Almonds Windmill, Lorna, *A British Achilles: The story of George, 2nd Earl Jellicoe KBE DSO MC FRS*, Barnsley, 2005.

Asher, Michael, *Thesiger: A Biography*, London, 1994.

Asher, Michael, *The Real Bravo Two Zero: The truth behind Bravo Two Zero*, London, 2003.

Asher, Michael, *Get Rommel: The secret British mission to kill Hitler's greatest general*, London, 2004.

Barber, Noel, *The War of the Running Dogs: How Malaya defeated the Communist guerrillas 1948–1960*, London, 1971.

Brown, George A., *Commando Gallantry Awards of World War II*, London, 1991.

Churchill, Winston, *The Second World War*, London, 1949.

Cole, Barbara, *The Elite: the story of the Rhodesian Special Air Service*, Durban, 1985.

Connell, John, *Auchinleck: A Biography*, London, 1959.

Connor, Ken, *Ghost Force – the Secret History of the SAS*, London, 1998.

Connor, Ken, *Ghosts: An illustrated story of the SAS*, London, 2000.

Cooper, Artemis, *Cairo in the War 1939–1945*, London, 1989.

Cowles, Virginia, *The Phantom Major*, London, 1958.

Dickens, Peter, *SAS: The Jungle Frontier: 22 Special Air Service Regiment in the Borneo campaign 1963–1966*, London, 1983.

Dillon, Martin, and Bradford, Roy, *Rogue Warrior of the SAS: The Blair Mayne legend*, London, 1987.

Dixon, Norman, *On the Psychology of Military Incompetence*, London, 1994.

Dorney, Richard, *An Active Service: The story of a soldier's life in the Grenadier Guards, SAS & SBS 1935–58*, Solihull, 2005.

Farran, Roy, *Winged Dagger*, London, 1948.

Ford, Roger, *Fire from the Forest: The SAS Brigade in France 1944*, London, 2003.

Fowler, Will, *SAS: Behind Enemy Lines: Covert operations 1941–2005*, London, 2005.

Geraghty, Tony, *This is the SAS: A pictorial history of the Special Air Service Regiment*, London, 1982.

Geraghty, Tony, *Who Dares Wins: The story of the SAS 1950–1992*, London, 1993.

Harrison, Derrick, *These Men are Dangerous*, London, 1957.

Hebditch, David, and Connor, Ken, *How to Stage a Military Coup: From planning to execution*, London, 2005.

Hoe, Alan, and Morris, Eric, *Re-enter the SAS: The Special Air Service and the Malayan Emergency*, London, 1994.

Jones, Tim, *SAS: The First Secret Wars: The unknown years of combat and counter insurgency*, London, 2005.

Jones, Tim, *SAS Zero Hour: The secret origins of the Special Air Service*, London, 2006.

Keegan, John, *A History of Warfare*, London, 1994.

Keegan, John, *The Second World War*, London, 1999.

Kemp, Anthony, *The SAS at War 1941–1945*, London, 1991.

Kemp, Anthony, *The SAS: Savage Wars of Peace*, London, 1994.

Keyes, Elizabeth, *Geoffrey Keyes VC*, London, 1956.

Ladd, James D., *SAS Operations: More than daring*, London, 1986.

Lewes, John, *Jock Lewes: Co-Founder of the SAS*, Barnsley, 2000.

Mackay, Francis, *Overture to Overlord: Special Operations in Preparation for D-Day*, Barnsley, 2005.

McClean, Stewart, *SAS: The History of the Special Raiding Squadron, 'Paddy's men'*, Stroud, 2006.

McCue, Paul, *SAS Operation Bulbasket: Behind the lines in occupied France 1944*, London, 1996.

McLuskey, Fraser, *Parachute Padre*, London, 1951.

Messenger, Charles, *The Commandos 1940–1946*, London, 1985.

Morgan, Mike, *Sting of the Scorpion: The inside story of the Long Range Desert Group*, Stroud, 2000.

Murray, Raymond, *The SAS in Ireland*, Dublin, 1990.

Parker, John, *Secret Hero: The life and mysterious death of Captain Robert Nairac*, London, 2004.

Perrett, Bryan, *Desert Warfare: From its Roman origins to the Gulf conflict*, Wellingborough, 1988.

Pitt, Barrie, *The Crucible of War: Wavell's command*, London, 1980.

Pitt, Barrie, *The Crucible of War: Auchinleck's command*, London, 1980.

Rooney, David, *Mad Mike: A life of Michael Calvert*, London, 1997.

Ross, Hamish, *Paddy Mayne: Lt. Col. Blair 'Paddy' Mayne, 1 SAS Regiment*, London, 2003.

Southby-Tailyour, Ewen, *Jane's Special Forces: Recognition Guide*, London, 2005.

Strawson, John, *A History of the SAS Regiment*, London, 1985.

Urban, Mark, *Big Boys' Rules: The secret struggle against the IRA*, London, 1992.

Warner, Philip, *The Special Air Service*, London, 1983.

West, Nigel, *The Secret War for the Falklands: The SAS, MI6 and the war Whitehall nearly lost*, London, 1997.

Williams, Jack, *The Rigger: Operating with the SAS*, Barnsley, 2001.

Wynter, H. W., *Special Forces in the Desert War 1940–43*, London, 2001.

Unpublished Sources

Almonds Windmill, Lorna (ed.), *Diary of Jim Almonds 1941*.
Asher, Michael, *The Real Bravo Two Zero*, Channel 4 TV, 2001.
BBC TV, *Great SAS Missions*, 2006
Channel 4 TV, *SAS: The Real Story*, 2003.
Fairweather, Clive, interview with Nigel Morris, 2005.
Jeapes, Major General Tony, interview with the author, 2006.
List, David, *The Birth of the SAS*, BBC radio documentary, 2006.

National Archives

WO 32/1236R Definition of SAS Regiment
WO 193/27 Formation of Parachute & Commando Units
WO 193/405 SAS & SS Files
WO 205/93 Operations in France 1944
WO 201/435 Benghazi Operation 1942
WO 201/747 1 SAS Operations October 1942
WO 201/772 Abeam (A Force) File
WO 201/785 Formation of L Detachment
WO 201/811 LRDG Prendergast Papers
WO 218/11 Commando War Diary
WO 218/223 David Stirling 1948 memo
WO 219/509Z Operations in France 1944
WO 305/0176 22 SAS in Oman
WO 1131/133/24E RAF Files

Notes

Prologue: 'I always knew you would do a good job, but I never knew it would be this good'

1. Robin Horsfall, *Fighting Scared*, London, 2002, p. 154.
2. Clive Fairweather, interview with Nigel Morris, 2005.
3. ibid.
4. ibid.
5. Horsfall, *Fighting Scared*, p. 154.
6. Clive Fairweather, interview with Nigel Morris, 2005.
7. Peter de la Billière, *Looking for Trouble: SAS to Gulf Command*, London, 1995, p. 126.
8. ibid., p. 164.
9. ibid., p. 328.
10. ibid., p. 331.
11. Horsfall, *Fighting Scared*, p. 167.
12. De la Billière, *Looking for Trouble*, p. 334.
13. Anthony Kemp, *The SAS: Savage Wars of Peace*, London, 1994, p. 153.
14. Horsfall, *Fighting Scared*, p. 170.
15. Horsfall, *Fighting Scared*, p. 171.
16. De la Billière, *Looking for Trouble*, p. 337.
17. Ken Connor, *Ghost Force – the Secret History of the SAS*, London, 1998, p. 173.
18. Horsfall, *Fighting Scared*, p. 173.
19. Everything 2: website: The Iranian Embassy Siege 2006.
20. Horsfall, *Fighting Scared*, p. 173.
21. De la Billière, *Looking for Trouble*, p. 335.
22. One possibility is that the dead hostage in the telex room was shot by the sniper while throwing the terrorists' weapons out of the window. This would explain why the grenade was not primed.
23. Cult of SAS article 2.

24. De la Billière, *Looking for Trouble*, p. 283.
25. Michael Asher, *Get Rommel: The secret British mission to kill Hitler's greatest general*, London, 2004, p. 76.

1. 'The sort of plan we are looking for'

1. The date of Stirling's meeting with Ritchie is disputed. The typewritten memo is dated 16 July. The message asking for authority to form the SAS is dated 18 July. Since Stirling said that the meeting with Auchinleck came three days after the initial meeting with Ritchie, process of deduction produces 15 July as the most likely date. If the original memo was written in pencil as Stirling claimed, it will probably have been typed up for the meeting with the C-in-C – hence the date 16 July.
2. Gordon Stevens, *The Originals: The secret history of the birth of the SAS in their own words*, London, 2005, p. 20.
3. Virginia Cowles, *The Phantom Major*, London, 1958, p. 15.

2. Bands of brothers, packs of hounds

1. Winston Churchill, *The Second World War*, London, 1949, pp. 46–7.
2. ibid., p. 466.

3. 'The landing of small parties by night will clearly be most effective'

1. John Lewes, *Jock Lewes: Co-Founder of the SAS*, Barnsley, 2000, p. 122.
2. Ernie Bond in BBC radio documentary, 2006, presented by David List.
3. National Archives WO7/122.
4. ibid.
5. ibid.

6. Carol Mather, *When the Grass Stops Growing*, London, 1997, p. 29.

7. Lewes, *Jock Lewes*, p. 203.

8. Alan Hoe, *David Stirling: The Authorized Biography of the Creator of the SAS*, London, 1992, p. 61.

9. Lewes, *Jock Lewes*, p. 247.

10. ibid., p. 220.

5. *'Jock wanted to be sure I was going to stay with it'*

1. Alan Hoe, *David Stirling: The Authorized Biography of the Creator of the SAS*, London, 1992, p. 193.

2. Carol Mather, *When the Grass Stops Growing*, London, 1997, p. 53.

3. John Lewes, *Jock Lewes: Co-Founder of the SAS*, Barnsley, 2000, p. 220.

4. ibid., p. 196.

6. *'An extremely truculent Irishman'*

1. Geoffrey Keyes, personal diary, Lord Roger Keyes Collection.

2. Keyes's diary proves conclusively that Mayne was not RTU'd for striking Keyes himself, as the accepted myth holds.

3. Michael Asher, *Get Rommel: The secret British mission to kill Hitler's greatest general*, London, 2004, p. 100.

4. Martin Dillon and Roy Bradford, *Rogue Warrior of the SAS: The Blair Mayne legend*, London, 1987, p. 216.

5. ibid., p. 238.

6. ibid., p. xvii.

7. Gordon Stevens, *The Originals: The secret history of the birth of the SAS in their own words*, London, 2005, p. 28.

8. This wasn't always the case, though: there are records in the 11 Commando diary of commandos being jailed.

7. *Wondering why he should be scared if Lewes wasn't*

1. Gavin Mortimer, *Stirling's Men – the inside history of the SAS in World War II*, London, 2004, p. 23.

8. *'The man is the Regiment'*

1. Alan Hoe, *David Stirling: The Authorized Biography of the Creator of the SAS*, London, 1992, p. 468.
2. Peter Ratcliffe, with Noel Botham and Brian Hitchen, *Eye of the Storm: Twenty-five Years in Action with the SAS*, London, 2000, p. 5.
3. Malcolm James (Malcolm Pleydell), *Born of the Desert*, London, 1945, p. 30.
4. Robert Pirsig, *Lila: An inquiry into morals*, New York, 1991, p. 140.
5. Lorna Almonds Windmill, *Gentleman Jim: The wartime story of a founder of the SAS & special forces*, London, 2001, p. 5.
6. Gavin Mortimer, *Stirling's Men – the inside history of the SAS in World War II*, London, 2004, p. 64.
7. Charlie A. Beckwith, *Delta Force – the Army's Elite Counter-Terrorist Unit*, San Diego, 1983, p. 12.
8. Roy Close, *In Action with the SAS: A soldier's odyssey from Dunkirk to Berlin*, Barnsley, 2005, p. 256.

9. *'A yellow streak a yard wide'*

1. Gordon Stevens, *The Originals: The secret history of the birth of the SAS in their own words*, London, 2005, p. 36.
2. Lewes, John, *Jock Lewes: Co-Founder of the SAS*, Barnsley, 2000, p. 199.
3. Stevens, *The Originals*, p. 36.
4. ibid., pp. 36, 47.

10. *'We tried not to think about it. But we did'*

1. Lewes, John, *Jock Lewes: Co-Founder of the SAS*, Barnsley, 2000, p. 207.
2. Philip Warner, *The Special Air Service*, London, 1983, p. 20.
3. Lewes, *Jock Lewes*, p. 207.
4. ibid., p. 224.

11. *'A nice little black pudding'*

1. Gordon Stevens, *The Originals: The secret history of the birth of the SAS in their own words*, London, 2005, p. 51.

13. *'We'll go because we've got to go'*

1. Alan Hoe, *David Stirling: The Authorized Biography of the Creator of the SAS*, London, 1992, p. 93.
2. National Archives WO7/122.
3. Gordon Stevens, *The Originals: The secret history of the birth of the SAS in their own words*, London, 2005, p. 63.
4. ibid., p. 64.

14. *Raining so hard it hurt*

1. Gavin Mortimer, *Stirling's Men – the inside history of the SAS in World War II*, London, 2004, p. 26.

15. *'Well crikey, if these people can penetrate this far . . .'*

1. John Strawson, *A History of the SAS Regiment*, London, 1985, p. 30.
2. ibid.
3. ibid.

4. Gordon Stevens, *The Originals: The secret history of the birth of the SAS in their own words*, London, 2005, p. 18.
5. ibid., p. 76.

17. 'You'll like him, and he's well placed to help'

1. Bryan Perrett, *Desert Warfare: from its Roman origins to the Gulf conflict*, Wellingborough, 1988, p. 126.
2. David List, private collection.
3. ibid.
4. Alan Hoe, *David Stirling: The Authorized Biography of the Creator of the SAS*, London, 1992, p. 107.

18. 'Advance and attack any suitable objectives'

1. H. W. Wynter, *Special Forces in the Desert War 1940–43*, London, 2001, p. 199.

19. Swallowed up by the huge dimensions

1. Philip Warner, *The Special Air Service*, London, 1983, p. 36.

20. 'I saw him rip the instrument panel out with his bare hands'

1. Martin Dillon and Roy Bradford, *Rogue Warrior of the SAS: The Blair Mayne legend*, London, 1987, p. 3.
2. Gordon Stevens, *The Originals: The secret history of the birth of the SAS in their own words*, London, 2005, p. 66.
3. ibid.
4. Alan Hoe, *David Stirling: The Authorized Biography of the Creator of the SAS*, London, 1992, p. 111.

21. 'Rommel must have had a headache'

1. Ian Wellsted, *SAS with the Maquis: In action with the French resistance June–September 1944*, London, 1994, p. 26.
2. Gavin Mortimer, *Stirling's Men – the inside history of the SAS in World War II*, London, 2004, p. 31.
3. J. V. Byrne, *The General Salutes a Soldier: With the SAS and Commandos in World War Two*, London, 1986, p. 16.
4. ibid.
5. Mortimer, *Stirling's Men*, p. 32.
6. ibid., p. 33.
7. Byrne, *The General Salutes a Soldier*, p. 17.
8. Mortimer, *Stirling's Men*, p. 33.
9. Virginia Cowles, *The Phantom Major*, London, 1958, p. 70.
10. ibid.

22. 'When they went up, they went'

1. Gordon Stevens, *The Originals: The secret history of the birth of the SAS in their own words*, London, 2005, p. 83.
2. ibid., p. 144.

23. 'The only one to be killed and it had to be him'

1. Lorna Almonds Windmill, *Gentleman Jim: The wartime story of a founder of the SAS & special forces*, London, 2001, p. 99.
2. In some versions it was Lilley.
3. Almonds Windmill, *Gentleman Jim*, p. 101.
4. Malcolm James (Malcolm Pleydell), *Born of the Desert*, London, 1945, p. 17.
5. ibid., p. 287.
6. ibid., p. 27.

7. John Lewes, *Jock Lewes: Co-Founder of the SAS*, Barnsley, 2000, p. 23.

24. 'The day the SAS was truly born'

1. Gordon Stevens, *The Originals: The secret history of the birth of the SAS in their own words*, London, 2005, p. 116.
2. Alan Hoe, *David Stirling: The Authorized Biography of the Creator of the SAS*, London, 1992, p. 123.
3. This may be another myth: the original Airborne colours were blue – representing the sky – and only became maroon in 1944. The SAS at one point wore field caps with blue facings: the blues incorporated into the wings may be simply a reflection of this.

25. 'Surrounded by bottles, reading James Joyce'

1. Cooper, Johnny, *One of the Originals: The Story of a Founder Member of the SAS*, London, 1991, p. 39.
2. Gordon Stevens, *The Originals: The secret history of the birth of the SAS in their own words*, London, 2005, p. 100.
3. Alan Hoe, *David Stirling: The Authorized Biography of the Creator of the SAS*, 1992, p. 158.
4. Lorna Almonds Windmill, *Gentleman Jim: The wartime story of a founder of the SAS & special forces*, London, 2001.
5. Martin Dillon and Roy Bradford, *Rogue Warrior of the SAS: The Blair Mayne legend*, London, 1987, p. xvi.
6. Gavin Mortimer, *Stirling's Men – the inside history of the SAS in World War II*, London, 2004, p. 72.
7. Dillon and Bradford, *Rogue Warrior*, p. 89.
8. Mortimer, *Stirling's Men*, p. 116.
9. Hoe, *David Stirling*, p. 138.

26. 'You can get away with it by sheer blatant cheek'

1. Alan Hoe, *David Stirling: The Authorized Biography of the Creator of the SAS*, London, 1992, p. 148.
2. Fitzroy Maclean, *Eastern Approaches*, London, 1949, p. 177.
3. ibid., p. 180.
4. Johnny Cooper, *One of the Originals: The Story of a Founder Member of the SAS*, London, 1991, p. 50.
5. ibid., p. 50.
6. ibid.

27. The most ambitious SAS project yet

1. Malcolm James (Malcolm Pleydell), *Born of the Desert*, London, 1945, p. 295.

28. 'Give them something to remember us by'

1. Gordon Stevens, *The Originals: The secret history of the birth of the SAS in their own words*, London, 2005, p. 125.
2. Anthony Kemp, *The SAS at War 1941–1945*, London, 1991, p. 52.
3. ibid., p. 53.
4. Alan Hoe, *David Stirling: The Authorized Biography of the Creator of the SAS*, London, 1992, p. 166.
5. ibid.
6. Martin Dillon and Roy Bradford, *Rogue Warrior of the SAS: The Blair Mayne legend*, London, 1987, p. 135.
7. Kemp, *The SAS at War*, p. 52.

29. 'The lorry kept spluttering to a halt'

1. Gavin Mortimer, *Stirling's Men – the inside history of the SAS in World War II*, London, 2004, p. 51.

31. 'We had finally emulated Paddy Mayne on our own'

1. Malcolm James (Malcolm Pleydell), *Born of the Desert*, London, 1945, p. 297.
2. Virginia Cowles, *The Phantom Major*, London, 1958, p. 154.
3. ibid., p. 155.
4. Johnny Cooper, *One of the Originals: The Story of a Founder Member of the SAS*, London, 1991, p. 54.
5. Cowles, *The Phantom Major*, p. 156.
6. Hamish Ross, *Paddy Mayne: Lt. Col. Blair 'Paddy' Mayne, 1 SAS Regiment*, 2003, p. 79.
7. Gordon Stevens, *The Originals: The secret history of the birth of the SAS in their own words*, London, 2005, p. 103.
8. Cowles, *The Phantom Major*, p. 171.
9. Ross, *Paddy Mayne*, p. 79.
10. Gavin Mortimer, *Stirling's Men – the inside history of the SAS in World War II*, London, 2004, p. 53.
11. Cooper, *One of the Originals*, p. 56.
12. Alan Hoe, *David Stirling: The Authorized Biography of the Creator of the SAS*, London, 1992, p. 169.
13. ibid.
14. Mortimer, *Stirling's Men*, p. 159.
15. Ross, *Paddy Mayne*, p. 180.
16. H. W. Wynter, *Special Forces in the Desert War 1940–43*, London, 2001, p. 320.
17. Cooper, *One of the Originals*, p. 57.
18. ibid.

32. *'The target was a fat and sitting bird'*

1. H. W. Wynter, *Special Forces in the Desert War 1940–43*, London, 2001, p. 412.
2. ibid.
3. ibid., p. 411.

33. *'I suppose you've had a good time then'*

1. John Keegan, *The Second World War*, London, 1999, p. 276.
2. Alan Hoe, *David Stirling: The Authorized Biography of the Creator of the SAS*, London, 1992, p. 171.
3. Gavin Mortimer, *Stirling's Men – the inside history of the SAS in World War II*, London, 2004, p. 54.
4. Gordon Stevens, *The Originals: The secret history of the birth of the SAS in their own words*, London, 2005, p. 126.

34. *'Our job was to constantly invent new techniques'*

1. Carol Mather, *When the Grass Stops Growing*, London, 1997, p. 82.
2. Stephen Hastings, *The Drums of Memory: An autobiography*, London, 1994, p. 49.
3. John Connell, *Auchinleck: A Biography*, London, 1959, p. 302.
4. Hastings, *The Drums of Memory*, p. 49.
5. H. W. Wynter, *Special Forces in the Desert War 1940–43*, London, 2001, p. 330.
6. Alan Hoe, *David Stirling: The Authorized Biography of the Creator of the SAS*, London, 1992, p. 183.
7. Johnny Cooper, *One of the Originals: The Story of a Founder Member of the SAS*, London, 1991, p. 65.
8. Gordon Stevens, *The Originals: The secret history of the birth of the SAS in their own words*, London, 2005, p. 148.
9. Wynter, *Special Forces in the Desert War*, p. 330.

10. Hoe, *David Stirling*, p. 186.
11. Cooper, *One of the Originals*, p. 60.
12. Mather, *When the Grass Stops Growing*, p. 91.
13. Cooper, *One of the Originals*, p. 60.
14. Mather, *When the Grass Stops Growing*, p. 91.
15. Hastings, *The Drums of Memory*, p. 64.
16. ibid., p. 65.
17. ibid., p. 66.
18. Malcolm James (Malcolm Pleydell), *Born of the Desert*, London, 1945, p. 160.
19. Cooper, *One of the Originals*, p. 65.

35. 'Mort au Champ d'Honneur'

1. Malcolm James (Malcolm Pleydell), *Born of the Desert*, London, 1945, p. 159.
2. ibid., p. 162.
3. ibid., pp. 242, 163.
4. Alan Hoe, *David Stirling: The Authorized Biography of the Creator of the SAS*, London, 1992, p. 190.
5. ibid., p. 196.

36. 'It looks rather that we are expected'

1. Fitzroy Maclean, *Eastern Approaches*, London, 1949, p. 189.
2. Malcolm James (Malcolm Pleydell), *Born of the Desert*, London, 1945, p. 233.
3. ibid., p. 242.
4. Maclean, *Eastern Approaches*, p. 190.
5. James, *Born of the Desert*, p. 242.
6. ibid.
7. ibid.
8. ibid.
9. Maclean, *Eastern Approaches*, pp. 190–91.

10. Carol Mather, *When the Grass Stops Growing*, London, 1997, p. 139.

37. 'Let battle commence'

1. Carol Mather, *When the Grass Stops Growing*, London, 1997, p. 138.
2. Lorna Almonds Windmill, *Gentleman Jim: The wartime story of a founder of the SAS & special forces*, London, 2001, p. 150.
3. Mather, *When the Grass Stops Growing*, p. 141.
4. Gordon Stevens, *The Originals: The secret history of the birth of the SAS in their own words*, London, 2005, p. 159.
5. Mather, *When the Grass Stops Growing*, p. 142.
6. ibid., p. 143.

38. 'This is going to be a shaky do'

1. Malcolm James (Malcolm Pleydell), *Born of the Desert*, London, 1945, p. 249.
2. Fitzroy Maclean, *Eastern Approaches*, London, 1949, p. 194.
3. Carol Mather, *When the Grass Stops Growing*, London, 1997, p. 145.
4. Gavin Mortimer, *Stirling's Men – the inside history of the SAS in World War II*, London, 2004, p. 69.
5. Maclean, *Eastern Approaches*, p. 197.
6. ibid., p. 199.
7. James, *Born of the Desert*, p. 265.
8. Gordon Stevens, *The Originals: The secret history of the birth of the SAS in their own words*, London, 2005, p. 162.

39. Talking out of turn over gin-and-tonics

1. H. W. Wynter, *Special Forces in the Desert War 1940–43*, London, 2001, p. 339.

40. The Regiment

1. Alan Hoe, *David Stirling: The Authorized Biography of the Creator of the SAS*, London, 1992, p. 210.
2. ibid., p. 211.
3. ibid., p. 213.
4. Carol Mather, *When the Grass Stops Growing*, London, 1997, p. 200.

41. 'A one-way ticket with no return'

1. Hamish Ross, *Paddy Mayne: Lt. Col. Blair 'Paddy' Mayne, 1 SAS Regiment*, 2003, p. 87.
2. Wilfred Thesiger, *A Life of My Choice*, London, 1987, p. 374.
3. ibid., p. 377.
4. ibid., p. 378.
5. Carol Mather, *When the Grass Stops Growing*, London, 1997, p. 202.
6. ibid., p. 202.
7. ibid., p. 203.
8. ibid., p. 204.

42. They had become invisible

1. Virginia Cowles, *The Phantom Major*, London, 1958, p. 276.
2. Wilfred Thesiger, *A Life of My Choice*, London, 1987, p. 380.

43. 'Mistakenly overconfident about our security'

1. Johnny Cooper, *One of the Originals: The Story of a Founder Member of the SAS*, London, 1991, p. 173.
2. ibid.
3. Gordon Stevens, *The Originals: The secret history of the birth of the SAS in their own words*, London, 2005, p. 174.

4. ibid., p. 84.

5. Alan Hoe, *David Stirling: The Authorized Biography of the Creator of the SAS*, London, 1992, p. 223.

6. B. H. Liddell-Hart (ed.), trans. Paul Findlay, *The Rommel Papers*, London, 1954, p. 393.

44. 'It's a bad one this time'

1. Gordon Stevens, *The Originals: The secret history of the birth of the SAS in their own words*, London, 2005, p. 211.

2. ibid., p. 212.

3. ibid., pp. 85, 213.

4. ibid.

45. 'Will you shoot my brother?'

1. Stewart McClean, *SAS: The History of the Special Raiding Squadron, 'Paddy's men'*, Stroud, 2006, p. 48.

2. Martin Dillon and Roy Bradford, *Rogue Warrior of the SAS: The Blair Mayne legend*, London, 1987, p. 88.

46. 'Paddy Mayne was the man'

1. Gordon Stevens, *The Originals: The secret history of the birth of the SAS in their own words*, London, 2005, p. 177.

2. Alan Hoe, *David Stirling: The Authorized Biography of the Creator of the SAS*, London, 1992, p. 230.

3. Stevens, *The Originals*, p. 188.

47. *Those bloody fools back at HQ will one day tell me who I'm talking to'*

1. Carol Mather, *When the Grass Stops Growing*, London, 1997, p. 71.
2. Gordon Stevens, *The Originals: The secret history of the birth of the SAS in their own words*, London, 2005, p. 196.
3. Derrick Harrison, *These Men are Dangerous*, London, 1957, p. 19.
4. ibid.
5. Hamish Ross, *Paddy Mayne: Lt. Col. Blair 'Paddy' Mayne, 1 SAS Regiment*, London, 2003, p. 129.
6. ibid.

48. *'The best crowd he had ever had under his command'*

1. Martin Dillon and Roy Bradford, *Rogue Warrior of the SAS: The Blair Mayne legend*, London, 1987, p. 88.
2. Hamish Ross, *Paddy Mayne: Lt. Col. Blair 'Paddy' Mayne, 1 SAS Regiment*, London, 2003, p. 105.
3. Roy Farran, *Winged Dagger*, London, 1948, p. 203.
4. Derrick Harrison, *These Men are Dangerous*, London, 1957, p. 199.
5. Farran, *Winged Dagger*, p. 203.
6. ibid.
7. Malcolm James (Malcolm Pleydell), *Born of the Desert*, London, 1945, p. 319.
8. Farran, *Winged Dagger*, p. 157.

49. *Never quite lived up to its promise*

1. Anthony Kemp, *The SAS at War 1941–1945*, London, 1991, p. 103.
2. ibid., p. 111,
3. ibid., p. 116.

50. 'We don't think about you at all'

1. John Strawson, *A History of the SAS Regiment*, London, 1985, pp. 121–2.
2. Johnny Cooper, *One of the Originals: The Story of a Founder Member of the SAS*, London, 1991, p. 83.
3. Ken Connor, *Ghost Force – the Secret History of the SAS*, London, 1998, p. 286.
4. Martin Dillon and Roy Bradford, *Rogue Warrior of the SAS: The Blair Mayne legend*, London, 1987, p. 93.
5. Derrick Harrison, *These Men are Dangerous*, London, 1957, p. 199.
6. Dillon and Bradford, *Rogue Warrior*, p. 126.
7. Cooper, *One of the Originals*, p. 84.
8. ibid.
9. Harrison, *These Men are Dangerous*, p. 108.

51. 'We just picked up our rucksacks and left'

1. Alan Hoe, *David Stirling: The Authorized Biography of the Creator of the SAS*, London, 1992, p. 260.
2. Roy Farran, *Winged Dagger*, London, 1948, p. 222.
3. ibid., p. 223.
4. Gordon Stevens, *The Originals: The secret history of the birth of the SAS in their own words*, London, 2005, p. 238.
5. Paul McCue, *SAS Operation Bulbasket: Behind the lines in occupied France 1944*, London, 1996, p. 117.

54. 'For the life of me I couldn't think what all the noise was about'

1. Gavin Mortimer, *Stirling's Men – the inside history of the SAS in World War II*, London, 2004, p. 211.

55. 'A marvellous killing-ground'

1. Fraser McLuskey, *Parachute Padre*, London, 1951, p. 151.
2. ibid.
3. Johnny Cooper, *One of the Originals: The Story of a Founder Member of the SAS*, London, 1991, p. 91.
4. ibid., p. 92.
5. Ian Wellsted, *SAS with the Maquis: In action with the French resistance June–September 1944*, London, 1994, p. 66.
6. Cooper, *One of the Originals*, p. 92.
7. Wellsted, *SAS with the Maquis*, p. 67.
8. Gavin Mortimer, *Stirling's Men – the inside history of the SAS in World War II*, London, 2004, p. 207.
9. Gordon Stevens, *The Originals: The secret history of the birth of the SAS in their own words*, London, 2005, p. 258.
10. Wellsted, *SAS with the Maquis*, p. 86.

56. 'Thank you, Madame, but I intend to attack them'

1. Roger Ford, *Fire from the Forest: The SAS Brigade in France 1944*, London, 2003, p. 115.

57. 'My wife will be furious if I get myself killed today'

1. Derrick Harrison, *These Men are Dangerous*, London, 1957, p. 185.
2. ibid.
3. ibid.
4. ibid.
5. ibid., p. 188.
6. Martin Dillon and Roy Bradford, *Rogue Warrior of the SAS: The Blair Mayne legend*, London, 1987, p. 129.

58. 'Why don't we just fuck off quietly because we're not going to do any good here'

1. Roger Ford, *Fire from the Forest: The SAS Brigade in France 1944*, London, 2003.
2. Gordon Stevens, *The Originals: The secret history of the birth of the SAS in their own words*, London, 2005, p. 240.
3. Anthony Kemp, *The SAS at War 1941–1945*, London, 1991, p. 190.
4. Hamish Ross, *Paddy Mayne: Lt. Col. Blair 'Paddy' Mayne, 1 SAS Regiment*, London, 2003, p. 164.
5. ibid., p. 168.
6. Johnny Cooper, *One of the Originals: The Story of a Founder Member of the SAS*, London, 1991, p. 104.
7. Ian Wellsted, *SAS with the Maquis: In action with the French resistance June–September 1944*, London, 1994, p. 219.
8. ibid., p. 120.

59. 'In the face of enemy machine-gun fire'

1. Martin Dillon and Roy Bradford, *Rogue Warrior of the SAS: The Blair Mayne legend*, London, 1987, p. 172.
2. ibid., p. 169.
3. Derrick Harrison, *These Men are Dangerous*, London, 1957, p. 223.
4. Dillon and Bradford, *Rogue Warrior*, p. 170.
5. ibid.
6. ibid., p. 176.
7. ibid., p. 172.
8. ibid., p. 174.
9. ibid.

60. He couldn't believe that he'd actually survived

1. Johnny Cooper, *One of the Originals: The Story of a Founder Member of the SAS*, London, 1991, p. 110.
2. ibid.
3. ibid., p. 113.

61. 'In peacetime a man born to battle has to change his ways'

1. Johnny Cooper, *One of the Originals: The Story of a Founder Member of the SAS*, London, 1991, p. 116.
2. Gordon Stevens, *The Originals: The secret history of the birth of the SAS in their own words*, London, 2005, p. 321.
3. Martin Dillon and Roy Bradford, *Rogue Warrior of the SAS: The Blair Mayne legend*, London, 1987, p. 147.
4. Stevens, *The Originals*, p. 321.
5. Tim Jones, *SAS: The First Secret Wars: The unknown years of combat and counter insurgency*, London, 2005, p. 24.
6. Dillon and Bradford, *Rogue Warrior* p. xv.
7. Michael Calvert, *Fighting Mad: One man's guerrilla war*, London, 1964, p. 200.
8. Dillon and Bradford, *Rogue Warrior*, p. 212.
9. Cooper, *One of the Originals*, p. 118.
10. Stevens, *The Originals*, p. 320.

62. 'The standard jungle-drills must have come out'

1. Johnny Cooper, *One of the Originals: The Story of a Founder Member of the SAS*, London, 1991, p. 127.
2. ibid., p. 129.

64. *A force that would 'live, move, and have its being in the jungle'*

1. Michael Calvert, *Fighting Mad: One man's guerrilla war*, London, 1964, p. 204.
2. Frederick Spencer Chapman, *The Jungle is Neutral*, London, 1951, p. 115.
3. Calvert, *Fighting Mad*, p. 205.

65. *'The Special Air Service, at last, was back in the regular army'*

1. Alan Hoe and Eric Morris, *Re-enter the SAS: The Special Air Service and the Malayan Emergency*, London, 1994, pp.64–5.
2. ibid., p. 60.
3. ibid., p. 59.
4. Michael Calvert, *Fighting Mad: One man's guerrilla war*, London, 1964, pp. 207–8.
5. Hoe and Morris, *Re-enter the SAS*, p. 67.
6. Hoe and Morris, *Re-enter the SAS*, p. 66.
7. David Rooney, *Mad Mike: A life of Michael Calvert*, London, 1997, p. 149.
8. *SAS: The Real Story*, Channel 4 TV, 2003.
9. Hoe and Morris, *Re-enter the SAS*, p. 73.
10. Peter de la Billière, *Looking for Trouble: SAS to Gulf Command*, London, 1995, p. 112.
11. Rooney, *Mad Mike*, pp. 102–3.
12. ibid., p. 151.
13. Mike Sinclair-Hill, *SAS: The Real Story*, Channel 4, TV 2003.
14. Rooney, *Mad Mike*, p. 152.
15. Calvert, *Fighting Mad*, p. 208.

66. 'Like a bunch of grapes hanging out of his slacks'

1. Johnny Cooper, *One of the Originals: The Story of a Founder Member of the SAS*, London, 1991, p. 121.
2. ibid., p. 124.
3. Lofty Large, *Soldier Against the Odds: From Korean war to SAS*, Edinburgh, 1999, p. 138.
4. ibid., p. 136.
5. ibid., p. 139.
6. Cooper, *One of the Originals*, p. 124.

68. 'The Regiment had got something. You could sense it from the moment you arrived'

1. Barbara Cole, *The Elite: The story of the Rhodesian Special Air Service*, Durban, 1985, p. 431.
2. Johnny Cooper, *One of the Originals: The Story of a Founder Member of the SAS*, London, 1991, p. 137.
3. John Strawson, *A History of the SAS Regiment*, London, 1985, p. 284.
4. ibid.

69. 'He was a coward and had surrendered to save his skin'

1. A. J. Deane-Drummond, *Arrows of Fortune*, London, 1992, p. 150.
2. ibid., p.154.
3. Peter de la Billière, *Looking for Trouble: SAS to Gulf Command*, London, 1995, p. 124.
4. ibid., p. 114.
5. ibid., p. 81.
6. Deane-Drummond, *Arrows of Fortune*, p. 160.
7. ibid.
8. De la Billière, *Looking for Trouble*, p. 126.

70. 'There will be nothing left for my squadron at this rate'

1. Johnny Cooper, *One of the Originals: The Story of a Founder Member of the SAS*, London, 1991, p. 145.
2. ibid.

71. 'Condition their frame of mind to the extent where negotiations will be successful'

1. A. J. Deane-Drummond, *Arrows of Fortune*, London, 1992, appendix.
2. Peter de la Billière, *Looking for Trouble*: *SAS to Gulf Command*, London, 1995, p. 142.
3. ibid., p. 139.
4. Deane-Drummond, *Arrows of Fortune*, p. 202.

72. 'We had done it in the nick of time'

1. Tony Jeapes, interview with the author, November 2006.
2. A. J. Deane-Drummond, *Arrows of Fortune*, London, 1992, p. 205.
3. Lofty Large, *SAS: The Real Story*, Channel Four TV, 2003.
4. Peter de la Billière, *Looking for Trouble*: *SAS to Gulf Command*, London, 1995, p. 147.
5. Lofty Large, *Soldier Against the Odds: From Korean war to SAS*, Edinburgh, 1999, p. 178.
6. ibid., p. 177.
7. De la Billière, *Looking for Trouble*, p. 147.
8. ibid., p. 148.
9. ibid., p. 149.
10. Deane-Drummond, *Arrows of Fortune*, p. 210.

73. 'A great success as a bloody idiot'

1. Peter de la Billière, *Looking for Trouble: SAS to Gulf Command*, London, 1995, p. 160.
2. ibid., p. 161.
3. Lofty Large, *Soldier Against the Odds: From Korean war to SAS*, Edinburgh, 1999, p. 217.
4. De la Billière, *Looking for Trouble*, p. 235.
5. Large, *Soldier Against the Odds*, p. 219.
6. ibid.
7. Ken Connor, *Ghost Force – the Secret History of the SAS*, London, 1998, p. 110.
8. Large, *Soldier Against the Odds*, p. 111.
9. Charlie A. Beckwith, *Delta Force – the Army's Elite Counter-Terrorist Unit*, San Diego, 1983, p. 39.

74. 'A battle for a man's mind and a test of his will to win'

1. Charlie A. Beckwith, *Delta Force – the Army's Elite Counter-Terrorist Unit*, San Diego, 1983, p. 17.
2. Peter Ratcliffe, with Noel Botham and Brian Hitchen, *Eye of the Storm: Twenty-five Years in Action with the SAS*, London, 2000, p. 41.
3. John Woodhouse, *SAS: The Real Story*, Channel 4 TV, 2003.
4. Nick Downie, *SAS: The Real Story*, Channel 4 TV, 2003.
5. Mac, *SAS: The Real Story*, Channel 4 TV, 2003.
6. Jimmy Ladner, *SAS: The Real Story*, Channel 4 TV, 2003.
7. Lofty Large, *Soldier Against the Odds: From Korean war to SAS*, Edinburgh, 1999, p. 216.
8. ibid., p. 213.
9. Ratcliffe, *Eye of the Storm*.
10. Ken Connor, *Ghost Force – the Secret History of the SAS*, London, 1998, p. 13.
11. Large, *Soldier Against the Odds*, p. 126.

12. Peter de la Billière, *Looking for Trouble: SAS to Gulf Command*, London, 1995, p. 99.

13. ibid., pp. 99–100.

14. Ken Connor, *Ghosts: An illustrated story of the SAS*, London, 2000, p. 14.

15. Robin Horsfall, *Fighting Scared*, London, 2002, p. 104.

16. ibid., p. 117.

17. Tony Geraghty, *Who Dares Wins: The story of the SAS 1950–1992*, London, 1993, p. 502.

18. De la Billière, *Looking for Trouble*, p. 235.

19. Geraghty, *Who Dares Wins*, p. 502.

20. Ratcliffe, *Eye of the Storm*, p. 51.

75. 'When fighting for your life, you've got to enjoy it'

1. Peter de la Billière, *Looking for Trouble: SAS to Gulf Command*, London, 1995, p. 217.

2. Ken Connor, *Ghost Force – the Secret History of the SAS*, London, 1998, p. 179.

3. De la Billière, *Looking for Trouble*, p. 215.

4. ibid., p. 217.

76. 'I think we should expect to fight to the death for this'

1. Peter de la Billière, *Looking for Trouble: SAS to Gulf Command*, London, 1995, p. 230.

2. ibid., p. 231.

3. Peter Dickens, *SAS: The Jungle Frontier: 22 Special Air Service Regiment :in the Borneo campaign 1963–1966*, London, 1983, p. 179.

4. De la Billière, *Looking for Trouble*, p. 234.

5. Dickens, *SAS: The Jungle Frontier*, p. 181.

77. 'One of the most efficient uses of military force in the history of the world'

1. Peter de la Billière, *Looking for Trouble: SAS to Gulf Command* London, 1995, p. 240.
2. ibid., p. 234.
3. ibid., p. 245.
4. ibid., p. 248.
5. ibid., p. 248.

78. 'The covert and clandestine actions for which it is world famous'

1. Ken Connor, *Ghost Force – the Secret History of the SAS*, London, 1998, p. 211.
2. Ken Connor, *Ghosts: An illustrated story of the SAS*, London, 2000, p. 143.
3. Connor, *Ghost Force*, p. 102.

80. 'Purely for training purposes'

1. Tony Jeapes, *SAS Secret: War Operation Storm in the Middle East*, London, 1996, p. 51.
2. ibid., p. 63.
3. Tony Geraghty, *Who Dares Wins: The story of the SAS 1950–1992*, London, 1993, p. 186.
4. Brummie Stokes, *Soldiers and Sherpas: A taste for adventure*, London, 1988, p. 103.
5. Peter Ratcliffe, with Noel Botham and Brian Hitchen, *Eye of the Storm: Twenty-five Years in Action with the SAS*, London, 2000, p. 98.
6. Jeapes, *SAS Secret War*, p. 97.

82. 'Close with the terrorists and kill them'

1. Peter de la Billière, *Looking for Trouble: SAS to Gulf Command*, London, 1995, p. 282.
2. Ken Connor, *Ghosts: An illustrated story of the SAS*, London, 2000, p. 143.
3. De la Billière, *Looking for Trouble*, p. 143.
4. Barry Davies, *SAS: Shadow Warriors of the 21st Century: The SAS Anti-Terrorist Team*, Staplehurst, 2002, p. 34.

83. 'Not a very pretty sight!'

1. Peter Ratcliffe, with Noel Botham and Brian Hitchen, *Eye of the Storm: Twenty-five Years in Action with the SAS*, London, 2000, p. 3.
2. ibid., p. 96.
3. ibid., p. 100.

85. 'Never a happy hunting-ground'

1. John Parker, *Secret Hero: The life and mysterious death of Captain Robert Nairac*, London, 2004, p. 161.
2. Raymond Murray, *The SAS in Ireland*, Dublin, 1990, p. 164.
3. John Parker, *Secret Hero*, p. 148.
4. ibid., p. 154.
5. Murray, *The SAS in Ireland*, p. 182.
6. Parker, *Secret Hero*, p. 163.

86. 'What the SAS are employed to do'

1. Lofty Large, *Soldier Against the Odds: From Korean war to SAS*, Edinburgh, 1999, p. 264.

2. Barry Davies, *SAS: Shadow Warriors of the 21st Century: The SAS Anti-Terrorist Team*, Staplehurst, 2002, p. 112.
3. Scott Graham, *Shoot to Kill: The true story of an SAS hero's love for an IRA killer*, London, 2002, p. 137.
4. ibid.
5. ibid., p. 139.
6. ibid.
7. ibid.
8. ibid., p. 269.
9. Mark Urban, *Big Boys' Rules: The secret struggle against the IRA*, London, 1992, p. 65.
10. Ken Connor, *Ghost Force – the Secret History of the SAS*, London, 1998, p. 281.

87. 'Blind or not, we're going in'

1. Nigel West, *The Secret War for the Falklands: The SAS, MI6 and the war Whitehall nearly lost*, London, 1997, p. 145.
2. Peter Ratcliffe, with Noel Botham and Brian Hitchen, *Eye of the Storm: Twenty-five Years in Action with the SAS*, London, 2000, p. 141.
3. Johnny Cooper, *One of the Originals: The Story of a Founder Member of the SAS*, London, 1991, p. 346.
4. Horsfall, *Fighting Scared*, p. 192.

88. 'Eleven, repeat eleven aircraft. Believed real'

1. Peter Ratcliffe, with Noel Botham and Brian Hitchen, *Eye of the Storm: Twenty-five Years in Action with the SAS*, London, 2000, p. 145.
2. ibid., p. 144.
3. ibid., p. 137.
4. ibid., p. 143.

89. 'Long nosed kamikazes'

1. Peter Ratcliffe, with Noel Botham and Brian Hitchen, *Eye of the Storm: Twenty-five Years in Action with the SAS*, London, 2000, p. 147.
2. Scott Graham, *Shoot to Kill: The true story of an SAS hero's love for an IRA killer*, London, 2002, p. 159.
3. Ken Connor, *Ghost Force – the Secret History of the SAS*, London, 1998, p. 399.
4. Robin Horsfall, *Fighting Scared*, London, 2002, p. 202.
5. ibid.
6. ibid.
7. ibid.

90. 'A bloody milestone in the struggle for freedom'

1. Scott Graham, *Shoot to Kill: The true story of an SAS hero's love for an IRA killer*, London, 2002, p. 264.
2. Raymond Murray, *The SAS in Ireland*, Dublin, 1990, p. 383.
3. Mark Urban, *Big Boys' Rules: The secret struggle against the IRA*, London, 1992, p. 234.

91. 'Unholy priesthood of violence'

1. Raymond Murray, *The SAS in Ireland*, Dublin, 1990, p. 410.
2. Tony Geraghty, *Who Dares Wins: The story of the SAS 1950–1992*, London, 1993, p. 303.
3. Murray, *The SAS in Ireland*, p. 415.
4. Geraghty, *Who Dares Wins*, p. 308.
5. Murray, *The SAS in Ireland*, p. 410.
6. Geraghty, *Who Dares Wins* p. 291.

92. *Sow fears in the mind of the enemy*

1. Michael Asher, *The Real Bravo Two Zero: The truth behind Bravo Two Zero*, London, 2003, p. 34.
2. ibid., p. 35.

93. *'If it comes to a firefight it could well save your arse'*

1. Peter Ratcliffe, with Noel Botham and Brian Hitchen, *Eye of the Storm: Twenty-five Years in Action with the SAS*, London, 2000, p. 199.
2. ibid., p. 199.

94. *'High possibility compromise'*

1. Michael Asher, *The Real Bravo Two Zero: The truth behind Bravo Two Zero*, London, 2003, p. 65.
2. ibid., p. 74.

95. *'No pain, only shock'*

1. McNab, Andy, *Bravo Two Zero: The true story of an SAS patrol behind enemy lines in Iraq*, London, 1993, p. 136.
2. ibid., p. 167.
3. Michael Asher, *The Real Bravo Two Zero: The truth behind Bravo Two Zero*, London, 2003, p. 147.
4. Mike Coburn, *Soldier Five: The real truth about the Bravo Two Zero mission*, Edinburgh, 2004, p. 115.
5. Asher, *The Real Bravo Two Zero*, p. 155.
6. ibid.
7. Coburn, *Soldier Five*, p. 185.

96. 'The right bloke to have around if it's action you're looking for'

1. Cameron Spence, *Sabre Squadron*, London, 1997, p. 127.
2. Peter Ratcliffe, with Noel Botham and Brian Hitchen, *Eye of the Storm: Twenty-five Years in Action with the SAS*, London, 2000, p. 212.
3. ibid.
4. Spence, *Sabre Squadron*, p. 169.

97. 'Shut the fuck up and keep shooting!'

1. Peter Ratcliffe, with Noel Botham and Brian Hitchen, *Eye of the Storm: Twenty-five Years in Action with the SAS*, London, 2000, p. 93.

98. 'The SAS had some new curtains to choose. Saddam could go swivel'

1. Cameron Spence, *Sabre Squadron*, London, 1997, p. 337.
2. ibid.

99. 'More than a Regiment'

1. John Lewes, *Jock Lewes: Co-Founder of the SAS*, Barnsley, 2000, p. 225.
2. Ken Connor, *Ghost Force – the Secret History of the SAS*, London, 1998, p. 526.
3. Gordon Stevens, *The Originals: The secret history of the birth of the SAS in their own words*, London, 2005, p. 338.
4. ibid.

Index